SOCIOLOGY

 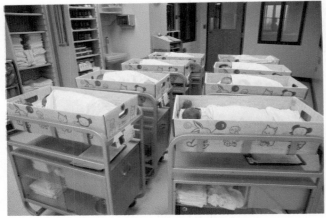

SOCIOLOGY

Robert Perrucci
PURDUE UNIVERSITY

Dean D. Knudsen
PURDUE UNIVERSITY

West Publishing Company
ST. PAUL   NEW YORK   LOS ANGELES   SAN FRANCISCO

COPY EDITOR   Elaine Linden
ARTIST   Barbara Hack
COMPOSITION   Parkwood

A study guide has been prepared by Spencer J. Condie to assist you in mastering concepts presented in this text. The study guide is available from your local bookstore under the title *Study Guide to Accompany Sociology*. If you cannot locate it in the bookstore, ask your bookstore manager to order it for you.

Library of Congress Cataloging in Publication Data

Perrucci, Robert.
    Sociology.

    Includes bibliographies and index.
    1. Sociology.   I. Knudsen, Dean D., 1932–
II. Title.   [DNLM: 1. Sociology. HM 51 P461s] HM51.P435
1983   301   82-23857
ISBN 0-314-69673-3

CREDITS—BLACK AND WHITE PHOTOS

xviii James Graschow. **2** Stock, Boston: Mark Antman. **10** Magnum: Reproduced from the collection of The Library of Congress. **12** The Bettmann Archive. **13** Magnum: Gilles Peress. **15** Stock, Boston: Peter Southwick. **18** Stock, Boston: Peter Menzel. **28** Robert George Gaylord. **37** Courtesy of University of Michigan Institute of Social Research. **39** Robert George Gaylord. **41** Stock, Boston: Cary Wolinsky. **54** Photo courtesy of the William L. McKnight 3M Omni Theater. **56** Myrdene Anderson. **61** Richard Harrington/FPG. **63** (2) Stock, Boston: Owen Franken. **71** Isiah Karlinsky/FPG. **75** Magnum: Bruno Barbey. **82** Stock, Boston: George Malave. **91** Stock, Boston: Owen Franken. **95** Photoworld. **100** Jeffry Myers/FPG. **105** Stock, Boston: Elizabeth Hamlin. **114** Natalie Leimkuhler. **119** Stock, Boston: Jean-Claude Lejeune. **123** Magnum: Leonard Freed. **131** Magnum: Hiroji Kubota. **133** Robert George Gaylord. **142** Natalie Leimkuhler. **147** Stock, Boston: Jean-Claude Lejeune. **148** Stock, Boston: Ellis Herwig. **151** Magnum: Burk Uzzle. **152** Robert George Gaylord. **161** Magnum: David Hurn. **170** Stock, Boston: Robert Eckert. **176** Stock, Boston: Bohdan Hrynewych. **177** (left) Magnum: Leonard Freed. **177** (right) David Margolin/Black Star. **188** (top) Jan Van Raay/FPG. **188** (bottom) Karen M. Kern/FPG. **190** Stock, Boston: George W. Gardner. **193** Magnum: Danny Lyon. **196** FPG. **212** Etching by Larry Welo. **214** Magnum: Inge Morath. **221** Nat Norman/Frederic Lewis, Inc. **227** (top) Robert George Gaylord; (bottom) Stock, Boston: Ira Kirschenbaum. **231** SOANDSO from Monkmeyer Press (Photo Service). **233** Ben McCall/FPG. **237** Magnum: Richard Kalvar. **250** Photo Researchers, Inc.: Stephen L. Feldman. **255** Stock, Boston: Peter Menzel. **261** Magnum: Danny Lyon. **266** AP: Wide World Photos. **269** Robert George Gaylord. **280** Natalie Leimkuhler. **292** Stock, Boston: Daniel S. Brody. **293** Stock, Boston: Jean-Claude Lejeune. **298** Stock, Boston: Elizabeth Hamlin. **306** Stock, Boston: Peter Vandermark. **317** Magnum: Paul Fusco. **323** Stock, Boston: Daniel S. Brody. **328** Magnum: Elliott Erwitt. **333** Stock, Boston: Peter Menzel. **342** Robert Kaufman. **344** Natalie Leimkuhler. **354** Dean Knudsen. **355** Renault Thomas/FPG. **357** Stock, Boston: Karen Rosenthal. **361** Stock, Boston: J. R. Holland. **365** Stock, Boston: Mark Antman. **376** Natalie Leimkuhler. **382** FPG: Keystone. **387** Magnum: Marc Riboud. **388** Stock, Boston: Cary Wolinsky. **394** Photograph by Ken Heyman. **399** Robert George Gaylord. **405** United Press International. **418** Magnum: Jean Gaumy. **423** Magnum: Rene Burri. **425** Carolyn A. McKeone © 1983/FPG. **426** United Press International radio telephoto. **433** © Henry Monroe—DPI. **442** Magnum: Hiroji Kubota. **454** Stock, Boston: Peter Southwick. **461** United Press International. **468** Magnum: Burt Glinn. **469** Stock, Boston: Peter Southwick. **475** David M. Doody/FPG. **478** Stock, Boston: Copyright © by J. Berndt/

(Continued on page 635)

CONTENTS

PREFACE

To the Students and Teachers Who Will Use This Book

After systematically studying the large number of existing introductory sociology texts we discovered many positive features, but we are convinced that several serious weaknesses exist that must be addressed.

First, is the failure to show the connection between sociological issues, as expressed in current sociological literature, and the social issues that people face in their everyday lives.

Second, is the failure to attend to the needs of most students who take only one course in sociology. What can we do in an Introductory text to show how sociologists actually look at the world?

We believe that we have written a book that is informative, interesting, and conveys a clear message about the sociological way of looking at the world. We further believe that students who understand and use the sociological point of view will be well prepared for further study in the area and better able to understand the social structures that will affect them throughout their lives.

This book emphasizes basic questions about the social forces that produce order, conflict, and change in human societies. This emphasis introduces students at the outset to the current social issues of the time: the use and abuse of political power; problems of population growth and depletion of resources; the way that giant corporations affect our lives; the increasing incidence of individual and group deviance from traditional standards of conduct. Sociological concepts, theories, and research findings can then be used to help us understand the nature and course of these social issues.

Our sociological perspective has led us to focus attention on some of the most fundamental and puzzling features of human society. (1) All human societies exhibit a degree of social order. There are forces that promote stability and continuity of patterns of social life. What are the sources of order, given the diversity of human motives, group interests, and collective human activities? (2) All human societies exhibit a degree of conflict among persons and groups that make up the society. Are there recurring sources of conflict that can be traced to inequalities in race, gender, wealth, and power that confront all societies? (3) All human societies experience social change, either through evolutionary development or social and political revolutions. What are the major forces for and against social change in modern societies?

If we have been successful, students who use this book will begin to understand how their personal beliefs, decisions, actions, and opportunities are shaped and limited by the larger social forces that surround them.

How to Use This Book

This book is organized into five parts. Part I introduces the field of sociology. The first chapter gives you an idea of what is special about how sociologists look at the world. We introduce you to basic concepts and perspectives used by sociologists in their study of society. Chapter 2 presents the objectives and methods of sociological research. We indicate how researchable sociological questions are formed, and the steps followed in gathering, analyzing, and summarizing data needed to answer such questions. The basic concepts, perspectives, and methods presented in these opening chapters will be used throughout the book to describe and analyze many different aspects of society.

Part II examines the relationships between individuals and their society. Culture—beliefs, values, norms, and rules shared by a group of people—provides the basic context and symbols of social life, and is discussed in Chapter 3. In Chapter 4, social organizations and social structures are considered as they affect the individual. The importance of groups is discussed in Chapter 5, especially those groups which provide intimacy, support, and care for the individual. How people from newly born infants to the aged learn the symbols, values, and expectations of their cultural settings is the focus of Chapter 6. Finally, the ways in which people adjust and adapt to or deviate from the norms and expectations of the society are considered in Chapter 7. In short, Part II concerns the interplay between the individual and society. How is the self created and maintained? How do social forces affect individuals and impinge upon them? How do people react to these forces?

In Part III we turn our attention to the main forms of inequality in society. Inequality is often the basis for conflict among social groups competing for scarce and valued resources, such as equal treatment, income, political power, and prestige. Chapter 8 discusses inequality in wealth, power, and prestige that results in structured inequality called social stratification. In Chapter 9 we look at formal organizations as places where much of the work of modern societies is carried out. People use organizations as the means of achieving their collective goals—economic, political, and social. Much social conflict takes place in and through organizations as people try to use organizations to serve individual and group goals. Chapters 10 and 11 examine inequality that stems from gender, race, and ethnic differences. Each of these forms of inequality has given rise to social movements designed to change society so as to eliminate inequality. Such efforts result in social conflict and social change.

Part IV is concerned with major areas of human activity found in all societies, which we refer to as social institutions. Institutions are based on shared values and beliefs and thus are resistant to efforts to change them. Family institutions, Chapter 12, illustrates social order in the patterns for control of love, sex, and childrearing. In Chapter 13, economic institutions and their impact on society are considered. Religious institutions and their effect on values and social life are examined in Chapter 14. Political and educational institutions are also discussed as they provide an orderly pattern for human activities. However, in each institutional activity, we examine the potential for conflict and order as appropriate to the topic.

Finally, Part V deals with two of the most important developments of modern life. One concerns the growth of cities in response to social, technological, and economic change. Chapter 17 examines different theories on how cities grow, as well as how city life affects people who live there. Chapter 18 examines worldwide patterns of population distribution and growth. Changes in the size and composition of populations can have important consequences for many different patterns of social life.

The parts of this book are logically interrelated.

Part I introduces the field, giving the student a basic vocabulary and overview of the sociological perspective as well as some tools for evaluating research and analyzing data. Part II begins with the consideration of people as biological beings and explores the social factors that make them social beings. Part III considers the social structures that produce and perpetuate inequality and differences among people, while Part IV examines the social structures that produce and perpetuate order and inhibit change. While the ordering of Parts III and IV reflect our view, it can be reversed to fit preferences of instructors. Part V attempts to assess two developments of modern life that will continue to be issues for societies for decades.

Similarly, we have attempted to provide an order within each chapter. Chapters start with topics or experiences with which students should be familiar. These topics provide the basis for analysis using sociological concepts and methods.

Special Features

Each chapter in the book follows a planned structure designed to develop student interest and assist learning.

- Chapters open with "At Issue" sections presenting a controversial sociological or social issue discussed from two different positions. Each "At Issue" was specially written by the authors to encourage students to think for themselves and interest them in using the sociological ideas in the chapter to develop their own views. Summaries follow each "At Issue" and serve as a link to the following chapter material.
- Each chapter begins with a listing of four or five "Questions to Consider." These questions orient the student to the chapter, spark interest, and suggest discussion topics.
- Chapters begin with high-interest openers drawn from news stories, popular literature, or specially written vignettes. They deal with situations that students may have read about, actually experienced, or with which they could empathize. These openers illustrate sociological concepts and concerns that will be treated in the chapter.

- Interspersed in chapters are boxed "Highlights" which provide a closer look at topics or ideas treated in the chapter.
- Chapter "Summaries," "Glossaries," and "Additional Readings" are designed to reinforce the main ideas of the chapter and give direction to students wishing to explore the topic further.
- The close of each chapter usually has two "Readings" that demonstrate how sociologists use their concepts and methods in understanding society. Readings are followed by specially written summaries and questions for further discussion.
- Several pages of attractive color photographs depicting "The Texture of Social Life" are placed at four locations in the book.

Acknowledgments

A great many of our colleagues were very generous in the time they gave to critical reading of the manuscript. Their careful, constructive comments revealed extensive knowledge of the field of sociology and a sensitivity to the needs of students and what does and does not work in the classroom. We are appreciative of their efforts to improve our book.

Adrian F. Aveni, Jackson State University
Paul Baker, Illinois State University
Spencer J. Condie, Brigham Young University
Ronald G. Corwin, Ohio State University
Edward Z. Dager, University of Maryland
John M. Day, Foote Hill College
William H. Form, University of Illinois at Champaign-Urbana
Charles E. Garrison, East Carolina University
James R. George, Kutztown State College
Richard Hall, State University of New York at Albany
Joseph S. Himes, University of North Carolina at Greensboro
Joan Huber, University of Illinois at Champaign-Urbana
Donald Irish, Hamline University
Stanley Kupinsky, Wayne State University
Calvin J. Larson, University of Massachusetts, Boston
Bebe Lavin, Kent State University
Dick Mathers, Western Illinois University

Paul T. McFarlane, North Carolina State
   University
Ephraim H. Mizruchi, Syracuse University
Kent G. Mommsen, University of Utah
Charles Mulford, Iowa State University
Fred C. Pampel, Jr., University of Iowa
Margaret Park, Florissant Valley Community
   College
Richard A. Peterson, Vanderbilt University
Michael Radelet, University of Florida
Ellen Page Robin, Western Michigan
   University
James Skellinger, Kent State University
Arthur B. Shostak, Drexel University
Cole V. Smith, San Antonio College
Robert F. Szafran, University of Iowa
Several first drafts of chapters were written, with
our collaboration, by James G. Anderson, Gary
Grossman, Russell Hamby, Mark LaGory, Michael
Micklin, and Ronald Westrum. Special thanks are
extended to Spencer Condie for his exceptional work
in developing the study guide and instructor's man-
ual.

We are greatly indebted to Mary Perigo and Maria
Broughton for preparation of the final manuscript
and their perseverence in obtaining needed per-
missions from authors and publishers.

Finally, we express our thanks to West Publishing Company for working with us on this book.
Our editor, Mary Schiller, was the moving force on
this project. She not only had the idea for a second
edition, but she challenged the authors with her
own views about how to produce a readable, attractive, intellectually sound book. We are also indebted to Lenore Franzen, West's production editor, who very ably kept this book on schedule and
made valuable contributions to art and illustra-
tions. William Stryker also provided creative and
attractive ideas for the design. Elaine Linden is a
copy editor without peer. She not only improved
the quality of the writing but she read the text as
well, making extensive suggestions for revision.
Elizabeth Hannan, marketing coordinator, with the
assistance of Larry Schneider, ably translated the
author's ideas into an attractive and informative
marketing program.

ABOUT THE AUTHORS

ROBERT PERRUCCI is professor of sociology at Purdue University. His main areas of teaching and research include *complex organizations*, with special emphasis on interorganizational relations; the *professions*, with special attention to engineers as salaried employees in large organizations and to career mobility; and *social networks*, with emphasis on their role in providing social support to persons with "troubles."

Professor Perrucci has published over fifty research articles and book chapters. He is author or coauthor of nine books, including: *Profession Without Community* (1968); *The Engineers and the Social System* (1969); *The Triple Revolution Emerging* (1971); *Circle of Madness: On Being Insane and Institutionalized in America* (1974); *Divided Loyalties: Whistleblowing at BART* (1980); *Mental Patients and Social Networks* (1982).

He has served as associate editor for the *American Sociological Review, Social Problems, Sociological Quarterly,* and *Sociological Focus.* In 1973 he was elected president of the North Central Sociological Association, and in 1982 elected president of the Organizations and Occupations section of the American Sociological Association.

DEAN D. KNUDSEN is Associate Professor of Sociology at Purdue University. He was educated at Sioux Falls College, South Dakota, the University of Minnesota, and the University of North Carolina at Chapel Hill, where he was awarded the Ph.D. He has taught at Augsburg College, The University of North Carolina at Chapel Hill, The Ohio State University, and Purdue University. He is the author or coauthor of articles and monographs in the areas of sociology of religion and family sociology, and of *Spindles and Spires: A Restudy of Religion and Social Change in Gastonia.* He has served as president of the North Central Sociological Association, has been active in the Society for the Scientific Study of Religion, the Family section of the American Sociological Association, and the National Council on Family Relations, and has been a member of the editorial boards of *Youth and Society, Sociological Focus,* and *Review of Religious Research.* His current research interests include child abuse, ethnic identification, and intergenerational relations.

PART I

The Field of Sociology

People who take the time to think about the society in which they live are often bewildered by the seeming chaos and confusion of events. Although social life is complex and often difficult to understand, human societies are also orderly systems of interacting individuals and groups. In many ways, human societies are remarkably similar, despite some of their extraordinary differences. The study of society and social behavior is both challenging and rewarding. There is the excitement of studying things that you have experienced and know first hand, and there is intellectual growth that comes with learning how other people see their society. Sociology is one discipline involved in the effort to study human society systematically. The chapters in this first part of the book deal with the theoretical and methodological tools used by sociologists to describe and explain the enduring patterns of social life and the way in which they change. Chapter 1 discusses some of the dominant theoretical approaches used by sociologists and some of their divergent ideas about the objectives of sociology as a discipline. Chapter 2 examines the research procedures used in studying society and social behavior. A combination of the key concepts, theories, and methods of sociology serve as the basis for the knowledge we can develop about our social world.

CHAPTER 1

The Nature of Sociology

CONTENTS

AT ISSUE

Is a science of society possible?

The debate over whether it is possible to have a *social* science has gone on for many years. One basis for disagreement is philosophical and concerns assumptions about human beings. Are they part of the natural order along with atoms, cells, plants, and animals, and therefore available to our knowledge, or are they basically different, presenting special problems for study? The second disagreement concerns whether or not the methods of science can be used in the study of human behavior and society. Is true science only possible in physics, chemistry, and biology?

YES   Science begins with the belief that there is pattern and regularity in the universe. This is true in physical science, natural science, and social science, even though they may be concerned with different phenomena; for example, the interaction of atomic particles, the process of cell division, and the structure of social relationships.

The goal of science is to *identify* the pattern and regularity that exists in the universe and to *explain* the relationships. Scientists pursue this goal by using the *scientific method,* which consists of logical and systematic procedures that are used to obtain knowledge. A basic procedure is observation, which allows scientists to make cause-and-effect statements (such as ''B invariably follows from A''). Scientists try to take what they learn from *particular* situations and make it apply to a more *general* set of situations. In short, they work from what is known to what is unknown.

Sociology is among the youngest of the sciences, but it has made great progress, especially in the last 50 years. The procedures for measuring human behavior have been greatly refined, and the techniques for collecting and analyzing large bodies of information are very advanced. There now exists a precise set of specialized terms that social scientists can use to communicate their observations.

The record is clear and the promise is great. Sociology can be a science of human behavior and society. It will continue to develop, as all sciences have, by improving its research methods and theoretical models to explain relationships in the social world.

NO   The ambition of sociology to be considered a science is shared by other disciplines like anthropology, political science, and psychology. Sociologists share a belief in the unity of all science and that the social sciences are no different from physical and natural sciences. There are, however, some major barriers facing the social sciences.

First is the fact that humans, unlike atoms, molecules, or cells, are self-conscious beings, aware of their actions and able to reflect on them. This makes it possible for humans to learn new patterns of behavior and adopt new ideas. Therefore, they do not act in fixed and predictable ways, as do atoms and molecules.

The second problem for the social sciences is that when they study people and groups they are in fact changing them. This happens in physics too (the phenomenon of the observer affecting the behavior of the observed is known as the Heisenberg principle), but we are especially aware of it in the study of social behavior because people are self-conscious and able to learn.

The third problem is the inability of sociologists to carry out true experiments with human beings. Without experimentation under highly controlled conditions it is not possible to establish cause-and-effect relationships.

In sum, sociology can never become a "real" science because it cannot apply the scientific method to the study of human society. What passes for scientific sociology today is little more than common-sense knowledge.

Many of the questions raised in this "At Issue" will be dealt with in this chapter. We will examine why sociology emerged as a special discipline to study human society and the major ideas sociologists use to guide their studies. In Chapter 2 we will examine how sociologists use the scientific method.

QUESTIONS TO CONSIDER

■ Why did sociology emerge as a discipline in Europe and the United States?

■ Is society real? How would you convince someone of this?

■ Can sociology be value-free? Should it try to be?

■ Is society based on common beliefs and values, or is it based on force, dominance, and conflict among persons and groups?

A SOCIOLOGICAL VIEW OF SOCIETY

Ralph stirred restlessly . . . What could they do? Beat him? So what? Kill him? . . .

The cries, suddenly nearer, jerked him up. He could see a striped savage moving hastily out of a green tangle, and coming towards the mat where he hid, a savage who carried a spear. Ralph gripped his fingers into the earth. Be ready now, in case.

Ralph fumbled to hold his spear so that it was point foremost; and now he saw that the stick was sharpened at both ends.

The savage stopped fifteen yards away and uttered his cry.

Perhaps he can hear my heart over the noises of the fire. Don't scream. Get ready.

The savage moved forward so that you could only see him from the waist down. That was the butt of his spear. Now you could see him from the knee down. Don't scream . . .

Five yards away the savage stopped, standing right by the thicket, and cried out. Ralph drew his feet up and crouched. The stake was in his hands, the stake sharpened at both ends, the stake that vibrated so wildly, that grew long, short, light, heavy, light again.

The savage peered into the obscurity beneath the thicket. You could tell that he saw light on

this side and on that, but not in the middle—there. In the middle was a blob of dark and the savage wrinkled up his face, trying to decipher the darkness.

The seconds lengthened. Ralph was looking straight into the savage's eyes.

Don't scream.

You'll get back.

Now he's seen you. He's making sure. A stick sharpened.

Ralph screamed, a scream of fright and anger and desperation. His legs straightened, the screams became continuous and foaming. He shot forward, burst the thicket, was in the open, screaming, snarling, bloody. He swung the stake and the savage tumbled over; but there were others coming towards him, crying out. He swerved as a spear flew past and then was silent, running. All at once the lights flickering ahead of him merged together, the roar of the forest rose to thunder and a tall bush directly in his path burst into a great fan-shaped flame. He swung to the right running desperately fast, with the heat beating on his left side and fire racing forward like a tide. The ululation rose behind him and spread along, a series of short sharp cries, the sighting call. A brown figure showed up at his right and fell away. They were all running, all crying out madly. He could hear them crashing in the undergrowth and on the left was the hot, bright thunder of the fire. He forgot his wounds, his hunger and thirst, and became fear; hopeless fear on flying feet, rushing through the forest towards the open beach. Spots jumped before his eyes and turned into red circles that expanded quickly till they passed out of sight. Below him, someone's legs were getting tired and the desperate ululation advanced like a jagged fringe of menace and was almost overhead.

He stumbled over a root and the cry that pursued him rose even higher. He saw a shelter burst into flames and the fire flapped at his right shoulder and there was the glitter of water. Then he was down, rolling over and over in the warm sand, crouching with arm up to ward off, trying to cry for mercy.

This chilling scene of pursuit and life or death struggle is from *Lord of the Flies*, a novel by William Golding (1962). The remarkable thing about this scene is that both Ralph and the painted "savages" pursuing him are English schoolboys. The Golding novel is about a large group of English schoolboys who are shipwrecked on an uninhabited desert island. The author uses the experiences of these children to comment on the nature of human society.

The novel begins with the boys being washed ashore along a beach covered with palm trees. After gathering together and getting over the initial shock of being without adult guidance, the boys set out to explore the island and to find a supply of food and water. Primitive shelters are constructed to provide protection against the night's menace.

Soon small groups of close friends form. Membership in these groups is based on emotional ties, and feelings of security and support are enjoyed by all who belong. Boys who are outsiders experience greater difficulty in coping with their new situation.

As the youngsters begin to realize that survival requires the regular performance of certain tasks, a division of labor develops. Some are responsible for gathering food and water; others get firewood; and still others prepare food and watch over their youngest members.

But not everyone is willing to do his share or to do it in ways that contribute the greatest good. Informal expectations of how the boys are to behave are not enough. Formal rules, publicly declared and publicly enforced, are needed. A legal system gradually evolves, with "police," "judges," and "trials." A formal system of social control combines with the informal influence of friendship to help shape the social order. At the top of this structure is a leader, elected by a majority of the boys because of his demonstrated skills in hunting. The leader appoints an "administrative staff" of his closest friends who are responsible for the formal machinery of social control.

Despite their success in providing for basic needs, the castaways have a great many fears of the unknown. Unexplored parts of the island are thought to be populated with life-threatening beings and animals. The dark, violent storms and the unpredictable sea represent unseen and uncontrollable forces. Collectively, the boys begin to shape stories to account for what is beyond their control. Group rituals and ceremonies are used to pacify unknown forces, seek protection against harm, or obtain special help in hunting for food.

All seems to be going better than one might expect as the boys have effectively adapted to their physical environment. But gradually the established social fabric starts to unravel. A sharp division develops among the boys over the way in which they are governed and how material goods (like food) and symbolic rewards (such as group recognition) are distributed among the group's members.

The small, informal friendship groups that are the basic units of this island society polarize over government policies and practices. One faction supports the leader in power. The second faction has a different view of how the society should be governed, advocating greater equality in the distribution of goods and less emphasis on formal social control of citizens. Their chosen leader has leadership qualities that contrast sharply with those of the existing leader. Conflict between the two factions eventually escalates into "civil war" threatening the entire society.

This fascinating little book by Golding contains, in miniature form, many of the basic features found in human societies. If a group of social scientists tried to analyze this fictional society, they would approach it from the perspective of their particular disciplines. Economists would be concerned primarily with the way that food and shelter are produced and distributed. They would also try to understand the way that the boys determined the value of different jobs (wages) and different products (prices). Political scientists would give special attention to the sources of social power among the boys and how that power is used. They would also be concerned with the way that rules and order are established and how they work. Psychologists would focus on the nature of the boys mental life—their personalities, intellectual capabilities, and interpersonal skills. They would look for the source of these individual traits and skills in early childhood experiences, stressful life events, or genetic inheritance. Anthropologists would be interested in the shared meanings and symbols developed by the boys as they adapt to their environment, especially their language and the way that it expresses their common values and problems.

We can see that each of the social sciences looks at society in a very selective way. The economist studies economic life as a particular subpart of the larger society. The political scientist considers the larger society as the social and historical setting in which political life develops. The anthropologist, although interested in the broad category of language, needs to live in the society to get a firsthand feeling for its meaning systems and is thereby allowed to see only a small segment of the entire society. The psychologist considers the influence of particular aspects of a society, such as its child-rearing patterns, on the psychological makeup of its members.

A sociologist looks at society in terms of the groups that make it up and the relationships among them. Particular aspects of a society may be studied, such as race relations or organizations, but they are considered as part of a more encompassing web of relationships. Sociology provides the concepts, theories, and methods to look at the island society as a society, rather than as a collection of individuals and their activities. Let us consider some of these basic ideas and illustrate the sociological viewpoint, or the way that sociologists look at the world.

1. *Human societies exist in a natural environment to which they must adapt if the society is to survive.* In the Golding novel the boys developed social patterns that enabled them to adapt first of all to their natural environment to satisfy basic needs for food, shelter, and security. Other social patterns developed later to deal with secondary needs for a stable social order.

2. *All human societies exhibit a high degree of pattern and regularity.* In our fictional society we observed that as the castaways adapted to their new environment they developed stable and recurring behaviors and shared expectations about behavior. Small groups of boys, "families"

or friendship groups, came into being and they provided emotional support and security. The pattern and regularity of an ordered economic life helped obtain and distribute needed goods and services. Conflicts among group members were moderated and a system of rewards and punishments developed to ensure that social rules were followed—producing an ordered political system. Fear of the unknown was handled collectively through rituals and ceremonies—a patterned religious life.

3. *Patterned and recurring social behavior of human beings is shaped by the social groups to which they belong.* The youngsters in Golding's novel often exhibit behavior that is quite foreign to their basic personalities and prior upbringing. We would not be able to predict very well their behavior on the island from knowledge of how they behaved as schoolboys in England. Their aggressive or cooperative or nurturant behavior is a product of the new social situations in which they find themselves. They do what they do because of influence, pressure, and control exerted by their new social groups.

4. *At the same time that human beings are shaped and constrained by the social settings in which they live, they also try to shape and change the patterned interactions and group relationships that affect them.* Not each boy or group of boys reacted to the new social environment in exactly the same way. Some boys found existing social arrangements very acceptable and therefore were inclined to allow the status quo to continue. Others began to feel that the existing system for allocating power or prestige or "income" (food) was not fair to all segments of the society. Pressures for change, as well as its speed and extent, were generated by the social conditions of the society.

5. *Some patterned and recurring forms of social life are the result of conscious planning, while others are unintended and unplanned.* In the boys' island society many of their economic and political activities were the result of planned efforts to construct social arrangements designed to further the interests of most members of the society. A specific division of labor and a

system of laws and social control are examples. Other patterns, such as the emergence of small groups characterized by face-to-face relationships, were not planned. They appeared not by design but apparently in response to an unspoken or unrecognized social need shared by all human beings.

The Reality of Society

Although our castaway English schoolboys were not always aware of what they were doing, they did in fact "construct" a **society.** *A society is interacting individuals and interrelated groups sharing a common culture and territory.* While pursuing short-term, individualistic goals related to survival and security, they produced, unintentionally, patterned and recurring forms of social life. The boys developed shared beliefs and expectations that served as guides for behavior. They also developed ways of influencing each other's behavior through a system of social rewards and punishments. Some collectively held expectations were applied to all members, and some applied to certain segments of the society (for example, persons responsible for food gathering, or rule enforcement).

Patterned and recurring forms of behavior were associated with different areas of social life. Obtaining, distributing, and preparing food was guided by socially constructed and enforced customs. Another set of customs shaped the way members of small friendship groups behaved toward each other as compared with outsiders.

The reality of society has two aspects. First, it is *external* to individuals. Customs, beliefs, expectations, and the recurring behaviors they produce exist apart from the life of any individual member of society. They precede individuals who are born into or join any society, and they persist after those individuals have died or left. Second, people perceive society or experience it as a **constraint** upon their lives. The influence of social groups is felt by group members when they (1) think about how the group would react to something they *might do* and (2) experience a reward or punishment from the group for something they *have done.* For example, housing units in college often have long-standing

dress code traditions or dating practices that members are expected to follow. Failure to do so may result in informal peer pressure or formal punishment of the nonconforming member, such as expulsion. Often, however, members will take group expectations or rules into account before they do something that might be contrary to group practices.

Students, Sociology, and Society

As a student in a new course, and perhaps a first course in sociology, you may wonder how it will be useful to you. Rather than elaborate on the ways that sociology can contribute to the dozens of careers or professions students enter, we will simply note that the most basic good answer is that sociology can contribute to your understanding of the society in which you live. Sociology provides the tools for analyzing and understanding the complex, and at times bewildering, society that you experience daily. Rapid advances in science and technology, the tremendous growth of large bureaucratic organizations, changing values that create gaps across generations, and the persistent divisions of class and race all contribute to the complexity of modern life—and often to the feeling of powerlessness of the average person.

Sociology is one of the social sciences that can increase your awareness of the world about you and improve your ability to analyze and understand it. Once you understand the world, you are better prepared to deal with it—and perhaps to change it.

THE EMERGENCE OF SOCIOLOGY

The discipline of sociology as the systematic study of society was established in the middle of the nineteenth century. The appearance of this new discipline can be traced to the rapid and far-reaching social changes that were transforming European society. Why is it that sociology has emerged only recently as a field of study? Why did rapid social change stimulate its appearance?

One reason why the study of society was ignored for so long is that throughout most of human his-

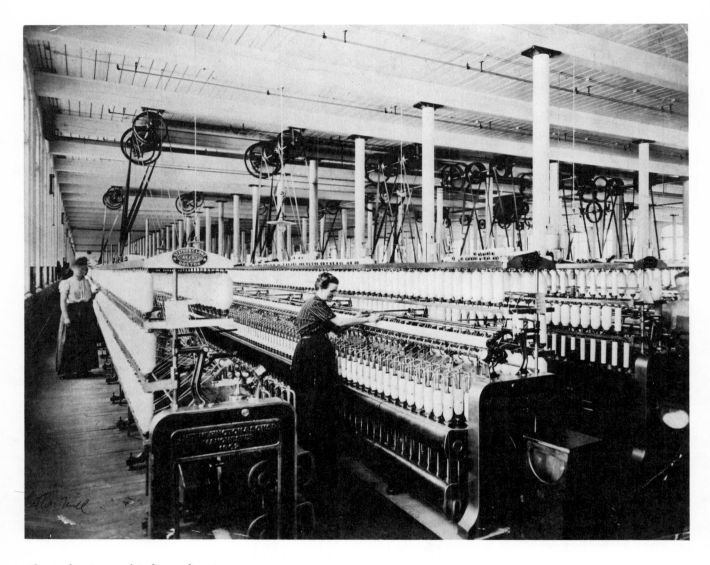

The early stages of industrialization
in the United States and Europe
were marked by dramatic changes
in the nature and pattern of work,
such as the factory system of
production. There was also child
labor, disrupted families, long
hours, and overcrowded worker's
housing as the demand for labor
attracted many people to
industrialized cities. The studies of
many of the early sociologists were
concerned with the changes
produced by industrialization.

tory social change was a very slow and gradual process. Patterns of living were passed on for generations through a seemingly unbroken chain of tradition. Even the most revolutionary discoveries in early human history resulted in social changes that took centuries to develop. For example, when people learned how to domesticate plants and animals about 8000 B.C., they were able to have a more stable and abundant food supply. This led to larger populations and settlements that eventually became cities. However, it took several thousand years between the domestication of plants and animals and the growth of cities.

Only within the past 300 years—a mere fragment of human history—did the pace of change begin to accelerate to the point where patterns of living are significantly altered within one person's lifetime. Beginning about 1700, the stable, argicultural society that existed in Europe gradually gave way to **industrialization,** that is, to the use of mechanical systems of production. Workers and their families who had been tied to the land for generations moved to towns and cities to learn new trades and to work in the competitive marketplace. Small shops appeared, in which five or six people worked together to produce something. This became the basis for the factory system that followed.

The shift of people and economic activity from the country to the city strengthened the political power of the central government, which increasingly administered the affairs of public life. In some cases political revolutions followed the changes brought on by industrialization. Royal families and ruling elites composed of clergymen and nobles were swept away by the newly developing and ever more powerful merchant and working classes. The new-found political and economic freedom that followed these revolutions further fueled the engines of social change.

The challenges to traditional institutions were of such scope and intensity that the social philosophy of the time was simply inadequate to cope with them. Philosophers, religious leaders, prophets, and tribal elders who throughout history had devoted their lives to understanding and explaining human affairs had not anticipated industrialization, the growth of urban life, or a decline in the power of the church.

During the seventeenth and eighteenth centuries in Europe, the main interest of the social philosophers was the impact of the **Industrial Revolution** and the French Revolution (1789) on society. They reflected on the new rights of citizens in their relationships with government and on the power of human reason, rather than tradition or superstition, for understanding human affairs. The conclusions of the social philosophers were often based on logical argument and on the way they felt social life *ought* to be organized. There was little systematic observation of how social life *is* organized.

Out of this period of social, political, and intellectual ferment sociology was born. **Auguste Comte** (1798–1857) is remembered as the founder of sociology and most frequently credited with coining the term. Comte emphasized observation and experimentation, combining the logical analysis of social philosophers with the data of firsthand experience—"facts"—in this new scientific study of society that he first called social physics.

Sociology was established in the United States in the late nineteenth century. Like its counterpart in Europe, American sociology developed in response to upheavals resulting from rapid social change. Industrialization, combined with the settlement of the western states, attracted immigrants to our shores and added to already large-scale population shifts from the farm to the city. By about 1860 one-half of the total United States labor force was employed outside of agriculture. In the decade 1850–1860 immigration reached 2½ million, a dramatic increase over the 150,000 figure of the years between 1820 and 1830.

These "new" people, both immigrants and migrants, formed a large working class living under marginal economic conditions in our cities. Unemployment, poverty, and overcrowding were endemic. Rising crime rates, broken homes, juvenile delinquency, political corruption, volatile race relations, and mental illness were only a few of the consequences that engaged the attention of sociologists.

Thus, American sociology in its early years was concerned with social reform, changing society to reduce or solve social problems. Before long, however, a new idea of what sociology should be like arose. This new idea held that the purpose of so-

Auguste Comte (1798–1857) is the founder of modern sociology. He called for the scientific study of society using methods of direct observation and the collection of social facts.

ciology was to develop a science of the social world, just as biology, for example, had developed a science of the world of living matter. Sociology, like physics or biology, should pursue knowledge for its own sake, regardless of whether that knowledge contributed to solution of social problems.

Today, sociologists continue to differ over the central purposes of sociology. Whether they are primarily interested in solving social problems or understanding how society works, sociologists begin their studies with some guiding ideas. The next section presents several of these ideas.

SOCIOLOGICAL MODELS OF SOCIETY

When sociologists carry out studies of society they are usually trying to answer specific questions or examine specific hypotheses, which can be thought of as "educated guesses." For example, they might seek an answer to the question of what factors influence academic achievement in high school by examining the effects of parental values, peer group pressures, and student aspirations upon grades. Often, their work is guided by a *theory*, which organizes a set of observations about, say, parental values, peer group pressures, and student aspirations and helps to explain the relationships among them. Thus, a theory would allow us to hypothesize a relationship—parents who value education will have children who get higher grades—and to explain the relationship. Without theories that organize and explain empirical (observable) facts, many research findings remain isolated and meaningless.

Yet the kind of questions that sociologists ask and the kind of research they pursue are often shaped by a broader set of assumptions about society and social behavior. We can call these broader assumptions a *model*, or mental picture of society. For example, in earlier times in Europe, society was imagined to work like a clock—a mechanistic image of interrelated parts, each of which has a fixed purpose and a specific relationship to the whole.

In sociology today there are three distinct models of society (or theoretical perspectives, as they are sometimes called) that guide the work of most sociologists. While these models help to organize concepts and questions about society, they produce quite different traditions of research and scholarship. The following sections discuss these three models: the structural-functional model, the conflict model, and the interactional model.

Structural-Functional Model: Society as a Moral System

The **structural-functional model** of society, exemplified in the work of Talcott Parsons (1951, 1971), stresses three main ideas. First, society is a system containing interdependent and interacting parts bound together in time and space. Second, shared values among members of the system are social "glue" that helps hold it together. Third, systems have a need for stability and therefore attempt to keep the parts working together harmoniously (that is, in balance or equilibrium). These ideas will be examined in the following paragraphs.

PART-WHOLE RELATIONSHIPS: INTERDEPENDENCE

The parts of a social system are social units like families, schools, ethnic groups, or social classes. The sum total of activities taking place in each part has consequences (which we can call an "output") for some other part of the system, for which it becomes an "input." When the outputs of one part of a system make important contributions to another part, there is a good fit between the parts of the system—a harmony or balance between outputs and inputs. When the outputs of one part do not contribute to another, there is a poor fit between the parts in question. For example, the economy has need for workers with certain motivations and skills, and the family and the school give people work aspirations and desire for training for employment. When such a situation exists we say that the parts of the system fit together and a stable

continuous relationship is established. If, however, families and schools produce peole who are not interested in economic life and work roles, but who instead pursue spiritual values, there will be a poor fit between these parts of society. This poor fit sets in motion pressures for change to reestablish equilibrium, or a good fit, between system parts.

The preceding description shows that parts of a system are neither isolated from each other nor self-sufficient. Each part must obtain the resources it needs to carry out its activities. Therefore, there is a high degree of interdependence among the parts of a system.

INTEGRATION THROUGH VALUE CONSENSUS

The structural-functional model stresses the important role played by **social values** in holding a society together. Values that are commonly shared by members of a society are the "glue" that binds people and activities into a unified whole. These values are expressed in shared expectations we have about how people are supposed to behave in certain situations. For example, there are widely shared expectations about the behavior of people in their marital roles (as husband, wife, mother, father, and

Many symbols and ceremonies in society serve to reaffirm widely shared values. They suggest a society with a unifying moral order and stable relationships among its members. Here we see an example of conventional political behavior by supporters of different candidates who nonetheless accept the "rules of the game."

so on) and in their business roles (as employer, employee, supervisor, and the like). People in these roles generally try to meet these expectations because they share the general belief in their worth or moral value. Most teenagers, who accept their parents' advice and guidance do so because they believe in their parents' moral right to do so, not because parents have the power to force them to do something.

The structural-functional model describes a society in which people from different social classes would agree that despite differences in wealth or prestige or power each has received a fair reward. Industrialists or physicians earning $200,000 a year view their income as a fair return for their investment of time or money to reach the positions they hold. Similarly, $18,000-a-year factory workers would also agree that the rewards of the industrialist or physician are fair because they all had an equal opportunity to compete for rewards by becoming industrialists or physicians. Thus, the shared *belief* in the existence of equality of opportunity, and the shared *belief* that those with long training deserve greater rewards, are the common values that bind a society together.

The assumption that dominant value patterns found in American society are the glue that holds it together has been questioned. Critics of the structural-functional model state that neither the values nor the behavior that results from the values are in any sense harmonious or compatible with one another. Pairs of values like freedom and equality or equality and individualism reflect conflicting patterns of thought and behavior that may be difficult to reconcile. Stressing the rights of individuals or guaranteeing freedom in economic activity may mean that those who start life with an advantage can limit the freedom or the opportunities of those who start life without the same chances. One person's freedom is another person's constraint. Given these contradictory and sometimes conflicting values, one may ask how it is possible to speak of society as having balance and equilibrium among its parts.

The structural-functional perspective emphasizes *shared* values and activities that integrate different parts of a society. Conflict, when it does

exist, is viewed as a temporary problem for a society. In contrast, the conflict model sees common binding values as the unusual feature of society and conflict as its central defining characteristic.

SYSTEM NEEDS: STABILITY AND EQUILIBRIUM

Another emphasis of the structural-functional model is on the sources of stability in a society rather than on the forces that produce change. Stability, which is essential for any society, results when societies try to develop routine ways of dealing with the less than perfect fit among its parts and the resulting conflicts and tensions. For instance, the labor-management conflict with its accompanying outbreaks of violence that was so marked a feature of American society in the early decades of this century is today handled through collective bargaining agreements, legal strikes, and government-monitored negotiations between conflicting parties. Similarly, people whose unconventional life styles may be a source of conflict with the larger society may form their own subcommunities, which diminish conflict by isolating their members to some degree from the larger society. The old-order Amish, the gay subculture, and religious communes are examples.

The reasons for this emphasis on stability rather than change are twofold: First, change in society is gradual. When one part of a system changes, there are step-by-step adjustments in other parts. For instance, the growth of two-career families (when both husband and wife are employed) has produced gradual changes in work organizations like the development of maternal leave policy, day care centers, and flexible work schedules. However, tensions between family patterns and the demands of economic life remain, and they will undoubtedly result in further gradual changes. Second, certain features of societies are seen as necessary for societies' survival, and maintaining these features becomes an overriding concern of the system. Because, for example, the family institution is seen as one of the essential parts of society, any threat to the survival of the family will result in efforts to strengthen and maintain it. Similarly, the existence of unequally rewarded occupations in society (which we discuss as "social stratification" in Chapter 8) is viewed as necessary because it helps motivate people to undertake the lengthy training needed to fill important jobs. Inequality, therefore, is held to be necessary for the survival of society and efforts to reduce or eliminate it will be resisted.

Conflict Model: Society as a Coercive System

The **conflict model** views society as containing basic inequalities in wealth, power, and prestige (Coser, 1967; Dahrendorf, 1959). Privileged segments of society are felt to benefit from a particular set of social arrangements, and they do so at the expense of less privileged groups. Feelings of injustice about unequal rewards and conflict between unequally rewarded groups are the basis of the Marxian form of the conflict model. Karl Marx's theory of social change described all human history as a conflict between opposing social classes.

When segments of society are in sharp disagreement over basic values or the means to achieve those values, conflict can escalate to the use of force and violence.

The history of all hitherto existing society is the history of class struggles. Freeman and slave, patrician and plebian, lord and serf, guildmaster and journeyman, in a word; oppressor and oppressed, stood in constant opposition to one another, carried on an uninterrupted, now hidden, now open fight, a fight that each time ended, either in a revolutionary reconstitution of society at large, or in the common ruin of the contending classes. (Marx, 1848).

PART-WHOLE RELATIONSHIPS: POWER

In the conflict model, different parts of a social system are interdependent, *not* because of common values, but because of the greater power of certain groups in society to achieve their ends at the expense of others. In short, the conflict model recognizes the central role of power as an explanation of how different parts of a society are interrelated and influence each other. In relationships between individuals, groups, or social classes there is a dominant party and a subordinate party. Dominance is based on the former's control of resources that the latter needs, which they obtain by being subordinate in the relationships.

Returning to the example used earlier, the $18,000-a-year factory worker may not view the wealth of industrialists or physicians as a fair or just return for their investment of effort (that is, education), but he or she is powerless to change the situation. Or, perhaps, the worker has been influenced by schools and mass media (controlled by privileged classes) to believe that a high income is a fair reward for people with extensive education. Thus, the power of privileged classes can be expressed by coercion (control over jobs, police, courts, and military) or by more subtle forms of socializing people to adopt the values and beliefs of dominant groups.

INTEGRATION THROUGH THE DOMINANCE
OF ECONOMIC INSTITUTIONS

Whereas the structural-functional model stresses common values and consensus among social groups, the conflict model sees society as composed of antagonistic economic classes, such as industrialists, financiers, and wealthy families who represent a ruling upper class and the mass of wage earners who represent the working class. Similar antagonisms exist in organizations of society between those who exercise authority (like management) and those who are subject to authority (wage earners, clerks). Antagonisms arise out of the opposed interests of different segments of society in the distribution of scarce resources such as wealth, power, and prestige.

Structural-functional theorists may recognize that tensions exist between different segments of society, but they see tensions as temporary expressions of competition for a larger share of the "social pie." Because society is composed of many groups involved in continuous efforts to influence each other, different groups will tend to dominate social life at various times. Sometimes, the influence of religious groups might crucially affect one aspect of social life because religious values are held to be of great importance. For example, in the congressional and presidential elections of 1980, the Moral Majority, a Christian fundamentalist group, was able to influence voters in many states to support candidates who shared their views. Yet on some other issues groups reflecting the interests of the military or of small businesses might have considerable influence. According to conflict theorists, influence is not shared by many groups but is exercised only by those who control economic resources.

The conflict model would lead one to hypothesize that economic institutions are dominant and relatively autonomous. Large corporations and financial institutions exert much greater influence on other institutions (for example, schools, government, church) than can be exerted on them in return. There is considerable evidence supporting this hypothesis, especially in the literature on the influence of giant corporations and research on national and community power structures (Barber, 1970; Galbraith, 1967; Perrucci and Pilisuk, 1970; Useem, 1979, 1980; Zeitlin, 1974). Individuals and groups that control large industrial and financial organizations are able to make sure that national and local governments do not pass legislation that is harmful to them. In 1980, groups representing business interests contributed an estimated $20 million to congressional candidates. In addition, the almost 15,000 lobbyists in Washington, D.C., are overwhelmingly representatives of economic interests, and they dwarf the small number of consumer and public interest lobbies.

The conflict model approach does not deny that social institutions are interrelated and influence each other, but rather it shows that some institutions have greater power than others and are therefore dominant in their relationships with other institutions.

SYSTEM NEEDS: THE NEEDS OF DOMINANT GROUPS

A final point of contrast between the structural-functional and conflict models is the meaning and importance attached to such ideas as "system needs" for stability or for survival. According to conflict theorists, system needs are little more than the needs of specific groups in society. Dominant groups, because of their economic and political power, are able to have their needs or value preferences defined as societal needs. For example, in discussing foreign policy or economic issues, political leaders will frequently assert that "it is in the best interests of the country" to do thus and such. In fact, proposed domestic or foreign policies may be seen as being in the best interests of groups that actively lobby for those policies.

Similarly, conflict theory defines "system survival" as the survival of particular social forms like religious values or private ownership that are in the interest of specific groups in society. Thus, the conflict model does not state that society has particular needs or goals or that society "requires" its citizens to be loyal, patriotic, hard working, or law abiding. Society does not have needs, but individuals and groups do. And not all individuals or groups have an equal chance to have their needs defined as system needs. For instance, people who are poor, black, or female have great difficulty in having their needs defined as system needs by legislators, the great majority of whom are well-to-do, white, and male.

Interactionist Model: Social Behavior as the Building Blocks of Society

Sociologists using a structural-functional or conflict model of society focus on the main characteristics of the overall society and the larger social units that are found in society. In contrast, the **interactionist model** looks at social interaction among individuals and the shared meanings that develop in the course of interaction. Society is not external to the individual but is located *within* the individual and is created by patterned interactions and shared interpretations of reality.

Interactionist theory sees society as in constant flux, rather than as fixed. This is because society is created by the innumerable small forms of social interaction and the meanings associated with interaction. Not only is society created in everyday social interaction but it is constantly being recreated in the same way. Let us try to illustrate this important difference between society as fixed and external to individuals and as constantly changing and within individuals.

Assume that you are interested in understanding the way that rules influence behavior in a school. A structural-functional or conflict theorist would start out by viewing rules as external to individuals. They are written down, they exist before particular individuals enter a school, and they will exist after they leave. Rules are part of a structure that is accepted by people because of shared values about the importance of rules (structural-functional view), or they are accepted because more powerful groups can impose their rules on less powerful groups (conflict view). Thus, rules are external to individuals and constrain them. An interaction theorist would say that rules in a school are recreated everyday in the interactions that take place between teachers and students. Participants in interaction take account of their previous actions when they confront each new situation requiring obedience to a rule. Whether or not a rule will be followed or ignored is a part of the interaction between student and teacher and not something external to it.

There are several major approaches used by interaction theorists. Some interactionists are interested in nonverbal and nonsocial forms of interaction, like eye contact and body movements. For example, research on doctor-patient interaction, using film and video techniques, has indicated how doctors control the medical interview through eye movements and body positions (Psathas, 1968). Pa-

People in face-to-face interaction, using the shared symbols of language, continually recreate the meanings that provide the pattern and regularity of social life.

tients learn when to speak from this set of non-verbal cues. This type of interaction theory, referred to as *ethnomethodology*, believes that the basic rules governing interaction are created in the process of interaction itself and not brought to interaction situations as shared expectations that guide the interaction in a prestructured way.

A second, more popular version of the interactionist perspective is **symbolic interaction** (Blumer, 1969). Sociologists holding this perspective view social life in terms of socially constructed symbols, such as language and gestures, to which people give

meaning in their everyday interactions. These meanings become part of the shared rules governing interaction. But interaction is not guided by a fixed set of meanings and rules that produce the same behaviors repeatedly. It is rather, a process whereby people continually interpret and reinterpret their own actions and those of others.

Another analyst of the symbolic nature of interaction is Goffman (1959, 1972) who often uses a *dramaturgical* model of interaction (using terms like staging, performance, audience). Everyday life, as experienced by individuals, is viewed as a series of performances in which individuals present themselves to others and then try to guide the impression that others form. An examination of "impression management" in interaction allows Goffman to isolate the particular techniques used by people in different situations.

Exchange theory is a view of social interaction (Blau, 1964; Homas, 1961) in which people are engaged in transactions, exchanging social goods of varying value, such as favors, assistance, or ideas. Some exchanges are reciprocal, involving a transfer of goods or services that are felt to be equal. An example would be if you asked your roommate to get you a book from the library in return for which you will include some of his clothes in your load of washing. Some exchanges are unequal and result in the creation of differences among those involved. If a classmate asks your help with a math problem, that person cannot reciprocate by helping you with a math problem. The person receiving help responds by acknowledging your superior talents as a student. You give your time and knowledge and your classmate gives you a superior position. However, the exchange is unequal because one student needs the math help more than the other student needs prestige. Over time, the student providing the math help may be able to extract greater payment without having to provide additional help.

Blau's use of exchange theory is especially important because he attempts to show how more complex forms of social groupings develop out of simpler forms of interaction. For example, unequal exchange relationships between individuals result in differences in power. If A has something that B needs, but A is not dependent on B for anything, then B's dependency makes A more powerful. Blau shows how there can be collective approval of this situation, which gives rise to the socially approved power held by persons in leadership positions. Thus, Blau links the microscopic level of interaction to the societal level of political and organizational power.

An interactionist perspective provides the tools for analyzing the face-to-face interactions of everyday life. As such, it reveals many of the basic features of social life that are ignored by other perspectives that focus on the broader structures of society.

The main characteristics of the three theoretical models discussed in this section are summarized in Table 1.1.

THE PROMISE OF MODERN SOCIOLOGY

Sociology is the scientific study of human society and social behavior. This very large subject is subdivided by sociologists as they study different aspects of social life. Some sociologists concentrate their attention on the way that individuals learn to become social beings (Chapter 6) and the importance of social relationships in small face-to-face groups (Chapter 5). They are also interested in understanding why some persons and groups behave in ways that are very different from the majority (Chapter 7). Social life in human society can also be studied in terms of the main areas of activity in which social relationships occur, such as family life, religion, education, and political and economic activities (Chapters 12 through 16). Finally, some sociologists are interested in the important differences among groups in power, prestige, and wealth, and the way such differences can lead to social conflict (Chapters 8 through 11).

The remainder of this book will examine most of the areas of social life that are studied by sociologists. In this section we will concentrate on the different objectives of modern sociology as they are expressed in the work of sociologists as teachers and researchers.

Sociology as a field is concerned with (1) describing the pattern and regularity found in social interaction and in the relationships among parts of society and (2) testing theories to explain the pattern and regularity of social life. *Some sociologists* are concerned with (3) changing existing social conditions that are felt to be contrary to social values. *Sociologists as educators* are concerned with (4) contributing to the personal liberation of students by expanding their awareness of forces that shape their lives.

The first two objectives are designed to contribute to sociology as a science and to develop a body

TABLE 1.1 Main Characteristics of Theoretical Models of Society

	STRUCTURAL-FUNCTIONAL MODEL	CONFLICT MODEL	INTERACTIONIST MODEL
What is society?	1. Society is a system of interdependent and interacting parts.	1. Society is composed of groups with differential power, wealth, and prestige.	1. Society exists in the face-to-face interactions of everyday life.
Is society real?	2. Society exists independent of, and external to, individuals.	2. Society is external to individuals and is most constraining to groups with the least power.	2. Society only exists when people are in social interaction.
What holds society together?	3. Shared values among individuals and groups are the "social glue" of society.	3. Dominant groups and institutions use coercive power to impose their values on others.	3. Shared meanings and values are created in everyday interaction and must continually be recreated.
What produces stability in society?	4. Society, as a system, has a need for stability and equilibrium.	4. Dominant groups in society have a need for stability of existing social arrangements that are in their interests.	4. Stability is the result of reciprocated exchanges in social interaction.
How is social change viewed?	5. Negatively, because stability and order are the main features of social life.	5. Conflict and change are defined as essential features of social life.	5. Positively, because society is continually changing as it is recreated and redefined in everyday interaction.

of knowledge about society. The third objective is to help contribute to a more harmonious and just social order by *applying* sociological knowledge to solve social problems. The fourth objective deals specifically with sociology's largest audience, the undergraduate student.

The objective of the sociologist as educator is to encourage the undergraduate student to use the study of society to achieve *personal liberation*. One sociologist, C. Wright Mills, suggests that sociology may help students see the connection between their private concerns or problems and the public or societal forces responsible for them. The selection from Mills's *The Sociological Imagination* (Reading 1.1 at the end of the chapter) tries to get people to "step outside of themselves" and view their private experiences in relationship to the wider society. Workers who experience unemployment, say, or young people who experience a sense of alienation from the adult world can come to recognize the societal forces linked to such experiences.

Not all sociologists would agree with the four objectives outlined here or with Mills's views on personal liberation, for these objectives and views reflect important differences in sociological thought. Most important is the difference between the objective of sociology as the pursuit of knowledge and the objective of sociology as social action. The intellectual roots of this distinction in the work of early European and American sociologists are discussed in the next section.

Dual Objectives of Knowledge and Action

Auguste Comte was greatly impressed by the achievements of the physical sciences in the seventeenth and eighteenth centuries and believed that such achievements could be realized in the social world as well. Comte was also influenced by the social philosophers of the time who were engaged in critical examination of all social life, especially political, religious, and social institutions. However, he sought a shift from the "criticism" and "negativism" of the social philosophers, which he viewed as destructive, to the "constructive principles of positive philosophy" (Zeitlin, 1968).

The work of Comte, as well as the work of two major sociologists of a later period, Max Weber (1864–1920) and Emile Durkheim (1858–1917), reveals the basic dilemma over the purposes of sociology and the uses to which it might be put. As we noted earlier, European sociology arose in response to the upheavals of the Industrial Revolution and the French Revolution that transformed the old social order. Comte, Weber, Durkheim, and also Karl Marx (1813–1883) did not simply seek to contribute to a fund of knowledge or to further the development of a discipline. Each hoped that his studies would help solve the social problems that followed the collapse of the old order. They differed, however, on how this was to be accomplished.

Of these giants of early sociology, only Marx was interested in the direct application of his own ideas. For example, Comte's theories and scientific methods were designed to reestablish the harmony and order that had been destroyed by the excessive criticism of the social philosophers. However, Comte cautioned against political action to further these ends, calling instead for changes compatible with the natural laws of evolutionary progress (Zeitlin, 1967). Weber was similarly cautious about the involvement of sociologists in actions based on their scientific studies (Coser, 1971). Marx, on the other hand, showed none of the caution and ambivalence of other European theorists. He viewed the application of theory through social action as fundamental to science. Marx spoke directly to this question: "Science should not be an egoistic pleasure. Those who are fortunate enough to be able to devote themselves to scientific work should be the first to apply their knowledge in the service of humanity" (Quoted in Lafargue, 1890).

The distinction between pure and applied sociology was between the pursuit of knowledge as an end in itself and the pursuit of knowledge to develop solutions to social ills. Discussion of this difference was most intense among American sociologists, for it is in the United States that sociology developed most rapidly as an academic discipline and as a profession. Sociology had to be distinguished from other academic disciplines before it could have a place in the university's structure of departments. Moreover, people who called themselves sociologists had to distinguish themselves from social workers, reformers, theologians, political scientists, historians, and psychologists.

The different views on whether the primary objective of sociology should be theory building (pure sociology) or social reform (applied sociology) may be seen in statements made by sociologists during the formative years of the discipline. William Graham Sumner (1840–1910), proponent of a philosophy called social Darwinism, believed that Charles Darwin's ideas of evolution, and the "survival of the fittest" in the struggle among animal species, could be applied to human societies; therefore, it was not possible to change or improve society through reform, since "laws" of social evolution would determine the course of social change.

In 1894, Sumner wrote an essay entitled "The Absurd Effort to Make the World Over," in which he expressed his view that knowledge should be pursued for its own sake. "I propose to define science as knowledge of reality because "truth" is used in such a variety of senses. I do not know whether it is possible for us ever to arrive at a knowledge of "the truth" in regard to any important matters. I doubt if it is possible. It is not important. It is the pursuit of truth which gives us life, and it is to that pursuit that our loyalty is due" (Davie, 1963, p. 10).

Lester Frank Ward (1841–1913), another influential figure in American sociology at the turn of the century, had very different views on the role of sociology as a science. Ward believed in the role of reform as an instrument of social change and as an active means of directing social progress. He stated: "The real object of science is to benefit man. A science which fails to do this, however agreeable its study, is lifeless. Sociology, which of all sciences should benefit man most, is in danger of falling into the class of polite amusements, or dead sciences" (Vol. 1, p. xxvii).

The sharp contrast between Sumner and Ward on knowledge versus action in sociology may be seen many times in the work of other sociologists in this century (Davis, 1940; Gelfand, 1975; Janowitz, 1972; Rossi, 1980; Young, 1955). Even though most sociological research is not labeled as pure or applied, there are important differences among sociologists in the kind of research questions that they ask and the intended audience for their findings, that indicate their position. Some research, because of the way it is designed, yields results that are useful to activist community groups involved in efforts to change legislation on school policies, to business organizations interested in worker productivity, or to welfare agencies trying to determine the needs of clients. Other research examines questions of long-standing concern to the discipline of sociology and is of interest primarily to academic scholars.

The fact that the question of the proper role of sociology is still being debated suggests that it is part of the very nature of sociology and perhaps also of the nature of people who become sociologists.

Should Sociology Be a Value-Free Science?

Another critical point of difference among sociologists centers on the question: Is it possible or even desirable for sociologists to carry out their scholarly work without being influenced by personal values? Those who argue for a **value-free** sociology often cite the views of Max Weber. Weber noted that sociologists often use a mixture of scientific criteria and personal values as a guide in the selection of research problems. A sociologist who chooses to study the effects of poverty upon the school performance of young children is probably expressing an interest in both the scientific question of how human behavior is shaped and a social concern about the existence of poverty in an affluent society.

However, Weber also stated that once a research problem is selected, sociologists must be concerned with "what is," not "what ought to be." Sociologists make "is statements" in their role as scientists. "Ought statements" are made in one's role as a citizen and must not be used in one's scientific work. For example, a sociologist may report the results of a study showing the positive and negative consequences of abortion ("is statements"). He/she

may not say that, based on the research findings, abortion ought to be permitted by the state or prohibited by the state. "Ought statements" are based on social and personal values, which may differ among sociologists as well as among different segments of society.

Adherents of a value-free sociology believe that personal values of sociologists can and should be excluded from their work. They also feel that sociology as a profession, embodied in the American Sociological Association, should not take positions on particular social issues such as busing, abortion, or disarmament. Allowing values to influence scientific judgments, they say, can lead to a loss of public support for sociology, a decline in its development as a science, and the reduction of sociology to little more than politics.

Most critics of a value-free sociology are not arguing for particular political values or for research that simply furthers social reform. They believe, however, that value neutrality is difficult, if not impossible, to attain—for sociologists, as well as for other scientists, scholars, or laypersons. As Alvin Gouldner (1962) pointed out, sociologists cannot divorce themselves from current political and social ideas. They must choose what to study, how to study it, what the most important findings are, what conclusions can be drawn, and who their audiences are—all of which reflect their values, biases, predispositions, and assumptions.

Obviously, no one wants sociologists to distort their research or to suppress findings that do not agree with their own values. There is little protection in scholarly research against falsification of findings. Scientists must rely on each other's commitment to the pursuit of truth *and* upon the possibility that attempts to repeat a given study will reveal unethical manipulation of results.*

---

*Replication of a study requires that each original procedure be repeated exactly to see if the results can be duplicated. True replication is easier to achieve in the physical sciences than in the social sciences, making the latter disciplines more vulnerable to "undiscovered errors," whether purposeful or accidental. An excellent example of how the physical sciences can detect efforts to falsify data may be found in the story of a young scientist who is alleged to have tampered with skin transplants on white mice so that he could falsely claim to have made certain discoveries. See "The Sloan-Kettering Affair" in *Science*, May 1974 and June 1974.

Perhaps the best that sociologists can do to protect their work against value "contamination" is to state their values explicitly so that readers may judge for themselves if the analysis is biased. The Swedish economist-sociologist Gunnar Myrdal (1944) took this position in his monumental study of race relations in the United States: "There is no other device for excluding biases in social sciences than to face the valuations and to introduce them as explicitly stated, specific, and sufficiently concretized value premises" (p. 1043).

Howard S. Becker (1967) seems to go somewhat further than Myrdal when he calls for sociologists to "take sides" in an issue. If, for example, sociologists are studying police-community relations, Becker believes they should conduct the study from the point of view of either the police or the community.*

Teachers of sociology are also not immune to the problem of introducing their own values in what they teach. Should sociologists 30 years ago have been more critical of the racist laws and beliefs that kept blacks and whites in two separate school systems? What about today? Should teachers take a clear value-based position in the classroom on such matters as gay rights, abortion, or the equal rights amendment? Or should they remain neutral, teaching only "what is" rather than "what ought to be"?

A final problem facing sociologists in trying to develop a value-free science is that establishing the "facts" ("what is" statements) is a complex process. Sociologists studying the same question, but using different theoretical models may obtain the same factual data but they will offer different interpretations and draw different conclusions. Structural-functional, conflict, and interaction theorists probably would agree on the amount of poverty in the United States, but they would have very different views on its causes.

The debate is far from over. However, the issue can be clarified by making a distinction between the discipline of sociology and the practitioners of the discipline when discussing value-free sociology. This position is stated most clearly by Peter Berger (1971):

*For a criticism of Becker's position and a discussion of the direct use of values in one's studies, see Gouldner (1968).

The discipline of sociology, I insist as emphatically as I can, must be value-free . . . The moment the discipline ceases to be value-free in principle it ceases to be a science and becomes nothing but ideology [and] propaganda . . . *The practitioner of the discipline*, the sociologist— a living human being—must *not* be value-free. The moment he is, he betrays his humanity and . . . transforms himself into a ghostly embodiment of abstract science. (p. 5)

The discipline of sociology can remain value-free because sociologists care about the quality of the information, that is, the data, that they use in their studies. All sociologists are concerned about whether people tell the truth when they are interviewed. They want to know that crime statistics collected by the Federal Bureau of Investigation accurately reflect the number of crimes committed. Unless sociologists can have some degree of faith in the data they use, they will be unable to make any systematic and reliable statements about the social world.

Concern over the quality of data has led sociologists to develop and share a body of techniques called a methodology for collecting, processing, and analyzing the data of experience. The methods are value-free in that they should yield the same results in the hands of a liberal or a conservative, of a theory-builder or a social reformer.

Chapter 2 discusses the methodology used in sociological research as well as the different objectives of research.

SUMMARY

The sociological way of looking at the world places special emphasis on society as a set of influences that are external to, and constraining upon, individuals. Human societies exhibit a high degree of pattern and regularity, expressed through recurring forms of social structure and social behavior. It is the task of sociological analysis to investigate the factors contributing to pattern and regularity and the forces that change them.

Despite this unifying concern of sociology, it is also clear that sociology is not a discipline with a single set of assumptions about the meaning and purpose of sociological work. Sociology was established amidst the social turmoil of industrialization, urban growth, and political revolution in Europe and North America. Some of the early sociologists were interested primarily in developing a science of society and searching for knowledge for its own sake. Others wanted to use the knowledge of sociology to solve social problems like crime, delinquency, and mental illness. Differences between the advocates of pure knowledge and the advocates of social reform continue in contemporary sociology and influence the kinds of research done by sociologists. In Chapter 2, for example, we examine the differences between basic research, which is concerned with developing sociological knowledge, and applied research, which is concerned with eliminating some social problem.

There is no single sociological view of how human societies are organized. We have presented three theoretical perspectives most frequently used by sociologists to guide their study of society: (1) the structural-functional model, which emphasizes the elements of cohesion, shared values, and equilibrium as bases of social order; (2) the conflict model, which views society as shaped by the interests of powerful and dominant groups and the antagonisms of opposing classes and groups struggling over the distribution of scarce resources; and (3) the interactionist model, which chooses to study the smallest units of social interaction in the hope that by discovering their basic laws it will be possible to understand the larger structure of social life.

The promise of sociology rests in (1) its potential for becoming a science of society, (2) the use of its theories and methods to solve social problems, and (3) the insight it provides in helping people to relate personal problems to the societal forces that produce them. Students of society must confront the question of whether it is possible or desirable for sociology to be a value-free science. Can sociologists carry out their research without being influenced by personal values? There are several answers to this question. Some say that values may influence one's choice of topics to study, but that they must be kept out of the research process itself.

Others feel that values influence every stage of the research process and it is therefore best to make one's values explicit.

GLOSSARY

Comte, Auguste   founder of sociology (1798–1857). He stressed the importance of obtaining factual data about society.

Conflict model   a view of society as made up of antagonistic groups with different amounts of economic power that relate to each other in patterns of dominance and subordination.

Constraints   pressures that groups exert on their members to make sure that their ideas and behavior are consistent with the groups' norms.

Exchange theory   a version of the interaction model that sees interaction in terms of transactions in which social goods like favors, time, or ideas are exchanged.

Industrialization   a shift of the labor force from agriculture to manufacturing.

Industrial Revolution   a shift from hand labor to the use of machine tools and mechanized production of goods, generally assumed to have started in late eighteenth-century England.

Interactionist model   a view of society as composed of elementary patterns of social interaction among persons.

Social values   goals and standards in which people have great emotional investment.

Society   interacting individuals and interrelated groups sharing a common culture and territory.

Structural-functional model   a view of society as made up of interdependent parts and common values, existing in stability and equilibrium.

Symbolic interaction   a version of the interaction model that sees interaction taking place through socially constructed symbols such as language and gestures.

Value-free   sociological research uncontaminated by influence of the investigator's personal values.

ADDITIONAL READINGS

Berger, Peter L. *Invitation to Sociology.* Garden City, N.Y.: Anchor Books, 1963.
A short, concise introduction to the field of sociology which emphasizes the "humanistic" side of the discipline. Examines different perspectives on the role of the sociologist.

Collins, Randall. *Conflict Sociology.* New York: Academic Press, 1975.
Chapter 1 provides a good introduction to sociology as a science in contrast to a variety of approaches not directed toward building an explanatory science. Chapter 2 contains a discussion of the conflict perspective in contemporary sociology.

Foss, Dennis C. *The Value Controversy in Sociology.* San Francisco: Jossey-Bass, 1977.
Students interested in the debate over whether sociology can be, is, or should be, value-free will find this book very useful. Opposing views on the question are examined and an alternative approach is presented that attempts to clarify the relationship between facts and values.

Horton, John. "Order and Conflict Theories of Social Problems as Competing Ideologies." *American Journal of Sociology* 71 (May 1966): 701–13.
Contrasts the major assumptions and approaches found in the two dominant, but conflicting, perspectives on contemporary society. Examines the implications of these perspectives for dealing with societal problems.

Inkeles, Alex. What *Is* Sociology. Englewood Cliffs, N.J.: Prentice-Hall, 1965.
A short, concise introduction to the field of sociology which emphasizes the "scientific" side of the discipline.

Lyman, Stanford M. and Scott, Marvin B. *A Sociology of the Absurd.* New York: Appleton-Century-Crofts, 1970.
This book challenges the prevailing assumption of sociology that the social world has an order and meaning that can be discovered with the methods of science. It holds, instead, the view that all meanings and beliefs, including those of sociologists and ordinary men, are arbitrary human constructions.

Paloma, Margaret M. *Contemporary Sociological Theory.* New York: Macmillan, 1979.
A collection of papers dealing with most of the major theoretical approaches used by sociologists today. Useful for students who want additional information on structural-functionalism, conflict, and symbolic interaction theory.

Williams, Robin M., Jr., *American Society,* 3rd ed. New York: Knopf, 1970.
An introduction to sociology. Basic sociological concepts are examined in Chapter 3. For a treatment of values and American value systems, see Chapter 11.

Wrong, Dennis H. "The Oversocialized Conception of Man in Modern Society." *American Sociological Review* 26 (April 1961): 183–93.
Criticism of major themes in sociology that see people as easily socialized and social and which ignore certain basic aspects of their nature.

READING

The Promise of Sociology
C. Wright Mills

Nowadays men often feel that their private lives are a series of traps. They sense that within their everyday worlds, they cannot overcome their troubles, and in this feeling, they are often quite correct: What ordinary men are directly aware of and what they try to do are bounded by the private orbits in which they live; their visions and their powers are limited to the close-up scenes of job, family, neighborhood; in other milieux, they move vicariously and remain spectators. And the more aware they become, however vaguely, of ambitions and of threats which transcend their immediate locales, the more trapped they seem to feel.

Underlying this sense of being trapped are seemingly impersonal changes in the very structure of continent-wide societies. The facts of contemporary history are also facts about the success and the failure of individual men and women. When a society is industrialized, a peasant becomes a worker; a feudal lord is liquidated or becomes a businessman. When classes rise or fall, a man is employed or unemployed; when the rate of investment goes up or down, a man takes new heart or goes broke. When wars happen, an insurance salesman becomes a rocket launcher; a store clerk, a radar man; a wife lives alone; a child grows up without a father. Neither the life of an individual nor the history of a society can be understood without understanding both.

Yet men do not usually define the troubles they endure in terms of historical change and institutional contradiction. The well-being they enjoy, they do not usually impute to the big ups and downs of the societies in which they live. Seldom aware of the intricate connection between the patterns of their own lives and the course of world history, ordinary men do not usually know what this connection means for the kinds of men they are becoming and for the kinds of history-making in which they might take part. They do not possess the quality of mind essential to grasp the interplay of man and society, of biography and history, of self and world. They cannot cope with their personal troubles in such ways as to control the structural transformations that usually lie behind them.

Surely it is no wonder. In what period have so many men been so totally exposed at so fast a pace to such earthquakes of change? That Americans have not known such catastrophic changes as have the men and women of other societies is due to historical facts that are now quickly becoming 'merely history.' The history that now affects every man is world history. Within this scene and this period, in the course of a single generation, one sixth of mankind is transformed from all that is feudal and backward into all that is modern, advanced, and fearful. Political colonies are freed; new and less visible forms of imperialism installed. Revolutions occur; men feel the intimate grip of new kinds of authority. Totalitarian societies rise, and are smashed to bits— or succeed fabulously. After two centuries of ascendancy, capitalism is shown up as only one way to make society into an industrial apparatus. After two centuries of hope, even formal democracy is restricted to a quite small portion of mankind. Everywhere in the underdeveloped world, ancient ways of life are broken up and vague expectations become urgent demands. Everywhere in the overdeveloped world, the means of authority and of violence become total in scope and bureaucratic in form. Humanity itself now lies before us, the super-nation at either pole concentrating its most co-ordinated and massive efforts upon the preparation of World War Three.

SOURCE: From *The Sociological Imagination* by C. Wright Mills. Copyright © 1959 by *Oxford University Press, Inc.* Reprinted by permission.

The very shaping of history now outpaces the ability of men to orient themselves in accordance with cherished values. And which values? Even when they do not panic, men often sense that older ways of feeling and thinking have collapsed and that newer beginnings are ambiguous to the point of moral stasis. Is it any wonder that ordinary men feel they cannot cope with the larger worlds with which they are so suddenly confronted? That they cannot understand the meaning of their epoch for their own lives? That—in defense of selfhood—they become morally insensible, trying to remain altogether private men? Is it any wonder that they come to be possessed by a sense of the trap?

It is not only information that they need—in this Age of Fact, information often dominates their attention and overwhelms their capacities to assimilate it. It is not only the skills of reason that they need—although their struggles to acquire these often exhaust their limited moral energy.

What they need, and what they feel they need, is a quality of mind that will help them to use information and to develop reason in order to achieve lucid summations of what is going on in the world and of what may be happening within themselves. It is this quality, I am going to contend, that journalists and scholars, artists and publics, scientists and editors are coming to expect of what may be called the sociological imagination.*

---

*The authors would like to point out the predominant use of the male pronoun in the article by Mills. The English language historically has used the male gender for individuals and general units ("Nowadays men often feel . . ."), and thus has presented certain social roles as sex-linked ("A doctor must serve an internship before he practices.").

Throughout this book we have tried to overcome this style, which in its own subtle way has perpetuated sexist attitudes. We have not always been successful, for the English language itself often does not allow construction of smooth, clear, gender-free sentences. However, wherever possible, we have tried to use (a) the phrase he or she, (b) neuter words, such as person or human, or (c) plural forms.

SUMMARY

The promise of sociology, according to Mills, is that in the chaos of modern life it can help us understand what is happening to us and why. To the extent that we can grasp our relationship to history, we may feel less trapped by personal problems. The realization of the connection between our biography and our history may indeed lead to a loss of the feeling of powerlessness and to greater participation in public affairs that have direct bearing on our private lives.

QUESTIONS

1. Why is it that people today feel increasingly powerless despite their greater access to information?
2. Can greater knowledge of the social forces that shape our lives increase our participation in public affairs?
3. What may society be like in the year 2000 if people continue to withdraw into their private lives?

CHAPTER 2

Sociological Research: Objectives and Methods

CONTENTS

Should some practices used in sociological research be prohibited?

Although there have been great benefits associated with scientific research, many people are concerned with the growing instances where the consequences of research to society and research subjects have not been considered. Some believe that the risks of research have increased and that something must be done to control new scientific developments. Others feel that science can only develop when there is great freedom for research and that only scientists can judge when controls are needed.

YES   In 1932 physicians from the United States Public Health Service devised an experiment to determine what the effects of syphilis were if the disease was left untreated. They traveled to Tuskegee, Alabama, where they identified 400 syphilitic black men from rural Alabama.* The illiterate sharecroppers were told that they had "bad blood" and were promised free treatment in return for their cooperation in the experiment. The "treatment" they believed they were receiving consisted, in reality, of diagnostic examinations and placebos, unmedicated preparations. For 40 years treatment was withheld from these subjects so the researchers could follow the progress of the disease until they died and autopsies could be performed.

The price of progress in medical science has often been paid for by human experimentation on the poor, imprisoned, women, and blacks. Despite the apparently benign motivation of physicians engaged in such experiments to help the poor and the sick, much of this research is ethically unjustified, or at least questionable.

Although sociological researchers are not likely to put their subjects of study in situations of physical risk, they often engage in the same unethical practices found in the Tuskegee experiment. Three practices are of special concern.

First, sociologists often use deception to gain access to social settings or to gain the cooperation of subjects. Researchers may misrepresent the true purposes of a study for fear that cooperation would otherwise be withheld. In some cases deception is essential for the study, for a fully informed subject would no longer be a suitable respondent. The second concern is that those persons being studied may not benefit, directly or indirectly, from their participation in the research. Third, subjects of sociological research are most likely to be members of vulnerable groups in society, with little or no ability to refuse to participate in studies when invited to do so. There are more studies of the poor than of the rich, of prisons and mental hospitals than of corporations, of street gangs than of the military, and of ethnic minorities than of high status groups.

The sociological profession should establish clear guidelines for researchers to follow when dealing with human subjects. People in institutions like prisons or hospitals, and those in vulnerable positions, like welfare recipients, should be protected against the subtle pressure that is often used to gain subjects' cooperation. In addition, subjects should receive some benefits from the studies in which they participate. Researchers should be obligated to contribute something from their research to persons or groups directly involved in the research or closely associated with the subjects. Without such guidelines, sociological research will continue to be exploitive and ethically unjustified.

*Source: James H. Jones, *Bad Blood: The Tuskegee Syphilis Experiment* (New York: Free Press, 1981)

NO   Science is a widely shared value in the United States. Most people have come to support science because they believe that scientific research can yield many benefits that will improve the quality of life for most citizens. Medical research has resulted in the ability to limit the effects of many diseases afflicting both the very young and very old. Social research has helped us to deal more effectively and humanely with persons served by public institutions such as schools, nursing homes, and hospitals. Agricultural research has greatly increased food yields. Research in the biological sciences on the mechanisms of heredity promises to eliminate many birth defects.

Most of these advances could not have been realized without some degree of direct or indirect risk to the people involved in the research. Medical research with organ transplants or cancer chemotherapy has been carried out on children and adults who consented to participate with the understanding that while they might not benefit, others might be helped in the future. Research in pesticides and insecticides was conducted with a probability of risk of contaminating food and water supplies. And social experiments designed to improve social institutions cannot fully inform their subjects without seriously damaging the scientific nature of the investigation. For example, income maintenance experiments were designed to see how welfare recipients would use different dollar amounts to supplement their income. Subjects could not be informed that supplements were of varied amounts and they were led to believe that everyone was getting the same amount of additional income. This deception made it possible to learn how much additional income was needed to produce some change in the recipient's behavior.

In most research, benefits, both direct and long term, far exceed the costs in the form of risk to subjects. Recently issued federal regulations governing research with human subjects require clear specifications of potential risk factors and "informed consent" procedures.

The extremely rare instances of questionable ethical practices in experiments involving human subjects should not be used as the basis for developing policies for all such research. Efforts to legislate ethical procedures are not only doomed to failure, but they will also do great harm to research in general. Scientific research flourishes best in an atmosphere of maximum freedom. Control over research, including the establishment of ethical standards of practice, must be in the hands of scientists themselves.

This chapter is concerned with the application of the scientific method to sociological research. The objectives of sociological research, the different questions that are asked, and the stages in the research process are discussed. The topic of this "At Issue" is treated in greater detail in a section on the ethical problems of research.

QUESTIONS TO CONSIDER

■ What is the difference between a sociological problem and a social problem?

■ Can applied social research contribute to the development of a science of society?

■ How do you protect against mistreatment of subjects in research?

■ What are the main stages in the research process and how are they interrelated?

Everyone knows that the crime rate in the United States has been on the increase in the last 20 years. Right? No, wrong!

Well, at least we all know that the typical family in America has a father who is the breadwinner, a mother who is a homemaker, and two children. Right? No, wrong again!

One last try. People who are poor in the United States do not have the same desire to work or hold the same aspirations for themselves and their children as do most Americans. Sorry. This is another false statement and another popular belief that is not supported by sociological research.

The knowledge that many of us have about human society is often based upon tradition or widely shared beliefs with little factual basis. The knowledge that sociologists try to obtain about human society is most often based on systematic observation of the social world. Sociologists, whether their objectives are to understand society or to change society, must carry out carefully planned investigations to develop new knowledge. Such investigations, or research studies, are guided by procedural rules that make up the **methodology** of research. This methodology, often referred to as the scientific method, is a set of procedures for making observations of the empirical world (facts) and for interpreting those observations (theories). Textbook descriptions of

scientific methods and empirical research are often idealized, probably to make it easier to describe scientific research. Unfortunately, such descriptions are written as if scientists were not people and the research process itself not a social activity.

Scientists select ideas to study in many ways. Some research ideas are simply attempts to test or modify ideas reported in previous research literature. Other studies may develop out of an intense personal interest in a question (Hammond, 1967; Koestler, 1964). Once an idea is chosen, the way in which the study is actually carried out can be understood only partly by the rules and logic of scientific inquiry. Competition among scientists to be the first to publish may be the most important consideration in choosing different research strategies. The competition to discover the structure of the DNA molecule, the code of genetic life, led to antagonisms and secretive behavior between research teams rather than collaboration (Sayre, 1975; Watson, 1968).

An excellent example of how the research process resists simple explanation is found in an account of the work of two distinguished medical scientists. Sociologists Bernard Barber and Renee Fox (1958) report that each scientist, working independently, was injecting rabbits with the same enzyme. Each scientist observed that the ears of the rabbits would "flop" following the injections. One scientist ignored the effect and continued the study as planned. The other scientist became interested in the effect and studied it, although it had nothing to do with the original research question. As a result, the second scientist made some important discoveries about the drug cortisone.

Some research, like that with the floppy-eared rabbit, is characterized by **serendipity**, or the chance discovery of outcomes that were not being sought (Merton, 1957). It is impossible to know how scientists will react to a serendipitous finding. Two scientists observed floppy-eared rabbits. One ignored the observation. The other went on to make a breakthrough in scientific knowledge.

Thus, textbook descriptions of sociological research can be poor representations of what sociologists actually do. The ideal description, however, is a useful beginning.

OBJECTIVES OF SOCIOLOGICAL RESEARCH

Although sociological research may satisfy multiple purposes, it can be described according to its primary objective as either basic or applied. **Basic research** is concerned with making contributions to a body of theoretical knowledge about human society, regardless of the possible usefulness of such theories. Such research is aimed at influencing a discipline or a group of scientists. This does not mean that basic research is not useful, for as someone has once said, "there is nothing so practical as a good theory." Rather, it means that the purposes of the researcher may have nothing to do with practical or useful knowledge. As Rossi (1980) has noted, basic research has often had very applied consequences, while applied research has often contributed to basic sociology.

Applied research is concerned with using sociological knowledge to answer questions of interest to a specific client. It may involve such things as consultation to business or government, evaluation of social programs, and designing projects to create social change. For example, the client may be a public agency, like a community mental health center. The center may be interested in knowing how well it is serving the mental health needs of clients in its area. The applied researcher tries to design a research study that will answer the client's questions. The researcher must work closely with the client when conducting research or using existing knowledge on behalf of the client.

Basic Research: Development of Empirically Based Theory

The primary objective of basic sociological research is to provide evidence of patterned social relationships and explanations of how and why these patterns develop. These explanations are called theories, which are, as we learned in Chapter 1, statements that help to organize and make sense of the patterns we observe in empirical facts. For example, suppose that you had obtained data (empirical facts) that students in certain housing units showed a consistent pattern of higher grades than students in other housing units. Without a theory to explain the facts, you would not know why the patterns occur. It could be because of differences in basic intelligence, or differences in the students' field of study, or differences in the dominant values (academic achievement or social activities) found in the housing units.

Basic research looks for answers to questions that interest a particular group of sociologists. For example, for some time sociologists have tried to determine the particular characteristics of groups that make the groups better able to control the behavior of their members. The size of the group and the interdependence of group members are two factors that have been identified. Basic research on this sociological problem would attempt to set up a study that models the relationship between these group characteristics and the group's control over its members. Sociological journals are the media for discussing this and others sociological questions.

Applied Research: Evaluation and Action

The second major type of research is applied research. Its purpose is to provide information about some social condition that is of interest to a particular client. The results of applied research are often used to solve a social problem—a condition that is contrary to the way some group would like it to be. For example, sociologists are frequently called upon to use their specialized knowledge in *evaluation research*, which obtains information on the actual or anticipated consequences of some existing or planned program. The results of such research may be used to improve the performance by public and private agencies on some existing or planned program.

Some years ago legislation was enacted by the U.S. Congress to establish alternatives to the state mental hospital system where most people with severe psychological problems were eventually committed. Community-based clinics were supposed to provide outpatient care for clients so that they could remain in their homes and at their jobs while still receiving medical care. Reducing admissions to state mental hospitals was expected to reduce the cost of care for mental health services and to improve the chances for effective treatment.

An evaluation research project could attempt to determine if there was a significant reduction in hospital admissions and in the cost of care as a result of expanding community mental health facilities. The results of such studies would be used to shape policy decisions affecting future programs giving assistance to psychologically handicapped people.

In evaluation research the sociologist provides knowledge and identifies the possible consequences of different courses of action to be taken by clients. However, the sociologist is removed from the final decision or action phase of the project. In some cases, the sociologist may not even have a personal interest in the particular course of action that follows from the evaluation project.

Action research, a subtype of evaluation research, brings the sociologist into a direct relationship with a specific program of change and in direct contact with the change agents. For example, a community action group may be concerned about the lack of medical care available to their low-income constituency. However, they do not know whether this is due to the cost of medical care, the availability of physicians, or the geographical location of care facilities. A sociologist could provide knowledge and research skills to answer these questions and thereby help the group put pressure on the medical power structure to create a low-cost community health clinic.

In this form of action research the sociologist is a member of the community action group and is identified with its objectives. It is clear that the role of the action researcher is not passive and it is not value-free. Some sociologists would not do this kind of applied research because it is contrary to their scientific or political values. (Some sociologists would not do policy research for the Republican or Democratic parties for the same reason.)

In Reading 1.1 William F. Whyte, president of the American Sociological Association in 1981, proposes that sociology should redirect its efforts in the area of applied research. In particular, he suggests greater study of social inventions, the things that communities and organizations do to solve some of their human problems.

ASKING AND ANSWERING SOCIOLOGICAL QUESTIONS

The most difficult and creative part of the sociological research process is asking a question that is important enough to study or phrasing a question in a way that makes it researchable. An important question has a way of shattering existing understandings and assumptions about a particular problem. A question clearly and unambiguously stated can more easily be translated into a researchable question by identifying the kind of data needed for the research.

After having asked an important or a researchable question, the investigator must determine the *level of analysis* that will be followed. Level of analysis refers to the particular social units that will be examined in the research and how abstract they are. Individuals are less abstract than groups because they can be more directly observed and measured. In the same way, groups are less abstract than organizations or social classes.

Choosing a level of analysis is not a trivial matter. The kind of knowledge that is gained will obviously be limited to the social units that have been studied. More important, in applied research studies the level of analysis chosen determines the kind of social changes that can be recommended to improve a particular social condition.

For example, assume that we are interested in why adolescents in high school differ in their ambitions, aspirations, and performance. Such a question can be of interest because it can contribute to basic knowledge of human behavior. It can also be of applied interest in that we might want to open up job opportunities for adolescents by improving school performance. There are three approaches that a sociologist might take in examining this question. Each approach illustrates a different level of analysis.

Individual Level of Analysis

One approach to the research question is to look for the role played by individual psychological and social characteristics in shaping ambitions and school performance of adolescents. For example, one might hypothesize that intelligence (IQ) in combination with an achievement-oriented personality are primarily responsible.

Another individual level approach might be to analyze the influence of social characteristics like socioeconomic status or sex roles in shaping ambitions and performance. Students from lower socioeconomic background are said to receive less encouragement from parents about school performance and may thereby develop pessimistic views of what the future holds for them (Han, 1969; Della-Fave, 1974; Hyman, 1953). In the same way, adolescent girls might be socialized to think of themselves in future roles as wives and mothers rather than as scientists or managers. Growing up under such circumstances may lead adolescents to develop lowered ambitions and to place less value on school performance.

Group Level of Analysis

The group level of analysis looks at the social groups in which people reside as the main influence upon social behavior. In the research question we are considering, the sociologist would examine adolescents' social groups and the role of group standards in shaping performance and ambition. Some researchers believe that the school performance levels of boys and girls are more strongly influenced by the norms and values of their social groups in the school than by their intelligence, personality, or socioeconomic standing (Alexander and Eckland, 1975; Hauser et al., 1976; Otto and Alwin, 1977).

An excellent example of this approach is a study by the sociologist James Coleman (1961) that examined 10 high schools in Illinois in search of the way group standards influence performance. Coleman found that each school was dominated by a "leading crowd," which emphasized sports, social life, and dating rather than academic performance. The norms and values of the leading crowd had greater influence on students than did their sex or socioeconomic standing.

Structural Level of Analysis

At the structural level of analysis the sociologist examines the social settings in which people live as a source of influence on their social behavior. For example, characteristics of a community like residential density or racial diversity can affect its residents' beliefs and behavior. Residents of a densely populated, racially integrated community will probably have different views on race relations than residents of rural or segregated communities.

When sociologists use this level of analysis to understand the ambitions and performance of students, they will examine the policies, practices, and resources of schools (Alexander, et al., 1978; Rosenbaum, 1978, 1980). Schools are known to vary in terms of the quality of their teachers. Experienced and better trained teachers, especially in specialty areas like mathematics, music, and science, may command higher salaries and better working conditions. If a school system lacks financial resources it may not be able to attract better teachers.

Schools are also known to vary in the quality of their equipment and laboratories. Student interest and knowledge in many subjects will be limited when they have to work with outmoded and poor equipment.

Finally, schools differ in their policies and practices in "streaming" or "tracking" students who are assumed to differ in ability. A student who is assumed to have low ability and is thereby placed in a vocational track in high school receives a very different educational experience than one who is in a college track. Such placement may result in a "self-fulfilling prophecy": A student is defined as having low ability, is placed in a situation that makes it difficult to prove otherwise, and therefore does in fact exhibit lower performance.

Conclusions of Individual, Group, and Structural Analyses

Let us assume that the research results of our sample question will be used to remedy the problem of reduced ambition and performance of adolescents. The three different levels of analysis will produce widely different actions. The first approach assumes that some individuals are deficient in intelligence or achievement or favorable perceptions of the future. Therefore, remedies might involve counseling students about their future or special programs to improve their ability and desire for achievement.

The second approach would seek ways to "penetrate" student groups and influence them to develop rewards for academic performance. Group influence on the individual would still prevail, but now it would be directed to encouraging academic achievement rather than social achievement. Student leaders and the leading crowd would exemplify norms and values that would produce improved student performance and greater ambition.

The third approach would emphasize changes in the way school districts obtain and distribute economic resources to specific schools. Schools in lower socioeconomic areas obtain less money from public taxes, while in middle and upper income areas there is more money available for better teachers and facilities. In addition, higher income communities provide a great many nonschool activities and resources that stimulate student's interests and indirectly contribute to school performance. Community libraries, museums, film programs, science fairs, and the like all contribute to a richer and more stimulating intellectual environment for children.

Thus, we see that the particular level of analysis selected by sociologists when doing basic or applied research shapes not only the kind of knowledge obtained but also the kind of social programs that might follow.

Studying Individuals, Groups, and Social Structures

In the previous section we used as an example of a research problem the question of why adolescents in high school differ in their ambitions, aspirations, and performance. Differences in the way adolescents behave in school is the social phenomenon that we want to explain. What we want to explain in research is called the **dependent variable.** The factors that we think are responsible for causing differences in the dependent variable are called **independent variables.** In the discussion of the three levels of analysis, we identified three different sets of independent variables that we thought could be responsible for variations in our dependent variable. Let us illustrate this in Table 2.1.

For each of these levels of analysis individuals are studied as the dependent variable. However, we are interested in adolescents as representatives of a social category, *not as individuals.* We are seeking to explain differences in the frequency of occurrence of some behavior, rather than why particular individuals exhibited the behavior. Sociologists who study crime are less interested in the life histories of individual criminals than in

TABLE 2.1   Levels of Analysis in Sociological Research

	INDEPENDENT VARIABLES	DEPENDENT VARIABLES
Individual level of analysis	Intelligence Achieving personality	School performance of adolescents
Group level of analysis	Peer group values Importance of peer group to students	School performance of adolescents
Structural level of analysis	Quality of teachers Quality of curriculum resources	School performance of adolescents

what makes certain groups of people more likely to engage in crime.

Sociologists are also interested in studying groups as dependent variables, that is, they may want to explain why social groups differ in some fashion. For example, groups such as families differ in whether they have rigid or flexible sex-based division of responsibilities. In some families males and females have sharply differentiated and non-overlapping responsibilities (for example, shopping, cooking, childcare, financial matters), while other families have less sex-based differentiation of tasks. Independent variables such as family size, employment status of members, and duration of marriage might be used to explain the variations in the dependent variable of sex-based divisions of labor in the family.

Finally, sociologists study larger social structures such as organizations, social classes, or cities as dependent variables and attempt to understand what is responsible for their variations. Examples of such research and of the kind of independent variables that are involved will be discussed in Chapters 8, 9, and 17.

THE RESEARCH PROCESS

All research projects are conducted with constraints of money, time, and personnel. During the course of the project, the sociologist makes related decisions about research design and procedures that have costs and benefits in terms of money, time, and the quality of the data obtained. Each decision also requires the sociologist to adapt to the conditions with which he or she is faced. Limited funds may require the researcher to interview fewer people than planned, to ask fewer questions, or to sacrifice depth of information for broader coverage of topics.

Selecting a Research Problem

Some research is born when sociologists get into discussions with students or colleagues or when they discover contradictory findings in sociological literature. The idea emerges out of a state of tension or disagreement between two logical arguments, two sets of research findings, or an alternate explanation for a widely held belief about reasons for

Large social research projects, especially those involving national issues like access to health care or the impact of unemployment are usually conducted at research centers with a staff of trained social scientists, statisticians, and data analysts. Here we see the building of the Institute of Social Research at the University of Michigan.

social behaviors that people have long assumed to be true but have never tested.

One of the authors recently conducted research on mental illness and the conditions for commitment to mental hospitals (Perrucci and Targ, 1982). The genesis of this research was a long-standing scientific dispute about the nature of mental illness. One theory holds that mental illness is a disease, like cancer or diabetes, and that the peculiar or unusual behaviors exhibited by persons who are mentally ill are "symptoms" of the disease. These symptoms can be diagnosed and a treatment can be prescribed. The other theory suggests that mental illness is a social role, not a disease. Our culture teaches us that persons who are mentally ill exhibit certain peculiar or unusual behaviors. But while many people may exhibit these behaviors, only a few of them are labeled as mentally ill. Therefore, the behaviors themselves cannot be the sole basis for being classified as mentally ill. It may depend on who is exhibiting the behavior, where it is exhibited, and what kind of problems the behavior creates for others. Being mentally ill, therefore, is a socially constructed role and not a clear cut medical category. Thus, out of the intellectual dispute between two views of mental illness emerges a research idea that attempts to provide a better explanation.

A second stimulant to research comes from federal agencies and private foundations that are interested in particular lines of inquiry. Federal agencies may seek answers to any number of problems related to the health, education, and welfare of citizens—crime rates, industrial alcoholism, and the effects of unemployment on family life. In some cases, the agencies define the problem to be studied and then ask sociologists to submit proposals, much as one would bid for a contract.

Private foundations have missions or goals that stimulate sociological research. The Rockefeller Foundation encourages research in human fertility in the United States and Latin America. The Ford Foundation solicits proposals for studies of unique problems in industrialized societies. The Johnson Foundation sponsors research aimed at improving health care for all citizens. These and other foundations and private corporations fund research on topics of special interest to them.

While the benefits of federal and private foundation funding of research are obvious, there are hidden problems. Not only do funding sources stimulate research, but they also *channel* research. Research priorities of public and private funding agencies may have little or nothing to do with the objectives of sociologists interested in developing a science of society or those interested in social reform. Those who subsidize and sponsor research do not always have benign objectives, and sociologists must become increasingly aware of how their research may be influenced or the uses to which it may be put. The most well-publicized instance of corruption of academic research by sponsors who had different objectives occurred during the 1960s. A large interdisciplinary social science project, called Project Camelot, was presumably concerned with studying the causes of social unrest and political instability in Latin American countries. This project was later found to have been funded by the U.S. Army for the purpose of developing paramilitary tactics for undermining popular protest movements in Latin America (Horowitz, 1965). A number of sociologists who were involved in what they considered to be legitimate research felt that they had been used by those who funded the research.

Research problems also are developed through the availability of large amounts of data collected by federal agencies and research organizations. For example, the U.S. Bureau of Census conducts periodic household surveys. Many sociologists, especially those in ecology and demography, use these data to study patterns of residence, migration, social mobility, suburban growth, and racial integration. Other data sources for sociologists are the National Opinion Research Center at the University of Chicago, the Survey Research Center at the University of Michigan, and the Gallup, Roper, and Harris public opinion polls.

Setting Research Objectives: Type of Study

The particular study developed by the sociologist may be classified as either **descriptive research** or **analytic research.** Descriptive research is an effort to obtain accurate information about some social phenomenon or in response to a specific question. For example, an interest in having very accurate estimates of the rate of crime in the United States led to *victimization studies*—surveys of the general population to obtain reports from a large number of citizens about whether they have experienced any form of crime. The purpose of such studies is not explanation but simply drawing a picture.

Analytic research is concerned with establishing the relationships between variables to identify their causal connections. Its goal is to explain why certain relationships exist, and it does this by testing hypotheses about such relationships. An **hypothesis** is a prediction about the relationship between a dependent variable and one or more independent variables. For example, hypotheses about job satisfaction might be as follows: (a) the more that workers control their own work, the greater their job satisfaction; or (b) the higher the income of workers, the greater the job satisfaction; or (c) the more friends one has at work, the greater the job satisfaction. Analytic studies could be designed to test the accuracy of these predictions. The findings could be used to develop a theory of job satisfaction that would explain why persons in certain kinds of occupations are more or less satisfied with their jobs than persons in other kinds of occupations.

Defining the Problem:
Conceptual Definitions

The concepts or key ideas on which the research is based must be so well defined that there is no question about what the researcher means when referring to these concepts or using such terms as job satisfaction, occupational prestige, control over one's work, or supervised personnel. For example, does job satisfaction refer to positive feelings about pay, retirement benefits, work conditions, supervisors, or all of these? If concepts are carefully defined, the hypotheses will correspond closely with the types of the study. Concept clarity will also make it easier to identify the procedures to be followed in measuring the concept.

Although precision in conceptual definitions is desirable, it is often not possible. Some concepts are "sensitizing" rather than "definitive" in nature (Blumer, 1954). They give the sociologist a general sense of meaning and serve as a guide for approaching empirical instances of the concept. "Mental

Sociological surveys obtain information by means of questionnaires and personal interviews. Here we see an interviewer in the field carrying out a formal interview with a person selected as part of the research sample.

health," "anxiety," "culture," or "social institution" are examples of sensitizing concepts. In contrast,. a definitive concept, like "occupational mobility" or "migration," provides clear and unambiguous identification of the class of objects to which it refers.

Measurement of Concepts: Operational Definitions

Each concept stated in the hypotheses or objectives of the descriptive or analytic study must be measured. Can job satisfaction be observed directly at the workplace or can it be determined by asking workers how they feel about their jobs? The conceptual definition of job satisfaction will indicate the aspect of reality that is to be measured. The operational definition will further specify the meaning of specific actions or answers. Suppose you choose to define job satisfaction as the degree of similarity between what a person thinks is important in a job and what the chances are of achieving it. You might decide to use a questionnaire to measure this degree of similarity and include items as shown in Table 2.2.

People answering the questionnaire would check how important each statement is to them and how much of a chance they perceive they have of achieving what the statements describe. The responses to each question would be given some number values, such as 1, 2, 3, and each person would receive a total score that showed the difference between the importance of the statement and the chances of its coming true.

On the other hand, you might decide to measure job satisfaction with a single question: "If you had a chance to start over again, would you get into the same type of job you are in today?" This approach is simpler, but it might be too crude to capture the

different shadings of job satisfaction that you might need to test your hypotheses.

Different ways to measure sociological concepts are described in handbooks of measurement (Bonjean et al., 1967; Miller, 1977). These handbooks report on the number of other studies that have used the measures, enabling the researcher to see how well the questions or scales have worked for other sociologists.

Unless the steps in an operational definition are spelled out carefully, the data collected may have little or nothing to do with the hypotheses or research objectives and therefore will not help answer the questions asked by the study.

Research Design

The objectives of research, or the hypotheses to be examined, must be placed within an overall plan of how the investigation will proceed. This plan is the **research design.** The sociologist must decide: (1) What will be the unit of analysis—will it be individuals, a group, an organization, or a census tract? (2) How are the data to be collected? (3) What kind of operations will be performed on the data after they are collected? Three types of research design are most frequently used by sociologists: the sample survey, the experiment, and direct observation.

SAMPLE SURVEY

A sample survey uses interviews or questionnaires to obtain information from a sample of persons who come from and are believed to represent a much larger population. For example, assume you want to know about the political beliefs and behaviors of college students at a particular university. Moreover, you want to know if their political beliefs and behaviors vary according to their sex, school year,

TABLE 2.2   Sample Questions for Measuring Job Dissatisfaction

IMPORTANCE TO YOU				CHANCES OF ACHIEVING		
Very	Some	Little		Good	Medium	Poor
_____	_____	_____	Freedom to set my own schedule	_____	_____	_____
_____	_____	_____	Opportunity for advancement	_____	_____	_____
_____	_____	_____	Variety in work assignment	_____	_____	_____
_____	_____	_____	Congenial coworkers	_____	_____	_____

Laboratory experiments in social research involve controlled observations of simulated real-life situations. Here we see two research workers observing a child through a one-way mirror and recording information.

religion, urban or rural origins, and social class background. These are the objectives of a descriptive study—that is, you merely want to describe some behaviors of a specific population according to certain subcategories of that population.

The **population** in this case is *all* students at the university. However, you do not have to interview or question all of the students to make reasonably accurate statements about that population. You can select a **random sample** of that population to be interviewed or to receive a questionnaire. A sample is random when each person in the population has the same chance (a known probability) of being selected in the sample. If your sample is *representative* of the population, then the distribution of characteristics in the sample (such as age, sex, political party preference) should closely correspond to the distribution of characteristics in the population. For example, if you have drawn a representative sample from a population of students and 50

percent of students in the sample who were questioned prefer "middle-of-the road" politics, you can be reasonably certain that about 50 percent of the entire student body at the university feels the same way. Thus, you can make an **inference,** or statement, about a characteristic of a population from knowledge of that characteristic in a sample drawn from the population.

You can use similar sampling procedures to make statements about other populations, such as all college students in the United States, or all adult residents of the state of Nevada, or all registered voters in a particular county, or all industrial organizations with 1000 or more employees in Los Angeles.

The advantages of a survey design are that (1) it produces large amounts of data from a relatively small sample of a large population and (2) it allows you to make reasonably accurate descriptive or analytic statements about that large population within a known range of error. Disadvantages include

(1) the costs of a survey in both time and money, which are high; (2) the limited depth of data collected with a questionnaire or interview; and (3) the bias of structured questionnaires and interviews; for example, they may "create" responses about matters on which respondents have no real position.

LABORATORY EXPERIMENTS

A laboratory experiment is a specially set up and controlled social situation that allows the sociologist to test and observe the relationships among a small number of variables. Experiments are almost always analytic in that they test specific hypotheses related to clearly stated theories. The relative ease with which experiments can be conducted, as compared with surveys that require more time and money, makes it possible to replicate research quickly and to develop a series of experiments that build on one another to support, elaborate, or modify a particular theory. However, there are a great many real-life situations that cannot be studied with the experimental method.

Derek Phillips (1963) used an experimental design to examine the question, How do persons become identified as mentally ill? Part of Phillips' theory was that other people's attitudes toward individuals who show symptoms of mental illness are related to something other than the individuals' behavioral symptoms. He hypothesized that people's attitudes were strongly influenced by knowing what particular help-source was used by the disturbed person. By "help-source" Phillips meant community figures and groups, such as "clergymen, physicians, psychiatrists, marriage counselors, mental hygiene clinics, alcoholism clinics, and mental hospitals . . ." (p. 963). In his experiment Phillips presented each person interviewed with five stories describing the behaviors of people exhibiting paranoid schizophrenia, simple schizophrenia, anxiety and depression, phobias and compulsions, and normalcy. Each story contained information about the help-source, if any, the person consulted—"He has been going to see his clergyman regularly about the way he is getting along" or "He has been going to see his psychiatrist regularly about the way he is getting along." This de-

sign allowed the researcher to change the combinations of behaviors and help-sources. (Such control would not be possible in sample surveys or direct observation studies.)

This experiment showed that the source of help sought by disturbed persons, rather than their behaviors, was most closely related to rejection by community members. "Individuals are increasingly rejected as they are described as utilizing no help, as utilizing a clergyman, a physician, a psychiatrist, or a mental hospital" (p. 971).

The sample survey and the laboratory experiment have the same bias. In both designs, it is assumed that the questions or social situations presented by the researcher have similar meanings for both the researcher and those who are responding, which is not necessarily so. Respondents or subjects do not participate in shaping the social reality presented to them by the researcher. Therefore, when faced with a similar situation in real life, a respondent or subject might see and react to the situation quite differently.

PARTICIPANT OBSERVATION

In the third major research design, the researcher-observer becomes involved in the activities of the group that is being studied. The observer enters into a natural social setting without determining in advance the data to be collected. The specific objectives of the study emerge from the behaviors exhibited and the meanings shared by those making up the group.

Participant observation does not mean that the researcher has no study ideas before the fieldwork begins. However, these ideas can be easily modified by field experience, which allows the observer to change the focus of the research. Such changes of focus are virtually ruled out in survey or experimental work.

Participant observation is used to uncover hypotheses and theories that can be pursued in further studies rather than to test hypotheses. Observation in natural settings allows the researcher to consider many more variables than structured designs do. This makes observational studies extremely fruitful in producing insights and ideas for further development.

Perrucci (1974), one of the authors of this text, carried out a one-year participant observation study in a mental hospital. He collected several hundred pages of "field notes," including detailed descriptions of specific events taking place on a particular day, as well as general summaries of each day's activities. These notes, along with formal interviews of patients and staff members, are the basic materials for a comprehensive picture of life in a mental hospital.

During one phase of the year's observation, Perrucci became interested in which patients on a ward had the most contact with hospital staff members, and what effect these contacts had on the patients. This idea emerged after several months of observation and turned out to be an important clue to the structure of social relationships in this setting.

The major shortcoming of participant observation as a research tool is the difficulty of generalizing the research findings to other settings. It is hard to know if what is true for one mental hospital is true for others. Good field researchers provide enough detailed data to permit other sociologists to corroborate or challenge their particular interpretation.

Direct observation designs are not substitutes for surveys or laboratory studies. The selection of design depends on the objectives of the research, and the ideal study might employ several techniques. For example, direct observation might be used to understand how persons living in the natural setting think about selected aspects of their lives. This information could be used by the researcher to develop questionnaires that will be more easily understood by respondents and perhaps less likely to impose a personal view of reality on respondents.

Data Analysis

Up to this point, we have stated research objectives or hypotheses, specified basic concepts, and identified the specific means to measure these concepts. We have defined the variables to be measured—those characteristics, behaviors, and conditions that can change in amount or degree. After the data have been collected in a statistical study they are summarized or compared to satisfy the research objectives or test the hypotheses. These statistical operations fall into three general types.

SUMMARIZING A SINGLE VARIABLE
The simplest way to classify data for a single variable is to calculate an average such as a mean or median score. For example, if your research objective is to compare the average income for male and female employees in a given community, you would first need to find the mean income for each group. You would sum the incomes of all females and divide by the number of females and then perform the same procedure for males. This would give you the mean average incomes of both groups and enable you to compare their averages.

Under some conditions using a mean score as the average measure of some variable may not be best. For example, the average income of rock musicians could be distorted if there were a few extremely high incomes, in the $100,000 range, while most incomes clustered around $15,000 to $20,000. Because the mean is sensitive to extreme values (a few high incomes) it could produce a higher mean income among rock musicians. In such cases, the median would be a better average measure. The median is that point in a distribution of scores (such as incomes or ages of respondents) below and above which 50 percent of the distribution is found. The median is calculated by listing all scores from high to low and counting down the list until you hit one-half of all the scores in the distribution. That score is the median.

DETERMINING THE RELATIONSHIP BETWEEN TWO VARIABLES
Often you will want to know if two variables are related and, if they are, how they are related. When two variables have a regular and recurrent relationship, there is **correlation** between them. If, when the average score on one variable increases, the average score on another variable also increases, the two variables are positively correlated. If, when one variable increases, the other decreases, the two variables are negatively correlated. If, when one variable increases or decreases, the other variable does not change, the two variables are probably not related. There is no correlation between them. There

are degrees of correlation; relationships between variables may be strong or weak.

For example, assume that we want to know about the relationships between work experience and job satisfaction, salary and job satisfaction, and education and job satisfaction. For each of these three pairs of variables, you could select a statistic to test for relationship. This would allow you to make statements about, say, length of work experience, worker's salary, and worker's education in relation to job satisfaction.

DETERMINING THE COMBINED AND SEPARATE
EFFECTS OF TWO OR MORE VARIABLES
ON A THIRD VARIABLE

Some studies try to unravel the relationships between one set of variables, independent variables, and another variable, the dependent variable, described earlier. For example, suppose you have a theory that links the work experience, salary, and education of workers (independent variables) to their job satisfaction (dependent variable). Then you could measure directly the combined effect of the three independent variables on job satisfaction.

Increasingly, sociological studies employ statistical analyses of large numbers of independent variables that influence a dependent variable. These studies rely on advanced statistical techniques and the use of large-scale computers for storing and manipulating hundreds of variables collected from thousands of persons.

Reporting Research Findings

The results of most sociological research are generally prepared for publication in journals and books, presented at meetings of professional social scientists, and summarized in reports to agencies that may have sponsored or cooperated in the research. Communication of research results to others has several important consequences: (1) it increases the development of a cumulative body of knowledge about human society; (2) it enables others to evaluate or try to replicate the findings; and (3) it reduces the likelihood that researchers will knowingly distort or misrepresent their findings for personal or political reasons.

In addition, sociological research has consequences for various public policies. Research on the effects of total institutions like mental hospitals has contributed to the movement away from their use. The growing interest of state and federal legislatures in the problem of child abuse has been stimulated by social research. Public policies and programs dealing with problems of alcoholism, gang delinquency, drug abuse, retirement, and health care, to mention a few, have been based partly on sociological research in these areas.

Thus, the communication of research findings contributes to the development of a body of knowledge about human society and also serves to maintain sociology as a study that is vital and useful to the society that sustains it.

The usefulness of social research to government and private corporations has enabled sociologists to fill many important positions in these institutions. However, social research has not always been able to produce the results expected of it. Reading 2.1, from a popular weekly news magazine, discusses some of the problems and prospects facing contemporary sociology.

ETHICAL PROBLEMS OF RESEARCH

All research, whether by sociologists, biologists, psychologists, or physicists, raises questions about the responsibility of researchers to the people they study and to society at large. Ethical issues have been of concern to scientists and lay persons for some time, but the importance of ethical issues was brought to the forefront during World War II when it was learned that doctors working in Nazi concentration camps engaged in inhumane experiments on people, which they justified in the name of scientific knowledge. After the destruction of Hiroshima and Nagasaki, some American scientists involved in developing the atomic bomb questioned the use to which their knowledge was put.

While scientists believe in the importance of research, they also recognize the need for guidelines to ensure that research does not threaten those who participate in it and to determine their responsibility for the outcomes of their work.

Two ethical issues are of greatest concern: treatment of subjects and responsibility for outcomes of research.

Treatment of Subjects

Most sociological research presents very little risk to its participants. People who participate in questionnaire and interview studies usually do so voluntarily and with knowledge of the objectives of the research. Federal agencies that fund sociological research and university research committees require that "informed consent" procedures be followed by the researcher. In addition to consent, researchers must guarantee privacy and confidentiality to participants who provide information.

The most serious ethical problems facing researchers often occur in connection with laboratory experiments and direct observation in natural settings. The problem is deception. In experiments participants are sometimes subjected to fear and extreme tension by being asked to inflict harm on others or being the recipient of potential harm. These contrived experiments do not inflict actual physical harm but they lead subjects to believe that this is actually what is taking place or will take place.

Observation in natural settings is sometimes carried out with the researcher deceiving the persons being observed. This can be as extreme as disguised observation, where researchers take on some other role to observe and record behavior. Rosenhan's (1973) research in a mental hospital was carried out by having project members admitted to the hospital as patients. Humphreys (1970) studied homosexual encounters in a men's restroom in a city park, serving as a "look out" while homosexual acts took place. The researcher also wanted to know something about the kind of people who engaged in such acts. He recorded automobile license numbers of the participants in homosexual acts, which he used to obtain home addresses. He then visited these persons in their homes by assuming the role of a survey pollster. In this way, he was able to gather information on the social, educational, and economic backgrounds of the men he observed in the restroom.

Some sociologists would argue that deceptive practices are necessary to carry out certain investigations and that these practices are justified because the data obtained is held in strictest confidence and the people involved are never identified. Balancing the interests of sociological research and the rights of citizens against intrusion in their private lives is a difficult task for the ethical researcher.

Responsibility for Outcomes of Research

While it is understandable that all scientists place a high value on research and are reluctant to see limitations placed on their freedom as researchers, it is also clear that it can no longer be assumed that the results of research are always beneficial. The ethical scientist must try to examine his or her own values when making judgments about whether to carry out a particular investigation. There are no hard and fast rules that can be applied to cover all situations.

There are also situations where the researcher is the one who has been deceived by research sponsors. Stephenson (1978) carried out research on Hungarian refugees who fled their country following the Hungarian uprising of 1956. This research was funded by what appeared to be respectable foundations. In fact, the research sponsor was the U.S. Central Intelligence Agency, who apparently had access to the interview data obtained.

Misrepresentation by sponsors of research, whether public or private foundations, does serious damage to the integrity of research. Sociologists must not allow their eagerness to obtain research funds to stand in the way of asking questions about why sponsors want the research to be done. Universities and professional associations also have obligations to protect the integrity of research. They might seek ways to extract contractual assurances from research sponsors about the source of funds and the sponsor's interest in the research.

The ethical problems that researchers face can be handled by following some general guidelines: first, to carry out research openly and without deceiving participating subjects; second, to avoid any practices that might result in harming participants;

and third, to consider the possible consequences of undertaking research in light of competing values of different groups and to accept responsibility for the course of action chosen.

SUMMARY

Sociological research has two general objectives. The first is basic research, which is concerned with developing a body of theoretical and empirical knowledge about human societies. The second is application of knowledge in ways that are felt to be useful in helping to remedy a variety of social problems.

Asking important and researchable sociological questions is the most important aspect of the research process. The way in which questions are stated will influence the conduct of investigations and their practical implications.

Despite the different purposes of research, sociologists carry out investigations by following many of the principles of scientific methodology in (1) selecting problems to study; (2) choosing appropriate approaches, whether descriptive or analytic; (3) developing conceptual and operational definitions in tests of the researchers' predictions and hypotheses; (4) designing research strategies, including the use of sample surveys, laboratory experiments, and participant observation to collect data; and (5) analyzing the data in light of the objectives of the study.

All research raises important ethical questions about how the investigation is being conducted and who is responsible for the way the results are used. The treatment of subjects in social and biomedical research is a matter of great concern. The ethical scientist must balance the value of freedom of inquiry with the protection of the rights of human subjects.

GLOSSARY

Analytic research a study to test hypotheses about the relationship between two or more variables and to identify causal connections.

Applied research attempts to use sociological knowledge to conduct research of interest to a specific client. The objective is more practical because it may result in social change.

Basic research attempts to contribute to a body of theoretical knowledge about human society. The audience is usually other scientists in the researcher's field.

Correlation a relationship between two variables; if, when one variable increases, the other variable increases, they are positively or directly correlated; if, when one variable increases, the other decreases, they are negatively or inversely correlated.

Dependent variable a variable measured by a researcher that follows in time, and changes as a result of changes in, an independent variable.

Descriptive research a study to obtain accurate information about some social phenomenon, for example, crime rate.

Hypothesis a prediction about the relationship between two or more variables that is derived from a system of explanation called a theory.

Independent variable a variable that may be manipulated by a researcher and that precedes in time, and produces changes in, a dependent variable.

Inference a statement about a research population based on information obtained from a probability sample of that population.

Methodology the total set of procedural rules used in collecting, organizing, and analyzing data in scientific research.

Population all persons who have one or more social characteristics in common; for example, college freshmen, bankers, snake handlers, blue-collar workers.

Random sample selection of persons from a population in such a way that each person has an equal chance of being selected. Such a sample is believed to represent the population.

Research design the plan for a scientific study that designates the unit of analysis, the method of data collection, and the method of data analysis. Three common research designs are the sample survey, the experiment, and direct observation.

Serendipity the chance discovery of positive outcomes that were not being sought.

ADDITIONAL READINGS

Cole, Stephen. *The Sociological Method.* Chicago: Markham, 1972.
An introduction to the sociological perspective and its relationship to the basic logic of research. Provides good examples of how sociological research is relevant for social problems.

Hammond, Phillip E., ed. *Sociologists at Work.* Garden City, N.Y.: Anchor Books, 1964.
Very readable, personal accounts by sociologists of specific studies they conducted. Provides realistic documentation of the research process.

Lindblom, Charles E., and David K. Cohen. *Usable Knowledge: Social Science and Social Problem Solving.* New Haven: Yale University Press, 1979.
An examination of the current problems in using social research to help solve social problems. Provides specific discussion of some ways social research could be done in order to have greater impact on real-life problems.

Marx, Gary T., ed. *Muckraking Sociology: Research as Social Criticism.* New Brunswick, N.J.: Transaction Books, 1972.
Examines the potential of sociological research for uncovering and examining contemporary social and political issues.

Phillips, Derek L. *Knowledge from What?* Chicago: Rand McNally, 1971.
A critical view of the methods of current sociological research and suggestions for alternative procedures.

Sjoberg, Gideon, ed. *Ethics, Politics, and Social Research.* Cambridge, Mass.: Schenkman, 1967.
Examination of how both scientific and nonscientific considerations enter into the decisions that one makes when doing sociological research.

READINGS

READING 2.1

Social Inventions for Solving Human Problems

William Foote Whyte

This is a time for rethinking sociology. In President Reagan's initial budget proposal for 1982, we were told, in effect, that what we (and other social scientists) do in research is of little relevance in solving national problems. On past performance, we do not warrant that judgment, but let us not expend our energies in defending past accomplishments. We must do better in the future to demonstrate the practical relevance of sociology.

We can meet that challenge if we reorient the way we do sociology. I suggest that we conceptualize this focus in terms of the discovery, description, and analysis of *social inventions for solving human problems*.

Let me start with a definition. A social invention can be

—a new element in organizational structure or interorganizational relations,
—new sets of procedures for shaping human interactions and activities and the relations of humans to the natural and social environment,
—a new policy in action (that is, not just on paper), or
—a new role or a new set of roles.

We can leave it to the historians to determine whether the social invention we study is *new* in the sense that nothing quite like it has ever been done before in the history of mankind. For sociologists, the important point is that the ideas underlying the invention are new to the people involved in developing and applying them. Even if they have consciously copied from elsewhere, at least they had to adapt the copy to their own social, economic, and cultural environment.

SOURCE: American Sociological Review 1982, Vol. 47 (February): 1–13.

Before going farther, let me distinguish between *invention* and *intervention*, two words that sound similar but have different meanings.

Whatever else it may be, an *intervention* is something brought into an organization or community from the outside. An *invention* is a new creation which may and often does emerge in a community or organization, without any direct outside influence. While an *intervention* may indeed involve the introduction from outside of what I would call a *social invention*, I am here primarily focusing on inventions more or less autonomously created within the organization or community in which they are utilized. Quite apart from concerns over terminological exactitude, I emphasize the autonomous creation of social invention to suggest that human beings have enormous resources of creativity that permit them to devise their own social inventions, without waiting for an outsider to intervene and invent what the community or organization needs. . . .

The study of social inventions involves more than a shift away from more traditional topics. It also involves major changes in research methods and theory development. Let us explore these implications, starting by contrast with what I take to be the standard model of social research taught to our graduate students.

According to that standard model, the researcher goes through the following steps. He reviews the literature and consults with his colleagues regarding the problem he would like to study. Then he selects hypotheses that he wants to test, arming himself with a combination of reasonably well supported hypotheses that involve conflicting evidence from past research, and perhaps a novel hypothesis or two that he can think up himself. With this theoretical armament in place, he picks out a target population for study—and with this research style, the "target population" is well named. He then moves in to persuade the gatekeepers controlling access to this target population that, if they let him do the study, somehow the information he gathers will be useful to them as well as to him. Having done the study, if he isn't too busy writing his scientific papers and proposals for new research, he may return to the gatekeepers with what he has learned.

Where did this research style come from? I suspect that sociologists have been unconsciously following a physics model. In physics, the phenomena under study are fixed, at least in the sense that, though they are in constant movement, they follow a reasonably standard orbit. The physicist is experimenting on the basis of a highly developed and coherent body of theory. And finally, since the phenomena are under the control of the investigator, he does not require their active participation in the experiment.

This model is much less appropriate in sociology or organizational behavior. The phenomena we study are in movement, and new combinations are constantly emerging. Our theory base is much less firm, and our links from data to theory are often exceedingly shaky. Furthermore, we are dealing with active human beings, who can contribute to our study if we allow them to participate. Under these conditions, before adopting the standard model, we should at least ask ourselves: Do we really know the territory we are investigating? Or are we just mechanically applying a given research instrument?

In the research strategy required for the study of social inventions, you do not start out with a pre-established research design. Of course, you don't start out with a blank mind either. You consult the research literature, but you refuse to be bound by it. In the first place you assume that the published literature is likely to be a decade behind the most interesting things happening in the field. Furthermore, while the literature may illuminate a problem, it may also impose intellectual blinders that guide you along traditional path-

ways. In many cases it is less important to gather new data than to develop a new way of organizing and interpreting data. . . .

Before preparing your research design, you go out into the field. Through interviewing and observation, you develop a rough map of the social, economic, and technological territory. You gain a preliminary idea of social processes—of the interactions and activities in which people are engaged—in order to diagnose and solve their problems.

After some period of immersion in the field, fortified by reading about it, you discover a general pattern along the following lines. The people you are studying have their own conventional definitions of the problems they are facing. Conventional solutions are proposed and sometimes tried out. More often than not, the conventional solutions don't work, and the problems remain—or else the conventional solution solves one problem but creates other equally intractable problems. . . .

Instead, let us assume that our preliminary diagnosis is accurate and then look for situations where actors are defining the situation differently and devising different solutions—in other words, where they are trying out social inventions.

Having discovered a social invention, you then move in to observe, interview, and gather documentary material so that you will eventually be able to provide a systematic description of that invention. You then seek to evaluate the invention or set of inventions. This is not simply a matter of judging the degree of success or failure. If the invention appears to work, this judgment does not tell us *why* or *how* it works. If we are to be able to describe a social invention in a way that makes it potentially useful in other situations, we must grasp the social principles underlying its effectiveness in the case under study. . . .

This research strategy has important implications for the choice and timing of research methods. The questionnaire or survey has long been the favorite method of sociologists, but you do not go out looking for social inventions by doing a survey. When it comes to evaluating success or failure, however, it is important to know the opinions and attitudes of the people who are affected by a social invention and here the survey can be an indispensable instrument.

This research strategy also has important implications for the relations between the researcher and the people he/she studies. It is folly to treat those who have created an important social invention as passive subjects of research. We need to learn from them the personal experiences and thought processes that led them to create the social invention as well as their theories of why the invention works or why it fails to work as well as they think it should. That is not to say that we function simply as reporters, passing on the wisdom of the social inventors. We must look for the underlying principles of social dynamics, whose discovery will enable us to describe and analyze a social invention in such a way that other human beings in other situations may be able to adapt and utilize it.

In seeking to apply the results of our research, we should think in terms of social inventions rather than in terms of attitudes, beliefs, and values. . . .

I am not denying the importance of subjective mental phenomena, but, we are rarely able to change behavior simply by telling people that they should change their attitudes. Attitudes, beliefs, and values do indeed change as people, in grappling with persistent social problems, devise creative ways of restructuring their activities and interactions and their relations to the physical and social environment. In studying the social inventions that enable people to bring about such changes, we can build a more useful applied sociology. And, as we study the implementation of social inventions in new socioeconomic and technological contexts we will also contribute to the building of sociological theory.

SUMMARY

Sociological research can be more relevant if it tries to discover and analyze social inventions that are developed for the purpose of solving human problems. Social inventions are new creations in a community or an organization that draw upon the creativity of people in solving a common problem. The study of social inventions will require changes in research methodology and theory development. Researchers will have to become closely involved with the people who develop and are affected by a social invention.

QUESTIONS

1. What are some of the special skills that a sociologist will need in order to study social inventions?
2. Is a food co-op a social invention? How would you try to learn something about how it got started?
3. What kind of social inventions are possible on a college campus or in a college town?

READING 2.2

Social Sciences: Why Doubts Are Spreading Now

George E. Jones with Carey W. English

A time of doubts and self-reassessment has begun for the nation's social scientists after years of nonstop growth in status and power. . . . The prestige enjoyed by the social scientists in other years has come back to haunt them today.

Failures in Vietnam and the war on poverty cast much doubt on their once claimed ability to diagnose and solve human problems in the mass. These days it is not just the politicians who get the blame for much of the nation's

SOURCE: Reprinted from "U.S. News & World Report" Copyright 1982 U.S. News & World Report Inc.

social and economic disarray—sociologists, economists and other scholars are becoming targets, too.

Surfacing also are old suspicions of such scholars as "social engineers" capable of applying their talents to mass control as depicted in such futuristic novels as *1984* and *A Clockwork Orange*. Other authorities, recalling the 1960s when some social scientists were backing student rebellions, add radical tendencies to their critique of the social professions.

All this comes at a time when recession and government cutbacks are reducing job openings for new professionals in the social sciences. Cuts in government payrolls have struck at a wide range of social scientists, from program analysts to economic statisticians, and business firms are going slow on hiring new professionals. On campus, teaching and research jobs are just as scarce—or more so. . . .

Generally, America's social scientists regard their professions as still influential in government and business decision making, and likely to become more so in years ahead. Yet doubts and concern in the new and unsettling era for social sciences are evident—especially so at vulnerable research projects on campuses. . . .

THE UNFULFILLED PROMISE

These conflicting doubts and hopes are bringing to a new turn an academic field that originated in the social research of Max Weber in Germany and Emile Durkheim in France before and after the turn of the century.

Today, it is not Europe but the U.S. that is the world's center of social-science research—not just in scholarly output but in the power represented by its solid links to older disciplines such as history and economics, and newer ones such as population, ethnic or urban studies.

What has evolved in the U.S. since World War II is a formidable academic bloc whose engagement in public issues and acknowledged achievements in the study of human behavior has enabled it to claim parity, though uneasily, with the natural sciences and humanities.

Yet many social scientists still envy the status and credibility of traditional disciplines. Says one well-known social scientist: "Sociology is much more interesting and useful than it was 25 years ago—but it hasn't gained much in respect and understanding."

Traditionalists keep alive an old complaint: That social scientists often cloak dubious premises or conclusions with jargon—what one critic calls "intellectual Swahili"—that clogs prose with arcane words or phrases such as *paradigms, hermeneutics, episteme,* and *thick description.* Critics point out that an outsider, David Riesman, wrote *The Lonely Crowd*—a work some rank with the study of *Middletown* by Robert and Helen Lynd, or C. Wright Mills's *The Power Elite* as a landmark in sociological study.

Some social scientists join in the criticism. "Social sciences always compare themselves with physical sciences and suffer from the misunderstanding that as far as possible they should be like the physical sciences," says Boston University's Peter Berger, a European-born sociologist: "Once you make this philosophical mistake, you think that if no one understands you, you will be just as respected as they are."

In-house critics find other defects worth studying. "I think the social sciences have gotten themselves into great difficulties," says Bard College President Leon Botstein, a historian. "They have become self-perpetuating enclaves of specific disciplines and have lost the sense of the larger picture where research comes into play. Their questions are increasingly narrow, where the great students of society were motivated by the large questions." . . .

In late 1981, the magazine *Public Opinion*

asked a panel of social scientists: "Is Social Science a God that Failed?" Opinions differed—but there was near consensus that its achievements had not met overblown promises.

"We and our teachers saw ourselves as part of a social movement that would raise social science to the standards achieved earlier by the natural sciences," wrote the magazine's coeditor, political scientist Seymour Martin Lipset. "We would play a role in reshaping society, both nationally and internationally. We were convinced that social science . . . was ready to take off intellectually to make breakthroughs that would transform society: Thirty years later, that promise is largely unfulfilled."

SHANTYTOWNS AND CORPORATE SUITES

In today's hard times, the social sciences are undergoing major shifts that could change profoundly their research methods and goals—a matter of interest and perhaps concern for their clients in government and business.

More and more, not only economists but many other social scientists try to validate their humanistic judgments with tabulations based on more or less relevant numbers obtained from surveys, financial records, personnel rolls, opinion polls and the like.

A sizable number of skeptics see perils in overreliance on this practice, which has surfaced in such guises as "econometrics" for economists, "cliometrics" for historians and "psychometrics" for behavioral scientists.

"In metrics, you can use lousy data on all kinds of assumptions and get very precise and misleading results," says a widely respected sociologist, S. M. Miller of Boston University. "Computers are one of our great disasters—if you multiply data at an enormous clip, you have very few ways of analyzing it. A famous study a few years ago came up with the most meaningless results you could imagine. Why? They threw every variable into the computer and cross-tabulated it. Fifty thousand correlations overwhelmed them—they had no sense of what was going on."

Also likely to reshape the profile of the social sciences in years ahead are job shifts toward the private-sector as opportunities for campus teaching and research decline. "We find that employers, increasingly, seem to want the kind of analytic skills our students tend to have," says anthropologist John Cole at the University of Massachusetts.

Social scientists are moving into such areas as industrial management, personnel evaluation, environmental-impact studies and consumer surveys. In the Far West, a utility hired an anthropologist to dicker with Indians for placement of power lines across their lands.

This trend, some scholars believe, could give the social sciences new momentum if harnessed to disciplined scholarship. "The social sciences are a pretty young set of disciplines—they haven't developed the kind of solidly tested, reproducible knowledge about human behavior that one would like to see," says Michigan's Juster.

Meantime, the social scientists still wield some top-level influence in the nation's affairs. Their ranks include such scholars as Murray Weidenbaum, head of the President's Council of Economic Advisers; political scientist Jeane Kirkpatrick, Ambassador to the United Nations, and sociologist Daniel P. Moynihan, a top Democratic spokesman in the Senate.

Federal, state and local bureaucracies still employ thousands of professionals—from psychologists in U.S. intelligence who profile the behavioral strengths and frailties of foreign leaders to staff economists who coach busy legislators on the likely impact of complex tax bills.

"Today, social-science research is almost an irreplaceable part of policymaking," says David L. Sills, the Social Science Research Council's executive associate. "You couldn't run the government without it. A lot of corporations couldn't make their plans without it. The social sciences are going to be around for quite a while."

SUMMARY
After a long period of growth and influence, the social sciences today are experiencing cutbacks in the need for their services in industry, government, and universities. Some attribute the decline to the failure of the social sciences to deliver results on ambitious programs to reshape society. Others see the problem to be the result of extreme specialization, with disciplines concerned with self-perpetuation. There is still optimism, however, because social science research is an indispensable part of policy making. But changes are occurring in the face of today's hard times as the social sciences adjust their research methods and goals.

QUESTIONS
1. Do the social sciences pose a threat as "social engineers" who can develop and apply mass control techniques?
2. Is social science research out of favor in government and corporate circles because it tends to be critical of powerful groups and to be pro-underdog?
3. How are the social sciences viewed on your campus?

PART II

Culture, the Individual, and Society

Every new-born infant enters a world already created for him/her and which will shape all aspects of human growth and development. Culture provides the norms, values, and ideas that become a part of the child's experience and personality. Society provides the basic pattern of human interaction that makes life predictable and orderly.

In this section, we will examine the ways in which individuals relate to society, the conditions which shape and change human social life, and the forms of structure and control that operate in society. Chapter 3 explores the world of ideas, norms, values, and beliefs that surround people and give meaning to social life. Chapter 4 describes the ways in which behaviors are structured and ordered in society. Chapter 5 continues the discussion of structures by focusing upon small groups as they affect individuals in various social situations. Socialization, Chapter 6, considers the process by which people—infants, children, youth, adults, and aged—learn the rules and behaviors of social life. Finally, in Chapter 7, we explore the ways in which people deviate from social norms, and the processes of social control that are designed to prevent such deviance and to punish the deviant.

CHAPTER 3

Culture

CONTENTS

AT ISSUE

Can "culture" explain the differences among human groups?

The characteristics that humans are born with determine their social behavior—or do they? The differences in values and behavior between Chinese and French, Iranians and Spaniards, or ghetto blacks and suburban whites are obvious, but why do these differences exist? Few students of human behavior would deny the influence of culture—the values, norms, and beliefs that people learn through social interaction. However, sociobiologists have recently challenged the view that culture largely determines how people think, feel, and act. Instead, they argue that genetic traits are the most significant factor in shaping the behavior of cultural groups.

YES Culture surrounds the child from birth. Not only does the child learn the language, ideas, and values of the culture; the meanings and interpretations of physical and verbal cues are also learned. What, for example, would happen to a child born into one cultural group but raised in another? Kroeber (1952) states:

Let us take a French baby, born in France of French parents, themselves descended for numerous generations from French-speaking ancestors. Let us, at once after birth, entrust the infant to a mute nurse, with instructions to let no one handle or see her charge, while she travels by the directest route to the interior heart of China. There she delivers the child to a Chinese couple, who legally adopt it, and rear it as their son. Now suppose three or ten or thirty years passed. Is it needful to discuss what the growing of grown Frenchman will speak? Not a word of French; pure Chinese, without a trace of accent and with Chinese fluency; and nothing else. (p. 27)

The physical features of this child of French parents would be different from those of the Chinese with whom he lived. Eyes, ears, nose, skin color, hair texture, and stature would set him apart from others, but his speech and culture would not. For practical purposes in living, he is Chinese—in thought, language, attitudes, and behavior.

This learning of language, values, and behavior is largely unconscious. The one fact that is important in understanding differences among humans is that culture is the source of language, values, ideas, and the meanings of symbols—in fact, all those things that we identify as different in others. Culture explains human differences.

NO There is a persistent belief that children are molded in much the same way that putty is molded into various shapes. The culture, it is argued, provides the materials and the context from which humans learn. In this view, human infants of any culture can be exchanged for those in another culture, and their behaviors would reflect the culture.

This view ignores the impact of heredity on behavior. Recent studies of behavior of newborns suggest that there are differences among cultural traditions that cannot be explained by conditioning, or learning. Infants of Chinese-American heritage tend to adjust to new stimuli and discomfort more readily, to calm themselves more quickly, and to be less disturbed by noise and movement than Caucasian-American infants. Similarly, Chinese-American children tend to be less noisy, less vocal and emotional, and less likely to be involved in disputes and arguments than their playmates of European-American heritage (Wilson, 1978).

Such differences suggest that culture is not an adequate explanation for behavior. A better explanation is the process of genetic selection that has occurred naturally in different parts of the world as people and culture developed in relation to their environment. For the Chinese, the personal traits or behaviors that have been important are cooperation, acceptance, and serenity. In contrast, the personal traits or behaviors important to Europeans are individuality, self-assertion, and control. The processes of selection, through the successful adaptation of some people and the failure of others, has produced distinctive genetic groups. In short, Chinese-Americans share a gene pool whose dominant traits are different from the dominant traits in the European gene pool and thus the behavior of people from these cultures is different.

Is culture the basic source of group patterns of belief and behavior? In this chapter we will attempt to answer that question and others by exploring the concept of culture. Culture is the process of adaptation by which people develop ways of dealing with issues of survival and social relationships. We will note the wide diversity of cultural beliefs, norms, and values that shape the behavior of humans and how these developed from the experience of various groups.

QUESTIONS TO CONSIDER

- Are people genetically programmed for loving or hating?

- How does living in a desert or a tropical forest shape cultural life?

- Can people think without language?

- Can ethnic or religious groups maintain distinctive cultures in modern societies?

On January 13, 1982, a jet airliner taking off from Washington National Airport failed to climb fast enough, hit a bridge, and crashed into the icy Potomac River. Only five of the 76 passengers aboard survived, and those who lived owed their lives to people who risked their own lives to save them. Four such heroes emerged: two members of the park police helicopter team who described their actions as "all in the line of work," a 28-year-old office worker who jumped into the water to pull a young woman out, and an unknown "man in the water" who passed lifelines and flotation rings to other survivors before he disappeared under the water.

Their actions brought praise and honor to the four heroes. Why? Airplanes crash regularly, rescue efforts to save people in danger are made daily, individuals frequently experience such accidents and survive, and violent death is a common occurrence in modern society. Attention was focused on these four people, not because they acted in routine ways, but because they took exceptional or unusual actions. In a similar way we rarely think about the events and behavior that are typical of our culture until we see people acting in ways that are unusual, strange, or different. At such times we may become conscious of cultural patterns—those ideas, beliefs, norms, and values that guide our behavior but which are unnoticed because most of our lives are routine and predictable.

It is the routine and pervasive character of cul-

ture that is important in shaping and guiding human social life. However, these same characteristics make it difficult for us to study or evaluate our own cultures. When we meet someone from another culture who acts in ways that are strange to us, we begin to think about the reasons for the differences in behavior between the other person and ourselves. By comparing our culture—beliefs, norms, values—with other cultures, we can better understand our own.

THE CONCEPT OF CULTURE

The term culture has been used in many ways. For many people, culture may refer to sophisticated tastes in art, music, or drama. For social scientists, however, **culture** refers to the shared knowledge, meanings, rules, and ideas that are acquired by humans through social learning and which we shall call beliefs, norms, and values throughout this chapter. Culture affects how we think, talk, make love, build our homes, deal with others, go crazy, and die.

Culture as a Process

Culture, learned, shared, and transmitted by language, is a process. It is constantly being modified by group organization, technological developments, environmental conditions, genetic traits, and population characteristics. Each of these factors shapes the way culture develops and is passed on to later generations. Culture is also cumulative. Each generation adds to the storehouse of knowledge and meaning that subsequent generations draw upon. The ability to store and transmit knowledge through culture is what distinguishes humans from animals and is the source of our domination as a species.

CULTURE AS LEARNING

Human culture has developed over millenia. As homo sapiens evolved from earlier hominid species, their brain size increased and consequently their capacity for symbolic behavior, or intelligence. Such changes meant the development of stone tools, the beginning of communication and planning, and the organization of people into groups and communities. These organized activities, symbolic forms of communication, and socially shared meanings are the essence of human culture (Keesing, 1981).

The history of human evolution is essentially the history of culture—the process by which humans developed and adapted to the demands of their environment. Unlike other species whose behavior is directed by biological (inherited) instinct, humans learn from their culture how to deal with their environment. The process of learning the symbols and rules of the culture and adapting them to new situations is crucial for human survival.

Culture is the accumulation and organization of shared beliefs, norms, and values and their expression in behavior. Culture refers to the meaning and value associated with materials, inventions, tools, and the world rather than to these things themselves: it is what humans learn in the process of becoming members of a society. What is available to learn in the culture sets the limits of a person's social behavior. From this perspective, all individuals may learn a wide range of behaviors, such as playing the violin, becoming a loan shark, or enjoying books, with equal ease, but what is learned depends upon the culture. As an alternative view, **sociobiology** suggests that the processes of human development and cultural transmission are inherited and that adaptation and variation are most important factors in producing distinctive behaviors.

BEHAVIOR AS BIOLOGICALLY BASED

While accepting culture as an important factor in shaping human life, sociobiologists emphasize "the biological basis of human behavior" (Wilson, 1975). In their view the genetic programming over which humans have little direct control is the dominant

Cultural differences are the result of many factors including geographic environment, weather, genetic inheritance, density, and level of technology. Every culture provides meaning, norms, and values for its members. Among the Chinese, the norms, values, and ideas associated with work are reflected in the involvement of women in hard physical labor but few men or women work at such physically demanding jobs in industrial societies.

factor in human adaptations, selection, and behavior.

Sociobiology emphasizes the role of genetic characteristics, which are transmitted from one generation to the next. Biological variation occurs through *mutation*, or change in genetic material, and *natural selection* acting on new genetic characteristics that are best adapted to the organism's environment. The most adaptive or most efficient genes are likely to survive and be reproduced, while the less capable genetic traits or characteristics will disappear because they are not adaptive for the individual. Over several generations, even a very slight advantage in adaptation will result in significant changes in humans and in their behavior and culture. According to sociobiology, evolution, or change by the process of natural selection becomes the primary factor in shaping not only new species but new patterns of human life. The distribution of genes in populations, especially those that are socially or geographically isolated, account for variations in human behavior. As a result, children of Chinese-Americans will be different from children of European-Americans, not simply because of culture, but because their gene pools are different.

Human behaviors like aggression, love, greed, or spite can therefore be explained in terms of genetically based adaptations to the environment (Wilson, 1975). Heredity and environment provide the basic materials of a culture. Over many generations, the survival or natural selection of genes may create a distinct population, adapted to the physical and social environment. Culture, as the symbols, language, and meaning attached to social behavior, is essentially the product of natural selection (van den Berghe, 1978). As a result, human behavior as well as ways of thinking differ in various groups of people.

Sociobiology is not simply a variation of the old argument about heredity versus environment, or nature versus nurture as it is sometimes called. Sociobiology makes no effort to describe individual behavior except as such behavior is shared by all members of the gene pool. The heredity-environment controversy focuses upon "bad" genes or "bad" environment as the reason for an individual's behavior.

CULTURE AS A SYSTEM OF SHARED MEANINGS

While genetic factors may account for some kinds of cultural adaptations, we must remember that cultural differences that exist among groups of people have emerged out of the social life of those people. These differences may be responses to the physical environment which provides materials for shelter and food supplies. They also reflect patterns of social relationships. However, regardless of the source of cultural differences, culture is the shared meanings that are attached to behaviors and symbols for a particular people.

An example of these shared meanings is the way different people view time and space. In industrial societies, schedules, clocks, and a keenly developed sense of time are important, and human activities are divided into hours, minutes, and seconds. In agricultural societies the most important time divisions are night and day. Space, too, may be perceived in different ways, as is evident in the following statement by Yi-Fu Tuan (1974), a Chinese scholar.

Americans have a sense of space, not of place. Go to an American home in exurbia, and almost the first thing you do is drift toward the picture window. How curious that the first compliment you pay your host inside his house is to say how lovely it is outside his house! He is pleased that you should admire his vistas. The distant horizon is not merely a line separating earth from sky, it is a symbol of the future. The American is not rooted in his place, however lovely: his eyes are drawn by the expanding space to a point on the horizon, which is his future.

By contrast, consider the traditional Chinese home. Blank walls enclose it. Step behind the spirit wall and you are in a courtyard with perhaps a miniature garden around the corner. Once inside the private compound you are wrapped in an ambience of calm beauty, an ordered world of buildings, pavement, rock, and decorative vegetation. But you have no distant view: nowhere does space open out before you. Raw nature in such a home is experienced only as weather, and the only space in the sky above. The Chinese is rooted in his place. When he has to leave, it is not for the promised land on the terrestrial horizon, but for another world altogether along the vertical, religious axis of his imagination.

Nostalgia is a recurrent theme in Chinese poetry. An American reader of translated Chinese poems may well

The adaptability of human cultures is evident in housing. Tents that are readily moved are used by the herders and nomads of Iran and houses on long poles are well adapted to the culture of Southeast Asians who exist on water and seafood. Each of these houses is very different from those found in North America, but each reflects and plays an integral part in the maintenance of cultural patterns.

be taken aback—even put off—by the frequency, as well as the sentimentality, of the lament for home. To understand the strength of this sentiment, we need to know that the Chinese desire for stability and rootedness in place is prompted by the constant threat of war, exile, and the natural disasters of flood and drought. Forcible removal makes the Chinese keenly aware of their loss. By contrast, Americans move, for the most part, voluntarily. Their nostalgia for hometown is really longing for childhood to which they cannot return: in the meantime the future beckons and the future is "out there," in open space. When we criticize American rootlessness we tend to forget that it is a result of ideals we admire, namely, social mobility and optimism about the future. When we admire Chinese rootedness, we forget that the word "place" means both location in space and position in society: to be tied to place is also to be bound to one's station in life, with little hope of betterment. Space symbolizes hope; place, achievement and stability. (p. 8)*

Differences between Chinese and American views of space are deeply rooted in the social life of each population. These shared views and meanings are communicated by one generation to another through various means, the most significant of which is language.

SYMBOLS AND LANGUAGE

Communication among people is made possible by sharing similar meanings for symbols that are used to express ideas. **Symbols** take many forms. They may be verbal or nonverbal. They may refer to objects like a chair or a car or to ideas like love or duty. We say, then, that symbols are concrete or abstract.

The common language of a small community will have similar meanings for symbols because people share common experiences. But what happens when people share a language such as French but have different experiences and therefore different meanings for the words or symbols that are used among French-speaking people in, say, Haiti, Paris, and Tunisia? Or, if the context of a symbol is not understood, as when a rural westerner with his easy informal manner attempts to strike up a conver-

sation with an urban woman waiting for a bus? Or, if the language is not adequate to express certain ideas or experiences, as in English where the single word *love* is used to express the concepts of sexual love (*eros*), brotherly love (*philos*), and self-giving love (*agape*). The Greeks had three words for it.

Let us look at an example of an English word that has multiple meanings, the word *body*.

* A *body* has a head, two arms, and two legs.
* He has a nice *body*.
* This coffee has real *body*.
* There is no*body* here.
* Laws em*body* the values of the people.
* Lake Huron is a large *body* of water.
* Different alphabets of *body* type are used in printing.
* The *body* of the letter is in paragraph three.

People living in English-speaking countries will understand the meaning of the word in its different uses. But how do they learn this?

In an effort to identify the processes by which the different usages of a word can be understood by members of a culture, scholars have attempted to find the underlying rules or patterns of language that operate during the act of speech or writing. This study is called linguistics. However, such rules and patterns cannot be understood apart from knowledge about people, situations, and language.

In short, culture and language are inseparable: human capacities to build traditions, to create conceptions of reality, and to transmit these perspectives and traditions to later generations require some form of symbolic communication which we call language.

Words, like other symbols, are abstractions. For most people born and raised in North America, the English language provides a shared system of meanings and an underlying structure or set of rules to describe social life and personal experiences. Another important aspect of language, however, is the fact that the ideas, the perceptions of reality, or the things we see are the things that we have learned through our cultural experiences. Conceptions of what is real, what is seen, and what is experienced, then, as well as our beliefs, norms, and values, exist because, through language, we have learned to identify, see, or experience these things. The significance of language in human life has been emphasized by the symbolic interactionist approach, described in Highlight 3.1.

Because language is a social process, meanings are created and shared between people in social life by the process of communication itself. This means

---

HIGHLIGHT 3.1
Symbols and Social Life: The Assumptions of the Symbolic Interaction Perspective

Assumption 1.   Man lives in a symbolic environment as well as a physical environment and can be "stimulated" to act by symbols as well as by physical stimuli.
Example: Reading a book that brings laughter, tears, anger, or joy. The words were only symbols on paper, but they caused the same reaction that observing the things that they described in real life would have caused.

Assumption 2.   Through symbols, man has the capacity to stimulate others in ways other than those in which he is himself stimulated.
Example: Frowns, smiles, body posture, fists, or changes in the tone of voice are stimuli to other people, express anger, love, pleasure, etc., and cause a reaction by others.

Assumption 3.   Through communication of symbols, man can learn huge numbers of meanings and values—and hence ways of acting—from other men.
Example: It is unnecessary for each generation to reinvent the wheel, or to reestablish social order, or most patterns of social life, such as families, churches or schools.

General Proposition (Deduction) 1.   Through the learning of a culture (and subcultures, which are the specialized cultures found in particular segments of society), men are able to predict each other's behavior most of the time and gauge their own behavior to the predicted behavior of others.
Example: When driving a car, it is expected that people will stop for a red light, and proceed on green. If such behavior could not be predicted, auto traffic would cause enormous problems for most people.

Assumption 4.   The symbols—and the meanings and values to which they refer—do not occur only in isolated bits, but often in clusters, sometimes large and complex.
Example: None of the symbols of space-age travel would have meaning to seventeenth-century humans or to preindustrial peoples; only by understanding the entire complex of modern technical language does any of these symbols have meaning.
General Proposition (Deduction) 2.   The individual defines (has a meaning for) himself as well as other objects, actions and characteristics.
Example: Words, such as nice, strong, beautiful, handy, or cute are often used to define people, not only in isolated situations, but are also used as self-definitions.

Assumption 5.   Thinking is the process by which possible symbolic solutions and other future courses of action are examined, assessed for their relative advantages and disadvantages in terms of the values of the individual, and one of them chosen for action.
Example: Decisions about which course of study to take or which word to use in conversation, as well as how to act in class, with a date, or at a game involve the use of symbols.

SOURCE: Arnold M. Rose, "A Systematic Summary of Symbolic Interaction Theory," in Arnold M. Rose, editor, HUMAN BEHAVIOR AND SOCIAL PROCESSES: AN INTERACTIONIST APPROACH, Copyright © 1962 by Houghton Mifflin Company. Adapted by permission. pp. 3–19.

that language may create new meanings without the experience that produced the language. For example, the new space-age terminology—module, satellite, interstellar travel, laser—is a cultural artifact of the industrialized world and would have little meaning to a person whose culture experience does not include knowledge of such objects and ideas. However, these terms do not mean the same to all members of a modern society, though hearing them will bring a cognitive response, even if the person has never seen a satellite. Similarly, the English word snow brings a mental picture to a person, though that word does not adequately describe the several types of snow that Eskimos identify with different words. Language, then, is not only a vehicle of communication; it also creates meanings by teaching people to see or to experience reality.

Components of Culture

All people store a vast amount of information that they use in social life: how to cash a check, how to use the subway, how to act in a classroom, how to respond when someone speaks to them, how to obtain food or shelter. This information, and thousands of other pieces of information, learned through social interaction, enable us to survive. The rules or guides for such behavior define what is appropriate or acceptable in various situations. These guides are called norms and values and they are found in all societies.

Norms

Norms are rules or expectations that define what is acceptable or required in a social situation. The behavior of individuals in such diverse social situations as dating, working, playing, driving a car, eating with others, and drinking alcoholic beverages is guided by norms that are accepted by most people in the society.

There are two types of norms. Norms that govern the consumption of alcoholic beverages, for example, may be **proscriptive,** or prohibited as among some groups like Mormons and Southern Baptists. Among other groups, such as orthodox Jews and college fraternities, the norms are **prescriptive—**

there are rules for the use of alcoholic beverages. Still other groups consider the drinking of alcohol "nonnormative"—that is, they provide no guidelines because the behavior has little meaning to the group.

No one in any society follows all of the norms all of the time. Thus, rape, murder, speeding in automobiles, alcoholism, embezzlement, and cheating on exams do occur, despite norms that proscribe such behavior. Social scientists often use the term **statistical norm** to describe the amount of actual behavior that is consistent with the norm. While marriage as a lifelong commitment has been an expectation in most societies, a large proportion—perhaps 40 percent—of the population does not follow this pattern. In this case, the statistical norm refers to the number of people, usually a majority, who actually behave in accordance with this expectation. Another term sometimes used to describe nonconformity to the social norm is "factual" behavior. The term norm, used alone, refers to the rule, standard, and general expectation about people's behavior and not to the behavior itself.

Values

Values are abstract standards that persist over time and serve as guides to what is right and proper for people in a society (Kluckhohn, 1962). Values may be inferred by observing ways that people choose to behave among the various options available to them in their social setting. In the United States, private ownership and use of guns are defended on the basis of the values of personal freedom and individual rights, while in most European countries gun control is based upon the values of community or corporate membership. Similarly, the world may be viewed as something to be mastered, typical of most modern, industrial societies, or as something to be accepted or adopted as it is, typical of many Native American cultures.

Like most modern societies, the United States is a complex mix of people from various cultural backgrounds. Many of these people have roots in Northern Europe, some in Latin countries, others came from Asia, Africa, or Eastern Europe. The diversity of these cultures and the resulting inconsistency of values are common features of the society. Because different values operate in various settings, people may subscribe to contradictory beliefs and may espouse values that are inconsistent with both related behaviors and other values. It is not surprising in such a diverse culture that all people do not share the same values or that the general values held by some people are in conflict with those held by others.

This diversity of cultural values and its significance for American society can be seen by examining the dominant themes of the culture and the variations or alternatives to them supported by other people. In 1970, Williams described 15 general values of people in the United States that guide their behavior: (1) achievement and success, (2) work, (3) moral integrity, (4) humanitarianism, (5) efficiency, (6) progress, (7) material comfort, (8) equality, (9) personal freedom, (10) external conformity, (11) science and secular rationality, (12) patriotism, (13) democracy, (14) individual personality, (15) racism and related group superiority themes.

An effort to evaluate the level of support people gave to each of these general values was made by Christensen and Yang (1976). Based on responses by over 3000 residents in North Carolina, these researchers found that moral integrity was ranked first, with personal freedom a close second. In general, patriotism, work, and efficiency were valued more highly than racial or sexual equality. This ranking held for whites of different educational and income levels; blacks tended to emphasize racial equality along with freedom and moral integrity.

The list of American values could be expanded to include other themes like violence, idealism, and professionalism (see Highlight 3.2). At the level of general values there is a high degree of agreement. At the level of specific applications, contradictions occur. For example, the value of efficiency might sanction the elimination of workers by businesses through automation to achieve greater efficiency, while the value of humanitarianism and belief in individual worth would preclude such an action.

Not all values are held equally by all members of all groups in our society. People kill, cheat, and steal, and society responds by applying negative sanctions, or punishments, as a means of social

---

HIGHLIGHT 3.2
What's Important to Americans?

(PERCENT RATING IMPORTANCE VERY HIGH OR HIGH)

Having a good family life	82%
Being in good physical health	81%
Having a good self-image	79%
Personal happiness or satisfaction	77%
Freedom of choice to do what one wants	73%
Living up to one's potential	71%
Having an interesting job	69%
Having a sense of accomplishment	63%
Following God's will	61%
Having many friends	54%
Helping people in need	54%
Working to better America	51%
Having an exciting, stimulating life	51%
Following a strict moral code	47%
Being active in church or synagogue	40%
Nice home, car, other belongings	39%
Having a high income	37%
Having enough leisure time	36%
Social recognition	22%

SOURCE: THE GALLUP POLL

---

control. However, individuals may belong to several groups within the larger society which support contradictory norms and each of which may attempt to influence the behavior of individual members in various situations.

SUBCULTURE

The term **subculture** often is used to describe the cluster of values, norms, and ideas that differs from those of the dominant culture. The unit that holds these values and ideas may be a juvenile gang, an ethnic community, a school club, a business group, or a wealthy elite. The common values, norms, and beliefs for such groups, like those for larger cultural units, emerge from unique experiences. Groups that desire to maintain their unique culture and identity have used several techniques to preserve cultural traditions. Some groups may choose social or geographic isolation or both. For example, Reverend Moon's Unification Church isolates its members socially by a rigorous discipline and also by geographic isolation, while the monastic orders of the Roman Catholic Church, involved social isolation but were often located among the lay people, and the Hutterites in rural areas of North America have geographically separated themselves to achieve social isolation. For the rich who live in "gilded ghettos," the technique of isolation serves to cut off meaningful social contact with the nonwealthy, though the former may interact with the latter as servants or employees. For the poor, social and often geographic isolation is often imposed by lack of money. The social isolation of various economic or ethnic groups is a major factor in the development of a subculture.

Oscar Lewis (1966) described the values, beliefs, and norms of the very poor as a distinct subculture, which he labeled "the culture of poverty." In his view, the culture of poverty is characterized by a lack of participation in the major institutions of the larger society, a lack of community organization, early sexual initiation, marriage at early ages without elaborate rituals, mother-dominated families, and strong feelings of isolation, marginality, helplessness, and dependency of individuals. Children learn the beliefs, norms, and values of the subculture in their early years. As a result, poverty perpetuates itself as people are unable to take advantage of opportunities for participation in the larger society when they do appear. This explanation of the culture of poverty emphasizes the importance of values, norms, and beliefs in adapting to the circumstances of life. When the larger society values wealth and thrift and blames poverty on personal inadequacy, the culture of poverty provides an alternative to the dominant norms, values, and beliefs.

Sociologists disagree about the source of the values, norms, and beliefs of subcultures. Is the subculture of poverty or the subculture of the wealthy maintained and transmitted from generation to generation regardless of objective social and economic conditions? Or, conversely, do the cultures of the rich and of the poor develop from the economic and social conditions of isolation and ghetto

life? To emphasize the culture of poverty as a culture that is transmitted across generations places the responsibility for poverty on the culture: people are poor because they learn to be poor. To emphasize the culture of poverty as an adaptation to objective social conditions suggests that people learn to be poor because they are poor.

ISSUES IN UNDERSTANDING CULTURE

Every human society has a distinct culture: beliefs, norms, and values that define appropriate patterns of behavior. The differences in the norms, values, beliefs, and behaviors of people in various cultures reflect the adaptations of the people and their ancestors to circumstances of their environment. To the social scientist, cultural diversity does not imply superiority or inferiority but simply adaptability. The ordinary experiences of individuals that are shared with others in the social group gradually become defined as normal and right. By contrast, other people's ways may be seen as strange and wrong. In some societies, cultural change is rapid, while in others there is little change in values, norms, and behavior for generations. Why do these differences occur? The following sections examine several concepts to help us understand these differences: diversity and variability, relativity and ethnocentrism, and persistence.

Diversity and Variability

The diversity of human cultures is obvious even within the industrialized world. One of the clearest expressions of cultural difference is the way groups choose to rear their children. Americans, for example, expect their children to be active and accept dirty faces and soiled clothes as a normal part of childhood. As children begin school, teachers are often faced with active children who cannot sit still; indeed, one of the important functions of kindergarten is to prepare children for later grades by teaching them to sit still for long periods of time. In contrast, French children are relatively immobile. Not only can French children play without becoming covered with dirt, but they have learned at young ages to remain quiet. One observer, in fact, reported that a child was sent to a school psychologist by a French teacher who concluded that, because the child would not sit still in class, he must be ill. As Berger and Berger (1979) note, "In other words, a degree of motor activity granted in an American school was looked upon as evidence for some sort of pathology in France" (p. 23).

Definitions of what is appropriate behavior for a child emerge from the general values and meanings associated with the culture. The desire to dominate and to control life that is common in America—even in children—is rooted in generations of living in a spacious continent; similarly, the ability to remain still for a French boy reflects the values of his society that have developed over generations.

Eating, attitudes toward food, expectations about hospitality, and even taste also are culturally defined. When a person of one cultural background is faced with a new and unknown set of cultural norms about these matters, problems can develop, as the following account by Keesing (1981) suggests:

A Bulgarian woman was serving dinner to a group of her American husband's friends, including an Asian student. After her guests had cleaned their plates, she asked if any would like a second helping—a Bulgarian hostess who let a guest go hungry would be disgraced. The Asian student accepted a second helping, and then a third, as the hostess anxiously prepared another batch in the kitchen. Finally, in the midst of his fourth helping, the Asian student slumped to the floor; but better that, in his country, than to insult his hostess by refusing food that had been offered. (p. 70)

These behaviors can be understood in terms of cultural traditions. Closely knit Asian families are the dominant groups in Asian societies and exist in an environment of scarcity and frugality. Sharing one's food is a sign of friendship and acceptance, and thus to refuse the offer is to reject the offer of friendship. Bulgarian culture emphasizes the responsibility of a host or hostess to place the guest first. To fail to attend to the guests' needs is to violate the cultural norms. Such contradictory traditions have emerged over many generations in a variety of social settings and environments. While the reasons why such norms, values, and beliefs first developed have disappeared from view, they continue to shape the perceptions and behavior of people who share the culture.

All cultures have emerged out of shared human activities focused on common concerns. These concerns may include the lack of food or shelter, a desire for order, fear of the unknown, control of sex, and the like. However, culture cannot be understood by examining only its parts. Culture must be seen as a symbolic system that provides beliefs about reality for the people who share it. This characteristic of culture leads us to the issue of cultural relativity.

Relativity and Ethnocentrism

The concept of **cultural relativity** requires that we examine each of the various elements of a culture in terms of its relationship to other elements, as part of the total symbolic system of the culture. Thus behaviors that have meaning in Islamic cultures, such as daily prayers while facing East, are seen as an important part of that culture, however strange those behaviors may be to a Christian in the United States. Similarly, television commercials are an integral part of the American culture and must be understood in the context of our commercially oriented society, however ridiculous they may appear to an outside observer. A loud belch after an excellent meal in some cultures conveys a guest's appreciation to the host, but such behavior would be offensive at a dinner party in the United States.

We can apply the concept of cultural relativity to an examination of the rituals associated with changing statuses, which have been described as "rites of passage" (Van Gennep, 1960) and which are characteristic of every culture. While these rituals may occur at several stages of life, we shall compare only two: the transition to adulthood and death. The rite of passage to adulthood is more clearly marked in preindustrial societies than in modern ones, though there are great variations even among preindustrial societies.

Rituals associated with the transition from childhood or youth to adulthood barely exist for most groups in the United States. Only among the wealthy is there a clear rite-of-passage, the debut, signifying that a young woman has reached marriage age. For most of the population adulthood means economic independence. At one time, high school commencement served as a ritual of transition to adulthood, because it signalled to others that young people were ready to work, to assume responsibility, and to marry. Now, many youth experience an extended period of education, which is required for entrance to many occupations. As a result, whatever ritual importance high school graduation once had has ended. In addition, neither marriage nor full-time work is clear evidence of adult status.

Contrast the situation in the United States to that of the Masai people of East Africa. Among the Masai boys between the ages of 12 and 16 underwent a rite of passage into adulthood—but only after each boy's father had performed a ceremony indicating his acceptance of the status of "old-man." Boys were isolated, their heads were shaved, and they were circumcised; after healing and the regrowth of hair, they received the status of warriors. Masai girls experienced excision of the clitoris and shaving of heads around the age of puberty; these actions defined the young woman as ready for marriage. The rites were not related to sexual initiation, however, since the girls had lived with the young warriors for several years and had had one or more lovers (Merker, 1904). Among the Masai, rituals must be seen as a part of the entire culture. Warriors were needed to protect the herds and people from raids by enemies and wives were essential to the domestic economy; the rituals ensured that boys would become warriors and that girls would marry at appropriate times.

Rituals of death and dying also illustrate cultural relativity. Among the Walbiri of Australia, the rites of death involved acts of self-mutilation by survivors. Men gashed their thighs, women cut off their hair and gouged their heads, and the deceased's widow and close relatives burned off their pubic hair. After a night of mourning and wailing, the corpse was carried by brothers into the bush, placed in a tree, and covered with branches. When the men returned, mourning ceased and life returned to normal. For the Walbiri death threatened the social order. The purpose of these rituals was to reestablish the relationships of the family into the larger group (Meggitt, 1962). In contrast, the Bara of Madagascar saw life as a tenuous balance between order and vitality. Death was viewed as an overdose of order that must be corrected by an increase in vitality. Rituals involved loud, extravagant expressions of grief, dancing, drinking, eating, and sexual activity. Later rituals and ceremonies focused on a communal gathering and a reburial which signaled the return to normal life (Huntington and Metcalf, 1979).

Rituals of death and dying in the United States are a part of a culture that emphasizes individualism and a religious belief in an afterlife. Most deaths occur in a hospital with a doctor presiding and few relatives or friends in attendance. At death, the family turns the body over to others. The embalmed corpse is made to look as natural as possible and at peace. The wake and the funeral are held in unfamiliar surroundings, and services are conducted only by a clergyman. While many people may attend the wake and the funeral, the survivors are largely left alone after a few days. These death rituals would be unacceptable to either the Walbiri or the Bara, but they clearly reflect dominant themes in the culture of the United States. The concept of cultural relativity enables us to examine and to define all behaviors and patterns of thought and meaning in terms of their particular cultural context. No behavior, belief, or value is acceptable or unacceptable by itself.

In contrast, **ethnocentrism** evaluates other cultures on the basis of familiar and commonly shared ways of thinking and acting. The term is a combination of the Greek *Ethno*, meaning "a group that shares a common culture," and *Centrism* meaning "at the center." Literally, ethnocentrism means "our people are at the center of the world." Such feelings and sentiments promote patriotism, group unity, and individual self-esteem. Ethnocentrism may strengthen group morale and bring unity and a sense of purpose to the group, as in the case of athletic teams, the British in the Falkland Islands, or an army in battle.

Death rituals exist in every culture. The traditional Jewish ceremony includes specific rituals that have developed out of the cultural experiences of the groups. In a similar way, death rituals in other cultures reflect shared experiences, and most redefine the social relationships of surviving kin members to the community.

Not all aspects of ethnocentrism are positive, however. In Germany in the Nazi era (1942–1945), an extreme view of ethnicity was developed. Hitler was able to convince a large proportion of the German people that they belonged to a superior Aryan race, which was destined to rule the world. The Jews, though not a race, were defined as inferior and dangerous, to be first segregated and then eliminated as a source of pollution of "pure" Aryan culture. Similar reasoning has led white South Africans to control and confine the black natives, and ethnocentrism has been a major factor in conflict among peoples of Southeast Asia.

Ethnocentric thinking leads to defining the ways and ideas of other peoples as inferior or wrong, rather than viewing cultural patterns as natural or the result of adaptation to particular conditions. This type of thinking underlay the white man's treatment of North American Indians. The early settlers defined Indian ways as savage, un-Christian, and "primitive," and therefore felt themselves justified in attempting to obliterate their culture. Such a view continues and has had important consequences for Native Americans and their cultures, as is evident from the following account by Witt (1980).

Take the way American Indians live—in large family groups. This is a preferred arrangement, not necessarily related to poverty. Thus, it is not unusual to find more than one child sleeping in a bed, a situation that was once common for all but wealthy American families. But times have changed, and an arbitrary ruling that the "proper" home has a bed for each child and has been used in some instances, as a lever to pry Indian children out of their homes and communities.

Not long ago, Bernice Appleton, an officer of the Native American Children's Protective Council chartered in Michigan, protested against the restrictions of the Michigan state social service agencies which, she contended, were denying foster home status to Indian families because they could not provide a separate room or half a room per child, nor a service bed for each child. She reported that:

"These agencies are going into Indian homes and telling them their homes are unfit because they have two children, or three children, sleeping in one bed. . . . It isn't necessary for Indian children to have one bed apiece. I don't even think it's good for children to sleep apart. Our children learn sharing right from the start."

Such requirements can force the breakup of families in a culture in which, traditionally, there is no such thing as an orphan or an illegitimate child. (pp. 24–25).

In recent years, Indian children have been sought by welfare, social service, and adoption agencies as one means of filling the need for adoptable children. In addition, church organizations have participated in removing Indian children and justifying their actions on moral grounds. So great is this activity that a 1977 study entitled "The Destruction of American Indian Families" estimated that 25 to 35 percent of all Indian children are removed from their families to be placed in foster homes, adoptive homes, and institutions. Another estimate by a former official of the Puyallup Nation in the state of Washington is that 40 percent of the Indian children are removed from their homes and raised as non-Indians, mostly whites (Witt, 1980). That such events could occur without public outcry is evidence of the ethnocentrism of the dominant whites, whose justification of such actions is that the children benefit from the "enriched" cultural experiences in their new homes.

Another consequence of ethnocentrism is that people who share a culture may seek to separate themselves from people or groups that have different ways of thinking and acting. While ethnocentrism creates a sense of unity among the group members, it also insulates them from outside influences, often to their disadvantage. Indeed, isolation from contact with different cultures may lead to cultural stagnation, while cultural contact often leads to innovation and adaptation.

Persistence and Adaptation

Cultures are identified with geographic areas. When such areas are isolated from one another, the cultures develop and continue independently, with unique beliefs, norms, and values. Historically, contact between people of various cultures has had both positive and negative results—on the one hand, for example, a transfer of technological knowledge; on the other, armed conflict.

Contact between cultures has occurred throughout history but has increased greatly in the past 200 years. The continued fighting among Laotians and Vietnamese; among Palestinians, Lebanese, Israelis, and Syrians, among Asians and Africans in Uganda; among Irish Protestants and Catholics, and among Moslems in Pakistan and Bangladesh indicate that culture conflict is not only history. However, for most cultural groups who have experienced contact with another culture, conflict has preceded some form of accommodation.

Cultural accommodation may be seen as one way by which a subculture satisfies the demands of the dominant culture while maintaining its own identity as a group. In most modern, industrialized societies, there is a general culture shared by the great majority of people. This general culture is created and maintained by mass communications and transportations systems. However, subcultures or distinctive cultural elements remain even in modern societies, fashioned around ethnic traditions, religious beliefs, or common experiences of a small group of people. Some subcultural groups, such as the Amish in the United States, share some of the same values as the larger culture—hard work, moral orientation, humanitarianism—but have rejected other attributes—technology, militarism, and secular rationality. Other groups, like the "Moonies" of the 1970s and 1980s, have sought to establish a cultural identity independent of the dominant American culture values. Native American groups in recent years have attempted to reestablish much of their earlier cultural heritage.

These accommodations or adaptations to the dominant culture may be subtle, and groups may maintain subculture values for many years. Perez (1980) has described the persistence of subculture values among the natives of the Andes Mountains in South America.

The Spanish conquistadors fought, conquered, and dominated the native Indians of South America in the 16th Century. Violence, superior arms, and religious passion were the central elements in their efforts to subjugate the natives. Their influence was obvious in the cultural developments since their arrival. When new cities were built, Spanish patterns of urban life provided the models. Faced with overwhelming military, cultural, and social power, the Indians gave up their gods, their language, their art, their freedom, and even their joy. Many were forced into heavy physical labor by the Spaniards, who sought to destroy the Indian culture rather than to harmonize the two cultural traditions. No cultural accommodation was possible because of the differences between the characteristics of the conquistadors and the Indians, and the violence which the newcomers used in seizing control of the lands. Even though the Spanish and Indians mated, there was no cultural marriage, and there are still millions of Indians without a trace of white ancestry.

The Spaniard's absolute dominion over the Indian withered his soul. However, his habits remained and his personality was not conquered. While European religion has been the dominant form of religious life for centuries, it has not penetrated deeply into the soul of the Indian. Similarly, the Spanish that the Indian speaks is laced with native words and expressions, despite the intensive and often brutal efforts of the Spaniards to eliminate them. The resistance to assimilation that characterizes the Andes Indians is subtle but persistent, and finds expression in the shrill notes of music, the monotonous beat of dance, the style of work, in masonry, in roads, and in handicrafts and agriculture. As Perez (1980) notes, the accommodation to Spanish culture has been superficial, and has not disrupted the close relationship of the Indian with the environment: no one is more at home with the geographical reality and no one belongs more to the earth than the Indians of the Andes with their love of the earth and a culture that brings meaning to that relationship.

This persistence of traditional Indian values and symbols through four hundred years of Spanish rule and influence suggests the power of culture. As in other situations where people of one culture have contact with people from another culture, each has adapted to the other to some degree. However, the type of accommodation that one culture makes to another is defined by several factors.

At least four conditions are important in shaping the outcome of cultural contact: (1) the degree of cohesion among people in the two cultures; (2) the level of technological development in each culture; (3) the number of points at which contact is made between the cultures; and (4) the adequacy of each culture's symbols to explain the new situation.

Regardless of the responses of leaders or adults to contact between two cultures, such contact will mean that children will experience a different culture from that of their parents. Cultural differences defined and evaluated negatively by parents may be accepted as socially valid by children. Only when a culture exists in isolation can it persist without significant change.

CULTURE AND SOCIETY

Differences among cultures are due to differences in the context of social life, including geography, ease of obtaining food, density of population, relative isolation of a group, level of technological development, even weather. These and many other social and environmental conditions shape the content of culture. People living in the tropics construct houses and fashion clothes appropriate to their hot climate, which would be unsuitable for people living in temperate and frigid zones. People who live near the sea, like Scandinavians and Japanese, develop diets that depend heavily on fish and seafood, while Americans living in the agricultural Midwest eat much beef and pork.

How do such environmental conditions affect the organized life of people?

Cultural and Social Patterns

Within every society, food production, family life, political and economic activities, and religious behavior are common concerns. The term society refers to the patterns of relationships among people in social situations. The symbols, values, and meanings that are shared by members of a specific culture reflect the common experiences of the people in a society.

Some activities are common to nearly every society and are expressed in similar ways. Religion, for example, whether monotheistic or polytheistic,

is expressed through prayer, singing, chanting, and other ritualistic behaviors. Similarly, mate selection rituals, marriage ceremonies, and rules of divorce are found in every society, though their form or content differ. In Western industrial societies, education and literacy are essential because individuals must compete in a complex economic system. In Shoshone Indian society, in contrast, where bartering or trading dominates, economic activities are communal rather than individual and cooperative rather than competitive. Also, the practices of individual choice in marriage mates and private ownership of land that characterizes modern Western societies would be unthinkable to a Shoshone Indian. Nomadic peoples emphasize authority of elders whose experience in decision making makes frequent moves to new pastures easier and more efficient. In industrial societies action and decisions by all individuals are required for optimal functioning.

Differences among cultures and societies are found in every area of social activity. Is there a pattern to these differences? Do similar physical environments lead to similar forms of marriage, government, religion, and the like?

Under similar environmental conditions, two entirely different cultures may develop. Indeed, the elements that make up the total culture of any population are the result of selections from a wide range of alternative solutions to human problems. Since there are many ways to deal with these problems, each culture responds differently within the general limits of its environment. Humans have created cultures throughout the world that reflect their adaptability. Environmental conditions, genetic heritage, and social relationships all affect adaptability.

The Integration of Culture

The contradictions within the values, norms, and beliefs of a group has important consequences for cultural integration, or unity. **Cultural integration** refers to the way in which elements of a culture like values, beliefs, and symbols are related to each other. In a well-integrated culture, the way people act is consistent with their beliefs and there are

Cultural contradictions exist in most societies, especially those with rapid social change. Modern harbor facilities and rice paddies which are planted and harvested as they have been for centuries exist side by side in many developing countries.
While many contradictions are not so obvious, in nearly every culture contradictory elements exist side by side.

few contradictions. Such cultures tend to be stable, slow to change, and relatively small.

By contrast, cultures of modern industrial societies may have many contradictory elements. These contradictory elements may exist at many levels and in many situations. At the personal level, one may hold a value of concern for others that conflicts with the self-assertion needed for job success. In organizations like churches or schools, there are people of diverse social and economic backgrounds who share a set of general values but whose symbols and rituals for specific events are not the same. This lack of cultural integration is illustrated in Reading 3.1, "Cultural Contradictions: A High School Homecoming."

Another type of cultural contradiction is found in family values. For example, sexual behavior, childrearing, and the provision of emotional support and intimacy for family members are all family functions. However, there is no single set of norms in modern, industrial societies that governs husband-wife or parent-child relationships. Apart from prohibitions against extreme physical brutality or exploitation, there are few specific norms that regulate marital behavior in the United States. Though all couples may subscribe to the value of equality, they may develop styles of marital relations that contradict this value. In a similar way, parents may

be very strict with their children or extremely permissive without violating the general family norm of responsibility for children.

In American society many values and symbols support "the family," without defining the form the family must take. Praise and attention is lavished on "the Mother of the Year," parents who are said to be a "good father and mother," and parents of children who succeed in athletics or in school. In short, families are good and have symbols to support them; at the same time there is a strong emphasis on individual achievement and personal happiness.

How can cultural integration exist in the face of such contradictory elements? How important is cultural integration to a society? Such questions must be considered in terms of human creativity and changing social conditions. Human relations both reflect and create shared meanings and symbols. Few Americans do not respond to the symbolism of the flag or national anthem, though they may not agree about what these symbols mean for race relations. In times of national danger these symbols have special power to motivate men and women to acts of patriotism and bravery. Cultural integration for modern nations means agreement about general values, symbols, and rituals. In such circumstances, cultural integration is fairly superficial and contradictions are inevitable; indeed these contradictions remind us that culture is a continuing process.

SUMMARY

Culture is the shared beliefs, norms, and values that humans acquire through social learning. The history of human cultural evolution is the history of adaptation to the demands of the environment and the development of shared meanings and symbols of human experiences. Sociobiology seeks to explain part of the adaptability of humans by genetic mutation and natural selection.

The development of language was a critical element in the evolution of human culture. Language—the ability to create and manipulate symbols—is the essence of human culture. Language not only provides a system of meanings, but it structures our perceptions of reality, that is, the way we perceive reality is affected by our cultural experiences, which are mediated through language.

The variability of human cultures reflects the adaptations of people to their environments. Each society has developed its own culture, with values, norms, and sanctions, that can be understood only within the context of that culture. The concept of cultural relativity suggests that all values and standards, when evaluated in terms of the culture in which they exist, are meaningful and valid. Conversely, ethnocentrism holds that one's own cultural values are superior to all others. While ethnocentrism fosters group unity and cohesion, it may also lead to negative judgments and exploitation of groups with different cultural values.

Contact between two cultures brings changes in both cultures. Accommodation of one culture to another may range from active to passive acceptance. Some subcultures persist in modern industrialized societies because they provide meaning to people who share social experiences. However, because culture changes continuously, no two generations hold exactly the same set of beliefs, norms, and values.

Contradictions among values and symbols exist in all cultures. Such contradictions may lead to conflict and change, emphasizing the dynamic aspects of culture as meanings emerge through new social experiences. Most people adapt general cultural values and beliefs to their own experiences, and contradictions may be muted.

GLOSSARY

Cultural accommodation the process by which a subculture satisfies the demands of the dominant culture while maintaining its own identity as a group.

Cultural integration the way in which the elements of a culture, such as values, beliefs, and symbols, are related to each other.

Cultural relativity a concept that encourages examination of a culture in terms of its internal cohesion, not its differences from other cultures; acceptance of validity of all cultures.

Culture shared knowledge, meanings, concepts, rules, and ideas that are acquired by humans through social learning.

Ethnocentrism an evaluation of other cultures on the basis of familiar and commonly shared ways of thinking and acting.

Norms rules or expectations defining acceptable or required behaviors of individuals in social situations.

Prescriptive norms social rules that require certain behavior.

Proscriptive norms social rules that prohibit certain behavior.

Sociobiology a perspective that emphasizes the biological basis of human behavior.

Statistical norm the number of people in a society who actually behave in accordance with a cultural norm.

Subculture values, norms, and ideals associated with smaller units of population that emerge as a result of that group's unique experiences in achieving particular goals or satisfying particular needs.

Symbols words, actions, body movements, and visual cues that stand for ideas and objects and to which members of a culture attach similar meanings.

Values abstract standards that persist over time and identify what is right and proper for people in a society.

ADDITIONAL READINGS

Alinsky, Saul. "The War on Poverty—Political Pornography." *Journal of Social Issues* 21 (January 1965): 41–47.
An examination of the effort to manipulate culture among the urban poor, with a critical view of the program.

Bell, Daniel. *The Cultural Contradictions of Capitalism.* New York: Basic Books, 1976.
Examines the assumption that human interaction can only be understood by a consideration of expressive symbols which create and recreate society.

Belmonte, Thomas. *The Broken Fountain.* New York: Columbia University Press, 1979.
A description of a small neighborhood in the slums of Naples, Italy.

Edgerton, R. B. *The Individual in Cultural Adaptation: A Study of Four East African Peoples.* Berkeley: University of California Press, 1971.

Ewen, S. *Captains of Consciousness: Advertising and the Social Roots of the Consumer Culture.* New York: McGraw-Hill, 1976.
Explores the role and impact of media in the development and spread of American consumer culture.

Hostettler, John A. "Persistence and Change Patterns in Amish Society." *Ethnology* 3 (April 1964): 185–198.
A sympathetic look at a subculture in American life that has persisted despite pressures from the modern world.

Kay, Shirley. *The Bedouin.* New York: Crane, Russak, 1977.
An examination of patterns of life among the desert Bedouins and the impact of the modern world on their culture.

Liebow, Elliot. *Tally's Corner.* Boston: Little, Brown, 1967.
A descriptive account of a black street corner society in Washington, D.C., and an analysis of the factors that promote cultural continuity.

Linton, Ralph. *The Tree of Culture.* New York: Knopf, 1955.
A classic description of the various cultural complexes that are found throughout the world.

READING 3.1

Cultural Contradictions: A High School Homecoming

Edgar Friedenberg

INTRODUCTION. *Adolescence is a period of contradictions. Teenagers face the demand to behave as adults; at the same time they are granted few adult privileges. The patterns of consumption urged upon youth can only be fulfilled by allowances from parents or through part-time, poorly paid jobs. Adolescents tend to hold the values of their parents, but not having their parents' experiences, they often do not understand why they hold them.*

The following description of a high school homecoming focuses on these contradictory elements of culture, especially for adolescents. The event is rich in cultural symbols, rituals, ethnocentrism and beliefs—as well as illustrative of diverse values in the culture at large.

The home team represented a famous public school, which has justly become distinguished for exceptional academic quality; before this game it had lost four in a row. The library has a collection of which a small college should be proud, excellent in both range and political audacity. It is a national center for imaginative curriculum planning and manages to provide an atmosphere of trust, respect and intellectual stimulation for students of a very wide range of ability. The model of scholarship it presents is both appealing and demanding and suggests as strongly as a school well can that intellectual interests are to be extended into daily life. Few if any of its students can be seriously hampered in using its resources by any anxiety or hostility caused by its treatment of them.

Efforts to arouse community enthusiasm, however, are artificial because the school

SOURCE: From Edgar Friedenberg, "Adolesence as a Social Problem," in Howard S. Becker, editor, *Social Problems: A Modern Approach.* New York: John Wiley and Sons, 1966.

serves a region of extreme geographical mobility. Many elderly people come there to retire and have no interest whatever in the school except as a possible basis for taxation. Economically, the area has exploded from near-destitution to a high rate of low-level employment in industries related to military and missile development. A high proportion of the inhabitants have moved into the area within the past few years, and many of the students are transfers from other high schools.

What the word "homecoming" means in such a context is unclear; it serves, however, as an occasion for remarkable ceremonial. At the half, the National Anthem was played. Afterward, the spectators remained standing and repeated the Pledge of Allegiance, while drum majorettes in gold lamé blouses and brief shorts held their batons rigidly in various positions of attention. There followed a small parade of five or six comic floats pulled by automobiles. The winning float depicted a large, papier-mâché bulldog—the symbol of the home team—dressed as a pugilist, revolving as it was towed along. The second prize winner seemed more imaginative and was certainly more elaborate. It bore three human figures, only two of which were visible at a time. A young athlete was ushered by another boy dressed in a white coat with a stethoscope and a big clipboard of charts into a large box labeled TERRORIZING MACHINE. (The visiting team was called "Terriors.") A puff of smoke and a flash were emitted from the box, and a third boy who had been concealed in it staggered out, smudged and rag-clad, in an attitude of extravagant decrepitude.

The comedy finished, the solemn feature of the homecoming ceremony began. A throne was erected in the middle of the field. The band disbanded and reassembled as an orchestra seated behind the thirty-yard line. As it began playing, in slow tempo, a series of familiar popular favorites of yesteryear—the first was "My Funny Valentine"—a procession of some twenty-five or thirty teen-age couples began to cross the field, the girls in elaborate formals, the boys mostly in summer jackets with a few dark business suits. Each of the girls had been nominated as a candidate for homecoming queen by the boys' organization whose president was now escorting her. The winner had been selected, though not publicly announced, at a pep rally that afternoon for which last-period class had been canceled.

The girl chosen was a French exchange student who was spending a year at the school; the choice evoked marked and clearly genuine enthusiasm, apparently for the international gesture, since school had been in session less than two months and this girl, unlike most of the candidates who were regularly enrolled in it, could not have been well known personally. She ascended the throne, flanked by the girls who had been chosen for second and third place. The captain of the football team, covered with the stains of the playing field, then advanced on the throne and handed her a huge bouquet of roses.

From the sidelines, then, a boy in summer evening dress drove a new, black, Pontiac convertible that had been lent by the local dealer across the field to the throne. The Queen entered it, sat on the folded canvas of the top, like a political candidate, and graciously saluted the spectators as she was driven slowly around and around the asphalt running track. Meanwhile, however, it began to drizzle. The Queen, captive, held her position royally; but the girls and their escorts, who had been standing as an honor guard in their vulnerable finery, slunk off to shelter. They missed the second half of the game, which the Bulldogs won by an impressive margin.

Tribal customs often seem grotesque to extraneous observers who do not understand them. But this homecoming ceremonial seems more grotesque if one does understand it: what is troubling about it is its utter lack of integration. Individually, each of the values symbolized in the successive parts of the ceremony is valid in the sense that it is indeed powerfully held by the community; some of them may be bad values, but all are conspicuous in our way of life. Every culture expresses in its ceremonial some values that are destructive and growth inhibiting even on its own terms. Every culture includes discordant values and expresses their conflict in symbolic terms. Every culture is ambivalent about many of its most cherished attitudes.

But not every culture lumps secular, religious, patriotic, and exhibitionist motifs into one electric mess. Not every culture confuses its occasions for outdoor, body-contact sport and for display of ballroom attire. Not every culture translates its generosity to a foreign visitor into commercial display. Behind this disorder and heterogeneity one senses genuine apathy, the kind of neglect that has created a neon strip along the thoroughfares leading into every major American city: expensive, banal, repetitive, and enervating. . . .

The teen-agers in the high school where the Bulldogs play have at their disposal, more abundantly than most high school students, intellectual and cultural resources adequate to inform them who they are and where they come from, and to help them decide where they wish to go. They use them with marked enthusiasm. But when they wish to project a public image of themselves they include nothing of this in it; nor do they use it more subtly to give order and discipline to their way of arranging this display. One can hardly avoid concluding that their smiling confusion and taste for chaos have become cultural principles in themselves, serving to reassure them that life is made of interchangeable, replaceable parts and can be plugged in anywhere.

SUMMARY
*Varied cultural elements are noted in this
high school event. They are secular, religious,
patriotic, and exhibitionist in character, all
a part of a ceremony that occurs yearly in
nearly every high school in the United States.
The combination of these varied, inconsistent
elements represents no unity or integration
of culture in which loyalty to a set of principles or beliefs is important.*

QUESTIONS
1. How are cultural values related to this
ceremony?
2. How important is cultural integration to a
society?
3. What does the combination of these diverse
symbols say about the values of American
society?

CHAPTER 4

Society and Social Structure

CONTENTS

Will society as we know it cease to exist in the postindustrial age?

Some analysts of advanced industrial societies like the United States believe that we are entering a time in which most goods and services will be produced by a very small proportion of the population. An overabundance of food for domestic consumption and export is already being produced by a handful of large-scale farms. Soon automated production and computer information systems will replace most blue-collar and white-collar workers. Society will be run by technical experts and there will be little need for many of the forms of social life that now exist.

YES   The social structures of modern society are changing so rapidly that we can begin to think in terms of a postindustrial society. This society has several distinctive features: (1) the production of goods by industrial plants will become less important to our economy; (2) manual workers and low-skilled white collar workers will largely be replaced by professional and technical workers; (3) the source of power in society will shift from property and wealth to science-based knowledge; and (4) the formulation of national policies on matters related to the economy and the health and welfare of citizens will be made by a new class of professionals, technicians, and scientists.

Some of the effects of this new society will be greater social and political passivity and more leisure for its members. In the postindustrial society all important decisions will be technical, not political. Elected officials like mayors, senators, and congressional representatives, who do not have the advanced scientific and technical knowledge needed for most important decisions, will simply ratify decisions made by the scientific and technical elite. People will no longer be involved in the political system as they will have no effective control over this elite. The community groups, organizations, and associations that people now participate in to express their social and political ideas about their society will have no function in the postindustrial society. What need will there be for labor unions, the League of Women Voters, political parties, the NAACP, Citizens for Nuclear Disarmament, the Moral Majority, or National Right to Life organizations? People will become increasingly isolated and increasingly unable to influence decisions that affect their lives.

Work will no longer be a lifetime commitment or a central life interest for most people. People will work in order to get money for food and shelter, but it may only be for two days a week. The productivity of our automated and computerized economy and our corporate farms will provide an abundance of goods to satisfy material needs. People will live a life of leisure that will enable them to seek greater personal development.

NO   It is very unlikely that technological advances in the form of computers, automation, and industrial robots will become so widespread that industrial plants and workers will be obsolete. Although such changes are theoretically possible, the cost of computerizing and automating most of the work now done by people would be more than any nation could afford. Postindustrial theorists have made the mistake of assuming that current scientific and technical advances will continue at the same pace and in the same direction. Change in society never occurs in an unbroken line. There are reversals, changes of direction, and syntheses of old and new ideas.

But even if many of these changes were to take place, would society as we know it be significantly transformed? Probably not. For one thing, new scientific and technical elites are not going to dominate national decision making. They will be subservient to political elites and to economic elites that control great wealth. These groups have always used the knowledge class to serve their own interests.

Thus politics will be alive and well even in postindustrial society. People will continue to form and join groups to advance their interests and to try and shape their communities, state, and nation through the political process. People will still be different in religion, race, ethnicity, age, and social class, and differences will remain the basis of social group formation for most people.

The question raised here will be considered in this chapter as we examine the different type of societies that exist in the world today, the different social groupings (social structures) in which people are involved, and the functions these groups fill. This chapter should help you consider whether a postindustrial society is possible and what its effects might be.

QUESTIONS TO CONSIDER

- What would be the advantages of living in a hunting and gathering society?

- In what way is life simpler in nonindustrial societies?

- How does social structure make social life more predictable?

- What are the different forms of social structure found in a college or university?

Human beings are social animals. They live in groups; they form clubs, associations, and clans; and they settle in territories called neighborhoods, towns, and cities. The social nature of human beings is due both to basic biological needs for sustenance and comfort and to the fact that many individual needs and wants can only be satisfied with the help of other people. The survival of newborn infants depends on the care of adults. Obtaining food and shelter for survival depends on relationships with others.

Yet the way in which children are cared for or food is obtained varies widely from society to society. In some societies socialization of the young is the responsibility of schools, while in other societies it is the responsibility of parents or an extended kinship group. The goal of socialization in some societies is to tie children more closely to the family unit by stressing lifelong obligations to kin, while in other societies children are socialized to be independent and to leave the family when they are adults. Thus socialization may be carried out within different social structures (families, kinship systems, or school organizations) and have different meanings and values (culture).

In this chapter we will try to do two things. First, we will examine differences in the broad outlines of society, which is a system of interacting individuals and interrelated groups sharing a common culture and territory, and the different types of societies that result from adaptation to their natural and social environment. Second, we will examine the idea of **social structure** as the patterned and recurring social relationships among individuals and groups in a society. Societies differ in the particular forms and degree of specialization of their social structures. Some societies, for example, may carry out economic and political activities as part of the kinship system; others may develop separate and independent social structures like factories and political parties. An understanding of the concept of social structure will help us to understand some of the differences that exist between societies.

SOCIETY'S ADAPTATION TO ENVIRONMENT

Human societies are part of the natural order. They share with a variety of animal societies the fundamental problem of adapting to their environment to increase their chances of survival. Human societies, of whatever size or complexity, must develop social patterns so they can fully exploit the environmental resources necessary to maintain life. An environment may have life-sustaining potential, but only with the application of technical and social skills can a society utilize that potential to produce what it needs. Many nomadic people move their herds within environments that have abundant game, yet they do not hunt the game. Some American Indians did not exploit available grains because they lacked the knowledge to convert them into usable products.

The success with which a society adapts to its environment is therefore the result of society's interaction with selected aspects of its environment. The culture & social structure of society will determine which aspects of the environment are defined as usable resources. The aspect of culture that represents techniques for transforming raw materials into usable products—that is, technology—"defines" those aspects of the environment that are viewed as resources. Another aspect of culture—religious beliefs—may prohibit certain natural resources as appropriate food for consumption.

A useful starting point in examining how societies adapt to their environment is to classify them according to how they satisfy basic material needs.

There are five types of societies, four nonindustrial and one industrial. The nonindustrial societies are hunting and gathering, pastoral, horticultural, and agricultural. These are, of course, very broad categories. Some analysts, like Lenski and Lenski (1982), have used a much more refined classification, but for our purposes these will suffice.

Each type of society represents a different kind of adaptation to its environment. Some adaptations result in very complex societies and some produce simpler societies. A technological advance in the way in which a society obtains its food opens up opportunities for further changes in social structure and culture. Many new occupations may develop, as well as new ideas about distributing food. Early human societies had primitive techniques for obtaining food, for example, the use of a club, throwing stick, spear, or bow and arrow. Food production was small, and as a result populations were small. Societies that depended on hunting were not likely to develop permanent settlements because the search for food had to be conducted across very large areas.

Such societies have very *simple social structures*, with few specialized roles and a limited division of labor. Political and religious activities may be tied to kinship roles; for example, only married males may be allowed to participate in certain religious ceremonies. There are no organizations, voluntary associations, stable territorial structures, economic classes, or ethnic subgroups.

With advances in the techniques of food production, as in the cultivation of plants and domestication of animals, more food is produced and a larger population can be supported. Stable settlements emerge, along with further elaboration of the social structure. As Lenski (1966) has noted, when a surplus of food is available, economic and political power differences emerge based on the control and distribution of that surplus. With even further advances in food production, more members of society are released from the tasks of producing food. There is a consequent elaboration of activities in religion, art, politics, and education.

This general view of the consequences of different kinds of technological advances was put forward by anthropologist Walter Goldschmidt (1959) and

has been neatly summarized by Lenski (1970):

First, technological advance means a more efficient utilization of the environment, and this usually leads to *population growth*. Second, technological advance reduces the need for migration, and *settlements become more permanent*. Third, technological advance leads to an *increased production of goods and services*, with all that it implies (e.g., the possibility of greater economic and political inequality). Fourth, technological advance fosters greater *specialization and division of labor and increased organizational complexity*. Fifth, technological advance makes possible increased "leisure" (i.e., time not consumed in providing for such basic material needs as food and shelter), which can be used for a wide variety of other activities—art, religion, politics, the production of nonessential goods and services, etc. . . . (pp. 101–102)

SOCIAL AND CULTURAL CHARACTERISTICS OF NONINDUSTRIAL SOCIETIES

Before discussing specific examples of nonindustrial societies, we must offer a note of caution about the meaning of the term nonindustrial and about our usage specifically. In discussions of economic life, social scientists and lay persons alike tend to contrast *peasant-primitive societies* (as examples of nonindustrial economies) with more advanced, modern societies. When making such comparisons many people imply that members of primitive societies lack those values and motives that are necessary for advanced economic activity; for example, that primitive people do not have the ability to plan for the future because their beliefs or their language emphasize the present. Supposedly, they lack the rational modes of thought needed for such economic behavior as investment, and they lack a view of the world as a place that can be controlled and shaped by human activities. In short, the basic reasons for the different levels of development in peasant and advanced societies can be found in the economic motives and values of their citizens, which are an expression of their ways of thinking.

We wish to make clear to the reader that our use of the term peasant or primitive to describe a society refers to a level of sociocultural adaptation and does not imply any less intelligent or rational approach to life. It also does not imply that there are important social-psychological differences relative to economic behavior between the members of peasant and advanced societies. Our use of the term **nonindustrial society** describes (1) a society whose labor force members are primarily involved in food production and (2) a society with a simple division of labor and little differentiation between the production and consumption units or between economic and noneconomic aspects of social life.

These features of a peasant economy are illustrated in the following description by Nash (1968) of the Bemba of Rhodesia, who have developed very ingenious techniques for raising food in a harsh environment with poor soil and weather conditions:

Men do most of the agricultural work of the Bemba, and one man is virtually as good as another in agricultural skill. The division of labor follows lines of sex and age. An occupational list in a peasant and primitive society is not a long one. Persons tend to learn their productive skills in the ordinary business of growing up, and within age and sex categories there is high substitutability of productive workers. Work and tasks are apportioned to the appropriate persons without much regard to functional differences in skill or productivity. (pp. 360–361)

The age, sex, and work roles of the Bemba are part of the relatively simple social structure they have developed for economic activities. In peasant societies the social units of production and consumption are commonly one and the same, namely, the family. Moreover, purely economic activities may serve as the means by which a person's place in the social structure is maintained and reinforced. For example, an exchange of animals can satisfy economic needs, as well as reinforce important political ties and allegiances. While it is also true that economic activities influence noneconomic activities in advanced societies, it is the combination of the two into a single pattern of activity that is characteristic of peasant economies. Entire families are involved in economic activities such as hunting or gathering, which also simultaneously satisfy religious or political objectives.

The existence of a simple division of labor (for

example, one based on age and sex) and the lack of clear demarcation between economic and noneconomic activities is characteristic of what have been termed **multifunctional** (or **functionally diffuse**) **role structures.** This term simply means that only a small set of differentiated roles exists in the society, and that these roles are not linked to specific activities. Bert Hoselitz (1968), an economist, has described such multifunctional role structures in the following way:

Functional diffuseness starts in direct contrast with specificity. The simple peasant in a nonindustrial society is a characteristic representative of the functionally diffuse. He not only performs all work connected with producing a crop but he also builds his house, makes his implements, and often produces his own clothes and other final consumption goods. (p. 424)

Because peasant societies have a relatively simple division of labor and because economic and noneconomic activities are more closely linked than in industrial societies, a closer look at examples of peasant societies should reveal a good deal about social structure.

Peasant societies, characterized by simple division of labor and functionally diffuse role structures, are most commonly classified on the basis of their economic life. There are four general classes, reflecting different kinds of "production" systems or technologies for extracting needed resources from the environment: hunting and gathering, pastoral, horticultural, and agricultural. Each of these forms of technology has important consequences for many aspects of social life outside of the economic sphere.

Hunting and Gathering Societies

People in **hunting and gathering** societies are foragers. They pursue available game and they gather fruits, nuts, roots, and berries. Whether foragers are sedentary or nomadic depends on the environment. Where game and plants are relatively plentiful, sedentary living is possible. In harsher environments it is necessary to move as game and plants become depleted. For hunters and gatherers, their physical strength and skills are their "technology"—their means of adapting to the environment.

As might be expected, hunting and gathering societies are small. The supply of game and plants is much too unpredictable to sustain a large population. As Bohannon (1963) has stated: "The whole Arctic area of the New World, however, supports only a few thousand Eskimos. The Kalahari Desert supports only a few hundred Bushmen, and the great deserts of Australia and America supported at most a few thousand aborigines or Indians" (p. 213). According to Hallowell (1949) the size of hunting groups does not increase in direct relation to the size of the hunting territory. He found that the larger the hunting territory the smaller the hunting group, due to the presence of other hunting groups that are attracted by the abundance of animals.

The abundance and type of game and plants will also have important implications for political organization. Techniques for obtaining food that can be utilized by a single individual or a family group alone will inevitably discourage the development of cooperative arrangements and reciprocal obligations that are necessary for developing political organization. Reading 4-1 describes collective hunting by the Shoshonean Indians and illustrates the features of peasant-primitive societies discussed earlier.

Pastoral Societies

A second form of adaptation to the environment is **pastoral**—the use of domesticated animals like goats, camels, reindeer, and cattle as the primary food supply. Pastoral people are found primarily in the Old World, in the broad grassland areas from eastern Russia to China, extending south through Iran and into Africa where the semiarid environment is unsuited for growing food. Their particular adaptation of domesticating animals to secure a food supply requires great sensitivity to seasonal change and to the patterns of weather and climate. The movements of pastoral peoples are not haphazard; they follow a fixed cycle of movement in accordance with the availability of water and of grazing land.

In contrast to hunters and gatherers, pastoralists demonstrate a greater capacity for concerted political and military activity. There are many examples of pastoral peoples dominating their settled neighbors through the use of organized military activities under centralized leadership. Their ability to use the horse, in particular, gave them great mobility in military pursuits. The most notable example is the Mongols, who, under the leadership of Genghis Khan, conquered large areas of Asia, as well as Eastern Europe.

The importance of animals to pastoralists is reflected in the way in which concern for their stock influences many of their social relationships. An example of this is seen in the description of kinship and friendship patterns among the Jie of East Africa in Highlight 4.1.

The social life of the Jie of East Africa is expressed in different patterns of exchange of livestock. Animal exchanges are used to create special bonds of kinship and friendships as well as being a part of economic life.

Horticultural Societies

Horticulture is essentially gardening with primitive hand tools like digging sticks and hoes. As a form of adaptation to the environment, horticulture permits a more elaborate social and political organization than hunting and gathering or the pastoralist domestication of animals. Moreover, horticultural technology has the potential for expanding into marginal agriculture, which has even greater possibilities for the elaboration of social structure.

A good example of horticulture can be found in the description by Carneiro (1968) of slash-and-burn cultivation among the Kuikuru of the Amazon basin in South America. The Kuikuru live on a plant called manioc, which is poisonous and must go through a complex processing to be made edible. The technology for cultivation is simple. Steel axes and machetes are used to clear garden plots of trees and underbrush, which are left to dry and then are piled up and burned. The wood ashes provide the fertilizer for the soil. Manioc cuttings are planted, cared for by weeding and hoeing, and the manioc tubers are harvested some 18 to 20 months after planting. Replanting of new cuttings takes place soon after.

The horticulture technology of the Kuikuru gives

them the opportunity to produce more food than they can consume, that is, surplus production. In addition, there is a greater possibility of permanence in the settlement area and of sustaining a larger population.

Settlement permanence, larger population size, surplus production, and leisure are important for the development of more complex forms of social and political structures. Some of these forms can be seen in another horticultural group, the Pima Indians of the American Southwest.

The horticultural activities of the Pima, although based on simple tools, extend into marginal agriculture. By means of irrigation and collective planting and harvesting, facilitated by the development of a more complex social and political structure, they were able to effect some control over their water supply. Hackenberg (1968) has described this process as follows:

The Pima alone made a promising start at preindustrial. It began late in their aboriginal history—after 1750—and the trend lasted little more than a century. During this period, however, the Pima developed the following patterns unknown to the Papago:

1. Concentration of settlement pattern;
2. Cooperative intervillage water management;
3. Tribal-wide political leadership in war and mobilization for defense;
4. Production of surplus farm commodities for sale and trade;
5. Escape from the need for wild foods except in years of poor water supply;
6. Commencement of social differentiation, as seen in the employment of laborers and the accumulation of wealth. (p. 151)

Agricultural Societies*

The fourth form of adaptation found among peasant-primitive peoples is **agriculture,** represented by the use of the plow, the use of animals as an energy source, and the domestication of food supplies. With the plow and draft animals very large areas can be

*This section draws heavily on Cohen (1968, pp. 315–322).

HIGHLIGHT 4.1
"The Jie of Uganda"

Each Jie man stands at the center of a particular network of formal, personal relations with certain other men. Some of these relations are established by birth . . . some by marriage—his own and those of his sister and daughters (affinal kin), and some by deliberate pledge (bond-friends). A man looks to these people for friendship, sympathy, advice, and affection. He often visits them and he gives hospitality and assistance to them. More than this, they are the people with whom he maintains reciprocal rights to claim gifts of animals in times of need. While never neglecting the initial basis of the relationship—kinship—Jie always lay greatest stress on the exchanges of live-stock at such times as marriage, shortage of milking animals, the desire for a particular kind of ox or goat, or the need to pay a judicial fine or to provide a specified animal for ritual purposes. For that reason I refer to these men as "stock-associates." A Jie refers to them collectively as "my people," but they do not form a corporate group since they act with respect to a particular individual, and seldom at all together.

Jie recognize two kinds of stock-associates: those with whom reciprocal rights involve cattle, and those involving only small stock. In the first category come . . . mother's full brothers and their sons, close affines (fathers and brothers of wives and sons' wives, sisters' and daughters' husbands and their brothers), and bond-friends. In the second category are more distant maternal and affinal kin and clansmen. The distribution is not precise and depends on the particular conventions established, but usual practice works out like that. . . . In emphasizing the rights and obligations over animals, I am following Jie conceptions. I do not wish to ignore the many other kinds of assistance or affections, but, like the Jie, I stress the most vital aspects of the relationships. (p. 272)

SOURCE: Philip H. Gulliver, in Yehudi A. Cohen, *Man in Adaptation* (New York: Aldine Publishing Co., 1974).

cultivated. Also, soils and grasslands that cannot be cultivated with the digging stick and the techniques of horticulture yield to the plow.

The cultivation of large areas, combined with control over the elements through fertilization and irrigation, results in more predictable food supplies as well as surplus production. Large populations and large settlements are made possible by greater productivity.

Agricultural societies also have a more diverse division of labor, extending beyond the simple age-sex division found in more primitive economic systems. Not everyone is involved in food-producing activities. Craftworkers provide the more complex

The use of draft animals and the plow is characteristic of agricultural societies. In contrast to horticultural societies, very large land areas can be cultivated with a more plentiful and predictable food supply. This results in larger human settlements and the development of a more complex social structure.

tools for agricultural production. Bureaucratic officials administer the political agencies that coordinate the activities of diverse groups.

Finally, agriculture is associated with more developed and persistent forms of inequality. Those who control land are able to acquire wealth and power. The largest segment of society—the peasant class—owns neither land nor animals; peasants cultivate the land for the owners, who may recompense peasants in kind or by renting them a small portion of land for their own production.

Reading 4.2 describes the relationships of peasant cultivators to their rulers and other groups.

The four forms of nonindustrial societies that we have examined—hunting and gathering, pastoral, horticultural, and agricultural—represent different ways in which human societies adapt to their environments. Each form of adaptation represents the interaction of society and environment, starting from relatively uncomplicated social forms and moving toward increasingly complex and differentiated activities. In the simpler societies of hunters and gatherers the economic aspects of life are virtually indistinguishable from the noneconomic. Each succeeding form of society represents a corresponding increase in the separation of economic and noneconomic activities. This separation, represented by specialized roles and a complex division of labor, does not mean that economic and noneconomic institutions no longer influence each other; rather there is both a separation of such activities and a growing centrality of economic institutions, which tend to dominate other areas of social life.

INDUSTRIAL SOCIETIES

One of the most significant social changes of the modern age was the transformation of agricultural societies into industrial societies. This transformation is associated with the Industrial Revolution, which began in England around the middle of the eighteenth century. The Industrial Revolution was marked by a rapid increase in the use of machine-based production systems and a shift in the labor force from agriculture to industrial production. Industrial societies have greatly increased both agricultural and industrial productivity. For example, in 1800 in the United States it took 373 worker-hours to produce 100 bushels of wheat, while it took only nine worker-hours in 1980. Between 1820 and 1970 the production of iron and steel in the United States increased 12,000 times (Lenski, 1982). As a result industrial societies have very high per capita incomes and greater abundance of goods and services for their members.

The following sections will examine the factors that changed agricultural societies and created the industrial factory system.

Agricultural Society in Decline

We have noted that in the simplest hunting and gathering societies there is no distinction made between production for the household and production for the community. In horticultural societies there is some tendency toward separation of the two spheres. In the fully developed agricultural society the household economy and the community economy are clearly distinguishable.

Feudalism, the social and economic system of the Middle Ages in Central and Western Europe was based on agriculture, landholding, and an elaborate system of rights and obligations associated with land. Landowners, or lords, of large estates enjoyed special rights over the peasants who worked the land. Peasants were allowed to till certain parcels of land, called fiefs, for which they were in turn obligated to furnish services to the lord, for example, protecting the lord's domain.

The feudal system underwent gradual decline. The self-sufficiency of agricultural life could not fill the growing demand for goods and services. Trade and commerce, encouraged by the travels of the Crusaders, stimulated interest in new products and materials. By 1700 feudalism was no longer the dominant social and economic structure.*

---

*We should be cautious in fixing specific dates to some of the gradual transformations that took place in England and Western Europe at this time. Wilbert Moore has referred to these transformations as a "history without dates," because change was uneven in different industries and regions.

Craftwork and the Guild System

Around the eleventh century cities emerged as important centers of commerce, encouraging the growth of a powerful merchant class. The existence of a money economy in the cities subverted traditional landlord-tenant relationships. Peasants carried their surplus production to the city markets and obtained money for what they sold. Payment in money meant a change in the rights and obligations that characterized the lord-vassal relationship.

Not only was the agricultural worker released from the traditional obligations of the feudal order, but the skilled craftworkers of the large manorial households (often trained by the proprietor) were also attracted to the cities where their services were in increasing demand by the new merchant class. Some craftworkers owned their own tools and raw materials and could therefore produce directly for a consumer. Others had only their skilled labor to sell to a fellow craftworker or to a merchant-entrepreneur who would provide the tools and raw materials. In some cases, it might be the consumer who provided everything the craftworker would need to produce the desired item.

During the eleventh and twelfth centuries associations of independent artisans who produced for the marketplace (rather than for a merchant-entrepreneur or a fellow craftworker) became established. They were known as **craft guilds**. The guilds had two main functions. The first was to provide for the regulation of the entire production process. This included the selection of raw materials, the use of specific work techniques, the training and use of apprentices, the tools to be used in the production process, and the quality control of the final product. The second function of craft guilds was to establish a monopoly over the production of certain products or sole jurisdiction in a particular geographical area. The guild's claim to exclusive jurisdiction was supported by public authority, but there was often conflict between the guild craftworker and independent artisans.

Regulation and monopolization of work by the guilds allowed them to limit competition among craftworkers and to provide equal opportunities to all guild members. Because of the concern over internal competition the guilds also sought to limit the accumulation of excessive capital by individual workers. It was recognized that capital accumulation might lead some artisans to become the employers of other craftworkers, thereby becoming entrepreneurs.

Despite all these efforts at regulation and the control of competition among workers, the guild system lost its force as an institution governing economic activities. The disintegration of the guilds occurred for the following reasons:

First, the attempt by the guilds to regulate all aspects of the production process and craftworker activities led them to hold on to traditional methods of production. Innovative production techniques were discouraged, despite the possibility of increased productivity or improved quality, because they might introduce unfair competition among guild members. Apprentices or journeymen who sought advancement to the next rank (journeyman or master) were discouraged because of regulations that determined the ratios of classes of workers within guilds. All in all, the very effectiveness of the guilds produced pressures on dissatisfied craftworkers to work outside of them.

Second, craftworkers and merchants who had accumulated capital emerged as the capitalist-employers of home workers. They provided the raw materials, and the home craftworker produced to their specifications. This eliminated the direct relationship between the craftworker and the consumer that prevailed under the guild system.

Third, some guilds became wealthy and powerful and were able to force other guilds into an employee position. Jurisdictional disputes among guilds increased as it became more difficult to avoid specialization in the production process. Under guild regulations, each guild specialized in terms of the final product, not in terms of parts of production process. Thus a guild that produced shirts was responsible for spinning, weaving, dyeing, finishing, and marketing. As new products that cut across traditional guild jurisdictions emerged, internal disputes became more frequent.

Although the guilds declined in importance, they did set in motion a number of forces that would continue to influence economic life. Most important was the creation of a labor force that worked for wages and produced goods and services for a competitive market.

The Domestic or Shop Production System

The decline of the guild system, which left the merchant-entrepreneur in a position to use the labor power of the craftworker, resulted in a new system of work called the **domestic or shop production system.** Raw materials, and sometimes tools, were brought to the home of the craftworker by the merchant-entrepreneur. The final product was collected by the merchant-entrepreneur and put on the market. In some cases, several workers were gathered in a shop provided by the merchant-entrepreneur.

Pressure on the craftworker also contributed to the rise of the new system. Individual craftworkers could no longer pay for costly raw materials and the increasingly expensive tools necessary for greater productivity. In addition, work became more specialized and standardized with the increased pressure for more and cheaper goods. The craftworkers in the shop became another unit of production.

The domestic or shop production system set in motion the following trends that would find their full expression in the factory:

First, task specialization and division of labor were more developed under the domestic or shop production system than under the guild system. This occurred because of the pressure for greater productivity and the inability of the craftworker to resist such pressure and also because the basic production unit was made up of a number of persons (whether household members or several craftworkers) with shared involvement for turning out a product.

Next, the independent status of the skilled artisan under the guild system gradually changed to employee status. The craftworker was no longer responsible for the total product. He no longer selected the raw materials, made the final judgment of the quality of the product, produced for an individual consumer, and owned the means of production, that is, his own tools. In short, the mer-

chant-entrepreneur exerted control over all phases of the production process.

Finally, under the conditions of shop production, household and industry functions became separated. Family members left the household to carry out their work, which was contractual in nature, rather than kinship based.

Domestic or shop production remained the major form of production until new and complex technology began to demand increasing amounts of capital. The capital investment in hand tools by the merchant-entrepreneur was relatively small compared with the cost of power-driven machines. The importance of this difference in investment was noted by Weber (1927):

> The ability of the [domestic or shop production system] to maintain itself so long rested on the unimportance of fixed capital. In weaving this consisted only of the loom; in spinning, prior to the invention of mechanical spinning machines, it was still more insignificant. The capital remained in the possession of the independent worker, and its constituent parts were decentralized, not concentrated as in a modern factory, and hence without special importance. (p. 160)

The use of expensive machinery in the production process meant an increase in the amount of capital that the entrepreneur had to invest. With the invention and use of this new technology, the domestic or shop production system gave way to the factory.

The Factory Production System

"A factory is a shop industry with free labor and fixed capital," wrote Weber (1927, p. 163). To this definition Moore (1946) adds the idea that the factory is based on shop production; that is, the shop, not the individual worker, is the productive unit. **Factory production,** in its fully developed form, is generally held to have emerged in England in the latter part of the eighteenth century. Power-driven machines and an abundance of labor—workers who had left or had been driven from the land—combined with the availability of entrepreneurs with capital, produced the early factory system.

Shop production was a transitional form that followed the guild system. Raw materials, tools, and a small number of workers were brought together by a merchant-entrepreneur in a small shop. They were sometimes referred to as "sweat shops" because of the low wages, long hours, and poor working conditions. Shop production, of the sort seen in this shop making dolls, laid the basis for factory production through its task specialization and division of labor.

Most new factories were built by men who started out with a great deal of capital, not by workers who had accumulated small savings. In a study of the Industrial Revolution in England, Foster (1974) shows that the first 42 cotton mills in Oldham (the center of England's cotton industry) were built by coal-mine owners, bankers, and wealthy merchants. He also argues that extensive capital was not needed simply for the purchase of the new machinery. As he puts it:

. . . machinery was only a small part of what was needed to build new mills. Far more important was competitive control over power, raw materials, labour and credit—and the men who built the first of the forty-two mills were not just men already in business but men coming from families in hatting and coal (industries demanding far larger capital than outwork manufacturing in either cotton or wood). A worker might be able to get credit for the machinery but the rest would be altogether beyond him. (p. 11)

The main features of factory production—shop production, fixed capital, and free labor—are discussed in detail in Reading 4.3.

It was not long after the emergence of the factory system that some of its negative features were recognized. The working conditions found in the early factories would be difficult to believe today. A long chapter of Karl Marx's *Capital* (1906) titled "Machinery and Modern Industry" contains a bitter denunciation of the factory system and a documentation of its destructive effects on the men, women, and children who worked there. Marx suggests that the factory system was quick to employ women and young children because their bodies were better suited to the work and their labor power could be purchased more cheaply. At the end of the 1700s and during the early 1800s children less than 13 years old were allowed to work only six hours a day, but the law was violated by both employers and parents. Orphans were taken out of workhouses for employment as factory workers. Provisions for the continuing education of working children less than 14 years old were required by law. The law was quickly circumvented, however, with the emergence of special "schools" that seem to

have done little more than sign the periodic "certificates of attendance" for working children that were required.

Some of the harshest descriptions of factory life in England in the early nineteenth century can be found in the periodicals of the time, which gave expression to a range of public opinion on the economic and social tensions of the first industrial society. These materials, such as those cited by Saville (1973), provide a grim picture of life in early industrial England.

WHAT IS SOCIAL STRUCTURE?

The term structure is used in many scientific disciplines. The biologist speaks of the genetic structure of DNA. The chemist describes the atomic structure of molecules. The neuropsychologist analyzes the neurological structure of the brain. In each case, structure invariably suggests a physical model, an orderly arrangement of parts that are interconnected and form a meaningful whole. Such a physical model might be represented by the familiar tinker toys, a building toy for children consisting of spools serving as the basic parts and dowels of various length serving as connecting links between the spools.

The concept of structure as an orderly arrangement of interconnected parts forming a meaningful whole is one that sociologists also find useful for understanding human society. As we have noted, social structure is (1) the patterned and recurrent social relationships among persons in human collectivities, and (2) the patterned and recurrent interrelationships of human collectivities. Most people live out their lives in human collectivities like families, friendship groups, organizations, and communities. The fact that social life within and between these collectivities is socially structured is what gives human society the pattern and regularity necessary for predictable social relationships.

This predictability is revealed in the fact that the experience of living in particular groups (such as families or organizations) can be generalized to living in other groups. In this way people can become members of many collectivities without extensive learning. For example, students can transfer from one university to another without special preparation. They will find the main features of student-student or student-teacher relationships, as well as expectations of social and academic behavior, to be very similar.

Positions and Roles

The pattern and predictability found in human groups is based on the existence of specific **positions** that their members occupy. A position in a human society is a "bundle" of activities that are important for the groups purposes or objectives. For example, in a university there are positions of student, teacher, dean, president, and so forth. In an industrial organization there are positions of lathe operator, foreman, accountant, shop steward, and so on. In a family there are positions of mother, father, wife, husband, daughter, and the like.

Positions precede and are independent of the people who may occupy them. Each position in a social structure has a set of rights and obligations that the position's occupant will be expected to fulfill. Rights include material rewards, authority over others, and freedom to act in certain ways. Obligations involve the activities that must be carried out for the group to continue to exist. People in groups learn what is expected of them and what to expect of others when they assume certain positions.

When positions are filled by people, the expectations are activated and applied to the position's occupant. Each position in a social structure is linked to some other position by its "bundle" of activities and by its rights and obligations. The positions of student and teacher are linked by reciprocal rights and obligations. The students' rights to clear, informative lectures and fair exams are the teachers' obligations. The teachers' rights to have students attend class and read assignments are the students' obligations.

When we describe a social structure in terms of positions, what we have is a "map" of behavior but not the actual behavior of people in positions. Positions occupied by actual people are transformed into roles. **Roles** are expectations about appropriate behavior for occupants of particular positions. Role expectations are held by both the role occupant and the people who interact with the role occupant. The actual behavior of people in positions is called **role behavior**.

There are three main reasons why role behavior may be different from the map of behavior obtained from knowledge of the positions. First, when people occupy a position they bring to the position their own personality, values, and unique life experiences. Role occupants may choose to interpret the position in a way that is different from the usual. For example, a new chemical engineer working on fertilizers may feel that she has a professional responsibility to refuse to work on products that may be potentially harmful. She does this even though her position as an engineer does not give her the right to choose between projects; her role is to follow orders and leave it to others to determine a product's safety.

The second reason is that role occupants may be exposed to multiple and conflicting expectations to which they must adapt. For example, a supervisor in a factory has role relationships with workers, managers, shop stewards, and other supervisors. In the process of reconciling conflicting or incompatible expectations his position as supervisor will be modified.

The third reason is that people occupy many different positions and are therefore called upon to play different roles that sometimes involve contradictory demands. For example, a person may occupy the position of mother in the family and chief engineer at work. The expectations that her children and husband have of her as mother may call for more time at home in the evenings or weekends. However, the expectations that her colleagues have of her as engineer may call for working evenings and weekends. This is a situation of **role conflict.** Such conflict makes it difficult to fulfill either role in a satisfactory manner.

Positions and roles, as elements of social structure, allow individuals to anticipate the behavior of others, to organize their own behavior and thus to provide pattern, regularity, and predictability to human behavior.

Social Institutions

All human societies face a common set of problems that must be dealt with if its members are to have a reasonably satisfying life. Basic material goods must be produced and distributed so that all members can sustain life. Disputes among members must be controlled and regulated. Sexual relationships and childrearing must be carried out in socially approved ways. Every society must deal with the training of the young by transmitting social traditions and needed skills. Every society must develop ways of dealing with the unknown.

The solutions to these problems are dealt with by institutions. **Social institutions** are clusters of values, norms, positions, and social roles that deal with the basic problems of human society and are the basis of a society's stability. The economic institution is concerned with the production and distribution of goods. The family institution is concerned with sexual liaisons and childrearing. The political institution regulates conflict among

members of society. The religious institution deals with questions of ultimate value and the meaning of life. The educational institution imparts knowledge to each new generation.

Social institutions are a combination of social structure and culture—the patterned and recurrent social relationships and the values and norms that give them meaning or content. Thus while all societies have economic institutions, the particular way in which goods are produced and distributed will vary from one society to another, depending on the values that a society places on different kinds of economic activity. One society may stress collective ownership of property and distribution of goods based on need, while another will stress private ownership of property and distribution of goods based on the ability to pay.

FORMS OF SOCIAL STRUCTURE

Social structure refers to social relationships in collectivities that are shaped by positions and roles that people fill. There are four major forms of social structure that are based on different human collectivities. Table 4.1 lists the four social structures

TABLE 4.1   Forms of Social Structure

GENERAL FORM	SPECIFIC EXAMPLES	MAJOR CHARACTERISTICS
Primary group structures (Chapter 5)	Family Friendship groups Work groups	Member identification Intimate interaction Frequent interaction
Purposefully organized structures (Chapter 9)	Voluntary associations Organizations	Goal directed Specialized tasks Hierarchy of authority Impersonal social relationships
Territorial structures (Chapter 17)	City	Political and psychological boundaries Interdependence Institutional completeness
	Community	Political and psychological boundaries Potential for intimate interaction Identification with community and its institutions
	Neighborhood	Psychological boundaries Great potential for intimate interaction
Latent structures (Chapters 8 and 11)	Socioeconomic structure Racial-ethnic groups	Members have a common attribute Potential for emergence of groups and organizations Members have common life chances

along with specific examples of each and some of their most important characteristics. The table also indicates the chapters of this text that deal with each type of structure.

Primary Group Structures

Primary group structures, such as families and friendship groups, are the smallest social units. Some analysts think of these structures as the "building blocks" of larger society (Olmstead, 1959). They are building blocks in the sense that all larger social structures, such as organizations or cities, can be viewed as made up of overlapping social groups. These small, face-to-face structures can also be seen as "small societies." In these small societies individuals learn about power, legitimacy, social norms, rights and obligations, and conflict resolution. This learning is generalized to, and often becomes the basis for, social life outside the smaller group. For example, children who have close, trusting relationships in their families are likely to establish similar relationships with friends, teachers, co-workers, and so on.

Highlight 4.2, an often-quoted statement by Charles H. Cooley (1909) describes the major characteristics of primary groups and their functions for individuals and society in quite lyrical prose. These can be listed as follows. The primary group is characterized by (1) intimate face-to-face association, (2) cooperation among group members, (3) identification with the group by the members, (4) each member's self-concept tied to the group, and (5) competition among group members controlled by mutual commitment to the group's continuity. The functions of the primary group include (1) socialization of group members, (2) emotional gratification of group members, (3) emotional development of group members, (4) development of social bonds that provide for the continuity of social institutions, and (5) mobilization of human resources and energies for use by other collectivities.

How are primary groups structured and how do they influence their members? Sociological studies of the family group, the friendship group, and the work group give us some answers.

HIGHLIGHT 4.2
The Primary Group

By primary groups I mean those characterized by intimate face-to-face association and cooperation. They are primary in several senses, but chiefly in that they are fundamental in forming the social nature and ideals of the individual. The result of intimate association, psychologically, is a certain fusion of individualities in a common whole, so that one's very self, for many purposes at least, is the common life and purpose of the group. Perhaps the simplest way of describing this wholeness is by saying that it is a "we"; it involves the sort of sympathy and mutual identification for which "we" is the natural expression. One lives in the feeling of the whole and finds the chief aims of his will in that feeling.

It is not to be supposed that the unity of the primary group is one of mere harmony and love. It is always a differentiated and usually a competitive unity, admitting of self-assertion and various appropriative passions; but these passions are socialized by sympathy, and come, or tend to come, under the discipline of a common spirit. The individual will be ambitious, but the chief object of his ambition will be some desired place in the thought of others, and he will feel allegiance to common standards of service and fair play. . . .

Primary groups are primary in the sense that they give the individual his earliest and completest experience of social unity, and also in the sense that they do not change in the same degree as more elaborate relations, but form a comparatively permanent source out of which the latter are ever springing. . . .

These groups then are the springs of life, not only for the individual but for social institutions.

Source: Charles H. Cooley, *Social Organization*, New York: Charles Scribner's Sons, 1909, pp. 27–28.

THE FAMILY GROUP
Many of the characteristics and hypothesized functions of primary groups are based on studies of the

The family represents the best example of a primary group because of the strong emotional bonds among members, the identification with the group as a basis of self-concept, and the mutual commitment to the group's continuity. It is for these reasons that the family is so influential in socializing its members and providing for their emotional gratifications and development.

family group with its traditional structure made up of a father, mother, children, and in some cases relatives. Relationships within the family were often idealized as reflecting strong ties, loving relationships, and an enduring, harmonious bond (Vincent and Small, 1961).

Conceptions of the contemporary family as a primary group will have to be reexamined in light of the changing permanence and structure of the family. The divorce rate has been rising steadily in the last twenty years, from a rate of 2.2 divorces per 1,000 population in 1962 to 5.3 divorces in 1980. As a result, more single-parent families face increased financial problems and emotional demands.

There are also fewer families that have older parents living with them. Increasing numbers of older people are living alone or in nursing homes. Why are recent generations not sharing their homes with aging parents? What does this say about the family

as a primary group with presumed bonds of closeness and support?

We must be careful not to assume too quickly that rising divorce rates and isolated aged signal the decline of the family. The high divorce rate is followed by a high remarriage rate, indicating that people still have a strong preference for marriage. Similarly, the declining coresidence of aging parents with adult children is balanced by evidence that aged parents live close to their adult children and maintains stable and supportive social relationships (Lee, 1980; Shanas, 1979).

Sociologists like Skolnick (1981) have reflected on the significance of current domestic patterns of single-parent households, childless marriages, divorce, and long-term liaisons without marriage. Research on these new family structures may tell us whether the family continues to provide the close, emotional support of primary group structures.

THE FRIENDSHIP GROUP

In contrast to the family, the friendship group is less involved with the intellectual and emotional development of its members and more often directed to providing members with social standing among their peers. Membership in a friendship group is a matter of choice, and therefore persons will move into and out of such groups easily, remaining only in those groups that satisfy their needs.

The importance of a friendship group for the psychological well-being of its members is revealed in Whyte's (1943) classic study of white street corner gangs in the Boston slums. Whyte describes how gang members who lost their standing in the group or whose patterns of interaction in the group were undergoing change experienced increased social stress, reflected in dizzy spells, sleeplessness, and nightmares. In each case, the stress seemed to be related to the loss of support by the group.

Another characteristic of friendship groups that is in sharp contrast to the family groups is the constant restructuring of the relationships within the friendship group. Friends are continually gained and lost. This gives the group an element of fluidity and also instability. Liebow's 1967 book, *Tally's Corner: A Study of Negro Streetcorner Men*, vividly portrays the instability of friendship patterns among the members of this group in a Washington, D.C., slum. This study, carried out almost 30 years after Whyte's study in Boston, did not find the same highly organized patterns of street life and strong bonds of friendship and mutual aid that Whyte found in the slum community in Boston.

What accounts for the different findings? Could the difference be caused by a general decline in the importance of primary groups in the 30 years separating the two studies? Could it be because the studies were based on different ethnic groups? Or could it be due to other factors associated with these communities, such as size, length of residence of its members, or cultural similarity of its members?

Thus friendship groups may offer the close personal relationships of a primary group, but the groups' instability may prevent enduring primary relationships.

THE WORK GROUP

Contributions to the study of primary groups by early sociologists like Cooley (1909) had limited impact on American sociology for many years. Renewed interest in primary groups came with the publication of a series of studies of industrial work groups. A work group can be a primary group when people who work together become involved in an active social life centered around their common job. The most important of the early research on work groups came to be known as the Hawthorne studies, after the Hawthorne plant of the Western Electric Company where they took place (Roethlisberger and Dickson, 1939).

The Hawthorne studies started out as an effort to discover how worker efficiency and productivity are influenced by factors like fatigue, piece rate pay, and heating and lighting conditions of the work place. Five female workers, whose job was extremely repetitive (it consisted of assembling telephone relays), were removed from the main plant and placed in the Relay Assembly Test Room, which was especially outfitted for the studies. Here researchers manipulated various conditions like illumination, temperature, humidity, rest periods, and even the payment system, to determine how these conditions affected the women's work behavior.

After 12 months the investigators concluded that there was not much effect upon worker output from physiological factors, economic incentives, or the physical environment itself. Instead, they made the unanticipated discovery that it was the character of the work group and the individual's satisfactions within that group that were the important determinants of output.

Working with the idea that workers do not respond to their work situation as individuals but as group members, further research found that the work group set and enforced norms about a fair day's work. The group, through its informal leaders, made sure that workers followed the norms, punished "rate busters," and instructed newcomers on what was expected of them.

The kind of social relationships that develop in a work group can be influenced by how people's work is structured. Some studies of assembly line and automated production systems indicate that the opportunities for socializing and for forming primary group bonds are very limited because of factors like noise, pace of work, and physical arrangements of the workers (Faunce, 1958; Walker and Guest, 1952). However, other research on automobile workers in four countries does not support the theory that assembly line work reduces the quantity and quality of social interaction among workers (Form, 1972; 1973).

We have encountered some contradictory evidence on whether we can generalize the primary group characteristics of families to other groups. Perhaps the problem lies in applying the concept of the primary group to situations where there is only the *appearance* of cohesive groups. Thus an important task for the sociologist is to reexamine the nature of the primary group and to better identify those conditions that encourage the formation of primary groups in both friendship and work settings.

Purposefully Organized Structures

The existence of large organizations in every area of social life is a relatively recent occurrence. Most people today are born in a large organization called a hospital. In earlier times childbirth took place at home. We are now socialized in organizations called schools. Most people work in large organizations called factories or corporations rather than on family farms or in small family businesses. Our social and civic activities take place in a variety of voluntary associations rather than through less formal friendship and community groups. Our movement through the significant stages of the life cycle, from birth to marriage to death, are recorded by government agencies or are ceremoniously acknowledged by religious organizations.

There are two general types of purposefully organized structures: the voluntary association and the organization. Although there are many similarities between the two, their differences are worth noting.

VOLUNTARY ASSOCIATIONS

The term **voluntary association** is generally used to refer to civic and service groups, fraternal clubs, occupational and professional groups, veterans associations, and a host of social, cultural, religious, and political associations. Sills (1968) defines voluntary associations as follows:

A voluntary association is an organized group of persons (1) that is formed in order to further some common interest of its members; (2) in which membership is voluntary in the sense that it is neither mandatory nor acquired through birth; and (3) that exists independently of the state. (pp. 362–363)

We can refine this broad definition by recognizing another aspect of voluntary associations. Members of voluntary associations do not make a living from the association. This factor excludes business firms, schools, and universities from our list of voluntary associations, limiting it to "spare-time, participatory associations" (p. 363).

People form or join voluntary associations because of common interests that can be advanced or achieved through collective action. Their commitment to the goals of the association and their identification with the group is generally greater than for members who work full time for the organization. This commitment and members' part-time nonsalaried participation result in a more informal internal structure than is characteristic of organizations. This occurs because committed members seek greater direct involvement in the association's activities, and they resist efforts to restrict their involvement to narrow roles.

ORGANIZATIONS

There are a number of distinctive features of **organizations** that make them a very important kind of social structure. These features produce the pattern and regularity of social relationships that take place within organizations and between organizations and other social structures, including primary groups, communities, and social classes.

The first distinctive feature of organizations is that they are deliberately constructed, goal-directed collectivities. The goals are formally stated, often written down, and a matter of public knowledge. Formally stated goals provide a clear link to the social environment surrounding an organization. The result of an organization's activities is a "product" or "output," which is in turn "consumed" by an individual or by a group or another organization in the environment. By having formally stated goals an organization establishes a basis for evaluating its activities and can therefore change things that are not working well, that is, not contributing to the organization's goals.

The second distinctive feature of organizations follows from the first one. A goal-directed collectivity will generally act to improve its chances for goal attainment. This means it must identify the specialized tasks necessary for goal attainment as well as recruit the people needed to carry out these tasks on the basis of their knowledge or training (often referred to as expertise).

The third distinctive feature of organizations is the existence of a hierarchy of authority that functions to coordinate, communicate, and control the behavior of its members. These activities are very important in large organizations. They are not so important to smaller ones, which may rely primarily on oral communication and personal relationships to carry out organizational functions.

The fourth important feature of organizations is that they are designed to operate through impersonal social relationships. The absence of emotion, whether of hatred or affection, is expected to result in a more equitable treatment of an organization's clients, and more rational control over the activities of the organization. Impersonality is possible because of the existence of specialized roles. The engineer in an aerospace firm and the social worker in a welfare office are not expected to introduce their domestic life, community activities, or religious or political beliefs into the organization. Of course, they often do.

In summary, the four major characteristics of an organization that are responsible for pattern and regularity are (1) goal direction, (2) specialized tasks, (3) hierarchy of authority, and (4) impersonal social relationships.

Territorial Structures

Each type of social structure discussed so far cannot meet all of people's needs. Primary groups do not generally provide the economic resources for survival. Nor do organizations generally provide the emotional resources necessary for human growth and development. Voluntary associations cannot be used to develop primary ties or to supply economic resources. **Territorial social structures,** however, include all social structures described so far. They provide a common physical location for primary groups, voluntary associations, and organizations.

The three types of territorial social structures discussed in this section are the city, the community, and the neighborhood. All are defined by a combination of spatial and social factors. For example people who are near to each other may be more likely to interact than people who are spatially distant. Over a period of time these interactions may lead to common values and to similar behavior patterns, which in turn give each territorial structure its own special character. Table 4.2 compares the territorial structures of city, community, and neighborhood in terms of seven spatial and social characteristics.

CITY

The term city may be variously defined (Taylor, 1980). The U.S. Bureau of the Census describes a city as a place where 2,500 or more people reside. Other definitions used by social scientists stress the spatial and social aspects of the city. For example, Mumford (1968) states: "The city is both a collection of architectural forms in space and a tissue of associations, corporate enterprises, and institutions that occupy this collective structure and have interacted with it in the course of time" (p. 447).

Neither of these definitions includes the characteristics that differentiate the city from rural areas and from other territorial structures such as community and neighborhood (Table 4.2). Noting these characteristics, we may define a **city** as a large human collectivity with recognized territorial bound-

TABLE 4.2 Spatial and Social Characteristics of Territorial Structures

	Formally Designated Territorial Boundaries	Common Political System	Institutional Completeness	Functional Interdependence	Unit Autonomy	Population Homogeneity	Intensity of Interaction and Identification with Unit
City	Yes	Yes	High	High	High	Low	Low
Community	Yes	Yes	Moderate	Moderate	Moderate	Moderate	Moderate
Neighborhood	No[a]	No	Low[b]	Low	Low	High	High

[a] The neighborhood is a distinct territory to its residents though it often has no formally recognized boundaries.

[b] Neighborhoods often have specific organizations, such as the church, commercial establishments (such as stores), schools, and perhaps social, civic, recreational, and political organizations (often church-related). However, they lack the full range of economic and political activities necessary to support a population to the same extent as communities and cities.

aries and a common political system, which enables it to make binding decisions for those who reside within its boundaries. The city has many elements of *institutional completeness*. This means that it can provide many functions necessary for sustained social life, including economic, political, religious, educational, and family activities. The institutional completeness of a city is related to the large amount of interdependence among social structures within the city.

Institutional completeness does not mean total self-sufficiency. For example, the city carries out many economic functions, but it cannot provide its own food. It must obtain its food from outside its territorial boundaries. Also, the city provides for the protection of its residents through police and fire-fighting services, but in times of disaster, like earthquake or flood, outside resources may be needed. Yet, while not totally autonomous with respect to its environment, the city has the highest degree of autonomy among the three territorial structures.

Finally, the city has a low degree of population homogeneity. Population is diverse with respect to socioeconomic strata, ethnic and religious groups, and age categories. This heterogeneity, combined with large size, contributes to the low intensity of interaction by its members. It also limits their sense of identification with the city.

COMMUNITY

In much sociological writing little distinction is made between the concepts of city and **community**.

Some writers refer to the "urban community" when they mean the "city," and when they refer to a smaller, less complex territorial structure they will speak of the "local community." In many respects a community cannot be distinguished from a city.

There is some research support for the hypothesis that small cities exhibit characteristics usually attributed to communities; that is, intimate social relationships and a sense of involvement in, and identification with, its territorial structure. Smith, Form, and Stone (1954) in their study of a midwestern city of 140,000 population report that residents maintain extensive intimate relationships with other urbanites. These intimate relationships are not limited to their immediate locality; in fact, the majority of friendships are formed with people outside of their neighborhood. It is possible that as the size of the city increases, intimate relationships become limited to the neighborhood because the extended space of the city reduces the opportunity for friendships outside the immediate locality.

As Table 4.2 indicates, the city and community are similar because they have recognized territorial boundaries and political systems. The smaller size of the community, however, reduces the extent to which it carries out all of the functions necessary for social life (institutional completeness) and reduces interdependence among social structures as well as the autonomy of the community relative to its environment. In addition, the community, in contrast to the city, has a more homogeneous population and greater intensity of interaction among the members of its territory.

The neighborhood is the immediate environment in which a person lives within a city or community. Its boundaries are subjective and personal, and people in neighborhoods interact frequently and identify with the area. Here we see a block party in an urban neighborhood that reflects a common identification with the locale.

NEIGHBORHOOD

Social science research has tended to emphasize the significance of large territorial structures to the neglect of smaller territorial structures like communities and especially neighborhoods.

The relative lack of attention devoted to neighborhoods may be related to some of its characteristics. The **neighborhood** does not have clearly marked boundaries or a formal political system. The territory called the neighborhood is usually subjective and personal in nature and often exists only in the minds of its members. For some, it may be "the block." For others, it can be an area with a "name" that has deep historical roots.

The neighborhood seldom has an economic function. Institutional completeness and interdependence are almost nonexistent. An obvious consequence is that the neighborhood is without autonomy with respect to its environment. What the neighborhood has that larger territorial structures do not have is a more homogeneous population, more intense social relationships, and a greater common consciousness of residential locale.

The research of Gans (1962) and Suttles (1968) described in great depth and rich detail the importance of the small territorial structure called a neighborhood to the lives of the urban poor. Gans studied a working-class area in Boston known as the West End, a tenement area of poorly maintained three- and five-story apartment buildings, some vacant stores, and other buildings. These buildings are populated by first- and second-generation ethnic households the largest group being Italian-American. Life in the West End is dominated by what Gans calls the "peer group society." The organizations and associations in the area, such as the church, parochial school, and social-civic groups, "exist outside the peer group society, but are linked with it if and when they can be used to meet group and individual needs" (p. 105). Peer group bonds were apparently so strong and pervasive in that territory that its inhabitants began thinking of themselves as "belonging" to a neighborhood called the West End only when the area was threatened with destruction by a redevelopment scheme.

Suttles studied the Adams Street area of the Near West Side of Chicago. The area is divided into four ethnic enclaves occupied by blacks, Italians, Puerto Ricans, and Mexicans. The Italians, because of their long residence in the area, have an extensive peer group culture that includes all age groups. Blacks, the most recent residents of the area, have the least developed and cohesive peer group structure. The separation of one black from another occurs more often than it does with other groups because blacks more often reside in public housing developments. Life in these "projects" inhibits the emergence of solidary relations and makes it more difficult for blacks to develop any control over local businesses.

In contrast, Italians control local commercial establishments. The Mexicans and Puerto Ricans are somewhere in between the Italians and blacks in peer group strength and control over local establishments.

Although the neighborhoods studied by Gans and Suttles differed in important ways, both studies indicate the significance of neighborhood structures for many of the people who live there as well as identify some of the social forces that make cohesive, solidary neighborhoods.

Latent Structures

Up to this point we have considered three types of social structures—primary group, purposefully organized, and territorial. Each of these types is either an explicitly recognized membership collectivity or a bounded territorial area. The people whose lives are carried out within these structures are generally aware of their involvement with others in the structure or at least of their proximity to others in a shared social and physical environment.

Latent structures are neither membership entities, as in groups or organizations, nor territorial entities, as in communities. However, latent structures have the **potential** of being transformed into either membership or territorial structures.

By definition, a **latent structure** is a collection of people who have a socially significant attribute in common. A collection of people, as used here, is a social category rather than a membership grouping. For example, all red-haired individuals form a social category because they have an attribute in common, namely, red hair. However, that attribute is probably not socially significant. For an attribute to be socially significant, it must be a meaningful symbol to the people who possess the attribute as well as to those reacting to it. The attribute must also be a constraint on the range of actions available to those who possess it.

In our example red hair would become a socially significant attribute if it carried the following meaning: all red-haired people are emotionally incapable of holding high pressure jobs. If individuals with and without red hair accepted this meaning and then acted upon it, we would soon have a structured inequality in our social system in which red-haired people would be denied access to positions of high responsibility and reward. Furthermore, children of red-haired parents, even if they did not have red hair, would also be at a disadvantage because they started life in a disadvantaged family.

Attributes that can be the basis of latent structures include sex, age, religion, socioeconomic characteristics, and race-ethnicity. People with these attributes may decide to establish organizations, like the older Americans who formed the Gray Panthers, or form communities, such the religious communes of American Zen Buddhists. Each attribute is important because it influences other aspects of social life and therefore produces a degree of pattern and regularity. A full discussion of the importance of these attributes is contained in Chapter 8 (Social Stratification), Chapter 10 (Gender Inequality), Chapter 11 (Minorities), and Chapter 14 (Religion).

SUMMARY

In this chapter we have dealt with the concepts of society and social structure. Different forms of society can be viewed in relation to the way in which they obtain life-supporting resources from the environment. The four types of nonindustrial societies—hunting and gathering, pastoral, horticultural, and agricultural—represent progressively more advanced or elaborate ways of adapting to the environment. They also represent increased complexity in their social structures, with greater role specialization and division of labor.

In Europe during the eleventh century the predominant agrarian social system of feudalism began to decline. With the rise of the cities and the ascent of a new merchant class, the emergence of the independent craftworkers, organized in protective craft guilds, presented a new economic pattern—formally free wage labor producing goods for the market. When the guild system was transformed by internal pressures into the domestic or shop production system, the merchant-entrepreneurs took the upper hand in the economic partnership, leading to the eighteenth-century social

and economic transformation known as the Industrial Revolution.

Social structure is one source of pattern and regularity in human society. Social structure refers to recurrent social relationships among persons who occupy positions and play social roles in different areas of human activity. Major areas of activity in human societies—such as producing and distributing goods and services—have clusters of values, norms, positions, and social roles that are called social institutions.

Four types of social structure are (1) primary group structures—families, friendship groups and work groups; (2) purposefully organized structures—voluntary associations and organizations; (3) territorial social structures—the city, community, and neighborhood; and (4) latent social structures, such as sex or racial-ethnic categories.

GLOSSARY

Agriculture domestication of food supplies with the use of the plow and the use of animals as an energy source.

City a large human collectivity with recognized territorial boundaries and a common political system.

Community a collectivity similar to a city but smaller in size, with a lesser degree of institutional completeness, a more homogenous population, and more intimate social relationships.

Craft guilds protective associations of independent artisans or craftworkers.

Domestic or shop production system system whereby a merchant-entrepreneur brings raw materials and sometimes tools to craftworkers in their homes or gathered in shops and then collects the finished products for sale on the market.

Factory production shop production with wage labor and fixed capital.

Feudalism an agrarian socioeconomic system based on an elaborate system of rights and obligations existing between landed lords and those who serve them.

Horticulture   gardening with primitive hand tools, such as a digging stick or a hoe.

Hunting and gathering   foraging for available game and plant foods in an environment.

Industrial Revolution   the change to the use of inanimate power sources in the production of goods and services, with an accompanying transformation of many aspects of social life, generally considered to have begun in late-eighteenth-century England.

Latent structure   a collection of persons who have a socially significant attribute in common that can become the basis for group formation, for example, age, sex, religion, race-ethnicity, or socioeconomic status.

Multifunctional (or functionally diffuse) role structures   the existence of only a small set of differentiated roles in a society that cover a wide range of activities.

Neighborhood   the immediate environment within a community or city in which one lives covering territory that is usually subjective and personal in nature.

Nonindustrial society   a society that has a labor force whose members are primarily directly involved in food provision and that has a simple division of labor and little differentiation between the production and consumption units.

Organization   a deliberately constructed, goal-directed collectivity based on impersonal social relationships and run by a hierarchy of authority whose purpose it is to produce something that is ultimately used or consumed by an individual or other groups or organizations.

Pastoral   a type of society based on the use of domesticated animals as a food supply.

Position   a social location in a system of activities undertaken by a group to attain its formal or informal objectives.

Primary groups   social structures that have intimate face-to-face association and cooperation among their members and which, because of their more permanent nature, give the individual his or her earliest and most complete experience of social unity.

Roles   expectations about appropriate behavior for occupants of positions.

Role behavior   the actual behavior of people in positions.

Role conflict   contradictory expectations placed upon a person in a single position, or contradictory expectations from occupying two incompatible positions.

Social structure   the patterned and recurrent social relationships among persons in organized collectivities as well as the patterned and recurrent interrelationships of the various parts (not persons) of organized collectivities.

Society   a system of interacting individuals and interrelated groups sharing a common culture and territory.

Social institutions   clusters of values, norms, positions, and social roles dealing with a basic problem facing members of a society, such as producing and distributing goods.

Territorial social structures   human collectivities based upon spatial and social factors, such as city, community, or neighborhood.

Voluntary association   a group of persons organized to further some common interest of its members and who participate on a voluntary, spare-time basis.

ADDITIONAL READINGS

Banfield, Edward C. *The Moral Basis of a Backward Society.* N.Y.: Free Press, 1958.
An examination of how the culture and social structure of a poor, rural town in southern Italy serve as barriers to economic improvement.

Bendix, Reinhard. *Work and Authority in Industry.* New York: Harper Torchbooks, 1956.
An analysis of the way in which ideas and beliefs about how to exercise authority over workers in factories ("ideologies of managment") played an important role in early industrialization. Especially interesting is the comparative framework that draws upon differences among England, Russia, and America.

Damachi, Ukandi G. *Nigerian Modernization.* N.Y.: Third Press, 1972.
An examination of the history of colonialism in Nigeria and the impact of the interplay of industrialization, urbanization, and Western values on the Nigerian class structure.

Hoebel, E. Adamson. *The Cheyennes: Indians of the Great Plains.* New York: Holt, Rinehart & Winston, 1960.
A good example of how the culture and social structure of a nonindustrial society are interrelated with its subsistence activities in hunting and gathering.

Lenski, Gerhard and Jean Lenski, *Human Societies: An Introduction to Macrosociology.* New York: McGraw-Hill, 1982.
An excellent introduction to sociology from the perspective of the evolution of total societies.

Smelser, Neil J., ed. *Readings in Economic Sociology.* Englewood Cliffs, N.J.: Prentice-Hall, 1965.
A collection of essays that serve as a good introduction to how sociologists study the interplay of economic activities and social life.

READINGS

READING 4.1

Shoshonean Indian Rabbit Hunt

JULIAN H. STEWARD

The principal collective hunt was the rabbit drive. It could be held fairly often, and it yielded not only meat which could be consumed during a short period but furs which, cut into long strips and twisted, were woven into robes and blankets. The only distinctive technical feature of these drives was a net of about the height and mesh of a modern tennis net but often several hundred feet long. A number of these nets were placed end to end to form a huge semicircle. Men, women, children, and dogs beat the brush over a wide area, gradually closing in so that rabbits which were not clubbed or shot by the drivers became entangled in the nets, where they were killed.

Custom determined the several crucial aspects of the drive and the division of game. Experienced men—in recent years called rather appropriately "rabbit bosses"—were given supreme authority to coordinate all activities in this fairly complex operation. They chose the locality of the drive, directed disposition of nets, regulated the drivers, and divided the game according to customary understandings. Anyone who killed a rabbit with a bow or throwing stick in the course of the drive could claim it. Since, however, only a few families owned rabbit nets, net owners received a somewhat greater portion of the rabbits caught in the nets.

In spite of the rather rigid direction of these drives, there were several reasons why they did not bring about permanent integration or cohesion of territorial or social groups of fixed membership. First, drives were held only when rabbits were sufficiently numerous in a particular locality. Second, participants in the drive consisted of families who, because of the rather fortuitous annual occurrence of seeds and other foods in one place or another, happened to be in the locality where the drive was worth holding. Third, the drive was held only if an experienced leader and families owning nets happened to be present. Since the occurrence of these factors was rather haphazard, since the place, the participants, and the leaders were never quite the same in successive years, the drives provided only temporary bonds between independent families. A given family was under no obligation whatever to participate in a drive with a fixed group of families under a permanent leader. And, since the "rabbit boss" held authority only during the drive, the family paid little heed to him in other times, places, and contexts.

SUMMARY

The collective hunting of the Shoshonean rabbit drive involves all family members of this hunting and gathering society. The social structure for carrying out this activity is relatively simple, in that there is little role specialization. Although leadership positions exist, they are temporary and do not extend beyond the hunt. The game is divided among all families. No permanent political organization results from the collective hunt.

QUESTIONS

1. Would it be possible in the rabbit hunt to have more private accumulation of game rather than communal sharing?

2. If rabbits were more abundant and their location predictable, would a more permanent political structure emerge?

SOURCE: Julian H. Steward, From Yehudi A. Cohen, *Man in Adaptation: The Cultural Present* (New York: Aldine Publishing Co., 1968), p. 74.

READING 4.2
Agricultural Societies
YEHUDI A. COHEN

Because peasants are the food-producing specialists of their societies and because they occupy subservient sociopolitical status, they hold values different from those of their rulers and of other groups. Thus in studying peasants it is important not only to understand their ways of life but also the ways in which their local patterns relate to, and are integrated with, the total organization of social relations in their societies. . . .

. . . There are many intrusions into peasant villages by urban institutions. It is in agricultural states, for example, that schools develop. While in most societies schools were initially confined to the ruling classes, who lived in urban centers, there are instances (as in ancient China and Japan during the Tokugawa Period, from 1600 to 1870) in which schools were established in rural areas. These were usually intended for the local nobility, however; and when an attempt was made to bring the peasants into the schools, an important step had been taken to identify them with national ideologies.

One of the first steps in a state's attempt to entrench itself is the establishment of courts; initially, these usually are circuit courts, but whether they are permanently established or make their appearance periodically, "the long arm of the law" (from the capital to the most remote village) enforces the ultimate authority of the centralized state. A central concern of such courts is the enforcement of national laws on land tenure, which often are different from, and in conflict with, local village patterns. Not infrequently, centrally promulgated and enforced land laws are

SOURCE: Yehudi A. Cohan, *Man in Adaptation: The Cultural Present* (New York: Aldine Publishing Co., 1968), pp. 320–321.

designed to benefit members of the ruling classes who want to add to their landholdings at the expense of the peasants. In some societies, laws are enacted that permit members of the nobility to buy land and deny this right to peasants.

Another important institution that affects the lives of a peasantry . . . is the nation's military organization. One source of the military's influence is that it recruits most of its foot-soldiers among the peasants, and military training and indoctrination expose the conscripts to new values (such as allegiance and obedience to the state) that they communicate to their families and friends in one way or another. . . .

Another aspect of the complexity of agricultural societies is the wide range of social relations in which every individual engages. . . . Every advance in adaptation is accompanied by an increase in the number and the types of groups with which each group interacts. Generally, a nomadic foraging group tends to interact primarily with other nomadic foraging groups; furthermore, the number of groups with which a band associates and on which it is dependent is very limited. This also tends to be the case among horticulturists, though in horticultural societies in which most of the diet is made up of domesticates, there may be an expansion and elaboration of trade relationships among groups and an increasing mutual dependency between cultivators and non-cultivators. In agriculture, this dependency is not only between societies, as between agriculturists and pastoralists, but also between cultivators and artisans and other specialists within the society.

Urban centers depend on cultivators not only for food but also for personnel; until very recently in history, cities have not been able to sustain necessary population growth without recruitment from rural areas. Political bureaucrats, generally urban, interact with a wide variety of groups: other political functionaries, priests, warriors, artisans, traders, representatives of commercial interests, peasants, pastoralists, and often with members of other societies. Reciprocally, each group looks—and is forced to subscribe—to the legal and administrative rules of the state bureaucracy. Indeed, one of the accompaniments of cultural evolution is that the individual must at every successive stage learn to cope with an increasing variety of social categories.

SUMMARY

Peasants in agricultural societies are food-producing specialists who are very important to those who live in urban centers. Because of the urban centers' dependence on peasants, efforts are made to extend the influence of the urban ruling classes into the rural areas. This may be done by bringing schools to peasant areas and teaching the young to identify with a national state. It may also involve using courts to enforce a central authority.

QUESTIONS

1. What is the relationship between rural and urban areas in the United States today?
2. How do urban elites try to dominate rural people?
3. Why don't rural people have more power since they produce food needed by everyone?

READING 4.3

Factory Production
WILBERT MOORE

Although economic historians tell us that forms of shop production (as opposed to home

SOURCE: Wilbert Moore, *Industrial Relations and the Social Order* (New York: Macmillan, 1946), pp. 22–24. By permission of the author.

industry) are very old and very common in human society, and often involved rather large numbers of workers, the essentials of the factory in the modern sense are: (1) shop industry, requiring (2) fixed capital, and (3) free labor.

SHOP PRODUCTION

Shop production means unified and coordinated production within a single establishment for that purpose. Although usually thought of as denoting a small establishment, shop in this sense might apply to manufacturing units ranging from the very small to the extremely complex. It is not even necessary that all the operations take place "under the same roof" as long as the units are located in close proximity, are interdependent, and are subject to a unified control.

There are certain inherent advantages arising from the centralization and close supervision provided by shop production, particularly for large-scale production or for manufacturing that entails a series of closely related processes. Among the advantages which early (and modern) factories enjoyed over domestic production were: minimizing the transportation of goods, especially those at different stages of completion; saving of time and effort of agents and "factors"; reducing irregularities of quality and quantity resulting from inadequate supervision. It does not follow that these advantages were in every case crucial; often they were outweighed by the failure of other necessary conditions for factory production. They are, however, sufficiently important to merit the attention of those who think that the use of natural power alone "caused" the industrial revolution.

Actually the first factories were not large, but did combine several processes in manufacturing or else brought a number of similar machines together for centralized supervision. Often the interests of the entrepreneurs were technical as well as commercial; the "capitalist" was frequently his own technical designer both for machines and for shop arrangement. Others relied chiefly on managerial ability. In any event, the impetus to further specialization and elaboration was provided by making the shop, not the craftsman, the productive unit in society.

FIXED CAPITAL

The term *fixed capital* refers to investments in productive goods that are not easily transportable from one locality to another, or broken up into small units. A water wheel, heavy machinery, or a series of smaller machines which can be effectively operated only as interdependent units are examples of fixed capital. It was the introduction of fixed capital which often prompted transferral of production from scattered homes to a unified productive establishment. . . .

The early development of textile manufacturing in England, which may be taken not as typical of industrial transformation, but rather as its vanguard, illustrates the early advantages gained through centralization of production. The introduction of the power loom, together with the utilization of nonhuman energy in the form of water power, made the decentralized [domestic or shop production system] definitely outmoded. . . . the establishment of the "factory system" was actually the the introduction of unified production with fixed capital in one manufacturing industry in one country—cotton production in England. . . .

FREE LABOR

The characteristic use of free labor saved capital investments in slaves, removed the risk of such investments, and made possible an insistence on technical efficiency in the labor force. This is one of the chief distinctions between the modern factory system and the "factories" of the ancient world. Actually, of course, enterprising capitalists in England and western Europe did not have to face this issue; they simply benefited, especially in England, from the presence of a large supply of cheap labor.

In the gradual disestablishment of feudalism in western Europe the lot of the peasant fell out in quite different ways. . . . the English freeman paid for his liberty by lack of economic security. . . . with the complete collapse of feudalism, tenants were evicted from their ancestral holdings. The extent of poverty and unemployment in England is attested by the famous Elizabethan Poor Laws of the sixteenth and early seventeenth centuries. By 1750 the tenant evictions and general agricultural poverty had created such a large unemployed population that labor supply was no problem, at least in regard to quantity. These same considerations also guaranteed that it would be cheap.

SUMMARY
The modern factory was made possible by the existence of shop production requiring fixed capital and free labor. Shop industries involved unified and coordinated production within a single establishment. The shop, and not the craftsman, became the productive unit. Shop production required capital investments in heavy machinery that was "fixed", that is, not easily transportable. With the collapse of feudalism peasants became a source of cheap labor for the factory system.

QUESTIONS
1. Is it possible for small shop production plants to flourish today?
2. What would be the advantages and disadvantages today of shop production compared with factory production?

CHAPTER 5

Small Groups

CONTENTS

AT ISSUE

Do social group ties need to be strengthened?

With the passing of traditional society and the emergence of modern urban-industrial society, the importance of small groups has declined. The cohesive role of kin groups, small communities, and tribal or ethnic identification seems part of a romantic past that cannot survive in today's mobile society and in the cosmopolitan culture spawned by mass media. Some have viewed this change with alarm and call for the strengthening of group ties. Others see a danger in encouraging strong group ties because they tend to stifle individuality and discourage social relationships with people different from ourselves.

YES   Traditional society provides its members with stable and secure ties to others through strong group affiliations. Kinship, religious, and community groups give people a sense of place in society and support their members throughout the life cycle. The very young and very old, who are the most dependent and vulnerable members of society, especially benefit from the care that the group extends to all its members.

In urban-industrial society many areas of social life are dominated by large organizations and impersonal urban centers, where people are less important as individuals. Supportive groups decline as family and community life changes under the impact of higher divorce rates, smaller families, and geographical mobility. People become isolated from one another because of the absence of an active group life that draws them into participation with others.

In such a society large, impersonal organizations carry out their activities without direct involvement of average citizens. Organizations like hospitals and schools do not reflect the needs of the people they are supposed to serve, but rather the interests of the organized professions (doctors and teachers) and of political and economic elites. Here we find the roots of alienation, where individuals feel that they are "numbers" or "cases" to be administered by impersonal bureaucracies. The major institutions also suffer since they lack the active support of the average person.

The modern life style of temporary relationships and personal gratification is essentially hollow. And only in a stable social order can people find meaning in their lives. The only way to combat the alienation of modern life is to strengthen groups built around the family, church, community, and ethnicity. These traditional groups are our only bulwark against chaos and our only assurance of stability.

NO   For the last decade or so we have been exposed to a barrage of statements by religious leaders, educators, and others that our civilization is threatened by the decline of strong group ties built on kinship, community, and religion—that modern, urban society has swept away many of the warm, supportive relationships so characteristic of traditional society.

The growth of communes, new religious groups, and encounter groups is based on the belief that people are desperate for close, intimate relationships. Many of these groups promise to give new meaning to a person's life by reestablishing the importance of the group over the individual. These groups also promise the love and security of close relationships that once existed but have been lost in the modern age.

This romanticized view of the past fails to recognize the fact that Americans have always placed a high value on privacy and self-reliance. Such values were found in the people who first settled in

116

this land and faced great hardship to help develop the strongest, most prosperous nation in history.

There is something to be said for the intimacy and security of the group. But what of the cost? What price is paid to return to the womb of the primary group? First, a person must be prepared to have his or her total identity shaped by group pressure and rendered synonomous with the group's identity. Second, a person must accept the pronouncements and dictates of a charismatic leader as the source of truth and morality. Third, she or he must forego the exercise of independent intellect and reason, which are discouraged as destructive, ego-centered values of modern life. Fourth, a person must learn to value conformity more than freedom of thought and expression and freedom to create and to make mistakes. Finally, there is a cost to society when the overriding importance of primary group ties discourages involvement in the larger community and a willingness to try to improve modern society rather than escape from it.

Having close, supportive ties is important, but people can not live their total lives in small, privatized primary groups. The solution to the problems of modern life will not be found in the security or tyranny of the group.

The small group has great influence on the ideas and behavior of its members. It can also be very effective in motivating members to achieve desired goals, such as winning a basketball game or meeting a production quota. This chapter examines the characteristics and functions of small groups and the way they are related to the larger society.

QUESTIONS TO CONSIDER

- How do groups influence a person's behavior?

- Is it possible to be a nonconformist?

- How are people recruited into religious cults?

- Can people be influenced by a group to which they do not belong?

Imagine that you are at a small social gathering attended by some of your close friends at college, some casual acquaintances, and some strangers. Someone tells a funny joke that is clearly disparaging to a minority group. There is considerable laughter in response to the joke, and there follows a quick series of similar jokes contributed by other group members. You are troubled by these jokes because you have always been uncomfortable with such forms of humor. What are you likely to do in this situation?

1. You can choose to do nothing despite the fact that you are upset about the joke telling. Your heart is beating a little faster then usual and you wonder whether people can see disapproval in your face even though you have not tried to show it. After a few minutes you are angry at yourself for not saying something about the joke being in bad taste. You consider making a statement, but by now the group's conversation has moved on to another topic.

2. You quickly blurt out your objection to such jokes, trying to be reasonable in describing what you think is wrong with racial and ethnic jokes. The group is stunned by your comments and after a moment of silence there are remarks made that are critical of you for "making a big deal out of a small joke." You feel your face getting flushed and you are embarrassed by the situation in which you find yourself. You

immediately start thinking of ways to restate your feelings without sounding so "high and mighty" or critical of your friends and acquaintances.

3. While your mind is racing with different thoughts about how to react to the offensive jokes, you notice another member of the group who also **seems** to be uncomfortable. You make eye contact and roll your eyes as if to say "how gross." The other person smiles. You soon pair off with this other like-minded person and move away from the center of the party's activities to share your common views on why both of you object to such jokes.

This hypothetical incident is probably similar to something that many people experience in social situations. What a person chooses to do in these circumstances is greatly influenced by the group in which they occur. Each of the possible actions just described had the same goal—to avoid being isolated from the group because of publicly announced differences. Let us consider some of the characteristics of groups that serve to bind their members together.

CHARACTERISTICS OF GROUPS

A **group** is an aggregate of people who define themselves as belonging together. Groups may differ on a number of characteristics such as size, emotional bonds among members, or reasons for the group's existence. In Chapter 4 we discussed *primary groups* like families and friendship groups. Primary groups are noted for the intimate, emotional bonds that develop among members in face-to-face contact. In Chapter 9 we discuss *task groups* like voluntary associations and organizations, in which relations among members are impersonal and often indirect. Task groups are formed to pursue a specific goal, and members participate in specific roles with limited emotional intensity.

Although primary and task groups are generally different, they do occasionally overlap. Some groups can be both primary and task, for example, work groups or athletic teams. Even families—the basic primary group—can also be organized for task at-

The family, like some friendship and work groups, is a primary group because of strong emotional bonds among its members, frequent interaction, and the "we" feeling that its members share.

tainment, such as being successful in a family business.

Group Size and Social Interaction

Group size plays an important role in changing the structure and culture of groups. In this chapter we will look at the effect of the **small** group. The smallest and simplest group is the *dyad*, a two-person group. The existence of the dyad is dependent on its members, since loss of either member will destroy the group. This dependence often encourages greater intimacy and more frequent interaction between members.

The addition of another person to the dyad will create a *triad*, or a three-person group. The triad creates new interaction possibilities and group structure that could not exist in the dyad. There can be majority resolution of conflicts, temporary withdrawal of one group member, and the assumption by one member of a mediator role to handle group disagreements. The addition of further new members brings a dramatic increase in the number of possible two-person (dyad) relationships within the group. For example, in a two-person group there is only one possible dyad; in a three-person group there are three possible dyads; and in an eight-person group there are 28 possible dyads. In fact, the number of possible relationships of all types in an eight-person group is 3025 (this includes dyads, individual to subgroup relationships, and subgroup to subgroup relationship) (Talazzolo, 1981).

The smaller a group, the greater the chance for development of intimate, face-to-face relationships. Not all small groups will be primary groups but there is a greater probability that they will. Many social scientists use *small* and *primary* as roughly equivalent terms. If they wish to put emphasis on the quality of relationships (close, emotional) they will use the term primary group. If they wish to emphasize the forms of interaction that are possible among members, they will use the term small group. We therefore define a **small group** as having (1) no more than 15 people who (2) have some emotional commitment, (3) some intimacy, and (4) some face-to-face contact with one another. Each of these four characteristics needs clarification.

SIZE

We say that a small group should contain no more than 15 people because feelings of commitment and intimacy are not likely to develop in larger groups. Some sociologists also argue that groups cannot number less than three because in dyads the withdrawal of one member can terminate the group. We will not insist on the triad as a minimum group, but the reader should be aware that the difference between dyad and triad has consequences for organizational features of the group.

EMOTIONAL COMMITMENT

The second characteristic of small groups is some emotional commitment. By some commitment we mean that members overall feel moderately positive about the group. This does not mean that members have no negative feelings about the group but rather that the difference between positive and negative feelings is moderately positive. The degree of overall positive feelings about the group defines **group cohesion.**

Cohesive groups exhibit a high level of motivation among members to achieve the groups' stated or implicit goals. If the balance of feelings is negative, group members will likely leave the group. Theoretically, if alternative groups are available that offer high levels of satisfaction, members also will leave a group that offers moderate levels of satisfaction. On the other hand, members may remain in a group that offers low levels of positive feelings if no better alternatives exist. Thus the meaning of moderate levels of positive feelings toward the group is relative to the person's alternative opportunities for group memberships.

INTIMACY

The third characteristic of small groups is some intimacy within the group. In a general sense intimacy refers to knowledge about the most personal aspects of others. We can define a continuum ranging from anonymity to intimacy. Some interactions, such as attending a large concert or being a member of a large college class, are anonymous. Other participants know nothing of our public or personal lives. Less anonymous is behavior in purely task-oriented groups like a political campaign com-

mittee, in which participants are known to each other on the basis of their public roles that are relevant to the group's task. More intimate are groups, for example, the board of directors of a community civic center, in which members are knowledgeable not only about each other's task-relevant roles but also about some of the other public and private roles of groups members. Still greater intimacy exists in friendship groups, in which group members know a lot about one another's personal lives, and relationships are most intimate when members know about each other's deepest feelings about themselves and their lives.

Note that intimacy may be of a purely personal nature and include little information about public roles. However, we will define intimacy as some knowledge about the variety of both social and personal roles, of both ideals and behavior, and of past and present influences and future aspirations. In this sense, the first meeting of a purely task-oriented collection of individuals does not yet constitute a group, but it provides an opportunity for the formation of a group to the degree that people in it learn about one another's lives outside the group.

FACE-TO-FACE CONTACT

The fourth and final characteristic of social groups is some face-to-face contact. Simply, it is difficult for members to establish feelings of commitment and intimacy without face-to-face interaction. Most of us are hesitant to reveal personal information about ourselves unless we see our audience, for only in face-to-face interaction can we judge the reaction of others to our personal revelations. Judging others' reactions is important because we use this information in deciding how much we can safely reveal about ourselves.

Face-to-face contact may be more or less important at different stages of a group's interaction and depending on the individuals. The potential for a group may be established by written or telephone communications, and subsequent face-to-face communication may cement group bonds. In addition, groups that once enjoyed face-to-face contact may be maintained by other modes of communication. Finally, some people are better communicators and better audiences or listeners in non-face-to-face modes of communication; these individuals may find face-to-face communication less important in defining their group memberships. For most of us most of the time, however, some face-to-face interaction is essential in maintaining membership in small groups.

SOME EXAMPLES

We have defined small groups in terms of four characteristics, each of which is modified by adjectives such as more or less, some, and moderate. Although one might conclude that the definition is vague, we think not. Considering all four characteristics interdependently usually allows us to decide whether a set of individuals constitutes a small group. Here are some examples. Consider a lynch mob. It may have a suitable number and face-to-face interaction. On the other hand, it lacks emotional commitment to the maintenance of the group (although other emotional feelings run high), and members of the mob tend to feel anonymous. Thus it is not a small group. The Pulitzer Prize-winning novel by Harper Lee and Hollywood movie, *To Kill a Mockingbird,* has a sociologically insightful scene in which a lynch mob is dissolved when the anonymity of its members is lost. The mob is before the jailhouse facing Atticus Finch, the hero-attorney (played by Gregory Peck in the movie), and they are bent on lynching a man being defended by the attorney. Atticus's young daughter, who is observing the scene, manages to destroy that anonymity through an exchange with the mob's leader. Highlight 5.1 is an excerpt from the novel that describes this crucial scene.

What about a work group? The chances are good that there is some emotional commitment and some intimacy among some members, thus meeting the criteria for small groups. Perhaps it is most difficult to establish this definition in cases in which we irregularly meet a small set of other people, we have mildly positive feelings toward them, and we have some knowledge about a few of the public or personal roles they perform. In these cases a criterion for determining the degree to which this set is a group is the amount of effort individuals would expend to be together. A person might be unwilling

to cross the street to speak to some sets of acquaintances while willing to cross the country to speak to others. This suggests that perhaps the most important characteristic of social groups is emotional commitment to the maintenance of the group. Certainly, internal problems like the social integration of individuals and problems that impinge on the group like adaptation to a changing environment and task-related problems are important also. Nonetheless, commitment to the maintenance of the group through changing internal and external conditions seems to be crucial.

Reading 5.1 presents a general statement of why the small group is viewed as sociologically important.

Social Control in Small Groups

The degree to which members are emotionally committed to the maintenance of a group is positively correlated with influencability. If a group is very important to us and we strongly want to maintain our membership in it, we are likely to accept attempts by other members to influence us. If, on the other hand, we are indifferent to the group and our membership in it, we are likely to reject group influence. In general, the influence process linking groups and members is part of the process of social control. **Social control** includes influences on a person by group members that increase the probability that the person will behave similarly to group members. The influence process may be direct, as in the case of parents who distribute rewards and punishments for their children's behavior, or it may be indirect, as with parents who teach their children table manners by their own example.

When social control efforts in a small group increase uniformity, that is, when one or more people change their beliefs or behavior to be more similar to those of other group members, we call this **conformity.** Some people view uniformity and conformity as evils, but these characteristics are essential to the maintenance of the group. In addition, uniformity may increase a group's ability to work together toward achieving common goals. For example, students who work on group projects for a class discover that everyone must accept common

HIGHLIGHT 5.1
Anonymity in a Lynch Mob

I looked around the crowd. It was a summer's night, but the men were dressed, most of them, in overalls and denim shirts buttoned up to the collars. I thought they must be cold-natured, as their sleeves were unrolled and buttoned at the cuffs. Some wore hats pulled firmly down over their ears. They were sullen-looking, sleepy-eyed men who seemed unused to late hours. I sought once more for a familiar face, and at the center of the semi-circle I found one.

"Hey, Mr. Cunningham."

The man did not hear me, it seemed.

"Hey, Mr. Cunningham. How's your entailment gettin' along?"

Mr. Walter Cunningham's legal affairs were well known to me; Atticus had once described them at length. The big man blinked and hooked his thumbs in his overall straps. He seemed uncomfortable; he cleared his throat and looked away. My friendly overture had fallen flat.

Mr. Cunningham wore no hat, and the top half of his forehead was white in contrast to his sunscorched face, which led me to believe that he wore one most days. He shifted his feet, clad in heavy work shoes.

"Don't you remember me, Mr. Cunningham? I'm Jean Louise Finch. You brought us some hickory nuts one time, remember?" I began to sense the futility one feels when unacknowledged by a chance acquaintance.

"I go to school with Walter," I began again. "He's your boy, ain't he? Ain't he, sir?"

Mr. Cunningham was moved to a faint nod. He did know me, after all.

"He's in my grade," I said, "and he does right well. He's a good boy," I added, "a real nice boy. We brought him home for dinner one time. Maybe he told you about me, I beat him up one time but he was real nice about it. Tell him hey for me, won't you?"

Atticus had said it was the polite thing to talk to people about what they were interested in, not about what you were interested in. Mr. Cunningham displayed no interest in his son, so I tackled his entailment once more in a last-ditch effort to make him feel at home.

"Entailments are bad," I was advising him, when I slowly awoke to the fact that I was addressing the entire aggregation. The men were all looking at me, some had their mouths half-open. Atticus had stopped poking at Jem: they were standing together beside Dill. Their attention amountd to fascination. Atticus's mouth, even, was half-open, an attitude he had once described as uncouth. Our eyes met and he shut it.

"Well, Atticus, I was just sayin' to Mr. Cunningham that entailments are bad an' all that, but you said not to worry, it takes a long time sometimes . . . that you all'd ride it out together . . ." I was slowly drying up. wondering what idiocy I had committed. Entailments seemed all right enough for living room talk.

I began to feel sweat gathering at the edges of my hair; I could stand anything but a bunch of people looking at me. They were quite still.

"What's the matter?" I asked.

Atticus said nothing, I looked around and up at Mr. Cunningham, whose face was equally impassive. Then he did a peculiar thing. He squatted down and took me by both shoulders.

"I'll tell him you said hey, little lady," he said.

Then he straightened up and waved a big paw. "Let's clear out," he called. "Let's get going, boys."

As they had come, in ones and twos the men shuffled back to their ramshackle cars. Doors slammed, engines coughed, and they were gone.

SOURCE: TO KILL A MOCKING BIRD by Harper Lee (J. B. Lippincott). Copyright © 1960 by Harper Lee. Reprinted by permission of Harper & Row, Publishers, Inc.

goals for the project and rules for achieving those goals. Failure to do this will likely result in a disorganized and inferior product.

Social control takes one of two forms: (1) individuals may try to believe or behave as they feel they ought to or (2) they may conform to obtain rewards or avoid punishment. For example, in a class where attendance is required some students attend because they feel that the rule is appropriate and therefore they should attend, whereas others go only because attendance affects their grades. Those who attend because they feel they should are **internally motivated** to conform, while those who attend only because their attendance affects their grades are **externally motivated** to conform.

In small groups individuals socialize one another to conform to group norms by using peer pressure. Groups are able to exert social control because members want very much to belong to the peer group. The withdrawal of group support can be very damaging to group members.

Groups whose members are internally motivated will develop normative rules, while groups with externally motivated members will have coercive rules.

NORMATIVE RULES

When members of a group accept a set of rules and are internally motivated to conform to them, sociologists refer to the rules as norms. **Norms** are rules governing beliefs and behaviors of group members that are considered essential to the group. Those who fail to conform to group norms often are negatively sanctioned, either by direct application of punishments, such as exclusion from group activities, or by more indirect methods, like sarcastic comments directed to the errant member. Groups usually apply negative sanctions to violations of norms because violations are perceived to threaten the group's ability to maintain coordinated activity among members and to achieve common goals.

The norms of a group are rules with a moral character. Members who conform to the norms do, of course, occcasionally receive social approval and other rewards, but primarily they believe and behave as they do because they feel these norms are right. A good example of how groups reward those who conform and apply sanctions against those who do not can be seen in a study by Schachter (1951). He recruited college students for case study clubs and radio clubs. Students in the case study clubs were interested in the subject, and thus the club and its norms were important to them. Those in the radio clubs were uninterested in the club and its norms. Both clubs met to discuss the case of a juvenile delinquent who had been convicted of a minor crime and was awaiting sentence. Without the students' knowledge Schachter had three actors in each group assigned to the following roles: (1) to conform to group opinion toward the delinquent, which was mild and nonpunitive; (2) to disagree with group opinion and take a harsh and punitive position; and (3) to first advocate a harsh sentence and then change that opinion to conform to that of the group.

Schachter found that in the case study clubs, nonconformers who refused to change position were excluded from the group discussion, while nonconformers who subsequently changed their opinion to conform were not. Further, after the discussion nonconformers were selected for the burdensome task of taking care of correspondence, while those who conformed or changed their opinions were selected for prestigious tasks like being on the executive or steering committees.

In the radio clubs, which were composed of uninterested members, differences in treatment of conformers and nonconformers were not great. Differences between the clubs resulted in part from differences in norms. Clubs with interested students felt a greater commitment to group norms and therefore rewarded conformers and punished nonconformers.

COERCIVE RULE

Social control can result from efforts to believe or behave as one should. Social control also can result from efforts to get rewards or to avoid punishments. Many teenagers conform to norms of politeness in their family group in order to avoid adult punishment. However, social control that is based primarily on rewards or punishments is ineffective for a number of reasons. First, if social control rests primarily on rewards or punishments, then the group must keep the individual under surveillance to reward appropriate beliefs and behaviors and to punish inappropriate ones. For example, teenagers who avoid using offensive language around their families to avoid punishment often use very foul language when the family is not present. When social control is based primarily on either rewards or punishments, those who reward or punish have power over the other members. Therefore, the basis of maintenence of the group is **coercion.**

Groups usually have both coercive power and moral norms that can be used to influence group members. In addition, groups often vary in the degree to which one is used over the other. Most sociologists agree with Shibutani (1961), however, who suggests that to work effectively all groups depend on a minimal amount of normative control in the form of politeness and cooperation.

GROUP STRUCTURE

In the previous section we discussed how small groups develop emotional commitment among their members and maintain the group through social control. Here we will discuss the group as a system with its own structure and dynamics, such as leadership, status, and communication patterns. **Group structure** consists of interrelationships of members that persist over time, and it is an essential characteristic of all groups. The structure of some groups is formal, with clearly specified positions, duties, and lines of communication or authority. Other groups have informal structures such as exists among college friends. There are no written rules or regulations, and although there may be leaders they are not referred to as such.

Leadership

A **leader** is someone who has more influence in the group than most of the other members. **Power** is the ability of a group member to get his or her way by coercing another member to do something either to obtain a reward or to avoid a punishment. Thus power is coercive but leadership is not. Social psychologists who have studied leadership often have been interested in the effects of leadership style, that is, in the way a leader exercises influence on group performance.

In a famous study White and Lippitt (1960) compared the behavior of children in three types of groups: (1) authoritarian, with a leader who dictated activities and remained aloof; (2) democratic, with a leader who encouraged discussion and choice about group activities; and, (3) laissez-faire, or a leader who was passive and allowed the group complete freedom. They found that the authoritarian groups were the most hostile, aggressive, and discontented, but also productive. Democratic groups were somewhat less productive than authoritarian groups, but intragroup relations were friendly. Laissez-faire groups did very little work and played a lot. The performance of the leaders was analyzed by observers who recorded how many times a leader used nonconstructive criticism (punishment) and

praise and approval (reward). Authoritarian leaders punished more than four times as frequently as democratic leaders, and they also rewarded twice as frequently as democratic leaders. To influence members to work together, democratic leaders gave guiding suggestions and tried to stimulate self-guidance. Democratic, or noncoercive, leaders seemed to produce higher satisfaction in members than coercive leaders, but did not stimulate as high group productivity.

People who have power are treated in special ways by other group members. Hurwitz, Zander, and Hymovitch (1968) found that group members who had little power liked those who had much power, overrated how much powerful persons liked them, spoke infrequently, and when they did speak, talked predominantly to members with high power. Jones and associates (1965) noted that subordinates often ingratiate themselves with superiors by trying to appear similar to them. Ingratiation usually fails when the ingratiator overconforms, appears unattractive, is dependent, or appears to be insincere. Unfortunately, little research has been done on the efficacy of ingratiation in different circumstances.

A psychological approach to leadership would stress the individual qualities or personality traits of group leaders. Hare (1976) reports that research has identified qualities of leaders like enthusiasm, dominance, self-confidence, and intelligence. Sociologists would be more inclined to consider such traits within the context of different groups, rather than seeing the traits as general indicators of leadership. Not all groups would judge these traits as equally necessary or important for the group. In addition, a group may have several leaders, each having qualities suited for different group needs.

Leaders can be identified as *instrumental*—those who are task-oriented—or *expressive*—those who provide social and emotional support to members (Hare, 1976). Although it may be desirable for the two leadership functions to be exercised by one person, this does not always occur. Leaders who are recognized for their task-related skills are not necessarily well liked. Research also indicates that groups without an expressive leader tend to find "scapegoats" as a way of dealing with some of the group's problems (Gallagher and Burke, 1974).

Status

Status is the amount of social honor or prestige a group member receives for filling a position in the group. Like power, status is distributed unequally, and people with high status are more likely to receive deference from others. Once attained, high status is relatively easy to retain. Wiggins and associates (1965) found that high status members who moderately decreased their group's winnings in a betting game were not devalued, while those who interfered greatly became intensely disliked. It is not clear why the latter members were rejected. Possibly, the resentment directed toward them was in inverse proportion to others' expectations of them.

In cases of national political scandal, leaders of formerly high status such as former Vice-President Spiro Agnew, who in 1973 was forced to resign over allegations of bribery and tax evasion, have been stripped of their honor. Apparently, some people felt that Agnew's punishment should be based on his not fulfilling their expectations, and others felt that his punishment should be commensurate with the honor of the vice-presidency. Since his punishment (in terms of fines and jail sentence) was not severe, perhaps Agnew's failure to live up to expectations was the important determinant of the public's reaction to his scandal.

The status of a group member can also be related to his or her external status. For example, women or blacks in a predominantly male or white group face a disadvantage in achieving high status in the group. Kanter (1977) has described the problems that face the "token" woman or minority member of a group, among them the exceptional performance pressures put on such people at the same time that they are denied the kind of group support needed for successful performance. Results of an experiment by Ridgeway (1982) indicate that females in male groups can achieve high influence in the group when they are perceived as working for the benefit of the group as a whole rather than for themselves alone. In contrast, males in a female group achieved high influence regardless of whether they were perceived as group or self-oriented.

A classic account of how a person's status in a group can influence performance can be found in

Whyte's (1955) study of a working-class gang of 13 young men in their early 20s in Boston's North End during the Depression. Whyte found the gang, known as "The Nortons" (after the leader), to have a clear status hierarchy reflecting each member's prestige and standing in the group. A member's status position imposed clear obligations toward other members about matters such as who to borrow money from, who could initiate activities for the group, or who had the right to call for group action in the absence of the leader.

Whyte describes how gang members' bowling scores and health were affected by their status in the group. When a skilled but low-status group member challenged a less-skilled but higher status member to a bowling match, the group exerted enough social pressure on the skilled bowler to "rattle" him and cause him to lose the match. Another high status member who lost his standing in the eyes of the group experienced dizzy spells and general *malaise* which he could not explain.

Communication

For positions of leadership and prestige to emerge in a group, members must have a clear understanding of where they and others stand. They achieve this understanding through communication. Communication is a process by which one person sends information to another, and a **communication structure** is the set of relationships defined by who communicates with whom. Imagine a sociometric chart of communication relationships like that in Figure 5.1. First we observe who initiates the communication, who receives it, and how frequently. Then we can draw lines between members to illustrate a communication structure.

Three types of communication structures in five-person groups are presented in Figure 5.2. In the all-channel structure everyone can communicate with everyone else; in the wheel structure only one person can communicate with everyone else; and in the circle structure each person can communicate with two others. In the wheel network the person who can communicate with all other members will probably coordinate the problem-solving

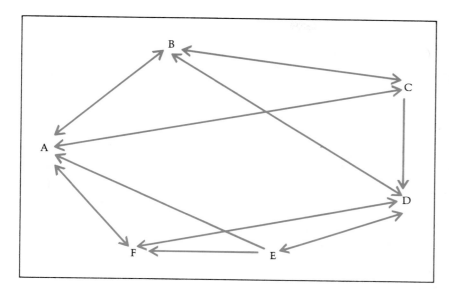

FIGURE 5.1   Friendship Chores among Six Persons

The lines between the individuals, who are represented by letters, mark friendship chores, which correspond to the direction of the arrow (for example, A chooses B, C, and F, and B chooses A, C, and D). Lines with arrowheads at both ends indicate reciprocal friendships. In this example, each person has chosen three friends, and when these choices are diagrammed, we can see the friendship bonds, which define the group's sociometric structure. Obviously A and D are liked by more members than anyone else, and E is liked the least.

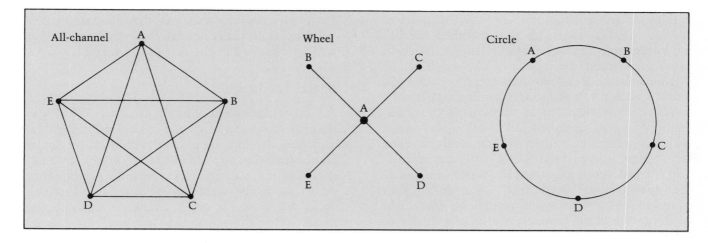

FIGURE 5.2   Communication Networks

activity of other members, and the group will or-ganize its activity around this person as leader. Wheel groups have also been found to make the fewest number of problem-solving errors. In the circle structure often no leader will emerge. Intermember agreement on individual jobs appears to be critical to the organization of groups with relatively open communication structures like the circle and all-channel. When agreement develops the open struc-ture that fails to develop intermember agreement on task expectations is less efficient than the closed structure, the members of which are organized by a central leader at the expense of morale.

The *centrality* of the network, or the total num-ber of channels needed to reach all other persons, tells us how fast, and by what paths, information can move through a communication structure. The important question is the relative effectiveness of different types of communication patterns. One communication structure may be especially well suited for meeting members' emotional needs but poorly suited to task needs. Highly centralized structures ("wheel") are more effective in com-pleting tasks but are not satisfying to members, while decentralized structures ("circle") have the opposite consequences.

GROUP DYNAMICS

It is much more difficult to identify dynamic or process variables than structure variables because the former consist of a series of changes that occur over time in a consistent pattern. The way in which a group makes decisions or completes tasks will involve all aspects of group structure (leadership, status, communication) as they shape the inter-action of group members on a day-to-day basis. Group processes also often are the result of many factors that are interrelated in a particular fashion. Certain situations, for example, seem to encourage the appearance of "groupthink"—the tendency for groups to seek consensus and avoid issues that might be disruptive to the group. It results in a collective pattern of defensive ideas and illusions that protect the group against criticism (Janis, 1972). Reading 5.1 contains an example of groupthink.

Janis and Mann (1977) suggest that groupthink usually occurs in a highly cohesive group. Because its members are more concerned about consensus than a realistic appraisal of problems groupthink is a negative consequence of high cohesion. Specifi-cally, characteristics of groupthink include lead-ership that assumes rather than asks for a certain position on problems; selective perception that as-sumes certain positions are unacceptable rather than discussing them; group blindness to the risks of preferred alternatives; simplistic positions that can be easily understood and shared by all group mem-bers; and people who play the role of "mindguards" and, in doing so, criticize and downplay any op-position to preferred alternatives.

An example of groupthink is President Johnson's decision to bomb North Vietnam in the mid-1960s in spite of intelligence reports advising against this course. Groupthink occurred in part because John-son's advisors began to see themselves as a special, elite group, which simply had to stick together in whatever decision they made. The result of having to stick together was simple solutions to complex problems. Advice about alternative solutions and the possible political consequences of aerial bomb-ing, both in Vietnam and the United States, were ignored by Johnson and his advisors. Furthermore, Johnson's concern for harmony in his "war cabi-net" reduced dissent and also reduced the consid-eration of risks and alternatives. The outcome was temporary military victories that alienated politi-cal support for the American position domestically, in Vietnam, and in the rest of the world.

Social Facilitation

An important aspect of group dynamics is the way that the group can shape the behavior of individual members through supportive relationships. **Social facilitation** refers to the degree to which an audi-ence facilitates or hinders a person's performance on a task. It also refers to coaction effects, which occur when people are working on tasks in the presence of others who also are working. Among other questions, social facilitation research asks what effects, if any, other people have on us when we are working on an individual task in the presence of others but are not interacting with them. Although the first experiment ever conducted in social psychology was on this question (Tripplett, 1896), 70 years of research produced results that did not explain why under these conditions performance was sometimes enhanced and sometimes impaired.

Zajonc (1965), after reviewing the research literature on these conflicting results, suggested that whenever individuals are in the presence of others they are more aroused (that is, have greater drive) than when alone. Borrowing a principle from the psychology of learning, Zajonc explained social facilitation by observing that for well-learned tasks the presence of others increases drive, which enhances performance, but for tasks that are being learned the presence of others decreases performance. These findings suggest that it may not be the presence of others but rather a person's perception of the importance of others' evaluation of her- or himself that affects arousal. When a person is learning tasks there may be greater concern about evaluation of performance than when the tasks are well learned. This principle implies that a variety of factors associated with an individual's perception of the group, including the amount of importance that the person attaches to the group's evaluation, determine whether the presence of others affects performance positively or negatively.

Trust and Cooperation

Related to emotional commitment in groups is the development of trust and cooperation, which are essential to optimal group functioning. We trust others when we feel confident that they are reliable, honest, and worthy of our confidence. With trust we are willing to tell others more things about ourselves that might be damaging to us. Trust also leads to the development of cooperative relationships among group members.

An interesting approach to the study of trust and cooperation is an experimental game called the "prisoner's dilemma" (Rapoport and Chammah, 1965). In the game two prisoners are charged with an identical crime. They are unable to communicate with each other because they are in separate cells. The state needs a confession from one or the other prisoner in order to get a conviction. Each prisoner (independently) is offered freedom and a reward if he confesses and implicates the other prisoner. Both are informed that they will be penalized if both confess, but not as severely if one confessed and the other remained silent. If both remain silent, they will both be set free.

Each prisoner is faced with the choice of confession or silence. Reasoning from self-interest, each prisoner concludes that confession is the best choice. Their reasoning is as follows: If I (A) confess and B doesn't I am free. If I confess and B does the same I am still better off than remaining silent because the punishment is less severe. If I remain silent and B confesses then I am doomed. The logic of each prisoner is to confess regardless of what the other does. Yet, while each chooses what seems to be best for himself, both are convicted.

Such experimental games can help to understand people's tendency to trust and cooperate, or to be fearful and to compete. Researchers using this game have attempted to study the effect of increases in the rewards and punishments on trust and cooperative behavior. Findings from this research indicate that (1) an increase in rewards for confessing reduces cooperative strategies; (2) the strategies followed by players are learned in the interaction of the game and are not related to the personal characteristics they brought to the situation; and (3) the choice of strategies by the same players after a series of games results in either repeated cooperative decisions (silence) or repeated destructive decisions (confession).

Thus, it appears that trust can be developed in temporary groups after players come to recognize trustworthy acts and respond in kind. This is consistent with the view that trust and cooperation are more common in primary groups than in temporary groups with brief interaction encounters (Scott and Lyman, 1968). People in groups with enduring social relationships develop norms of reciprocity that obligate members to explain the reasons for their behavior or beliefs. Disclosures, in the form of excuses or justifications, can lead to feelings that someone is trustworthy, calling for a trusting response.

Deindividuation

Deindividuation occurs when people in groups lose inner restraints and act toward others in ways that deny their individuality—when people treat others as objects rather than as social others. An example of deindividuation is crowd violence at sports events. Supporters of opposing teams may indiscriminately attack any person seated in the section set aside for supporters of the rival team.

Zimbardo's (1969) experiment illustrates the effects of deindividuation. Some subjects were given name tags, spoken to by name, and treated personally. Others were not referred to by name and were given hoods and lab coats to wear. Zimbardo then asked all subjects to "teach" a female student and to deliver electric shocks when the student erred. Experimenters arranged that all subjects would deliver the same number of shocks but subjects were free to control the shocks' durations. Half of the female students acted pleasantly and half acted obnoxiously. Zimbardo found that the "anonymous" subjects delivered longer shocks than "named" subjects and delivered them to nice and obnoxious students alike, while the "named" subjects delivered longer shocks to obnoxious students than to nice students. Here, people who had deindividuation thrust upon them (by the experimenters) acted similarly toward others.

When deindividuation occurs in a group, members behave in an unrestrained and uninhibited manner. They also often exhibit egocentric behavior by failing to listen or pay attention to what other group members are doing (Hamby, 1976). Sometimes this egocentrism results in aggression (Zimbardo, 1969); it also can result in a relaxation of sexual inhibitions. Gergen and Gergen (1971) made students unidentifiable by putting them in a dark room in which they could not see each other. With the use of special low-light equipment, and without their knowledge, the students were observed touching and hugging each other. Unlike other enjoyable experiences in cohesive groups, however, the students did not want to know who their partners were. Since the students' behavior violated cultural norms it is possible they did not want to expose themselves to the likelihood of social control from other group members.

Deindividuation clearly is a complex phenomenon, but we might question whether it truly is a small group phenomenon. After all, small groups are defined as including some degree of intimacy, and anonymity is the opposite of intimacy. We include it as an example of group processes, however, because deindividuation can occur in interpersonal relations in task-oriented groups; that is, in a goal-directed task situation the specialized roles of group members can lead to anonymity.

RELIGIOUS CONVERSION IN CULTS: A GROUP PHENOMENON

A group process that has gained recent national attention is religious conversion in cults. Although religious cults are often large, the practice of getting converts usually takes place in small, intimate groups composed of cult members and potential converts. Many people feel that conversion practices in cults resemble brainwashing, and some make a living as specialists in "deprogramming" individuals, usually young people, who have been converted to cults. In religious conversion a person becomes deeply and emotionally committed to new values, attitudes, and norms—often to a completely new way of life within a community of believers. Cult conversion typically takes place within such a community. Religious conversion can take different forms. While some religious groups use methods that resemble brainwashing, others offer instruction that appeals to reason. Further, we should remember that conversions sometimes last only for a short time or are "unsuccessful." Even highly effective indoctrination procedures will not work with all people all of the time.

One of the most successful conversion procedures is that of Reverend Sun Myung Moon's Unification Church, or the "Moonies." The essential belief of the inner circle of the Unification Church, which distinguishes it from that of established churches, is that Reverend Moon is Christ in His Second Coming. However, this belief typically is not revealed to the potential convert. Instead, potential converts initially are invited to a weekend retreat in a tranquil setting, with transportation,

Religious cults often use the power of primary relationships to socialize new members. Here we see converts to a religious group being brought into intense interaction with etablished members of the group. Successful conversion is dependent upon identification with the group.

shelter, and food provided. A committed believer then accompanies the potential convert, introduces him or her to friends, and in general shepherds the person around. The atmosphere is peaceful, the people are congenial, and potential converts often are impressed by the warmth and serenity of the believers. Potential converts also are invited to drop by a center or house in which the church members live, either for a weekly discussion group or whenever the potential convert feels like visiting. These contacts reinforce the impression of commitment of the believers and the serenity that results. Group discussions often focus on the failure of established churches to be deeply committed, and they emphasize the importance of emotional commitment as a component of true belief.

If the person appears to respond to these discussions, he or she is led along the path of additional spiritual and material commitment. Spiritually, as the convert progresses in understanding and commitment to the positions of the Unification Church, belief in a millenium and in Reverend Moon as the messiah is introduced. The group encourages and supports the convert in open discussion of these beliefs. Materially, converts are encouraged to move into homes with other Moonies, to work with other Moonies, and to spend their spare time with other Moonies. Converts who make good progress may be invited to spend months or years at church centers, such as the one in New York State, which are isolated in the country and staffed only by the most committed members. Here, work, leisure, and spiritual belief are integrated. As an index of their commitment converts give up their material possessions to the church, which in turn provides for them.

Thus conversion to belief in the Unification Church is a step-by-step process. These steps foster commitment by encouraging the potential convert to come to decisions with the support of a small group of true believers. Theological beliefs that distinguish Moonies from members of established churches are revealed only gradually, as the convert becomes more involved in contact with other believers and more isolated from contact with nonbelievers. Eventually, the Unification Church becomes like a family, supplementing previous families, and offering not only the support of other family members but also the integration of the convert's spiritual, social, and material existence.

In a study of how persons are recruited to religious cults and sects Stark and Bainbridge (1980) report that the most important factor in recruiting and holding new members is the social ties that they have to leaders and other group members. Defections from the group are most likely to occur among those lacking strong interpersonal bonds with group members.

The Moonies did not devise the strategy overnight of using small groups to develop commitment to cult beliefs. In fact, two decades ago there were only a handful of believers in Rev. Moon's Unification Church in the United States. Some were in New York and some in California. John Lofland (1968) decided to study the California group, which numbered less than a dozen, and to describe the group's procedures in his doctoral dissertation. He spent many months attending group meetings, and observing the group's successes, its failures, and how strategies for conversion were modified by these outcomes. Little did he know at the time that the Moonies would become one of the most successful and feared cults in America. Lofland's documentation of changes in membership and changes in procedures for conversion are interrelated, the former usually preceeding the latter but occasionally the latter being tried experimentally. The result eventually was a conversion procedure utilizing small group support with the integration of work, leisure, and spiritual activities. Furthermore, revelation of the doctrine of Rev. Moon as Christ reincarnate seemed to be most effective if it occurred slowly, and if the convert was encouraged to suggest this belief first.

Contemporary groups like the Moonies can be contrasted with examples of nineteenth-century communes. Kanter (1972) studied these utopian communities, most of which had a religious basis and most of which were seen as deviant by the dominant culture. Results of a comparison of successful communes, which lasted 25 years or longer, with unsuccessful ones revealed consistent differences in commitment-producing mechanisms. Successful communes more frequently had mech-

anisms for sacrifice, investment, renunciation, communion, mortification, and transcendence than unsuccessful ones, and these mechanisms were a form of social control. In Reading 5.2 Kanter discusses the dilemma posed by the awesome power of social control in utopian communities and of its dangers and opportunities.

LINKAGES BETWEEN GROUPS AND SOCIETY

Small groups can be viewed as the building blocks of society. Charles Horton Cooley (1864–1929), the distinguished social psychologist, believed that a person's values derive from small groups with their intense, personal relationships—that small groups are the source of beliefs, values, and norms that define the basic institutions of society. Thus individuals' beliefs in societal institutions are mediated by small groups, which encourage and support the development of individual identities based on values and norms that are similar to the group's values and norms.

Identity and Behavior in Groups

When we enter into social relationships we present to others our **identity,** or the way we conceive of ourselves in terms relevant to the values and norms of the group, we define ourselves in terms important to others. The claims to an **identity** made by a group member are especially important in interaction since identity represents a commitment to normative standards. When we present an identity to others they can infer our motives and goals from our commitments and trust or expect us to behave accordingly. If we behave inconsistently people do not know what to expect of us, coordinated group activity is made more difficult, and others are likely to mistrust our motives. However, motives are not visible and they are not the sole determinant of our behavior. As a result, inferring motives from what others do and say is difficult.

In public groups, individuals spend much time presenting and clarifying their motives.

How our judgment of motive gives meaning to behavior can be seen in reactions to two Supreme Court justices who, during the years of the Warren court (1953–1969) reportedly never attended viewings of allegedly pornographic films, although they participated in Court decisions about them. Both nonviewing members behaved similarly, one because he felt that the films were disgusting and the other because he felt that all films are protected by the First Amendment. Our own feelings about the two justices probably are dictated more by the differences in their motives than the similarities in their behavior.

Nonverbal behavior also can communicate information about identity. An example is appearance, which includes clothes, hair, and makeup. Appearance is an important aspect of identity, which is partly based on an image of how people think they look. Stone (1962) suggests that in creating our appearance four processes are involved: (1) we announce identity so that the audience can place us in relation to others; (2) we show values so that others can appraise them; (3) we express mood so that others can appreciate it, and (4) we propose an attitude so that others can anticipate our behavior. In all cases the meaning of our appearance is in part determined by our audience, and both performer and audience take appearance seriously. In the early 1960s longer hair on men was unusual, and many men who had long hair were drug users. As both nonusers of drugs and narcotic agents became unidentifiable in long-hair groups, long hair ceased to be a sign of drug-user identity. In a research study (Form and Stone, 1967) several men were told about a man named John who did excellent work and was promoted from foreman to division head. He continued to wear work clothes to his new office and many people, including former friends, began avoiding him. Eighty percent of the men who read the case study predicted that he would be fired, demoted, or receive no further promotion. One man even thought that John might kill himself. Clearly, many people think that fancy clothes do not make the person inside them, but inappropriate clothes can hurt the person's presentation of self.

Even in large, bureaucratic organizations, primary type relationships exist among employees that serve to satisfy individual needs. Here we see workers sorting corn on a "moving belt" while still enjoying social interaction on the job.

Reference Groups and Social Networks

People are brought into active social life through other types of groups that are similar to small groups except that their members may not have face-to-face contact.

REFERENCE GROUPS

A **reference group** is a group whose norms an individual uses to evaluate and judge his or her own beliefs and behaviors. It is often a group that a person aspires to join. Unlike small groups the individual may not meet in face-to-face situations with members of the reference group. There are two types of reference groups: comparative and normative.

A reference group is **comparative** when a person judges the distance between her or his own and the group's beliefs and behaviors to obtain information about the relative distance between personal beliefs and those of others. For example, Stouffer and associates (1949) found that American soldiers in World War II who held safe stateside posts sometimes compared themselves with other stateside soldiers rather than with soldiers in combat zones. As a result this group had lower morale and more feelings of deprivation than soldiers who compared themselves with soldiers in combat zones.

Sometimes a good student in high school may compare her academic performance with a group of exceptional students with the result that she underestimates her true abilities. Some research (Davis, 1966) on academic performance suggests that students in groups of highly talented persons may have lower aspirations for themselves because of poor estimates of their abilities. However, if they were with students who had a range of abilities (exceptional, average, below average), they would develop a stronger academic self-concept.

A **normative reference group** is one in which a nonmember conforms to the norms of the group to which he would like to belong. For example, high school graduates who are eager to go to college often are also eager to conform to college norms. Sometimes students buy new clothing in styles they think will be popular on campus in an effort to conform to the collegiate reference group. As we may anticipate, a person who attempts to conform to reference group norms may err in judging the norms. The student who buys a new college wardrobe may discover that other students wear old jeans and workshirts. The person already belonging to the group is more likely to judge accurately and to conform to the group's norms than one who holds the group as a normative referent.

Also, the person who holds the group as a normative referent is more likely to conform to the group's norms than one for whom the group is not a referent. For example, Siegal and Siegal (1957) studied students who wanted to live in housing units whose members held authoritarian, rigid beliefs. Students who wanted to join the units were less authoritarian than the members in the units. Subsequently, some of the new students were randomly chosen for membership. Those who had become members of the housing units developed authoritarian beliefs similar to unit members. However, the group that did not live in the unit but still wished to become members, were less authoritarian and less similar to members of the housing unit than those who became members. Those who did not live there and no longer wanted to were the least authoritarian and the most dissimilar to the unit members. It appears that the authoritarian beliefs of groups in the housing units produced the most conformity within the membership group and the least conformity among those for whom the unit had ceased to be a reference group.

In a study by Lieberman (1956) investigators looked at a group of factory workers with similar attitudes toward management and labor unions. Later some workers secured management or union positions. As a consequence of their membership in the new groups, those in management positions supported management more strongly than before, while the other group became more prounion. Cutbacks later forced both groups to leave their new positions and return to the factory as workers. When that happened, ex-managers became less promanagement and exstewards became less prounion. Both developed attitudes that supported their reference groups of the moment.

SOCIAL NETWORKS

A **social network** is a set of people who have direct and indirect ties to each other, but not all individuals in the network know each other or have face-to-face relationships. For example, Harry may have *direct* ties with Dena, Carolyn, and Bob, who in turn have *direct* ties with several other people. However, only some of these other people have direct ties with each other, or with Harry, Dena, Carolyn, and Bob. The rest of the ties are *indirect*: Bob is tied to Harry's friends but only through his ties with Harry. Thus people can be influenced by others with whom they have no direct contact but who are in the same social network.

Perrucci and Targ (1982) studied how different kinds of social networks reacted to the unusual behaviors of one of their members, which did or did not result in speedy hospitalization of the member for psychological problems. Networks with more frequent interaction among members and with a recognized leader were more likely to define a member's unusual behavior as a psychological problem requiring medical attention. Networks without these characteristics tended to see the unusual behaviors as some other kind of problem, such as a marital dispute or "growing up pains," and to do nothing about it. As a result people with problems in the first kind of network were hospitalized sooner, received quicker care, and were more likely to be released from the mental hospital than were people in the second kind of network.

SUMMARY

We have discussed characteristics of small groups and emphasized the importance of emotional commitment to the maintenance of the group. Social control in groups serves to bind its members to each other and to the group. Social control may be based on internalized norms and on rewards and punishments. When individuals internalize norms they conform because they feel that conformity is morally right. Coercive social control results from efforts of group members to get rewards or to avoid punishments. Groups usually have both normative and coercive power to influence members.

The internal structure of groups, involving leadership, communication, and status, is important for maintaining the commitment of its members and for social control. A number of group processes also operate to defend the group against outside threats and to provide supportive and trusting relationships among its members. There are, however, situations in which highly cohesive groups with strong emotional commitments among its members can have negative consequences for the group. Group members may cease to relate to each other as individuals with unique differences. This results in deindividuation and may encourage unrestrained behavior that can be harmful to others.

An example of how group processes can be used to develop commitment among members is religious conversion in cults. Cult conversion takes place within a small group of believers and a potential convert. Close, trusting relationships are developed and the convert is guided to make an emotional commitment to new spiritual beliefs. Support for the convert's new beliefs also comes from greater involvement with members in work, leisure, and common residence.

Small groups are building blocks of society because they are important sources of social control. Groups promote internalization of norms through the commitment of members. Groups are sources of personal identity because of the bonds of affection and intimacy they foster.

GLOSSARY

Aspirations   goals and hopes shared by group members that they wish to realize.

Coercion   social control based on the power of some group members to reward or punish other group members.

Communication structure   the set of relationships defined by who communicates with whom; three types of structures are all-channel, wheel, and circle.

Conformity changes in one's beliefs or behaviors, making them more similar to those of other group members and usually occurring in response to efforts to increase group uniformity.

Deindividuation loss of inner restraints and failure to pay attention to others as individuals.

Group an aggregate of people who define themselves as belonging together.

Group cohesion the degree to which members feel positively about the group.

Group structure positions of members of a group relative to each other and differentiated according to criteria relevant to the group's activities.

Identity a commitment to normative standards that allow observers to place us in relation to others and to expect certain behaviors from us.

Leader someone who has more influence in the group than most of the other members.

Nonverbal communication behavior that is understood without verbal explanation.

Norms rules governing the beliefs and behaviors of group members that members agree are essential to group maintenance.

Power the ability of one group member to coerce another member to do something either to obtain a reward or avoid a punishment.

Reference group a group whose norms an individual uses to evaluate and judge her or his own beliefs and behaviors.

Reference group, comparative a group used by individuals to judge the relative distance between their own and the group's beliefs and behaviors.

Reference group, normative a group to whose norms a nonmember conforms because he or she would like to belong.

Small group a group of no more than 15 people, characterized by some emotional commitment, intimacy and face-to-face contact.

Social control influences on individual behavior that increase the probability that a person will behave similarly to other group members.

Social facilitation the degree to which an audience facilitates a person's performance on a task; also, the effects on a person of working with others on a task.

Social network a set of people who have direct and indirect ties to each other but not all of whom necessarily know each other or have face-to-face relationships.

Status amount of social honor or prestige a group member receives for filling a position in the group.

ADDITIONAL READINGS

Argyle, Michael, ed. *Social Encounters: Readings in Social Interaction.* Chicago: Aldine, 1973.
A collection of 28 articles on social interaction collates recent research, especially in nonverbal interaction, with areas of traditional interest in small groups.

Birenbaum, Arnold and Edward Sagarin, *Norms and Human Behavior.* New York: Praeger, 1976.
A discussion of group norms, which are social processes that produce conformity and deviance as outcomes of social interaction.

Kanter, Rosabeth. *Commitment and Community: Communes and Utopias in Sociological Perspective.* Cambridge, Mass.: Harvard University Press, 1972.
This book presents a survey of the correlates of success and failure in nineteenth-century communes in America and a study of some twentieth-century communes, also.

Ofshe, Richard, ed. *Interpersonal Behavior in Small Groups.* Englewood Cliffs, N.J.: Prentice-Hall, 1973.
The articles represent the works of sociologists and psychologists in areas of mutual interests, such as attraction, status, power, and leadership processes in small groups.

Talazzolo, Charles S. *Small Groups: An Introduction.* New York: Van Nostrand, 1981.
A basic introductory text that covers the major theoretical approaches to the study of small groups. Contains an excellent synthesis of current research on small group structure and process.

Phillips, Gerald M., and Eugene C. Jackson. *Interpersonal Dynamics in the Small Group*. New York: Random House, 1970.
A special feature of this book is an excellent set of individual and group projects described at the end of each chapter that should be of interest to students.

READINGS

READING 5.1

The Small Group As a Sociological Phenomenon

Howard L. Nixon II

On December 3, 1977, the Ohio State University varsity basketball team visited Burlington, Vermont, for a game against the University of Vermont team. Local sportswriters in Burlington described the Ohio State team as young, explosive, and extremely talented. It was supposed to be a powerhouse in the making, with all six of its freshmen ranked among the top 100 high-school players in the nation the year before. In fact, Ohio State had been quite impressive in winning its first three games of the 1977–78 season, with its very highly regarded 6'11" freshman center averaging 26 points and 10 rebounds in those games.

Vermont was also undefeated in its first two contests of the new season, but even its most loyal supporters seemed to dismiss the team's chances of victory against its more talented and quicker opponent. Furthermore, many basketball fans in the area wondered why Vermont scheduled teams like Ohio State that were clearly "out of their league" and could humiliate them on the court. Of course, Vermont won the game, 77–76. When asked which individual or individuals on the Vermont team mainly had been responsible for this victory, the losing Ohio State coach commented, "I can't single out any individual because this was certainly a team victory."

While it may be easy to see an inspirational quality in this story, it may not be quite so easy to see its relevance to the sociology of small groups. Viewing a basketball team as a small group, though, may begin to bring the relevance of this story into focus. As a small group, a basketball team combines the individual skills, feelings, beliefs, and actions of

SOURCE: Howard L. Nixon II, THE SMALL GROUP, © 1979, pp. 3–5. Reprinted by permission of Prentice-Hall, Inc., Englewood Cliffs, N.J.

group members into patterns of group interaction and collective effort that often differ from the types of behavior we would expect from the group members if we looked at them merely as a collection of individuals. For example, most would not have predicted the Vermont victory just by looking at the individual abilities of the Vermont players in relation to those of the Ohio State players. On the other hand, the reverse often happens, too. Groups with outstanding individuals may perform miserably, or much worse than we might have expected from looking at the membership of the group.

In this latter regard, consider the case of the men who made up President Kennedy's inner circle of advisers and helped formulate the decision to support the Bay of Pigs invasion of Cuba in 1961. We might reasonably ask how intelligent people, in positions of high responsibility, could arrive at such a disastrous and seemingly unintelligent decision. This question was addressed by Janis (1972), who concluded that the Kennedy Administration's top policy makers were victims of "groupthink"; that is, this policy group had become so tightly knit and friendly that its members were reluctant to engage in the tough, critical appraisal of policy alternatives that was necessary, but might have disrupted the group's esprit de corps or its normal patterns of interaction.

In clarifying the meaning of "groupthink," Janis wanted to draw attention to the idea that its source was not to be found in the individual nor in the organizational setting, but in small group interaction. He proposed that:

. . . Beyond all the familiar sources of human error is a powerful source of defective judgment that arises in cohesive groups—a concurrence-seeking tendency which fosters overoptimism, lack of vigilance, and sloganistic thinking about the weakness and immorality of out-groups. This tendency can take its toll even when the decision makers are conscientious statesmen trying to make

138

the best possible decisions for their country and for all mankind.

I do not mean to imply that all cohesive groups suffer from groupthink, though all may display its symptoms from time to time. Nor should we infer from the term groupthink that group decisions are typically inefficient or harmful. On the contrary, a group whose members have properly defined roles, with traditions and standard operating procedures that facilitate critical inquiry, is probably capable of making better decisions than any individual in the group who works on the problem alone. And yet the advantages of having decisions made by groups are often lost because of psychological pressures that arise when the members work closely together, share the same values, and above all face a crisis situation in which everyone is subjected to stresses that generate a strong need for affiliation. . . . (Janis, 1972:13).

. . . [T]he cases of a successful basketball team performance and policy groups victimized by "groupthink" enable us to dramatize some important ideas about the small group as a sociological phenomenon. First, they demonstrate that small groups can exist for different purposes and their interaction can have very different consequences. Second, they show that groups can have a character of their own, distinct from the personalities or qualities of their individual members. And third, they reveal that this "group character" can have a significant impact on how individual group members feel, think, and act, both individually and collectively.

SUMMARY
Small groups are of interest to sociologists because they can help to understand how patterns of social relationships in groups have different consequences for the performance of individual members and the total group. It can help us to explain why a basketball team with talented individuals can lose to a team with average players, or why one work group

is more productive and has higher morale than another.

Groups have a special character that is different from the characteristics or personalities of individual members. The beliefs and behavior of people are greatly influenced by the groups in which they hold membership.

QUESTIONS
1. How do people experience the influence of group pressure on their beliefs and behavior?
2. Why is it that some groups can have great influence on its members while others do not?

READING 5.2
Group Pressure and Social Control
Rosabeth M. Kanter

The final important critical question about communal groups concerns their internal organization, particularly the role of group pressure and social control. If communal orders do succeed, critics contend, it is because they substitute one form of coercion for another. The argument runs that when communal groups effect harmony between members and develop a smooth, intimate, cooperative life, they often achieve this at a terrible cost to the individual. Though communes may remove the repressive control of distant, impersonal institutions, they replace it with the control of the intimate, face-to-face group of peers, which is perhaps a more benign kind of coercion, but coercion nonetheless. Such critics also point out that in the past the longest-lived communes have been those apparently most "authoritarian" in the sense of having strong leaders or a leadership hierarchy, many formal

SOURCE: Reprinted by permission of the publishers from COMMUNITY AND COMMITMENT: COMMUNES AND UTOPIAS IN SOCIOLOGICAL PERSPECTIVE, by R. M. Kanter, Cambridge, Mass.: Harvard University Press, Copyright © 1972 by the President and Fellows of Harvard College.

rules or informal group norms, and continual demands on the individual for "spiritual improvement" as defined by the group.

Some of this concern is legitimate, and all communal groups are subject to the danger of crossing the point at which a close, warm, loving group becomes an instrument for inducing conformity. But part of the concern also lies in the American fear of being swallowed up by a group, a fear of suffocation of the individual, a fear of loss of freedom and privacy. Americans are generally pictured as friendly, gregarious, and expansive, but other evidence suggests that instead they shy away from intimacy. D. K. Weisberg presented data to indicate that Americans maintain more physical distance in interaction than French or Latin Americans and do much less touching. Abraham Maslow cited Kurt Lewin's and Walter Toman's arguments that Americans need so many more therapists than the rest of the world because they just do not know how to be intimate. As Philip Slater forcefully argued in *The Pursuit of Loneliness*, it is this very American protection of individualism to the exclusion of cooperation and community that may be in large measure responsible for many of the psychological crises in our society today.

It is true that those communities have worked best which manage to generate commitment and loyalty in their members, which immerse people in a strong group that often asks them to make sacrifices, renounce other relationships, and open themselves to criticism by the group. In some cases the community stops there, having created the conditions for harmony and cooperation, and desires little more than to retain its members. Other groups wish to promote self-reliance and responsibility as well, so as to develop strong individuals capable of meeting or suspending their own needs in the context of a loving community. Synanon, for example, has transformed some former drug addicts into responsible members

of the community. Carl Rogers suggested that the end states of encounter groups are "more personal independence, fewer hidden feelings, more willingness to innovate, more opposition to institutional rigidities."

But the issue need not necessarily be phrased as the group versus the individual, as community or privacy, as organization or freedom. Rather, the question for the future is how to promote the growth of the individual and to respect his privacy in the context of a close loving community that also has the degree of organization needed to continue to meet the needs of the individuals within it. There are trade-offs to be made here: a certain amount of one thing may be exchanged for a measure of the other. For example, many members of contemporary communes have reported in interviews that they did give up some of their privacy when they joined the communes. However, they also assert either that they do not miss it, that they do not need as much privacy as they had thought, that they have learned to live without it, or most significantly, that the rewards they find in intimacy and closeness far outweigh the cost in privacy. All human groups may need to strike balances, for social life is full of such trade-offs.

SUMMARY
The intimate, face-to-face relations in small groups can be just as coercive as the formal social control found in impersonal institutions. The friendly, cooperative life found in many communes is achieved at the expense of individuality and privacy. Yet many close communities that generate loyalty and commitment among members are able to develop self-reliant, responsible persons capable of suspending some of their needs to benefit the group.

QUESTIONS
1. Is it possible for groups to promote individ-

ual growth in the context of intimate relationships and group loyalty?

2. Is privacy an important value for most Americans?

3. How does an emphasis on independence and privacy work against cooperative, close communities?

The Texture of Social Life

CHAPTER 6

Socialization

CONTENTS

AT ISSUE

Should children be reared "scientifically"?

During the last 50 years, a large number of books and articles have been published to assist parents in rearing children. They contain information on a range of childrearing problems from diet to feeding schedules, dealing with fussy children, toilet training, and discipline. These books have been greeted enthusiastically, by new parents especially, and accepted widely. In fact, some claim that several generations have now been reared by "the book"—Dr. Spock's *Baby and Child Care, Infant Care* by the U.S. Children's Bureau, or others. However, social scientists disagree about the value of much of this expert advice. Basically, the issues are whether scientific childrearing is valid and if it is desirable.

YES At one time childrearing practices were the same generation after generation. Both the good and bad methods that parents used were repeated by their children in the same way. What were thought of as inherited characteristics really were only traditions and patterns of socialization that had similar results over many generations.

Research evidence now suggests that toilet training can be accomplished without undue stress in one day, that a child's IQ score can be raised by 15 to 20 points with intensive effort by parents, and that personality characteristics can be modified, if not changed, by direct action. These possibilities indicate that a science of childrearing is nearly a reality.

Through the use of rewards, children can be taught bladder and bowel control in a very short time. The advantages of this approach for the child and parent are many: there is no prolonged conflict over dirty diapers; parents are freed from diaper chores—saving time, energy, and emotions; the child learns self-control early; and early success for a child in this area may lead to other successes and high achievement.

In a similar manner, stimulation and intense interaction with a young child can increase her or his intelligence, creativity, and curiosity. These highly structured patterns of interaction provide many benefits: the child will have the intellectual ability to achieve greater success; parents will have fewer problems in relating to the child during childhood because of the established pattern of contact; curious, creative, and intelligent people tend to be happier and have more fulfilling lives than others.

Personality characteristics also can be subjected to scientific manipulation. Rearranging patterns of feeding, fondling, or other care, will affect the frustration level of the child and consequently whether the child will be easy going or aggressive, and intense. Not only would society benefit from such scientific application, but people themselves would be happier and better adjusted if they were programmed to societal expectations and needs.

We have sufficient knowledge about childrearing that if it were applied, it would benefit both society and individuals. Why not use this knowledge?

NO Raising children is time consuming, emotionally draining, and unpredictable in its effects. The attempt to apply scientific findings to childrearing is inhumane, immoral, and bound to fail. Let us look more carefully at the three examples given to buttress the claim for scientific childrearing.

The claim that rapid and stress-free toilet training is possible must be qualified, if not rejected. Success in such efforts assumes that the child values cleanliness and is motivated to be clean. As in the case of other learning in early childhood, toilet training is likely to be successful only when the child is ready—not when the parent becomes tired of changing diapers. It should be remembered that it is the parent who benefits most from toilet training.

144

The desire to increase IQ scores often is based on the good intentions of parents, who desire high achievement for their children. However noble such a goal, the increase in an IQ score does not necessarily mean higher achievement or greater happiness for the child. It may only mean that the child has learned to manipulate the symbols that are used in IQ tests. In addition, creativity and curiosity are often destroyed by the rigid program that is needed to increase a child's IQ score. The benefits to the child are questionable in the light of such a tradeoff.

Perhaps the most dangerous idea of scientific childrearing is that personalities of infants and children may be programmed according to some adult's plan or scheme rather than being allowed to develop naturally. If given the choice, many parents would likely select those personality characteristics that make a child easy, tractable, and conforming. To make parents—or a committee of the larger society—responsible for choosing which personality a child should have would be a denial of most of our democratic values. Fortunately, the ability to do such programming does not exist; no one can actually predict how a child will develop. There are even fashions in childrearing advice. For example, the expert advice of one era that infants should be fed according to schedule gave way to the advice for demand feeding of another era.

The case for scientific childrearing rests upon partial evidence, upon questionable assumptions about human nature and society, and upon a denial of our basic values. Children should not be the crucible for scientific experiment!

Most new parents feel anxious and uncertain about childrearing. Their desire for help in dealing with the many problems of infancy and childhood has created a new industry of experts who promote techniques that will bring quick and painless toilet training, higher IQs, and better adjustment. However, not all people agree that scientific data exist to support such methods of rearing children, and some challenge the use of these methods even if they are available. Clearly, new parents are faced with problems for which they often do not feel prepared and fear that they may do the "wrong" thing in raising their children. Are such fears valid? How do children learn? How important is parents' behavior on the child's development? Can people learn how to act in new situations at any age?

QUESTIONS TO CONSIDER

- How important is human care, contact, and attention for an infant?

- How does socialization occur in games and play?

- How do the potential human qualities of infants develop?

- Are adults socialized as well as children?

LAS VEGAS, 24 APRIL 1982 (AP)—Six young children who never learned to talk and were starved for affection while being secluded in a dark room for most of their lives have been taken away from a couple who "didn't know how to be parents," juvenile officials say. The plight of the children—a 6-year-old boy, 4-year-old twin girls, a 3-year-old girl, and an 8-month old twin boy and girl—was disclosed Thursday by authorities.

Authorities said the children feared toys and small animals and communicated among themselves by gibberish when they were found in February. They are making an excellent adjustment, officials said, although they still must learn to talk. The children are very affectionate, authorities said, often hugging each other and adults. The five younger children have been placed in foster homes and the 6-year-old remains with juvenile authorities.

Juvenile authorities said the children were found after a policeman saw the 6-year-old wandering along a street. The officer took him to Child Haven because the boy couldn't talk. There, workers recognized the boy from a previous visit by the child and his mother. Officials said they had come in to inquire about benefits, but never returned. No physical abuse of the children can be substantiated, . . . although the signs of emotional neglect are very prominent.

. . . A report said the children were "fearful of toys, of males, afraid of other peers, did not

know trees or swings, would hide from overhead sounds, were unreceptive to most foods, had a difficult time using eating utensils," and probably had been locked and fed in a dark room.

When the oldest boy was taken to Child Haven, the mother was called. She told officers she had two other children at home and agreed to turn them over to authorities. Ten days later, she called to say she had three more children. Welfare officials said the mother worked at low-paying jobs and the father was unemployed and was supposed to watch the children. . . . officials have been unable to find the father.

The incidents recounted here, in addition to their social implications, raise many questions about human growth and development. How important are contact, affection, and emotional stimulation for the newborn child? What are the long-term consequences of lack of contact and stimulation? How does language influence human development? What are the processes of human development? How do children learn to follow rules?

THE PROCESS OF BECOMING HUMAN: SOCIALIZATION

Human babies are totally dependent at birth. Not only are they unable to sit, crawl, walk, or feed themselves, but they cannot speak, think, or otherwise act in ways that we identify as distinctively human. While children even if isolated may learn to walk and feed themselves, they need contact and attention from other people to develop human characteristics.

The process by which such learning occurs is called socialization. Specifically, **socialization** is the process through which a person acquires the skills and behaviors necessary for social living. This process draws on the child's culture, the child's biological inheritance, and the interactions of the child and the other humans who provide care and attention. We can see how these elements are related in examining the effects of isolation on child growth and learning.

Frequent social and physical contact between parents and children is essential if infants are to develop human traits. The regularity of parental care, feeding, and touching enables the child to develop relationships with others and to learn new social roles.

Isolated Children

Several cases of **feral children,** who failed to develop language and other intellectual and physical skills through being isolated from human contact from very early ages, have been reported. One case, "Anna," was an illegitimate child whose grandfather kept her in a small, dark attic room for her first six years. When discovered, she could not talk or walk, and appeared to be blind, deaf, and mentally retarded. However, special care and attention during the four remaining years of her life helped her to learn some language, to identify colors, and to do some simple tasks. In another case, "Isabelle," who was discovered at age six living alone with her deaf-mute mother, had no verbal language. However, during the first two years of special attention her development was very rapid and she had achieved normal levels of skills by the age of eight and a half (Davis, 1940, 1947, 1948).

Other accounts of children isolated from human contact have been reported, though not all have been verified. Among the most notable cases are those of Kamala and Amala, the "Wolf Girls of Midnapore" who were "adopted" and reared by a pack of wolves in India, and Victor, the "Wild Boy of Averon" (Lane, 1976). Apparently, these children were abandoned by, or separated from, their families at an early age. They were discovered later by people who thought the children had been raised by an animal species; presumably, the animals saw the children as infants of their own species. Malson (1972) says that 53 cases of feral children were reported between 1944 and 1961. These children allegedly were raised by wolves, apes, cattle, sheep, bears, or leopards. Typically, these feral children were unable to talk and walk. Instead, they grunted, made other animallike noises, and "walked" by using their arms as a secondary set of legs. They ate their food raw, often gulping it down, and used their teeth to defend themselves. In addition, their habits apparently were nocturnal for they often withdrew during the day. Finally, they seemed more at ease in the company of animals than that of humans.

One of the most famous of the feral children was "Victor", discovered and named by a French physician named Jean Itard. Itard found Victor, a 12-year-old boy, wandering in the woods of Averon. He took charge of the child and systematically attempted to overcome his early learning deprivation. His work with the boy was documented extensively and won for Itard a government grant. (Two reports were published in 1801 and 1806 and reprinted in 1962). Although Victor developed a simple vocabulary, elementary arithmetic skills, and some writing ability, he never learned to read or speak before his death at age 40. Itard's reports

about Victor have been used recently by educators who teach deaf-mutes and by scientists who teach sign language to chimpanzees. All of these reports emphasize the necessity of human contact for children to learn survival and language skills.
who teach deaf-mutes and by scientists who teach sign language to chimpanzees. All of these reports emphasize the necessity of human contact for children to learn survival and language skills.

The Cultural Context

An important element in human development is the cultural context within which language and ideas are learned. Culture, as the expression of socially shared meanings, provides ideas, values, and norms, which are learned. Concepts about human nature, about the ways children should be fed, handled or disciplined, or about how children should relate to adults are rooted in the culture.

The potential for learning language, sharing symbols and symbolic meanings, and adapting language to express new ideas and concepts is unique to humans. This potential is only realized when the infant receives attention, physical contact, and stimulation from others. How such attention and contact are provided is defined by the culture. To understand the development of human potential, let us examine some ideas about biological inheritance and about human nature and human growth.

Instincts, Repression, and Social Learning

Before about 1920, many students of human behavior held that instincts were the basis of human behavior. **Instincts** are biologically predetermined behaviors characteristic of a species. These behaviors, often complex, are always performed the same way, regardless of circumstances. Instinct as applied to humans, however, meant a predisposition to act in certain ways rather than a predetermination to act. Instincts, or unlearned drives, were the reason why humans acted as they did—why, for example, they went to war, amassed wealth, or dominated others. Perhaps the most famous effort to explain behavior by unlearned drives was that of Freud, the founder of psychoanalysis, who pro-

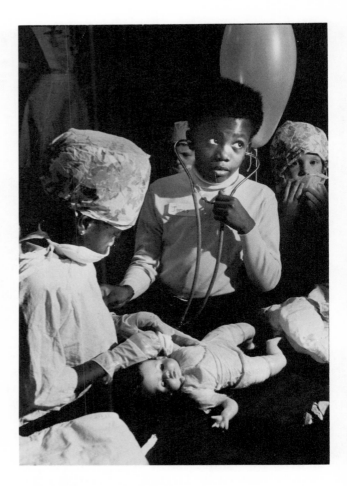

Early childhood learning involves imitation of others and learning culturally defined roles. These children in the United States play the role of medical doctor, but children of nomads in Saudi Arabia or of Zaire do not play such roles because these roles are not a part of their culture.

posed that sex was a basic human drive. For Freud, the infant seeks (sexual) pleasure through sucking and feeding (oral behavior), as a toddler through defecation (anal behavior), and as a preschooler through masturbation (phallic behavior). The biological drives of this pleasure-seeking creature were described as the *id*, the unconscious drive for self-gratification. Society, through parents, seeks to control these drives by scheduled feeding times, toilet training, and punishment for masturbation. As a result, the *ego*, or the conscious self emerges. Conscience, or the *superego*, develops as young children incorporate their parents' ideas about correct behavior and repress their drives for self-gratification. Freud argued that repression, or refusing to allow individuals to express these drives, caused guilt, anxiety, and failure in later male-female relationships. In this view, society is a negative force on individual self-expression.

Some psychoanalysts continue to accept Freud's basic views; others have modified his theories. As our knowledge of human cultures began to grow, however, it became apparent to many researchers that instincts were an inadequate explanation for varied behavior patterns, not only in these cultures, but for human beings generally.

Human behavior is not comparable to that of birds, bees, or other animals. A peregrine falcon, for example, which never has seen a prey-killing by its own species, will attack and kill a prey in a manner appropriate to the size and weaknesses of the prey and then will pluck and eat it. Another complex instinct governs the reproductive behavior of salmon which, at the appropriate time in their life cycle, will swim upriver to lay their eggs and then die. Instinctual behaviors, like these, are usually a complicated and extended chain of acts arranged in a specific order or pattern. In contrast, humans survive, build houses, work, mate, and enjoy pleasure in a variety of forms not through instinct but by learning—by the process of socialization.

The socialization process begins with the newborn's reflex behavior. A **reflex** is an inborn tendency to perform specific, simple, and undifferentiated behavior. For example, the sucking of human babies is a reflex. The newborn's sucking reflex does not differentiate between a source of food, like the breast or bottle, and other objects, like the infant's fist. Food is given to the infant while it sucks; then, after several days of feeding, the infant learns to seek the food source. Depending on the way in which food is supplied, the infant's reflex is modified and extended to more complex chains of behavior. Most of the social behaviors of young infants are probably the result of the modification of reflexes.

Processes of Social Learning

The experiences of hunger, physical discomfort, or cold are part of the infant's world. Another part of this world is people who modify and mediate the nonsocial, biological aspects of the child's experience. The satisfaction of a child's needs are the result of the actions of others: hunger that is assuaged by feeding, discomfort that is alleviated by a change of diapers, a sense of cold that disappears when the infant is wrapped in a blanket.

It is the actions of others, especially parents, that establish regularity in the world of the infant. This regularity enables a child to develop a relationship with the surrounding world. In other words, the process of feeding on schedule, changing diapers, or responding to some cries but not others creates a structure to the relationship that the child has with the things and people surrounding him or her. These patterns shape the development of the child, not only socially but biologically. Berger and Berger (1979) give an example of this process:

The most obvious illustration of this is the timetable of feedings. If the child is fed at certain times, and at certain times only, the organism is forced to adjust to this pattern. In making this adjustment, its functioning changes. What happens in the end is not only that the infant is fed at certain times but that he is hungry at those times. Graphically, society not only imposes its patterns upon the infant's behavior but reaches inside him to organize the functions of his stomach. The same observation pertains to elimination, to sleeping, and to other physiological processes that are endemic to the organism. (p. 5)

The general processes of social learning have received much attention. How does the child learn from others? How important are the child's relations with others in her or his development? Bettleheim (1959) argued that some children never develop the capacity to relate to others in a human way because of prolonged early emotional deprivation. He noted that such children, like feral children, had never experienced love and warmth from a caretaker. For example, some parents have locked babies in closets for hours. Others have beaten their children with closed fists to punish them for such acts as urinating in their clothes. These children later displayed fear of other human beings and pathologically aggressive behaviors.

Some of the strongest needs of the infant are for love, warmth, and affection from its caretakers. In a famous series of experiments, the Harlows (Harlow, 1959; Harlow and Harlow, 1962), a husband and wife team of psychologists, replaced the parents of some infant monkeys with a variety of surrogate, or substitute, parents. Some of the surrogate parents were made of wire, others of terrycloth; some fed the infant from an attached bottle, some did not. The Harlows found that the infant monkeys, when given a choice, preferred the terrycloth surrogate to the wire one, even when the wire one had a bottle of food and the terrycloth one did not. To the Harlows, this suggested that the softness of the terrycloth surrogate was a more important quality to infant monkeys than food when the latter was associated with the wire surrogate. In addition, they found that the monkeys who had wire surrogates did not learn how to play with the other monkeys; when they were with other monkeys, they became withdrawn and tense.

Although we must be cautious in applying these findings to humans, Spitz's (1945) work with infants who were less than a year old supports the Harlow's findings. Spitz compared babies in the nursery of a women's penal institution to babies being cared for in a foundling home. Although health and sanitary precautions were adequate in both institutions, the infants in the women's penal institution received more attention from their caretakers than those in the foundling home. Partly because of this lack of attention, 37 percent of the infants in the foundling home died of common childhood diseases, while none of the children in the penal nursery died from these diseases. These are dramatic results. They provide very strong support for the argument that caretaker contact is essential for an infant's optimal functioning.

THE LOOKING-GLASS SELF

The learning process involves both the social world and the child's responses. The child, through contact with others, gradually sees him- or herself as an object that reflects this process. Charles H. Cooley, an early sociologist, described the development of **self** on the basis of social contact with others as the "looking-glass self."

According to Cooley (1909), humans develop a sense of personal identity by observing the way other people react to them. Gestures, verbal responses, and other reactions present a person with an image of him- or herself to which the person responds. One's self-identity, then, is shaped in large measure by the way in which a person perceives, understands, and responds to the people around him or her. The reflection one sees in the mirror held up by others becomes the basis for self-identity.

Despite the importance of Cooley's insight, many questions remain unanswered about the development of a sense of self. How do children learn to interpret the cues and reactions of others? Why do people select some responses of other people and ignore other responses? How does an individual develop a sense of personal identity if the images that he sees are contradictory or inconsistent? Further examination of such issues led some researchers to define the processes of socialization more precisely. Two concepts are especially important: "role taking" and "significant others."

ROLE-TAKING AND SIGNIFICANT OTHERS

Role refers to the behavioral expectations associated with a particular status, or position. People have multiple roles. For the role of a parent, these expectations include obligations—feeding, teaching, and providing for children—privileges—respect and appreciation from spouse and children—and norms about appropriate behavior—not leaving children alone at night or physically abusing them. For each status—male or female, father or daughter, employer or student—society defines expectations that guide the behavior of the person in that position.

How does one learn these expectations? How does one learn to play the role of son or daughter, boyfriend or girlfriend, employer or employee? In the process of learning to play a role, other people react to one's behavior. People whose reactions are most important, for example, a father for the young boy learning the role of son, are **significant others.** In short, people learn roles through relationships with significant others.

Children often act out roles of parents and in so doing rehearse and organize their conception of the social world. This young man is acting out an adult male role taking the role of the other—and is learning the expectations associated with that role.

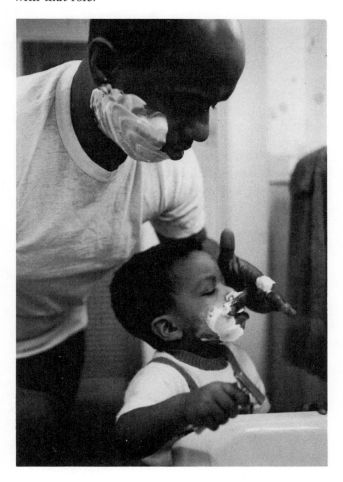

In an effort to explore the development of the self or self-identity, George H. Mead (1934) noted that, in learning language, and in particular grammar, children not only are socialized in one of the most important skills of living but also they learn to distinguish between the self as an active subject (the "I") and the self as an object of the actions and attitudes of others (the "me"). For example, in the sentence, "I see me in the mirror," "I" is the subject which sees and "me" is the subject which is seen.

Two important points are reflected in Mead's distinction between "I" and "me." First, the development of the self as subject implies an ability to separate oneself from other people and things. Second, the development of the self as object implies the ability to see oneself through the eyes of others—to look at oneself from their viewpoint. Seeing oneself from another's perspective, or "taking the role of the other" as Mead described it, increases the one's ability to communicate and to share activities with others. Mead noted that the development of the concepts of self as subject and as object corresponds to the child's developing ability to use these concepts' grammatical equivalents correctly. At the same time children learn to conceive of themselves as distinct from others, they also learn to think of themselves both as social objects and social subjects.

People who are particularly important in influencing our self-images are significant others, those who stand in special relation to us. To small children, parents are the dominant others and later, close friends may assume this role. Also important to self-image is the *generalized other.* This concept refers to our impression of society's expectations of our behavior, which we are made aware of not only through relationships with family and friends but also through acquaintances, strangers, media, and other sources of information about society.

To Mead, role taking, especially of significant others, was an extremely important means of socialization. Mead suggested that young children, especially during the preschool years, learn in their play to adjust their own behavior to the expectations held by others. While much play is relatively aimless, children during play often practice various roles that they have observed. In doll play children may act out the roles of mother, father, baby, doctor, storekeeper, and so on. Doing so, they rehearse and organize their conception of the social world. Indeed, role playing may allow children to act out feelings that, because of emotional blocks or lack of vocabulary, they are unwilling or unable to talk about. During World War II in London, Anna Freud (Freud and Burlingham, 1943) found that many children were not able to talk about their fears of bombing raids although they were clearly disturbed by these raids. Later, through doll play, the children were able to reenact the bombing raids, after which they could discuss their fears.

Learning to participate in games is another way that children learn the roles of society. A game has rules; and that players usually have a goal; namely, to win; and in team games players have teammates with whom they cooperate while competing with their opponents. Finally, in many games, teammates have different positions, for each of which different activities are specified, and on the basis of which players have expectations that help them to predict the behavior of other game players. Learning childhood games thus becomes a model for socialization.

COMPLIANCE, INTERNALIZATION, AND BEHAVIOR

Most of our discussion thus far has involved behavior that occurs in the presence of others. But what happens when no one is watching? Do the values, expectations, and norms that we have learned operate only when others are around? To the customer in a store who is unobserved and knows it, shoplifting is an easy and perhaps tempting crime because no punishment will result. Why, then, do most of us, most of the time, choose not to shoplift?

Socialization is the acquisition of motives and values as well as knowledge and meaning. When a person is socialized so that he or she will perform appropriately whether or not rewards for that behavior are forthcoming, we say the person has **internalized** the moral values into her or his self-concept (Brim, 1966). These internalized values become an intrinsic part of our identities. To return to our example of shoplifting, one reason that many of us refrain from shoplifting is because to shoplift would damage our image of ourselves as honest

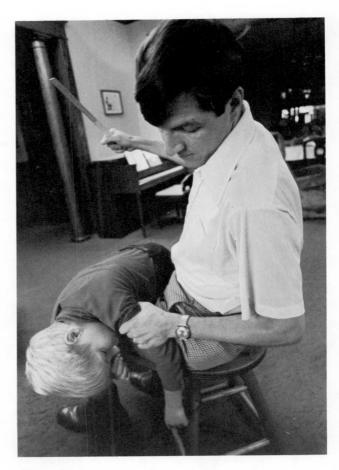

Spanking is a common form of punishment and usually is effective in obtaining a child's compliance in a specific situation. However, spanking has little long-term effectiveness and is not effective in developing appropriate behaviors in other situations.

people. Most of us do not shoplift no matter how easy the opportunity and attractive the booty because we have been socialized in the values of our society and we have internalized the prohibition against stealing. Also, the risk and embarrassment of exposure if caught would damage our self-image and serve to keep us from shoplifting.

Another reason for compliance to social norms is to obtain rewards or to avoid punishment. It is clear that rewards and punishments affect learning, but there is controversy over their effectiveness in socialization. Do rewards and punishments help a person learn behaviors that will persist over time? When and how much punishment or rewarding should be used?

Punishment appears to be one of the least effective methods of socializing children for a variety of reasons. First, punishing a child for performing a particular behavior does decrease the probability that the child will do it again and thus is effective in controlling inappropriate behaviors. However, the overall effect of punishment is negative because it does not assist in developing appropriate behaviors. For long-term learning, teaching a child what not to do usually is less effective than teaching the child what to do. Second, frequent punishment is subject to the **law of marginal utility;** that is, the effect of frequently applied punishment diminishes over time. To maintain the effectiveness of punishment, its severity must be continually increased. Third, punishments that are physically aggressive, like spanking, can teach the child to be physically aggressive. Parents who want to teach children to control their aggressiveness may find that physical punishment is counterproductive.

Punishment applied at the beginning of misbehavior appears to be more effective than punishment applied later, perhaps because early punishment prevents the child from reaping any rewards that are attached to the completion of the transgressing act (Walters and Demkow, 1963). Also, mild punishments are more effective than severe punishments in obtaining compliance. For example, a parent may inflict severe punishment on a child for jumping on the furniture. Such punishment will inhibit the child's tendency to jump on the furniture—but only when the parent is present and is prepared to punish the child. When the parent is not around or is not prepared to punish the child, the child still may jump on the furniture. Festinger and Freedman (1964) suggest that **sufficient deterrence,** a severe punishment, will stop the child from jumping on the furniture, but this compliance will occur only as long as the child knows there is

someone to administer the punishment. By contrast, if parents give mild punishments, or **insufficient deterrence,** the child may lack justification for not jumping on the furniture. However, in an effort to understand his or her own behavior, the child who is mildly punished internalizes a moral code that says not jumping on the furniture is the good behavior parents desire. The child uses the increased positive value of good behavior to justify not jumping on the furniture; thus mild punishment is more effective in long-term learning.

In contrast to punishment, rewards seem to have a direct, positive effect on behavior. In general, the greater the reward and the frequency of the reward for a particular behavior, the more likely it is that the person will perform the behavior. However, some conditions seem to slow down the learning of a behavior but will lead to internalization. Internalization will be more likely to occur if the appropriate behavior is rewarded only sometimes rather than every time, if there is a delay between the behavior and the reward rather than no delay, and if the response is hard to learn rather than easy to learn. The effects of these three conditions are well documented in psychology through experiments with both animals and people. This research suggests that the conditions under which behaviors are learned in the shortest time may not be the same conditions that produce internalization.

Investigators explain the effects of the first and second conditions by noting that when a behavior has been learned under conditions of **intermittent** or **delayed reward,** the person cannot easily tell when the rewards have stopped coming. The effect of the third condition in socialization may be explained in much the same way as insufficient deterrence explains the effects of mild punishments (Lawrence and Festinger, 1962). Children who are frequently and extravagantly rewarded for good behavior have no doubts about why they should behave well. They behave well for the rewards. Children who must work for small rewards that are given only part of the time learn behaviors more slowly than the other children. They lack the justification for their effort that the more highly rewarded children have in the reward. The children who worked hard for the rewards must find another justification for working so hard. One way to do this is to increase the value of the behavior itself. Thus the modestly rewarded child comes to value the behavior rather than the reward. As a result, when rewards are unavailable these children are more likely to perform the behavior than are the highly rewarded children. In other words, modest rewards are more effective than great rewards for internalization of behaviors.

The processes of learning involve both internalization and compliance through punishment, and society depends on the learned values as well as public shame or ridicule to obtain conformity. Thus, as a result of internalized social values, many of us feel guilty when we violate social norms—even in private—and tend to follow the norms when we are in public.

Socialization to Social Positions

Much socialization of children is similar across a culture because people share general values about children. Thus most children are fondled, fed, and carefully tended, and cases of extreme abuse or neglect shock and anger most of us. However, within every society there are various sets of relationships that demand different behaviors of people and have specific norms and values attached to them. These relationships can be defined in terms of positions or locations in a general system of social activities. Learning these norms and values is the process of socialization to a social position. This process is analogous to learning to play the various positions of a baseball team.

Baseball depends upon cooperation among the players. The pitcher knows that the catcher expects him or her to throw the ball past the batter to the catcher. In another game, the pitcher might be the catcher; in any one game, however, a person cannot play both of these positions at the same time. The positions of pitcher and catcher are dependent upon each other and upon the other seven positions on the team. Each player must learn what is expected of the person in every position.

Children joining Little League must learn this interdependence. If we observe beginning players

we will see that players initially think only of their own positions, like first baseman or outfielder. Only with experience does the first baseman learn that his or her position has wider role expectations than being on the base to catch balls thrown by other players. The rules of the game are such that the pitcher, the catcher, and the other seven players all have certain rights and obligations that make the game possible. The pitcher, for example, must know how the rights and obligations of the position— what to do when the ball is hit to third base or the outfield or how to play if there is only one out compared with two outs—relate to the rights and obligations of the other players on the team. While pitching, a person will attempt to conform to the team's expectations and to surprise the opponents. If the pitcher violates the rules of the game by, for example, balking on the pitcher's mound, he or she is not "playing the game."

Positions in the larger society similarly have both general and specific expectations attached to them. The positions of president, foreman, personnel manager, and payroll clerk in a large company have some common values and expectations but also have many different expectations for each position. Other socially defined positions that have different norms and values are organized around expertise, wealth, power, and age. To facilitate age-appropriate socialization, schools have been organized into age categories for educating children and youth. However, we must remember that socialization as a process begins at birth and continues until death, as individuals are faced with new expectations at every stage in the life span.

Socialization Through the Life Span

Over our life span, the changes in the roles we play correspond with socialization experiences. In childhood we learn our roles through the expectations and examples of our parents. In adolescence the opinions of our peers rather than those of our families are important to our role learning. In adulthood work and parental roles are learned, and in old age we learn new roles on the bases of our experiences with, say, retirement, widowhood, or failing health. Learning these roles is not easy; in fact, successful role performance usually depends upon the expectations not only of experts and superiors but also of peers, inferiors, and audiences. For example, the successful military officer's performance satisfies bosses, peers, subordinates, and observers. With each change in rank the constituents of the position changes, and therefore one must become socialized to a new role.

Of course, socialization is not a one-way street in which recipients simply absorb information from agents of socialization. Those who are socialized are active participants in the process and affect or even change it. One way participants affect the socialization process is through anticipatory socialization. **Anticipatory socialization** occurs when a person who foresees becoming a group member attempts to assume the attitudes and behaviors appropriate to group membership. For example, the high school graduate who is college-bound may shop for clothes that are perceived by the graduate to be appropriate to college life. The anticipatory socialization may be based on either accurate or inaccurate perceptions of the roles; thus the new college student may be right or wrong in the choices of clothing. Nonetheless, if a substantial percentage of new students buy clothes and dress on the basis of these perceptions, the appearance on campus of these students so dressed will have some effect on campus clothing styles. Anticipatory socialization, then, is one way in which those who are members of a group can affect the group to which they are socialized.

The changes that occur over the life span as a result of socialization to different roles in various groups develop in sequence; that is, to learn some roles, others must be mastered first. For example, to be a college undergraduate student, a person usually must have been a satisfactory high school student. To be a graduate student, she or he usually must have been a good undergraduate student. In short, socialization is a continuous process, and learning experiences at earlier ages prepare a person for future roles.

Another important factor in socialization is the change in expectations at different ages. In infancy and childhood we typically are socialized to the skills and behaviors that are important to virtually all the roles in society that we might perform. In adolescence and adulthood socialization processes focus more on specific roles, while in old age role requirements in American society once again are more diffuse.

CHILDHOOD SOCIALIZATION

Childhood is idealized as a time of carefree play, self-indulgence, and unrestrained freedom. However, as Denzin (1977) suggests, children actually find themselves under constant surveillance. Adults, believing that children will avoid work and serious activities at all costs, accept the responsibility to remake these nonserious children over into serious adults.

For most children this effort to socialize them is carried on in three social units: the family, the school, and the peer group. The child's first observations of adult behavior are usually that of parents, who serve as role models and whose behavior the child imitates. Parents encourage children's imitative behavior by, for example, providing them with role-appropriate toys—giving boys hammers just like daddy's or giving girls pots and pans like mother's. (Such actions are a part of the sexist pattern of childrearing illustrated in Reading 6.1) Eventually, children begin to act independently of parental behaviors.

Children whose behavior, values, and beliefs are similar to those of parents, even when the child is removed from parental control and stimulation, have identified with the parent. **Identification** is the internalization of the values and behaviors of the parental model. By contrast, **imitation** is simply copying the behavior of the model without internalizing it.

Parental dominance may not be complete in a child's early years. Mass media—especially television—play an important role in the socialization of most young children. For example, "Sesame Street" was created to be a source of cultural enrichment and stimulation for young children; other children's programs have also attempted to provide new experiences. The impact of mass media—radio, television, magazines, records—is in dispute.

However, there is no doubt that these media must be considered influential in the socialization of children and youth.

While we cannot define the conditions under which a child internalizes the values and behavior of a model, there is evidence that a warm and affectionate adult is more likely to be imitated by a child than an aloof adult. Bandura and Houston (1961) asked children to play with an adult for 15 minutes on two different days, five days apart. Half of the children played with a person who acted in a reserved and standoffish manner; the other half played with one who was warm and affectionate. After the second play period, each child and adult pair was taken to another room where they were asked to choose which of two boxes contained a decorative sticker with a picture on it. A doll sat on the top of each box. All of the adults who chose first knocked the doll from the top of the box, opened the lid, removed a sticker, pasted it on the wall, and replaced the doll on the box. The way in which the model chose the box was incidental to the experimenter's instructions. However, in both the play and the task situations, children who observed the warm and responsive model imitated more of the model's behaviors than children who observed the aloof model; and children who had been rated as highly dependent imitated the model's incidental behaviors more frequently than children who were low in dependency. In short, the warm, nurturing parent may be more effective than the aloof parent in socializing children, whether the parent's behavior is intentional or incidental. Also, children of affectionate parents quickly learn to imitate not only their parents' good habits but also their bad ones.

The process of child development has been examined by many researchers. Freud, as we noted earlier, emphasized the innate, selfish drives of the child. He defined these drives in terms of oral, anal and phallic stages for young children, a latency (nonsexual) period for older children, and a genital stage for adolescents. Parents' hostile reactions to a child's behaviors in any one stage may create conflict in parent-child relationships. Parental power generates fear and antagonistic feelings on the part of children toward parents, but since moral standards do not permit them to express this antagonism, they repress it. Repressed antagonism produces feelings of guilt, and identifying with parents is one way of coping with such feelings. Thus, for Freud, guilt-induced identification is an important process through which both males and females acquire their parents' attitudes.

Erik Erikson, though a student of Freud, emphasized that human development involves social as well as psychological growth. Socialization for Erikson develops through eight stages, from birth to old age, each of which is characterized by specific psychosocial crises that must be resolved before the stage can be successfully completed. Until about age one, the basic crisis is "trust versus mistrust." The child, who receives regular, consistent and predictable care will develop trust; the lack of such care will result in mistrust and delayed development. For the toddler, the crisis is "autonomy versus shame and doubt," for the preschool child it is "initiative versus guilt," and for the elementary school child, "industry versus inferiority." Adolescents face "identity versus role confusion," and young adults, the crisis of "intimacy versus isolation." Finally, for adults, the crisis is "generativity versus stagnation" and "ego integrity versus despair" for older people. Mastery of the crisis at each stage leads to the development of personal identity, growth, and maturity, while failure to resolve the crisis cripples growth or development.

A third view of early childhood, that of Jean Piaget, emphasizes cognitive factors, that is, thinking and reasoning, in the development of personal identity. Piaget describes four stages of cognitive development, which begins at birth. Personal identity emerges as the child acquires an understanding of the objects that surround him or her (sensory-motor stage), learns language (intuitive preoperational stage), discovers cause and effect (concrete operational stage) and finally reasons with abstract concepts (formal operational stage). These stages are sequential.

Though the family is the primary socializing force during early childhood, the school and the peer group also are important, especially among older children. However, it is during adolescence that these agents of socialization have their greatest impact.

ADOLESCENT SOCIALIZATION

When children reach adolescence, expectations about their behavior become similar to those for adults. In the United States teenagers begin to develop strong heterosexual relationships through "dating" and to assume occupational roles by taking part-time jobs. In Western, industrialized society, adolescence is a time when youth makes the transition from childhood to adulthood. The study of adolescence in different societies is a study of the way in which agents of socialization encourage youths to transfer their allegiance from the family to the society as a whole. Industrial societies typically have a variety of specialized work roles, which must be filled by skilled and educated workers. Few families are equipped to teach their children these specialized skills, and thus nonfamilial agents, like schools train youth in occupational roles.

The basic social and economic unit of most nonindustrial societies is the family. There is little occupational specialization and the family often assumes most of the responsibility for socializing the young to adult roles. In addition, the roles of adulthood in nonindustrial societies, like the roles of childhood, often are determined by one's family's position in society, and one's own position in the family. As a result, the period of adolescence is marked by fewer drastic changes and consequently less conflict and stress than in industrial societies.

Margaret Mead's *Coming of Age in Samoa* (1928) describes a society in which the stress that we usually associate with adolesence did not exist. Certainly life in Samoa during the time of her study was idyllic. Coconuts, breadfruits, and fish were plentiful, easily obtained, and sufficient for sustenance. Occupational distinctions, and wealth, status, and power distinctions were few and those that existed were often determined by kinship. In most social respects, members of the society were homogeneous, and the demands of adulthood did not represent a radical change in a person's life. Since adults roles in Samoa were continuous with childhood roles, there was little need for formal socialization during adolescence as preparation for adult roles. For the Samoan adolescent life was calm and carefree.

Contrast adolescence in Samoa with the same age-sets in the United States. We typically see adolescence as a time of conflict, confusion, turmoil, and discontent. (Reading 6.2, "Growing Up Confused," describes the sources of some of this conflict.) Much of the family's influence over the child is relinquished to other agents of socialization. The school has an increasing impact on teenagers through the teaching of skills necessary for adult life and as a social environment for age-based peer groups.

One of the most important arenas in which adolescent socialization occurs is the peer group. For many youth in industrial societies, the most significant reference group and source of evaluations about one's activities and values is a group of peers of similar age (Eisenstadt, 1956). In nonindustrial societies the group to which one belongs is more age-heterogeneous, even in societies in which age grading throughout the life span is an important part of the society's social organization. The Karimojong of northeastern Uganda, for example, base the political organization of their society on age-sets, but the only distinction between a boy of any age and a man is whether one has undergone an initiation ceremony. In the United States, in contrast, adolescent peer groups are so homogeneous in respect to age that, to a group of 16-year-olds, someone 15 or 17 would be seen as much younger or older in social age than one year. The degree of age homogeneity in adolescent peer groups undoubtedly is related to the educational system, where children are grouped by age as soon as they enter school on the highly questionable assumption that mental and social development correspond exactly to age.

The organization of age-homogeneous groups helps to identify the steps toward adulthood in industrial societies and to assist adolescents in this transition. The universalistic values associated with industrial societies are more effectively taught by age-homogeneous peer groups than by families, which tend to be particularistic in the way they treat members. In addition, adolescent peer groups give their members opportunities to practice for adulthood with others who also are learning the new roles. The relative isolation of adolescent group from the influence of the family in the United States often encourages the adolescent to form a strong emotional attachment to the peer group. As a result, adolescents are easily influenced by pressures to conform to the group and their identity as a group member is very important.

The transition to adulthood is gradual in most industrial societies. In the United States, for example, it is composed of a number of small steps: the first driver's license, high school graduation, voting, buying liquor, getting married, the first full-time job, and so on. For many people adolescence may be prolonged through college or postgraduate training, which extends economic dependency, eliminates meaningful involvement in social organizations, and hampers a person's ideas being taken seriously. In many nonindustrial societies, however, the transition to adulthood is clear-cut, often marked by an initiation ceremony or a rite of passage. The ceremony confers on the child an adult role in the society with its attendant rights and obligations, it interrupts the youth's dependency on parents, it increases adolescent identification with the adult role, and it encourages peaceful acceptance of the transition.

By focusing upon the expectations for children and adolescents within families in contrast to those of adults in work settings, it may appear that the problems of adolescents in industrial societies can be explained simply in terms of change from the particularistic values of the family to the universalistic values of society. Such a view assumes, however, that industrial societies are more homogeneous than most actually are. For example, while most of us in the United States hold the universal value of religious freedom, many also question whether it applies to cults. Most of us also hold the value of free speech but many question whether Communists, Nazis, and those who reveal the identities of U.S. Secret Service agents

should be included as its beneficiaries. In other words, there are great differences of opinion on value-related issues. The successful transition to adulthood does not simply result in similarity of values between parents and their adult children. While there is considerable evidence for value similarity between parents and adult children, especially of religious and political values, different social experiences make real value similarity impossible. Conflicting values, both within the adolescent and between generations, means that the storm and stress of adolescence does not derive solely from a role transition. Not only does such value conflict cause trouble for the adolescent but it also disrupts society as a whole. Indeed, to the degree that values are diverse, there is no real way to eliminate the stress in the adolescent's search for adult roles and values.

It is important also to remember the effects of the rate of social change on the values and roles in industrial society when examining adolescence. Rapid change, compounded over a generation, means that social institutions, norms, values, and roles in which the young must learn to participate differ from those learned by their parents, just as the parents' social world differs from what they had expected as youth. Rapid change in social institutions that does not correspond with adaptive changes in socialization creates special problems for the adolescent.

ADULT SOCIALIZATION

While it is easy to observe the process of socialization in childhood and adolescence, we may overlook the importance of the socialization that takes place throughout our adult lives. For example, important adult socialization occurs in work activities. Business firms often assign new employees to training programs designed to socialize them in the organization's standard operating procedures. In the military services initial socialization occurs in basic training. In monasteries the new member assumes the title of "novice" while learning the ways of the group. In all of these organizations the new participant formally learns new roles and expectations.

In addition, the participant learns the informal system of interpersonal relations and how they modify or extend the requirements of the formal training program. With each promotion or transfer, participants must assume new roles and adjust to new expectations. This process continues throughout adult life, at times demanding greater change than at others.

One of the most obvious role changes in adulthood is parenthood. The arrival of the first child adds the parent role to the spouse role, and this addition creates a new constellation of emotional relationships in the family. Socialization to parenthood requires changes and adaptation; it begins with preparations for the first child but continues throughout life.

Studies of people's adaptations to parenthood illustrate a lack of anticipatory socialization to the new role. Study of 48 middle-class couples found that 83 percent reported that circumstances following the birth of the first child could be described as a "severe" or "extensive" crisis (LeMasters, 1957). Couples who reported a crisis following the birth of their first child were less likely than others to have been prepared for parenthood, had romanticized parenthood, and had overemphasized the positive aspects of parenthood. In short, there was a greater discrepancy between the expectations and the reality of parenthood for couples who saw the birth of the first child as a crisis than for those who did not.

While more studies by Hobbs (Hobbs, 1965; Hobbs and Cole, 1976) have not supported the notion that the transition to parenthood is necessarily difficult, they reported that the most bothersome item to new parents was the interruption of habits of sleep and leisure-time activities. The extensive changes in the new parents' schedules and types of activities are difficult to anticipate, few experiences offer any real socialization for them, and their impacts are frequently underestimated prior to parenthood.

Recognizing the need for socialization to parenthood, many hospitals, clinics, and community groups have developed education programs for parents-to-be in recent years. To the degree that experiencing the birth of the first child as a crisis is associated with a lack of or inappropriate anticipatory socialization, education programs that increase the accuracy of anticipatory socialization for parenthood should assist in the socialization of people to this role.

A recent study of the "empty-nest" syndrome (Borland, 1982) suggests that the period after the last child has left home can result in depression, confusion, role loss, and a lowered sense of well-being, especially for women. Some women resolve the problem by entering the labor force or by turning their energies to the care of grandchildren. White, middle-class women who had prepared for nonparental roles, such as by involvement in community activity, travel, or pursuing other personal interests, were likely to be healthier and better adjusted than those whose attention had been exclusively on the parental role. Black and Mexican-American women tended to be better adjusted than Anglo women, perhaps because of closer family ties.

Anticipatory socialization also is an important part of socialization of adults into occupational roles. Socialization may occur after a person assumes a role, it may be initiated and flow down a hierarchy from boss to subordinate, or it may involve peers in a working setting. Socialization of superiors also can be accomplished by subordinates in a hierarchy. A new boss in an office often has expectations for changes he or she would like to make. To make the transition to new ways easier, however, management experts usually suggest that new managers ask the workers with longer tenure about problems that exist, what changes need to be made, the best ways of improvement, and the like. In other words, the effective new office manager involves subordinates in planning for change, and the subordinates help socialize new managers into their roles.

Even in a work hierarchy subordinates have ways to reward or punish a boss. Workers may refuse to cooperate when cooperation is not required but is needed. For example, when a heavy workload demands that a worker arrive early, take a shorter lunch period, or stay after official hours, the worker can reward or punish a boss by accepting or refusing his or her requests for overtime. Workers who are unhappy with their bosses also tend to be absent from work more often, and such absenteeism may lower organizational effectiveness. Thus cooperating or not cooperating when cooperation is optional is one way that subordinates influence the socialization of their superiors.

Currently, social scientists in several disciplines are studying adulthood to identify some of the role changes that occur throughout this period. One such change is menopause. A study by Neugarten and her associates (1963) found that expectations about menopause in a sample of middle-class women were inconsistent with reality: more expected other women to define it disagreeable than actually experienced it as disagreeable, and older women found that the experience of menopause was less disagreeable than anticipated by premenopausal women.

As in the case of the birth of the first child, expectations about menopause acquired in anticipatory socialization may be an important factor affecting the role transition. For some women the discrepancy between expectations and the reality of menopause may result in a relatively pleasant disconfirmation of expectations when menopause occurs. For other women the anticipatory socialization of negative expectations of menopause may result in a more negative transition than otherwise. In these cases more accurate anticipatory socialization might reduce the detrimental effects of menopause.

Many other role changes requiring socialization occur in adulthood. Some researchers are investigating the idea of a midlife crisis for men as well as women. Others are studying role changes following heart attacks or other debilitating illness. Still others are examining divorce as an event requiring role changes in adulthood. Many of these role changes are stressful and appropriate socialization may reduce their detrimental effects and enhance opportunities for positive change. Research indicates that negative experiences occur most frequently with unexpected role transitions over which a person lacks control. Events that occur at times in the life span that are not typical for most people, for example, teenage pregnancy or first marriage or first parenthood in midlife, also seem to produce more stress.

SOCIALIZATION TO OLD AGE

An emerging area of interest in the field of sociology has been retirement, or withdrawal from occupational roles. The number and percentage of Americans who live to retire continues to increase. Many adults find that quitting work poses difficult problems, because roles for the retired are both poorly defined and negatively evaluated. The loss of the work role not only creates unused time but it reduces the number of social activities of the retiree as well. Thus while retirement means termination of the work role, it often involves other role losses. Finally, retirement signifies a transition in which future role losses like widowhood are anticipated.

Many newly retired men find retirement to be a negative experience. Their expectations of time to rest, relax, and do all things they never had time to do while working are not met. Instead of engaging in meaningful leisure activities, they find themselves wondering how to fill empty hours. Pollack (1969) has suggested that, in response to the changed role demands from external sources, the goal of socialization in old age should be to develop a self-image that is separate from one's occupational role. Retirement is a process of disengagement from normal activities of the working adult, but it should not mean disengagement from social contacts. Social isolation need only occur if one has failed to develop interests outside the occupational and familial roles of adulthood.

We should note that the bad effects of retirement often are overstated, and for some retirement may be enthusiastically anticipated and thoroughly enjoyed. Neugarten and her associates (1965), in a study of older people in Kansas City, found some respondents, called "rocking-chair" types, who enjoyed the freedom from schedules as an opportunity simply to sit and think. Research also suggests that while many people may find it difficult to adjust to retirement at first, this distress is temporary and lasts only a year or so (Chatfield, 1977). Those who adjust most effectively to retirement seem to be those who replace lost roles with new leisure activities or those who increase their participation in activities enjoyed before retirement.

Although most role transitions in old age imply

Just as adults are socialized to new roles, like parenthood and work, older people may learn new roles appropriate to leisure. These retirement community women are adding roles that are usually associated with adolescence to adult roles and those of old age.

the possibility of loss, the role of grandparenting is often associated with increased activities at this time. Neugarten and Weinstein (1964) found that nearly three-fourths of their grandparent respondents did not feel remote from this role and frequently felt that it gave them a sense of biological renewal or continuity and emotional self-fulfill-

ment. Indeed, approximately 60 percent thought that the grandparent role was comfortable and pleasant, compared with about 35 percent who experienced difficulty and discomfort.

The finding that satisfaction with life in old age is positively correlated with activity level in the majority of older people contradicts some widely held stereotypes of the aged. Most older people are not rocking-chair types. Only a small percentage of the elderly are psychologically disoriented or disorganized and few are in nursing homes. Most are happy, healthy, active individuals, living independently and enjoying themselves. In fact, one recent study reported that morale is not affected by contact with siblings or children (Lee and Ellithorpe, 1982); apparently good health, friends, and activities with people generally are the most important aspects of adjustment to old age.

There is much left unsaid in our treatment of socialization in old age. Some role losses, such as the loss of the spouse role through widowhood, have negative effects on most elderly persons. Other role losses occur because of income limitations in old age, often in conjunction with retirement or widowhood. The simultaneous loss of two or more roles may have a greater impact than the sum of the effects of the losses independently. Add to all this the decreased activity that may result from failing health and one easily can understand why some of the negative expectations for old age have developed. Still, to transform negative expectations into negative stereotypes of the fastest growing age aggregate in our society is foolish and short-sighted. **Ageism,** or prejudice against the elderly, is the only common prejudice in which those who hold it eventually wind up as members of the group that they stereotype.

SUMMARY

Socialization is the process through which a person acquires the behaviors and skills that are essential for social living. The cultural context provides the basic knowledge, values, and expectations—in the models or social roles—and the child's genetic heritage provides the potential for human development. From the evidence derived from cases of isolated children, social contact, care, and nurture are necessary for a person to develop human characteristics.

A person learns about him- or herself from the reactions of others and develops an identity based on these responses, especially of significant others.

Mead emphasized the importance of distinguishing between the subjective self "I" and the objective self "me" and also the importance of play for learning social roles.

When a person acts on the basis of rewards or punishment, we say that compliance occurs; when a person acts appropriately whether or not rewards are given, we say that the person has internalized the values and norms of the culture. Punishment is important in establishing compliance but is not directly related to internalization. Socialization is both general, or culture-wide, and specific to a position and social relationships. Anticipatory socialization occurs when a person seeks to develop behaviors, attitudes, and values appropriate to a future role.

Socialization occurs throughout a person's life. Age-specific expectations are defined in the culture. For children and adolescents most socialization takes place in the family, the peer group, or the schools. Several researchers have noted the importance of consistent, stable care in childhood for resolving ambivalence for the young child that will enable him or her to develop and mature. Adolescence is a time for practicing adult roles and gradually assuming adult responsibilities. For adults, roles of work, spouse, and parent dominate. Although these roles may be lost with age, socialization continues as people adjust to new life circumstances.

GLOSSARY

Ageism   prejudice against older persons.

Anticipatory socialization   the learning of parts of a role by an individual who expects to occupy the role in the future.

Feral children   children whose mental, physical, and social growth has been cut off because of being reared in total, or nearly total, isolation from other humans.

Identification   in socialization, the internalization by the learner of beliefs and behaviors characteristic of a model who is unusually attractive to the learner (compare with *imitation*).

Imitation the copying of beliefs and behaviors characteristic of a model who is unusually attractive to the person doing the copying (compare with *identification*).

Instincts inborn tendencies within a species to perform a complex set of behaviors in a predetermined, systematic way.

Insufficient deterrence mild punishment, insufficient to inhibit prohibited social behavior; may lead to internalization of positive value for not performing the behavior.

Intermittent or delayed reward reward for making a desired response that is given only part of the time or after a delay; leads to slower learning but greater internalization.

Internalization willingness of individual to perform socially approved role behaviors in the absence of any external rewards.

Law of marginal utility condition of loss of effectiveness of frequently applied punishment; to maintain effectiveness, severity of the punishment may have to be increased over time.

Reflex an inborn tendency to specific, simple, and undifferentiated behavior.

Role behavioral expectations associated with a person's status.

Self A person's identity, which develops when an individual sees or experiences his or her behaviors as they appear to other individuals as well as how they appear to the person.

Significant others those people who are particularly important in influencing the development of self-identity.

Socialization process of learning by which members of a society acquire the behaviors and skills that are essential for social living.

Sufficient deterrence severe punishment sufficient to justify inhibiting behavior as long as the threat of punishment is present; condition for compliance.

ADDITIONAL READINGS

Clausen, John, ed. *Socialization and Society*. Boston: Little, Brown, 1968.
Thorough and sophisticated reviews of socialization theory and research by Clausen, Brown, Inkeles, Lippitt, Maccoby, and Smith.

Elkins, Stanley. *Slavery: A Problem in American Institutional and Intellectual Life*. New York: Universal Library, 1963.
The controversial argument is advanced that black slaves brought to America, in comparison with black slaves sold elsewhere in the Western Hemisphere, were socialized into a Sambo personality by the unique structure of the American institutions of Slavery.

Goffman, Erving. *Behavior in Public: Notes on the Social Organization of Gatherings*. New York: Free Press, 1963.
The social etiquette of everyday encounters is analyzed to uncover the basic rules governing social interactions.

Scarr-Salapatek, Sandra, and Philip Salapatek, eds. *Socialization*. Columbus, Ohio: Merrill, 1973.
A discussion with readings of the socialization that occurs to people in various situations and how this socialization affects expressive, instrumental, and normative aspects of behavior.

Spiro, Melford. *Children of the Kibbutz: A Study on Child Training and Personality*. Cambridge, Mass.: Harvard University Press, 1958.
The kibbutz in Israel is researched to determine the effect of communal socialization on the personalities of children who are reared within it.

READINGS

READING 6.1

The Case for Nonsexist Childrearing
Letty Cottin Pogrebin

"It's a baby!" Obviously, that is not the sentence you hear in the delivery room.

Sex is the first noun attached to a human life at the moment of birth. Sex is the first self: "It's a girl!" or "It's a boy!" In that primal instant, gender is being and being is gender. Then as the minutes and hours pass, your baby is given elaboration: it is "a healthy baby," "a 7-pound 4-ounce baby," a "restless," "docile," or "alert" baby.

Days go by. Adjectives are added. As you feed, hold, touch, kiss, cuddle, coo to, gaze at, change, dress, bathe, burp, stroke, comfort, and love your baby, this unknown creature gradually becomes defined, like a sculpture emerging from a lump of clay.

You get to know your baby's look, feel, and smell; the way your baby cries, sleeps, nurses, reacts to light or music; the grip of your baby's tiny hand on your finger; the gummy little smile that rewards you for materializing beside the crib.

Weeks turn into months. Your baby develops more personality, more individuality: you know the funny way she turns over, the expression on his face when he eats his peach puree, her favorite song, his beloved toy, her creep-and-crawl locomotion, his gurgling monologues. This is no longer a baby born to thus-and-so parents on such-and-such date; this is a person, with a discernible temperament and special qualities all his own.

Or so you think. But how much of your baby's uniqueness is really developing freely? And how much is a result of that first fact duly noted by all—"It's a boy" or "It's a girl"—and all the unconscious acts of "genderizing" that flow from there?

SOURCE: Letty Cottin Pogrebin, *Growing Up Free*, Chapter 7, McGraw-Hill, 1981. Used with permission.

Watching an adult with an infant, you may not notice what systematic research observation has proved to be true. From the first millisecond after its sex is known, people act and react, think, speak, and move differently with a baby girl than with a baby boy. Many parents say, "It would be 'unfair' to treat boys and girls differently," and insist, "I treat all my children the same."

ARTIFACTS, ACCOUTREMENTS, AND CUSTOM

Why is gender so important in babies? For the same reason people are afraid of adult "unisex" fashion, of a journey without signposts, of a wine without a label, of having to make judgments without first reading the reviews. Once a person is presented to the world as female or male, everything else follows.

In the fable Baby X, a government "x-periment" requires a chosen set of parents to refuse to divulge the sex of their baby to the outside world. The child, too, keeps its gender identity to itself. Because no one knows if X is a girl or a boy, X is allowed the entire range of girl-type and boy-type activities. Baby X grows to be a happy, well-rounded, loving child, but friends, neighbors, relatives, and school authorities are outraged and confounded because they do not know "what" X is. You don't know how to treat it if you don't know what it is.

In the hospital the swaddling blanket, the wrist identification bands worn by mother and baby, or the name card on the nursery bassinet gives a pink or blue sex identification signal.

Floral arrangements in maternity wards announce what "kind" of baby each woman had. Sex is proclaimed on the bands of cigars dad hands out, on the gift-wrappings, in the baby book, and by the color of the booties and blankets presented by visitors.

Congratulations cards parents receive from friends are among the most extreme sex discriminators. "Excitement," "fun," "noise," and action fill the congratulations cards for boys; "enchanting," "angel," "charmer," "sugar-sweet," and "precious treasure" describe the delights of girls.

Besides the differences in active verbs and passive nouns, the cards foretell that a boy will "bring a lifetime of joy," be a winner, become an inventor, a leader; a girl will become a little "lady."

A printing company dares to imagine your child's future. A friend feels free to tuck such predictions into an envelope. And parents display these cards proudly. Why? Because the values embodied in their corny rhymes are shared values. In this culture it's perfectly all right to tell parents that their children will be like everyone else as long as the generalizations are based on sex, not race or ethnic stereotypes. The "winner" and "lady" don't raise an eyebrow. But let a greeting card company publish a couplet about the black child who will become a good dancer or the Jewish child who will grow up to be a clever money-lender, and watch the fur fly.

If you receive sexist greeting cards from close friends, you may not want to embarrass them with your objections, but at least send the cards back to the printing company with your criticisms. If enough new parents protest, the publishers may have to create more non-sexist messages, such as "One little baby . . . so much happiness! Congratulations!" That says it all.

DIFFERENCES IN INTERPRETING INFANT BEHAVIOR

Home from the hospital. The visitors have gone, the celebrations are over, and the baby's life is in your keeping. But how do you raise a free child if sex stereotypes are so deeply entrenched that few of us can even recognize them without help? Where do you start?

I think you start by becoming aware of how others treat girls and boys. Just as we speak better once we notice other people's speech affectations, when you're alert to other parents' sex prejudices, it's almost impossible to fall into those habits yourself. At first, you'll be hyper-conscious, but soon enough nonsexist attitudes will be second nature, and you'll know what to watch for.

People react differently to the exact same baby behavior (a movement or sound, say) depending on the baby's sex. That's how life becomes an entirely different experience for girls and boys; that's why the "live in two different worlds" and "don't speak the same language": a different world has been created for them by their parents and a different language has been spoken to and about them from birth.

AT ONE DAY OLD.   Within 24 hours after the birth of their first child, 30 sets of parents were asked to "describe your baby as you would to a close friend or relative." They, fathers especially, rated sons as "firmer, larger-featured, better-coordinated, more alert, stronger and hardier. They described daughters as softer, finer-featured, more awkward, more inattentive, weaker and more delicate."

Were the parents being particularly alert to the looks and behavior of their own babies? Quite the contrary. Just because they knew the sex of their baby, they saw in him or her sex-appropriate characteristics that were not there at all: *hospital records show that the 15 boys and 15 girls were virtually indistinguishable from one another in terms of weight, height, muscle tone, reflexes, and general level of activity.*

AT THREE MONTHS.   In another study a small rubber football, a Raggedy Ann doll, and a flexible ring were placed on the floor for the adults to "use" while interacting with a three-month-old baby dressed in yellow.

Researchers found that when the adults were told they were playing with a girl baby, they used the doll. When they weren't told if the baby was a girl or boy, the men took the "safest" course and played with the neutral toy (the ring) while the women chose either the football or the doll.

AT SIX MONTHS.   The "Adam/Beth" experiment tested the same principle with a child who was old enough to provide feedback. This time, a six-month-old was dressed in blue pants when introduced as "Adam" to half of a group of young mothers and in a pink dress when presented as "Beth" to the other half. The toy choices here were a fish, a doll, and a train.

Results: When the women thought they were playing with "Adam," they handed him the train more often; when they thought they were playing with "Beth," they gave her the doll. The mothers also tended to smile more when playing with "Beth."

Before the experiment these mothers had said that they do not treat their own children differently by sex. After the experiment the women did not recognize that they had actually treated "Adam" and "Beth" differently. If people are totally "unaware of their stereotyping" under supersensitized laboratory conditions, imagine how biased they can be in casual, everyday life.

AT NINE MONTHS.   After watching a videotape in which a nine-month-old baby responds to a teddy bear, a jack-in-the-box, a doll, and a buzzer, many people saw different attributes in the baby depending on whether they were told they were watching a girl or a boy: ". . . When the infant cried, 'the boy' was seen as angry and the girl as afraid. Further, both men and women considered the boy to be more 'active' and 'potent' than 'the girl'!"

Same film, same baby, same behavior, but what a difference a label makes.

DIFFERENCES IN MOTHERS' TREATMENT OF INFANTS

Girl and boy infants do the same amount of vocalizing (babbling), fretting and crying, smiling, and moving about. Accordingly, you cannot tell the sex of a baby from watching the baby. However, the skilled observer can tell from a mother's behavior with her child whether it is a girl or a boy. In fact, several key differences in mothers' behavior seem to be determined by the sex of their infants, and nothing more.

What accounts for these differences and where do they lead? We can follow some educated guesses. Michael Lewis, director of the Institute for the Study of Exceptional Children in Princeton, New Jersey, says mothers may touch boys more at first because boys are more valuable in this culture, but by age six months, "mothers start to wean their sons from physical contact with them," because "mothers believe that boys rather than girls should be independent and encouraged to explore and master their world."

Female infants are allowed to touch and stay close to their mothers throughout early childhood because females are being "socialized" for dependency. (Socialization is the way children are trained to think about themselves and act with others in their environment.) When these more clinging infant girls become women, no wonder they are less confident about their autonomy.

Another result is that American males do not learn to be comfortable with touching behavior except in such defined situations as sex or contact sports, while American females are raised to need the touching behavior most men cannot give them.

The cry and the smile are forms of social communication at which females are thought to excel. If mothers respond to these behaviors more readily and enthusiastically in girls, crying and smiling are reinforced "in keeping with cultural expectations."

Similarly, the additional time spent babbling to girl babies and encouraging their vocalizing in response, tips the developmental scales in favor of girls' becoming more verbal and word-oriented than boys. If mothers treated boy babies to more "conversation" in infancy, perhaps Johnny would be able to read better later in life.

DIFFERENCES IN FATHER-INVOLVEMENT

Fathers, too, touch male infants more than females; they are more attentive to first-born boys and more active playing with year-old sons than with year-old daughters. New fathers tend to get more angry and irritated with female infants for no apparent reason; they roughhouse with boys but treat girl babies "like porcelain."

Such preferential treatment may be explained in various ways. For example, like attracts like; therefore, the father is drawn to the miniaturized version of himself. (That theory would not explain mothers' preferential treatment of sons.) Others say that the father values his special relationships as a "role model" for the son's manly behavior; but what is so man-to-man about relating to a newborn?

I'd say the preference emanates from the father's unconscious evaluations of the two sexes. Boys Are Better: better babies to touch, play with, and whittle into chips off the old block. And if daughters happen to miss out on the full energy of a man's fathering attentions, oh well, Girls Are Meant To Be Mothers anyway, and that's not something a Dad can teach a girl. The perfect alibi for the crime of sex preference.

It's not new that parents talk baby-talk to babies. But did you ever notice that fathers talk to babies differently than mothers do, and both parents talk differently to girl babies than to boys?

According to one study, fathers address their sons in "a sort of Hail-Baby-Well-Met style; while turning them upside down, or engaged in similar play, the fathers said things like, 'Come here, you little nut!' or 'Hey, fruitcake!' Baby girls were dealt with more gently, both physically and verbally." Fathers also tend to talk in a high-pitched voice to little girls and a deep bass voice to little boys.

From this combination of hardy handling and mock rough talk, perhaps boys are toughened up for the real world, while girls, being "dealt with more gently," are readied for vulnerability.

On the other hand, perhaps the withholding of physical and verbal gentleness to boys is what rears unexpressive adult men who equate a soft world with "femininity" and weakness. Can parents learn to speak in a full range of voices to each child, regardless of gender? Yes, if we learn to hear sexism before it rises in our throats.

SUMMARY
Socialization is not the same for boys and girls. Because of the ideas people hold about boys—rough and tumble, aggressive, active—they are treated in a different way from girls, who are seen as fragile, accepting, and quiet. Pogrebin questions these views about boys and girls and also the patterns of childrearing associated with them.

QUESTIONS
1. Can boys and girls be socialized without a sex label attached to them?
2. Does socialization create the differences in behavior that we associate with the concepts of male and female?
3. Is nonsexist childrearing better than sexist childrearing? For whom?

READING 6.2
Growing Up Confused
Richard Flacks

A final source of parental confusion derives from the sense perhaps shared by most people in the culture—that the world in which children will be adults will be substantially different from the world in which they are children, in ways that are considerably obscure. Parents generally conceive of themselves—perhaps more than at any time in history—as inadequate models for their children because they are already obsolete. In this situation, the parental tone of voice lacks conviction, parental guidance has overtones of fatuousness, and parental authority is undermined by the parents' own lack of confidence. This particular source of cultural incoherence may not be directly related to the structure of the nuclear family itself, but it is a rather obvious consequence of a culture that values technological change and development as one of its central priorities. Presumably, a child-rearing program that emphasizes independence, flexibility, and openmindedness meshes with a culture that values change. But as we have seen, such virtues are more easily espoused than instilled in a culture that places such heavy reliance on isolated and morally confused mothers and fathers to implement such a program.

It should not be hard to envision from our depiction of the built-in "strains" associated with the middle class nuclear family some idea of the consequences for young people. Briefly, such a family situation is likely to generate considerable confusion over values, goals, roles, and aspirations for the youth who experience it. More specifically, we can suggest that the "new" family is likely to impart a number of dispositions and personality

SOURCE: Richard Flacks, "Growing Up Confused." *Youth and Social Change,* Markham, 1971, pp. 30–32.

"trends" in its offspring—traits or potentialities that predispose such youth to be restless with, skeptical of, or alienated from certain crucial aspects of conventional culture and, consequently, ready for certain kinds of cultural change.

A listing of some hypotheses concerning certain tendencies that the middle class family situation seems to generate in its offspring follows (I term them hypotheses, which await persuasive empirical tests, because for the most part, there is little direct evidence that these tendencies are clearly linked to childhood socialization):

1. Confusion and restlessness with conventional definitions of success. Such feelings would derive from the types of paternal ambivalence we have described, from the psychological distance of the father's work role from those of his sons', from the parental value confusions we have called attention to, and from the pattern of maternal domination. Even youths who have strong motivations to achieve and who may act these out in school would be likely to entertain doubts about whether material success, status-striving and careerism constitute appropriate avenues for expressing their desires to "do well." But neither conventional parents nor the conventional culture provide very many clues about how one can achieve in ways other than the economic. The consequences of this combination of predispositions to question material success coupled with predispositions to achieve include profound indecisiveness about vocation (what Erik Erikson has called "role confusion"), vague yearnings for recognition and fame, a restless search for alternative vocations and life styles.

2. Restlessness under conditions of imposed discipline. These derive from such features of the family as parental indulgence and permissiveness and are related to feelings of discontent with conventional definitions of vocation and achievement. Some consequences are discontent with classroom drill and learning situations requiring rote memorization; tendencies to feel bored and restless when concentration is required; avoidance of school subjects requiring discipline and attention to detail; and a generalized resistance to tasks that do not appear to

be personally rewarding or are set without reference to goals determined by the self. These feelings are accompanied by intense desires for immediate pleasure and release and immediate experience, often coupled with guilt.

3. Restlessness with conditions of arbitrary or coercive authority. Such feelings might derive from expectations developed in the family for authority structures based on egalitarianism—expectations derived from parental fostering of participation, independence and autonomy and parental refusal to use physical punishment or coercion. Children raised in this way, we can speculate, may grow to expect that authority *outside* the family will be similarly responsive, democratic, nonpunitive and permissive. A consequence of such dispositions and expectations about authority is the tendency to be unusually trusting of teachers and other adults, but vociferously and unusually upset, angry and rebellious when such authority figures betray expectations that they will be egalitarian, democratic, and so forth. Or one might expect such children to be capable of more active expression of opposition and resistance to authority when it appears arbitrary, more skeptical of its claims in general, more likely to ask embarrassing questions, and more ready to systematically test the limits of its tolerance.

4. Discomfort with conventional sex-role definitions. Boys who have ambivalent fathers or who tend to identify with their mothers and have accepting, nonpunitive parents are likely to define masculinity in ways that are quite untraditional. They are likely to be less motivated for dominance, less physically aggressive and tough, less physically competitive, and more emotionally expressive and aesthetically inclined. Presumably, many girls raised in these ways are likely to be less submissive, more assertive, and more self-assured and independent. Insofar as parents continue to expect conventional sex-role performance on the part of their children—and insofar as such performance is expected by the schools and by peers—confusion and feelings of inadequacy can be the result.

Speculation on the kinds of traits, dispositions, and feelings that might be expected to be pattened outcomes of the family structure and childrearing practices we have been

discussing could go on indefinitely, but the main line of our argument should be clear: certain major changes in social structure and economy have had a direct impact on the structure of the family, especially in the "middle class." These changes have also had a profound impact on the values and practices of parents. The result is a mixed one: on the one hand, the "new" family appears eminently suitable as an instrument for creating the "right" kinds of people for technological society; on the other hand, inherent in the same family situation are tendencies to generate profound feelings of dislocation and discontent with established values, institutions and roles. Thus, the American family, especially the middle class, suburban American family with its confusions and ambivalences, reflects the general crisis of American culture. At the same time, it contributes to that crisis by generating in the next generation aspirations, expectations, and impulses that are not compatible with established norms and institutionalized patterns. It creates the psychic grounds for new identities in a society that provides no models, roles, or life styles around which such new identities can crystallize.

SUMMARY
In this reading, Flacks has identified sources of strain in childhood socialization, created by the speed of social change. Definitions of success, discipline, arbitrary authority, and conventional sex-role definitions are no longer accepted as valid, and the family is confused by these changes.

QUESTIONS
1. What values should the family seek to instill in its children?
2. Can parents teach children appropriate values if the parents themselves are discontent about the dominant society?
3. What are the consequences of cultural confusion for children?

CHAPTER 7

Deviance and Social Control

CONTENTS

Is society responsible for crime?

According to a recent poll, more Americans are concerned about crime than about any other issue, including inflation, unemployment, and the threat of war (*Los Angeles Times*, Aug. 8, 1982). Many citizens feel like prisoners in their own neighborhoods, reluctant to go out after dark and afraid to use public parks and transportation. Reactions to this social problem are divided. Some seek to solve the problem by stronger law enforcement, more convictions, and longer prison sentences. Others stress the fact that crime is a product of a society's values and social structures and that the solution to the crime problem lies in changing society.

YES   Japan is an urban, industrialized society like the United States, but it has a dramatically lower crime rate. It is a society that places great emphasis on the family, community, work, and other traditional values that bind people together in social groups. Japanese society is also more supportive of all its citizens. It has a full employment policy and a stronger commitment to secure jobs for its workers. Japan does not have a permanent "underclass" of people without hope of ever having a decent life. In the United States, inner-city crime rates are astounding, but so is the rate of unemployment. When 40 to 50 percent of inner-city youth are unemployed and have no prospect of employment, it is no wonder that many of them turn to crime.

The breeding ground for crime is the overcrowded and deteriorating centers of American cities and the dehumanizing life of poverty and despair found there. Children born and raised in such conditions may be neglected by parents who are demoralized by poverty and grow up with a clear feeling that no one cares for them. Children growing up in middle-class homes may also experience neglect, although here the source is not poverty. Parents who give their children "things" but are indifferent to their needs for love and guidance are also conveying the message that nobody cares.

But in the main, crime is widespread in America because we have allowed ourselves to become a society where being poor or unemployed, or alone and old, is *your* problem and not *our* problem. We have trumpeted the values of success so loudly that all people—the rich and powerful as well as ghetto youth—can think about is "get it when you can and get as much of it as you can. If you don't the next guy will."

Society is responsible for crime, and only by changing society can we deal with this immense danger to our civilization.

NO   In American cities today can be found a criminal class of young men who are unwilling to take the kind of jobs that society offers people without training or skills. In past generations young people faced the choice of taking a low-paid job in, say, a laundry or grocery store or turning to hustling and street crime, which promised the chance of a "big score." In the past more young people chose to work at whatever jobs were available, but today inner-city youth are ignoring this option.

In every society, in every age, young people make choices that produce a lifetime of honest work and respectability or a life on the fringes of civilized behavior. Many young people start out in low-paying, dead-end jobs, and many rise far above these beginnings. Many who begin life without fathers or with alcoholic parents do not make that an excuse for their own failures. Certainly, injustice exists and there is prejudice against minorities. But enough people have survived hatred and injustice to show that opportunities are there for those willing to work.

Crime will not go away until we recognize criminals for what they are and not as sociological casualties. Crime will not go away by efforts to show the greater danger of corporate crime committed by the wealthy and powerful as compared with street crime. Corporate criminals do not threaten you with a knife, or put a gun to your head. They do not engage in senseless acts of brutality and humiliation of their victims. No, crime will not go away until we recognize that criminals can only be controlled if we raise the cost to the criminal of getting caught. Punishment must be swift and certain. Habitual criminals and those who are vicious and violent should be imprisoned for very long periods without promise of parole.

The crime problem in America can be solved. It requires as a first step the recognition that criminals are not ordinary human beings and that they are responsible for their criminal acts.

In this chapter we examine many forms of deviance including criminal behavior. Competing theories on crime provide different insights into its causes. The way a society reacts to different forms of deviance and crime touches on a number of questions raised in the previous pages; for example, the reasons given for punishing deviants may vary according to the deviant acts or to the persons committing them.

QUESTIONS TO CONSIDER

■ What factors determine whether a deviate becomes a deviant?

■ What are the functions of deviance in society?

■ How is social inequality responsible for deviance?

■ What is the justification for punishment through the legal system?

CASE 415: *The patient is a 46-year-old white, divorced female with one child. The interview is with a close relative of the patient.*

Question: *When did you first notice any thing unusual about her behavior?*

Answer: *She would say things happened out where she worked that were so hard to believe; yet I believed her, I believed her all the way. I thought she was really telling me the truth and other people don't . . . can't understand this . . . because I've worked in plants and I figured, "I do know things do happen like this." She thought that the doctor gave her a shot of dope and she swore up and down that he gave her a shot of dope. Her employer sent her to a doctor . . . I can't remember his name or anything because she's been to several doctors. I suppose he was a company doctor. He gave her a shot and it swelled all up and there were several different reactions that she had of it. He gave them to her in her leg and she couldn't understand this. She thought that was a weird thing right there. Usually she would have them in the hip or the arm, but he gave it in the leg. It swelled up and got black and blue. Different things like this had happened and she started reading up about dope and stuff in magazines and any article she could get her hands on she'd*

read about. After reading this stuff she said that she was having the very same symptoms . . . something about her throat and her tongue and so forth and she just swore up and down that the doctor gave her a shot of dope. And she'd tell things about the plant that she said nobody would believe her. They were all picking on her.

Question: *Did you think she had a problem? Did you do anything about what she said, like try to get her to a doctor?*

Answer: *Some of what she said made me wonder but generally there were a lot worse people walking around the streets—worse than she was. Still, I've worked out at plants and I know that a lot of times they have favortism and they might put the oldest person on a rough job if they don't like this person. I've seen it happen myself and so I believed her. I thought, well, golly, maybe that doctor is crooked. I don't know, there are a lot of quacks around. You never know, you read in the paper all the time where strange things happen. Stranger things than that has happened, that's for sure.*

CASE 105: *The patient is a 44-year-old black female, married with two children. Interview is with patient's husband.*

Question: *When did you first notice anything unusual about her behavior?*

Answer: *Oh, about the first of July I came home and the house is wide open. She was nowhere in sight. Then she said, "We have a cat named Bambi and I killed that cat, I don't trust that cat." Well, we don't have a cat. Then she started to pack my clothes up and packed my daughter's clothes up. She said her mother was dead and I asked how did she know. I asked her if she called and has checked if her mother is sick. She said no. So I said, "Call her." She called, she was having trouble getting her 'cause she changed her number. After that she was walking around the house hollering and screaming at us and at the kids. On top of all this she claimed that everyone was against her, for some kind of reason. She ran out of the house, hollering.*

174

Question: *Did you think she had a problem? Did you do anything about what she said, like try to get her to a doctor?*

Answer: *I knew it was serious. I wanted to take her to a doctor, but she refused to go. We got the doctors to come here and we had her committed.*

In Case 415 (Perrucci and Targ, 1982), almost three years passed before the woman was committed to a mental hospital. The people whom she saw daily—family, friends, coworkers—all attempted to "normalize" her unusual behavior by finding plausible explanations, as did the relative who was interviewed.

The woman in Case 105 was taken to a doctor immediately following the incident in question and was committed to a mental hospital within a week. The people she saw daily immediately "medicalized" her problem behaviors; that is, they defined her problem in medical and psychological terms.

What accounts for the different reactions of people to the unusual behavior of these two women? Why was one immediately defined as mentally ill and hospitalized, while the other was not? Was it because the unusual behavior they exhibited was so different, with the woman in Case 105 being *obviously* "crazy." Or was it because of the different social circumstances of the two women—one a married housewife with problems that may have been a burden to her family and the other an employed woman who was supporting herself and her child.

As we noted earlier, social life is expressed in patterned and regular social relationships. When individuals and groups disrupt social relationships—when they violate social norms—society's reactions may be to punish the violator or to take some action that will reduce the chances that the disruptive behavior will occur again. Some people and some types of behavior are responded to by others with fear, disgust, or anger, creating social categories of "offenders" and "offensive" behavior. The question facing sociologists who study deviance is: What is the process by which people are defined as having violated social norms?

DEVIANCE AND DEVIANTS

Deviance is the process by which those who violate group norms are identified as norm violators. **Deviants** are people whose behavior diverges from group norms and calls forth negative sanctions from the group. **Deviates,** on the other hand, also display divergent behavior but, for one reason or another, they are not identified as norm violators. By maintaining a distinction between deviation and deviance, sociologists may study ways in which groups define some deviates as deviants.

Deviant behavior may be broken down into four components: (1) the *act* or unit of action, (2) the *actor* who exhibits the behavior, (3) the social *situation* in which the act is exhibited, and (4) an audience of *definers* of that act. The study of deviance, both within and outside of sociology, is often concerned with only a single aspect of deviant behavior, such as some characteristic of the actor. For example, a biologist might seek to explain deviant behavior patterns, like mental illness or alcoholism by studying the actor's biochemical and genetic makeup, and a psychiatrist might seek explanations for deviant acts by examining the actor's personality.

To understand why certain behaviors are defined as deviant and why certain persons become identified as deviants, we must look at the way in which the act, the actor, the situation, and the definers are interrelated. A person's social acts may be evaluated differently by different audiences of definers. Some acts are defined as deviant because they are extremely repugnant to the group. These acts will be considered deviant regardless of the actor, the situation, or the audience. Father-daughter and mother-son incest are the best examples. Killing is also felt to be repugnant and threatening to the group, but it is permitted for certain actors in certain circumstances, such as soldiers in wartime or police in pursuit of a fleeing felon. Other acts of killing may be permitted, depending on the definers, such as political assassination of one country's leaders by the government of another country. By understanding the position of the actor in the social situation and the relationship of the act to the audience of definers, sociologists can explain condi-

Some social scientists have suggested that forms of sexual deviance, such as prostitution and pornography, provide an outlet for sexual activity that is not approved within family roles. Here we see prostitutes looking for customers, a female impersonator preparing for his performance in a nightclub, and an X-rated theatre.

tions under which killing is acceptable and conditions under which it is deviant.

Since deviance varies according to the relationships among the four components, acts may be viewed as more or less deviant. Examples abound. Physicians who are addicted to morphine but able to obtain pharmaceutical maintenance doses are considered less deviant than addicts who must steal to buy from illegal suppliers. A number of borderline offenses in criminal law like prostitution, pot smoking, and other so-called "victimless" crimes are tolerated more than crimes like theft or rape (Schur, 1965). Embezzlers and other white-collar criminals also are often perceived as less of a threat

to society than armed robbers. Regardless of whether we agree that some violations threaten social values less than others, we cannot deny that variations in actors, situations, and audiences affect the degree to which most people view a given act as a threat to society.

Since cultural values differ, it is not surprising that an act often considered deviant in one culture is not so considered in another. Variations in the rate of deviance among cultures also probably exist. In many simpler societies deviate acts by members who otherwise are integrated into the society are accepted, for example, the male members of certain Plains Indians tribes who thought of and dressed

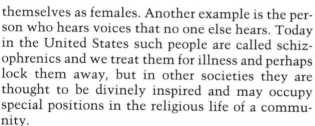

themselves as females. Another example is the person who hears voices that no one else hears. Today in the United States such people are called schizophrenics and we treat them for illness and perhaps lock them away, but in other societies they are thought to be divinely inspired and may occupy special positions in the religious life of a community.

Table 7.1 reports results of research on comparative perceptions of different forms of deviance of audiences in six countries. Respondents were asked to give their reactions to different acts by selecting the social sanction that should be applied ("treatment," "punishment," or "nothing"). There was considerable agreement on disapproval of the "traditional" crimes of robbery and appropriation. However, for borderline offenses like drug taking, homosexuality, and abortion there was great disagreement. Cross-cultural differences are also apparent in opinions about the kind of sanction that should be applied. A society like the United States is generally more inclined to choose treatment as a sanction than other societies. Thus, we find that

some acts of deviance are culturally relative, while others are universally disapproved.

Lower rates of deviance in simpler societies are no doubt partly a reflection of different audience perceptions of acts, actors, and situations. It may be that people's extensive familiarity with each other (and each other's family history) may produce greater toleration for idiosyncracies. Related to toleration is the fact that simpler societies compared with complex societies may have fewer norms and therefore fewer opportunities for breaking them. If there are fewer laws to break, there probably will be fewer lawbreakers and, conversely, the more laws there are making activities criminal, the more criminals

TABLE 7.1 The Preferred Societal Sanctions[a] (Percentages)

ACT AND SANCTION	INDIA (N = 497)	INDONESIA (N = 500)	IRAN (N = 475)	ITALY (SARDINIA) (N = 200)	U.S.A. (N = 169)	YUGOSLAVIA (N = 500)
Robbery						
Treatment	6.2	0.8	5.4	7.0	16.8	0.6
Punishment	85.6	89.6	87.0	92.0	79.6	94.8
Nothing	8.0	5.2	7.6	4.0	0.0	1.8
Incest						
Treatment	29.3	12.4	17.2	41.0	62.7	41.4
Punishment	45.7	55.0	82.3	62.5	12.4	50.8
Nothing	24.9	25.4	2.8	4.5	16.0	2.2
Appropriation						
Treatment	2.0	0.4	4.4	4.0	6.0	0.0
Punishment	93.1	87.4	82.1	91.0	85.7	90.2
Nothing	4.9	7.6	13.6	4.5	1.8	2.0
Homosexuality						
Treatment	26.9	14.4	26.8	65.5	33.7	58.8
Punishment	20.2	21.6	60.9	22.5	5.9	17.4
Nothing	52.9	57.6	12.3	9.5	60.4	13.0
Abortion						
Treatment	5.6	6.4	13.5	15.0	14.9	1.0
Punishment	9.2	43.8	48.4	32.0	4.0	11.2
Nothing	85.1	45.2	38.1	52.5	77.5	80.8
Taking drugs						
Treatment	23.0	19.8	68.9	63.0	78.1	68.4
Punishment	21.4	25.4	15.8	4.0	15.4	18.2
Nothing	55.8	48.0	15.1	15.0	1.2	5.6
Factory pollution						
Treatment	3.0	2.6	1.1	2.0	1.2	0.2
Punishment	82.3	46.8	78.2	62.5	87.0	76.2
Nothing	14.7	42.2	20.8	26.5	6.5	14.8
Public protest						
Treatment	1.6	3.6	5.3	1.5	3.0	0.2
Punishment	19.2	10.6	22.6	7.5	5.3	21.2
Nothing	79.4	73.2	71.9	85.5	91.7	60.4
Not helping						
Treatment	5.4	2.4	7.1	2.5	11.6	0.2
Punishment	15.2	8.4	22.6	59.0	14.7	42.6
Nothing	77.3	84.0	70.1	38.0	56.2	55.4

SOURCE: Graeme Newman, *Comparative Deviance: Perception and Law in Six Cultures.* New York: Elsevier, 1976, pp. 142–143; reproduced with permission.

[a] "Treatment" = Choice of probation, mental hospital, other treatment.
  "Punishment" = Choice of prison, fines, corporal or capital punishment, other punishment.
  "Nothing" = Choice of "nothing" or "warning only."

will be defined. For example, laws making possession of marijuana illegal create criminals. Eliminate these laws, and we reduce the rates of deviance in society by the number of those people found guilty of violating them.

Another reason for seemingly lower rates of deviance in simpler societies may be the extreme nature of the sanctions in those societies for transgressions of important societal values. In many simpler societies the ultimate penalty for deviance is exclusion from the group. This extreme punishment means not only psychological isolation but also physical isolation that may result in slow and painful death.

In contrast, in complex and hetergeneous societies such as the United States, deviants excluded from the larger society often form their own societies or subcultures. The obvious example is prison society, in which inmates create their own values, norms, and roles.

SOCIAL CONTROL

Broadly speaking, **social control** refers to all those attitudes and behaviors originating in the social environment that have the effect of directing or restricting the attitudes and behaviors of an individual or group. External social control uses such methods as physical restriction, ridicule, and ostracism. Internal social control is influenced by other people's belief systems about appropriate behavior. Socialization, discussed in Chapter 6, is internal social control because it directs a person to acquire motives and behaviors appropriate to the roles and norms of a given society. Internal social control depends upon self-control, one result of socialization.

In this discussion we will emphasize external rather than internal processes of social control, since the latter are discussed in chapters on socialization and small groups. Also, in cases of deviance, external forms of social control play a more obvious role. Note the typical processes involved in a criminal violation. When apprehended for a crime, a suspected criminal may be arrested or not, and the police officer's attitude toward the suspect is an important element in the process of social control. Suspects who are poor, black, or Chicano, arrogant or offensive—in other words, who deviate from the characteristics of respectable citizenship—in the eyes of the police officer are more likely to be arrested than their middle-class, Anglo, or meek counterparts.

After arrest, another opportunity for external social control is the setting of bond. The avowed purpose of bond is to ensure that the accused show up for trial, and again the person who owns property and has a job usually is presumed to be more reliable than the indigent or unemployed.

The trial is a third phase in the imposition of external social control on suspects, and the court represents a formal agency charged by society to render verdicts of guilty or not guilty. Suspects who receive guilty verdicts are formally labeled by society as convicts, or deviants. Further, the options available to the court in sentencing convicts also represent different approaches to the social control of criminal behavior. Fines, suspended sentences, probation, and jail give the court substantial latitude in how convicts are treated, and this latitude results in a good deal of variation in the sentencing of criminals convicted for the same crime. One's race, occupation, and other social symbols of respectability help to explain a significant portion of these variations in criminal sentences.

Once a person has been convicted of a crime and has served time in jail, the label of "con" is forever attached to the person. This often results in further sanctions, and these sanctions may also be applied against all those who become enmeshed in the criminal justice system. For example, Schwartz and Skolnick (1962) found that employers discriminate in hiring against persons convicted of a crime and also against those arrested for a crime even if found not guilty. In this study, three groups of prospective employers were given files on job applicants. One group of employers read that an applicant had been convicted of assault, another group read that an applicant was arrested for assault but found innocent, and a third group did not receive any information on the record of criminal charges against an applicant. The employers were nine times less likely to respond positively to an applicant who was convicted than to one about whom they had no knowledge of an arrest record, and those who were arrested and tried but found innocent were only one-half as likely to receive a positive response from prospective employers as those without an arrest record. This research suggests that each step in the process ranging from arrest to conviction may increase the probability of negative reactions of external agents of social control toward deviants.

Figure 7.1 describes the different stages in the criminal justice system that a person may encounter following violation of a criminal law. Each point in the process of being handled by the police, courts, and correctional system gives authorities the option of applying or withholding sanctions against offenders. For example, after being arrested for a crime a young offender can be sent to the juvenile unit. At an intake hearing a decision can be made to send the youth to a residential center without making a formal charge or to institute a formal court procedure, followed by either probation or sentencing to a correctional facility.

The adult offender may be processed through even more stages in the criminal justice system. Again, the options available to police, courts, and correctional institutions at each stage give them great discretion in decision making. The term "discretionary justice" describes this system. It gives the system flexibility but at the same time it creates decided inequities in the way people of different classes and races are treated in our legal system.

Crime Rates

Effective social control depends upon maintaining a high level of public concern about the undesirability of certain acts. If the social control of drug use is to be effective, the laws prohibiting the use of drugs must be supported by public attitudes; if a law is not supported by social norms it will be violated widely.

Crime is the violation of formal laws. The dissemination of crime statistics collected annually by the Federal Bureau of Investigation is one way in which public concern about crime is encouraged,

especially particular kinds of crime. Each year the FBI collects criminal statistics from reports of about 8000 local police departments, which are published in the *Uniform Crime Reports* (UCR). The UCR is based on "crimes known to the police," and it gives special attention to the Crime Index: eight offenses selected because of their seriousness and frequency of occurrence. The offenses are murder, forcible rape, robbery, aggravated assault, burglary, larceny of $50 or more, auto theft, and arson (arson was added to the Crime Index in 1979 and annual figures for arson were not available for the total United States in 1980.) Table 7.2 reports crime statistics from the *Uniform Crime Reports* for 1980.

Another way that the public's attention is focused on crime is by the UCR's publication of the "Crime Clock," which is frequently picked up by magazines and newspapers around the country. Figure 7.2 is the crime clock for 1980. Although crime clocks are not a very good indicator of the crime problem, they do have some shock value. As a public relations device they maintain a high level of public concern and they encourage greater financial allocations for crime-fighting agencies.

Data reported in the *Uniform Crime Reports* cannot be used as measure of the "actual" amount of crime. There are a number of reasons for this.

1. The reports sent in to the FBI by local police agencies are not uniform. Each state has its own criminal code and court procedures, which are administered by local criminal justice agencies. This produces a great deal of variation in how criminal offenses are reported and makes it difficult to compare information from one reporting unit to another.

2. Many crimes are never reported to the police because of fear, embarrassment, and lack of knowledge of the law, among other reasons (Clinard, 1963). Surveys of victims of unreported crimes in eight American cities found that about one-third of the victims did not report because they felt "nothing could be done," and another one-third felt it was "not important enough" (National Crime Panel, 1974).

3. Statistics for use in official reports are not collected for many types of crimes, including violations of tax reporting, commercial and industrial

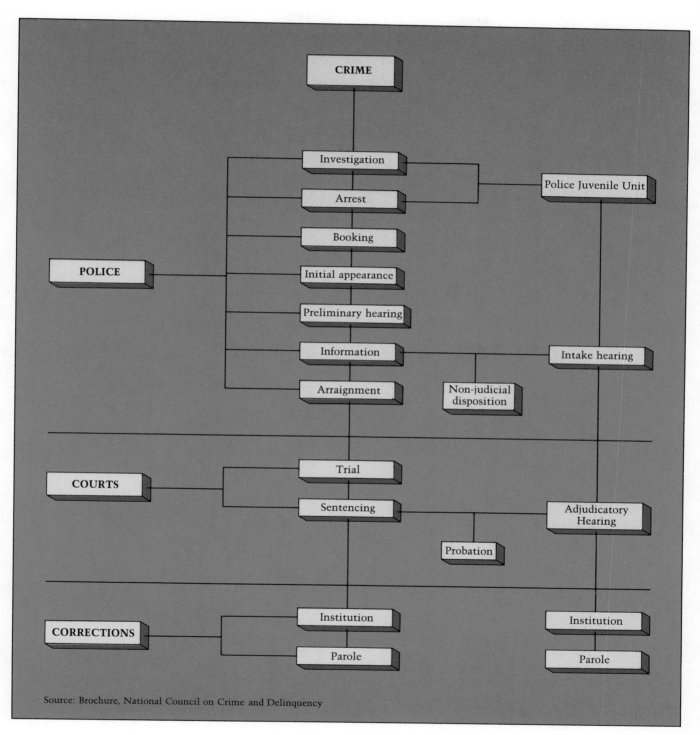

FIGURE 7.1   The Criminal Justice System

TABLE 7.2 Index of Crime, United States, 1980

AREA	POPULATION[1]	CRIME INDEX TOTAL	VIOLENT CRIME[3]	PROPERTY CRIME[3]	MURDER and NON-NEGLIGENT MANSLAUGHTER	FORCIBLE RAPE	ROBBERY	AGGRAVATED ASSAULT	BURGLARY	LARCENY-THEFT	MOTOR VEHICLE THEFT
United States Total	225,349,264	13,295,399	1,308,898	11,986,501	23,044	82,088	548,809	654,957	3,759,193	7,112,657	1,114,651
Rate per 100,000 inhabitants	....	5,899.9	580.8	5,319.1	10.2	36.4	243.5	290.6	1,668.2	3,156.3	494.6
Standard Metropolitan Statistical Area	164,403,285										
Area actually reporting[4]	98.8%	11,023,600	1,148,179	9,875,421	18,818	70,870	522,806	535,685	3,118,617	5,763,638	993,166
Estimated total	100.0%	11,109,721	1,154,322	9,955,399	18,915	71,330	524,377	539,700	3,143,078	5,811,428	1,000,893
Rate per 100,000 inhabitants	....	6,757.6	702.1	6,055.5	11.5	43.4	319.0	328.3	1,911.8	3,534.9	608.8
Other Cities	25,432,244										
Area actually reporting[4]	96.1%	1,316,318	86,442	1,229,876	1,427	5,022	15,765	64,228	308,658	857,824	63,394
Estimated total	100.0%	1,372,261	89,795	1,282,466	1,482	5,247	16,438	66,628	321,276	894,993	66,197
Rate per 100,000 inhabitants	....	5,395.8	353.1	5,042.7	5.8	20.6	64.6	262.0	1,263.3	3,519.1	260.3
Rural	35,513,735										
Area actually reporting[4]	93.5%	771,560	61,008	710,552	2,438	5,184	7,477	45,909	278,361	387,236	44,955
Estimated total	100.0%	813,417	64,781	748,636	2,647	5,511	7,994	48,629	294,839	406,236	47,561
Rate per 100,000 inhabitants	....	2,290.4	182.4	2,108.0	7.5	15.5	22.5	136.9	830.2	1,143.9	133.9

SOURCE: U.S. Department of Justice, *Uniform Crime Reports*, Washington, D.C., Superintendent of Documents, U.S. Government Printing Office, 1980, p. 41.

[1]Populations are Bureau of the Census preliminary census counts as of April 1, 1980 and are subject to change.

[2]Collection of arson as an Index offense was begun in 1979. Tabulations are not available for inclusion in this table. However, limited summary data are presented on pages 35–37 and the number of arsons reported by individual law enforcement agencies are displayed in tables 6–9 of this publication.

[3]Violent crimes are offenses of murder, forcible rape, robbery, and aggravated assault. Property crimes are offenses of burglary, larceny-theft, and motor vehicle theft. Data are not included for the property crime of arson.

[4]The percentage representing area actually reporting will not coincide with the ratio between reported and estimated crime totals, since these data represent the sum of the calculations for individual states which have varying populations, portions reporting, and crime rates.

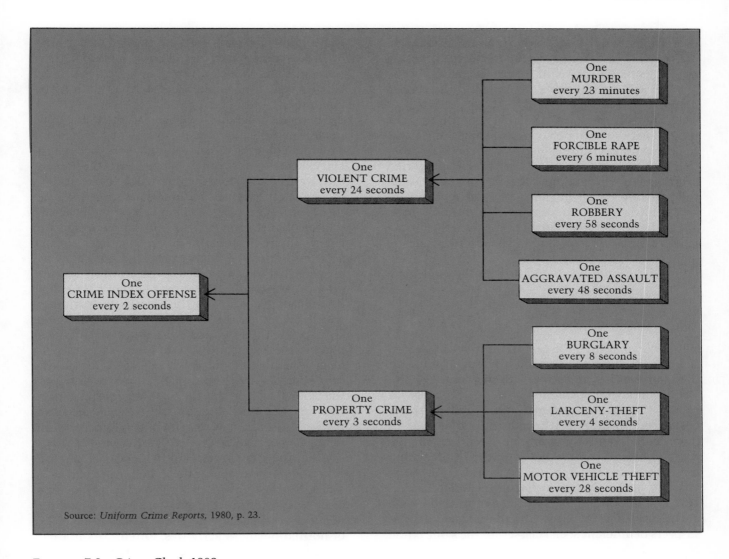

FIGURE 7.2 Crime Clock 1980

The crime clock should be viewed with care. Being a summary representation of UCR data, it is designed to convey the annual reported crime experience by showing the relative frequency of occurrence of the Index Offenses. This mode of display should not be taken to imply a regularity in the commission of the Part I Offenses; rather, it represents the annual ratio of crime to fixed time intervals.

regulations, and laws regarding union-management relations. Failure to report such crimes in official statistics results in misrepresentation of the *kind* as well as the *amount* of crime in the United States.

The FBI's crime statistics tell us something about the rates of criminal behavior and something about the behavior of criminal justice agencies. The problem is that we do not know how much of reported crime is due to criminal behavior and how much is due to how that behavior is counted. As Quinney (1979) has stated: "It is impossible to know from any statistic the 'true' rate of crime. Whether crime is increasing or decreasing in the United States is a question that can never be answered objectively without considering the politics of the times" (p. 65).

White-Collar Crime

White-collar crime is "a crime committed by a person of high respectability and high social status in the course of his profession" (Sutherland, 1949; p. 9). The financial costs of such crime probably far exceed that of conventional crime, and its social costs are also high as it creates public distrust of professionals and corporations. However, the reactions of social control agents to white-collar crime may not be as strong as it is to assault or robbery, possibly because white-collar crime, such as embezzlement or fraud, is typically committed by the "respectable" citizen. The differential treatment of suspects of different social classes for the same crime is related to the differential treatment of crimes that are class related. Stock swindles are an excellent example. In 1973 an investment company called Equity Funding reported its assets as $143 million. Its actual worth was a negative $40 million, a fact revealed in the stock market that year. Eighteen executives were charged with fraud. One received an eight-year sentence, two received five years, three received three years, and three received two years. Other executives got suspended sentences and probation, and auditors involved in the fraud received three-month sentences (Blundell, 1976). These swindlers defrauded thousands of small investors

of millions of dollars, yet had they robbed a bank of far less money they would have received harsher sentences. As Woody Guthrie in a Depression-era ballad phrased it, some folks rob you with a six-gun, others with a pen.

There are several other observations that can be made about the punishment or lack of it meted out to white-collar criminals. Some people believe society ought to deal more harshly with those committing armed robbery than those who commit theft by pen because armed criminals are more likely to injure or kill people. Others, however, believe that white-collar criminals who rob the poor and the elderly injure by directing scarce resources of their victims from food, shelter, and health care purchases. This issue involves political values and not science. Politically liberal people argue, for example, that those who sell the elderly useless insurance policies, worthless land, or misrepresented stock while their victims live in substandard housing, eat a substandard diet, and reduce heating to dangerous (for the elderly) levels are killing a certain percentage of their victims just as surely as the armed robber. Liberals also argue that crimes like breaking and entering and burglary are often treated as if they were crimes of violence while white collar crimes are not. Conservatives would say that there is a world of difference between robbery and white-collar crime. The former occurs as direct, personal intrusions into people's private lives, often with the threat of physical harm. The latter is impersonal and often occurs within the context of normal business activities. Often, it is not perceived as a crime by either the perpetrator or the victim.

Second, white-collar crimes are associated with lower rates of recidivism than other crimes and this may result in lesser sentences. **Recidivism** occurs when previously convicted criminals are convicted of crimes committed after their first conviction. White-collar crimes like fraud and accepting bribes are dependent on trust. Once violated, trust is difficult to reestablish. Further, white-collar criminals often lose their occupational positions, incomes, and friends, resulting in a general loss of social status. Thus, they seldom enjoy the positions from which their former crimes were perpetrated. All in all, white-collar criminals seldom repeat their crimes.

Third, when sentencing is considered for certain crimes, judges may feel that the white-collar criminal, especially one who violates the law in a spectacular way, is being tried and punished by the mass media as well as the court and that punishment meted out by the former is perhaps sufficient. One can be tried in the media as well as the courts and even be found guilty by the former while found innocent by the latter. High status people who violate group norms are likely to receive strong public condemnation. Indeed, some findings suggest that, while group members will tolerate some errors on the part of high status members, when the errors are severe and consistent, the group is especially hostile in its reactions (Wiggins, Dill, and Schwartz, 1965). The colloquial observation about white-collar graft may be correct; namely, a little bit of graft spread around among a number of persons is accepted, but a lot of graft for the benefit of a few is not.

Fourth, white-collar crime may be treated leniently by employers who regard it as a kind of payment to their employees. There are many forms of employee theft or improper use of company equipment, marking down merchandise as damaged so that the employee can purchase it more cheaply, repairing personal possessions on company time and with company tools and materials, taking office supplies for personal use. In a study of three chemical plants, Dalton (1959) noted that management tolerated extrasalarial payments to workers because the practical considerations of controlling some forms of employee theft were too complicated to be handled formally. In addition, the ability to use company resources for personal ends served as an informal reward system, especially for those who did not participate in the formal extrasalarial reward system through, say, having an expense account and using of a company car. Employee theft at lower levels of an organization serves a function similar to formal perquisites at higher levels, namely, to increase commitment to the organization by providing nontaxable, extrasalarial benefits to em-

ployees. However, in some cases employee theft is the result of job dissatisfaction and not an extra-salary reward (Hollinger and Clark, 1982).

The social control of white-collar criminality is extremely complicated. So much white-collar crime occurs and is never prosecuted that one wonders if it is deviant or if it is the norm. While white-collar crime, like other forms of deviance, may contribute to the preservation and maintenance of a society by making it more flexible, the way our criminal justice system discriminates in favor of the white-collar criminal negatively influences people's perceptions of the system.

Reading 7.1 discusses the ideas that are used to justify use of legal punishment in the United States.

FUNCTIONS AND SOURCES OF DEVIANCE

Sociological approaches to the study of deviance have been influenced by ideas derived from the two models of society discussed in Chapter 1, namely, the structural-functional model and the conflict model. The former model, it will be remembered, emphasized the role of shared values and norms in providing the "social glue" that keeps society together. It also emphasized the equilibrium-seeking tendency of society that produces a harmonious balance among its different parts—social roles, groups, and organizations.

Applied to the study of deviance, the structural-functional perspective stresses the *functions* of deviance, or the effects that deviance has on the stability of a society. It tends to view deviance as a normal aspect of society that can serve to relieve individual tensions at the same time that it reaffirms group values.

According to the conflict model, society contains basic inequalities in wealth, power, and prestige. Groups that are more powerful or privileged are more likely to be in positions where they determine the nature of education, politics, or the law. Groups that define what is or is not deviant behavior do so not on the basis of widely shared values but on the basis of their power to impose their values on less powerful segments of society. Thus if the dominant groups in society are economic elites, the legal system will be designed to protect the interests of those elites. Deviant behavior, whether it be a violation of law or of social norms, exists because of conflicting values and beliefs about behavior and differential power to establish the standards of behavior that define deviance.

The next section examines deviance from the structural-functional point of view. This is followed by a section that links deviance to group differences in values and power, as stressed by the conflict model.

Structural-Functional Perspective on Deviance

Although rates of deviance may vary among societies, Durkheim (1938) noted that deviance is a persistent social pattern. By this, he meant that all societies have socialization processes that affect individuals differently and thereby produce deviations from the normative pattern. Durkheim argued that, in all societies, if deviations from norms are reduced, smaller deviations will be negatively sanctioned with the vigor previously reserved for larger deviations.

According to Durkheim, deviation and deviance serve two major functions. Deviation from social norms produces not only the sinner but also the saint, the idealist, and the innovator. To adapt to changing environmental conditions, societies must produce innovators, yet the same tolerance for deviation that is needed to produce innovation also produces criminality. Moreover, under some conditions crime itself is an innovation that prepares the way for social change. Thus one function of deviance is to introduce flexibility into the moral system and thereby enable the society to change and adapt.

The second function of deviance is to allow groups to demonstrate support for and allegiance to the existing moral order and to identify the boundaries of "normality." Whenever a group defines a person's act in a particular situation as deviant, the act is denounced in terms of group norms and it reinforces the group's "we-feeling," or collective

identity. The deviant's behavior is shown to be deficient in some moral quality that is accepted by the audience of definers as important to group membership. The denunciation separates the deviant from other group members who, by applying negative sanctions to the deviant, reaffirm their own commitment to the norms that have been violated. Dentler and Erikson (1959) suggest that groups tend to institutionalize deviance and to incorporate the deviant into the group. Ultimately, the group's ability to define its norms depends upon the presence of a deviant member. The deviant's behavior can be used as an index of the group's expectations for normative behavior.

The strength of the sanctions applied to deviance is not the same for all acts. By varying the sanction members of a society demonstrate the degree of importance they attach to the violated norm (Davis, 1961). Studying the sanctions against deviance gives us an idea of the structure of norms that control most people's behavior most of the time. Davis uses prostitution as an example and analyzes its variations through history to determine how social norms regulate sexual behavior. He argues that the number and status of prostitutes are higher in societies in which sexual relations are strictly regulated and sex is unavailable. For these societies prostitution has a safety-valve function by providing for sexual release outside of marriage. Since a relationship with a prostitute is commercial, not personal, people can use prostitutes to increase sexual variety without threatening the institution of marriage. The safety-valve role is a third function of deviance in society.

Polsky (1967) applies Davis's analysis of prostitution to pornography, and he concludes that pornography serves the same function in society as prostitution but often for more deviant types of sexual behavior. Polsky argues that both prostitution and pornography provide nonfamilial sexual outlets in which a wide range of perversions are permitted, such as sadomasochism, that may be condemned in the marriage relationship. This safety-valve function particularly applies to pornography because its customers can vicariously enjoy activities in print and on film that may be unacceptable in interpersonal relations. The vicarious enjoyment of the voyeur, or peeping Tom, is a safety valve, not only for the society, but also for the individual. Through pornography, the voyeur can obtain gratification which, if obtained through observing real people, might produce guilt feelings.

The safety-valve theory of sexual deviance suggests that use of pornography should be directly related to the degree of repression (Gray, 1982). If so, people whose sexual inclinations have been repressed most strongly should be the heaviest users. In a study that compared convicted male rapists, homosexuals, transsexuals, frequent consumers of pornography, and a group of control subjects, Goldstein (1973) found that the control subjects reported a greater exposure to pornography in adolescence than the other groups. Furthermore, the rapists and transsexuals reported low rates of pornography use in adulthood. These data support the idea of a safety-valve function for pornography.

Additional support for the safety-valve theory is provided by Howard (1973). Twenty-three subjects viewed pornographic films for 90 minutes a day for 15 days. Although personality tests revealed no discernible change in the general predispositions of the subjects, both behavioral and physiological measures obtained during the testing indicated a significant reduction in both interest in and sexual response to the films. Increases in exposure to pornographic films apparently decrease their appeal.

The safety-valve theory of prostitution and pornography can be criticized on two points. The first concerns the research indicating exposure to pornographic materials seems to decrease their appeal. The viewer of pornography who becomes satiated and loses interest may be like the alcoholic who easily swears off liquor while suffering a hangover. What do these people do two weeks later when they are no longer satiated with erotic images, or alcohol and their resolve is tested?

Second, the safety-valve theory can be used to support the idea that prostitution and pornography are essentially benign. Both are considered victimless crimes because they are entered into without coercion by adults in search of pleasure or income. Yet it is possible to view prostitutes as victims of a society that has offered them few opportunities for other jobs and of the pimps who use and abuse

them. There are also the costs to society as a whole. Both prostitution and pornography help to maintain sexist attitudes that contribute to the subordination of women, a cost to society that has many ramifications.

To summarize, the structural-functional perspective maintains that deviance serves three functions: (1) to create flexibility, (2) to reaffirm group norms, and (3) to provide a safety valve.

Conflict Perspective on Deviance

The conflict perspective asserts that to understand deviance it must be placed within the broader context of (1) political and economic inequality and (2) the agencies of social control (police, army, prison officials) that have a monopoly over the means of coercion. Society is composed of groups that are struggling to control scarce resources and to gain advantage by defining the activities of other groups as "dangerous," "deviant," or "criminal." Groups of workers would like to have strikebreaking defined as a crime, and corporate executives would like to have strikes so defined. Groups in conflict try to influence the agencies of social control (the government) to use their power on their own behalf. Corporate executives try to get the courts and the police to help break strikes, while unions try to get the government to allow strikes to be used against employers.

Consider the situation of South Africa, a society with an official policy of racial separation (apartheid). Whites, who make up one-fifth of the population, make the laws that keep black people from voting, restricted to certain occupations, and prevented from living where they choose. A black person may be held by the police without charges or jailed for speaking or publishing ideas critical of the government. Clearly, the black person is defined as deviant for violating the laws developed by whites for the purpose of controlling blacks (Report of the Study Commission on U.S. Policy Toward Southern Africa, *Africa: Time Running Out* (U. of California Press, 1981).

Another example can be drawn from American society where criminal laws seem heavily weighted toward protecting private poverty. As Sherman and

Reactions to deviance are often influenced by the social status of the person involved in the deviant behavior. The criminal justice system—from the police through the courts—is more likely to be lenient when confronting middle- and upper-class citizens. Poor people are more likely to be arrested, convicted, and jailed for violations than are citizens who are more comfortable financially.

Wood (1979) point out: "Laws make it a crime to force a hospital to care for someone at gunpoint, but do not make it a crime to turn away a sick man with no money from the hospital door" (p. 303). Also, as we noted earlier, the poor and less powerful are more likely to be arrested, convicted, and sentenced than are persons of higher social standing (Quinney, 1979).

What these examples indicate is that conflicting values and interests, and inequalities in power and wealth are at the basis of our system of criminal justice. Laws are developed by representatives of dominant groups to protect their interests and meet their needs. If laws were made by representatives of subordinate groups we might have stricter laws against corporate price fixing, false advertising, union-busting activities, or shutting down factories in one part of the country to seek greater profits elsewhere.

The existence of conflicting values and the differential distribution of power produces a struggle among social groups to influence each other's conduct. Dominant groups attempt to establish and enforce a particular set of values for the entire society. This conception of conflict and power has been used to develop a theory of crime that can be expressed in the following propositions put forward by Quinney (1970):

1. "Crime is a definition of human conduct that is created by authorized agents in a politically organized society."
2. "Criminal definitions describe behaviors that conflict with the interests of the segments of society that have the power to shape public policy."
3. "Criminal definitions are applied by the segments of society that have the power to shape the enforcement and administration of criminal law." (pp. 15–18)

These propositions stress the fact that crime is *socially created* by defining certain behaviors as criminal. Since any behavior can be defined as deviant or criminal, the values and interests of persons who create definitions of crime is of central importance. Individuals and groups that are better able to have their interests represented in public

policy will play a greater role in defining the behaviors that are called criminal.

A Marxian version of the conflict perspective identifies capitalism as the specific source of inequality that helps to define deviance or criminality. Capitalist society is divided between the capitalist class, which owns and controls the means of production, and the working class, which is exploited by capitalists. The social and political institutions of society, including the use of governmental power, are under the control of the capitalist class, which also controls the means of consciousness, that is, the capitalist class is able to manipulate ideas, including those about crime. As we saw earlier, a society's sensitivity to different types of crime can be manipulated by the kind of official statistics that are collected and published.

The objective of the conflict perspective is to investigate the way that a capitalist society shapes the nature of law, crime, and deviance. This perspective shifts attention from the study of deviance to the study of social control.

THEORIES OF DEVIANCE

Deviance is a complex process based on the interrelationships of act, actor, situation, and definers. Different explanations of deviance emphasize different parts of the process. In general, two views have emerged. The first view, which includes anomie theory, subculture theory, and differential association theory, tries to explain why different parts of the social structure, such as lower-class neighborhoods, have higher rates of deviation than others. The second view, labeling theory, tries to explain why some deviates are thought of as deviants and negative sanctions are applied to their behavior.

Anomie Theory

A classic general theory about the structural sources of deviance is that of Merton (1957) presented in his essay "Social Structure and Anomie" (originally published in 1938). Merton was interested in how much deviation from existing standards of expected or appropriate behavior occurs and under what circumstances. Merton suggested that, because cultural goals and the institutionalized means to carry out the goals are not perfectly related, groups located in positions in the social structure that experience stress from the lack of integration of goals and means should have higher rates of deviance. For Merton, deviance is an adaptation by members of a group to structural strains. For example, one cultural goal is economic success, and legitimate means to this goal include education for an occupation and hard work. There are other means to the same goal, such as robbing or embezzlement, but these are not culturally legitimate. If a society emphasizes the goal of financial success more heavily than the means of education and hard work, groups that lack access to legitimate means may use illegitimate ones. Thus those groups that lack legitimate means to success will have higher rates of deviance than other groups. Moreover, the type of deviance is related to the type of strain. If the strain is associated with economic success, the deviant will tend to rob or embezzle to acquire money.

Based upon this theory of deviance as an adaptation to strain, Merton devised the typology presented in Table 7.3. When a person uses institutionalized means to achieve cultural goals, the result is conformity. **Conformity,** as a model of adaptation, is acceptance of both culturally approved goals and means. **Ritualism** results when a person adheres to institutionalized means long after cultural goals have been forgotten or have declined in importance. People who do not expect to achieve economic success but who still extol the virtues of hard work and education as a way of "making it" are ritualists. Neither the conformist nor the ritualist is a norm violator.

Innovators endorse cultural goals but, unlike conformers or ritualists, do not employ institutionalized means. **Innovation** is the use of illegitimate means to achieve cultural goals. Criminal acts of juvenile delinquents in lower-class neighborhoods are examples of innovation. Cloward and Ohlin (1960) studied this group of innovations. Delinquents are socialized to value economic success just as others are in our society. However, delinquents have few opportunities to attain success

Many cases of juvenile delinquency involve behaviors that are defined as inappropriate for young people but not for older persons. Adults can engage in drinking, smoking, sex, and staying out all night without consequence. For juveniles, the same behavior can result in a juvenile court hearing.

through institutionalized channels. Their education is probably inferior, and their families and neighborhoods offer little assistance toward upward mobility. The probabilities that slum-dwelling juveniles will become doctors or lawyers are very small. Nonetheless, in the slums these juveniles see pimps, gamblers, dope dealers, and prostitutes who dress well, drive expensive cars, go to expensive restaurants, and display other signs of material success. The delinquents also see members of the wealthier class in society buying the services of gamblers and prostitutes. So, while juveniles may realize that these activities are illegal, they see them as one of the few means of economic success open to them.

The other two categories that Merton identifies are **Retreatism** and **Rebellion.** Retreatists reject both the institutionalized goals and the means to them. Typically, people who respond to stress by rejection of goals and means tend to isolate themselves from the rest of society, for example, drug addicts and some of the mentally ill. Rebellion, according to Merton, is rejection of existing goals and means combined with endorsement of them in principle. Rebels come to feel that while cultural goals in themselves may be valuable, the system in which goals and means are interrelated is a source of frustration and dislocation. Rebels therefore seek new values and new means—a new institutional system—to replace existing ones.

Criticism of Merton's anomie theory has stressed three major points (Davis, 1975; Lemert, 1967; Schur, 1979):

1. Merton assumes that there is a shared value system that emphasizes success that is embraced by most members of society. It is possible that many Americans do not share the cultural goal of success and therefore are not likely to become "innovators" to achieve the goal.

2. Merton's typology deals with *individual* adaptations to the problem of trying to achieve cultural goals. However, many forms of deviant behavior (innovation) involves collective actions based on group values. Marijuana smoking, some professional crime, and prostitution, for example, are all supported by groups that value the particular deviant behavior and support its members who exhibit the behavior.

3. Anomie theory assumes the existence of higher crime rates among lower socioeconomic groups where the institutionalized means for achieving cultural goals are not available. However, recent research indicates that there is considerable deviance and crime in the middle classes, even though their members are able to achieve cultural goals (Quinney, 1979).

These and other weaknesses of anomie theory have given rise to other theories of deviance, which will be examined in the following sections.

Deviant Subcultures

Merton's theory of deviance helps explain the behavior of people who become "innovators" in order to succeed economically. However, the theory fails

TABLE 7.3   A Typology of Modes of Individual Adaptation

MODES OF ADAPTATION	CULTURE GOALS	INSTITUTIONALIZED MEANS
I. Conformity	+	+
II. Innovation	+	−
III. Ritualism	−	+
IV. Retreatism	−	−
V. Rebellion	±	±

+ signifies acceptance of the goals or means
− signifies rejection of the goals or means
± signifies rejection of prevailing goals and means and
   substitution of new ones

SOURCE: Robert Merton, "Social Structure and Anomie," in *Social Theory and Social Structure,* rev. ed., New York: Free Press, 1957, p. 140.

to account for many deviant acts that have nothing to do with the use of illegitimate means to economic success. For example, there are delinquent gangs that seem to be involved mainly in random acts of violence, petty theft of worthless objects, and destruction of property. How can we explain such economically unrewarding behavior?

Cohen (1955), who studied delinquent gangs, started with a view much like Merton's. He saw that American males are encouraged to value upward mobility, which becomes a measure of personal worth and success. The means for achieving upward mobility include academic skills and personal traits like good manners, proper speech, self-discipline, and cooperativeness. The working-class male, according to Cohen, is poorly equipped to achieve upward mobility because these are the means that are taught to middle-class, not working-class, children.

Thus we have working-class male children faced with a discrepancy between cultural goals (success) and legitimate means (education, proper behavior) to those goals. While Merton would assume that these young men would retain the goal but alter the means for its achievement, Cohen believes that working-class males band together and repudiate middle-class standards of success. They create a new status system that allows them to compete successfully for rewards. The result is a gang subculture that turns middle-class virtues into vices and vices into virtues. Polite speech and manners, respect for property, acceptance of authority figures, academic achievement, and nonaggression are replaced by drinking, truancy, gambling, sexual promiscuity, use of foul language, physical aggression, and destruction of property.

The main weaknesses of subculture theory are that it does not account for middle-class delinquency and it does not consider the fact that many lower-class juveniles are sometimes involved in delinquent acts and sometimes in conventional ones. As Matza (1964) has noted, the delinquent's actions are not determined by a subculture that is opposed to conventional norms and values but that "he drifts between criminal and conventional action" (p. 28).

Differential Association

Sutherland (1947), as Merton and Cohen, is concerned primarily with reasons for high crime rates among certain groups. Sutherland, however, emphasizes common historical factors in the backgrounds of deviant individuals. From these he devised a theory of differential association and social learning that states: criminals associate with other criminals who teach novice members the techniques, motives, and attitudes that favor criminal activity. Sutherland summarized his theory in nine propositions.

1. Criminal behavior is learned.
2. Criminal behavior is learned in interaction with other people in a process of communication.
3. The principal part of the learning of criminal behavior occurs within intimate personal groups.
4. When criminal behavior is learned, the learning includes (a) techniques of committing the crime; (b) the specific direction of motives, drives, rationalizations, and attitudes.
5. The specific direction of motives and drives is learned from definitions of the legal code as favorable or unfavorable.
6. A person becomes delinquent because of an excess of definitions favorable to violation of law over definitions unfavorable to violation of law.
7. Differential associations may vary in frequency, duration, priority, and intensity.
8. The process of learning criminal behavior by association with criminal and anticriminal patterns makes use of all of the mechanisms used in any other learning process.
9. While criminal behavior is an expression of general needs and values, some noncriminal behavior is an expression of the same needs and values.

The research of Cloward and Ohlin (1960) on delinquent gangs supports and extends Sutherland's theory. Cloward and Ohlin agreed with Merton that not all of society's members have equal access to roles that are culturally valued. They also point out, however, that there are differences in

Deviance by groups (as compared to individual deviance) involves support for the behavior of its members and rejection of the norms and values of the larger society. Here we see a motorcycle group that has accepted the societal definition of their deviance by describing themselves as "outlaws."

access to illegitimate roles as well as legitimate ones. The availability of both illegitimate and legitimate roles make up the "opportunity structure" for working-class youth. Thus young people living in neighborhoods in which there is an organized criminal subculture with criminal role models will have the highest access to illegitimate roles. Residents have opportunities for interpersonal relationships in which they can learn to be criminals. Disorganized slum neighborhoods that lack a stable criminal subculture will not offer youth opportunity for this type of success, rather, youth may be drawn into the destructive, purposeless gang activity described by Cohen.

How do people view their own deviant behavior? Sykes and Matza (1957) suggest that delinquent groups learn to deny their deviance "in the form of justifications for deviance that are seen as valid by the delinquent but not by the legal system or society at large (p. 666)." These justifications, which they call *techniques of neutralization*, include (1) the denial of responsibility for one's behavior, (2) the denial of injury to the victim, (3) the denial of the victim's innocence, (4) the condemnation of the condemners, and (5) the appeal to higher loyalties.

There are other examples of deviants using stigma-neutralizing techniques as rationalizations for their actions to help them maintain their self-respect. Bryan (1966) reported the following statements by call girls:

I could say that a prostitute has held more marriages together as part of their profession than any divorce counselor.

I don't regret doing it because I feel I help people. A lot of men that come over to see me don't care for sex. They come over for companionship, someone to talk to.

[If] they didn't have girls to come to like us that are able to handle them and make it a nice thing, there would be so many rapes . . . (p. 443)

These justifications typically serve to lessen the effects of internal as well as external forms of social control over the deviant. What is not well known is whether such beliefs precede deviant behavior and therefore make it possible or whether they are after-the-fact justifications.

Labeling Theory

Theories of deviance proposed by Merton, Cohen, and Sutherland all hold that certain groups in our society are under special pressure to engage in deviant acts because of social and cultural constraints. People who are young, male, and poor are believed to exhibit higher rates of deviance than those who are old, female, and nonpoor because the former face more barriers to achieving valued goals.

The labeling theory of deviance begins with a different idea: persons in all social categories, regardless of age, sex, education, ethnicity, or social class, engage in acts of deviance at one time or another, for example, petty theft, underage drinking, illicit sex, stealing from an employer, illegal gambling, bizarre personal behaviors, and income tax evasion. The number of people who have violated laws and standards of public morality is far greater than the number of official deviants who are in prisons, mental hospitals, and juvenile halls. To labeling theorists, the important question is why some people are labeled and punished as deviants and others are not.

According to labeling theory, the difference is not in the acts themselves but in the reaction of others to those acts. (This is the fourth component of deviance described earlier.) In short, deviance is not something a person does but something created by people who respond to a particular act. Deviance is created when the reaction to norm violation is such that the violaters are forced to play the role of deviants and to think of themselves as deviants. One becomes a deviant, therefore, not from the initial act of norm violation, but as a result of definition by others as a deviant. When others respond to one as a deviant, the possibilities for defining oneself as nondeviant are reduced.

The process by which labeling leads to deviance is described in Figure 7.3. After a deviant act has taken place and has been perceived by others, the

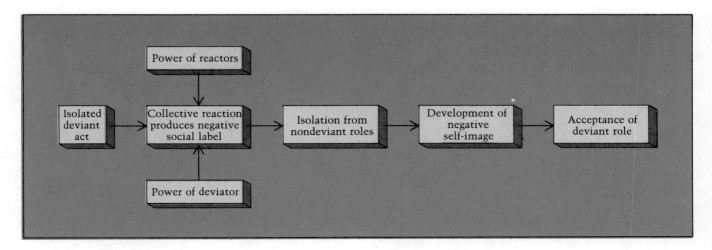

FIGURE 7.3   Labeling Model of
Deviance

nature of the collective reaction is determined by the balance of social power between the reactors and the deviator. If the deviator has limited power he or she will have limited ability to resist the imputation of a negative social label. The negative label results in the deviator being isolated from opportunities to fill "normal" social roles; for example, he or she may be avoided by friends and relatives and excluded from normal social relationships. The deviator, unable to avoid the stigma of the negative label, starts to develop a negative self-image. The result is acceptance of the deviant role.

Reading 7.2 indicates how deviant identities can be applied to persons with unusual physical attributes. Thus conditions for which a person is not responsible or that are beyond personal control, such as blindness or disfigurement, can also result in stigma and the creation of deviant roles.

Two examples will illustrate how the labeling process creates deviance. First is the case of a high school student who is observed by a police officer to possess a small amount of illegal narcotics. The deviant act is established, but the officer has at least two options. The officer may choose to treat the incident as minor and hope to control further acts of deviance through admonishing the offender and drawing the offender's family into the process of control. The boy is given a lecture and taken home to his family, who are warned of the dangers of their son's behavior. The boy is not officially labeled as a drug user. Assuming the cooperation of his family, neither they nor authorities will see him as a drug user. He will not label himself as such and he will not be cut off from conventional society.

If, however, the police officer decides to arrest the boy for possession of narcotics, he is then stigmatized with a deviant label. He may be shunned by his friends and sought after by other drug users in school. Thus begins the construction of a deviant role that results in the student's eventually identifying himself as deviant.

Our second example involves unusual behavior rather than illegal acts. Consider a manager in a large corporation who feels that his career is not going well. He has been passed over for promotion and suspects that someone has been spreading rumors about the quality of his work. Although he continues to perform satisfactorily at work, at home he is either edgy and irritable, at times giving way

According to labeling theory, most people violate a law or important social norm at some point in their lives. However, the societal reaction to the violation varies according to the social standing of the actor. Here we see average, "law-abiding" citizens involved in looting a store in the aftermath of a natural disaster.

to violent anger, or he is moody and depressed. His family may decide that he is simply discontented and going through "male menopause." They may adapt to his moods and accept the fact that he is, and will continue to be an unhappy, angry man.

Suppose, however, that the man's family becomes greatly concerned about the change in his behavior. They fear that he may harm himself or other family members. One time when he is particularly upset he makes seemingly suicidal statements and locks himself in the bathroom. His family calls the police. When the police arrive, the man is further upset by their presence. He resists their efforts to talk to him and orders them out of the house. A fight ensues and he is subdued by the police. He is taken to jail, where he continually shouts about his rights, his privacy, and the invasion of his home by police. In court the next morning the judge recommends a psychiatric interview. Assuming that the interview isolates the manager from his family and his friends, this incident could well mark the beginning of his career as a mental patient.

These examples are simplifications of the labeling process, which takes place over a period of time and is affected by the actor and the situation, as well as the audience. For example, Winick (1964), who studied physicians addicted to narcotics, found that they were useful and effective members of their communities, unlike many other addicts, and they did not experience the same difficulties as other addicts. Schur (1964) noted that addiction in Britain, which has a liberal addiction treatment program, is less of a problem than it is in the United States. Ray (1961) found that former addicts in the United States tend to return to drug use because nonaddicts seem to doubt their new identity as abstainers. Since unreformed addicts do not treat reformed addicts as "cured," the latter are likely to reestablish old friendships and habits.

The deviant label can be attached to an individual in varying degrees. Becker (1963) points out that when a deviant actor is caught and punished for a crime, the label is more firmly attached than previously and the deviance becomes a **master status.** Lemert (1951) distinguishes between **primary de-**

viance, which occurs when one deviates originally, and **secondary deviance,** which occurs when the person uses "deviant behavior or a role based on it as a means of defense, attack, or adjustment to the overt and covert problems created by the consequent societal reaction to him ... (p. 76)." The degree of labeling varies according to the deviant's status and the deviant's willingness to use the labels; that is, the degree to which the deviant's behavior affects him or her. When secondary deviance becomes characteristic of a deviant, **role engulfment** may occur (Schur, 1971). Labeling is composed of both self-definitions and others' definitions of the deviant. With role engulfment the deviant comes to perceive self in the same way as others do. Lemert (1967) gives us an example of role engulfment in his study of the habitual check forger, who is constantly moving from town to town, a social isolate without friends. When he accepts the views that others have of his life as meaningless, he attempts to develop a more stable life style. Unfortunately, for a check forger, remaining in one location too long makes arrest inevitable.

Deviant behavior also can result in **disavowal.** Cameron (1964) suggests that when the criminal does not think of self as a criminal and can conceive of no supportive group for the criminal behavior, the deviant label is rejected. She studied shoplifters who typically are women from families with modest incomes. Generally, they do not think of themselves as thieves, even when arrested. Moreover, they expect their parents, friends, spouses, and employers to be appalled by their behavior. Expecting no support for their crime, the shoplifters would repudiate their behavior if given the chance and offer to pay for the stolen items. According to Cameron, shoplifters will reform rather than accept the shoplifter's label.

Causes of Deviance: A Summary

There are important differences among the four theories as to how deviance is caused. Both anomie theory and subculture theory locate the cause of the motivation to violate norms in the blocked opportunities for achieving success goals. The motivation for deviance is *caused* by the poor fit between cultural goals and the socially structured opportunities to achieve them. Figure 7.4 illustrates the causal sequence.

In anomie theory, groups with fewer opportunities to achieve success goals (working-class youths) will have greater motivation to violate norms and higher rates of deviance. In subculture theory, the greater motivation to violate norms will result in different patterns of deviance depending upon the availability of illegitimate opportunities in the neighborhoods of working-class youths. Neither of these theories pays much attention to how social control agents (police, courts) help to define deviance.

Differential association theory, as developed by Sutherland, is also more concerned with the factors that cause deviant behavior than with social reactions to deviance. Deviant and nondeviant behavior is learned by the same process. The specific direction of a person's motivations and actions depends upon the frequency and intensity of interactions with others who express definitions that are favorable and unfavorable to violation of law. The differential association with persons who hold

procrime and anticrime views is shaped by the social organization of areas in which people live. Figure 7.5 summarizes this theory.

As Davis (1975) points out, Sutherland's assumption that some groups hold procrime values and others anticrime values does not show how value conflicts and differential power are involved in the formulation of laws. Both powerful and vulnerable groups have an interest in maintaining a view of the law that is in their own interests. However, only the powerful have the resources to have their views transformed into laws to control what they consider undesirable behavior.

Labeling theory assumes that most people commit deviant acts at one time or another. The key question is how social definitions of these initial acts vary with the interests and values of powerful groups, particularly how agents of social control stigmatize deviants and influence them to accept a deviant identity. The theory does not explain why people display initial deviant behavior.

These theories differ primarily in the fact that they tend to focus on different stages in the process of becoming deviant. A more integrated theory would explain the motivation to violate norms

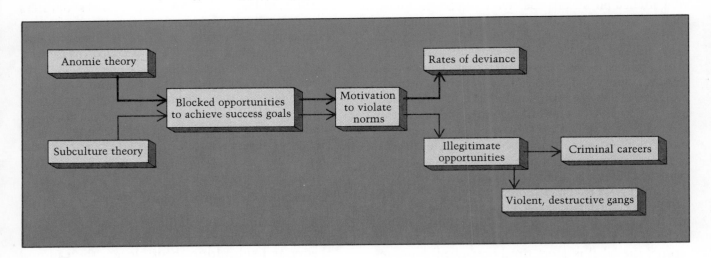

FIGURE 7.4   Anomie and
Subculture Models of Deviance

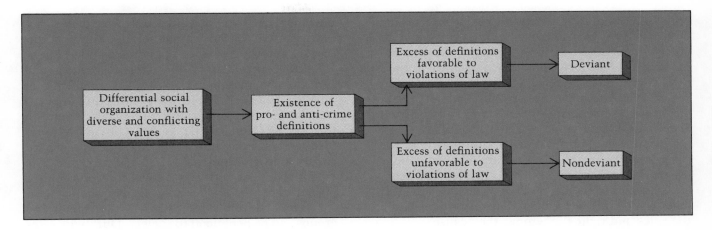

FIGURE 7.5 Differential
Association Model of Deviance

among different groups and how norm violations become transformed into deviance and deviant careers to provide a fuller understanding of deviance.

DEVIANT GROUPS AND MOVEMENTS

Groups of deviants, for example, drug users, whose behavior is proscribed by the larger society, may develop a community with norms, values, and roles that differ from those of the wider society, which will attract other deviants. Thus the community develops a social structure of its own that contradicts the rules of society at large but serves to regulate interpersonal behavior within the community.

Deviant groups, like other groups, have leaders, followers, and interrelated roles. Furthermore, they have institutionalized means and goals. There are informal and formal deviant groups and groups that try to accommodate to society to some degree as well as those that try to change it. The behavior of those in deviant groups can be thought of as responses to forms of interpersonal social control just like the behaviors of people in primary and membership groups, discussed in Chapter 5.

For example, Becker (1963) notes that, to join a group of marijuana users, a person must learn to smoke the right way, to perceive the drug's effects, and to enjoy the effects. Weinberg (1970) observes that nudists must learn to avoid the appearance of being sexually oriented. Learning how to smoke marijuana or how to look unconcerned about sex is not theoretically different from learning the techniques of other roles or the norms of other communities.

Role definition also occurs in deviant groups. In a study of male homosexuals who paid to participate in sexual activities with young boys, Reiss (1961) found that the boys defined their role as play-for-pay-only and that boys who participated without receiving pay were excluded from the group. In a more extensive study of male homosexual activity, Humphreys (1970) noted that homosexual groups distinguish four separate homosexual roles. Two variables—marital status and occupational status—seemed to influence the choice of one role over the others and affected the number of constraints and the amount of secrecy exercised in the different roles. The four homosexual roles Humphreys observed were as follows: (1) *trade*—those who resort to tearooms for sexual satisfactions they no longer derive from marriages that they still do not want to end; (2) *ambisexuals*—those who enjoy both homosexual and heterosexual contacts and who usually have both the time and income to have both family and lovers; (3) *gay guys*—the true homosexuals of society who participate fully in their own community and seek more lasting relationships with other homosexuals, and (4) *closet queens*—those who are somewhat socially isolated and afraid of detection.

Deviant groups often try to accommodate to the social structure of the larger community and thereby lessen the probability of being "hassled" by agencies of social control. However, when deviants feel that existing rules are unjust, they may try to change the rules and right the wrongs they cause.

Although deviant movements have tended to be conservative in the changes they seek, in recent years a number of deviant group movements have formed to liberalize attitudes and laws. Two such groups are the Gay Liberation Front and Coyote. The first seeks acceptance of homosexuals in society, the second unionization of prostitutes.

Sagarin (1969) sees the strong tradition of association in the United States as one of the reasons why deviant movements flourish. In the early twentieth century, for example, many associations developed to help the large number of immigrants of diverse ethnic origin and to serve as a bridge to their new culture. The new immigrants were analogous to deviants in that they shared the common stigma of being foreigners. The anonymity of urban life allowed the immigrants to meet with others with similar problems for the purposes of mutual support and protection. Sagarin notes the similar function of the associations and the functions of emerging movements of such deviant groups as alcoholics, gamblers, homosexuals, drug addicts, convicts, dwarfs, and mental patients.

SUMMARY

Deviates are people whose behavior violates social norms but who are not identified as such. When they are identified as violators and sanctioned they become deviants. The distinction between deviates and deviance allows us to study the process by which

norm violators are identified and sanctioned. That process involves the deviant act, the actor, the situation, and the audience of definers.

Social control refers to all those attitudes and behaviors originating in the social environment that have the effect of directing or restricting the attitudes and behaviors of an individual or group. In the area of crime, social control is found to differ for violent crime and white collar crime and for suspects from different social backgrounds. The criminal justice systems allows for considerable discretion in the application of sanctions.

Deviations from some norms by individuals and groups can be beneficial to society. Durkheim cites two social advantages of deviance: (1) it is a source of flexibility in the moral system and (2) it is evidence of the true support and allegiance society pays to the existing moral order. To these, we may add a third—the safety-valve function, particularly as it relates to prostitution and pornography.

Sociologists have been primarily concerned with two issues—why deviance occurs more frequently in certain parts of the social structure and why some deviates are labeled and punished as deviants and some are not. Merton attributes deviance to the attempts of society's members to adapt to structural strains. He cites five modes of individual adaptation—conformity, innovation, ritualism, retreatism, and rebellion. Merton's typology does not account for socially nonutilitarian behavior, such as random acts of violence or destruction of property. Cohen suggests that those who are denied opportunities for achieving cultural goals establish subcultural status systems of their own that value the vices of the dominant culture. Another theory of deviance seeks the answer to high crime rates among certain groups in differential access to social roles.

Finally, labeling theory suggests that deviance is not defined by the behavior itself but by others' reactions to the behavior.

Recently, some deviant groups have attempted to change the norms of the dominant society that give rise to the identification of their behavior as deviant—to seek their "rights" as groups of individuals within the larger group.

GLOSSARY

Conformity acceptance of culturally approved goals and means as a mode of adaptation.

Deviance the process by which those who violate group norms are so identified and whose behavior receives negative sanctions by the group.

Deviants those who violate group norms and are so identified and whose acts are negatively sanctioned by the group.

Deviates those who violate group norms but are not identified as norm violators and whose acts are not negatively sanctioned by the group.

Disavowal refusal by a deviant to perceive self as deviant, particularly in the absence of any group support for deviant behavior.

Innovation use of illegitimate means to achieve cultural goals.

Master status firmly established identity as a deviant attached to individual who has been caught and punished for deviance.

Primary deviance initial act of deviation from group norms.

Rebellion rejection of existing cultural goals and means, combined with endorsement of cultural goals in general; attempts to establish a new institutional order.

Recidivism conviction for a crime committed after a first conviction.

Retreatism rejection of both institutionalized goals and the means to them.

Ritualism adherence to institutionalized means long after cultural goals have been forgotten or have declined in importance.

Role engulfment acceptance by deviant of others' perceptions and definitions of self.

Secondary deviance use of "deviant behavior or a role based on it as a means of defense, attack, or adjustment to the overt and covert problems created by the consequent societal reaction" to one's deviance.

Social control all those attitudes and behaviors originating in the social environment which have the effect of directing or restricting the attitudes, behavior, and emotions of an individual or group.

ADDITIONAL READINGS

Clinard, Marshall. *Sociology of Deviant Behavior.* 4th ed. N.Y.: Holt, Rinehart and Winston, 1974.
An extensive, well-organized, well-referenced, and comprehensive analysis of deviant behavior.

Davis, Nanette. *Sociological Constructions of Deviance: Perspectives and Issues in the Field.* Dubuque, Ia.: Brown, 1975.
The utility and character of pathological, disorganizational, functional, anomic, conflict, labeling, and social control theories of deviance are compared.

Farrell, Ronald, and Victoria Swigert, eds. *Social Deviance.* N.Y.: Lippincott, 1975.
Various theoretical approaches are considered in articles that represent the historical development of the theories, and major criticisms of the theories also are presented.

Geis, Gilbert, and Ezra Stotland, eds., *White-Collar Crime: Theory and Research.* Beverly Hills, Calif.: Sage, 1980.
A collection of articles that attempt to synthesize the latest theory and research on different forms of white-collar crime. Topics include computer-related crime, home repair fraud, corporate crime, and consumer abuse.

Johnson, John M., and Jack D. Douglas, eds., *Crime at the Top: Deviance in Business and the Professions.* New York: Lippincott, 1978.
An interesting and readable collection of articles that indicate how pervasive deviance is at the top. Especially valuable are the discussions of how deviance and nondeviance overlap, and the in-depth accounts of routine forms of middle-class deviance.

Lofland, John. *Deviance and Identity.* Englewood Cliffs, N.J.: Prentice-Hall, 1969.
A detailed discussion of the process of becoming

deviant, which compares normals and deviants in terms of their histories.

Rubington, Earl, and Martin Weinberg, eds. *Deviance: The Interactionist Perspective.* N.Y.: Macmillan, 1973.

This collection of articles with commentary emphasizes the relationships among social control, *deviant subcultures, and deviant identities.*

Simmons, J. L. *Deviants.* Berkeley, Calif.: Glendessary, 1969.

Discussions of deviance are linked to current examples, such as drug users, and original research is reported, as in the discussion of religious cults.

READINGS

READING 7.1

*Why Punish?**

Andrew von Hirsch

Decisions about the disposition of offenders after conviction are decisions about *punishing*—so our inquiry must be into the rationale of punishment.

We need, first, a simple working definition of punishment. *Punishment (for our purposes) means the infliction by the state of consequences normally considered unpleasant, on a person in response to his having been convicted of a crime.* The definition of punishment ought not to be confused with its purposes. Is the measure unpleasant, and is it inflicted because of conviction for crime? If so, it qualifies as punishment regardless whether the purpose is to visit the offender with his deserts, deter him or others, incapacitate him from doing further harm, or provide him with treatment. The use of the old-fashioned word "punishment" should be a reminder of the painful nature of criminal sanctions, whatever their claimed objectives are.

In speaking of the rationale for punishment, we shall make use of a distinction . . . between (1) the *general justification*—that is, the reason or reasons why punishment should exist at all; and (2) the rationale for *allocation*—that is, for distributing penalties of different severities among convicted offenders. To develop an allocation theory we must first examine the general justification, for it is the logically prior question: we need some idea of what the criminal sanction is supposed to accomplish before we can decide how much punishment different offenders should receive.

SOURCE: Reprinted by permission of Hill and Wang, a division of Farrar, Straus and Giroux, Inc. "Why Punish?" is a slightly adapted version of "Why Punish at All?—The General Justification of Punishment" from DOING JUSTICE by Andrew von Hirsch. Copyright © 1976 by Andrew von Hirsch.

*Footnotes omitted.

GENERAL DETERRENCE

It seems almost a truism that criminals should be punished so there will be less crime. Why penalize murderers, speeders, and tax evaders, if not to deter killing, reckless driving, and tax fraud? This idea of general deterrence had prominence in the criminological literature of a century and a half ago . . . By the end of the nineteenth century, however, the idea had come into disfavor: as criminologists began attributing crime to offenders' background or biological makeup, they became convinced that criminal behavior could not be influenced by the threat of penalties. Yet, in recent years, largely under the influence of the Norwegian criminologist Johannes Andenaes, the question has been reopened; general deterrence, never forsaken by law-enforcement officials, is again a topic of interest to scholars.

By "general deterrence," we mean the effect that a threat to punish has, in inducing people to refrain from prohibited conduct. The warning that "speeders lose their licenses" is a deterrent if it causes some persons to obey the speed limits who otherwise might not have done so. The actual imposition of the punishment is a deterrent insofar as it makes the threat credible; in Oliver Wendell Holmes's words: "The law threatens certain pains if you do certain things. . . . If you persist in doing them, it has to inflict the pains in order that its threats may continue to be believed." Essential to an understanding of the concept are these features:

Even though a punishment does not alter the behavior of the particular individual who is penalized, it still is a general deterrent if the example of his punishment induces *other* persons to comply. This has been overlooked by some critics, who point to high recidivism rates among convicted offenders and assert that, since such persons have not been deterred, punishment has no general deterrent effect. But recidivism among convicted offenders shows only that they have not been deterred, and indicates nothing about the effect of their punishment on the rest of the population. In the absence of any punishment, a much larger number of persons—who now refrain—might have committed crimes. General deterrence, it should be emphasized, is measured not just by the recidivism rate but by the *overall* offense rate (including first offenses).

When it is asserted that a penalty is or is not a deterrent, one must ask: *Compared to what?* Consider the much debated question whether the death penalty "deters" murder. That question makes no sense unless one asks what the death penalty is being compared to. A number of studies have found that the death penalty yields no measurable reduction in homicide rates, when compared to sentences of prolonged imprisonment. These studies, if correct, support the conclusion that the death penalty is no *greater* deterrent than long-term confinement. But were penalties reduced drastically or eliminated altogether, an increase in the rate of homicide might well result. To that extent, penalizing murder has some deterrent effect. . . .

Most empirical studies of deterrence concern the effect on crime rates of varying the severity of penalties. The results have been mixed . . . with some studies showing that increases in severity have a modest effect, and others showing no effect at all. But even if the crime rate is not particularly sensitive to variations in severity of the penalty, a penalty still may deter better than none. . . .

Assuming that punishment has some deterrent effect, it should be apparent why deterrence helps justify the existence of the criminal sanction. By means of the criminal law, the state proscribes various kinds of injurious conduct. The conduct is prohibited so that people will refrain from it. But were the prohibition not backed by sanctions, violations might become commonplace. The threat and imposition of punishment is called for in order to secure compliance—not full compliance, but more compliance than there might be were there no legal penalties at all.

Does that mean that deterrence is a *sufficient* justification for the existence of punishment? We think not, for reasons we shall explore next.

DESERT

In everyday thinking about punishment, the idea of desert figures prominently. Ask the person on the street why a wrongdoer should be punished, and he is likely to say that he "deserves" it. Yet the literature of penology seldom mentions the word. Instead, there is usually listed—along with the three traditional utilitarian aims of deterrence, incapacitation, and rehabilitation—a fourth aim of "retribution." We do not find "retribution" a helpful term. It has no regular use except in relation to punishment, so that one is precluded from learning about the concept from the word's use in other contexts. It also seems somewhat narrow. The Oxford English Dictionary, for example, defines retribution as "recompense for, or requital of evil done; return of evil"; this suggests a particular view of why punishment is deserved, namely that the offender should somehow be "paid back" for his wrong. Yet, as we will see presently, there are other explanations of deserved punishment which do not rely on this notion of requital-of-evil. Finally, the word is, perhaps through historical accident, burdened with pejorative associations.

We prefer the term "desert." Its cognate, "to deserve," is widely used: rewards, prizes, and grades, as well as punishments, are said to be deserved or undeserved. And the word "desert" is somewhat less emotionally loaded.

To say someone "deserves" to be rewarded or punished is to refer to his *past* conduct, and assert that its merit or demerit is reason for according him pleasant or unpleasant treatment. The focus on the past is critical. That a student has written an outstanding paper is grounds for asserting that he deserves an award; but that the award will yield him or others future benefits (however desirable those might be) cannot be grounds for claiming he deserves it. The same holds for punishment: to assert that someone deserves to be punished is to look to his past wrongdoing as reason for having him penalized. This orientation to the past distinguishes desert from the other purported aims of punishment—deterrence, incapacitation, rehabilitation—which seek to justify the criminal sanction by its prospective usefulness in preventing crime. . . .

Punishment differs from other purposefully inflicted deprivations in the moral disapproval it expresses: punishing someone conveys in dramatic fashion that his conduct was wrong and that he is blameworthy for having committed it. Why, then, does the violator deserve to be *punished*, instead of being made to suffer another kind of deprivation that connotes no special moral stigma?

To answer this question it becomes necessary, we think, to focus specifically on the reprobation implicit in punishment and argue that *it* is deserved. Someone who infringes the rights of others, the argument runs, does wrong and deserves blame for his conduct. It is because he deserves blame that the sanctioning authority is entitled to choose a response that expresses moral disapproval: namely, punishment. In other words, the sanction ought not only to deprive the offender of the "advantage" obtained by his disregard of the rules . . . but do so in a manner that ascribes blame . . . This raises the question of what purpose the reprobation itself serves. Blaming persons who commit wrongful acts is, arguably, a way of reaffirming the moral values that were infringed. But to speak of reaffirming such values prompts the further question: Why should the violator be singled out for blame to achieve that end? The answers must ultimately be that the censure is itself deserved:

that someone who is responsible for wrongdoing is blame*worthy* and hence may justly be blamed.

With this much preliminary explanation of the idea of deserved punishment, we turn to the main question: whether desert is necessary to justify the criminal sanction.

FROM DETERRENCE TO DESERT.   We have already suggested one reason for punishing: deterrence. The criminal sanction is called for to prevent certain kinds of injurious conduct. Why is it not sufficient to rely on that simple argument—and get on with deciding how punishment should rationally be allocated? Why bring in desert, with all its philosophical perplexities?

On utilitarian assumptions, deterrence would indeed suffice. The main utilitarian premise is (roughly) that a society is rightly ordered if its major institutions are arranged to achieve the maximum aggregate satisfaction and the minimum aggregate suffering. On this premise, punishment would be justified if it deterred sufficiently—because, in sum, more suffering would be prevented through the resulting reduction in crime that is caused by making those punished suffer. Our difficulty is, however, that we doubt the utilitarian premise: that the suffering of a few persons is made good by the benefits accuring to the many. A free society, we believe, should recognize that an individual's rights—or at least his most important rights—are prima facie entitled to priority over collective interests.

Given this assumption of the primacy of the individual's fundamental rights, no utilitarian account of punishment, deterrence included, can stand alone. While deterrence explains why most people benefit from the existence of punishment, the benefit to the many is not by itself a just basis for depriving the offender of his liberty and reputation. Some other reason, then, is needed to explain the suffering inflicted on the offender: that reason is desert.

The offender may justly be subjected to certain deprivations because he deserves it; and he deserves it because he has engaged in wrongful conduct—conduct that does or threatens injury and that is prohibited by law. The penalty is thus not just a means of crime prevention but a merited response to the actor's deed, "rectifying the balance" . . . and expressing moral reprobation of the actor for the wrong. In other words: while deterrence accounts for why punishment is socially useful, desert is necessary to explain why that utility may justly be pursued at the offender's expense. . . .

THE CONVERSE: FROM DESERT TO DETERRENCE.   The route of argument just taken is the more familiar in current philosophical literature on punishment: begin with deterrence as a reason for punishing, then consider whether it must be supplemented by desert. However, the logic can be reversed: one can start by relying on the idea of desert. But again, the interdependence of the two concepts—desert and deterrence—will quickly become apparent.

Desert may be viewed as reason in itself for creating a social institution. This is evident in the case of rewards. Most societies, including our own, reward those who have done deeds of special merit. Rewards may serve utilitarian ends (e.g., as an incentive for desired conduct); but, even disregarding such utility, a case for rewarding merit can be made simply on the grounds that it is deserved. Good work and good acts ought to be acknowledged for their own sake, and rewards express that acknowledgment. A parallel argument might be made for punishment: those who violate others' rights deserve to be punished . . . A system of punishment is justified, the argument runs, simply because it is deserved.

However, there are countervailing moral considerations. An important counterconsideration is the principle of not deliberately causing human suffering where it can possibly be avoided. With rewards, this principle does not stand in the way: for rewards per se do not inflict pain (other than the possible discomforts of envy). It is otherwise with punishment: while wrongdoers deserve punishment, it is necessarily painful. Arguably, the principle against inflicting suffering should, in the absence of other considerations, override the case for punishing based on wrongdoers' deserts.

It is at this point in the argument that the idea of deterrence becomes critical—for it can supply an answer to the countervailing concern about the infliction of suffering. When punishment's deterrent effect is taken into account, it may cause less misery than not punishing would. Moreover, not only might total misery be reduced, but its distribution would be more acceptable: fewer innocent persons will be victimized by crimes, while those less deserving—the victimizers—will be made to suffer instead. Deterrence thus tips the scales back in favor of the penal sanction. To state the argument schematically:

Step 1. Those who violate others' rights deserve punishment. That, of itself, constitutes a prima facie justification for maintaining a system of criminal sanctions.

Step 2. There is, however, a countervailing moral obligation of not deliberately adding to the amount of human suffering. Punishment necessarily makes those punished suffer. In the absence of additional argument, that overrides the case for punishment in step 1.

Step 3. The notion of deterrence, at this point, suggests that punishment may prevent more misery than it inflicts—thus disposing of the countervailing argument in step 2. With it out of the way, the prima facie case for punishment described in step 1—based on desert—stands again.

The case for punishing differs, then, from the case for rewards. With rewards, it is sufficient to argue that they are deserved: since rewards are not painful, there is no need to point to their collateral social usefulness to excuse the misery they cause. Punishments, likewise, are deserved; but, given the overriding concern with the infliction of pain, the notion of deterrence has to be relied upon as well.

The foregoing shows the interdependence of the twin concepts of deterrence and desert. When one seeks to justify the criminal sanction by reference to its deterrent utility, deserts is called for to explain why that utility may justly be pursued at offender's expense. When one seeks to justify punishment as deserved, deterrence is needed to deal with the countervailing concern about the suffering inflicted. The interdependence of these two concepts suggests that the criminal sanction rests, ulimately, on *both*.

SUMMARY

The justifications for punishment are (1) that it will serve as a **deterrence** *to encourage people to refrain from some prohibited conduct. (the threat of punishment is a warning for those considering illegal acts, and the actual punishment of offenders makes the threat believable), and (2) to give offenders a punishment they* **deserve** *for past conduct. The ideas of deterrence and desert are interrelated and both are needed to justify punishment.*

QUESTIONS

1. When students are punished for cheating, should the purpose of punishment be to deter similar future behavior or to attach a deserved moral stigma?

2. Should punishment be primarily for deterrence or to reaffirm the moral values that have been violated?

3. Is it possible to use deterrence as the reason for punishing certain crimes, and desert as the reason for punishing others?

READING 7.2

The Presentation of Shortness in Everyday Life—Height and Heightism in American Society: Toward a Sociology of Stature·
Saul D. Feldman

Physical stature is a variable that has generally been ignored by social scientists. American society is a society with a heightist premise: to be tall is to be good and to be short is to be stigmatized. This paper will examine the heightist emphasis within American society as it is manifest in aspects of everyday life.

VOCABULARY

The rhetoric of the joys of being tall and the evils of being short are well demonstrated in our daily language. When we degrade people we "put them down" or "belittle" them. Even when we inquire about an individual's physical stature, we ask, "How tall are you?" The ideal man is viewed as *tall*, dark and handsome. Impractical people are "shortsighted," dishonest cashiers "short-change" customers, losers get the "short end of the stick," electrical failures are known as "short circuits," and individuals with little money, no matter their height will state of their impecuniousness, "I'm short." A few years ago, a well-known politician spoke at a midwest liberal arts college and referred to a former head of the Federal Bureau of Investigation as "that short little pervert in Washington." It is rare that one hears of tall perverts for in many respects, just to be short is to be a "pervert."

SOURCE: S. D. Feldman and G. W. Thielbar, eds., *Life Styles: Diversity in American Society*, second edition. Boston: Little, Brown and Co., 1975.

*Footnotes omitted.

MALE-FEMALE RELATIONSHIPS

Sociologists of the family have demonstrated that most marriages are homogamous with regard to race, ethnicity, religion, social class, age range of partners, etc., but most marriages are also homogamous by height. After similar ethnicity, age or social class, probably what most individuals seek in a mate is an individual of compatible height. For a woman, it means marrying an individual somewhat taller than she, and for a male it means being certain that he may be able to look down upon his mate. For many short males, courtship becomes problematic. Unlike taller males, they feel that their range of potential partners is a lot more limited and generally does not include females of even equal height. Problems are created as well for short females and a new variety of heightism may be fostered as illustrated by this statement from a short female at a midwestern state university.

I don't like going out with short guys. It's not that I have anything against them but I think they're only going out with me because of my height and nothing else. . . .

The relationship between height and mate selection is indicative of the status of women in our society. Males are supposed to be more dominant and to have more power than females, and one way that a man may express his dominance is by being taller than his mate. If the women's movement has an impact, it may be manifested in such aspects of everyday life as the comparative heights of couples. In the future, if no sex will dominate, then more and more couples should not be matched on height. Tall couples tend to have tall children, and short couples tend to have short children. If height does become more of a random factor in mate selection, children of future generations may become "average" in height—i.e., not particularly tall or short.

POLITICAL LIFE

Height has been an important aspect of the American political scene. Is it by chance that almost every American president elected since 1900 has been the taller of the two major candidates? It has been hypothesized that the more favorably disposed people are toward an incumbent of a political office, the taller they will think he is.

At another level, the American political ideology has been one of domination of shorter peoples and societies. The United States has attempted to express its dominance over shorter peoples in Vietnam, the Philippines, and in Latin America. It has however been unsuccessful in dominating taller peoples. Witness for example, its lack of success with tall African nations.

Within the United States there are height regulations concerning becoming duly authorized agents of political authority—namely policemen and firemen. In Washington D.C., for example, all policemen and firemen must be at least 5'7" while in Washington state policemen and firemen under 5'8" are ineligible for pension coverages. Height is viewed as the badge of authority and in fact from elementary school on, children are taught to "look up" to policemen and firemen. There is nothing inherent in the duties of either occupation that really requires their incumbents to be tall. . . .

ECONOMIC LIFE

The fact that the short man has been discriminated against is no more evident than in the business world. A survey of University of Pittsburgh business graduates found that tall men (six feet two inches and above) received a starting salary 12.4% higher than graduates of the same school who were under six feet. The Wall Street Journal reported on a study which demonstrated that shorter men may even have more difficulty in obtaining a job than taller men:

David Kurtz, an Eastern Michigan University marketing professor, asked 140 recruiters to make a hypothetical hiring choice between two equally qualified applicants—one six feet one inches tall and the other five-five, for a sales job. Seventy-two percent "hired" the tall one, 27% expressed no preference, and 1% chose the short one.

The short man who becomes successful in politics or business is often viewed as an anomaly. Thus, a review of a book on the life of Andrew Carnegie began, "When he rose up to his full majestic height, he was all of five feet three inches tall." It is so rare for a short male to become a success in the business world (or political life) that his success is coupled with his height. Assumption of political or economic power for a tall individual is considered admirable, but let an individual of less than average stature, such as Andrew Carnegie or Fiorello H. LaGuardia, assume power and he is viewed as having a Napoleon complex.

POPULAR CULTURE

Perhaps nowhere is America's obsession with height more evident than in the area of popular culture. Games such as basketball glorify height. Few baseball or football players are short. Boxing interest is not among flyweights or bantam weights but among taller middleweights and heavyweights. The one sport that is associated with short people is horse racing—the most popular spectator sport in America. In this sport, however, the short jockey is given second place to a horse, is bet upon by taller individuals, and despite the great popularity of horse racing, a jockey's face has never appeared on a bubblegum card. (Jockeys, unlike football, baseball, or basketball players, however, do appear across the nation as plaster lawn ornaments.)

In the movies the short actor is rarely the romantic lead. The average American cannot identify with the hero unless he rides "tall in the saddle." Thus, the short actor is reduced to playing the buffoon (e.g., Mickey Rooney), the arch-villain (e.g., Peter Lorre), or the small tough guy with the big Napoleon complex (e.g., Edward G. Robinson).

CONCLUSION: HEIGHT AND DEGRADATION OF THE SELF

An article in a major metropolitan newspaper dealt with revitalizing urban centers throughout the United States. The article stated in part:

In Chicago, pudgy little Mayor Daley has been so concerned by the industrial exodus, he has taken the political stump to get a new airport near the city line to get firms that want to have easy access to air travel.

In an attempt to discredit Richard Daley and his program, comment in this article was directed not toward his politics but toward his physical stature. The media cannot make adverse comments about a person's race, religion, sex, or ethnicity but they can make adverse remarks about their height. Thus one newspaper referred to Lt. William Calley, commander at the My Lai massacre, as a "stubby little former platoon commander" while another paper called George Wallace a "bumptious little governor."

People do react strongly to an individual's height and make invidious distinctions on this basis. In a social psychological experiment, five groups of students were asked to judge the height of the same individual. In each of the five groups, he was introduced as having a different academic rank. The higher the academic status attributed to this person, the taller the student subjects thought he was. Status and height were highly correlated. . . .

Since height and lack of it, is such a visible variable, it is surprising that sociologists have not dealt with it to this point. In a society directed toward overabundance and glorification of anything above average, individuals of less than average height are almost universally known as "Shorty," short adults purchase much of their clothing in children's departments, and in short, are stigmatized. Stigmatization did not begin as an adult. As short children they were often lined up in elementary classrooms according to height. As teenagers, they learned the courtship problems of short people. As adults, discreditization of their stature became magnified in economic and political life, in popular culture, and in other aspects of daily life.

Shortness may be a virtue in academic papers, but as we have pointed out, to be of less than average height in American society is to fall short of the mark in almost all aspects of everyday life.

SUMMARY

To be short in a society that values tallness is to be stigmatized. Our language, male-female relationships, political and economic life, and our popular culture demonstrate the deviant nature of shortness. This article illustrates that the deviant label can be affixed to any segment of society and not only those who exhibit offensive behavior. Short people have violated identity norms that define desirable attributes. As Goffman (1963:128) has pointed out, any male in America who is not "a young, married, white, urban, northern, heterosexual Protestant father of college education, fully employed, of good complexion, weight, and height, and a recent record in sports" is likely to view himself at one time or another "as unworthy, incomplete, and inferior."

QUESTIONS

1. What are some of the behavior norms and identity norms on your campus? What is the source of such norms and how are they maintained?
2. Who benefits from the existence of these norms?

212

PART III

Structures of Inequality: Bases of Conflict

In South Africa, the black majority is economically and politically oppressed by the white minority who control the government and the economy. In Northern Ireland, Catholics do not have the same opportunities for jobs and housing as do Protestants. In the United States, unskilled workers have limited incomes and are thereby denied access to health care, decent housing, job security, and a quality education. In every part of the world some segment of a society is oppressed, exploited, or mistreated by some other segment. Social inequality is a structured, systematic part of a society and can be traced to its economic system, its history of conquest or immigration, or its political system.

Inequality can be an effective way of controlling some groups in a society, but it cannot last forever. Eventually, an oppressed people learn to strike back at oppressors and they try to change the conditions under which they live—sometimes peacefully, sometimes violently.

CHAPTER 8

Social Stratification

CONTENTS

Is America the land of opportunity?

Sociologists disagree about how easy it is for children with talent and ambition to achieve a high position in American society. Some emphasize the achievement of the "American Dream," where any child, regardless of social origins has the opportunity to rise in the social scale, and point to the absence of legal barriers to upward social mobility. However, others note that equality of opportunity may exist in the law but not in social fact. Children born to families of modest means have little or no chance to improve their circumstances in life despite their motivation and talents.

YES The United States is unusual among advanced industrial societies in not having an aristocratic tradition. England, France, Italy, Germany, and Japan were all, at one time, societies with rigid class barriers in which an individual's status was determined by his or her social position at birth. Such traditions do not die easily, and they continue to influence the opportunities available to people of modest social origins in these countries.

In the American revolutionary tradition equality of opportunity has been a central goal of our society. All children, regardless of their social position at birth, have the chance to rise as high as their ability and motivation will carry them.

Of course, some problems still remain. Black Americans, Spanish-speaking Americans, women, and other minorities may still not have attained complete educational and occupational equality. However, this is not due to built-in, artificial barriers, but because these groups are relatively new members of the urban occupational structure, as were immigrant groups before them. Indeed, the educational and occupational gains of young black men and women, compared with those of their parents, have been substantial in the last quarter century. Similar gains will undoubtedly be made by other groups who have recently entered the labor force.

Slowdowns in economic growth may produce temporary setbacks to the realization of the American Dream. It may become more difficult for a young person to get the money to go to college or to get the kind of job she or he desires after college. But these temporary problems cannot alter the fact that the United States remains a country that is committed to the ideal of equality of opportunity. Ability and hard work will eventually prevail over the accident of birth.

NO There is great inequality of wealth and power in American society. This inequality is permitted and justified by the belief that the opportunity to become rich is open to every American and therefore those who do not succeed are incapable or lazy. Thus "equality of opportunity" is an ideology that conveniently allows the rich and powerful to hold on to what they have and pass it on to their nondeserving children.

The central feature of American society is not equality of opportunity but corporate capitalism. The main features of American institutions are dominated by the one percent of the population that own and run the nation's largest industrial and financial corporations. They also control the mass media, give financial support to elite colleges and universities, and dominate the major professions. Because of their financial resources they are able to play a major role in national politics by supporting candidates and legislation that will advance their interests.

When there is an expansion of educational or occupational opportunities, it occurs precisely because it is in the best interests of corporate America. For example, when the U.S. government, whose interests often match those of corporations, realized that more scientists and engineers were needed to compete with the Russians in space technology, it expanded programs of support for science education in high schools, financial aid for college students, and research fellowships for advanced degree work. In all these efforts equality of opportunity was a goal, for business and government wanted the most talented people that could be found.

Most social science research indicates that children do tend to rise above their parents' station in

life—but they do not move very far. Children of farmers become factory workers; children of skilled blue-collar workers become white-collar clerks; and children of clerical workers become schoolteachers. While all this "upward" social mobility is taking place, the upper one percent of Americans continue to transmit their wealth and power from generation to generation without experiencing any mobility at all.

To answer the question "Is America the land of opportunity?" it is necessary to understand something about inequality in society and how inequality

influences the lives of people with different amounts of wealth, power, and prestige. In this chapter we first examine the two major forms of stratification found in contemporary societies—caste systems and class systems. We then focus on class inequality in the United States and consider the structural-functional and conflict views of why class inequality exists. The consequences of class position for people's ideas and behavior are considered next. The different consequences experienced by rich and poor people are related to their chances for enjoying the good things that a society has to offer, which is often called social mobility.

QUESTIONS TO CONSIDER

- Is there stratification in all societies?
- Can any person with ability and ambition "make it"?
- How do social classes differ?
- Is social mobility increasing or decreasing?
- What are the consequences of class?

In 1955, Dudley Gardiner, a retired English major in the Indian army decided to devote his energies to feeding the poor people of Calcutta. Every day since that time he distributed milk, macaroni, and curry to 5800 of the poorest "pavement people" of Calcutta, who literally live on the streets. They are without money or hope.

Gardiner expressed his views on his work and experiences to Christopher Mullin (1973):

"I don't know what will happen to India in the end. There is always talk about a revolution, but Hindus will only riot about politics or religion, not poverty. Maybe if you took all the children and gave them some kind of elementary education, they would revolt against their condition. Children here are abnormally bright. They have to be to survive on the pavement."

We were parted by a high wall, and in the darkness it was just possible to make out the figures of pavement people and their little bundle of possessions squatting along the base.

"Behind there," said the major, "lives a very rich businessman. Every day when he drives out in his Impala, he throws coins to the poor people who live on the pavement outside his wall.

"He despises them for their poverty, but the men on the pavement who receive the coins say that he is a good man. The pavement man does not envy the businessman or want to loot his big house. He believes he is poor because he has done something wrong, and when he puts it right, he believes he will be rich like the businessman. That is why there will be no revolution in India." (p. 57).

This brief description of life in Calcutta illustrates many of the central characteristics of a system of social stratification. It also contains a number of very good guesses (hypotheses) about what kinds of things lead to changes in a system of stratification.

First, the statement recognizes the existence of a *material* aspect of stratification. There are rich people and poor people because of the way that the objective factors of income and wealth are distributed in a given society. Other objective factors by which people in a society could be stratified are color, religion, and ethnicity.

The second element to note is the *beliefs* that people develop about a system of stratification; that is, people who are different according to objective factors also develop a shared set of beliefs that tries to explain their favorable or unfavorable standing. For example, we learned that the pavement people (the poor) do not blame the businessman (the rich) for their plight but blame themselves for their poverty. We see, then, that people's collective reactions to their material conditions of existence determine the extent to which the stratification system is seen as "just," "fair," or "legitimate." If people do not view the system as just, they will become dissatisfied, discontented, and angry and may then make efforts to change the system.

In addition to identifying the material (income) and cultural (beliefs) aspects of stratification, Gardiner's description of life in Calcutta also contains a number of sociological hypotheses that are stated in everyday language. For example, when Major Gardiner commented that the pavement children are abnormally bright, he seemed to be suggesting two things: (1) that the reason why the children of the poor remain poor has little or nothing to do with their intellectual capacities and (2) that whatever differences there are between the rich and the poor, they do not differ in their intellectual capacities. These suggestions form the basis for a general question that has engaged the attention of sociologists for some time; namely, what is the role of inherited characteristics, compared with environmental factors, in determining a person's position in a stratification system?

Major Gardiner also speculates about when people will become sufficiently dissatisfied to want to change a society's stratification system. The major suggests that Hindus will never revolt against poverty, but, if they had "some kind of elementary education, they would revolt against their condition." The major's hypothesis about the effects of a little education is one answer to a long-standing sociological question: What conditions must exist before people will engage in collective action to change an existing system of inequality? Some believe it is the condition of *extreme* poverty that drives people to revolt. Others, as does Major Gardiner, believe revolution takes place when people experience some improvement in one area of their life but not enough to change all of it. Therefore, giving the poor "some kind of elementary education" might only result in raising their aspirations while not being able to satisfy them.

NATURE AND TYPES OF SOCIAL STRATIFICATION

We have indicated the way in which observations of social life made in everyday language raise the same questions that have concerned sociologists for some time. We turn now to these questions and to the nature of social stratification itself.

Social Differentiation and Social Rank

All human societies are characterized by an inequality in the distribution of scarce, socially valued things, such as power, wealth, and prestige. This inequality is not the same as social stratification but is a necessary condition for it.

Consider the hypothetical case of a relatively small hunting-and-gathering society operating at a subsistence level. The environment is harsh, leaving only a small surplus of goods after the basic needs of all its members are met. The activities people must engage in for survival are assigned according to an age-sex division of labor. Men hunt, women gather, young people assist the women in gather-

ing, and old people take care of the children and help prepare the food. This particular society is characterized in its early stage by a simple form of **social differentiation** in which positions are allocated on the basis of age and sex and are not differentially rewarded with power, wealth, and prestige.

Now let us assume that several of the hunters in this hypothetical society develop their natural talent in the use of weapons and this results in their being more successful in the hunt. Given the importance of food for survival, the hunters with special talent would likely receive special recognition. First, they would probably assume positions of authority with respect to hunting and possibly other activities. In other words, they would achieve power. Second, they might receive special recognition and honors for their special talent from other members of the society. This would result in greater personal prestige. Third, they probably would be able to claim a larger share of the results of the hunt, or of any surplus that the society has accumulated. This would result in greater wealth.

Our hunting-and-gathering society began with a simple social differentiation of equivalent positions, but because of individual differences in native talent, the social rewards of the society are no longer equally distributed. What we have now is *personal inequality,* as the rewards go to particular individuals with particular talents. These rewards will be bestowed only as long as the talented hunters live or as long as they maintain their skills. Their rewards cannot be used to give their offspring a special advantage, although the offspring undoubtedly will enjoy the rewards received by their parents.

What we have in our hypothetical society so far is social differentiation and personal inequality but *not* social stratification. Before we can have a system of stratification rewards must be associated with positions, producing *social ranks.* Assume that instead of there being only a few hunters with exceptional talents, many hunters can learn the skills needed in hunting, like knowing the habits of animals, how to make hunting weapons, and how to organize the hunt. The possibility now exists that in the next generation many people with minimum native abilities may aspire to become hunters by learning the technology of hunting; they will aspire to fill the *position* of hunter because of the special rewards that go to hunters.

The question of how one becomes a hunter suddenly assumes great importance. Since it is no longer simply a matter of exceptional native ability, the selection and training of new hunters becomes a new activity to be undertaken by established hunters. At this point we have laid the basis for the development of vested interests on the part of established hunters. For one thing, they might try to maintain the importance of the position of hunter in the society by, for example, restricting the number of individuals allowed to become hunters. This action would increase, or at least maintain, the present level of dependence of the total society on the hunters' special knowledge. The hunters might also oppose any new developments in hunting technology that might reduce their hunting monopoly. This could be achieved by having the existing hunting technology sanctified by sacred authority or maintained by secular authority.

Another practice hunters might engage in to maintain their control over hunting would be to transmit their advantages as hunters to others of their choice, more often than not to their own children. Through law or tradition the sons of hunters might be favored in the selection and training of new hunters. In addition, hunters would be able to transmit advantage to their sons by using their rewards to pay for their sons' special training. This would give the sons a better chance of becoming hunters, which is similar to the offspring of wealthy families in modern societies who attend prestigious schools that gives them a special advantage in their own careers.

In summary, we can say that all societies are characterized by social differentiation, which is the division of activities engaged in by a society. Differentiation, which is nonhierarchical in nature, often leads to inequality in the distribution of social rewards. Inequality may occur because certain people have skills that are of special importance to a society. These rewards are temporary

and go to particular persons, which is described as personal inequality. Rewards may also be attached to positions, which results in a system of social ranks.

Social Stratification: Caste and Class Systems

When unequal social rewards are allocated to positions rather than to persons, we find the occupants of privileged positions acting to maintain them and to provide their offspring with special advantages in competing for positions that are similarly privileged. Thus we arrive at the following definition:

Social stratification exists when there is a hierarchy of positions with differences in wealth, power, and prestige, and when there is intergenerational transmission of advantage or disadvantage stemming from one's location in the hierarchy. The two major types of social stratification in modern societies are the caste system and the class system.

THE CASTE SYSTEM

The caste system is the most rigid form of social stratification, most often associated with the country of India. A **caste system** is made up of religiously sanctioned and hierarchically ranked groupings in which membership is fixed at birth and is permanent. An individual may not change his or her caste in the course of a lifetime; there is no social mobility.

Hindu India is composed of five major hierarchically ranked social groupings. These include four major castes and a fifth category of people who are without caste affiliation, referred to as untouchables or outcastes. The four castes, in rank order, are first the Brahmans, composed of a literate class of priests, teachers, and philosophers; then the warriors, military leaders, and large landholders; then artisans and merchants; and finally the laborers (Barber, 1957; Gould, 1971). Within each major caste are a very large number of subcastes, which are basically occupational categories.

The caste system is characterized by a series of religiously based rules governing one's occupation,

The caste system placed people into
rigid categories from which they
could not escape. Those at the top
must avoid contact with those
below them, especially the
outcastes. Those in the lowest
castes are often without
possessions, opportunities, or hope
for an improvement in their lives.
Here we see a beggar on a Calcutta
street trying to get the resources
needed for survival.

clothing, food habits, and patterns of association with individuals from other castes. These rules result in caste differences in such social rewards as wealth, power, and prestige. In addition, castes are culturally distinct groups that prescribe a whole series of relationships, from who may eat with whom to who may marry.

The traditional caste system in India is changing. Following Indian independence after World War II, castes were legally abolished. However, there remains a de facto caste system which is resistant to change. The impact of industrialization, modern communications, transportation, and education have put great stress upon the caste system because rigid caste hierarchies are poorly suited for an industrializing society.

Although caste systems are associated with old societies such as India, some features of a caste system are also found in newer ones. For example, South Africa has a system of rigid racial segregation (apartheid) where a small white minority dominates a black majority in all areas of social, economic, and political life. Relations between blacks and whites in the United States also have many castelike features.

THE CLASS SYSTEM

A **social class system** is composed of economic groups that are based upon similarities in occupation, income, and wealth. In contrast to castes, a class system is not founded in law or on religion. Legal restrictions on individual mobility or intermarriage between members of different social classes do not exist. A class system, therefore, is more open than a caste system.

In a class system, social position at birth is held to be temporary and "accidental." The system provides avenues of opportunity for the individual that can lead to positions with different rewards. All people are encouraged to believe that they have an equal chance to use these avenues to future positions by means of their natural talents, acquired abilities, and willingness to work hard.

The most frequently used indicators of class position in industrialized societies are a person's occupation, education, amount of income, and source of income (wages, interest and dividends, rents, fees,

and so on). The best single indicator, however, is occupation (Gilbert and Kahl, 1981). Knowledge of a person's occupation tells one something about his or her education, income, whether the work is physically hard or dirty, whether the work is secure, whether the person is in a dominant or subordinate position, and the degree of social prestige associated with the occupation.

Class Inequality

All social class systems are characterized by inequality in income and wealth among different classes. The extent of inequality, however, can vary, with some societies having wide income differences while others have smaller differences.

There are two frequently used measures of class inequality. First is the proportion of a society's population that is living in poverty. **Poverty** is a condition of living below an income level that provides minimum satisfaction of material needs. In the United States, the Social Security Administration computes the cost of a minimum standard of living, which includes food, rent, clothing, and other essentials. This figure is the official poverty line. Although the poverty line may be adjusted upward to reflect inflation, many people feel that the poverty line is unrealistically low and underestimates the cost of needed goods and services. An improvement or a deterioration of economic conditions may change the number of poor people below the poverty line.

The second measure of class inequality is the *income share* that goes to different segments of a society. A useful measure of inequality in income share is the percentage of total income earned by all Americans that goes to the poorest one-fifth of the population, the richest one-fifth, and the middle one-fifth. This method permits us to see if the share of income going to different segments has increased, decreased, or remained the same over a period of time.

Tables 8.1 and 8.2 present information on the two forms of inequality just described. Table 8.1 reports the percentage and number of persons that were below the poverty line in the United States between 1959 and 1980. It can be seen that the

TABLE 8.1   Persons below poverty level: 1959–1980

YEAR	NUMBER (MILLIONS)	PERCENTAGE OF TOTAL POPULATION
1959	39.5	22.4
1960	39.9	22.2
1965	33.2	17.3
1967	27.8	14.2
1968	25.4	12.8
1969	24.1	12.1
1970	25.4	12.6
1971	25.6	12.5
1972	24.5	11.9
1973	23.0	11.1
1974	24.3	11.6
1974	23.4	11.2
1975	25.9	12.3
1976	25.0	11.8
1977	24.7	11.6
1980	29.3	13.3

SOURCE: U.S. Bureau of the Census, *Statistical Abstract of the United States: 1977*, Washington, D.C., Current Population Reports, P-60, No. 131: p. 4.

percentage of poor people dropped sharply between 1959 and 1968. This was due to the federal government's "war on poverty," which provided a combination of direct income and assistance (such as food stamps and public housing) sufficient to bring millions of Americans above the poverty line. Since that time, however, the number of persons living in poverty has not changed very much.

In Table 8.2 we see the percentage of total income that goes to each one-fifth of American families and to the highest 5 percent from 1950 to 1979.

These percentages have changed relatively little in the last 30 years. The highest one-fifth of families continues to receive just about 44 percent of total income, while the lowest one-fifth receives about 4 percent.

No matter what the absolute level of income attained by the lowest one-fifth of families, their income share relative to that of the top fifth could remain the same. They may not be facing starvation or be without housing, but they will not be full members of a society able to enjoy its many benefits. Thus it is possible to reduce the level of absolute poverty (the proportion of people living below an official poverty level) without reducing the degree of relative poverty (the share of income going to different segments of society).

The degree of income inequality between the poorest and richest fifths of population varies for countries in different regions of the world. Table 8.3 reports the percentage of gross national product received by the richest and poorest fifths of the populations of these regions. The income gap is obviously much greater in some regions of the world than in others. It is much less in Eastern European countries than in Africa or Latin America, although it is clear that income inequality is universal.

In addition to the inequality that exists within countries, as measured by poverty and income share, there is also considerable inequality between nations. Dramatic differences exist between industrialized countries in the "developed" Northern Hemisphere and those of the "developing" South.

TABLE 8.2   Percentage of aggregate income received by each one-fifth and highest 5 percent of families and unrelated individuals: 1950–1979

FAMILIES, BY INCOME RANK	1950	1955	1960	1965	1970	1975	1979
All families	100%	100%	100%	100%	100%	100%	100%
Lowest one-fifth	3.1	3.3	3.2	3.6	3.6	3.9	3.8
Second one-fifth	10.6	10.6	10.6	10.6	10.3	9.9	9.7
Middle one-fifth	17.3	17.6	17.6	17.5	17.2	16.9	16.4
Fourth one-fifth	24.1	24.6	24.7	24.8	24.7	24.9	24.8
Highest one-fifth	44.9	43.9	44.0	43.6	44.1	44.5	45.3
Highest 5 percent	18.2	17.5	17.0	16.6	16.9	17.0	17.4

SOURCE: U.S. Bureau of the Census, Current Population Reports, Series P-60, 1980, No. 129, p. 54.

TABLE 8.3   Income Distribution by Region: Percentage of GNP in Poorest and Richest Fifth of Population (1979)

	EAST EUROPE	FAR EAST & OCEANIA	NORTH AMERICA	WESTERN EUROPE	SOUTH AMERICA	MIDDLE EAST	AFRICA	LATIN AMERICA
Poorest Fifth	10	9	3	5	3	3	2	2
Richest Fifth	32	41	42	45	50	52	58	61

SOURCE: Ruth Leger Sivard, *World Military and Social Expenditures*, 1979 (Leesburg, Va.: World Priorities, 1979). Adapted from Chart 16.

Table 8.4 presents information on differences in **life chances** between these two groups. People's life chances, determined by their income and wealth, refers to opportunities throughout the life cycle. The data in Table 8.4 clearly indicate that children born in developed or developing nations differ sharply in their chances of being alive at birth, having access to a physician, enjoying good health care, having safe water to drink, having adequate food, being able to read and write, and living a long life. These differences, reported for 1976, were reported as increasing when last examined in 1978 (Sivard, 1980). Clearly, class inequality reflects a wide gap between the rich and poor both within and between countries.

THEORIES OF SOCIAL CLASS

Though the concept of social class has been crucial to sociological thought, sociologists have defined and measured the concept in different ways. This section examines the treatments of social class by Marx, Weber, and some contemporary thinkers.

The Development of the Concept of Class: Marx

The first modern attempt to delineate the meaning of class was made by Karl Marx (1818–1883). He believed that economic relationships were the basis of social and political life. Marx defined class

TABLE 8.4   The Development Gap, 1976

	DEVELOPED NATIONS	DEVELOPING NATIONS
Annual income per capita	$5,191	$479
Annual government health expenditures per capita	$ 209	7
Life expectancy	72 years	57 years
Infant mortality rate[a]	19	111
Physicians per 10,000 population	21	3
Daily calories per capita	3388	2320
Percentage of population with safe water	93%	39%
Adult literacy	98%	55%

[a]Number of deaths per 1000 children one year of age or less.

SOURCE: Ruth Leger Sivard, *World Military and Social Expenditures*, 1979 (Leesburg, Va.: World Priorities, 1979).

as a group of people who hold the same position in relation to the means of production. He argued that there were two basic positions in capitalist society: owner and worker, or bourgeoisie and proletariat (Anderson, 1974).

Owners control the factories, the raw materials, and the machines, and thus are able to dominate the economic institutions and live off the labor of others. Workers, on the other hand, are without capital and have only their labor to sell. These observations led Marx to conclude that owners would always seek to increase their profits at the expense of workers until the workers were impoverished. Within this context, Marx predicted that a powerful sense of **class consciousness** would develop over a period of time. Class consciousness refers to an awareness of one's position in the process of production and of one's class interests. It also includes awareness of the political and social consequences of one's position in the productive enterprise. When Marx wrote of a false class consciousness, he was referring to the failure of workers to act and think in terms of their own best interests. Thus any worker who supported the owners in political matters had a false class consciousness.

According to Marx, a **social class** was a collection of persons with the same relation to the means of production, with an awareness of their common interests and a willingness to engage in political action to advance their interests. The position people occupied in the productive enterprise—whether owner or worker—was the primary factor in shaping their lives. The basis of existence was economic, and it determined all other aspects of life, including political, social, and familial institutions.

Class, Status, and Party: Weber

The German sociologist Max Weber (1864–1920) did not agree with Marx's idea that a person's economic position, or class, determined all other aspects of life. Weber viewed stratification in three dimensions instead of one: in addition to class, there were the political and status dimensions, which were relatively independent of the economic order. A **status group** is a group of people with a similar life style and a strong sense of group identity. The position of a status group in society may not necessarily correspond to their class position. For example, persons involved in activities like gambling or crime may have great wealth but would still be considered to have low status. On the other hand, a formerly wealthy family may still have high status while having little wealth.

Party refers to a collection of people with common interests who accrue political power to advance these interests. The political dimension of stratification may also be inconsistent with the dimensions of status and economic class. A powerful big-city mayor, such as the late Mayor Richard Daley of Chicago, usually has more power than status or wealth.

To Weber, social stratification is not only multidimensional, consisting of wealth, prestige, and political power, but these dimensions are unequal. Since all powerful people are not always rich and all rich people are not always honored, it is obvious that one factor alone is inadequate as an explanation of class and status in modern society. Class, or economic position; status, or prestige and honor; and party, or political power are all features of the system of stratification in a society. Nevertheless, there is a tendency for the three dimensions to be consistent because they influence each other. Money can sometimes buy status, or power can sometimes be used to get money.

The Concept of Class in Modern Societies

Weber's concepts have been influential in research on stratification, particularly the development of a measure of socioeconomic status, or **SES**, which is based on a person's income, wealth, education, and occupation. Marx's concepts have generated a separate research tradition that emphasizes differences between ownership classes and working classes. As a result, there are different ways to look at class inequality, and they involve such basic issues as the inevitability of stratification, the character of classes, the distribution of power, and the degree of consensus found among people about class inequality. Some of the differences on these issues are reflected in the structural-functional and conflict views of stratification.

THE STRUCTURAL-FUNCTIONAL VIEW

The structural-functionalists argue that stratification is both universal and necessary for societies. The argument rests on two assumptions. First, some positions in society are more important than others. They must therefore carry sufficient rewards so that people will want to fill them. Second, some positions require more extensive training and skill than others. Therefore, people who fill these positions must be compensated for their long and difficult period of training (Davis and Moore, 1945). In short, the greatest rewards will accrue to those people who are in positions that are most important to society as a whole and who are the best equipped to fill those positions. Thus doctors must be more highly rewarded than clerks, because the position of the former group is more important to the society as a whole and there is a scarcity of people with the talent and training to become doctors.

Support for the structural-functional view can be found in studies of how people rate the prestige of occupations. In 1947 the National Opinion Research Center interviewed a national sample of Americans to obtain their views on the relative prestige of 90 occupations. Based on ratings of each occupation's "social standing," a prestige score (ranging from 0 to 100) was assigned to each. Ranked number one with a score of 96 was U.S. Supreme Court justice, followed by physician and state governor in ranks two and three. At the other extreme, with ranks of 88, 89, and 90, were garbage collector, street sweeper, and shoe shiner. Examples of occupations in the middle of the rankings include public schoolteacher and electrician.

This study was repeated nearly two decades later with nearly identical results (Hodge et al., 1964). Similar studies were carried out in other industrialized countries and the results compared with those obtained in the United States (Hodge, Treiman and Rossi, 1966; Inkeles and Rossi, 1956; Trei-

man, 1977). The conclusion of all this research is that occupations have been given similar prestige ratings by people at different times and in different parts of the world. Structural-functional theorists have used these findings as evidence that some occupations are more important than others in all societies and that people agree on the occupations that should receive the greatest rewards. The fact that people in different industrialized countries rate occupations the same way is also seen as evidence that these societies are guided by a common value system that binds its members together.

THE CONFLICT VIEW

The conflict view emphasizes the way that the existence of structured inequality can perpetuate privilege among certain groups. Inequality is maintained by the use of force and deceit by privileged groups. There is not a natural tendency toward consensus among all members of society, but rather fundamental disagreement about basic values and goals; stability is maintained through coercion by the dominant group.

Conflict theorists would view the studies of occupational prestige discussed earlier as evidence that dominant groups perpetuate inequality. Occupations like scientist, educator, engineer, or technician are accorded high prestige, income, or power because such occupations serve the interests of groups in society that benefit from a high-technology industrialized society, not because a common value system defines these occupations as the most important for the society and therefore deserving of the highest rewards.

Suppose, for example, that Americans adopted Schumacher's (1973) "small is beautiful" philosophy and began to dismantle large technology-based enterprises in favor of small-scale technology ones that emphasize human over machine labor and are local in scope (such as community-based electrification systems using water power rather than oil, gas or nuclear power). In such a society, scientists, engineers, or managers, while still important, would not have as much income or power because their rewards would be in the form of social honor and pride in their work.

Where and how a family lives is a
consequence of their available
economic resources and the values
that determine how those resources
are used. The dwelling unit is both
a symbol of a family's position in
the socioeconomic structure and a
determinant of their access to such
public services as fire and police
protection, sanitation, and
recreation.

The same argument could be advanced about the power, income, and privilege of doctors in American society. Suppose, for example, that greater stress was placed on preventive medicine compared with exotic medical and surgical technology. Midwives, nurses, and paramedical teams would become much more important relative to physicians and surgeons as community clinic care replaced high-cost hospital stays, CAT scanners, and heart transplants.

Conflict theorists have decided views about how society should be ordered. They point out that when a society invests in complex technology rather than in workers or allows its medical system to stress technology over primary health care, those decisions are made by only a small segment of the population that will directly benefit. Citizens are not able to choose between having a different standard of living to secure the benefits of full employment or to give up advances in heart transplants in order to have better access to routine medical care.

EVALUATION OF THE TWO VIEWS

The differences between the functionalist and conflict views of stratification are substantial. They reflect two different models of inequality and theories about why it exists. A summary of these differences is presented in Table 8.5.

Both the functional and conflict views of stratification are partially valid statements about social inequality. Functionalism does a good job of accounting for why there are inequalities of income, power, and prestige associated with different occupational positions. As we noted, if a society has great need for persons to fill military, or religious, or scientific roles, because such roles are important for survival, (for example, the need for military leaders in wartime), then some way must be found to attract people to fill such positions. That way is to provide exceptional rewards.

What the functionalist view cannot help us see, however, is how persons who are in highly rewarded positions act in ways to perpetuate those rewards even when the positions are no longer as important as they once were (such as when the war is over). Also functionalist theory explains why doctors are so highly rewarded but not why doctors perpetuate those rewards by controlling the supply of new physicians or by monopolizing medical services that could be provided by others.

Conflict theory, on the other hand, explains how different segments of a society compete for scarce resources through attempts at domination and control. It also shows how power and coercion are the forces that produce a high degree of stability

TABLE 8.5   Differences Between Two Views of Stratification

THE FUNCTIONAL VIEW	THE CONFLICT VIEW
1. Stratification is universal, necessary, and inevitable.	1. Stratification may be universal without being necessary or inevitable.
2. Social organization (the social system) shapes the stratification system.	2. The stratification system shapes social organization (the social system).
3. Stratification arises from the societal need for integration, coordination, and cohesion.	3. Stratification arises from group conquest, competition, and conflict.
4. Stratification facilitates the optimal functioning of society and the individual.	4. Stratification impedes the optimal functioning of society and the individual.
5. Stratification is an expression of commonly shared social values.	5. Stratification is an expression of the values of powerful groups.
6. Power is usually legitimately distributed in society.	6. Power is usually illegitimately distributed in society.
7. Tasks and rewards are equitably allocated.	7. Tasks and rewards are inequitably allocated.
8. The economic dimension is subordinate to other dimensions of society.	8. The economic dimension is paramount in society.
9. Stratification systems generally change through evolutionary processes.	9. Stratification systems generally change through revolutionary processes.

SOURCE: Roach, Gross and Gursslin, editors, *Social Stratification in the United States.* (Englewood Cliffs, N.J.: Prentice-Hall, Inc., 1969), p. 55.

and order in society. Conflict theory assumes a society with a class structure of two antagonistic groups—owners versus workers, propertied versus propertyless, positions of domination versus positions of subordination. In reality, however, there are other, often overlapping classes in between the major antagonistic classes. These classes may be made up of individuals who are owners and workers (such as small farmers), or wage earners who are also owners of the means of production (like workers who own corporate stock), or people who occupy positions of domination and subordination at the same time (for example, a production supervisor in the factory who has a boss). All of these intermediary groups serve to minimize the possibility of sharp class divisions that could result in conflict and revolutionary change.

CONSEQUENCES OF SOCIAL CLASS

We now turn our attention to the consequences of social class. The central question is this: Do people in the same class have similar life chances and life style and do these differ from the life chances and life styles of other classes? We are especially interested in those values and behaviors that help to maintain or change the class structure. Change in a class structure can occur when there is an increase in the chances for individual upward mobility for people in lower classes. Change can also occur when shared beliefs and political ideologies lead to collective action for altering the way in which social rewards are distributed.

Figure 8.1 illustrates the different consequences of social class for life chances and life style. Let us review the figure carefully, because it contains a restatement of the nature of social class as well as a summary of the way in which social class membership shapes selected values and life styles.

The primary dimension of social class is occupation and the income yielded by it. People in certain occupations, such as upper- and middle-level corporate management, professionals, and small business proprietors, will actively participate in local and national decision making to protect their economic interests. At the local level, these interests may be affected by decisions about taxes, land development, or zoning regulations. Sometimes the formal definition of occupations, particularly in large

FIGURE 8.1 Social Class
Membership and Its Consequences

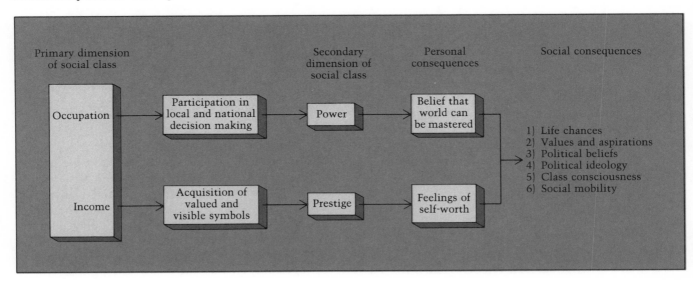

corporations, may include involvement in the political process. The average worker, on the other hand, who also has an interest in such decisions, must pursue it on his or her own time and not as part of the work role. This fact is a significant impediment to participation of blue-collar workers in civic and social affairs.

Figure 8.1 shows that the income of an occupation allows a person to obtain valued goods like an expensive car, stylish clothing, foreign travel, a quality education, and the like. These are visible symbols of success, and it is their visibility and the knowledge that they are obtained because of the income yield of an occupation that results in the high prestige accorded to certain occupations and not to others.

People in families in which the members are active in public decision-making activities are likely to develop a belief that the world external to the family is a place that can be mastered, controlled, or brought "into line" with one's personal desires. Such a feeling of personal control can have important consequences for the way in which a young person's life develops. In the same way, living in a family that enjoys prestige in a community will probably increase the feelings of self-worth of its members. Conversely, a study by Rosenberg and Pearlin (1978) found that respondents with less education, lower occupations, and lower income had lower self-esteem than respondents with greater socioeconomic resources. A more personal account of how social class position affects feelings of self-worth is presented in Reading 8.1.

Next in our model are the social consequences of social class. These comprise the experiences of individuals and groups in relation to the socioeconomic circumstances in which they find themselves. The consequences include life chances, values and aspirations, political beliefs and consciousness, and beliefs about, and involvement in, social mobility. The following sections examine these consequences.

Life Chances

One of the most immediate consequences of social class is the experiences that directly follow from a person's income and wealth. At practically every stage of the life cycle, from birth to death, people with more income will enjoy better experiences, better services, and a better quality of life than will those with low income.

We can think of life as a train ride in which very rich people occupy the first set of cars, middle-income people the next set of cars, and low-income people the last cars. The necessities of life like food and clothing will go first to the occupants of the lead cars with the remainder distributed in diminishing amounts to the last cars. The comfort level of cars—heating, cooling, and furnishings—would also diminish as one moves from the front to the rear of the train. In case of natural disasters, like floods or fires, passengers in the last cars are more vulnerable to injury and death because their cars are made of poor materials. When there is a war among nations more people are drafted into the military from the rear cars, and they are more likely to be wounded or killed than persons traveling on the front cars. Doctors and dentists do not spend much time helping persons in the back cars because they are less comfortable and attractive than lead cars. Children riding in the last cars have lower quality educational facilities and tend not to be encouraged to stay in school as long. Finally, passengers in the back cars do not ride on the train as long as those in the front cars, and they are less likely to reach their destination. Apparently, the combination of poorer food, shelter, medical care, and natural disasters takes its toll on riders in the end cars. The moral of a class society is: If you must travel, it is better to go first class!

Values and Aspirations

One of the earliest and most influential studies of the relationship between social class and selected values and aspirations was reported in a paper by Herbert Hyman in 1953. Hyman put forward the view that persons in different social classes had different values and aspirations and that the values and aspirations held by lower classes played an important part in their failure to achieve any improvement in their lives. In other words, while poor people are hampered by the fact of their poverty, they

Life styles of people reflect their ability to gain access to resources. The two styles of water recreation pictured here illustrate different resource levels—street showers by a fire hydrant and a luxurious private pool.

are further penalized by the values they hold, values that actually reduce their chances for social mobility.

Hyman examined data collected in nationwide surveys on class differences in three areas: educational values, motivation for economic advancement, and perceptions of the opportunity structure. He found that members of lower socioeconomic groups have less belief in the value of a college education for upward mobility, and are therefore less likely than the middle and upper classes to desire a college education for their children. Also, when adult and young respondents were asked to indicate the most important consideration in choosing a life's work, lower-class respondents emphasized security and wages, whereas middle and upper class respondents stressed the congeniality of the career pattern to the individual's personality, interests, and qualifications.

Hyman concludes:

To put it simply the lower class individual doesn't want as much success, knows he couldn't get it even if he wanted to, and doesn't want what might help him get success. Of course, an individual's value system is only one among many factors on which his position in the social hierarchy depends. Some of these factors may be external and arbitrary, quite beyond the control of even a highly motivated individual. However, within the bounds of the freedom available to individuals, this value system would create a *self-imposed* barrier to an improved position. (p. 426)

Although this statement was made more than 20 years ago, we should recognize the contemporary nature of the argument and current debate over it. Are people poor because of external conditions over which they have little control? Or are they poor because they do not value planning, saving, smaller families, education, discipline, and the like? Would the poor be able to improve their lives if given opportunities, such as stable jobs and college education, or would they be incapable of taking advantage of them?

It may be that the values and aspirations expressed by lower SES people are simply realistic adaptations to their limited opportunities rather than strongly held values (Perrucci, 1967). If people

are asked their *wishes* for more education or a good job, rather than their *expectations* of ever achieving it, we may find less difference among social classes.

Several sociologists have recognized the importance of distinguishing between wishes and expectations when trying to see if there are class differences in values (Della Fave, 1974; Han, 1969). The results of research in this area are inconclusive. Some researchers have found that high school students from low, middle, and high social class backgrounds do not differ in their wishes for future achievement; other researchers have found that differences do exist. Some conclusions of these studies are as follows:

1. The values exhibited by persons in the lower classes are in large part adaptations to the circumstances in which they live. Such values are not "deeply rooted" in their personality but can be discarded and replaced by other values that are better adapted to different circumstances (Liebow, 1967; Rodman, 1963).*

2. The differences in values and behavior between the upper and lower classes can be traced directly to the relative incomes of different classes (Rossi and Blum, 1968).

3. Both the poor and nonpoor have the same high aspirations for their children to achieve and excel in school and at work (Kriesberg, 1970).

Thus, research indicates that differences among the social classes are primarily in economic resources, power, and prestige and not in their values and aspirations. The persistence of class structures and the restriction on upward mobility are best understood as results of material inequalities among the social classes, not as individual deficiencies.

Political Beliefs

A second important consequence of social class membership for the maintenance or change of the class structure is the political beliefs people develop about the society in which they live. These

---

*For a less optimistic perspective on the ease with which persons can shed values and take on new ones, see Ulf Hannerz (1969, Chap. 9).

beliefs include views about how the formal political process works, how income and power are distributed, the chance for improving one's position
in society, the degree of trust in elected political
officials, as well as feelings about the need for radical change in American institutions.

Research by Alves and Rossi (1978) attempted to
answer the question "Who should get what?" by
seeing how Americans make judgments about the
fairness of earnings that go to individuals and
households. They found that judgments about the
fairness of earnings are based upon a set of norms
that attempt to balance merit (for example, years
of education) and need (such as number of children). High-status respondents placed greater weight
on merit, while low-status respondents emphasized need when making judgments about whether
incomes were fair.

There are also different perceptions of the class
structure itself. Some see American society as essentially classless, because there are no sharp divisions between occupational categories such as
white-collar and blue-collar jobs. Society is viewed
as a continuous hierarchy of occupations, each
differing slightly from the other in prestige. Others,
however, find a distinct class structure with substantial differences between members of each class
and virtually insurmountable barriers against
movement between classes (that is, very little social mobility).

Vanneman and Pampel (1977) have pointed out
how the continuous hierarchy model "justifies the
position of the successful" because it is "consistent
with the belief that persons move along the continuum through individual effort." On the other
hand, "subordinate groups are more likely to hold
a dichotomous class image in which society is
structured to prevent the lower class from rising
to the position of the dominant class" (p. 423).

If, as we concluded in the previous section, the
different social classes are more alike than different
in their basic values and aspirations, then we must
try to understand their reactions to their differential
achievements. For example, a lower-class person
and a middle-class person may value similar things
and have similar aspirations for themselves and
others. Yet, the lower-class person does not realize

*Some people who live their lives in
poverty develop political beliefs and
ideologies that hold existing
institutions responsible for their
situation. They may join social
movements in order to change
social conditions. Others withdraw
from social life, seeking solace in
fatalistic ideologies or religious
faith.*

his or her personal values and aspirations while the middle class person does. What are the likely reactions to the differences in achievement and what are the political consequences of these reactions?

Rytina, Form, and Pease (1970) conducted a study to examine the relationship between income and what they called "stratification ideology." This ideology consists of a set of beliefs that justifies the way in which social rewards are distributed in a society. The authors classified a sample of people in Muskegon, Michigan, according to whether they were "rich" (annual family income of $25,000 or more), "poor" (less than $3500 income for a family of four), or "middle" (the remainder of the study population).

People in each income class were asked the following questions about four areas of stratification ideology: (1) Do you believe the United States is a society with an open opportunity structure? (2) Do all social classes have access to education as a way to increase their social mobility? (3) Does the political and legal system operate in an impartial manner? (4) Is the individual or are the various social institutions primarily responsible for her or his economic standing in American society?

The authors found that, first, the rich were more likely than the poor to see equality of opportunity in the United States as a fact and, second, higher income classes were more likely to believe in the existence of equal access to education. Third, rich people believed that both rich and poor can influence government, while poor people believed that only the rich can do so. Only about one-fifth of both rich and poor people believed that the law and courts operate equitably. Finally, the rich were more likely than the poor to believe that a person's wealth is the result of personal attributes like self-discipline, hard work, and intelligence. The rich were also more likely than the poor to see undesirable personal qualities as the cause of poverty and to believe that poor people do not want to get ahead as much as everyone else does.

Although these data are limited, we see that the rich may be more likely than the poor to endorse a set of beliefs that justify existing inequalities in power, wealth, and opportunity in American society. This is important because it is the rich who

own or control the communication and educational channels that greatly influence the beliefs of the public. Reading 8.2 is an expanded discussion of the different beliefs that people have about the American class structure.

Class Consciousness

A third important consequence of social class membership is the possible development of **class consciousness.** Class consciousness refers to the recognition of class-related interests by members of a class and to the belief that such interests are in conflict with those of all other economic classes. Before class consciousness can develop, however, people must first have developed an awareness of (1) a total class structure, (2) the existence of differences in wealth, power, and prestige, and (3) the unequal opportunities and barriers that exist because of class structure. When people are aware of class inequality and its causes, and believe that it is possible for them to accomplish change, they are more likely to join groups trying to change the political or economic system to benefit themselves.

The specific conditions in American society that would encourage the development of a class consciousness are still a matter of speculation. Economic crises like depression and unemployment often encourage greater political action for change. Recent research by Schlozman and Verba (1980) examined the effect of unemployment upon political activism. They studied 1370 middle and working-class men, half of whom were unemployed, to see if the hardship of being unemployed leads to greater class consciousness. Their findings indicate that both the employed and unemployed were confident about their personal opportunities, believed in the American Dream ("Hard work is the route to success"), and were similar in their class consciousness ("Workers must stick together" and "Management and workers have conflicting interests"). These writers conclude that the experience of unemployment does not influence class conscious ideology or increase political activism, such as voting. However, the unemployed do show the highest degree of political alienation (belief in the statement that "Government is controlled by big interests"), which may be responsible for their lack of political activity.

Class consciousness might also be increased by the centralization of economic and political power (discussed in Chapter 13), which makes differences between the powerful and powerless much more visible. Such developments might lead to an awareness of inequalities and a polarization of interests, which are preconditions for class consciousness.

Another factor affecting class consciousness is the opportunities for individual mobility and whether such opportunities are increasing or decreasing. If there is a growing pessimism about the opportunities for mobility as well as an actual drop in the rates of mobility, awareness of social classes and class consciousness would likely increase.

SOCIAL MOBILITY

"Getting ahead" or "making it" are well-established themes in American life and literature. In sociological terms, we would say that achievement and success are important American values, urging each new generation to attain social positions above those into which they were born. Young men, and to a lesser extent, young women are encouraged to seek more education, higher income, and more prestigious occupations than those of their parents.

Social mobility refers to changes in one's social position over a period of time and can be measured in terms of occupational position and income. One type of social mobility is **intragenerational mobility,** or change in a person's position during his or her lifetime. For example, a comparison of people's occupations when they first entered the labor force with their present occupations would indicate whether they had experienced upward, downward, or no intragenerational mobility. Social mobility may also be studied as **intergenerational mobility,** or change in a person's position relative to parent's position. For example, one could obtain a sample of men in the labor force and compare their present occupations with those of their fathers at some earlier point in the sons' lives.

Figure 8.2 is a hypothetical intergenerational mo-

bility table that compares the occupations of a sample of sons with those of their fathers. The entries along the diagonal (the boxed cells) represent occupational inheritance, or immobility. If our hypothetical society did not permit any social mobility, all the sons would be in the same occupations as their fathers and all entries in Figure 8.2 would be the diagonal cells. Entries off the diagonal represent mobility; the upper segment is downward mobility (sons in occupations below their fathers), and the lower segment is upward mobility (sons in occupations above their fathers).

An intergenerational mobility table could be constructed for samples of people at two different points in time. This would allow us to see if there is more or less upward social mobility for the current sample compared with the earlier one. For example, Rogoff (1953) looked at the occupations of all males who got married in Indianapolis, Indiana, in 1940 and the occupations of their fathers (data were obtained from marriage license applications). She repeated this for the year 1910. From a comparison of the two intergenerational mobility tables, Rogoff concluded that there was little change in the rates of mobility between 1910 and 1940.

Similar comparisons could be made for samples of blacks and whites, males and females, or people from different cities or countries. This would allow for group comparisons in the total amount of mobility, the amount of upward and downward mobility, and the "distance" of the mobility that is experienced (such as mobility between adjacent occupational categories or mobility spanning several categories).

Until recently, most studies of mobility have focused on men, to the neglect of intergenerational mother-daughter or father-daughter mobility. This was no doubt due to the now-outdated belief that the socioeconomic status of women is determined by their husbands.

Recent research indicates that the mobility process is very similar for men and women (DeJong et al., 1971). This means that the present occupational positions of both men and women are influenced in a similar way by their parents' socioeconomic level, amount of schooling, and occupational level of their first job. In spite of this, women work-

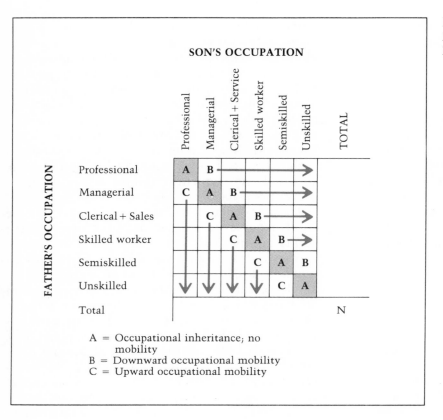

FIGURE 8.2   An Intergenerational Mobility Table: Comparison of Father's and Son's Occupations

A = Occupational inheritance; no
     mobility
B = Downward occupational mobility
C = Upward occupational mobility

ers tend to be concentrated in a narrower range of occupations than men (Oppenheimer, 1970), and the income of working women is far less than that of men with similar occupational characteristics (Treiman and Terrell, 1975).

The amount of intergenerational mobility found in a society is affected by several factors:

1. Changes in the occupational structure. Economic and technological changes may result in a decline in farm and unskilled occupations and an increase in skilled and sales occupations. Such changes would influence the sons and daughters of farmers or unskilled workers to seek positions in expanding rather than contracting occupations.

2. Access to education. As educational requirements for all jobs increase, the ability of people to fill these jobs becomes increasingly dependent on their access to higher education. Much of the upward occupational mobility following World War

II was due to the G.I. Bill of Rights benefits that paid tuition and monthly stipends to veterans who attended college. The increased cost of higher education in recent years and the reduction of federal loans to students from lower income families may severely limit opportunities for upward mobility in the future.

3. An expanding economy. The motivation to seek additional education is a form of risk-taking behavior. It is based upon the belief that the investment of time and money in education will be repaid in future benefits of income, prestige, and job satisfaction. Widespread pessimism about the economy or the value of additional education would lead many people to avoid investing in additional education if future rewards are uncertain.

4. Different rates of fertility. If higher status individuals fail to at least reproduce themselves, then people from lower social classes will have to be

recruited for higher status positions. On the other hand, if upper social classes have high fertility rates it will reduce the chances of persons from lower social classes to fill such positions.

Increasingly, in advanced industrial societies, the channel for upward mobility is through education. The college degree is necessary for most upper-level jobs and postgraduate training is required for the higher status professions. Whether the increased educational requirements are really essential for the work done in higher status occupations is a matter of some debate (Berg, 1970, Collins, 1971). Escalating "credentialism" can also be viewed as a means to control entry into high status occupations and thereby control the supply of people with such skills. The power, prestige, and income of professionals, for example, are closely related to the

One of the main avenues for upward mobility in American society is via education. The attainment of advanced degrees is a necessary credential for entry into the most prestigious high-paying occupations. Access to a quality education, and the ability to pay for it, is an important life chance in our society.

skill monopoly held by them and to their ability to control the supply of practitioners (Perrucci, 1971). Thus a clue to patterns of mobility can be found in the patterns of involvement in higher education by different segments of society.

Social Mobility in Industrial Societies

Modern industrial societies are often described as *open-class societies*, in which a high value is placed on success and all people, regardless of social origin, are expected to be able to take advantage of existing opportunities for social mobility. Because there are no legal barriers or restrictions placed on access to opportunities, all segments of society can experience mobility. Modern industrial societies emphasize merit in filling occupational positions compared with such nonmerit or nonachievement factors as religion, sex, race, or social origin.

Yet even in open-class societies with equality of opportunity and mobility based on merit, the influence of social origins is strong. Families differ in their power, wealth, and social esteem, and the advantages or disadvantages of social origin are transmitted through the family to each new generation.

Lipset and Bendix (1962) were interested in seeing to what extent social origins influenced mobility in modern industrial societies. They were also interested in seeing whether societies with an aristocratic tradition and a history of legally sanctioned class differences (like England and France) would have lower rates of mobility than societies without the tradition of a rigid class structure (like the United States).

These researchers compared countries in terms of differences in the occupations held by fathers and their sons. Upward or downward movement between manual and nonmanual occupations by sons was used to determine how much mobility there was from the fathers' generation. Lipset and Bendix concluded that all industrial societies have high rates of upward social mobility and that there is relatively little difference between the United States and other advanced industrial societies. In fact, in European societies the rates of "long-distance" mobility (people of very low origins rising to very high positions) were greater than in the United States. The belief that the United States is the most open society appears to be more myth than reality.

Most studies of occupational mobility have noted that there has been a vast expansion of technical, service, and white-collar occupations in industrialized countries and a decline in farm and blue-collar occupations. It is therefore easy to confuse changes in the occupational structure with the kind of mobility that reflects greater equality of opportunity.

Social Mobility in the United States

There are two questions that bear on whether the United States is a land of opportunity: (1) How much mobility actually takes place and has it been increasing or decreasing? (2) Is there equality of opportunity so that people can achieve mobility regardless of their social origins?

RATES OF MOBILITY

Studies of the amount of mobility in the United States indicate that there is a great deal of change in the occupations filled by sons in comparison to their fathers' occupations. Some studies show that as many as three out of four males are working in occupations different from their fathers (Vanfossen, 1979), while others report that mobility occurred for approximately one-half of those studied (Jackson and Crockett, 1964). These overall rates of mobility have neither increased nor decreased in the period between the 1940s and 1970s (Featherman, 1979).

Most of the mobility that occurs is upward rather than downward, meaning that mobile sons are in higher prestige occupations than their fathers. However, most mobility covers a very short distance; sons of unskilled laborers become semiskilled factory workers rather than schoolteachers or managers.

OPPORTUNITIES FOR MOBILITY

The idea of equality of opportunities is based on the existence of established avenues for moving into high-level positions. If one wishes to be a nurse or doctor or lawyer, it is necessary to obtain the appropriate educational credentials. Since education is one of the main avenues of mobility in American society, we are interested in whether people have equal access to educational opportunities. We are also interested in seeing if those who do obtain access to higher education enjoy the rewards that are supposed to follow. The denial of access to opportunities or rewards is usually the result of artificial barriers that affect poor people.

A large body of research evidence indicates that students from lower socioeconomic origins do not attend college to the same extent as those from higher origins. This is the case even when they have high measured intelligence, high grades, and the motivation to attend college (Bowles and Gintis, 1976; Sewell, 1971; Kahl, 1953). One study of 9000 Wisconsin high school students showed that among students from higher SES groups 91 percent of those with high intelligence and 58 percent of those with low intelligence went to college. Among students from lower SES groups 40 percent of those with high intelligence and only 9 percent of those with low intelligence went to college (Sewell and Shah, 1968).

The barriers to college attendance among talented, motivated young people from lower SES groups are partly related to these individuals' limited financial resources and partly to the expectations that schools have of them. A number of studies have indicated that teachers expect less of lower-class students and that such expectations can be self-fulfilling (Becker, 1953; Rist, 1970, 1977; Rosenthal and Jacobson, 1968). Lower-class students can also be programmed for failure by placing them in noncollege tracks in high schools (Alexander and McDill, 1976). Track membership (college or vocational) has a substantial impact on students' plans for college and on their self-esteem. Consider the following response by an entering junior high school student when asked "Did you think the other guys [in the college track] were smarter than you?" (Schafer and Polk, 1967):

Not at first—I used to think I was just as smart as anybody in the school—I felt it inside of me . . . I wanted to get a diploma and go to college and help people and everything. I stepped into there in junior high—I felt like

a fool going to school—I really felt like a fool. . . . I started losing faith in myself—after the teachers kept downing me, you know. You hear "a guy's in basic section, he's dumb" and all this. Each year—"You're ignorant—You're stupid."

For people of lower socioeconomic origins who manage to hurdle these barriers and go to college, we can then ask: Where do they go to college? Higher SES students are more likely to attend the most prestigious private and public colleges and universities, while lower SES students go to two-year community colleges and less prestigious four-year colleges (Medsker and Trent, 1965). Where one goes to college can have a significant impact on income and career success. Those who attend the most prestigious schools will have higher incomes and achieve higher administrative positions in their organizations (Perrucci and Perrucci, 1970).

New Directions in Mobility Research

The approach to studying mobility that has dominated research in the last decade emphasizes the role that an individual's resources play in contributing to, or limiting, occupational or income mobility. These resources include (1) social background, including parents' occupation and education; (2) academic ability, or performance in school; (3) extent of educational attainment; and (4) first occupation upon entering the labor force. These resources may be displayed graphically as in Figure 8.3.

This model of mobility assumes that children with parents who are better educated and in high status occupations receive greater encouragement and reward for their school performance. Thus an upper-level social background is a positive resource that can be converted into greater educational attainment. In the same way, education is a resource that converts into a better first job, which finally converts into a better present job.

The problem with the individual resources model of mobility is that it ignores the actual settings in which these resources are developed and converted into greater mobility (Kerckhoff, 1976; Rosenbaum, 1975). For example, academic performance

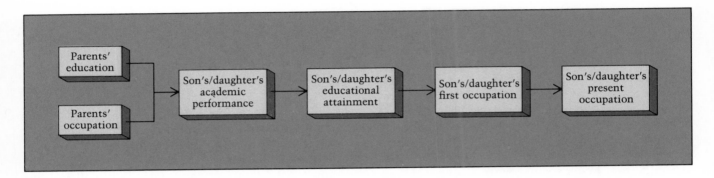

FIGURE 8.3   Status Attainment
Model

and educational attainment take place in organizations called schools. These organizations have policies that locate students in curriculum tracks that may determine their school performance and attitudes and the amount of education ultimately attained. Such decisions, which affect the fate of students, may have little to do with the resources held by individuals and their ability to use such resources effectively.

In much the same way, occupational achievements take place within work organizations, which have promotion policies and practices that may have nothing to do with individual resources. Certain occupations have built into them a linked sequence of job changes that unfold as part of an organizational career and not as the result of the educational resources a person brings to the job (Spilerman, 1977).

The only aspect of parents' and children's occupations that are considered in the individual resources model is prestige. But there are many other aspects of occupations besides prestige that may influence mobility (Robinson and Kelley, 1979). For example, occupations can be found in different sectors of an economy and this location can determine mobility. An engineer employed in an industry sector that is vital and expanding has better chances for advancement than an engineer in a declining industry, no matter how talented he or she may be (Bibb and Form, 1977).

The future direction of mobility research must be to combine the individual resources model with those organizational factors that shape educational and occupational careers. We may then begin to learn exactly how schools and work organizations knowingly or unknowingly build artificial barriers to mobility.

SUMMARY

A society is stratified when there is a hierarchy of positions that receive different rewards and when the advantages or disadvantages associated with positions are transmitted to the next generation. The two major types of social stratification are castes and classes. A caste system is made up of religiously sanctioned and hierarchically ranked groupings in which membership is fixed at birth and is permanent. Castes are culturally distinct groups marked by different occupations, food habits, clothing, patterns of social relationships, and marriage rules. A class system is made up of economic groupings based on similarities in occupation, income, and wealth. While a person's class position is set at birth, classes are "open" in that it is possible to move upward or downward with changes in occupation and income.

The extent of inequality found in a class system is determined by the proportion of the population living in poverty and the share of a society's total income that goes to different segments of society. When structural-functional theory is used to understand why class inequality exists, the conclusion is that inequality is necessary for all societies. Inequality serves as a device that societies use to get people to fill the positions that are most important. Also, there is a general consensus that existing inequality is fair because everyone has an equal chance to compete for high rewards.

Conflict theory does not view class inequality as necessary; neither does it see evidence of consensus among people that rewards are distributed equitably. Inequality exists, and persists, because privileged classes that dominate the corporations, educational system, media, and the government are able to shape society in their interests.

The consequences of social class include a wide range of life chances and life styles. Experiences at every stage of the life cycle are shaped by people's income and wealth. Poor people have greater health problems, poorer housing and education, shorter life spans, greater chances to become victims of crime, and poorer access to public services that are supposed to be available to all citizens.

Members of different social classes are more alike than different on values and aspirations related to success, advancement, hard work, and educational achievement. Often, class differences that are found can be traced to people's relative incomes and to adaptations to limited opportunities. If poor people do not rate a college education as very important, it may be partly because they lack the money needed to go to college.

The beliefs that people have about the class structure are related to their economic position. Poor people are less likely to believe that equality of opportunity exists or to believe in the existence of equal access to education. The rich are more likely than the poor to hold beliefs that justify existing inequalities.

Opportunities for upward social mobility are influenced by an expanding economy and changes in the occupational structure. The rates of upward mobility in all industrial societies are high, with little difference between the United States and other industrial societies. There are artificial barriers to mobility for persons from lower socioeconomic groups, and they are exhibited in the way that schools often treat students from lower SES groups.

GLOSSARY

Caste system a social order that is made up of religiously sanctioned and hierarchically ranked groupings in which membership is fixed at birth and is permanent.

Class consciousness the recognition of class-related interests by members of a class, and the belief that such interests are in conflict with those of all other economic classes.

Class system a social order with hierarchical economic groupings based on similarities in occupation and wealth and in which people may move up or down over their lifetime.

Intergenerational mobility the income, occupational, or educational attainments of children relative to their parents.

Intragenerational mobility social mobility of an individual during his or her own lifetime.

Life chances opportunities, determined by income and wealth, for long life expectancy, good health care, adequate food and housing, and quality education.

Poverty the condition of living below an income that provides minimum satisfaction of basic needs for food, shelter, and clothing.

SES abbreviation for the term *socioeconomic status.*

Social class a collection of individuals with the same relationship to the means of production, with an awareness of their common interests, and who engage in political action to advance their interests.

Social differentiation the process by which activities in a society are allocated to different persons, such as a division of labor based on age and sex. Such differentiation is not vertical since the positions do not have unequal rewards.

Social mobility changes in position in the stratification system over time that is measured by occupation, income, prestige, or other measure of social standing.

Social stratification a hierarchy of positions with different amounts of wealth, power, and prestige and intergenerational transmission of advantage or disadvantage stemming from one's location in the hierarchy.

Status group a group of people with a similar life style and a strong sense of group identity.

ADDITIONAL READINGS

Agee, James. *Let Us Now Praise Famous Men.* New York: Ballantine, 1966.
A study of the personal consequences of the Depression on various people, based on research sponsored by the U.S. government.

Aronowitz, Stanley. *False Promises.* N.Y.: McGraw-Hill, 1973.
A history of the failure of various efforts by labor unions to improve human life and a consideration of economic and political structures which preclude meaningful changes.

Baltzell, E. Digby. *Philadelphia Gentlemen: The Making of a National Upper Class.* New York: Free Press, 1958.
A study of the historical rise and persistence of the rich and powerful in America.

Feagin, Joe R. *Subordinating the Poor: Welfare and American Beliefs.* Englewood Cliffs, N.J.: Prentice-Hall, 1975.
Examines current American attitudes toward poverty and the poor. Criticizes the myth that the poor are lazy and promiscuous by showing that most of the poor are work oriented but can-

not work because of age, disability, or lack of jobs.

Gilbert, Dennis, and Joseph A. Kahl. *The American Class Structure: A New Synthesis.* Homewood, Ill.: Dorsey Press, 1982.
A textbook for the beginning student interested in an introduction to the American class structure, including the theories of Karl Marx and Max Weber and an analysis of the variables that affect the way that stratification operates.

Keller, Suzanne. *Beyond the Ruling Class: Stategic Elites in Modern Society.* New York: Random, 1963.
An analysis of the role of elites in societies, with a consideration of their origin and functions in modern societies.

Kohn, Melvin L. *Class and Conformity: A Study in Values.* Homewood, Ill.: Dorsey Press, 1969.
An in-depth study of social class differences in parent-child relationships. The book examines the way that social class affects parents' values and how these values affect parents' behavior toward their children.

Matthews, Mervyn. *Privilege in the Soviet Union: A Study of Elite Life Styles under Communism.* Boston: Allen & Unwin, 1978.
An examination of inequality in a society dedicated to an egalitarian ideology. The author looks at elite privileges and life styles within a historical perspective and compares social mobility in Soviet Russia and other societies.

Vanfossen, Beth E. *The Structure of Social Inequality.* Boston: Little, Brown, 1979.
A comprehensive introduction to social stratification. Provides excellent coverage and synthesis of recent research on the determinants and consequences of inequality. Especially valuable is the author's attempt to use a conflict perspective to interpret empirical findings.

READINGS

READING 8.1

The Hidden Injuries of Class
Richard Sennett and Jonathan Cobb

The terrible thing about class in our society is that it sets up a contest for dignity. If you are a working-class person . . . being treated by people of a higher class as though there probably is little unusual or special about you . . . if you resent this treatment and yet feel . . . it reflects something accurate about your own self-development, then to try to impugn the dignity of persons in a higher class becomes a real, if twisted, affirmation of your own claims for respect. Class . . . as a problem of day-to-day existence rather than as an abstraction, creates a hidden content in a wide variety of social issues, so that while people . . . seem to be fighting over general principles, they are in reality fighting for recognition from each other of their own worth. . . .

. . . Class society takes away from all the people within it the feeling of secure dignity in the eyes of others and of themselves. It does so in two ways: first, by the images it projects of why people belong to high or low classes— class presented as the ultimate outcome of personal ability; second, by the definition the society makes of the actions to be taken by people of any class to validate their dignity— legitimizations of self which do not, cannot work and so reinforce the original anxiety.

The result of this, we believe, is that the activities which keep people moving in a class society, which make them seek more money, more possessions, higher-status jobs, do not originate in a materialistic desire . . . of things, but out of an attempt to restore a psychological deprivation that the class structure has effected in their lives. In other words, *the psy-chological motivation instilled by a class society is to heal a doubt about the self rather than create more power over things and other persons in the outer world.*

Ricca Kartides emigrated twelve years ago from a small city in Greece, a town in which everyone knew everyone else . . . and life proceeded at a slow and traditional pace. More educated and affluent than most of the towns-folk, Kartides held a teacher's degree. He was disliked, however, . . . by certain important members of his community who controlled all well-paying jobs. Finding himself in daily fear of losing his teaching post . . . he decided at age twenty-four that he had to leave. Like many immigrants before him . . . he chose not so much to come here as to leave an intolerable state of affairs at home.

Kartides arrived in America with $12 in his pocket, no understanding of English, and no recognized skills. He went to work in a factory . . . while he learned English. However, he found himself stuck doing unskilled labor; having to work long hours to provide for himself and his family, he had neither the time, the money, nor the energy to return to school for the credentials that would get him into a white-collar job in America.

"If I am an unskilled man, where else can I go but to clean? You don't need a degree to clean." A naturally gregarious man, Kartides first began to understand his decline through the coldness with which people once his equals now treated him. In contrast to the old country, he feels, the culture of Americans permits no sense of reciprocal respect across class boundaries . . . He finds in America an absence of rituals by which people might transcend class lines.

Ricca describes his situation as one of having many acquaintances but no close friends. The lack of friendship, he says, "doesn't bother me at all, since my really close friends are my family. I'm the kind of person who, if I feel I'm not wanted I'm not getting involved at all. . . .

When Kartides first began work as a maintenance man, he lived in an apartment where he received strict instructions to use the back door, and never let his children play on the empty lawn surrounding the building. He reacted to this impersonality by making heroic efforts of time, work, and personal sacrifice so that he could own a home of his own . . . It was not to own, not for economic gain, that he worked so hard for a private house; it was to gain a sanctuary. . . . The home is therefore for him the center of freedom, "and what I mean by freedom is my children can play without nobody telling them what to do."

Yet this search for sanctuary has left Kartides in a difficult position. He has bought property in a nearby suburb of Boston in order to be free, yet must work fourteen hours a day at two jobs in order to pay for his "freedom," leaving him scant time to enjoy his home. . . .

He understands the trap in which he is caught. He knows that the actions he has taken are not yielding the promised rewards; yet to do nothing, to be just "Ricca the janitor" . . . is unbearable. . . .

"It seems to me," the interviewer observes, "that you really regret leaving Greece. . . . Let me ask you something—do you really think you have to be a rich man to go back? Couldn't you go to another town there?"

"Well, you see . . . now I am what I am, a family man, a daddy, and . . . I feel I have a duty to them . . . a duty to make something of myself here in America where the children are born . . . so that they can respect me, you see. . . ."

One senses, however, that Ricca has given up on himself. He feels his life to be pretty much over (he is now thirty-six); the station he occupies he believes he will remain in the rest of his days. Even so, he is not resigned, for there seems one path of hope left: his children. . . .

Kartides is proud, yet somewhat defensive, of the old-fashioned way in which he rears these children, teaching them manners, respect for their parents, and courtesy to others. He takes pride in not being a "permissive" parent, although he says he is more lax in his discipline than his parents ever were with him. . . .

His humiliation—that is part of his strictness, but so also is a revulsion at the gulf between classes. His kids will treat all men with dignity: "If this is a world where you have a rat race, let it be. But at least *my* kids is going to be the way I want them." But don't those who refuse to join the rat race lose, aren't they beaten down by the more aggressive? This thought too has occurred to him, and there is a fear in Ricca that in making his kids humane he might also be condemning them to remain in his station.

It is difficult for Ricca Kartides, even as he creates some measure of material security in his life to feel that his quantitative gains translate into the emotional sense of independence and assuredness he wants from these material improvements. . . . He feels vulnerable and inadequately armed, but what has he done wrong?

SUMMARY

Class in U.S. society sets up a constant contest for dignity. People fight one another for recognition of their own worth rather than over general principles. Class society takes away people's dignity by suggesting that their class is the outcome of their personal abilities and that this self is legitimate. This reinforces the original anxiety and drives people to acquire money and things to heal a doubt about self rather than to create more power over things and persons. An example of such a person is Ricca Kartides, an immigrant from a town in Greece. Dissatisfied with his life as a teacher and in fear of losing his job as well, at age 24, he came to the U.S. with his wife. He was stuck, in time, with a job as a janitor. Now, some twelve years have passed. He has a home, a car, and some money in the bank for his children's education, but he feels his life has passed him by. He feels that people do not respect him because of his job as a janitor. He is rearing his children to have respect for all people and all classes. Yet, he feels vulnerable and inadequately armed in his home and job and life in general, but he does not know why or what, if anything, he has done wrong.

QUESTIONS

1. How do low-status jobs strip people of their self-respect?
2. Why is it that in some countries people accept jobs like servant or street sweeper without feeling humiliated?
3. Do people seek more possessions and higher status jobs because they are caught up in the "rat race"?

READING 8.2

The American Culture and the Reality of Class Stratification
John Dalphin

The facts of inequality in America are very disturbing. How do Americans rationalize such tremendous concentration of power and wealth? A major part of the answer can be found in the traditional American culture which praises individual success, diverts attention from class stratification, and locates blame for the excesses of inequality in nonthreatening places.

THE AMERICAN DREAM PACKAGE

A core part of the culture is the American Dream Package—a set of values, beliefs, and

SOURCE: John Dalphin, "The American Culture and the Reality of Class Stratification," in *The Persistence of Social Inequality in America* (Cambridge, Mass.: Schenkman Publishing Co., Inc., 1981), pp. 55–65.

rationalization which defend the existing stratification system. Included are the approval of equality of opportunity, individualism, competition, hard work, deferred gratification, social mobility, and success.

The belief in equal opportunity conveys the notion that everyone should be able to have an equal chance to get ahead, achieve, and be successful. This does not mean that most Americans believe that everyone actually should be equal in what they earn, own, and possess: that is, enjoy equality of condition. Indeed, it is more typical for Americans to think that people should be rewarded according to what they do or produce. Both this phenomenon and other aspects of the American Dream Package have been explored by a variety of scholars.

Such disparate social analysts as Williams (1970) and Slater (1976) have observed that individualism is at the heart of the traditional American culture. Each person ultimately is responsible for the development and growth of his or her own life. What one makes of one's equal opportunity to succeed depends upon what the individual does with his or her chances. This means that one must be competitive if one is to maximize personal achievement and success. The traditional American culture views the world as being a Darwinian jungle where survival of the fittest is the rule. . . .

Regardless of whether or not the motivation is conscious or unconscious, upward social mobility has been held up as a goal ever since America began to serve as a land of opportunity for the first European settlers. Rags to riches mobility is to be accomplished by hard work according to the work ethic. If a person works hard, he or she can go as far as desired because the opportunities for success are there. Survey results (Rytina, Form, and Pease, 1970) indicate that both rich and non-rich Americans today still hold the same beliefs. Of course, the culture does not say that upward mobility will be easy. One is supposed to defer gratification—or sacrifice now for future satisfaction—along the way. Staying in school for a longer period of time or delaying marriage until later ages are often pointed to as examples of deferring gratification. Once upward social mobility has been achieved, personal success has been achieved. The two are as one. Then, the traditional American culture encourages one to demonstrate the achievement of personal success by the consumption and display of material possessions that signify the status of success. Prestigious cars and homes, luxurious vacations, and leisurely pursuits are the appropriate grist here. Also, the consumption behavior of the successful usually determines what is considered "in" or "trendy" by most Americans.

Closely related to the foregoing is the belief held by many that most Americans have done well by the American Dream Package. This is exemplified by the conviction that America has a large "middle class" predominantly made up of white-collar workers. Such people have "made it" and enjoy a very comfortable, affluent existence, so the stereotype goes. This tends to reinforce the belief in equality of opportunity for all people and in the rest of the American Dream Package. The "system" works.

BLAMING THE INDIVIDUAL

The system works, but many people, if not most, in America are upset with the stratification position that they personally "achieve." A sense of frustration develops because one has not gone further in the structure, that is, experienced rags-to-riches mobility. Who is one to blame; the upper class; the poor; the individual person?

Let us consider the last option first, namely, the individual person as scapegoat. The individual person who is upset with his or her stratification position is encouraged by the culture's emphasis upon individualism and equality of opportunity to blame the self for

not achieving more success. "It's my own fault. If I'd tried harder and had more stick-to-itive-ness, I'd have gone further. I wouldn't be where I am today," reason many individuals. How often do we hear the above or some variation said explicitly or implicitly? A garbage man from a study by Sennett and Cobb speaks:

"Look, I know it's nobody's fault but mine that I got stuck here where I am, I mean . . . if I wasn't such a dumb shit . . . no, it ain't that neither . . . if I'd applied myself, I know I got it in me to be different, can't say anyone did it to me" (1972:96).

Self-blaming for not going further in the stratification system has been a part of America's cultural baggage since the first European immigrants sought this fabled land of opportunity. The opportunity is there for those who want it. Those who do not take advantage of it have only themselves to blame. The open frontier of the West was especially interesting in this light. If one had a low stratification position in the East, one could always go West and start over again in an attempt to leap from rags to riches. Of course, most of those who tried this did not improve their situation much, but how could they complain? Now they had failed again. It was their own fault. Self-blaming was reinforced. . . .

It is important to note also that individuals who blame themselves for not going further in the stratification system do develop a variety of mental defenses. These defenses can minimize the sting of self-blame by covering up the gap between real achievement and imagined opportunities. As research dating back to that done by the Lynds has shown, a very important mental defense has been to think less and less of one's own stratification position and refocus attention upon the social mobility chances open to one's children. Such mobility can be shared vicariously by the parents and hence serve to make partial sense out of their own stratification position. Unfortunately, there is often a tragic underside to this scenario. The children in such families often suffer from the resulting pressure upon them and wind up resenting it. Even more poignant, however, is the fact that the parents of these families frequently tell their children either explicitly or implicitly not to be like them because they are failures. . . . [A]nother means of coping with the self-blaming dilemma is to consume status items that represent success even though one has not directly experienced the success of social mobility. This means that one can fail to acquire some important elements of the American Dream Package and still try to share in its ultimate rewards by buying the right material possessions. The automobile industry provides a good example. One can buy a moderately priced, large car that looks like a Mercedes (and therefore signifies success) for slightly more money than one pays for an "economical" subcompact car. It is no secret that Detroit has been trying to sell the average white-collar worker such cars by promising them the psychological sense of success in its advertising. There is much evidence of the efficacy of "success" advertising for many consumer products. The ultimate role of the resultant consumption is to divert attention away from the fact that people haven't really been as successful in the stratification system as they had hoped. It does this by making them *feel* like they actually have been successful. Of course, there are other escape valves for one's frustrations besides the consumption and display of the appropriate material objects.

BLAMING THE POOR

Enter the poor. People in the white-collar and blue-collar worlds, who have not gone as far in the stratification system as the American Dream Package tells them they should have gone, can also draw significant comfort from the fact that a relatively large group of poor people have not achieved as much as they have. This tends to inflate the stratification position of the non-poor. The following line of reasoning is typical of this attitude: "I may not have gone as far as I could have gone, but at least I've accomplished more than these people."

Why are the poor in their position? Many assume the stratification position of the poor to be the result of their not bothering to open up the American Dream Package containing the opportunity for social mobility and success. They blame the poor for not taking advantage of the opportunities available to all. They view the poor as failures because of their laziness, shiftlessness, and immorality. Such negative interpretations of the poor have been characteristic of the traditional American culture throughout our history.

Most Americans have assimilated the traditional culture well and are very adept, in the words of Ryan (1976), at "blaming the victim": The poor have bad housing because they do not take care of it, rather than the poor have little money for housing. The poor don't do well in school because they do not try to learn, rather than the poor don't succeed in school because there is inadequate funding for their schooling. In the above cases, the poor are victims who are blamed for their difficulties. The "system," the social structure and upper-class America are not blamed.

Blaming the poor does not stop with blaming them for their own situation. The poor also are blamed for the frustrations felt by white-collar and blue-collar people. Perhaps the most glaring example of how the poor serve this function is illustrated by the following reasoning: "Most of the poor are on welfare. Most people on welfare are chiselers." Both statements are false, but they are more than obliquely implied when we hear frustrated folks in the middle of the stratification system say, "I had to work for what I've got." Such sentiments are played upon when newspapers place the telephone number of the welfare office on their front pages with the accompanying suggestion that anyone knowing of a welfare chiseler should call the number and inform the authorities. . . .

Another way in which the poor are blamed for frustrations felt by blue-collar and white-collar Americans is related to crime, one of the prime concerns of many. Crime is identified with "crime in the streets" which, in turn, is equated with crimes committed by poor people, especially poor blacks. This is important for two reasons. First, the poor once again provide a favorable frame of comparison for people in the middle of the stratification system. They can feel good about themselves by saying, "Well, at least I haven't sunk that low." Secondly, crime is seen as something that poor people do. Poor people are blamed for most crimes. Attention is shifted away from white-collar crime, or "crime in the suites." There is no question that the upper-class dominated media play a critical role in perpetuating this interpretation of crime. Upper-class crime, for example, is rarely considered to be front-page material. As a result, people in the middle tend to blame the poor for one of their biggest worries—crime. This fits the overall pattern where those in white-collar and blue-collar America are encouraged by the traditional American culture to point the finger of blame downstairs at the poor rather than to look upstairs at the upper class for the source of their frustrations.

BLAMING THE UPPER CLASS

. . . Why, then, is not the upper class blamed for stratification frustrations felt by non-upper class people? . . . [T]he following reasons seem to be important for those non-upper class people who do actually perceive the existence of an upper class in America.

A belief held by some is that upper-class people deserve their position because they have worked hard to earn it. They have opened up the American Dream Package correctly. They have followed the rules of the game, so natu-

rally they are where they should be. . . . It pays off those who do work and get to the top. Such arguments and beliefs, however, overlook the fact that most large incomes in America are based upon the inheritance of unearned income sources (Lundberg, 1968). Such knowledge, though, is not part of the conventional wisdom. Rather, Horatio Alger rags-to-riches stories are presented to the non-upper class by a variety of upper-class dominated institutions.

Another interpretation of the upper class is that it provides the non-upper class with a fantasy world. Non-upper class members can vicariously enjoy the life-style of the more visible segments of the upper class. One can see ample evidence of this in contemporary society. The "people" sections of newspapers and television news programs draw heavily upon this "reality" by keeping us aware of the latest doings of a variety of upper-class members. . . .

Some members of the non-upper class also defend upper-class people by praising them for their philanthropy. They feel that the rich give their wealth away to charitable causes from which non-upper class people benefit. . . . Indeed, a considerable amount of so-called philanthropy is not only a means of defending and maintaining the position of the upper class but also a tax write-off to boot. As a prime example, Nicholas von Hoffman notes that "Hughes' only charity, the Howard Hughes Medical Institute, was a philanthropic fraud whereby the tax laws were manipulated to keep the tycoon yet richer and more powerful" (von Hoffman, 1979:21). . . .

A final defense of the upper class by the non-upper class is the reasoning that the upper class, because of its position, can and does help the rest of the population in ways other than philanthropy. For example, it can provide political leadership. . . . [T]he upper class does play a significant role in the political process, but it seems clear that this role is one of either protecting or furthering upper-class interests rather than non-upper class interests. A similar rationalization holds that the upper class helps the non-upper class by providing it with jobs in the corporations that the upper class owns and controls. This is a version of the formula that business success ultimately means success for all—via a gradual trickle-down effect. . . .

By the way of summary, some of the rationalizations discussed above defend the position of the upper class in America. For example, parts of the non-upper class believe that the upper class has earned its position and deserves it, and that the upper class provides the non-upper class with jobs, material for fantasies, political leadership, and charitable contributions. Such lines of reasoning encourage non-upper class people to admire the upper class and, perhaps, to model themselves after the upper class. "Work hard, become successful, and you can become part of the upper class yourself" is an opinion voiced by quite a few members of the non-upper class. Certainly such arguments do not lead many into a position of wanting to blame or challenge the upper class. . . . Finally, there also are interpretations of upper-class people that show resentment. These views see them as extravagant robber barons who exploit the working man.

There is no doubt that many Americans harbor such thoughts that, indeed, do blame the upper class. That there is not more blaming of the upper class that gets openly and politically expressed is surprising.

SUMMARY
Americans are able to accept inequality because they have accepted the American Dream package. This includes a belief in rags-to-riches mobility, a belief that equal opportunity exists, and a belief that people are ultimately responsible for their own success or failure. Even those who are unhappy with their position in society are more likely to blame themselves for their failure. They also blame the poor for their deficiencies and, as a result, feel somewhat better about their own situation. Rarely do people who have failed blame the upper class.

QUESTIONS
1. What is the source of such beliefs in the United States? In schools? Television? Books?
2. Have worsening economic conditions changed people's beliefs in success?
3. How do college students today feel about success goals and their ability to achieve them?

CHAPTER 9

Formal Organizations

CONTENTS

Do American organizations need fewer experts and more whistle blowers?

Many American organizations are in deep trouble because of their failure to achieve the goals they set for themselves. Corporations produce goods that are of poor quality and find they cannot compete with foreign firms. Mental hospitals do not cure the people sent to them for treatment. Police departments are unable to obtain the support and allegiance of the communities they serve. Schools fail to teach students the fundamentals of reading and arithmetic. These failures occur at a time when organizations have the most highly trained and best educated personnel in their history. Are these experts part of the problem? Are the experts more concerned with protecting their jobs than in exposing the reasons for their organizations' failures?

YES Organizations in America today are run by people who have highly specialized knowledge about a narrow area of activity, knowledge gained for the most part in the classroom rather than on the job. These people are accountants, economists, professional managers, quality control engineers, market analysts, public relations specialists, penologists, industrial psychologists, psychiatric social workers, and reading specialists, to name but a few. We call them experts.

Organization experts are people who know a great deal about a limited field of activity and little or nothing about the things that other people in the organization are doing. Experts have a gigantic blind spot that keeps them from seeing the "big picture," or how all the activities of organization members are supposed to contribute to some desired outcome. One reason why some American industries are unable to compete successfully with their Japanese counterparts is that U.S. firms are dependent on professional managers who have been hired at the top, while Japanese firms have managers who have spent most of their lives in the same firm and have been promoted up the ranks after years of "getting their hands dirty" as workers (Reich, 1981).

Experts are also career-centered persons who will not do anything that might jeopardize their positions or chances for advancement. They are conservative, organization team players, not inclined to "rock the boat" or "make waves." Experts cannot be relied upon to expose inefficient, unethical, immoral, or illegal activities of their employing organizations either because they are insulated by their specialties from such knowledge or their concern about their jobs creates a blind spot.

Whistle blowers, on the other hand, have specialized knowledge and also a strong sense of social and ethical responsibility. They call down their employing organizations for producing harmful or unsafe products, for environmental pollution, for cost overruns on government contracts, and for actions by coworkers that harm patients, inmates, or others. Whistleblowers are often fired for attempting to act in a professionally responsible manner. Perhaps if we had more whistle blowers in organizations, and fewer experts, many of the current problems in American organizations might be corrected.

NO Large organizations are one of the most remarkable social inventions. They have introduced greater efficiency and effectiveness into many areas of social life. Large factories produce goods in abundance and more cheaply than do small shops. Large schools serve students with better services and staff than do small ones. Large research hospitals provide higher quality medical care and a variety of diagnostic, medical, and surgical services that would be impossible for a small health care facility to duplicate.

Such organizations could not exist without highly specialized professional and technical personnel. Experts in economics, management, science, engineering, social work, and so on provide the knowledge that is essential to deal with complex technology and complex social relationships.

Highly specialized experts are also essential to deal with the knowledge explosion that has occurred in the last 50 years. It is no longer possible for people to be generalists and know enough economics, marketing, psychology, and public relations to fill the information needs of their firms.

The problem with whistle blowers is that they are not team players. They are not willing to work together with others and to make a small contribution to a project that is too big for any one person to understand. They are frequently prima donnas or malcontents.

The problem facing organizations today is not that they have too many experts, but that they have not always found the best way to get experts to work together. Organizations must be redesigned in order to encourage self-directed and highly motivated employees to become effective team players.

This chapter considers the important part that experts play in modern organizations, as well as some of the negative consequences of their activities. The rationality of organizations rests, in part, in its ability to use specialized knowledge to achieve objectives with efficiency. Yet it may be difficult to depend on the loyalty and allegiance of experts because they often identify with colleagues rather than with the organization.

QUESTIONS TO CONSIDER

■ What are the characteristics of the modern bureaucratic organization?

■ How are bureaucratic and nonbureaucratic organizations different?

■ What are the positive and negative features of bureaucratic organizations?

■ Who among employees are most dissatisfied with their jobs?

■ What are the reasons for job dissatisfaction?

PRISON INMATE WHO WOULDN'T EAT DIES: FEARED 'FOOD WAS POISONED'

VETERANS ADMINISTRATION PROBES CASE OF LOST HOSPITAL PATIENT

MENTAL HOSPITAL STAFF TRIES PATIENT'S LIFE: REPORT "THERE'S SOMETHING HARMFUL ABOUT HOSPITALIZATION"

The first newspaper headline is about a prison inmate who did not eat for 10 days, who lost more than 40 pounds, and who remained unnoticed by prison personnel. How is it possible that no one noticed that the inmate had stopped eating and was losing weight before he became critically ill?

The second headline tells of a patient, unable to speak and confined to a wheelchair, who was "misplaced" for 27 hours. The patient had been strapped in his chair and wheeled out of his ward by a hospital worker assigned to take him for therapy. He was found the next day in an elevator in the hospital basement. This happened in an institution with 3000 employees, 1300 patients and about 600 daily visitors. How is it possible for a patient to get "lost" by an organization designed to give him 24-hour care?

The story behind the third headline has to do with a group of "normal" people who easily got themselves committed to a mental hospital and, once there, could not convince the staff that they were not really patients. The experiences of these "mock patients" are vivid testimony to the lack of clearly defined criteria for mental illness. How is it possible for mental hospitals to operate without being able to distinguish between sick and healthy people?

These headlines are about only a few of the large organizations that affect the everyday life of the average person. Advanced industrial societies like the United States are often called **organizational societies.** While large-scale organizations have existed for thousands of years, it is only recently that they have become dominant because of the scope of their activities and their centrality to people's lives. The growing centrality of organizations is reflected in the importance of their activities for the health and welfare of millions of persons. Hospitals, police departments, welfare agencies, armies, factories, prisons, mental hospitals, nursing homes, and schools are only a few of these organizations.

The increased scope and centrality of organizations in contemporary societies make news stories like those just described a matter of concern to social scientists and laypersons alike. Organizations are established because they are an effective and efficient means to some desired goals. Yet organizations often do not achieve their goals and may in fact have an opposite effect. Prisons designed to rehabilitate inmates may produce hardened criminals. Government agencies designed to uphold the Constitution of the United States may operate in ways that subvert it. Police departments that are supposed to protect and serve the public may generate fear and hostility rather than support. Health and welfare organizations often neglect the needs of the people they are intended to serve.

One of the reasons why large organizations in contemporary society often fail to do what they are designed to do is that the way they are structured produces a reaction in employees that psychologists have called **deindividuation.** Deindividuation, or loss of personal identity, occurs when people working in large organizations ignore individual differences in their coworkers and in the clients their organizations serve—when workers come to see others as part of a large homogeneous group of people rather than as individuals with their own special needs and problems. Deindividuation is also reflected in the tendency of organization members

In an organizational society many functions once carried out by families and communities are now handled in large, impersonal settings. One example of this is the growth of nursing homes where an increasing number of older citizens spend their final years.

to deny personal responsibility for their actions. "Don't blame me, I'm only following the rules" is a typical justification for an action that has unpleasant consequences for another person.

In this chapter we will first examine the central features of formal organizations and some of the variations among types of organizations. By understanding the structure of organizations, we can begin to understand those features that help them achieve their goals and satisfy the needs of organizational members, clients, and society at large. We can also begin to identify the conditions that produce many of the undesirable consequences of living in an organizational society.

Whether you are interested in preserving individual freedoms, maintaining democratic institutions, producing more goods for a profit, protecting society from its dangerous members, or fighting an enemy army, you can better pursue your concerns if you understand the workings of large-scale organizations.

THE NATURE OF ORGANIZATIONS

A **formal organization** is a deliberately constructed social unit with explicitly coordinated activities designed to contribute toward the attainment of a stated goal. An organization is distinguished from other human groupings, such as families and friendship groups, by its internal structure—its authority ranks and formal system of communication and social control—which coordinates and continuously monitors the activities of members to achieve goals.

The term "bureaucracy" is often used in place of "formal organization." We will use *bureaucracy* to refer to a specific type of formal organization. Some formal organizations are bureaucratic in form, while others have only a few of the characteristics of bureaucracies.

Historical Context of Formal Organizations

Although the rise of large organizations is often identified with the industrialization of Western Europe, there is considerable evidence of large organizational activity in the pre-European experience. Egypt, China, and the Incan empire all had extensive administrative groups to manage selected tasks in their economic and political lives (Albrow, 1970). Through systems of regulations and networks of officials, such organizations were used, for example, to collect taxes, to operate an elaborate canal system, and to undertake large-scale agricultural activities.

It was not until the decline of feudalism and the advance of industrialization, however, that the large formal organization became a major form in many areas of social, economic, and political life. Wealth and power based on landed property gradually gave way to wealth and power based on production and distribution of commodities in a money economy. As a consequence of the new economic base, towns began to grow, challenging the traditional power of the feudal lords and the traditional symbol of the manor as the center of power. New towns developed systems of officials and regulations to deal with trade, crafts, finance, and the law.

Conflicts between the traditional social order represented by the feudal lords and the emerging social order of the growing middle class encouraged centralization of authority in the state. This marked the beginnings of modern bureaucracy, whose quasi-governmental functions were carried out by salaried officials rather than by traditional rulers.

Max Weber (1864–1920), German sociologist and foremost student of the history of organizations, observed that the decline of the feudal order and the emergence of the modern state were signaled by (1) the changing nature of authority, (2) the bureaucratic organization, and (3) the bureaucratic official. Each phenomenon, Weber argued, represented a sharp break with the feudal order and started the slow and still continuing process of the rationalization of social life.

From Traditional to Rational-Legal Authority

If someone holds a gun to your head and tells you to do something and you comply, that person has

power over you. Power is the ability of a person to achieve his or her purposes by controlling others or getting others to perform acts they would not ordinarily perform. If the only reason you comply with the order is the threat of death and if the person holding the gun has no other claim to power over you, then he or she is exercising illegitimate power. If, however, someone tells you to do something and you comply because you feel that person has a right to so direct you, then you are involved in a relationship of **authority.** Authority, therefore, is legitimate, or justified, power.

We can distinguish between different types of authority. The feudal order of the Middle Ages was based primarily on the existence of **traditional authority.** Relationships between lords and vassals, kings and lords, clergy and nobility, men and women, parents and children were justified or guided by the past, by "the way things have always been done." According to Weber (1920; English translation, 1947), traditional authority is based on belief in the "sanctity of the order and the attendant powers of control as they have been handed down from the past . . . " (p. 341). Obedience to traditional authority is based not on a set of written rules or laws but on the people who are the carriers of tradition. In short, one does not obey the rule, one obeys the person.

Traditional authority in the feudal order declined with the emergence of towns, merchants, craft workers, and markets. When workers in towns entered into contractual agreements for their labor, in contrast to honoring earlier traditional bonds with a particular lord, traditional authority was replaced by **rational-legal authority,** which is based on "belief in the 'legality' of patterns of normative rules and the right of those elevated to authority under such rules to issue commands" (p. 328). Rational-legal authority requires two conditions: (1) a system of enacted abstract rules that are binding upon all parties and (2) special knowledge possessed by the person in authority that can be demonstrated to be important for the organization's activities. For example, when you follow your instructor's assignment to read certain material and take a quiz each week, you do so because you accept a set of rules that give the instructor the right to quiz you, and you believe that her/his special knowledge justifies using quizzes as a teaching technique.

Obedience under rational-legal authority is not to a person but to a rule. Obedience to rules rather than people is possible because people who exercise rational-legal authority do so through a particular position that they occupy. Their areas of rational-legal authority are well defined. For example, the factory manager exercises rational-legal authority by issuing orders to workers about work-related activities. The manager's authority would not extend to the worker's family or political life. Those who exercise traditional authority, however, may not be so restricted.

The Bureaucratic Organization

As noted earlier, a bureaucracy is a particular type of formal organization. Weber, in his study of the political and economic organizations that emerged in the postfeudal period, developed the concept of an ideal-type bureaucracy. The ideal type is a composite of all of the elements of bureaucracy as they might exist in one "pure" form. Weber used the ideal type as a "measuring rod" to compare different countries according to their degree of bureaucratization.

According to Weber, the **ideal-type bureaucracy** consists of the following elements.

1. There is a clearly ordered hierarchy of positions or offices, each above and below another in authority.
2. Each position or office has a clearly defined "sphere of competence"; that is, there is a specified jurisdiction for each position that prohibits an official from overstepping his or her authority when acting in that position.
3. The activities of the bureaucracy depend upon the maintenance of written records. All rules, regulations, and procedures are written down, as are all orders or directives.
4. Positions are filled on the basis of expert training. The object is to have each position filled by the person with the highest qualifications.
5. The operation of the modern bureaucracy is based upon a system of general rules. These rules are designed to cover all situations the organization might face in its daily operations. It is further assumed that these rules can be learned and that such knowledge is a form of technical expertise.
6. Relationships among people within a bureaucratic organization should be impersonal; emotional bonds have no place in it. Impersonality is felt to be protection against arbitrary action by an official and protects all members equally.

Weber felt bureaucracy to be a superior form of organization, of controlling and coordinating human activities in selected areas of social life. He stated (1920): "The decisive reason for the advance of bureaucratic organization has always been its purely technical superiority over any other form of organization ... Precision, speed, unambiguity, knowledge of the files, continuity, discretion, unity, strict subordination, reduction of friction and of material and personal costs—these are raised to the optimum point in the strictly bureaucratic administration (p. 214).

Let us look at the way a modern bureaucratic organization conducts its daily business compared with that of a preindustrial organization. In the bureaucratic organization affairs are managed on a continuous basis by officials who have specialized knowledge. The authority of each official is clearly defined and limited to a particular area of activity. The position of the official is contained within a hierarchy of authority and responsibility. Officials do not own the resources of their office nor can they appropriate these resources for their own use. All business is conducted by following written rules, and all business transactions are recorded in written documents.

Under the nonbureaucratic organization of the feudal system, business is conducted when the "ruler" feels like it. The ruler resists efforts to restrict the scope of his or her authority, recognizing only unwritten tradition or custom. All members of a ruler's staff are viewed as part of his or her household. They are personally selected and owe their loyalties to the ruler, not to abstract rules. The resources of the office and the household are not separated but are combined and used by the ruler for both personal and official activities. Com-

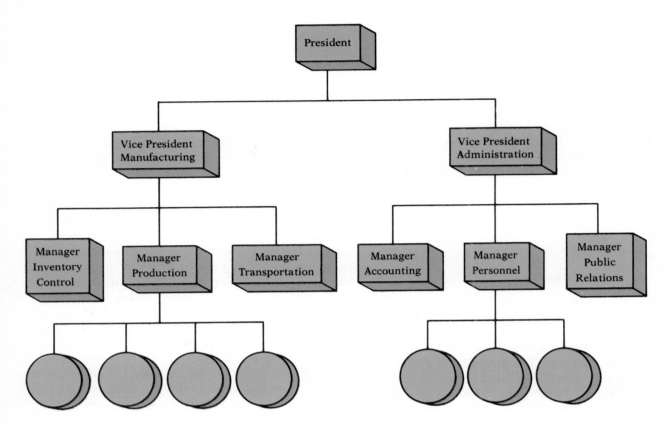

FIGURE 9.1   Sample organization Chart for a Manufacturing Company

The structure of large organizations is made up of hierarchically arranged positions, each with its own special responsibilities and area of authority. This organization chart shows the division of tasks at the upper management level and the lines of authority showing who reports to whom. A complete organization chart would extend downward to include production supervisors and blue-collar workers.

munications dealing with official activities are oral and there are generally few files or records. All in all, business activity in nonbureaucratic organizations is neither calculable nor predictable, making arbitrary actions by the ruler or official a common practice.*

Bureaucratic organizations have been viewed as one of the most effective and efficient ways of organizing the activities of many people to achieve a goal. What people frequently call "red tape" in organizations—rules that do not allow exceptions, impersonal treatment—are precisely what makes organizations most efficient. However, an important unanswered question is whether all types of organizations, regardless of their size or their goals, should be organized in a bureaucratic form. Is it possible that particular types of organizations are more effective and efficient without formal rules, impersonality, and a hierarchy of authority?

*See Chapter 13 for a discussion of the ability to predict the results of actions as a requirement of the modern corporation.

TYPES OF ORGANIZATIONS

There are thousands of organizations in modern society carrying out many different activities. One way to begin to understand their diversity is to group or classify organizations according to some characteristic they have in common. Such classification schemes are called typologies, and they are designed to reduce various characteristics (whether of plants, animals, or organizations) to a smaller and more manageable set of categories. Moreover, the classification should identify important differences among the types or classes. Thus a good typology might identify a group of organizations for which Weber's bureaucratic model would be an excellent description.

What characteristics have been used to develop organizational typologies? We can identify four of these typologies by their dominant characteristic: goal typology, who-benefits typology, compliance typology, and a total-institutions typology.

Goal Typology

Organizations can be classified by the kind of goals they pursue or the kind of output they produce. Parsons (1960) and Katz and Kahn (1966) identify four types of organizations that are roughly similar. First is the *economic* organization, which provides goods and services to the public. Second is the *maintenance* organization, such as schools and churches, which socializes people to their roles in society. Third is the *integrative* organization, which settles conflicts among individuals and groups and ensures the necessary degree of harmony for social order, such as the courts, prisons, and mental hospitals. Fourth, is the *political* organization, which allocates power to different groups to enable society to achieve its goals. The best example is government.

The main problem with goal typologies is the difficulty in classifying organizations according to a single criterion. The larger the organization the greater the chance that it can pursue several goals. For example, IBM is an economic organization, but it also uses its wealth to support educational programs and cultural institutions, as well as to shape political decisions through lobbying and support of political candidates.

Who-Benefits Typology

Blau and Scott (1962) developed a typology of organizations based upon the question of "who benefits" (*cui bono*). They suggest that each type of organization serves a prime beneficiary and that this service creates a special problem. In the *mutual-benefit* organization the members of the organization are the prime beneficiaries. Examples are voluntary associations like the YWCA, professional associations, social clubs, and labors unions. Their problem is membership apathy. The *business* organization has its owners as the prime beneficiary. The central problem of such organizations is efficiency, profits, and surviving in the marketplace. Next is the *commonweal* organization, which has the public at large as the prime beneficiary. Police departments, prisons, and government agencies are commonweal-organizations. The central problem facing such organizations is how to avoid too much interference from the public, which often seeks accountability and greater control. Finally, in the *service* organization clients served by the organization are the prime beneficiaries. Examples are schools, hospitals, and human service organizations. Conflict between service to clients and administrative procedures is the overriding problem of such organizations.

Classifying organizations by the *cui bono* typology also presents difficulties. Organizations may have several prime beneficiaries and their interests may conflict. For example, hospitals may find it difficult to serve their clients with high quality medical care at the same time that the medical directors are trying to enhance their own careers. Which group, then, is the prime beneficiary? We can ask the same question about business organizations, where stockholders as owners may have little to say about their organization in contrast to managers who run the organization.

Compliance Typology

All organizations have different levels of employees or members. Etzioni (1961) believes that the key problem facing organizations is how to get co-operation from its lower-level members, like hourly wage employees, parishioners, students, inmates, or patients. Each of these groups must be motivated to comply with organizational expectations of their performance on the assumption that compliance will increase productivity, efficiency, and goal at-tainment.

Compliance is a result of the kind of power used by an organization to get desired behavior from lower-level participants and the type of involve-ment that these participants have in the organi-zation. Power can be *coercive*, through, for exam-ple, use of physical force or deprivation of food and shelter; *remunerative*, through giving wages; or *normative*, through recognition of performance by bestowing esteem, honorific titles, and other sym-bolic rewards. The involvement of lower-level par-ticipants can be *alienative*, as is the negative ori-entation of prisoners, *calculative*, where one's interest in the organization is mainly financial or *moral*, where one has a strong positive orientation toward the organization and its goals.

Etzioni sees the three forms of power as linked to the kinds of involvement that lower-level par-ticipants have with their organization. This pro-duces three consistent organization types: coer-cive-alienative, remunerative-calculative, and normative-moral. In organizations where lower-level participants are very negative toward the organi-zation (alienative), coercive power is probably most effective. For example, it is not likely that prisoners could be motivated to comply by using normative power, any more than parishioners could be mo-tivated by remunerative power.

There are also mixed organization types in which we find organizations using more than one kind of power because of different kinds of involvement among lower-level participants. For example, in higher education student involvement is primarily moral, although there are undoubtedly some who exhibit a calculative orientation and a small num-ber who are extremely alienated. The power applied to students is primarily normative (in the form of grades, awards, honors, and so on), although some power may be remunerative, like loss of a schol-arship. Coercive power is infrequently wielded as

the extremely alienated students rarely remain in college very long.

A weakness of Etzioni's typology is that it ig-nores the largest proportion of people who work in organizations, namely, all those who are not at the bottom of the hierarchy. Another problem is that the typology assumes that lower-level participants are without power in organizations. This is con-trary to evidence. For example, studies have de-scribed how patients and attendants in a mental hospital develop power by making superiors de-pendent upon them (Mechanic, 1962; Perrucci, 1963; 1966; Scheff, 1961). Many patients do jobs like ward cleanup, run errands, and escort less mobile pa-tients around the hospital. If patients did not do this unpaid work it would create an added burden for attendants and nurses. Some patients become indispensable and therefore very powerful. Simi-larly, attendants control a great deal of information about patients, which they use to extract favors from physicians.

Total-Institution Typology

Another type of organization is the **total institution** (Goffman, 1961), in which members live for a pe-riod of time in isolation from the rest of society and whose lives are subject to the control of the organization. The best examples are prisons, men-tal hospitals, and military institutions.

Upon entering the total institution the prior life of the inmate may be systematically stripped away. Individuality is discouraged. The new recruit in, say, boot camp is given standardized clothing that resists individual identity, extreme haircuts that alter physical appearance, and psychological abuse that tears down the recruit's self-image. The recruit is then resocialized to new values, new symbols of authority, and a new self-concept.

Although the goal of total institutions may be to provide humane care or custody, they are inade-quately funded and staffed for such purposes. They therefore rely on means that provide order while subverting the original goals. According to Goffman, this increases the ability of prisons or mental hos-pitals to control a large number of inmates with

relatively few staff, thereby maintaining effective social control in potentially volatile situations.

DILEMMAS OF MODERN ORGANIZATIONS

The positive aspects of the modern organization is its ability to organize its activities in an efficient and predictable manner to better achieve its goals. This is the result of its emphasis on written rules, specialization, and hierarchical authority. However, each of these positive features of organization also has negative consequences, either for its members or for its ability to achieve stated goals. The dilemma of the modern organization is that its very strengths can also be the source of its weakness.

The desire for efficiency in "total institutions" sometimes results in treating inmates or clients as standardized and interchangeable. Any recognition of individual needs and differences introduces inefficiencies in organizational operations. Here we see prison inmates experiencing a routine "strip search."

In the four sections that follow we shall examine some of these negative consequences.

Impersonal Rules and Close Supervision

One way that organizations try to get predictable results is through a system of general rules. Rules reduce ambiguity by informing workers about appropriate behaviors in a variety of situations. Rules also take the place of direct supervision and the use of orders in face-to-face relationships. As a result there are fewer visible authority relations. Rules are impersonal and a subordinate can follow the rules without feeling that he is a subordinate. This leads to less tension between workers and supervisors and therefore more effective operations (Gouldner, 1954).

These are the intended, positive consequences of rules. However, rules also result in certain unanticipated negative consequences that do not contribute to the organization's efficiency. Rules inevitably establish a standard of minimally acceptable behavior. Because the rule applies to a large number of people, it must reasonably allow for a wide range of possible behaviors. If the standard set by the rule is high, some people will follow the rule but most will not, making the rule irrelevant. Thus to ensure compliance there is a tendency to state rules in terms of minimum standards. When rules reflect low standards of performance, there will be a discrepancy between an organization's performance goals and its achievements; many workers will appear to be unmotivated, goofing off, or making trouble.

Gouldner illustrates this point:

The rules served as a specification of a minimum level of acceptable performance. It was therefore possible to remain apathetic, for he knew just how little he could do and still remain secure.

For example, after Peele [the manager] had ruled that workers could not "punch in early" and accumulate a little overtime in that way, one mill worker said acidly, "Well, if that's the way he wants it, that's the way he wants it. But I'll be damned if I put in any overtime when things get rough and they'd like us to."
Said another worker:

" 'O.K., I'll punch in just to, and I'll punch out on the nose. But you know you can lead a horse to water and you can lead him away, but it's awful hard to tell just how much water he drinks while he's at it." (pp. 174–175)

Thus rules in a bureaucratic organization can have both intended, positive consequences and unintended, negative consequences for the attainment of organizational goals.

Specialists and Subgroup Interests

As we noted in the "At Issue" section of this chapter, positions in modern bureaucratic organizations are filled on the basis of specialized knowledge. When authority is delegated to persons in a bureaucracy, it is assumed that they can carry out their assignment because of their specialized knowledge. The intended result is greater effectiveness of an organization's operations.

The unintended consequence of authority based upon specialization is the development of a sharp division of interests among different subgroups in the organization. Technical specialists, sales specialists, management specialists, and accounting specialists often make decisions that are in the best interest of their subgroup rather than of the total organization. Many conflicts within organizations may have less to do with operating more effectively than with protecting the prestige or power of different subgroups. In addition, specialists tend to see problems from a narrow perspective, and the solutions they propose may be inadequate or unworkable.

Cosmopolitans and Locals

A related problem is the tendency of specialization to create *dual allegiances* in organization personnel (Kornhauser, 1963; Marcson, 1960; Gouldner, 1957, 1958). Specialists, who frequently receive their training in universities, also are often members of professional associations outside their employing organizations. These professional associations may embrace values, norms, and work standards that conflict with those of the organizations in which the specialists work. Specialists who try to maintain "dual allegiances" to their professions and their employing organizations may experience enough conflict to impair their effectiveness in the organization (Perrucci, et al., 1980).

In some cases, however, the problem is not maintaining allegiances to two organizations but choosing one over the other. Gouldner (1957, 1958) has examined two different types of people in organizations, cosmopolitans and locals. The main difference between the two types is whether they think of themselves primarily as belonging to the organization in which they work or as belonging to a body outside the organization. The **cosmopolitan** emphasizes loyalty to professional groups outside of the organization, while the **local** emphasizes loyalty to the employing organization and thinks in terms of advancement within the organization rather than among a national group of specialists.

Bureaucratic Authority and the "Cheerful Robot"*

The smooth functioning of bureaucracy is aided by conformity to written rules and by formal, impersonal social relationships. Nevertheless, these behaviors can have a number of unintended consequences. In a classic essay, "Bureaucratic Structure and Personality," Merton (1957) analyzes the relationship between rules and discipline, on the one hand, and rigidity and ritualism on the other. Following the rules, a behavior originally designed to further an organization's goals, can become an end in itself or a way of feeling secure in one's position. The overall result, according to Merton, is a *displacement of goals*, "where the primary concern with conformity to the rules interferes with the achievement of the purposes of the organization . . ." (p. 199).

An organization's emphasis upon rules and obedience to authority may also impair a person's ability to resist unjust authority, or authority directed toward destructive ends. Perhaps the most infamous example of this is the behavior of Nazi ci-

vilian and military personnel who rationally and systematically exterminated millions of civilians who were viewed as undesirables. Their defense when they were tried for these crimes at the end of World War II was simply that they were "following orders." Not to have followed the orders of military and civilian officials, they argued, would have been unpatriotic, illegal, or treasonable.

Alternatives to Bureaucratic Organization

Some modern organizations exhibit characteristics of Weber's ideal-type bureaucracy, while others do not. Some organizations, like factories, are hierarchically organized along clear lines of authority. Research laboratories usually have "flat" structures based on colleague control rather than administrative authority. Hospitals and universities usually have "mixed" structures containing administrative control of financial affairs and colleague control of academic affairs. Much of the theory and research on organizations in the past 20 years has been directed to the question of why this is so. Does it have to do with the size of the organization (Blau, 1970; Hall, Haas, and Johnson, 1967)? The technology an organization uses (Aldrich, 1972; Perrow, 1967; Woodward, 1965)? The organization's clients or members (Etzioni, 1961)? Its goals (Etzioni, 1964; Perrow, 1961)? Or does it have to do with those who control and benefit from the organization's activities (Blau and Scott, 1962)?

There are still no firm answers to these questions. Rather, there has been an accumulation of evidence about how organizations differ in size or in type of technology. Large organizations with production systems that are closely integrated, like an automobile production line, are more likely to have bureaucratic structures of hierarchical authority, formal rules, and a large administrative staff. Production systems that use only loosely related work groups and tasks, like designing a new type of building based on solar energy, are more likely to have "flat," nonbureaucratic structures that require work groups to meet frequently for joint decision making. In general, the more that work can be planned and controlled away from the production line, the more bureaucratic the organization. If teaching could

---

*Mills (1959) called attention to individuals in large organizations who become so adapted to rules and routines that they willingly give up their freedom to become "cheerful robots."

be reduced to a set of specifically prescribed acts, or done by teaching machines, colleges and universities would be no different than automobile plants.

Other investigators, such as Bennis (1965), believe that bureaucracy as a form of organization is no longer suited to our advanced industrial society. Major changes in the environment, increased levels of education, and changing work values will be responsible for the decline of bureaucracy and the emergence of new forms of organization. Bennis predicts that the organization of the future will be less like a machine and more like a living organism, responding quickly and easily to innovations in science and technology. Jobs will be more involving, calling on greater tolerance of ambiguity, on reserves of imagination, and on problem-solving abilities of workers. Authority relationships and rules will be kept to a minimum as workers will be more self-directed.

In Reading 9.1, Joyce Rothschild-Whitt reports the results of research on organizations that have rejected a rational-bureaucratic structure in favor of a collectivist-democratic structure. Free schools, community health centers, food cooperatives, law collectives, and alternative newspapers are examples of hundreds of alternative organizations that appeared during the 1970s, some of which continue to thrive today.

ENVIRONMENT AND ORGANIZATIONS

All organizations interact with segments of their environment to obtain needed resources (Aldrich, 1979; Zey-Farrell and Aiken, 1981). Business organizations must establish favorable relationships with the suppliers of labor, capital, and material. Colleges must attract students and faculty and funds from state legislatures or alumni. Community mental health centers must have good relationships with physicians, clergy, schools, welfare agencies, and hospitals from whom they get referrals or with whom they work to place former patients. Each of these organizations must also interact with agencies of government that are responsible for regulating activities in their area: the products of pharmaceutical organizations are tested for safety and efficacy by the Food and Drug Administration; financial transactions of corporations are regulated by the Securities and Exchange Commission; and so on.

All organizations try to reduce uncertainty in their relationships with elements of the environment. Large and powerful organizations are able to establish long-term agreements for supplies of labor, capital, or material. They also are able to influence legislation and agencies of government to create a favorable climate for their activities through lobbying and political contributions.

In their efforts to control their environment to obtain resources and reduce uncertainty, organizations also try to shape societal values and the way the general public thinks about broad issues. Thus we may see "public service" advertisements or "town meetings" sponsored by IBM, or Exxon, or United Technologies to bring before the American public discussion of such topics as how to deal with the United States' energy dependence, or the decline of the work ethic or the need to increase productivity, or the importance of defense spending to national security.

A specific example of such efforts to create a favorable "value climate" or "opinion climate" is a number of public opinion polls sponsored by Union Carbide Corporation, the nation's second largest chemical manufacturer (Kinsley, 1981). The subject of one poll was what Americans think about hazardous chemical wastes; of another, how the public views corporate profits; and of a third, American attitudes toward the relationship between business and government in connection with economic growth. The purpose of such polls is to give the impression (through a specific choice of topics) that there is a consensus in America on important national issues that happens to be favorable to corporate interests and to shape political debate on these issues.

Another way in which organizations try to increase their control over the environment is by establishing ties with other organizations that have needed resources. Industrial corporations heavily dependent on capital for their growth often appoint executives from financial institutions (banks, insurance companies) to their boards of directors. Community hospitals will invite influential political and civic leaders to sit on their boards to obtain needed community support to attract clients, physicians, nurses, donations and supportive legislation.

The ties established by large organizations with other organizations in their environment may be extensive, forming a "web of ties" that we can call an **interorganizational network**. Figure 9.2 is a hypothetical health network concerned with the delivery of services to a city (Perrow, 1979). The "nodes" in this network are organizations, and the connecting lines represent a "tie." Flowing through these ties are resources like information, personnel, funds, tax legislation, and regulatory decisions.

Some organizations have both direct and close ties. The five hospitals in the network are directly related to each other, and the length of the lines

between them indicates the closeness (the importance to each other) of the relationship. Other organizations are indirectly related, such as the state university's tie to the hospitals, which is through the medical school. Mapping ties among organizations and describing the nature of those ties, can help to identify the flow of needed resources to and from organizations. In addition, mapping out relationships of dominance and subordinance among organizations can help to identify centers of influence and power and the way that important decisions are shaped (Galaskiewicz, 1979; Laumann and Pappi, 1976; Mardsen, 1981; Perrucci and Pilisuk, 1970).

Network analysis is an emerging specialty in sociology that has the potential for increasing our understanding of the complex relationships among organizations at the national and international level. The way that power is used to shape national decisions has been one subject of network analysis

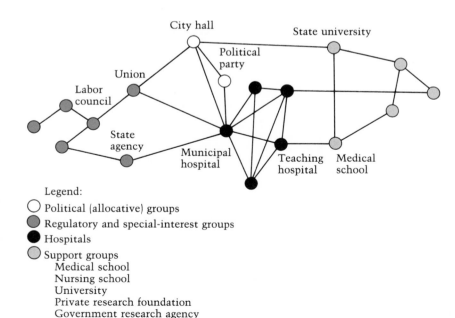

FIGURE 9.2 Imaginary City Health Network

Legend:
○ Political (allocative) groups
⬤ Regulatory and special-interest groups
● Hospitals
◐ Support groups
    Medical school
    Nursing school
    University
    Private research foundation
    Government research agency

Source: C. Perrow, *Complex Organizations*, Glenview, Ill.: Scott, Foresman, 1979.

(Burt, 1980; Moore, 1979; Useem, 1979). Similar efforts are underway in the study of multinational corporations (Hymer, 1979; Wallerstein, 1979).

TYPES OF ORGANIZATIONAL INVOLVEMENT

An important aspect of organizational effectiveness is the motives that people bring to the organization when they become members. Successful organizations are those that are able to satisfy member needs and still meet organizational requirements. An effective organization must (1) attract and hold members (2) who will perform their roles dependably and (3) who will occasionally engage in spontaneous behavior beyond role requirements that helps the organization achieve its goals (Katz and Kahn, 1966). The degree to which an organization is meeting these requirements is measured by absenteeism and employee turnover in the first case; by productivity in the second case; and by cooperativeness, willingness to make suggestions, and self-training to increase job skills in the third case.

All organizations make use of four general motivational patterns to satisfy member needs. They are as follows:

1. *Rule compliance.* Acceptance of organizational rules is most effective when the authority of people in leadership positions is widely accepted. Rules must be clear-cut, and penalties for violations must be specific and enforced. Rule compliance will produce dependable, though minimal, role performance. It will reduce absenteeism, but it will also reduce innovative behavior.

2. *Instrumental rewards and satisfactions.* Rewards and satisfactions include financial rewards to individuals (such as a piecework rate of pay) or to work groups (such as a bonus to all workers for finishing a project early) and peer-group approval. Rewards and peer-group satisfactions can reduce turnover and absenteeism, but they probably will not increase cooperativeness and innovation.

3. *Self-expression and accomplishment.* This motivation is closely tied to the nature of the job. People in complex, highly skilled, responsible, and autonomous positions, for example, skilled furni-

In some organizations, members closely identify with its goals and purposes, gaining satisfaction from the mere fact of membership. It is often said that Japanese employees think of themselves first of all as a member of a particular organization and secondly in terms of their occupation. Here we see employees of Bendix Corporation joining a rally in support of their firm when it was involved in a merger fight with two other firms.

ture makers or architects, have a greater chance for self-expression, which can motivate them to do a good job. This motivational pattern will reduce absenteeism and increase productivity. It may also increase a worker's exceptional and innovative behavior.

4. *Internalized organizational goals.* Identification with the organization occurs when the work is hazardous (FBI, CIA, and certain forms of police work), when the leader is charismatic, or when the members themselves participate in organizational decisions and rewards. This motivation reduces turnover and absenteeism and increases productivity and cooperative, innovative behavior.

Individual motives for joining organizations, the conditions under which those motives are facilitated, and their consequences for the organization are summarized in Table 9.1. We must note that these consequences do not take into account in-

dividual differences. For example, regardless of motivation, a highly skilled worker may meet organizational goals better than an unskilled recruit. Also, a person's motivation may be so high that it produces anxiety, which interferes with both performance and innovation on the job. As Vroom (1965) points out, work performance probably is highest when the worker's ability is high and motivation is only moderately high.

It is likely that internalization, the most effective motivational pattern for the organization, characterizes relatively few organizational members. However, we would expect that those who internalize an organization's goals or those who are able to express themselves in their work would be happier and more satisfied in their jobs than those who work only for rewards. The data in Table 9.2, which relates occupational status and job satisfaction, indirectly supports the latter hypothesis.

TABLE 9.1   Worker Motives and Organizational Behavior

MOTIVE	FACILITATING CONDITIONS	ORGANIZATIONAL CONSEQUENCES
I. Legal compliance ("I just follow the rules. No more, no less.")	Legitimate authority Clear rules Specific penalties for rule violations	Dependable role performance Low absenteeism High employee turnover Little innovation
II. Rewards (a) Organization rewards, e.g., pay, retirement benefits ("If they want more work out of me, they'll have to pay me more.")	Rewards must be large in size Rewards must be immediate Rewards must be dispensed uniformly	Low turnover Low absenteeism
(b) Peer group rewards ("The only reason I stay here is because I like the guys I work with.")	Must be a cohesive work group	Depends on whether group's norms do or do not support organization's norms
III. Self expression ("This job gives me a chance to realize my potential.")	Work must be complex and challenging Workers must be autonomous	High productivity Low absenteeism
IV. Identification with organization ("What's good for General Motors is good for America.")	If work is hazardous e.g., police, military If there is a charismatic leader If members participate in decision-making	Low absenteeism Low turnover High cooperation Innovation

SOURCE: Adapted from table in Daniel Katz and Robert Kahn, *The Social Psychology of Organizations*, New York: John Wiley & Sons, 1966.

TABLE 9.2   Amount and Sources of Job Satisfaction as Related to Occupational Status

	PROFESSIONALS, TECHNICIANS	MANAGERS, PROPRIETORS	CLERICAL WORKERS	SALES WORKERS	SKILLED WORKERS	SEMISKILLED WORKERS	UNSKILLED WORKERS	FARMERS
Job Satisfaction								
Very satisfied	42%	38%	22%	24%	22%	27%	13%	22%
Satisfied	41	42	39	44	54	48	52	58
Neutral	1	6	9	5	6	9	6	4
Ambivalent	10	6	13	9	10	9	13	9
Dissatisfied	3	6	17	16	7	6	16	7
Not ascertained	3	2	—	2	1	1	—	—
TOTAL	100%	100%	100%	100%	100%	100%	100%	100%
Number of men	(119)	(127)	(46)	(55)	(202)	(152)	(84)	(77)
Sources of Satisfaction								
Mention only ego satisfactions	80%	68%	39%	60%	54%	40%	29%	58%
Mention both ego and extrinsic satisfactions	16	20	35	29	28	31	26	17
Mention only extrinsic satisfactions	2	9	24	7	14	24	29	17
Mention no reasons for liking job	—	—	2	2	2	3	8	1
Not ascertained	2	3	—	2	2	2	8	7
TOTAL	100%	100%	100%	100%	100%	100%	100%	100%
Number of men	(119)	(127)	(46)	(55)	(202)	(152)	(84)	(77)

SOURCE: Table 6.8 "Relationship between Occupational Status and Sources of Satisfaction with the Job (among Employed Men)" from AMERICANS VIEW THEIR MENTAL HEALTH: A Nationwide Interview Survey, by Gerald Gurin, Joseph Veroff, and Sheila Feld (Joint Commission on Mental Illness and Health Monograph Series/No. 4). © 1960 by Basic Books, Inc., Publishers, New York. Reprinted by permission of the publisher.

Professionals, who can express themselves in their work, and managers, who are likely to internalize organizational goals, are more likely to be satisfied with their jobs than employees in any other occupational categories. In addition, professionals and managers are more likely than others to report ego satisfaction and less likely to mention extrinsic satisfactions in relation to their jobs. Employees who are highly paid mention ego satisfaction more than extrinsic rewards as motivating factors, while those who are paid less mention extrinsic rewards over ego satisfaction.

Job Satisfaction and Worker Alienation

The results presented in Table 9.2 are typical. In almost every study, job satisfaction is directly related to the status of the job. Persons in high status jobs report more job satisfaction than persons in low status jobs (Gruenberg, 1980). Wilensky (1966) has drawn together data from his own studies and others on the question of whether workers in different occupations would choose the same type of work if they could start all over again. In the upper professional occupations, about eight or nine persons out of 10 indicate that they would pursue the same job if given an opportunity to make their career choice anew. Seven out of 10 engineers and fewer than five out of 10 white-collar employees would choose the same occupation again. Of those in blue-collar occupations only two to four out of 10 would choose the same job again.

The reasons for greater job satisfaction in higher level occupations seem fairly clear. Higher status jobs yield more income, greater psychological satisfaction, greater freedom from supervision, more opportunities for social relationships with coworkers, and greater security. These reasons are often classified as a job's intrinsic rewards (in the nature of the work itself) and its extrinsic rewards (income).

Much early research on job dissatisfaction among blue-collar workers focused on assemblyline work in the automobile industry (Walker and Guest, 1952; Faunce, 1958; Kornhauser, 1962). There are four prominent features of assemblyline work: (1) the work pace is machine controlled; (2) the work is extremely repetitive; (3) the work requires only minimal skill or training; (4) there are few opportunities for social relationships with coworkers.

Consider the following typical comments by workers on the "moving belt" of an assemblyline, reported by Walker and Guest (1952):

The bad thing about assemblyline is that the line keeps moving. If you have a little trouble with a job, you can't take the time to do it right.

On the line you're geared to the line. You don't dare stop. If you get behind, you have a hard time catching up.

The line speed is too great. More men wouldn't help much. They'd just expect more work out of an individual. There's an awful lot of tension.

I don't like running all the time. . . . I don't mind doing a good day's work, but I don't like to run through it.

The work isn't hard, it's the never ending pace. . . . the guys yell "hurrah" whenever the line breaks down. . . . you can hear it all over the plant.

These statements reflect the workers' response to machine-paced work but also their concern with the repetitiveness of tasks and their lack of variety. Walker and Guest tried to measure variety by looking at the number of operations performed in a job. About 32 percent of the workers had jobs consisting of a single operation. Thirteen percent had jobs requiring two operations; 23 percent, three to five operations; 16 percent, five to 10 operations; and the remaining more than 10 operations.

The most repetitive, machine-paced jobs produced higher absenteeism and greater turnover than other jobs. In general, those who worked off the line and whose jobs required more skill and discretion tended to have more favorable reactions to their work. It is probably the combination of work repetition and machine-controlled work pace that is most distressing for the worker in the automated plant.

Many of the conclusions drawn from early research on the effects of mechanization on workers have been challenged in more recent studies. Form (1973) compared reactions of automobile workers in a modern industrial society (United States), an established industrial society still undergoing de-

The assembly line involves repetitive, machine-paced work, requiring only minimal skills or training, and little opportunity for social relationships with coworkers. Job dissatisfaction is highest among workers employed in such settings.

velopment (Italy), an industrializing society (Argentina), and a large country with few but recent industrial experiences (India). Form wanted to know the following: "Do auto workers hate working and seek to escape it? Do they despise the factory environment? Do they find their job so monotonous as to deprive them of their sense of human worth? Does increasing mechanization in advanced industrial societies make automobile workers more discontented with their jobs? Do workers with equal skills evaluate their jobs in the same way irrespective of the recency of industry in the country?" (p. 1)

The results of Form's research directly challenges many ideas about the negative consequences for workers in mechanized production systems. He reports that auto workers in all four countries do not hate their jobs and they expect to find satisfaction in their work. Although they seek more variety in their jobs and greater opportunities for sociability, they are only mildly distressed by the noise and monotony of factory work.

The traditionally alienating jobs have been those where workers have little control over their work (Blauner, 1963). However, these jobs have been declining to the point where in 1974 it was estimated that they accounted for only 2 percent of jobs in the United States (O'Toole, 1974). At the same time there is evidence of growing job dissatisfaction among white-collar workers and middle-level managers. Such dissatisfaction may be due to the inability of workers to realize their aspirations or to see any opportunities for job mobility (See Sheppard and Herrick, 1972, Chap. 2). The American labor force, better educated and trained than their predecessors, expects that their work should be interesting and that they should be able to continue to rise in the occupational scale.

Job dissatisfaction can stem from a number of sources, have different consequences and require different solutions. Workers who feel that the monetary rewards and benefits of their job are limited may be more attracted to unionization and collective bargaining efforts to secure these. Workers who have few opportunities for challenging jobs may be more interested in programs that give them a chance

to explore and train for new jobs or in efforts to redesign jobs so that they are less fragmented and specialized.

It is possible that all forms of job dissatisfaction will increase workers' efforts to have a larger voice in how they work as well as how much they earn. The recent examples of employer-owned firms will give us an opportunity to see how workers respond to their work when they not only receive a larger share of their productive labor but also have a greater say in how their work is organized.

Worker Participation, Worker Control, and Worker Ownership

As the discontent of workers in industrialized nations has grown, firms have begun to look for ways to involve workers more fully in their work organizations (Silver, 1981). Worker participation is the most well-established form of worker involvement, but the worker's role has been limited to decisions at the production level of the organization. For example, job enlargment programs, designed to give workers a greater sense of identification with their work, assign workers larger and more complete tasks. Small teams of workers may be responsible for assembling, inspecting, and approving an entire product, such as an automobile or a television set, rather than repeatedly working on only one of a dozen or more assembling operations. A similar innovation is job rotation. In this situation the work itself is not changed, but workers are encouraged to switch from one job to another from time to time, thereby reducing the boredom of repetition.

Worker participation in the form of job enlargement and job rotation gives workers a chance to help redesign their work tasks and choose the tasks on which they wish to work. It represents a modest form of worker involvement. However, there are other forms of involvement that can alter workers' relationships to their jobs by increasing their control over many aspects of the work process. At present, work schedules, pacing, quality standards, productivity, income plans, and the location of the work place are all matters that are decided upon not by the worker but by others who plan, organize, and supervise the work process.

There is a prevailing belief, as yet unsupported by research, that the success of Japanese firms in improving productivity and product quality is related to the special character of labor-management relations (Ouchi, 1980). Japanese workers have more job security, better opportunities for advancement, and greater involvement in co-decision making with management. It seems plausible that more secure, involved workers will be more motivated and committed to their organization's goals.

Increasing worker involvement by increasing control expands the worker's role to making decisions at the managerial level. These decisions have traditionally been the exclusive province of owners and managers, and the latter are loath to give up their rights in this area. However, there are some small "cracks" in this tradition, represented by the appointment in 1980 of a member of the United Auto Workers to the board of directors of Chrysler Corporation.

While in theory it may be possible to expand workers' control over many aspects of the work process, the description of a worker's typical work day in Reading 9.2 indicates that the prospect is not bright.

The most recent and most significant form of worker involvement is the worker-owned enterprise. Woodworth (1981) reports that there are from 1000 to 3000 worker-owned firms in the United States, and that they seem to be more profitable than comparable firms. The circumstance of plants relocating or closing because of bankruptcy has been prominent in stimulating workers to form or acquire their own companies.

It is still too early to know how workers will respond to working in firms that they own collectively. One might expect greater satisfaction with work and the emergence of new organizational structures and new values emphasizing consensus and cooperation. On the other hand, we may find that the demands of technology and organization are the same for worker-owned firms as for traditional firms.

SUMMARY

In industrial societies large organizations touch the lives of every person from the cradle to the grave. Throughout history, there have been groups devoted to large-scale human endeavors, but not until the decline of feudalism and the rise of the city did a new form of organization and a new form of authority appear. The feudal system, which rested on the traditional authority of individuals, was replaced by the hierarchical bureaucratic organization based on rational-legal authority.

Ideal-type bureaucracy, as described by sociologist Max Weber, consists of a clearly ordered hierarchy of positions or offices that are well defined in terms of authority and specialization. Abstract rules rather than tradition guide and bind the behaviors of all parties in the bureaucratic system. Those occupying positions of power and authority do so on the strength of specialized knowledge and training. Records are kept of all activities of the bureaucracy, and relationships between persons in the organization are impersonal. Such conditions often lead to deindividuation, or loss of personal identity, for those in the system, but they also protect members from arbitrary acts of individuals in positions of authority.

Bureaucratic officials devote their energies to a lifetime career in return for the security of a fixed salary, protection against arbitrary dismissal, and the promise of job advancement. The distinct advantages of bureaucracy are calculability of individual actions and predictability of outcomes.

The now familiar bureaucratic form seen in large schools, hospitals, businesses, and governmental agencies has negative as well as positive consequences. Rigid adherence to rules, conflict among experts, dual allegiances of experts, and unquestioning acceptance of rules and authority are among the problems facing the modern bureaucratic organization.

Just as bureaucracy replaced traditional forms of organization, so sociologists look for the emergence of other organizational forms in the future. Impetus for change will come both from member motivations as well as from changing conditions in the social, political, and technological environment. There are indications that less bureaucratic organizations are able to draw upon a greater emotional and moral commitment of their members. Such organizations may provide a glimpse of things to come.

GLOSSARY

Authority   legitimate or justified power; the ability of a person to elicit compliant behavior from another because both recognize the person's right to do so.

Cosmopolitan   a person low on loyalty to the employing organization, high on commitment to specialized role skills, and likely to use an outer [professional] reference group orientation.

Deindividuation   loss of individual identity, which occurs when people working in large organizations ignore individual differences in their coworkers or clients.

Formal organization   two or more persons in a deliberately constructed social unit whose explicitly coordinated activities are directed toward the attainment of a specifically stated goal.

Ideal-type bureaucracy   a large organization characterized by a clearly ordered hierarchy of positions or offices with clearly defined "spheres of competence" that are filled on the basis of expert training. Bureaucratic activities are carried out in a spirit of impersonality, carefully recorded in writing, and guided by general rules.

Interorganizational network   a set of organizations that are directly and indirectly linked to each by formal and informal ties.

Local   a person high on loyalty to the employing organization, low on commitment to specialized role skills, and likely to use an inner [organizational] reference group orientation.

Organizational societies   societies in which the health and welfare of most of the population is defined and controlled by large organizations.

Power   the ability of a person to achieve his or her own purposes by controlling others.

Rational-legal authority   legitimate power based on the "legality" of patterns of normative rules and the right of those elevated to authority under such rules to issue commands.

Total institution   an organization like prisons or mental hospitals where members live in isolation from the rest of society for periods of time and whose lives are subject to the control of the organization.

Traditional authority   legitimate power based on the sanctity of the order and the attendant powers of control as they have been handed down from the past.

ADDITIONAL READINGS

Blau, Peter M., and Meyer, Marshall W. *Bureaucracy in Modern Society.* 2d ed. New York: Random, 1971.
   An excellent introduction to the nature of bureaucracy and its implications for modern societies.
Coleman, James S. *Power and the Structure of Society.* New York: Norton, 1974.
   A series of lectures on the modern corporation as a "corporate actor" and the private person's loss of power in dealing with them.
Goffman, Erving. *Asylums.* Garden City, N.Y.: Anchor, 1961.
   The chapter on "total institutions" provides an excellent introduction to the basic features of organizations like prisons and mental hospitals.
Knoke, David H., and James R. Wood. *Organized for Action: Commitment in Voluntary Associations.* New Brunswick, N.J.: Rutgers University Press, 1981.
   A look at how organizations like the Urban League, League of Women Voters, ACLU, and NOW develop and use their influence.

Lipsky, Michael. *Street-Level Bureaucracy: Dilemmas of the Individual in Public Services.* New York: Basic Books, 1980.
A close-up examination of relationships between human service bureaucrats and their clients.

Zwerdling, Daniel. *Workplace Democracy.* New York: Harper & Row, 1980.
Describes the attempts of different firms in different countries to humanize work and increase worker participation and worker control.

READINGS

READING 9.1

The Collectivist Organization: An Alternative to Rational-Bureaucratic Models*

Joyce Rothschild-Whitt

This article represents a first approach to a model of collectivist organization, a model that is premised on the logic of substantive rationality rather than formal rationality. To date, theories of organizational action have assumed, explicitly or implicitly, that norms of formal rationality prevail . . . Indeed, in a modern society they almost always do. This decade, however, has given rise to a wide array of work organizations that self-consciously reject the norms of rational-bureaucracy and identify themselves as "alternative institutions." The emergence of these contrabureaucratic organizations call for a new model of organization that can encompass their alternative practices and aspirations. . . .

This paper aims to develop an ideal-type model of collectivist-democratic organization. It is an attempt to delineate the form of authority and the corresponding mode of organization that follows from [nonbureaucratic] premises. As such it is grounded in observations of counter-bureaucratic organizations which aspire to being "collectives." . . .

Table 1 summarizes the ideal-type differences between the collectivist mode of organization and the bureaucratic. Democratic control is the foremost characteristic of collectivist organization, just as hierarchal control is the defining characteristic of the smoothly running bureaucracy. Thus, collectivist-democratic organization would transform the social relations to production. Bureaucracy maxi-mizes formal rationality precisely by centralizing the locus of control at the top of the organization; collectives decentralize control such that it may be organized around [an] alternative logic.

SUMMARY

During the 1970s many alternative organizations were invented that were parallel to, but different from, established organizations. They sought to fill social needs for education, medical care, food, and legal assistance without relying on bureaucratic structures. Businesses such as bookstores, food cooperatives, newspapers, and medical clinics, to name but a few, were collectively owned and managed.

QUESTIONS

1. What social conditions are responsible for the emergence of such organizations?
2. Do collectivist organizations have much of a chance surviving in a society with competing bureaucratic organizations?
3. Are there any collectivist organizations in your community?

READING 9.2

Workplace Authoritarianism

Richard M. Pfeffer

Employees in American factories work under an authoritarian regime, based upon private ownership of the means of production, whose main function is to produce for the profit of owners. The attitudes and practices of the managers of this system of production toward workers reflect its purpose, as do workers' responses to management and to their jobs.

*Footnotes have been deleted.

SOURCE: Joyce Rothschild-Whitt, "The Collectivist Organization: An Alternative to Rational-Bureaucratic Models," *American Sociological Review*, Vol. 44, August 1979, pp. 509, 510, 518, 519.

SOURCE: Richard M. Pfeffer, *Working for Capitalism*, New York: Columbia University Press, 1979, pp. 91–96. Reprinted with permission.

TABLE 1   Comparisons of Two Ideal Types of Organization

DIMENSIONS	BUREAUCRATIC ORGANIZATION	COLLECTIVIST-DEMOCRATIC ORGANIZATION
1. Authority	1. Authority resides in individuals by virtue of incumbency in office and/or expertise; hierarchal organization of offices. Compliance is to universal fixed rules as these are implemented by office incumbents.	1. Authority resides in the collectivity as a whole; delegated, if at all, only temporarily and subject to recall. Compliance is to the consensus of the collective which is always fluid and open to negotiation.
2. Rules	2. Formalization of fixed and universalistic rules; calculability and appeal of decisions on the basis of correspondence to the formal, written law.	2. Minimal stipulated rules; primacy of ad hoc, individuated decisions; some calculability possible on the basis of knowing the substantive ethics involved in the situation.
3. Social Control	3. Organizational behavior is subject to social control, primarily through direct supervision or standardized rules and sanctions, tertiarily through the selection of homogeneous personnel especially at top levels.	3. Social controls are primarily based on personalistic or moralistic appeals and the selection of homogeneous personnel.
4. Social Relations	4. Ideal of impersonality. Relations are to be role-based, segmental and instrumental.	4. Ideal of community. Relations are to be wholistic, personal, of value in themselves.
5. Recruitment and Advancement	5.a. Employment based on specialized training and formal certification.	5.a. Employment based on friends, social-political values, personality attributes, and informally assessed knowledge and skills.
	5.b. Employment constitutes a career; advancement based on seniority or achievement.	5.b. Concept of career advancement not meaningful; no hierarchy of positions.
6. Incentive Structure	6. Remunerative incentives are primary.	6. Normative and solidarity incentives are primary; material incentives are secondary.
7. Social Stratification	7. Isomorphic distribution of prestige, privilege, and power; i.e., differential rewards by office; hierarchy justifies inequality.	7. Egalitarian; reward differentials, if any, are strictly limited by the collectivity.
8. Differentiation	8.a. Maximal division of labor: dichotomy between intellectual work and manual work and between administrative tasks and performance tasks.	8.a. Minimal division of labor: administration is combined with performance tasks; division between intellectual and manual work is reduced.
	8.b. Maximal specialization of jobs and functions; segmental roles. Technical expertise is exclusively held; ideal of the specialist-expert.	8.b. Generalization of jobs and functions; wholistic roles. Demystification of expertise; ideal of the amateur factotum.

The authoritarian quality of production relations at work is central, rather than coincidental, to the American political culture, which is a liberal-capitalist culture. Some of the society's nonwork institutions serve to obscure, soften, and distract Americans from that fundamental authoritarian reality so crudely exposed in the workplace. But it is hard to imagine that the shaping to which workers are subject when they look for jobs and on the job itself could be as effective as it is if Americans before they entered the job market had not, for example, been taught to be deferential to authority, to treat consumption as an end, and to respond individually rather than collectively. The authoritarian relation in the factory could not be maintained, in short, if it were not supported by other institutions in our political economy to legitimate, facilitate, and enforce the continuing existence and development of capitalist relations in production.

Capitalism means, in part, that working men and working women are treated as a factor of production, like land and raw materials, to be purchased as cheaply as possible and exploited as much as possible under the circumstances to produce profit. Management's main task within this system is to manipulate the factors of production to maximize profit. This requires that management use its authority and power over workers to mold them to its own ends.

Exercise of power by some over others is predicated upon relative strength. In American factories it is predicated upon the weak bargaining position of individual workers, upon workers' feeling dependent on management for a livelihood, and upon their consequent sense of vulnerability. Power in American factories generally is seen as legitimately held by management. Rather than challenging managers' orders and forcing managers to exercise their power directly, therefore, workers, while keenly aware of that power, obey management directives in no small part because they accept management's authority to give direction. This acceptance implies deference by workers to management in the belief that in some sense management and the property owners it represents have the "right" in very broad areas to make decisions that affect workers' lives. From the point of view of those who rule the factory, exercising authority rather than power is a more efficient and satisfying means to achieve their ends. The exercise of authority normally avoids open struggle and confrontation, allowing power to be conserved and hidden until needed.

Power and authority are organized hierarchically, with management engaged in tasks that incorporate more power and authority. Partly in reflection of this allocation of power and authority and partly in support of it, there are observable patterned differences in the command behavior of managerial personnel at different levels.

Take my foreman and superintendent for example, the only managerial figures with whom I had much contact. My foreman, Sam, like foremen in general, was the link between producers and managers. He was the lowest-level line employee in management and the person immediately in charge of all manual laborers within his department. As a crucial middleman, he had to face both ways: down, in personally directing and coordinating the work of those below him, and up in dealing with Ron Merritt, the superintendent, and higher levels of management to develop and implement their directives. As a man required to spend most of his time with workers in order to direct them in their tasks, he needed to be someone who could relate reasonably well to workers. As the lowest rung on the managerial ladder of power and authority, one who did not spend much time in committee meetings and dealing with outside businessmen, he did not need to be too sophisticated or polished.

In fact, my foreman, like most foremen I know, gave the appearance on the job of being "working class." Although I sensed that he might have had some technical training and perhaps some higher education, his style, even as he exercised power and authority over us, was working class. He dressed more or less like a worker—no tie or jacket—mingled easily with workers, cracked jokes, got angry, swore, typically used slang, and as a personality seemed fairly open. His outward behavior, however, obscured important facets of his managerial role that he nonetheless performed. Like other foremen, for example, he no doubt kept information from workers that might well have dramatically affected their lives, such as future layoffs, for they were conceived as having no right to such information.

By contrast, my super, Ron, gave the appearance of being decidedly ruling, not working, class. He oozed quiet confidence, almost to the point of arrogance, walked ramrod erect, was extremely courteous, spoke crisply, and dressed formally, and rarely if ever observably lost his cool. Although he related reasonably well to workers, always it was at a measured distance and openly instrumentally. If he spent considerable time with workers and foremen, he spent considerable time also with upper-level management and with men from outside the plant who came in to discuss business. If Sam's outward bearing obscured central aspects of his managerial role, Ron's epitomized his role as manager. Like a military officer, he gave off the aura of self-discipline and command. Like other successful business, academic, and political entrepreneurs, he gave the intimidating impression without actually ever saying so that it was his time that was most valuable, and that it was his judgment that most mattered. . . . Like men and women who rule us in various fields, he knew how to use information, silence, secrecy, and half-compliments to keep those below him with whom he dealt in place. He already embodied the rationalized traits of the American ruling class. He was attractive, purposeful, seemingly humane, and liberal, but in achieving his purposes he would be as ruthless as his role demanded. . . .

On the job, workers are trained to be compliant to management's wishes. The man who only half-jokingly said that he'd decided after repeated trouble with his foreman during his first years on the job to "jump off the roof" if his foreman told him to because he was getting paid to obey, caught the spirit of the kind of cooperation expected by management of workers. Another man who refused to "cooperate" and complained during work time to his union safety committeeperson about a machine that had just injured him received a warning slip for doing so. He was told that, according to contract rules, he was required to get permission from his foreman before speaking to the safety person. Still another worker, who was trying without union support to get his wage grade raised since he often was assigned to do work not in his job category, which he believed was above his grade, was told by his foreman, "you got to do as you're told." To which the worker replied, "I know that. Any child knows that, but fair's fair."

There it is, still perhaps somewhat hidden from view. Workers are surrounded by rules and treated and disciplined as if they were schoolchildren. What is "fair" is not a matter of abstract justice, but a function of rules in the company-union contracts. To perform their jobs, to retain their self-respect and dignity and/or to protect themselves from being exploited too much, workers are regularly likely to break some of those many rules. But rule breaking in turn leaves them vulnerable and liable to being disciplined. The whole arrangement is psychologically and politically destructive of what little sense of self-respect and control of their own lives workers in our system are able to build up.

Moreover, in a society in which the search

for approval from authority figures seems to be almost a way of life, at least for the better educated and for the characters on TV shows, workers have to live in a political work environment in which their authority figures rarely if ever show approval or appreciation for the job they do. Authority and power are normally exercised in the factory to organize and discipline, rather than to approve. So if factory workers also seek approval and appreciation, theirs is a deeply frustrating work life. Brought up to be such a seeker, I found my own need to be appreciated as a "good trashman" consistently unfulfilled, which often made me feel worthless and depressed. If, on the other hand, workers have learned from their experience not to seek or expect approval from workplace authority figures, their work, generally without inherent meaning, also largely is without extrinsic satisfaction. Either way, workers are made to feel not like valued men and women but like things to be manipulated and replaced if necessary for purposes of production.

SUMMARY

Relationships between managers and workers in American factories are very authoritarian. Workers are very dependent upon management for their jobs, and therefore accept management's authority without challenge. Authoritarian relationships in the workplace are reinforced by other social institutions that socialize Americans to be deferential to authority and to deal with one's problems as individuals rather than collectively.

QUESTIONS

1. What do Americans learn at home and in school that prepares them for work in authoritarian structures?
2. What would happen in factories if there were no formal authority figures?
3. Are there any authoritarian relationships at your college?

CHAPTER 10

Gender Inequality

CONTENTS

Does anatomy define social roles?

The idea that the different biological characteristics of men and women should be the basis of social roles has a long history. These real and perceived differences are the source of much current controversy about the roles of men and women in society. The disagreement revolves around the significance of childbearing, particularly for women, and the responsibilities of men for childcare.

YES   Differences between the sexes is the most fundamental condition of life. The most meaningful events in our lives are based on sexual differences— marriage, conception, childbearing, childrearing—and these events perpetuate society.

Sexual differences are related to social roles. The roles of mother- father, husband-wife are critical to families, to children, and to society. However, in sexual terms there is little equality in these roles. The male role is largely trivial for birth and dispensable after conception. Now artificial insemination can make even this level of participation unnecessary. The woman conceives, bears, and feeds the child, while the man can only participate in the last activity if the infant is bottle fed and to the degree that his interest and social pressure dictate. Male bodies have fewer erogenous zones, and men devote relatively less time to specifically sexual activity during their lives. Sexual experience for males is limited to erection and ejaculation, and the primary sexual drive is fulfilled in copulation. In contrast to the intimate involvement women have with birth, as well as their socially indispensable and psychologically crucial roles as mothers, men's roles are subordinate and minor.

The role of father is a social creation, based on marriage and other cultural requirements. As Gilder (1973) notes, "There is no biological need for the father to be around when the baby is born and nurtured, and in many societies the father has no special responsibility to support the children he sires; in some, paternity isn't even acknowledged.

Without long-term commitments to and from women—without the institution of marriage—men are exiles from the procreative chain of nature" (p. 42).

Social roles reflect the anatomy of men and women. If social roles no longer continue to do so—if we deny the validity of sexual differences—social life will become artificial and contrived and human potential will not be realized.

NO   A person's understanding of sex is based on the biological differences between men and women. While we all recognize that only men can sire children and only women can bear them, the social and political significance of these differences is not obvious.

Some people suggest that gender should serve as a guide to social institutions, with clear distinctions between male and female roles. However, it must be remembered that women are more involved with home and family as a matter of convenience and because they have been socialized into this role since childhood. At home both boys and girls learn traditional gender roles. In school, children are taught that most household chores and childbearing are women's work while earning money is man's work.

Why, just because women bear children, should women be primarily responsible for taking care of the family? There is nothing natural about a division of labor in families or societies that defines roles by biological inheritance. Fathers who have the task of providing for their family's material needs and mothers who are assigned the task of childrearing and household management can alter these roles without harm to anyone.

Biological and other supposedly natural differences need not confine women to certain social roles. In fact, throughout history women have played nearly every role that is defined as male by our culture. The role of woman as childbearer, while inevitable in preindustrial societies, is today a matter of choice with the aid of modern methods of birth control and advances in reproductive technology. The frequently drawn analogy between pregnancy and disease is no longer valid, if it ever was. Now diseases can be cured and prevented; so can pregnancy.

Women alone can bear children, but now we have the ability to control conception and birth. Women can fill many social roles, just as men can. Why not liberate both sexes from the slavery of anatomy?

Biological differences between men and women are important in defining sexual behavior, but do they shape or limit social roles? Those who answer affirmatively argue that the ability to have babies influences women's attitudes and behavior, making it impossible for women to fill the same roles as men in society. Those who believe that gender behavior is learned, not biologically inherited—that, for example, women are taught to be dependent, submissive, and emotional—also believe women can achieve equality with men in all roles that do not involve sexual activities and reproduction. Who is correct? To evaluate these views, in the following pages we will examine biological evidence about sexual differences and also the cultural traditions and social structures that reflect gender differences. We will compare achievements of men and women in work, income, and education, and explore the reasons for gender differences. We will look at gender roles in family, religious, and political institutions in an effort to trace the social sources of the women's movement. Finally we will consider the question: Is gender equality possible?

QUESTIONS TO CONSIDER

- Is real equality between men and women possible?

- Are women naturally more caring and nurturing than men?

- Why do women only earn about 60 percent of what men earn?

- How does society encourage men and women to enter different occupations?

- How important are sex differences in modern society?

"Unto the woman [God] said, I will multiply thy sorrow and thy conception; in sorrow thou shalt bring forth children; and thy desire shall be subject to thy husband, and he shall rule over thee."—Genesis 3:16

"What are little boys made of? Snaps and snails and puppy-dogs' tails. What are little girls made of? Sugar and spice and everything nice."—Old Nursery Rhyme

". . . a woman's function, a woman's way, a woman's natural bent, is motherhood. Every woman is called to be a mother."—Pope Pius XII

"Woman's intellectuality is to a large extent paid for by the loss of valuable feminine qualities; it feeds on the sap of the affective life and results in impoverishment of this life . . . All observations point to the fact that the intellectual woman is masculinized; in her, warm intuitive knowledge has yielded to cold unproductive thinking."—Helene Deutsch (quoted in Deckard, 1975)

These ideas about male-female differences are a part of the cultural history of modern, Western society. Few social distinctions among humans have been as widespread, obvious, and persistent as those between men and women. In every human society some roles and positions have been assigned to women and other roles and positions have been assigned to men. Often these positions have involved dominant-submissive or superior-inferior relationships, usually favoring male dominance and control. However, during the past 50 years, many people have begun to question sexual inequality.

What are the basic differences between men and women? Are these differences important, especially in modern society? How do some roles and activities become defined as appropriate for females and others as appropriate for males? Answers to these and similar questions requires us to examine the historical, biological, and social evidence for inequality based on sex.

SEX AND GENDER: SOURCES OF DIFFERENTIATION

The terms sex and gender are often used to describe male-female differences in social life and behavior. **Sex** refers to biological differences or characteristics that distinguish males and females. **Gender** refers to the social aspects of sex or to the socially defined expectations, roles, feelings, or concepts associated with sex (Sandler et al., 1980). Babies of the female sex learn gender roles, that is, they learn to be feminine, just as male children learn masculine gender roles, according to the definitions of gender in their cultures.

Sex and its social definition—gender—have had important consequences for work, family, politics, and even play relationships in nearly every culture. The traditional definitions of gender assume that cultural patterns based on sex differences are natural or inevitable due to the male biological attributes of strength and speed. To **feminists**—people who believe that sex or gender is not a legitimate basis for social roles and who seek to change current patterns of inequality—and others, the current pattern of gender roles has developed out of particular cultural settings; its traditions have little current validity.

However the roles of women and men are defined, biological factors, cultural traditions, and social relationships all contribute. Each must be examined to understand gender inequality in modern society.

Biological Factors

The essential biological difference between females and males involves reproduction. Women menstruate, become pregnant, give birth, and provide nourishment for infants, while men only can impregnate (Sandler et al., 1980). Genetic sex—male or female—is determined at conception, but the process of sexual differentiation occurs throughout the pregnancy as hormones influence the development of sex organs in the fetus. Biologically, babies are either male or female at birth, based on sex organ differentiation.

The assignment of a baby to a sex category is made on the basis of the appearance of external sex organs, at which time social and cultural gender influences come into play. However, research done during the past two decades suggests that such sex classification based on physical appearance is neither simple nor perfect. Because the fetus has the potential for developing both male and female sex organs, hormone imbalance during pregnancy has resulted in genetic females appearing to be males at birth, being misclassified and even reared as the opposite sex. Opposite-sex childrearing also occurred when a seven-month-old boy, who had his penis accidentally burned off during circumcision, was raised successfully as a girl after corrective surgery, even though he had an identical twin (Money and Ehrhardt, 1972). Such examples emphasize the importance of social factors in shaping the ability of newly born infants and children to adapt to socially defined sex categories.

Behavioral differences among infants are often cited as evidence of inherent male-female abilities. However, there is no real agreement about how much of these differences is biologically determined. Differences in cognitive abilities and social behavior between the sexes not only remain to be documented (Williams, 1977) but they appear to be as much the result of socialization as biological inheritance. Aggression, though found among both sexes, is more physical for boys and covert or verbal for girls: however, is this primarily because of differences in socialization or differences in biology?

In short, while there are sex differences in reproductive functions and characteristics like strength, height, and weight, it is not clear that biology also accounts for differences in behavior between men and women in our society. How are the biological differences related to social definitions of sex and to social relationships? Clearly, the cultural context and social structure are important in helping to define appropriate behavior for and attitudes toward each sex.

Cultural Factors

Men and women have distinctive social roles in all societies. However, activities and roles associated with sex are not viewed the same way in all societies: what is seen as masculine by some cultures is defined as feminine by others. What is the basis of sex roles in various cultures?

CROSS-CULTURAL EVIDENCE

Although specialization of work and social roles by sex has existed among hunting and gathering people, small-scale agricultural societies, and industrialized societies, there are some important differences among them. Early anthropological work by Mead (1935) among peoples of New Guinea suggested that sex roles typical of industrialized United States are not universal. In one of the three cultures that she studied, the Tchambuli, women were dominant and impersonal and had economic responsibilities, while men were nurturant, emotionally dependent, and supportive. In another, the Mundugumor, both men and women were aggressive and ruthless, while in the third society, the Arapesh, both men and women were trained to be cooperative and responsive to others. Too much should not be made of these differences, since men dominate in most societies. However, they do indicate that male dominance is not inevitable.

As evidence from other cultures has accumulated it has become obvious that gender roles are largely defined by the culture rather than by biological factors. The social and cultural conditions that have produced the current patterns of gender inequality in the United States are important in understanding the controversy about women's roles in modern society.

HISTORICAL CONDITIONS AND TRADITIONS

White people who settled in North America were predominantly from English, French, or Spanish cultures, all of which share the Judeo-Christian heritage. Male dominance and protection of women is a theme carried from traditional Judaism through Christianity and into the secular culture of the twentieth century. Though some scholars and leaders like Thomas More (1478–1535) or Thomas Paine (1737–1809) argued for women's equality in education or work, for the most part women of all social classes were viewed as the property of husbands and fathers. Legally women were under the control of men and socially they were subject to the double standard of sexual behavior, which demanded virginity of them but sexual experience for men. Only men could vote, hold public office, or obtain college educations. These conditions were consistent with society's ideals about marriage and family.

The ideal woman was chaste, obedient, dependent, and proper, supported by her husband and protected from the harsh world outside the home. This view was strongly supported by religious and political leaders—nearly all of whom were men. However, the conditions for this ideal did not exist in reality, except for a small number of wealthy families. For most of American history a large proportion of women have worked outside the home as well as maintaining the household.

On the frontier women worked as hard as men, tending fields and gardens, making clothing and other household items, preparing food, caring for babies, and teaching older children. During slavery black women worked at a large number of jobs, all of which involved hard labor. Immigrant women, lacking education, money, knowledge of the language, marketable skills, or—often—employed husbands, were a ready-made labor pool for the new industries. By 1850 the textile industry employed more than 200,000 women, often for 12 or more hours a day at very low wages. Throughout most of the 1800s women worked in industries, on farms, and in jobs requiring physical labor, but were denied access to college educations until the 1860s and 1870s.

Table 10.1 shows the amount of female employment from 1870 through 1980.

Many women workers in the period 1880–1910 were in service occupations such as domestic servants or laundry workers and in textile or clothing factories. There was no job security, pay was low, working conditions were often dangerous, and hours were long—a far cry from the ideal female role proclaimed by religious and political leaders.

In 1920, after a long, difficult struggle, the Nineteenth Amendment was ratified, giving women the right to vote. The number of women employed outside the home rose gradually, from 4,000,000 in 1890 to nearly 11,000,000 in 1930. During this period about one in five workers was a woman, though most were still in low-paying jobs or in labor-intensive industries as clerks, secretaries, seamstresses, or textile workers.

Educational opportunities for women expanded during the 1920s, though there was a shift to home economics courses preparing women for marriage and motherhood, away from the broad comprehensive training of earlier years. Women who could not attend college continued to work. By 1940 one worker in four was a woman. With World War II and the unprecedented demand for workers to re-

TABLE 10.1   Female Employment, 1870–1980

YEAR	NUMBER OF WOMEN	PERCENTAGE OF LABOR FORCE
1870	1,836,000	13
1880	2,647,000	15
1890	4,006,000	17
1900	5,319,000	19
1910	8,076,000	23
1920	8,550,000	21
1930	10,752,000	22
1940	12,887,000	25
1950	15,552,000	31
1960	22,410,000	35
1970	30,547,000	42
1980	41,283,000	42

SOURCE: Statistical Abstracts for various years.

place those drafted into the armed services, married women with and without children and single women responded, and female participation in nearly every occupational category increased the proportion of working women to more than one in three by 1944. Public approval of women working also increased: more than 70 percent of Americans in 1942 thought more married women could and should be working (Chafe, 1972). At the end of the war, however, appeals for women to return to their "natural" position signalled an effort to replace women with returning veterans, despite the fact that two-thirds of women desired to keep their jobs (Deckard, 1975).

THE RETURN TO NORMALCY: SOCIAL SCIENCE, IDEOLOGY, AND INEQUALITY

From 1945 to 1947 the number of employed women decreased by four million, primarily because of women voluntarily leaving the workforce, though some coercion was used. Media, religious groups, and business and community leaders sought to reestablish the previous ideals of women and family. Career women were labeled as "unfulfilled" sexually, working mothers were told they were damaging their children, and even social scientists found the traditional mother-homemaker role for women to be more efficient and more functional for society than working mothers or dual-career families. Parsons and Bales (1955) defined the female role as "expressive" and the male role as "instrumental." The **expressive role** of women focuses upon providing emotional satisfaction, care, and nurturance for children and an efficiently run home for family members. The **instrumental role** of men emphasizes achievement, assertive leadership, and dominance, especially in the home and to a lesser degree in all social roles involving male-female relationships. The female role is seen as complementing the male role.

Despite such an analysis of social roles, throughout the 1950s women continued to enter the labor force. However, the economic expansion of the postwar era did not lead to an expansion of the kind of jobs that were available to women. In fact, by 1966 women occupied relatively fewer professional positions than before World War II; not until 1976 was the proportion of professionals who were women

as high as in 1940. In 1980 44 percent of all professional workers were women, although they were still concentrated in teaching and nursing, the lower status and lower income categories of the professions.

Attitudes have changed, however. There is now widespread support for equality of educational opportunity, for equal pay for equal work, and for participation in the labor force by mothers of young children (Mason et al., 1976; Spitze and Huber, 1980). The impact of these changes on young men and women appears to be only related to the right to work. One recent study (Herzog, 1982), found that female high school seniors have different values and orientations to work—they view work as a temporary and supplemental activity—than males, who define work as lifelong and a primary activity. Whether these values reflect a view of their chances in the world of work or individual preferences due to socialization, their impact is the same. "Before young women and men have ever entered a full-time job and faced the constraints of the labor market, they have already 'lined up' for different kinds of jobs" (p. 10). Highlight 10.1 discusses the related issue of sexual differences in ability.

VARIATIONS ON A THEME: "THE TOTAL WOMAN," "SUPERWOMAN," "THE NEW WOMAN"

American women are currently confronted with many role models, ranging from traditional wife-subservient family roles to antimale, economic success, antifamily roles. Few have stated the traditional view more directly than Morgan (1973) in *The Total Woman:*

Man and Woman, although equal in status, are different in function. God ordained man to be the head of the family, its president, and his wife to be the executive vice-president. Every organization has a leader and the family unit is no exception. There is no way you can alter or improve this arrangement. On occasion, families have tried to reverse this and have elected a woman as president. When this order is turned around the family is upside down. The system usually breaks down within a short period of time. Allowing your husband to be your family president is just good business. . . .

It is only when a woman surrenders her life to her husband, reveres and worships him, and is willing to

HIGHLIGHT 10.1
Who Is Really Better at Math?

"It is well known that teen-age boys tend to do better at math than girls, that male high school students are more likely than their female counterparts to tackle advanced math courses like calculus, that virtually all the great mathematicians have been men. But why? Are women born with less mathematical ability? Or does society's sexism slow their progress?

"In 1980 two Johns Hopkins University researchers tried to settle the eternal nature/nurture debate. Julian Stanley—who is well respected for his work with precocious math students of both sexes—and Camilla Benbow had tested 10,000 talented seventh- and eighth-graders between 1972 and 1979. Using the Scholastic Aptitude Test, in which math questions are meant to measure ability rather than knowledge, they discovered distinct sex differences. While the verbal abilities of the males and females hardly differed, twice as many boys as girls scored over 500 (on a scale of 200 to 800) on mathematical ability; at the 700 level, the ratio was 14 to 1. The conclusion: males have inherently superior mathematical reasoning ability.

"Benbow and Stanley's findings, which were published in *Science*, disturbed some men and not a few women. Now there is comfort for those people in a new study from the University of Chicago that suggests math is not, after all, a natural male domain. With Researcher Sharon Senk, Professor Zalman Usiskin, a specialist in high school mathematics curriculums and an author of several math texts, studied 1,366 tenth-graders. They were selected from geometry classes and tested on their ability to solve geometry proofs, a subject requiring both abstract reasoning and spatial ability. Says Usiskin: "If you're a math whiz or a computer bug, you're going to pick up equations and formulas that will help you with tests like the SAT. But geometry proof is never learned outside of school." The conclusion reached by Usiskin and Senk: there are no sex differences in math ability.

". . . the Chicago researchers decided to take a few swipes at the recent Johns Hopkins findings. They argued that Benbow and Stanley had measured performance, not ability. Says Usiskin: 'To assume that the SAT has no connection with experience is poppycock.' Replies Stanley, who now has 50,000 subjects to bolster his conclusion: 'People are so eager not to believe that there is a difference in mathematical reasoning ability between boys and girls that all kinds of people are taking potshots.'

"The Chicago study, says Stanley, is 'irrelevant' because it tests knowledge of mathematics rather than raw ability. He points out that the students were receiving geometry instruction at the time of the test. 'What they've done,' says Stanley, 'is to show that when you teach boys and girls together in math classes, the girls learn quite well, and we've known that for 50 years.'

"While the critical volleys fly between Baltimore and Chicago, some educators believe that both sides are missing the real target. University of Wisconsin Professor Elizabeth Fennema, who has been studying sex-related differences in math for twelve years, maintains that most female mathematical disabilities result from environment. Says she: 'Neither study has collected a bit of data on the genetic evidence. Neither is measuring innate ability.' She discourages debate over mathematical genetics, since she believes it is insoluble and burdens one sex with an implied deficiency for which there is no remedy. Indeed, the researchers agree on one important fact: if boys and girls are given capable teaching and comparable attention, both will achieve."

SOURCE: *Time*, March 22, 1982, p. 64. Reprinted by permission from TIME.

serve him, that she becomes a priceless jewel, the glory of feminity, his queen. (pp. 70, 80)

Another model for women has been described as **superwoman.** This model encourages women to be nurturant and supportive wives and mothers, *and* to pursue careers, *and* to be involved in social activities, *and* to be successful in all of these roles. However, most women—like most men—are not successful in pursuing several careers at once. As a result this model may be of limited value. One woman (Rabiner, 1976) who tried it reported that "the superwoman who knits marriage, career, and motherhood into a satisfying life without dropping a stitch is as oppressive a role model as the airbrushed bunny in the Playboy Centerfold or 'That Cosmopolitan Girl' " (p. 11).

Other models seek equality—in work, family, play, sex, and politics. Some radical feminists, emphasizing the gender inequality of traditional family patterns, have argued that the family institution creates and endorses inequality. Others have noted that the capitalist concepts of ownership and private property extend to the family's possession and control of its members. The reform-oriented woman seeks to alter the basic economic and political structures of social life that produce and maintain inequality, especially family structures; the radical woman is more interested in values and personal change (Arafat and Yorburg, 1976). The women's movement is devoted to the goal of equality, although there are differences in defining equality and selecting the means to achieve it.

The consequences of such diverse role models for women who are uncertain about their roles may include frustration, guilt, a sense of inferiority, failure, and conflict. Nevertheless, social structures and the cultural beliefs about men and women continue to assign them to separate and distinct roles. What are the processes of socialization that affect gender roles?

Socialization

As we noted in Chapter 6 socialization begins at birth and continues throughout life. Socialization to gender roles is reflected in behaviors, preferences, and attitudes. By age four or five sex-stereotyped play activities have developed, with boys preferring guns, trucks, tractors, and fire engines and girls preferring dolls and tea sets (Maccoby and Jacklin, 1974). In addition, a sense of gender identity usually has developed by the age of five or six; if you call a young boy a girl, or mistake a girl for a boy, he or she will react vigorously to the error in sex identity.

Gender identity begins to be shaped at birth by adult attitudes. Pink is for girls and blue is for boys. Boys are expected to be more active, stronger, and more aggressive than girls. Girls are expected to be more reserved, dependent, and charming than boys. These beliefs have significance for socialization. From infancy boys and girls are treated differently. Boys receive more contact from mothers and fathers during early infancy, and they are taught independence and self-assertion at earlier ages than girls (Lewis, 1972). (See Reading 5.1, "The Case for Nonsexist Childrearing.") However, the family is only one source of gender-role socialization.

Children's books and television, two important influences in the lives of young children, tend to foster sex-role stereotypes. Not only are men and boys more common as major figures in books and TV programs, they tend to be more active and more likely to work outside the home. Girls and women tend to be portrayed as mothers and homemakers and dependent on males (Weitzman and Eifler, 1972). Family-oriented TV shows, like "The Brady Bunch," "Little House on the Prairie," and "Walt Disney," as well as the crime-detective or variety shows, use traditional gender roles for major characters. In this way the cultural attitudes of society are reinforced.

Another view of gender socialization is offered by Nielsen (1978), who suggests that sex-typed behavior is specific to situations. The process of social learning is general, so that when role demands override sex and gender, individuals can and do act as the opposite sex would act. As Nielsen notes, "many women routinely drive, brush the snow off their cars, scrape the ice off their windshields, and open car and garage doors for their children. . . . Yet when they are with their husbands, it is he who usually does these things. To the extent that the role demands are sex specific, then individual behavior is sex specific" (p. 120).

In Nielsen's view social behavior is not based on sex or gender but is dictated by the social role being played. Thus if both boys and girls are socialized to be active, assertive and skillful, their behaviors will be similar in all social situations. Nielsen believes that such socialization may be appropriate in industrial societies where sex and gender are no longer important in adult roles.

Clearly, socialization continues to be different for boys and girls. How important such patterns are is an unanswered question. In modern society with its multiplicity of social and work roles, it may be limiting and nonproductive to continue to define these roles in terms of gender. Under such circumstances traditional gender socialization, for both men and women may have serious consequences, especially in the competitive world of work. Women who learn to defer to men, to withdraw from competition with men, and to be supportive, warm, and expressive will find it difficult to achieve occupational success. Similarly, men who learn assertiveness and leadership skills and expect women to defer to them and to work noncompetitively with them will be ill-equipped to relate to women as colleagues. Many people think that **androgyny,** a role that selects from "masculine" and "feminine" behavior whatever is appropriate to a particular situation, is a desirable role for both men and women.

SOCIAL ORGANIZATION AND GENDER ROLES

The traditional model of families no longer fits American family life. The entry of a majority of women into the labor force and the development of the welfare state reflect changes in economic conditions and personal expectations that have upset the traditional pattern of male-female relations in every sphere.

Laws that deprived women of the right to own property, to vote, to divorce, or to act on their own behalf no longer exist in most industrialized nations. Legally, women have equal access to education, occupational opportunities, and public office; in fact, there are great differences in achievements in these areas. These differences have often been explained by socialization and personality factors—women are taught to be less aggressive, less ambitious, more emotional, more willing to accept low pay, dead-end jobs than are men, and so on. Such explanations, combined with women's responsibility for childdrearing, which interferes with continuous work, may account for part of the differences in achievement between males and females. However, other factors like discrimination, inflexible work rules, legal restraints, and family demands undoubtedly influence the lower achievements of women compared with those of men.

Work

As we noted earlier at least 30 percent of all women have been in the labor force since the 1940s. This proportion increased to over half of all women age 16 and over in 1980. As Table 10.2 indicates, the increases have been greatest for married women with children at home, though their labor force participation is still below that of widowed, divorced, or separated women with children.

There are several important questions to be asked about these increases in women's work for pay. Why has the proportion of all women working increased? Is this increase motivated primarily by economic needs or desires or the desire for personal achievement? Does the large increase in mothers in the labor force indicate dissatisfaction with traditional family life or is it a response to demands and opportunities in the job market? Is the current pattern of women working for most of their lives, except for childbearing years, only a temporary response to economic circumstances or will it continue?

Such questions are not easily answered. Several efforts to explain these changes have emphasized both pull and push factors—a pull from the labor market and push from changes in the family.

The history of pull factors is as follows. The traditional pattern for women was to work before marriage, typically from ages 18 to 22. During the 1920s and 1930s the birthrate declined consistently, and

TABLE 10.2   Labor Force Participation, 1960–1980 (in percent)

	1960	1970	1980	DIFFERENCE: 1960–1980
Males, 16 years and over	78.1	78.0	76.8	−1.3
Single, never married	55.5	60.7	70.7	+15.2
Married, wife present	88.9	86.9	81.0	−7.9
Widowed, divorced, married-spouse absent	59.3	54.2	67.0	+7.7
Females, 16 years and over	34.8	42.6	51.1	+16.3
Single, never married	44.1	53.0	61.2	+17.1
Married, husband present	30.5	40.8	50.2	+19.7
No children under 18 years	34.7	42.2	46.1	+11.4
Children 6 to 17 years	39.0	49.2	61.8	+22.8
Children under 6	18.6	30.3	44.9	+26.3
Widowed, divorced, married-spouse absent	40.0	39.1	44.1	+4.1
No children under 18 years	35.7	33.4	35.2	−.5
Children 6 to 17 years	66.2	67.3	74.3	+8.1
Children under 6	39.8	50.7	59.2	+19.4

SOURCE: U.S. Bureau of the Census, Current Population Reports, Series P-20, No. 363, "Population Profile of the United States: 1980."

as a result the female labor pool shrunk. By 1940 there were not enough young, unmarried women to fill even the typical "female" occupations in the clerical and retail sales areas. The problem increased with the need for women workers during World War II. Following the war the baby boom stimulated the expansion of services that traditionally were dominated by women, like education, nursing, and recreation. As a result there was a great demand for women workers, which, combined with the experiences of work during the war, provided a pull for mothers to seek paid employment (Oppenheimer, 1973; Waite, 1976).

Push factors came primarily from changes in family patterns, especially during the 1960s. After World War II the impact of labor-saving technology on domestic life allowed women to complete their housekeeping responsibilities much more quickly than in earlier years. Automatic washers and dryers, vacuum cleaners, electric kitchen appliances, prepared and frozen foods, and so on, combined with the new option to have fewer or no children, gave women a larger amount of free time than had been available in the past. Women could devote this new free time to their children, to volunteer activities, or to paid employment, and with the demand for women workers increasing numbers sought out-of-home employment (Hayghe, 1976).

Such explanations stress the impact of economic and social factors on the family, leading to changes in family patterns that allowed women to work outside the home. These changes appear to be permanent, at least if the commitment of working wives is considered. Iglehart's (1979) comparative study of employed wives in 1957—a period of strong social support for the housewife role—and 1976—a period influenced by the feminist movement, documented some changes in attitudes toward employment. In 1957 22 percent of working wives preferred to devote full time to housework compared with only 3 percent in 1976. Work commitment also changed. In 1957 58 percent indicated that they had a noneconomic commitment—they were working for personal satisfaction—compared with 82 percent in 1976. At all educational levels, all family income levels, and all ages of children, women in 1976 expressed higher noneconomic work commitments than in 1957.

Despite such impressive gains in employment outside the home, women tend to be concentrated in certain occupations with low pay. Nearly 80 percent of clerical workers and 60 percent of service workers were women in 1980, compared with 20 percent of managers, 44 percent of professionals, and 5 percent of crafts and kindred workers. Within the professional category, however, women are more

In recent years, there has been an effort to teach mechanical and buildings skills to girls and homemaking skills to boys. The effects of such classroom experience appears to increase the confidence of girls and the gentleness of boys.

likely to be in lower pay occupations, like elementary school teaching, nursing, social welfare, and library work, while men tend to be in the higher pay categories, such as engineering, law, surgery, accounting, and college-level teaching.

These differences reflect the emphasis on traditional gender roles, especially during the late 1940s and the 1950s. Because some work roles are defined as expressive or supportive, like elementary teaching or social work, women were encouraged to prepare for these fields if they intended to seek work, while men were directed to other areas. In addition, the pressure to educate men, especially war veterans, delayed equal educational opportunities for women, making them less able to compete in the modern work setting.

Education

Education, occupation, and income are closely related in modern societies. Educational achievement is important in obtaining access to many careers and professions, especially those that involve management or decision making. In addition, much education is specialized. For example, the developments in computer technology and its applications to many occupational settings requires special skills in mathematical understanding and reasoning, an area in which females have not achieved equality with males.

Boys and girls are encouraged by peers and teachers to pursue different courses early in their school experiences. By junior high school, which coincides

with the onset of the teenage years for most students, many gender-oriented courses are offered. Shop, metal, or woodworking, cooking, and sewing are offered as practical arts, with clear male-female preferences. A recent study (Wexler, 1980) in Los Angeles schools focused on the consequences of coed classes in such courses, with interesting results:

Students in the coed classes saw fewer differences in male and female personalities than did their counterparts in the traditional school. . . . [they] saw men and women as being more nearly alike in assertiveness, kindness, inventiveness, and adventurousness. The girls saw themselves as being not only good at cooking and sewing but also at building things and working with tools and ma-

chines. Boys saw themselves not only as active and forceful but also as domestic and gentle. (p. 32)

The significance of such educational experiences is not yet clear. However, it is evident that girls and boys have different school experiences and perceive education differently, especially in post-high school contexts.

When comparing educational data for men and women, the effect of post-World War II neglect of women's education is evident. Table 10.3 gives some comparative data. In 1960 nearly two-thirds of college students were male. By 1980 the numbers of men and women were the same among whites, though black women continued to outnumber black men in college. At nearly all levels of education

TABLE 10.3   Educational Comparisons by Race and Sex

COLLEGE STUDENTS, AGED 14–34

	TOTAL NUMBER	BLACK PERCENT MALE	PERCENT FEMALE	TOTAL NUMBER	WHITE PERCENT MALE	PERCENT FEMALE
1960	227,000	44.9	55.1	3,342,000	66.3	33.7
1970	522,000	48.5	51.5	6,759,000	60.2	39.8
1980	1,007,000	43.4	56.6	8,875,000	50.0	50.0

PERCENTAGE OF HIGH SCHOOL GRADUATES ENROLLED IN COLLEGE

	BLACK MALE	FEMALE	WHITE MALE	FEMALE
1960	20.8	16.5	31.1	17.9
1970	28.7	24.1	42.3	25.6
1980	26.4	28.8	34.0	30.2

COLLEGE AND ADVANCED DEGREES AWARDED

	BACHELORS MALE	FEMALE	MASTERS MALE	FEMALE	DOCTORATE MALE	FEMALE
1950	330,000	104,000	41,000	17,000	6,000	600
1960	256,000	139,000	51,000	24,000	8,800	1,000
1970	487,000	346,000	126,000	83,000	25,900	4,000
1980	530,000	480,000	151,000	148,000	23,100	9,700

SOURCE: Statistical Abstract, 1981.

the gap between men and women is closing, though men still receive most of the bachelor's, master's, and doctor's degrees. Since 1950, however, the proportion of dental, medical, and law students who are women has increased dramatically, partly because of active recruitment of women by professional schools.

The impact of education is obvious: women and men who are not well trained are treated as marginal workers who can be hired or dismissed at the desire of the employer. Especially in labor-intensive industries like the garment trades women without educational credentials provide a pool of cheap labor that enables these industries to survive and sometimes flourish. As one analyst describes it, "Women have traditionally been paid less than men, reflecting both their subordinate position in society and the assumption that women are never the principal source of family income, but are dependent on men as providers" (Safa, 1981; pp. 419–420).

Within this cultural context women face continued discrimination both because they are perceived to be less qualified and because of traditional norms about female roles. Unless women are educated to compete effectively with men, they will continue to occupy marginal positions and continue to lag behind men in earnings.

Income

In 1970 the average woman earned about 60 percent of what the average man earned; in 1980 the figure was still the same—60 percent. Comparisons of income for men and women within broad occupational categories shows few changes from 1960 to the present in the income differential between the sexes.

Much of the difference in income is due to the fact that men and women are concentrated in different specific occupations, though they share a common, broad occupational level. Men are overrepresented in higher-level professional—like physicians and surgeons—and wholesale sales categories, while women are overrepresented in lower-level positions—like nursing and parttime retail sales. Despite some modest shifts it is likely that these occupational patterns will continue, with the same economic consequences, noted in Table 10.4.

Lower incomes for women are often justified by the idea that women are less likely to work from necessity than are men. However, nearly one-fourth of the female labor force consists of women with husbands having incomes under $10,000, and nearly half of the female labor force is single women or women divorced or separated from husbands. While many women may not have the same pressures to work as men, it is clear that the income earned by most women is an important if not the primary contribution to the maintenance of family units.

Work within the household usually is not considered as a source of income, though a recent estimate of the value of the typical homemaker/housewife was over $18,000 per year. Obviously, this figure is arbitrary, and few men or women have been forced to pay—or could afford to pay—such a salary to the spouse. However, if this figure is included as income, the economic contribution of women in families but not working outside the home is very large. This contribution is especially important when children are present, because of their long-term dependency and the impact children have had on gender roles.

Family

Traditional definitions of gender roles emphasize the economic responsibilities of men and the homemaking responsibilities of women. This pattern no longer is characteristic of most American families, since wives are usually in the labor force before and after marriage and after the birth of children. However, the impact of children upon marriage still reinforces the traditional female role of nurturance and emotional support, even when the wife is employed outside the home. Some couples, seeking to reduce the impact of such sex-based roles, have developed formal marriage contracts or agreements spelling out the nature of the responsibilities of each spouse regarding household and childcare. The concept of contract is derived from common law and is implicit in all marriage relationships; the formal agreement, often signed before marriage, is a supplement to it. For the most part, marriage

TABLE 10.4   Median Income of Males and Females by Occupational Category (in dollars)[a]

	1975			1980		
	MALE	FEMALE	DIFFERENCE	MALE	FEMALE	DIFFERENCE
Total	$12,758	$ 7,394	$5,254	$18,612	$11,197	$ 7,415
Percent[b]		58.8			60.2	
Professional, technical and kindred workers	16,133	10,639	5,494	23,026	15,285	7,741
		65.9			66.4	
Managers and administrators, except farm	16,093	9,125	6,968	23,558	12,936	10,622
		56.7			54.9	
Sales	14,025	5,460	8,565	19,910	9,748	10,162
		39.8			49.0	
Clerical and kindred workers	12,152	7,562	4,590	18,247	10,997	7,250
		62.2			60.3	
Crafts and kindred workers	12,789	7,268	5,521	18,671	11,701	6,970
		56.8			62.7	
Operatives, including transport workers	11,142	6,251	4,891	15,702	9,440	6,262
		56.1			60.1	
Laborers, except farm	9,057	6,937	2,120	13,097	7,892	5,115
		76.6			60.9	
Service Workers, except private household	9,488	5,414	4,074	12,757	9,747	3,010
		57.1			76.4	

[a]Data are for persons 14 years old and over working full time, at longest job during year, 1975; 15 years and older, 1980.
[b]Female income as a percentage of male income.
SOURCES: Current Population Reports, Series P-60, No. 105 and No. 127.

contracts specify the time and tasks that the husband and wife are to assume in the family. Many types of contracts exist, but nearly all of them seek to establish equality in all aspects of family life.

While contractual arrangements that define rights and responsibilities of parties in various relationships are common in many phases of modern life, formal contracts do change the character of marital relationships. The primary focus on love and affection in traditional marriage is formalized into a relationship that places a value on each activity and attempts to balance the relationship in terms of these values. The goal of the contract is to modify traditional gender roles to secure equality in the assumption of responsibility for valued tasks.

Androgyny, in which social roles are not identified with or defined by gender, emphasizes the sharing of household and childcare responsibilities. **Role reversal**, in which the husband becomes the homemaker and the wife becomes the provider, is another alternative to the problem of traditional gender stereotyping. These patterns of marriage relationships have developed from changes in the economic and social conditions of modern society, reflect the equalizing effects of female employment, and have important consequences for males and females.

Marital roles are created and enacted in terms of personal definitions of the relationship, as well as the personal and economic resources that the man and the woman bring to it. In preindustrial societies male dominance was based on economic power and physical force. The woman, lacking independent resources, was viewed as sexual property to be controlled, protected, and guarded. In industrial societies, especially today, women have a broader range of resources—sexual, emotional, and economic—that have enabled them to have greater control over their lives. Increased legal and social sanctions against male use of physical force, combined with economic independence has produced—or eventually will produce—a general equality of males and females in family relationships (Collins, 1971).

Such an interpretation suggests that recent efforts by conservative political groups to reestablish the traditional family ideal are not likely to succeed.

Regardless of the ultimate fate of the Equal Rights Amendment, the contradictions between present reality and the traditional ideal will likely increase rather than lessen.

Religion and Politics

Women historically have been more active in religious organizations than have men, probably because of their greater role in socialization and moral education of the young. However, few women have held positions of leadership in Protestant denominations or the Catholic Church. Women in Roman Catholic religious orders have been teachers, community service workers, and assistants to priests, but cannot be ordained to serve in pastoral roles. Within Protestantism many of the mainline groups, such as American Baptists, United Methodists, and United Church of Christ, have ordained women during the last 20 years, though the issue has been the source of much controversy among most church bodies.

In the summer of 1974, 11 women were ordained to the priesthood by three bishops of the Protestant Episcopal Church. Soon thereafter the House of Bishops declared their ordinations to be invalid. The bishops reversed their position in 1976, though their decision was not popular. The Episcopalians are not alone in their miniscule representation of women as priests or ministers. Women make up less than 5 percent of ordained clergy in America, and most of them are assistants to men or have special, nonpastoral responsibilities. In fact, as of 1978 more than half of the church bodies still did not allow women to have full credentials as clergy (Thompson, 1979).

Religion helps to maintain traditions; thus resistance to change is not surprising. However, some women are challenging both the organization of religious life and the beliefs and ideas about God as male in Judeo-Christian tradition (Daly, 1973). Clearly, the issue of women's role in religious organizations will be a point of dispute for many years.

In contrast to their limited role in religion, women have played a significant political role since the American Revolutionary War, when the "Daughters of Liberty educated women to boycott British goods, keep the farms going during the war, and supply clothing to the army'' (Deckard, 1975, p. 245). However, they were denied the vote, had limited educational opportunities, and had no public voice until the middle of the nineteenth century. The idea that both women and blacks were being denied basic rights inspired agitation against slavery and for woman's suffrage.

Post-Civil War amendments to the Constitution ending slavery, granting citizenship, and extending the right to vote were restricted to men: women continued to work in often dangerous conditions in the new industries for low wages, but had no political power. After 1850 many women's organizations emerged to agitate or educate for women's rights. In 1890 Wyoming became the first state with women's suffrage, and by 1914 11 states had granted women the vote, thanks largely to women's developing political skill and organization. However, it was not until August, 1920, that the Nineteenth Amendment passed, extending the vote to women. This was achieved over the opposition of the liquor interests, big-city bosses, the Catholic Church, southern whites, and big business, which was apparently motivated by fear of prohibition, political reforms, or social change (Deckard, 1975).

The right to vote did not bring women to leadership in political organizations. Montana had elected a woman to the U.S. Congress in 1914, but of the few women who ran for public office, still fewer succeeded in being elected, and hardly any served for more than one term. Both Republicans and Democrats included women in their party organizations but continued to nominate men for office, except in rare situations, until after World War II.

The election of several women to a wide range of political offices in the postwar years as state senators, representatives, governors, and U.S. representatives and senators has enabled women to challenge traditional ideas about leadership roles. During the 1960s and 1970s the names of congresswomen—Edith Green, Martha Griffiths, Patsy Mink, Shirley Chisholm, Elizabeth Holtzman, Barbara Jordan, Patricia Schroeder, Bella Abzug—and senators—Margaret Chase Smith and Muriel Humphrey—became identified with political leadership

at the national level. As of 1981 there were 908 women state legislators, and more than 14,000 women elected officials. In 1982 in the U.S. Congress 19 of 435 representatives and two of 100 senators were women (*Time*, July 12, 1982, p. 20). However, like other areas of male-female relations, the political establishment has been slow to allow women to assume positions of leadership in politics and government. The positions that women have achieved reflect their new power to challenge traditional patterns of male-female relationships. Can such power be directed to other areas? What changes in other institutions are likely to occur as women unite and exert influence on social structures?

SOCIAL CHANGE AND THE FUTURE OF GENDER ROLES

During the past decade women have directed much of their energies to the ratification of the Equal Rights Amendment. This amendment failed to be ratified by 38 states by June 30, 1982, the date set for final approval. However, many organizations that have emerged to support its passage or to prevent its ratification continue to influence public opinion and political decision making.

The Women's Movement and Women's Roles

Until the 1960s most efforts by women to change traditional patterns were made by individuals or temporary alliances of political or issue-oriented groups. During the 1830s the Female Anti-Slavery Society was created; in 1845 a woman's union called the Lowell Female Labor Reform Association was formed to upgrade working conditions in the textile mills; in 1868 a working Womans Association emerged; the National Woman Suffrage Association was organized in 1869—later to merge with the National Woman Suffrage Association (in 1890); the Women's Christian Temperance Union was founded in 1874; and a National Women's Trade Union was formed in 1903. Each of these organizations had significant influence, but most were

The Equal Rights Amendment failed to be ratified by June of 1982, though public support remains strong for this amendment. Protests and demonstrations in support of the amendment occurred in many cities and states in an effort to influence state legislatures.

organized around special issues; even suffrage did not result in the development of a women's bloc vote (Deckard, 1975).

During the 1920s the **women's movement**—a general term encompassing both formal and informal efforts by women to achieve equal rights—was unsuccessful in extending equal rights but one development is worthy of note: the Women's Party did succeed in having the Equal Rights Amendment introduced in Congress in 1923. Though it failed to pass Congress the ERA was reintroduced every year from 1923 until 1972 when it was passed and sent to the states for ratification.

The women's movement was quiescent for much of the 1930s and 1940s and nearly disappeared after World War II until the 1960s. About the time Betty Friedan published *The Feminine Mystique* (1964), several diverse groups of women came together, having experienced the continued refusal of government to enforce the law governing equal opportunity. The National Organization of Women (NOW) was founded in 1966, followed by others like Women's Equity Action League (WEAL), Federally Employed Women (FEW), Radical Women, Redstockings, and the National Women's Political Caucus. With the passage of the Equal Rights Amendment by Congress in 1972, attention focused on ratification of this amendment by the states. By April 1977 35 states had voted for the amendment, three short of the number necessary for adoption. Congress voted an extension to June 30, 1982, for final ratification, though no other state ratified the ERA after 1977 and five states attempted to rescind their earlier positive votes. However, according to surveys, public support remains high: the Gallup Poll of July 1980 indicated that the amendment was favored by 58 percent of Americans—the same percentage as in 1975—while opposed by 31 percent—up 7 percent from 1975 (*The Gallup Opinion Index*, June 1980).

The goals of the women's movement enjoy the support of a majority of Americans, though there is not agreement on the means to achieve these goals. One recent study in Massachusetts (Mueller and Dimieri, 1982) clearly identifies the different social circumstances of women leading the efforts for ratification of the ERA. Among these leaders

the ERA supporters were more likely to have never been married, to be younger, to be employed full time, to hold professional or technical positions, and to be better educated and less religious than those opposed to ERA. However, among women voters generally, there were few important differences between opponents and supporters in attitudes about feminist goals, such as equal pay, more women in public offices, keeping maiden names, day care centers, and even rights to abortion and paternity leave.

Whether or not the ERA is eventually ratified by the necessary two-thirds of the states, the widespread support for women's rights has important consequences for marriage, children, and for individual men and women. What have been the effects of the women's movement thus far?

The impact of the increase in women's labor force participation is clearly evident in declining fertility rates, delayed marriage, and lower female participation in voluntary organizations. The women's movement has fostered greater awareness of inequalities in work, income, and family responsibilities. However, research suggests that the effects of such awareness is largely limited to the relationships within the family.

A 10-year study of women in the labor force (Huber and Spitze, 1981) found that few changes occurred in behavior within the family. As the authors state:

Wives do market work [hold jobs] because the family needs money; their husbands do a little housework to enable the household to continue to function. Approval of married women's employment increases because, otherwise, the wife's daily market work would make both spouses uncomfortably aware of inconsistency in belief and behavior. And both spouses come to approve married mothers' employment—the idea that such work harms children declines. The husband's attitude toward his own wife's employment is more favorable. (pp. 165–166)

They note, however, that such employment does not give women equal decision-making power or change many behavior patterns based on traditional gender roles within the family.

Similar results were obtained from a study of professional women and their families (Yogev, 1981)

Faculty women expressed contradictions in their ideas: they wanted to continue the traditional pattern of responsibilities for housework and childcare, but they also perceived themselves as equals to their husbands. These women appeared to accept an expansion of their roles to include occupational activities, rather than redefining them.

One contribution of recent research has been to clarify the impact of children on marital happiness. It is traditionally assumed that children bring fulfillment to marriage. Yet in their research during the past decade Spanier and Lewis (1980) have accumulated evidence that children tend to have negative effects on marital happiness. Glenn and McLanahan (1982) reviewed the evidence and claimed that this finding is "about as nearly conclusive as social scientific evidence on any topic ever is" (p. 70).

This conclusion suggests that the decision to have children will become more problematic in the future, despite cultural values endorsing parenthood. Further, if employed women have better mental health than unemployed women, as some studies have suggested (Kessler and McRae, 1982), the problems of defining appropriate gender roles will become more complex for young men and women.

Men and Changing Gender Roles

As women's roles have changed, men's roles have changed as well. In the traditional family, expectations of men centered on the roles of provider and protector. The traits that were seen as important in the world of work—aggressiveness, strength, responsibility, and persistence—became defined as masculine characteristics. Today not only has the application of modern technology made physical strength less relevant, but so-called masculine traits have been adopted by women who have entered the work place in competition with men.

While market conditions still favor male dominance in the work setting, the ability of women to compete has reduced the impact of one of the key ingredients maintaining this relationship—economic power. Men tend to be favored in many aspects of public life, however. As the data on education illustrate (Table 10.3) men are more likely

to complete college and receive graduate training; also family resources are more likely to be directed toward a son than a daughter. Men also have more opportunities to develop skills and talents through sports and a social environment that encourages curiosity and exploration.

The impact of changing gender roles has been more direct in some areas of men's lives than in others. No longer is childcare only a woman's function, economic support only a man's. These changes represent an increased opportunity for men—and women—to choose the roles they wish to play. The concept of women's liberation, a freeing from traditional roles, inevitably involves men's liberation. To be able to select from a wide range of possible relationships in marriage is to be liberated from the traditions and the rigid rules that have prevented people from achieving their potential.

The significance of such liberation is perhaps most evident in the area of sexual relationships, both before and after marriage. Traditional masculine roles involve heterosexual prowess and domination. Men are constantly involved in competition with each other to prove their masculinity. Men are assumed to have a strong sex drive; women are sexually passive. Women are idealized and protected or exploited, sometimes both. There is no assumption of equality between men and women. Liberation from this role definition for men enables them to accept women as people who can achieve, experience life, and make choices just as men are able to do. Protection is immaterial and exploitation is immoral.

Clearly, human liberation is still an ideal rather than reality. While some men object to changes, others welcome freedom from traditional definitions of masculinity. There is obviously a high degree of failure among American males to achieve these ideals. There are also inherent role conflicts in traditional gender roles, such as work "versus" family, strong "versus" caring, aloof "versus" loving, leading to much confusion for men. Some scholars have suggested that *machismo*—a concept of masculinity based on dominance of females through physical prowess, violence, or threats—is a cover for underlying feelings of insecurity and self-doubt that men experience (Aramoni, 1972).

The stress of work life is, in this view, complicated by cultural definitions that require men to act in aggressive and domineering ways toward women.

Obviously, equality between men and women is neither easily defined nor attained. Given the economic and social forces at work in modern societies, efforts to achieve equality will continue. But will they succeed?

IS GENDER EQUALITY POSSIBLE?

Equality may mean many things. For some, equality requires the same level of involvement by men and women in all aspects of social life: family, work, politics, education, religion. For others, equality means equal access to economic and occupational opportunities regardless of sex. For still others, equality means equal recognition, esteem, prestige, or honor for different social roles. In this view a woman should receive the same recognition for her achievements in rearing children as her husband for his achievements in work or career. Still a fourth group of people may argue that the question itself is wrong: women and men are so different—biologically and psychologically—that equality is not even an issue.

Any definitive answer to the question of gender equality may be impossible because of the various attitudes about gender roles that people bring to the issue. However, a review of the ways in which economic and prestige rewards are distributed in our society may suggest some reasons for the persistence of the dispute.

In the United States, as in most industrial societies, economic rewards are given to positions, or, more correctly, to people who occupy those positions. The incomes of most workers are set by the work they do rather than by their personality traits or abilities. Prestige also accrues to occupations. In general, prestige and income are closely related. It is the promise of high status, high income, and high authority that creates the intense competition for careers in medicine, law, or politics.

For the most part the mother-homemaker position is nonpaid, low status, and low in authority, except for control over children. While women may bring pride to their work and draw admiration from husbands for their skill in home management, no money is paid directly for their services, no formal education is required for entrance into homemaking or for giving birth, and no power over family decisions is inherent in the position. This does not mean that the mother-homemaker position is unimportant; it simply indicates that in a society in which money, education, and authority are criteria for measuring status and success, the position of mother-homemaker is not a part of the reward structure of society.

Those who argue that men and women are so different that the issue of equality is irrelevant offer little hope for people who desire equal job opportunity and equal wages for equivalent work. Presumed or actual differences become the basis for decisions about who is hired—"women can't be bosses, because they're too emotional," or "you really can't depend on women; first thing you know they get married and quit to have babies," or "men just don't have the physical ability to run sewing machines"—rather than the individual's ability. The issue is not simply that an individual is denied equal wages or opportunities, but that women or men are given or denied opportunities on the basis of sex or gender alone.

Is gender equality possible? Clearly, new patterns of gender roles have developed and exist along with older patterns. Whether these changes will develop even further is unknown. However, some factors continue to force changes in work and social roles, for example, changes in number of children, expectations of equality by women, economic pressures on married couples and increased educational requirements for jobs.

In most industrial societies gender is no longer an essential consideration in defining work roles; few jobs remain requiring such strength that only men can do them. Yet for some occupations gender remains an important issue because of presumed qualities related to sex, like emotionality or aggressiveness. However, as more women pursue educational credentials and obtain access to all occupations, their economic rewards will increase. Whether economic equality will bring basic equality within the family is difficult to determine.

However equality is defined, the issue will not be easily resolved because it concerns patterns of human relationships that are defined by basic human values and sanctioned by tradition.

SUMMARY

Sexual differences—real or assumed—have been the basis of different gender roles for men and women in every human society. Sex refers to physical differences while gender refers to social aspects and behavior associated with sex. Traditionally, in Western societies women have been assigned primarily to roles of homemaking and childrearing in the home and to lower-level occupations outside the home. Such assignment is made on the basis of perceived differences in ability or personality based on sex.

Biological differences between men and women focus on reproduction. Women become pregnant and give birth; men impregnate. Genes determine sex, and male or female sexual organs develop in the fetus as a combination of genetic and hormonal influence. However, few if any other differences between males and females appear to be based on biology.

Cultural traditions are very important in defining gender roles. Evidence from other societies indicates that men and women may have opposite roles, depending on the cultural context. In American society women had few legal rights until about a century ago; the social ideal was that men were to protect and support them. However, reality was never close to the ideal for most women—especially those on the frontier or in slavery or those who immigrated to the United States. Even with expanding work opportunities that came with World War II, women did not achieve equality with men in education, occupation, or income. Instead, women were encouraged to pursue expressive roles within the family, while men filled instrumental roles of leadership and control. The current confusion that many women feel about their roles reflects the competing models for their behavior. The traditional role of mother-homemaker, the role of superwoman, or the career-no marriage role are only three of many alternatives available.

A child is socialized from early infancy to his or her gender role. Girls are expected to be dependent and to prefer dolls and tea sets, while boys are expected to be aggressive and to prefer tanks and trucks. Appropriate behavior is rewarded and encouraged; boys quickly learn not to be "sissies" or "babies" just as girls learn that "tomboys" are not feminine.

In modern society all of these factors combine to create gender inequality. In work, women are concentrated in lower pay occupational categories. In part this is due to lower educational levels, especially in training for skills that are needed in modern technological enterprises. Not surprisingly, the median income of women is about 60 percent of men's median income, with few differences by occupational category.

Family roles have been slow to change, with traditional patterns supported by religious beliefs. However, a declining birth rate and increased out-of-home employment of women have altered family arrangements; these changes are likely to continue as more families need or want a two-spouse income. Religious organizations have been extremely resistant to change, though some groups have begun to include women among the ordained clergy. Women have been involved in political activities for many decades; their organizational efforts have effected legislative changes in women's status and have been instrumental in opening new educational and job opportunities for women. Men also may benefit from changing gender roles by being freed from narrow definitions of appropriate behavior in work and family life.

Is gender equality possible? The failure of the Equal Rights Amendment does not mean that the forces of change have been stopped. As long as economic rewards and prestige are awarded only to positions outside the home, there will be gender inequality. Clearly, gender equality will be an issue for many years.

GLOSSARY

Androgyny role that is characterized by behavior appropriate to a situation, regardless of traditional gender definition.

The Texture of Social Life

Expressive role a set of expectations, behaviors, or norms that provide emotional satisfaction, warmth and support to others; traditionally seen as more appropriate for a woman than for a man.

Feminists people who believe that sex or gender is not a legitimate basis for social roles and who seek to change current patterns of inequality.

Gender social aspects of sex, such as the expectations, roles, feelings or concepts associated with being male or female.

Instrumental role a set of expectations, behaviors or norms that emphasize achievement, leadership, dominance and self-assertion; traditionally seen as more appropriate for a man than a woman.

Role reversal the assumption of the male role of provider by the woman and the female role of homemaker by the man.

Women's movement a general term encompassing both formal and informal efforts by women to achieve equal rights.

Sex biological differences or characteristics that distinguish males and females.

Superwoman model the ideal which encourages women to combine the roles of nurturant, supportive wives and mothers, career women, and socially active people.

ADDITIONAL READINGS

Aronoff, Joel, and William D. Crano. "A Re-examination of the Cross-Cultural Principles of Task Segregation and Sex-Role Differentiation in the Family." *American Sociological Review* 40 (February 1975): 12–20.

Examines the idea that men are predominant in productive activities in various societies; offers no support for differential role idea.

Balswick, Jack O., and Charles V. Peck. "The Inexpressive Male: A Tragedy of American Society." *The Family Coordinator* 20 (October 1971): 363–368.

Attempts to identify one problem of being male and the socialization that produces it.

Eisenstein, Zellah R. "The Sexual Politics of the New Right: Understanding the 'Crisis of liberalism' for the 1980s." *Signs: Journal of Women in Culture and Society* 7 (Spring 1982): 567–588.

Explores the effect of the current political situation on women and families and the antifeminist stance of the New Right.

Huber, Joan, ed. *Changing Women in a Changing Society.* Chicago: University of Chicago Press, 1973.

A collection of articles that focus on women's roles in various phases of modern society.

Dubbert, Joe L. *A Man's Place: Masculinity in Transition.* Englewood Cliffs, N.J.: Prentice-Hall, 1979.

An examination of the history of concepts about masculinity in America, from 1800 to the present.

Rossi, Alice. "Equality Between the Sexes: An Immodest Proposal." *Daedalus* 93 (Spring 1964): 607–652.

A provocative article that examines the possibility of genuine social equality of the sexes.

Weitz, Shirley. *Sex Roles: Biological, Psychological and Social Foundations.* New York: Oxford University Press, 1977.

A general overview of the various sources of sex and gender roles; a careful review of evidence.

READING

READING 10.1

My Dinner with Five Silverware Salesmen

Maggie Scarf

I really used to believe in those Virginia Slims ads—the ones that say, "You've come a long way, baby!" Since a certain recent evening, however, I haven't been so sure. We may not have come much farther than half a block from Grand Central. The Grand Central area can grow eerily quiet on a Sunday; the whole neighborhood seems to shut down. That night, even though it was only 8 p.m., the streets were so empty that you could almost believe that nerve gas had been sprayed, silencing anything that breathed. I must confess that I ran, rather than walked, to the nearest restaurant (I was in from out of town, staying at the Yale Club, whose dining facilities were closed). It was on 44th Street. I hurried inside, my heart beating rapidly, and walked down the long, wide corridor to the hostess's desk. She glanced up at me and I asked for a table for one. She stared, her mascara-ringed eyes bulging, her lipsticked mouth forming an astonished "Oh." It was the look I would have expected to see on her face if I'd just run in there with a smoking gun in my hand, gasping: "Here, I've just killed someone. He's out on the sidewalk. Get the police!" Her reaction took me aback—so much that I literally stepped back. In doing so, I gave way to a couple who had just come in behind me. "Wait," the hostess said to me, taking a sheaf of menus from her stand. She led them into the dining room, and then returned. In the interim, she seemed to have undergone a plastic drenching, like the wax spray you gave your auto during a car wash; her face and en-

tire body posture were set in a smiling, umoving neutrality. She asked me, blandly, whether or not I had a reservation. "Well, no," I answered uncomfortably. "But—don't you just have a small table for one?" "Wait," she said again. This time she went down the long entryway toward the front door, and disappeared into a room off to the right. I stood there, shamefaced, like a pupil whose teacher has gone off to complain to the principal. In the meantime, the restaurant door kept opening and shutting, and a line of new patrons was forming. Where had they come from? I wondered. Cabs? The world outside had been so dark and deserted. I realized that I was the object of curious glances, for I wasn't quite in the line, and I tried to avoid meeting anyone's eyes. I found it disquieting, waiting for the hostess's return. But when I saw her, her unchanged expression told me that a decision had been made, and that it was not in my favor. "I'm sorry," she said, with brisk impersonality, "but we really can't seat you if you haven't any reservation." "Listen," I said reasonably, "there isn't any place around here that's open, is there? Everything looks dark." Her only response was a shrug. "Do you know of a place that *is* open?" I appealed to her. She shrugged again: "There's Arthur Treacher's, over on 43rd, or maybe it's 42nd. . . ." But, brandishing her menus, she was beckoning to a party of four. "On *42nd*?" I cried after her, dismayed—I, who had run around the relatively safe and respectable corner of 44th and Vanderbilt. "That's the only one I know of," she turned back to say, as she led her party into the dining room.

"She won't seat you because you're a woman alone," murmured a voice close to my ear. I turned to see a pleasantly balding man in a tan business suit. He touched my elbow and said kindly, "You come with us." I followed him. I was now one of a large group led by the hostess, and I didn't realize, until we were seated, who "us" was. "Us," as it turned out, was a

SOURCE: *The New Republic*, vol. 186, no. 22 (June 2, 1982): 42 Reprinted by Permission of THE NEW REPUBLIC, © 1982, The New Republic, Inc.

group of five wholesale silverware salesmen. The hostess, who had treated me like an escaped leper a few moments earlier, now seated me with a great show of friendliness, handed me my menu, and gave me a warm smile. I looked around the dining room, and saw at least five small tables that were empty. "Did you really refuse to seat me because I am a woman alone?" I asked, touching the sleeve of her dress, indicating those empty tables with a nod. "Oh," she answered, blinking her false eyelashes, "those are set for two." "Yes," I said, "but usually, when *one* person comes in, they take a setting away." She blinked again, smiled with professional warmth: "We find it doesn't pay. And besides, those tables are all reserved . . . for two." I contemplated making a scene; but felt it would be rude to my knights in shining armor, or wholesale silver, in this instance. My hosts were polite. They were friendly. Nevertheless there was something absurd about the situation: I'd been forced to have supper with five unknown silverware salesmen because I couldn't be seated in this restaurant on my own. Was this really New York City, the center of the women's liberation movement? Betty Friedan, I silently cried, where are you? Gloria Steinem, *au secours!* Was this really happening a half-block away from Grand Central? The salesmen paid for my dinner. I contemplated making a scene about that, too, but they made it clear that any other arrangement would have been insulting.

The following morning, on the telephone, I said to my husband: "You'll never be able to guess whom I had dinner with last night!" We pondered the hostess's motivations: my husband believed she'd refused to seat me because she thought I was a lady of the night. "A middle-aged mother of three?" I responded incredulously. "In a white wool suit with a mandarin collar?" Was it possible that because of the recent styles—suburban matrons dressing in low-cut blouses and skirts with high slits—that the real hookers had taken to dressing up as suburban matrons? Or is there a "no woman alone" rule that is so inflexible that even if I'd walked in there wearing a nun's habit I could not have been seated without the aid of my salesmen/protectors?

I'll never know. Nor will I know what role geography—the restaurant's proximity to the sleazy Times Square area—may have played in making unaccompanied females suspicious. What I do believe, though, is that a solitary male diner would have been seated without a raised eyebrow, and allowed to eat his dinner in peace. He wouldn't have needed the assistance of five traveling saleswomen in order to render himself an acceptable patron.

SUMMARY

Discrimination against women may be very subtle. As Scarf has illustrated, women and men may be treated very differently, especially in those areas traditionally defined as masculine. Much change has occurred in some areas, but male prerogatives remain dominant in much of public life and especially in business.

QUESTIONS

1. What other areas of social life persist with subtle but different treatment of men and women?
2. Is the effectiveness of such discrimination increased because both men and women "play the game?"
3. Do men experience similar forms of subtle discrimination?

CHAPTER 11

Racial and Cultural Minorities

CONTENTS

AT ISSUE

Should immigration to the United States be stopped?

For more than 200 years people have come to the United States to find better economic opportunities, to secure religious freedom, or to escape political repression. While white Europeans provided the bulk of the immigrant population during most of this period, since 1950 increasing numbers of immigrants have come from Mexico, Latin America, the Caribbean, China, Vietnam, and other Asian countries. During the 1970s large numbers of refugees from Vietnam, Laos, and Cambodia were brought to this country, while thousands of Cubans and Haitians sought freedom here at about the same time. Some people believe that the large number of immigrants—refugees and others—have created economic and social strains in American society. Others feel that the United States, as a nation of immigrants and a symbol of freedom, must continue to keep its doors open. Should immigration be stopped?

YES   Since its beginning the United States has been open to immigrants and refugees from other countries. However, circumstances have changed and the doors must now be closed. There are several reasons for this.

First is the economic problem. Most refugees and immigrants have few technical skills to bring to the U.S. labor market. Increased automation has eliminated many jobs that were traditionally performed by unskilled laborers and higher levels of skill are now required for most jobs. The result is that immigrants either cannot find work or they successfully compete with citizens for the remaining low-wage jobs because they are willing to work for less money. As a result the pool of unemployed increases, as do welfare costs and the frustration and anger of those who see their employment undercut by recent immigrants.

Second is the problem created by the tendency of immigrants to group together and isolate themselves from the dominant society. Rather than adapting to American society, they try to maintain the culture and language of their ethnic or national groups. While all immigrant groups have followed this pattern for some period of time, the goal of earlier immigrants was to become American.

Third, it is time to recognize that, as a matter of principle, we should not accept everyone who wishes to come to the United States. Other countries should be encouraged to expand their economic opportunities, freedoms, and rights making those countries more attractive to immigration. The entire world would benefit from such a development, and the pressure on the United States would decrease.

Immigration should be stopped, especially immigration of people who will compete with those already unemployed for the few available jobs. Doesn't the United States have a responsibility to protect and aid its citizens before providing a haven for those of other countries?

NO   Alarmists have been trying to close the door to immigrants for more than 100 years. Fortunately, they have failed, and their efforts to stop immigration now should be resisted for several reasons.

First, it is immigration that has made the United States what it is today. The mixture of races, linguistic and national backgrounds, religious experiences, and ethnic traditions has been the source of our prosperity, freedom, and democracy. The need for people to compromise because other citizens behave, believe, or think differently brings a vitality to cultural life not found in societies without such diversity. To stop immigration would eliminate one of the basic catalysts of change and growth.

Second, it is common for those who have privileges to want to protect and maintain them. However, our country's growth has been based on the contributions of diverse groups. People cannot protect their privileges by stopping immigration; we should remind those who want to do so that they are also descendants of immigrants who made good.

Third, the principles to which we as a nation adhere are freedom, opportunity, and personal choice. The words of Emma Lazarus engraved on the Statue of Liberty express our commitment to these principles: "Give me your tired, your poor, your huddled masses yearning to breathe free, the wretched refuse of your teeming shore, send these, the homeless, tempest-tossed to me: I lift my lamp beside the golden door." Throughout the past 200 years this country has been a symbol of opportunity and a light of hope for the poor, persecuted people of the world. Those who seek freedom and opportunity today should be given the same choice as our parents and grandparents.

The light on the Statue of Liberty means hope for the immigrant; to put it out would harm ourselves and the entire world. Immigration should not be stopped!

The issues about immigration are complex, but the major issue revolves around the rights of U.S. citizens to work at a decent wage. On the one side are those who believe that by allowing large numbers of refugees or other immigrants to enter the country, wages are lowered and jobs are lost because the newly arrived work at whatever is available. The other side believes that immigration mixes populations and produces a new creative society that benefits all people. Should people who take jobs from citizens be allowed to come to the United States? Is it true that immigrants depress wages? Can immigration be stopped without harming the creativity and growth of our society? Are racial or ethnic problems an American creation? Can such problems be solved?

In an effort to answer some of these questions, we will examine the processes by which racial and ethnic groups accommodate to one another and to society, and we will identify the role of power and privilege in shaping the relationships between these groups, both in the United States and throughout the world.

QUESTIONS TO CONSIDER

- Is race a scientific or a social concept?

- Why are some ethnic groups more successful in work and school than others?

- Is racial integration possible in America?

- How is ethnic identity maintained in modern society?

The bright morning sun sparkled off the plumed metal helmets of the Blues and Royals troopers of the Queen's Household Cavalry as they left their barracks for the daily mounting of the guard at Whitehall. . . . The cavalrymen never reached their destination. At 10:43 . . . a deafening explosion ripped through the detachment, filling the air with 4- and 6-inch nails and blowing the flesh of both men and horses yards around. . . . less than two miles away, the 30 man Royal Green Jackets Band was in the midst of playing a medley from the musical **Oliver!** *when an equally powerful bomb pulverized the bandstands. . . . The toll: ten soldiers killed; 32 soldiers, two policemen and 21 civilians injured. [Later the Irish Republican Army claimed responsibility.]* (**Time,** *August 2, 1982)*

For over the past 33 years, the South African government has uprooted between 2 and 3 million black people and placed them in impoverished rural tribal reserves. The people involved in this mass relocation were, for the most part, not consulted. Moreover, they have virtually no legal way to oppose what amounts to their own dispossession. The process is continuing even now, and constitutes one of the largest forced relocations of humanity in recent history.

The goal goes beyond the mere physical removal of black people from proximity to whites: *the eventual aim is to denationalize them, stripping them of any claim to political rights within South Africa. (Gary Thatcher, "South Africa's Archipelago,"* **Christian Science Monitor,** *September 14, 1981, p. 1)*

My mother had not been back to the city of her birth since 1962; my father's return to Palestine had taken 32 years. This was the first time I had trod the stones upon which my family has lived for thousands of years, the soil upon which I would have been born and raised had they not been forced to flee.

My aunt's house lies within the walls of the Old City of Jerusalem. Here, in this house, for 400 years, my family has lived. Walking through the limestone streets, my mother was more than a tourist. For her, every street was filled with a memory, an experience, an intimately familiar sight. For me, it was a return to my roots . . . a return to aunts, uncles, and some 60 first cousins; people descended from the Canaanites and the Philistines who had occupied this land for 10,000 years, long before Moses and David. (Maher Ahmad, "Palestine, My Home," **Chicago Tribune,** *June 20, 1982)*

ETHNICITY AND RACE: SOURCES OF INEQUALITY

Conflict among racial, religious, and ethnic groups is not only a problem in the United States. In Northern Ireland, Protestants and Catholics have turned their country into a battleground. In Russia, Jews who seek to emigrate are confronted with threats and loss of livelihood. Vietnamese and Cambodians have waged intermittent war on each other for centuries. In short, throughout the world, race and ethnicity play a prominent role in economic, political, and social relationships. In this chapter we will examine racial and ethnic groups, the history of their emergence and identity, and the social structures that define relationships between minority and dominant groups.

Minorities, Dominant Groups, and Relationships

A **minority** is a group or category of people who can be distinguished by special physical or cultural traits, which are used to single them out for differential and unequal treatment (Wirth, 1945). Differential treatment may involve discrimination and other acts of hostility directed against all people sharing the traits that are used to identify the minority. The minority, in turn, is relatively powerless to avoid this treatment.

Minority groups differ considerably. Minority status may be assigned on the basis of race, nationality, religion, and ethnicity or even sex or marital status. However, whatever the source of assignment to minority status, there are some common themes that emphasize minorities' relative powerlessness. **Powerlessness** refers to the lack of rights or power on the part of the minority groups to determine their own fate in political, economic, or social matters. It is this attribute that distinguishes minorities from the dominant group (Himes, 1974).

While powerlessness is the basic condition of minority status, other conditions such as **visibility** (easily seen) and **size** of the group (large enough to be defined as a special category) are important as well. The Indians on a South Dakota reservation have little power, are clearly visible, and are numerous enough to be seen as an ethnic population. Mexican Americans in cities like Chicago, Cleveland, and Pittsburgh also are relatively powerless and are culturally distinct. The dominant group is able to maintain control through its ability to use economic, political, and social resources to identify and isolate these groups.

The existence of a "minority group" implies the presence of a majority or dominant group. The term **dominant group** is preferable to the term majority group, since dominance is based upon higher status, more privileges, and greater power, rather than upon numerical superiority. The dominant group defines all members of the minority in terms of religion, ethnicity, physical traits, or the like. The individual cannot alter his or her status by personal merit or achievement and is forever trapped in a social "category."

Dominant-minority relations refers to patterned interactions that can be described in terms of dominance and control of one group by another. Dominance may be expressed through direct legal or political action, for example, by slavery or assignment of Native Americans to reservations. Dominance may also be maintained through structured interactions in schools, neighborhoods, or churches that legitimize discrimination and inequality. The behaviors and attitudes of the dominant group are viewed as normal or modal in a society. By tradition and custom, and even by law, these patterns of behavior have been made legitimate. In addition, the traditional dominant-minority relationship is usually defined by the dominant group as essential to the preservation of society.

Ethnicity and Culture

Ethnic minorities are groups defined by national origin, language, and cultural patterns that are different from the dominant group. Ethnicity may at times include race or religion, though for most ethnic groups cultural factors are the most salient.

IMMIGRATION: ETHNIC AND CULTURAL BACKGROUNDS

There is a close tie between ethnic background and cultural traditions, particularly among newly arrived immigrants. Dress, family customs, language, and social behavior all distinguish members of ethnic minority groups, even if skin color is similar to that of the dominant group.

Minority status based on language or culture is now or was at one time a fact for a large number of people in the United States. Waves of European immigration in the late nineteenth and early twentieth centuries brought many ethnic groups with distinctive characteristics. These characteristics have gradually disappeared in succeeding generations. Whether their loss indicates genuine identification with the dominant group remains unanswered: St. Patrick's Day and Columbus Day parades, Chinese New Year festivals, and other public expressions of ethnicity suggest that vestiges of ethnic identification remain. In 1980 less than 20 percent of the U.S. population was either foreign born or had at least one parent who was foreign born, though if grandparents were included the proportion would be considerably larger.

Several factors have influenced the patterns of U.S. immigration. Before 1850 most Africans arrived as recruits for slave labor. The political upheavals across Europe in the 1840s and the potato famines in Ireland in the same years sent thousands fleeing to this country. Before 1840 no country provided such large numbers of immigrants to clearly dominate the population, but from 1850 to 1890 over half of all immigrants came from Germany, Scandinavia, and the British Isles. Since World War II an increasing proportion of immigrants have come from Asia and Latin America. Changing patterns of immigration are illustrated in Table 11.1.

The first immigrants from Asia were attracted by work on the railroads in the western United States. Agitation for legislation against Asians came from white workers, beginning in the 1860s, though fewer than 50,000 Chinese had entered the country. In 1882, following a large influx of Chinese during the 1871–1880 period, Congress passed a law to suspend all Chinese immigration for 10 years. As a result of this and subsequent limiting legislation, there was little immigration from China until 1951 when refugees from Communist China were admitted.

The immigration act passed in 1921 limited entrance by national origin to 3 percent of the number of persons of that nationality who were here in 1910. The 1924 act was more restrictive, setting the quota at 2 percent of the 1890 number of foreign born of such nationality, with no quota less than 100 persons. The effect of these acts was to limit the flow of southern and Eastern Europeans and Asians to only a small fraction of the number who had arrived from 1900 to 1920. As a result, children of earlier immigrants from Northern Europe were able to maintain their dominant position in the United States. Changes in immigration laws in 1952 and 1965 substituted occupational skills for national origins as a basis for quotas, though political refugees and displaced persons have been admitted above the quotas for normal immigration.

TABLE 11.1   U.S. Immigration by Continent of Origin to the United States and Percent from Various Areas, 1820–1979 (number and percent)

	1820–1880	1881–1900	1901–1920	1921–1950	1951–1970	1971–1979
Total Immigrants	10,189,429 (100.0%)	8,934,177 (99.9%)	14,531,197 (100.0%)	5,670,679 (100.0%)	5,837,156 (99.9%)	3,962,500 (100.0%)
Continent of Origin:						
Africa	1,006 (0.0)	1,207 (0.0)	15,811 (0.1)	15,403 (0.3)	43,046 (0.7)	66,700 (2.0)
Asia	230,689 (2.3)	144,804 (1.6)	570,779 (3.9)	160,500 (2.8)	577,877 (9.9)	1,352,100 (35.3)
Australia, New Zealand,	9,992 (0.1)	9,757 (0.1)	24,323 (0.2)	24,335 (0.4)	31,068 (0.5)	21,600 (0.4)
Europe	8,989,253 (88.2)	8,290,836 (92.8)	12,377,927 (85.2)	34,318,870 (60.5)	2,449,003 (42.0)	728,200 (18.4)
North and Central America	744,489 (7.3)	462,860 (5.2)	1,446,380 (10.2)	1,959,708 (34.6)	2,363,736 (40.5)	1,660,000 (37.4)
South America	8,726 (0.1)	3.079 (0.0)	59,179 (0.4)	71,849 (1.3)	349,582 (6.0)	118,300 (6.2)
Other	204,316 (2.0)	21,634 (0.2)	36,798 (0.2)	7,014 (0.1)	16,377 (0.3)	15,800 (0.4)

SOURCE: Compiled from Annual Reports of U.S. Immigration and Naturalization Service.

Ethnic minorities are numerous in the United States. European immigrants, averaging slightly more than 100,000 per year since 1950, have various cultural traditions: Italian, Greek, English, German, Portuguese, Spanish, Russian, Turkish, Polish, and others. Asian immigration has increased dramatically since 1950. During the period from 1971 through 1979, 141,400 immigrants came from India, 235,400 from Korea, 312,700 from the Philippines, and 109,500 from Hong Kong. Even after the conclusion of U.S. involvement in Vietnam, the continued conflict among Vietnam, Cambodia, Laos, and Thailand has created thousands of refugees and immigrants as well: during 1971–1979, 129,300 came from Vietnam. Immigration from other countries near the United States, especially Mexico, Canada, Cuba, and the West Indies, totals about 200,000 people yearly; from 1971 through 1979, Cuban refugees and immigrants numbered 249,700 and Haitian refugees and immigrants, 49,800. Since 1979 refugees and immigrants from these two countries have continued to arrive. In fact, nearly 500,000 have come since 1970. By contrast, only 5,000 people have arrived from Africa in a typical year, and only 80,000 have immigrated here in the past 30 years. Table 11.2 shows which countries contributed most heavily to U.S. immigration at various periods.

ETHNICITY AND ETHNOCENTRISM

Ethnic identity and ethnocentrism—the belief that one's own cultural traditions are best—are closely related. To maintain an ethnic community requires large numbers, isolation from the dominant culture, and a strong identification with one's own culture. Because of their large concentrations Irish and Italian groups were able to maintain an ethnic identity in New York, Japanese and Chinese an ethnic identity in San Francisco, and Greeks and Poles an ethnic identity in Chicago, each with its distinctive language, holidays, foods, and customs. Recently, except for displaced national groups, such as Cubans in Miami and Vietnamese in Los Angeles, too few immigrants of one nationality exist to create new ethnic communities. In the United States unless groups are socially isolated—by their

TABLE 11.2   U.S. Immigration by Country of Origin, 1820–1979

	TOTAL NUMBER	NUMBER DURING PERIODS OF GREATEST IMMIGRATION	
Germany	6,985,000	3,930,000:	1850–1890
Italy	5,300,000	3,807,000:	1891–1920
Great Britain	4,914,000	1,355,000:	1871–1890
Ireland	4,724,000	3,223,000:	1841–1890
Austria-Hungary	4,316,000	3,042,000:	1901–1920
Canada	4,125,000	1,667,000:	1911–1930
Soviet Union	4,476,000	2,519,000:	1901–1920
Mexico	2,177,000	459,000:	1921–1930
		(1,034,000:	1961–1979)
Sweden	1,273,000	868,000:	1881–1910
Norway	856,000	462,000:	1881–1920
West Indies	758,000	1,206,000:	1961–1979
France	754,000	154,000:	1841–1860
Greece	661,000	352,000:	1901–1920
China	540,000	123,000:	1871–1880
		(175,000:	1971–1979)
Cuba	539,000	519,000:	1961–1979
Poland	520,000	228,000:	1921–1930
Portugal	453,000	90,000:	1911–1920
Philippines	431,000	318,000:	1971–1979
Japan	411,000	130,000:	1901–1910

SOURCE: Annual Reports of U.S. Immigration and Naturalization Service.

own choice or through rejection from others—and treated with hostility by the dominant population, education, participation in social life, and intermarriage will eliminate most distinctive ethnic characteristics by the second or third generation.

The close relationship between ethnicity and religion is evident among several populations, especially the Irish, Italians, and Jews. Not only were Italian and Irish Catholic immigrant groups culturally distinctive, but their religious commitments were in conflict with those of the Protestant majority. Similarly, Jewish religious and cultural life has differed considerably from that of Protestants.

Religion in America has no social visibility unless it is associated with racial or ethnic/cultural factors. Thus it is possible to affiliate with a new religious group to avoid minority status if no other minority condition is present. In an effort to maintain their ethnic traditions and beliefs, some religious groups of all faiths have sponsored schools. Not all such efforts are successful, however. For example, there continue to be conflicts between Amish parents and state officials in Iowa and Ohio over minimum standards of education as well as health and sanitation (Rodgers, 1969). The desire of the Amish to maintain German as the dominant language, and the view that eight or nine years of formal education are sufficient have caused many problems for these groups. Clearly, this is a complex issue involving cultural as well as religious facts.

Race: Myths and Realities

Biologically, black populations in America are mixtures of gene pools from Africa and Europe, as are many whites. A person who claims to be black or who can be shown to have black ancestry is defined as black, regardless of the distance of the ancestor. Indeed, one of the folk myths associated with race is the idea that individuals who are white can have black babies if there are black genes in their background; however, no one believes that blacks can have white babies if there are any white genes or white ancestors in the family. The difference in these views "reflects a crude racism in which the 'return' to blackness is seen as a throwback, or a return to a 'primitive' trait" (Alland, 1980, p. 168).

Among the myths about race none is as persistent as the idea that certain abilities or traits are characteristic of a group and are genetic in origin; for example, Jews are financial wizards, Japanese are talented imitators, and blacks have musical talent. Not only have such ideas been disproved but efforts to define and to identify racial groups or populations on the basis of genetic differences have been unsuccessful. Variation within racial groups is as great as variations between them (Dobzhansky, 1973). In short, all humans share a common genetic background, physical differences are due to both heredity and environmental influences, and there is no evidence to support the ideas that genetic differences produce different cultures or that pure races exist (UNESCO, 1952).

THE SOCIAL DEFINITION OF RACE

Is it possible to define the term race? Clearly, the concept of race refers to a social category, not a biological one. The term originally was applied to populations on the basis of visible characteristics like skin color, hair form, type of body or head shape. While all these characteristics are genetically based, they can be modified by environmental conditions.

However, it is not genetically based characteristics that are important to the concept of race, but the meanings and values applied to them. *Race*, then, is a social category constructed to fit populations that share characteristics assumed to be genetically distinct. Races are significant because visible differences between racially defined groups are seen as important; these differences are illustrated by the language of racism.

THE LANGUAGE OF RACE AND RACISM

Use of the term race to describe people with distinct genetic or biological traits is scientifically invalid, though such use is common. Perhaps the most flagrant abuse of the concept occurred in Nazi Germany during the 1930s and 1940s. As Alland (1980) states:

Hitler . . . chose to emphasize the Aryan myth of German ancestry. Yet the word "Aryan" refers to a linguistic group originating in India. Ironically, the only ethnic group living in Europe and speaking an Aryan language is the Gypsies. Yet Gypsies were classified by the Nazis along with Jews as inferior people and were subject to genocide. (p. 169)

During the 1970s a new controversy developed about the relationship between race and intelligence. In a 1969 article, Jensen presented data that indicated consistently lower IQ scores for blacks than for whites. Noting also that there is a low average difference in IQ scores of identical twins raised apart, Jensen argued that these data offer additional evidence that genetic factors rather than social conditions are responsible for the lower IQ scores of blacks. While few scholars would deny that genetic inheritance shapes intelligence, there has been considerable controversy about Jensen's work. Some have challenged his use of IQ scores as a measure of intelligence, arguing that the close tie between such tests and educational and middle-class values makes them dubious measures of intellectual ability. Others have challenged the use of racial categories, which assume distinctive gene pools producing racially pure stock; such gene pools do not exist. Criticism of Jensen's views and his response continue; clearly the issue is far from being resolved (Loehlin, John C., et. al., 1975).

Failure to recognize that race is a social rather than a biological category has had serious consequences in human history. The practice of using race as an explanation for all variations in human behavior as well as a measure of worth arose in the eighteenth century as an adjunct of nationalism and colonialism, justifying domination of one people by another. The exploitation and subjugation of peoples by the colonial powers needed a moral justification; color or race provided it. Colonialism became the "white man's burden"—a moral duty to Christianize and thus civilize the backward, nonwhite peoples of the world. As an ideological and moral justification for a system that perpetuates the power of a dominant group, "race" has continued to justify inequality.

To summarize, the establishment and maintenance of dominance depends upon the ability of the dominant group to identify minority members.

Traits that assist this identification are physical type and color or cultural facts like language, dress, and behavior. The significance of racial and ethnic differences is in the evaluation and judgments of others, not in the differences themselves. This significance is social—not biological.

ETHNIC DIVERSITY

Minority groups in the United States are identified by two sets of criteria: (1) race or color and (2) language or culture. While some groups are distinguishable by both color and culture, the visibility of color makes it more likely to be used as a basis for defining a person as a member of a minority. A third type of minority category is based on religion. Religion in the United States is a distinctive factor only when it is associated with racial or ethnic/cultural factors, however.

Minority Groups in the United States

Nonwhite populations in the United States include blacks, Chinese, Japanese, Filipinos, Vietnamese and other persons of Oriental background, and Native Americans. Other minority people, such as Mexican Americans, are considered culturally distinct from the dominant population rather than from different racial backgrounds.

BLACK AMERICANS
No discussion of blacks in the United States can ignore their history of slavery, repression, exploitation, and deprivation. This history can be divided into several eras. During the period from 1619 to 1865, most blacks who lived on the continent were legally slaves, and most lived in the South where slavery became institutionalized. The second era, between the end of the Civil War and until about World War I, was largely characterized by the establishment of a legal and social system of segregation, designed to maintain blacks' servile status. Since World War I blacks have sought greater participation in American society and greater rewards, culminating in the militancy and activism of the 1960s, when the term black became a symbol of racial pride.

Although the first permanent black settlers arrived in 1619 at Jamestown, probably as indentured servants, those arriving after 1690 came as slaves to fill the demand for agricultural workers in a plantation economy. Estimates of the number of blacks captured in Africa and sent to the North American continent on slave ships range from 500,000 to several million.

Most blacks who were captured by slave traders in Africa were taken from societies in which the cultural level and social organization were at least as sophisticated as those of their captors (Elkins, 1959). However, systematic efforts by whites to destroy the slaves' African heritage and to enforce their own language, customs, and religion produced a new culture. Slave culture in the United States became distinctively non-African, predominantly Christian (Protestant), English speaking, and similar in many of its outward manifestations to the culture of the white slaveowner. However, slave culture lacked the economic or social supports that sustained white culture. The significance of this slave culture should not be underestimated: the similarity of language, religious values, and social attitudes of blacks and whites meant that whites were able to define color or race as the crucial factor in shaping behavior. Blacks' color or race, as biologically ordained, made them innately inferior and justified their negative treatment by whites.

Slavery was abolished in 1865 but inequality of blacks was enforced by Jim Crow laws, which required separation of the races in public facilities—schools, restaurants, theaters, hotels, and transportation. Blacks remained in inferior positions; their status was perpetuated by a legal system that denied them the vote through literacy tests and by economic sanctions, intimidation, and violence. Segregated schools, economic deprivation, and social repression produced the desired stability based on black submission to white supremacy. The frequent violence of whites against blacks—there were 3116 lynchings between 1882 and 1921—was a constant reminder to blacks that the caste system was not to be violated.

During slavery many blacks had worked as skilled craftsmen, and some black workers were engaged in every class of occupation listed in the U.S. cen-

suses before 1900. However, with the growth of labor organizations and the exclusion of blacks from union ranks (Logan, 1965), along with general social discrimination, blacks were faced either with working at unskilled jobs or being scabs—that is, hiring on as ununionized workers in industries that opposed unionization. By 1900, as a result of discriminatory policies by employers and unions and lack of educational opportunities, the proportion of blacks in agricultural and domestic work was about twice that of the total population and the percentage in manufacturing and professional categories was less than half that of the entire labor force. Those in manufacturing, trade, and transportation were typically relegated to menial, poorly paying positions. Not surprisingly, the 1890–1920 period has been described as "the most explicitly racist era of American history" (Pettigrew, 1966). The systematic deprivation of this period led to structured economic inequality and subservience, the basis of social segregation and discrimination today.

Patterns of legally enforced segregation were not greatly altered until the end of World War II. In July 1948 President Truman officially abolished segregation in the armed forces. By 1953 more than one million southern blacks were registered to vote, constituting a 400 percent increase in eligible voters (Matthews and Prothro, 1966). However, it was the Supreme Court decision of May 17, 1954, in the case of Brown et al. *vs.* Board of Education of Topeka, Kansas, that dealt segregation a fatal blow by declaring that segregated schools were inherently unequal. This decision reversed the 1896 Supreme Court ruling on "separate but equal" schools. The change in views marked by the Brown decision has had important consequences. What was the basis for this new view of equality? In essence, the 1954 decision rested on a variety of sociological data and theories about social groups and the way they interact. Research documenting comparable levels of academic achievement for blacks and whites in integrated schools created serious questions about racial inferiority and pointed to segregation as a major source of educational inequality. Interpretations of research emphasized the impact of such social and structural factors as segregated schools,

The Ku Klux Klan is a white supremist organization that emerged after the Civil War to enforce the social norms governing relations between the races that existed before the war. Through threats, violence, and killing directed toward blacks, Jews, and Catholics, they sought to continue patterns of segregation. In recent years, the KKK has sought to influence public life by rallies and public meetings, though most of their beliefs and activities are rejected by a majority of citizens. Thus, meetings such as this one require police protection for the safety of the KKK.

discrimination in hiring and promotions, and lack of political access rather than personal characteristics as the major causes of the position of blacks in society.

In subsequent years, other court decisions extended desegregation orders to public facilities and interstate commerce, though compliance has been slow. The civil rights acts promulgated since 1957 have been designed to prevent racial discrimination in employment, education, and public facilities. Of particular importance was the omnibus Civil Rights Act of 1964 which spelled out the equal rights of all persons regardless of race.

In industrial-urban societies, education is the means by which occupational opportunities and economic rewards are obtained, and thus access to education has great significance. No other effort to desegregate facilities has encountered the same degree of resistance and hostility—both in the North and in the South—as efforts to eliminate dual school systems or to desegregate schools attended predominantly by blacks. Two major factors account for this resistance: (1) fear of interracial social contact and marriage and (2) fear of economic competition. The direct effect of unequal educational experiences for blacks and whites can be seen in their unequal participation in various occupations. Nearly twice as large a proportion of white as nonwhite workers are employed in white-collar occupations, while nonwhites are more often found in blue-collar or service occupations or are unemployed but looking for work.

There are three general factors believed to be responsible for the continuing relative disadvantage of minorities generally and of blacks specifically in the labor market. First is the benefits derived by employers and middle and upper income groups in a capitalist economy from a marginal work force (Baran and Sweezy, 1966). A large supply of cheap labor means a divided working class competing for jobs that are necessary for survival. This marginal work force is exploitable in many ways: they hold wages down, they are a market for staple goods like food and clothing, they can be used as examples of the failure of legislation by candidates for political office, they can be forced to pay high rents for overcrowded and deteriorating housing.

A second explanation is that the changing technology of advanced capitalist economies has resulted in less need for unskilled labor (Baran and Sweezy, 1966; Willhelm, 1971). Automated and mechanized production systems have replaced thousands of unskilled and semiskilled workers, creating a large underclass of unemployed and unemployable. As continuing technological advances are applied to factory and office settings, they will displace still more lower-level workers—many of whom are black. Thus technological displacement reinforces the historic disadvantaged position of blacks.

The third approach to explaining the persistent high rates of unemployment and underemployment for black workers is the split labor market interpretation (Bonacich, 1976). A split labor market "refers to a difference in the price of labor between two or more groups of workers, holding constant their efficiency and productivity. . . . The price differential includes not only wages but any costs incurred by the employer connected with his labor supply, such as housing, recruitment, training, and discipline. A racially (black/white) split labor market began with slavery . . . and persisted well into the twentieth century in industrial America" (p. 36). Bonacich's analysis indicates that blacks were more desirable workers than whites during the 1920s because they were paid lower wages for the same work and because they were available as strikebreakers in a period of labor-management strife. During the 1930s new labor legislation undercut the use of strikebreakers by companies and established wage standards that equalized the cost of labor for both blacks and whites in the same job. The immediate effect of this new legislation was a sharp growth in the labor movement, involving both black and white workers; however, the long-term effect of the new legislation was to increase the cost of labor. The response of owners included relocating their companies overseas to obtain cheaper labor and mechanizing their operations. Both of these responses resulted in increased unemployment for all workers, but especially for blacks. Since about the mid-1950s the black unemployment rate has been twice the white rate and that pattern persists today.

During the last three decades while nonwhites generally have experienced increased incomes, for most black families the net increases have been less than the increases for whites, resulting in greater discrepancy of spendable income by race. In 1980, median family income was $21,904 for whites and $13,843 for blacks and other races, or 63 percent of white income; in 1950, the comparable figures were $11,792 for whites and $6,398 for blacks and other races, or 54 percent of white income. However, the *difference* between black and white incomes has increased from $5,394 to $8,061 during this period, despite the larger percent of white income earned in 1980. At such a rate of increase, equality of income will take over 120 years.

Much of this income difference is a consequence of occupational distribution, since the number of people earning professional and other white-collar income has increased more rapidly than other categories. However, even at comparable educational or occupational levels, nonwhites receive less than whites, as documented in Table 11.3.

Unfortunately, the attention focused on blacks in recent years has produced a stereotype of blacks as poor, unemployed, undereducated, and having female heads of household. As with most stereotypes, there are some elements of truth in this picture; however, a majority of black families are stable, headed by employed men, and have aspirations and goals similar to those of whites (*Current Pop-*

ulation Reports Series P-20, No. 371, May 1982). Indeed, there is a growing middle-class black population that is socially mobile, economically successful, and claiming its share of America's benefits. However, in housing, health care, employment, and income a large number of the 25 million blacks have not begun to achieve equality with whites; for them, the gap between blacks and whites appears to be widening.

ASIAN AMERICANS
Asian Americans are a diverse group. While most Asian Americans trace their ancestry to China or Japan, since World War II there have been large numbers of immigrants from Korea, the Philippines, Vietnam, and other Asian countries. In 1980 there were 3,500,636 Asian Americans in the United States. This figure includes Asian Indians, Indonesians, Cambodians, Laotians, and Thais, not all of whom are correctly defined as of Asian origin.

People of Japanese Heritage. Japanese immigration began in the 1890s, at the height of American hostility toward its Chinese population. Anti-Japanese laws were enacted in California, one of which prohibited ownership or long-term lease of land by foreigners. Many Japanese working in agriculture moved to the cities, where they entered whatever occupations were open to them; many of these became successful businessmen.

TABLE 11.3   Average Family Income for Whites, Blacks, and Spanish-Origin Populations By Occupation of Head of Household, 1979

	WHITE	BLACK	SPANISH ORIGIN
Total: All Families	$23,288	$14,604	$17,168
Occupation of Household Head			
Professional, technical, and kindred workers	33,576	25,027	27,769
Managers and administrators, except farm	33,950	26,222	26,667
Sales	28,597	20,503	——
Clerical and kindred workers	22,291	16,235	19,219
Crafts and kindred workers	24,090	21,154	21,086
Operatives, except transport workers	20,783	17,863	16,374
Transport workers	22,445	20,294	19,421
Laborers, except farm	18,531	16,194	16,896
Farmers and farm managers	20,419	——	——
Farm laborers	14,337	——	——
Service workers	18,876	13,314	14,712

SOURCE: Current Population Reports, Series P-60, No. 129.

In 1942, two months after the Japanese attack on Pearl Harbor, the federal government ordered all people of one-eighth or more Japanese ancestry, 113,000 of the 126,000 Japanese Americans in the United States, to relocation centers, a term many considered a euphemism for concentration camps. Economically, the Japanese Americans lost nearly everything. After nearly three years in these centers, they were allowed to return to their homes; the U.S. Supreme Court had decided that the relocation of an entire race was illegal, and the shameful event was officially ended.

It was not until 1952, however, that Japanese could become U.S. citizens. The post-World War II era has seen impressive Japanese-American achievements. Compared with other ethnic groups, Americans of Japanese heritage have been more successful by U.S. standards of achievement, despite hostility from the dominant population. Fortunately for them, their reintegration into American society after release from the relocation centers coincided with a period of unprecedented economic expansion and provided opportunities that have not been experienced by other minorities. The success of the 600,000 Japanese Americans illustrates the ambivalent attitudes regarding minorities held by the dominant population. On the one hand, other groups such as blacks are told that they should be able to succeed as the Japanese have; on the other hand, Japanese Americans are distrusted because they have succeeded too well, perhaps, some feel, at the expense of others.

People of Chinese Heritage. Chinese immigration in the 1850s was a response to the American demand for cheap labor. However, by 1858, the Chinese began to feel the effects of racial hostility. Chinese workers were taxed, they were excluded from many occupations, both officially and by informal agreements, and finally prohibited from immigrating by federal law in 1882. Not until 1943, when sympathy for our Chinese allies in World War II was running high, was the law changed.

Many large cities have had concentrations of Chinese in central cities, or "Chinatowns," which once provided protection for new immigrants and a sense of stability for older residents. The social and cultural importance of these Chinatowns has declined as occupational and social structures have been opened to minority populations.

Chinese Americans still tend to be concentrated in particular occupations as a result of earlier discrimination. Before World War II, laundries, restaurants, and hotels were a dominant source of employment. When educational and occupational opportunities became available to them, during the 1950s and 1960, Chinese Americans quickly moved into the professions (Department of Health, Education and Welfare, 1974).

Chinese Americans have been more passive in the face of rejection by the dominant population than have the Japanese, for several reasons. The Chinese arrived earlier than the Japanese and were isolated and less well organized to combat prejudice and discrimination. They also received little support from the Chinese government compared with the actions taken by Japanese government to support its citizens (Schaffer, 1979).

People of Other Asian Backgrounds. Korea, the Philippines, Vietnam, and other Asian nations are well represented among U.S. minorities. Korean Americans probably total 150,000 at present, and are concentrated in the Los Angeles area. About 350,000 Filipino Americans also reside mostly along the Pacific Coast.

After the U.S. withdrawal from Vietnam in 1975, more than 130,000 refugees left their country. Most of them came to the United States. The government and various church groups took on the responsibility of finding them sponsors, employment, and helping them settle into their new communities. Unlike most other recent immigrant groups, there were no existing ethnic communities into which Vietnamese could move. Initially, they were settled throughout the United States, though many have relocated in California and the southwestern states. Unfortunately, many mixed-race children fathered by U.S. soldiers stationed in Vietnam remain there. Faced with rejection in Vietnam and excluded from the United States, their future is bleak, as noted in Reading 11.1.

During the early 1980s, the plight of the "boat people"—Asian refugees from Laos, Thailand,

Cambodia, and Vietnam, whose lives were so desperate that they left their homes for unknown shores under the most dangerous conditions—helped to swell Asian immigration. Their number continues to grow as conflict between ethnic populations continues.

NATIVE AMERICANS

The term Native Americans refers to a population of diverse geographical and cultural backgrounds. At first, the word *Indian* was applied to all native peoples of the Americas, despite the fact that there was at least as much difference among the languages, cultures, and practices of various Indian groups, or nations, as existed among African societies or even European nations. That one term could apply to so many diverse peoples reflects the inferior status to which all strangers were assigned by the Europeans who came to America (Wax, 1971).

The Native American or American Indian population occupies a unique position in American society. Unlike Africans who were brought by force and European or Asian immigrants who came by choice, Native Americans were conquered and subjected to minority status in their own country. This conquest of the Indians by Spaniards, French, and English was accomplished by a combination of (1) superior technology for waging war, (2) a belief in the superiority of their own cultures over those of the natives, and (3) a concept of religious responsibility for exploiting the earth's resources for human benefit.

Native American tribes dealt with Europeans in various ways. The Yaqui of New Mexico converted to Roman Catholicism and established a dynamic society. The Iroquois of the Northeast became involved in the fur trade and blocked the westward advance of agriculturally oriented whites until the new U.S. government established after the Revolutionary War destroyed their society. The Plains Indians ranged widely for food and trade, harassing other tribes and whites until the military subdued them and took their land for cattle ranching and farming. The metis (half-breeds) in the Red River area of Canada were forced to accept government terms for their existence by the power of repeating rifles, Gatling guns, and artillery (Wax, 1971).

Probably most whites believed that Indians should simply be exterminated; certainly, both the army and the settlers made serious efforts to eliminate them. To obtain land, Indians were moved with or without treaties or promises. Ultimately, the government created reservations for the relocation of the Native American population. Usually these settlements were many miles from the tribe's native territory, which had special religious significance, and almost always were on land that had little if any agricultural value. However, the reservations did provide geographic and social isolation from whites.

The reservation has been a place of social and cultural isolation for Native Americans, and the consequences have been both beneficial and detrimental for Indian life. Positive consequences include a reversal in the decline of the Indian population: from 600,000 in 1800, to 250,000 in 1850, to about 1,000,000 in 1980. However, the reservation has bred poverty, despair, and enforced dependency. Incomes of Indian families are extremely low and jobs are few on the reservation. Those jobs available to Indian workers, who are often without transportation, may be located many miles away; as a result, only half of those desiring work are employed. Education has been organized and administered by whites, and many textbooks have offered "white" history and have denigrated Native American culture. Native American youth have had to choose between the security and traditional culture of reservation life or trying for occupational and social integration in the larger, still discriminatory, society. Health facilities have been poor, legal rights have been ignored, and relations with whites nearby are often based on mutual dislike and distrust.

AMERICANS OF SPANISH HERITAGE

Persons of Spanish (Hispanic) background are a very diverse group, including Mexican Americans, Puerto Ricans, Cubans, and Central and South Americans. Much confusion exists about this group. Use of the Spanish language identifies a set of cultural patterns but does not denote any racial distinctiveness. Even cultural elements are varied due to adaptations of Hispanic populations to particular environmental, political, economic, and social conditions. Of the 14,600,000 Americans of Spanish origin in the United States in 1980, nearly 7 million claim Mexican and 2 million claim Puerto Rican backgrounds, with other Spanish populations distributed among the other Latin American countries.

Puerto Rican Americans. Puerto Rico was governed by Spain until 1898, when it became a territory of the United States after the Spanish-American War. U.S. citizenship was granted to all Puerto Ricans in 1917. After having been neglected as a colony for years, in 1952 Puerto Rico became a self-governing commonwealth but was bound to the United States by a common currency and strong economic ties. Easy migration between the island and the mainland has resulted in a large Puerto Rican population on the mainland, which has continued to grow during the past 30 years.

There are now probably more than 2 million people living on the U.S. mainland who trace their ancestry to Puerto Rico. Of this number, most live in the East, with more than two-thirds living in the greater New York City–Newark–Jersey City area, though Chicago, Philadelphia, and Los Angeles have sizable populations.

Reasons for migrating to the United States include better employment, schools, and health facilities and family ties. Many of those coming to the United States are young, while those returning are older. While arrival on the mainland often results in reestablishment of family ties, the reverse of the coin is the ghettolike residential areas into which Puerto Ricans are crowded and generally poor economic opportunities. Lacking skills to compete for the higher paying jobs, Puerto Ricans form a large proportion of the unskilled labor force of New York City. Under such circumstances, it is not surprising that median income for Puerto Rican families was low, $7669, in 1977, or about 48 percent of the median for all families (U.S. Bureau of the Census, *Current Population Reports*, Series P-20, No. 329).

Like other minorities, Puerto Ricans have experienced prejudice and discrimination by the dominant group. Their visibility rests primarily on lan-

guage and culture, although racial or color differences may also be apparent. Awareness of these differences is evident in the various terms sometimes used by Puerto Ricans in referring to themselves such as *blanco* (white), *indio* (Indian) or *de color* (colored) (Padilla, 1958). The core of Puerto Rican cultural values is the family, with its strict code of family expectations and obligations; an expression of this is male dominance and protection of women. Cultural values also support a sense of fatalism and joyfulness that is reflected in Puerto Rican social life. Still, traditional patterns slowly erode in the cities of the mainland. Opportunities for education, access to birth control and family planning, and social and geographic mobility have undercut the traditional concepts of group welfare and loyalty that existed in Puerto Rico and among early immigrants.

Mexican Americans. Mexican Americans trace their ancestry to a mixture of Spanish and Indian peoples and cultures. Most reside in the southwestern states of Texas, Arizona, New Mexico, California, and Colorado; in fact, the ancestors of many lived there when the territories were under Spanish or Mexican control. As Anglos seeking farmland entered the area, the Mexican culture and society was gradually destroyed. The new political and economic order brought changes in land ownership and land taxation (see Reading 11.2). Such changes, accompanied by threats and violence, reduced the Mexican population to minority status, a condition that continues today.

Contrary to the stereotype of the rural Mexican seen in movies and on television, Mexican Americans are predominantly an urban population, concentrated in metropolitan areas (Moore, 1976). Differences among them persist, partly as a result of differing social environments, and are reflected in the terms with which they identify themselves. For example, the "Latins" of South Texas are predominantly rural and traditional in culture, but the "Mexican-American" community in greater Los Angeles is urban, uses the English language, and follows Anglo patterns of educational and occupational achievement. At the same time, "Spanish Americans" in New Mexico and rural Colorado may

Minority workers often are forced into poorly paid positions with few benefits and no long-term security. Efforts to organize unskilled minority workers are directed toward improving pay and working conditions. While there have been some contracts between growers and Cesar Chavez's United Farm Workers Union shown here, most minority workers continue to experience severe problems in employment.

reject both the newer Mexican-American and the Anglo cultures, while "Chicanos" and "Indians" seek distinctive cultural identities based on earlier periods of history (Grebler, Moore, and Guzman, 1970).

Many Mexican immigrants or Mexican Americans are employed as unskilled workers, experiencing the same economic conditions as blacks. There have been some successful efforts to unionize agricultural workers, notably through Cesar Chavez's United Farm Workers, but these have been limited. Evidence of economic discrimination can be found in low wages for seasonal labor and non-union jobs in, for example, the garment industry. Neighborhoods and schools are segregated, though not by law, and school personnel rarely retain children of migratory laborers for entire school terms, often because the children are employed themselves or because the family moves frequently. In addition, inadequate access to health care and unequal law enforcement serve to remind Mexican Americans of their inferior status.

People of other Spanish Backgrounds. Cubans are the third largest U.S. group of Spanish-speaking immigrants, totaling about a million in 1980. Most of them have come since 1960, technically as refugees from the Cuban Revolution. Many of this group were well educated, with professional or managerial skills, and have been economically successful in their new country. While many large urban areas have sizeable Cuban populations, Miami's "Little Havana" is the largest and best organized community of Cuban Americans in the United States.

Spanish-speaking populations from other Central and South American countries total about one million. Other Spanish total one and a half million. Because of distance from the United States and the difficulties in entering for short-term employment or illegally, Spanish-origin people from Central and South America tend to be better educated and of higher occupational status than Mexicans or Puerto Ricans (CPR, Series P.-20, No. 329). Typically, they enter under the immigration quotas established for special occupational or professional personnel. However, the cultural and ethnic characteristics that distinguish them from the dominant popula-

tion attract the hostility and prejudice directed toward Spanish-origin groups generally.

JEWISH AMERICANS

The experiences of Jews as a minority group have ranged from destruction by the extermination programs of Czarist Russia and Nazi Germany to loss of distinctiveness and absorption into the dominant population. A continuing question concerns the identification of Jews: What makes one a Jew? Is Jewishness religious, cultural, racial, or political in character?

The **diaspora** (dispersion) began long before Christ and continued during the early Christian era. When the Romans destroyed Jerusalem in 70 A.D., the Jews were scattered from their homeland throughout the world. Their survival as Jews depended on living in closely integrated communities, or ghettos, often created by the dominant society, where their language and religion could be maintained. For 1800 years this basic pattern continued. Isolation and separation from the dominant population not only provided the means for controlling the Jewish population, it also provided the basis for a continued religious and ethnic identity among Jews.

While numerous punitive and discriminatory political, social, and economic programs had been directed toward Jews during these centuries, Nazi extermination of 6 million Jews before and during World War II produced a new sense of Jewish identity and a successful demand by the Jews for their own country. The State of Israel was born in 1948.

In the United States no physical traits distinguish Jews from other citizens. Jews have been among the earliest white settlers of North America. During the eighteenth and the nineteenth centuries, Jews from Western Europe dominated Jewish immigration and quickly adapted to American life and its dominant values. Between 1880 and 1924 Eastern European Jews came to the United States in large numbers. Their language (Yiddish), foods, and customs have largely contributed to what is thought of as distinctively Jewish in American life.

We do not have exact information about the American Jewish population because of the lack of questions identifying religion in the U.S. Census and the difficulty of defining who is a Jew. Estimates place the number of Jews at about 6 million, most of whom live in urban areas, primarily in the Northeast. Over half of U.S. Jews live in the greater New York City area.

One factor that has affected Jewish life in America to a larger degree than it has other groups was, and is, the immigration of entire families. Family immigration has meant easier transition to the new culture and less personal disorganization. The historic cohesiveness of Jewish families has been reaffirmed by social and economic structures in the United States as well as by the Jewish religious traditions.

Jews as a group have emphasized education and achievement. Evidence shows that Jews on the average are much better educated than the population generally. In fact, they have the highest educational level of all religious groups except Episcopalians (Goldstein and Goldscheider, 1968). Jewish males are heavily concentrated in business and professional occupations, in part because of their high occupational skills.

WHITE ETHNICS

White immigrants of Southern and Eastern Europe were limited by the 1924 legislation, which established quotas based on the national origin of residents who were in the United States in 1890. From the perspective of the older, established populations from Northern and Western Europe, the new immigrants were inferior in culture and biological inheritance. The *Poles, Italians, Greeks,* and *Slavs*—labeled PIGS by Novak (1972) in a sarcastic reference to the attitudes of the older ethnics toward these groups—were defined as undesirables who could not be expected to make a significant contribution to American life.

The reaction by the dominant population to people whose appearance and culture was different was based upon fears of being engulfed by these new groups. Immigration patterns had changed: in 1882, about two-thirds of immigrants were from Northern Europe—Britain, Ireland, Germany, Denmark, Norway and Sweden; by 1907, nearly three-fourths of immigrants were from Eastern and Southern Europe—Austria-Hungary, Italy, Russia, and the Balkan states. Set apart by language and culture, these new immigrants, like those before them, created urban settlements that were isolated from the dominant culture. After several generations few differences remain between these groups and others in terms of occupational or economic success. Greeley (1976) has noted the success of descendants of foreign stock, especially Irish, Italians, and Poles, but he also points out that these groups continue to be labeled negatively by the dominant population.

World Ethnic Relations

As we noted at the beginning of this chapter, ethnic hostility and conflict are not only characteristic of the United States. In Brazil, for example, slavery was more common during the 1700s than in the United States, but there race did not imply innate inferiority, and blacks have been recognized for their contributions to society. However, dark skin color is a social and economic barrier, despite government action to outlaw discrimination, for both blacks and native Indians.

In Great Britain, many non white people from former colonies like Uganda, India, Pakistan, and Jamaica have been refused entry in recent years, despite a long history of unrestricted movement among peoples of the Commonwealth. Racial disturbances in London and other cities have brought the issue to public attention, but the problem continues.

Perhaps no nation of the world has as brutal and rigid a system of racially defined social relations as South Africa. Apartheid, the official policy of total separation of racial groups, has reinforced poverty and has stripped blacks—the majority of the population of South Africa— of property and civil rights. Whites make up about 20 percent of the population, colored or mixed race about 10 percent, and Bantus or native blacks about 70 percent. Two other, small categories are Indian and Chinese. The official government policy of resettlement of blacks into undeveloped, unproductive reserves is enforced by a massive police force with virtually unlimited power. Failure to carry a government-issued pass may result in a long-term jail sentence. Though blacks have not passively accepted apartheid, immense military power on the one hand and some economic improvements on the other have thus far prevented a revolution.

Other examples of ethnic conflict are not difficult to find. Black-Asian relations in Uganda, Iranian-Iraqi battles, Cambodian-Vietnamese border skirmishes, Asian-Malayan hostility in Singapore, and Muslim-Christian conflict in Lebanon offer evidence that ethnic groups retain powerful loyalties in the modern world. How do ethnic groups create and maintain such loyalties? How can these conflicts be understood? What are the bases of ethnic conflict?

PREJUDICE AND DISCRIMINATION

Prejudice and discrimination are forms of hostility directed primarily toward minority populations by the dominant groups. **Prejudice** is an attitude or judgment that is unfavorable to an entire category of people; **discrimination** is an act of unequal treatment, usually directed toward a minority population, that deprives people of political, economic, or social opportunity.

Attitudes and Values

Personal prejudice is a common individual response in many situations, such as those calling upon school loyalties or food or music preferences. These preferences lead to discrimination when spaghetti rather than sauerkraut is chosen for a meal or when a tape of a Bach oratorio is bought instead of a Who recording. However, such attitudes and actions are not socially relevant because they are not based upon judgments about entire groups or categories of people. The social significance of prejudice and discrimination derives from the use of judgments about all members of groups or categories, often based upon stereotypes rather than upon accurate information. For example, when the immigration flow of the mid-nineteenth century brought Irish peasants to the United States, the stereotypes of the lazy, heavy-drinking Irishman became the basis for discriminating against all Irish immigrants. The result was the concentration of Irish workers in the lowest occupational categories.

Institutional Discrimination

Discrimination refers to actions and behaviors that deny political or legal rights or opportunities for education or jobs to individuals based on group membership. Even where laws prohibit such discrimination, differential treatment may be subtle and difficult to eliminate. Several examples might be cited.

In education the use of IQ tests as a basis for ability groupings in schools creates different opportunities for various groups. Selective enforcement of laws concerning crime and public behavior precludes equal justice for blacks. Private agreements that prevent minority members from buying houses in certain neighborhoods are discriminatory; so are social pressures that effectively prevent Indians from leaving reservations or employment patterns that bar Puerto Ricans from higher level positions. These actions are based on categorical rather than individual differences—the essence of discrimination. Whenever a group of people who share an easily defined characteristic, such as race, sex, age, or ethnicity, are systematically excluded from participating in all aspects of society, we may say institutional discrimination exists. The actions do not need to be intentionally discriminatory; indeed most institutional discrimination occurs without specific intent to discriminate against a minority person. Wilson (1978) suggests that social class, not race, is now the most significant factor in the discrimination faced by American blacks. As a result, the institutionalized social patterns that affect all members of an underclass affect blacks as well.

Institutional racism or discrimination includes actions based on administrative rules or procedures that effectively discriminate against categories of people. For example, the use of minimum income criteria for purchase of houses in an area is discriminatory, as is "redlining"—the practice of excluding residents of lower income neighborhoods from qualifying for home mortgages. When IQ scores are used to place minority members into vocational instead of college preparatory curricula, discrimination occurs. Such institutionally based discriminatory actions may be legal, but their effect is to bar categories of people from employment, educational opportunities, or residential choice.

The Relationship Between Prejudice and Discrimination

Obviously prejudice and discrimination are closely related in most cases. However, as Simpson and Yinger (1972) note: (1) there can be prejudice without discrimination; (2) there can be discrimination without prejudice; (3) discrimination can be among the causes of prejudice; (4) prejudice can be among the causes of discrimination; and (5) probably most frequent, prejudice and discrimination are mutually reinforcing.

Some efforts to specify the relationship between prejudice and discrimination have focused upon personality factors that underlie prejudice. Prejudice has been defined as a manifestation of particular personality "needs." In an early study Adorno and his colleagues (1950), attempted to identify clusters of personality traits that were related to prejudice. While the findings of this and other studies have not been entirely consistent, the original thesis that an *authoritarian personality* type is related to prejudice generally has been supported. However, there is some evidence that prejudice is activated by certain situations; that is, it is the situation rather than the attitude or personality trait by itself that produces the behavior we call discrimination. Factors that appear to activate discrimination include significant pressure by reference groups, the expressed hostile attitudes of important friends or other people, and the public character of the minority behavior (Allport, 1958; Simpson and Yinger, 1972).

It is not surprising, then, that type of group contact is an important factor in shaping dominant-minority group responses. These contacts define the character of ethnic relations in society.

PATTERNS OF GROUP CONTACT

The most important fact of dominant-minority group relationships is that the groups share a common national identity. Thus while patterns of relating to each other may range from open hostility to accommodation, their proximity requires some strategies by which they may achieve their objectives. Control and maintenance of their favored position are the objectives of most dominant groups; objectives of minorities may vary depending on the situation as defined by the dominant group.

Strategies of Dominant Groups

Dominant groups have a large degree of control over the relationships that exist between them and minority groups. Their power to classify, regulate, and police minority populations enables them to structure social relations as they wish. Not all designs are successful, because minority groups may not accept and follow the rules, but several strategies have been developed.

EXPULSION AND EXTERMINATION

Expulsion and extermination are efforts to eliminate all contact with a minority population or to secure their possessions, either by forcing them to move through threats, violence, or legal means or to practice **genocide**, the systematic destruction of a people. Numerous examples can be cited throughout the world: South Africa's expulsion of blacks from cities and towns to reservations, the attempt of one Cambodian population to destroy another, and the continued mistreatment of Native Americans in North America.

One example of a minority group that was expelled from its lands is the Cherokee, the largest and most important single Indian tribe in the southeastern United States. They had established an advanced agricultural society in Georgia, the Carolinas, and Tennessee. The discovery of gold in their territories created pressure for their removal, and in 1838 the tribe was deported by military force to what later became Oklahoma. Expulsion from their lands effectively destroyed their culture. The

Cherokees disbanded as a tribe in 1906 and became U.S. citizens.

Throughout the world, expulsion and extermination have been used to "solve" minority problems. Jews were scattered in the diaspora, were exiled from Brazil in the nineteenth century, and were the object of Hitler's extermination program in the 1930s and 1940s. Various native populations have been ousted from Africa by whites and others and Indians have been expelled from Uganda. The use of these means of control shows no signs of decreasing.

ISOLATION AND SEGREGATION

Dominant groups have often isolated minorities, thereby avoiding all but the minimum amount of social contact. The usual avoidance pattern is some form of segregation (setting apart or separating). **Segregation** is the practice of eliminating a defined minority from social interaction with the dominant group, usually by separating their areas of contact—schools, residential areas, and public facilities. The segregation of blacks and whites in the South during the nineteenth and early twentieth

centuries was **de jure segregation**, or segregation based on legal restrictions. In the North **de facto segregation** has been the pattern, that is, segregation based on residential or occupational patterns; some forms of de facto segregation are today illegal.

The result of segregation is nearly always to deprive the minority its appropriate share of services and benefits. This deprivation is reflected in housing, health, education, the law, and public services like street maintenance, sanitation, and transportation, resulting in a generally inferior quality of life and poorer life chances for minority members. In the post-Civil War South, the black minority was denied access to education and employment and prohibited from social contact with the dominant white group as equals. A caste system developed complete with elaborate rules that governed all social relations. These rules made clear who was in a superior position and who was in an inferior position. Blacks did not eat at the same table with whites. Blacks were expected to address all whites as "Mr." and "Mrs." and to show deference in all social relations, regardless of relative status. Blacks were to enter houses occupied by

Segregation in the South during the "separate but equal" era rarely meant equality. Not only were facilities and opportunities for blacks inferior to those for whites, but severe sanctions were used to enforce racial separation in social situations.

whites only through the rear or side door, and black men were to avoid all social contacts with white women. A biracial society was created with separate (and unequal) institutions.

Another example of isolation and segregation is the removal of Native Americans to reservations. Events of the 1970s at Wounded Knee on the Pine Ridge Reservation, as well as among the Navahos and other groups, have pointed to the high level of dissatisfaction of many reservation Indians, who face discrimination and are denied access to the opportunities for work and respect among the dominant population. While reservation life may be a means of preserving a Native American culture, few Indian societies have prospered under the direction of a dominant society that has defined their role in narrow and negative terms.

ASSIMILATION

Assimilation is the end of a process in which minority groups lose their distinctiveness and are absorbed into the dominant population. It depends on the degree to which dominant groups are willing to open their ranks to minorities. As individuals acquire the behavior, attitudes, values, and appearance of the dominant group through **acculturation**, it becomes no longer possible to identify them as members of a minority. In the United States the loss of ethnic characteristics like color or language and educational and economic achievement are evidence of assimilation.

In most societies assimilation is a slow process, since it involves interaction of minority and dominant groups along several dimensions. Gordon (1964) has identified several forms of assimilation, of which four are particularly important in the United States: (1) *cultural*—change of cultural patterns to those of host society; (2) *structural*—entrance of large numbers of minority members into cliques, clubs, and institutions of the host society on a primary group level; (3) *marital*—intermarriage of minority and dominant group members; and (4) *identification*—development of sense of peoplehood based exclusively on the host society. These types of assimilation are obviously related, since intermarriage and identification are unlikely without some degree of cultural change; however,

structural assimilation is probably the most important factor in the process leading to the elimination of discrimination and prejudice.

Intermarriage is perhaps the best measure of the level of assimilation of a group. The concept of amalgamation or the "**melting pot**," has been used to describe the process by which minority populations merge with the dominant group to form a new population that has most of the attributes of the dominant group.

Intermarriage occurs most frequently among the minority groups that are least different from the dominant group, not segregated by residence, and not of depressed status. In the United States newly arrived immigrants from a specific country tend to cluster together, having minimal contact with people of other ethnic or cultural backgrounds. Intermarriage with those of other groups rarely occurs until the second or third generation. The idea that the United States is a melting pot appears to be inappropriate. There are at least three distinct religious groups—Catholics, Jews, and Protestants—with relatively little intermarriage in the past. Color is the primary bar to assimilation and religion reinforces this bar.

Marriage between people of different races and ethnic groups on a large scale would eventually create a relatively homogeneous population, both culturally and physically. The strength of both structural and cultural patterns of racial and ethnic segregation is evident in the fact that, except in Hawaii, interracial marriages are rare in the United States, occurring in less than 2 percent of marriages in any year. However, there are more than 125,000 black-white marriages in the United States and the number appears to be increasing.

Assimilation is at best a painful process, since it denies the validity of familiar, personal values and experiences and substitutes new ones. Minority group members face a fundamental question: Is the ethnic group worth preserving, or should people try to become assimilated into the larger society?

Strategies of Minority Groups

If minority groups accepted discrimination and prejudice, race and ethnic relationships would be simple and uncomplicated. However, individuals, groups, and society would suffer from the unfulfilled dreams and hopes, the undeveloped abilities and talents of significant segments of the population. Few if any minority groups are passive in the face of hostile actions by dominant groups. Strategies of dealing with the dominant groups vary widely, from avoidance to integration.

ISOLATION AND AVOIDANCE

Groups, especially those that are small and cohesive, may isolate themselves to maintain their own cultures and avoid contact with the dominant groups. **Avoidance** may be forced or self-imposed. For example, Hutterite and Amish communities were intentionally created by their members to provide barriers between them and the rest of society. Similarly, the territorial separation of Native Americans affords a degree of continuity of tradition and allows individuals to avoid direct confrontation with the dominant group. Such avoidance would not be possible without social isolation.

ACCOMMODATION AND ACCULTURATION

Accommodation occurs when both minority and dominant groups accept the relative positions of each group. It is a strategy that offers some stability to the relationship. The long-term consequences of accepting the relationship between the dominant and minority groups is that individual members of the minority group are drawn into the dominant culture. Such movement may be rapid or slow, but it requires that the minority members develop the behaviors and language of the dominant group; that is, it essentially forces them to acquire another culture (Shibutani and Kwan, 1965). While some aspects of the culture are learned by sheer necessity, like learning how to buy food or to use public transportation, much of the culture is learned as children are socialized and educated into the language and values of the dominant culture. Thus, unless the adult minority population takes steps to prevent it, the process of *acculturation* (changing to the dominant way) leads to depreciation of past values by minority group children and acceptance of those held by the dominant group.

The acculturation process frequently creates problems between generations. Among Puerto Ricans, the emphasis of the dominant society on education, family planning, and occupational mobility often undercuts traditional ties to family and the Roman Catholic Church. Similarly, Native Americans may face a difficult choice between traditional culture or dominant culture. For many, acculturation has meant the loss of personal identity as an Indian; such "white Indians" may succeed as individuals but lose contact with their heritage. Perhaps most difficult for most Indians is adaptation to the individualistic, competitive values of dominant population, since their traditional values emphasize cooperation and respect for authority and sharing.

REBELLION AND PROTEST

The promise of equality in the United States has been a spur to minority groups seeking acceptance and justice, and ethnicity has been the common bond. For blacks, ethnic pride developed despite diverse experiences among various black groups in dealing with dominant populations. For years the National Association for the Advancement of Colored People and other groups had sought to abolish laws that maintained segregation, in both the North and the South. In the 1950s and 1960s ethnic protest based on race became a powerful force in changing laws and breaking up old patterns of discrimination.

Discrimination and segregation were regularly practiced throughout the South, and feelings of anger and despair among blacks had reached a critical point, especially the young and well educated. When four college students "sat in" at a lunch counter in Rock Hill, South Carolina in 1960, it signaled a new form of protest. Within days the movement spread and blacks were sitting at lunch counters and in public facilities that refused to serve them throughout the South. Demonstrations and boycotts in support of the sit-ins took place throughout the country, and the activist phase of the civil rights movement had begun.

From 1960 to 1965, a variety of techniques for establishing equal rights were developed, including "freedom rides," demonstrations, sit-ins at libraries, swimming pools, and parks, and marches. The response of the dominant population was frequently violent. In the summer of 1963 alone, 35 homes and churches were bombed or burned, at least 10 people were killed, and more than 20,000 demonstrators were arrested; thousands of demonstrators were attacked by police dogs, beaten, shocked by cattle prods, or doused and bruised by high-pressure fire hoses, all wielded by the police (Pinckney, 1969).

It is not surprising, under such conditions, that the idea of **black power** should emerge as a unifying concept among militant blacks. In the words of Stokely Carmichael and Charles V. Hamilton (1967):

Black Power . . . is a call for black people in this country to unite, to recognize their heritage, to build a sense of community. It is a call for black people to begin to define their own goals, to lead their own organizations and to support those organizations. . . .

The racial and cultural personality of the black community must be preserved and that community must win its freedom while preserving its cultural integrity. Integrity includes a price—in the sense of self-acceptance, not chauvinism—in being black, in the historical attainments and contributions of black people. No person can be healthy, complete and mature if he must deny a part of himself; that is what "integration" has required thus far. This is the essential difference between integration as it is currently practiced and the concept of Black Power. (pp. 44, 55)

Perhaps the most controversial demonstrations of black power were the raised-fist salutes by American blacks on the awards platform in the 1968 Olympic games, a symbolic gesture of defiance and anger at the oppression of blacks by whites. At a different level were the nonviolent, massive protests of blacks in Selma, Montgomery, Birmingham, and across the South, organized by Martin Luther King and others. Activities of black power advocates and nonviolent demonstrators are similar in their use of protests to force social change; they may differ in their objective, separation and isolation on the one hand and integration and full participation in the larger society on the other.

INTEGRATION

Integration assumes the complete participation of minorities in the larger society. Such participation, based on acceptance of all groups without regard to race, color, ethnic/national background, or religion, would result in assimilation and loss of ethnic or racial identity.

Complete integration is unlikely and would be unacceptable to many people, even if it were possible. Many ethnic group members desire to maintain their distinctive cultural traditions; integration may seem a heavy price to pay for equality. As a response to groups that push for a measure of integration, a technique of the dominant group in the United States has been to select a few minority members as representatives or "tokens" for inclusion in activities of the dominant group. Such actions may defuse anger among minority groups but offer no real evidence of integration.

Clearly, integration and assimilation mean loss of ethnic identity. Should ethnic traditions be eliminated for the sake of a national identity? While no consensus has emerged in the United States, cultural pluralism may be one answer.

Cultural Pluralism: Mutual Respect?

Cultural pluralism is the coexistence of different ethnic groups whose cultural differences are respected and protected as equally valid. There appears to be little support for cultural pluralism among the dominant group in the United States. Even minority group members often appear to be ambivalent, with some persons seeking assimilation and others seeking recognition of their cultural heritage. The line between cultural pluralism and separatism may be difficult to maintain. Efforts by Hutterites, Hasidic Jews, Amish, or other religious communities in the United States and actions by the French Canadians to maintain both language and cultural traditions in an Anglo-Protestant culture are separatist attempts to preserve cultural/ethnic traditions. A pluralist society, while supporting the right of many ethnic groups to preserve their own culture without fear of unequal treatment, also demands joint participation in the larger society.

Cultural pluralism, in which there is respect for the traditions of all groups, rarely if ever has been achieved. In most modern societies with mass communication and transportation facilities, the ideal of acceptance and encouragement of differences has been compromised by an emphasis on individual achievement and social mobility and by political pressures and conflict among groups. Switzerland probably remains the best example of a culturally pluralist society: a society of "equals" among French, German, Italian, and Swiss cultures.

Can cultural pluralism exist in a society that is stratified by race or ethnicity? Can respect for differences be maintained if minorities are powerless? Such questions will continue to confront modern societies as people of various racial and ethnic groups confront each other in competition for resources and power.

ISSUES OF ETHNIC INEQUALITY

The changing patterns of dominant-minority relations are most apparent in the decline of colonialism, the development of Third World nations, and the growing self-consciousness of ethnic and racial populations throughout the world. In the United States blacks and Native Americans are changing the pattern of centuries-old oppression by legal challenges to existing traditions.

The Americanization of ethnic groups has meant accepting the values and culture of the dominant group. As long as the social order was stable, a facade of unity was maintained. However, the rapid social changes of the 1960s and 1970s created new questions about values and legitimacy of traditions in the United States. The effect of these questions upon many Americans was a new search for identity. One phase of that search culminated in a reestablishment of ethnicity and ethnic identity; another, in a nativist response represented by the reemergence of white supremacist groups; a third, in the desire for complete identification with the dominant group and a consequent discarding of eth-

nic traditions. How does the reestablishment of ethnic identity fit into modern American life?

Emergent Ethnicity: A Search for Identity?

Although ethnic diversity has been a fact of American life from earliest times, for most of our history ethnicity has been viewed as a threat to the common culture. The "melting pot" idea suggested that efforts to maintain cultural or ethnic distinctiveness were misguided at best and disloyal at worst. As a result, in the effort to become American the ethnic language was not taught to children, family traditions were dropped because they appeared to conflict with those of the dominant culture, and many children became estranged from their foreign-born parents as they found themselves facing decisions about school and life that their parents were unable to understand. However, not all ethnic groups were quickly assimilated.

The ethnic groups that have continued to be identified as minorities in the United States—blacks, Mexican Americans, Native Americans, Orientals, Puerto Ricans—are visible ethnics, who have maintained their traditions in part because of their exclusion by the dominant group on the basis of their physical distinctiveness. The recent emergent ethnicity involves "invisible" ethnics, people and groups who have maintained a distinctive culture despite apparent, external signs of assimilation. Having a good job, two children, a house in the suburbs, and two cars may indicate an acceptance of American culture. However, as Novak (1971) argues, the dominant culture provides a barrier context for the intimate, primary relations of families and friends, where attitudes toward pain, joy, children, authority, money, or loyalty are developed. In times of crisis these attitudes emerge in distinctive ways among people of Greek, Polish, Italian, Slovak, Armenian, or Hungarian backgrounds. Crises draw together people who share the common meanings and close relationships forged by ethnic identity.

Greeley (1971) suggests that the changes associated with modern urban society have neither destroyed the need for nor the existence of communities based on a consciousness of kind or a sense of ethnic identity. All cultures are valid and important. Black is beautiful and so is Irish, Polish, Italian, Slovenian, Greek, Armenian, Lebanese, and Luxembourger. As such, efforts to seek ethnic identity may lead to a new appreciation of other ethnic groups. Indeed, Novak suggests that people who are clear about their own ethnicity have a sense of worth and self-acceptance that is likely to be translated into greater tolerance of others.

If such interpretations are correct, the strength of ethnic identity may increase in modern society. However, marriages between members of various ethnic groups tend to reduce ethnic loyalty. What is the relative strength of these opposing tendencies?

Equal Access or Individual Merit?

Equal opportunity in education and work has been an important goal of civil rights legislation in the past 25 years. There is, however, controversy over the meaning of equal opportunity. Does equal opportunity mean that all people should have equal access to education and employment regardless of their abilities, or does it mean that, while all have an opportunity to compete, positions should be assigned solely on the basis of individual merit?

If equal opportunity means equal access, new standards for evaluation are required. In addition, family resources that give some people preferential access to positions of power and influence will no longer be effective. Those whose educational experiences have been deficient and those to whom occupational success has been denied by discriminatory action might be given preference in selection or provided with additional resources to assist them in educational achievement. Head Start and other programs of compensatory education, offices of equal employment opportunities, and legal aid, among others, have been developed to provide an equal level of access to opportunities for minority group members. Though there is no consensus about the effectiveness of these programs, they represent new approaches to remedying past inequities.

The issue has become focused through legal suits challenging the actions of universities that have set quotas for admitting blacks *because they are*

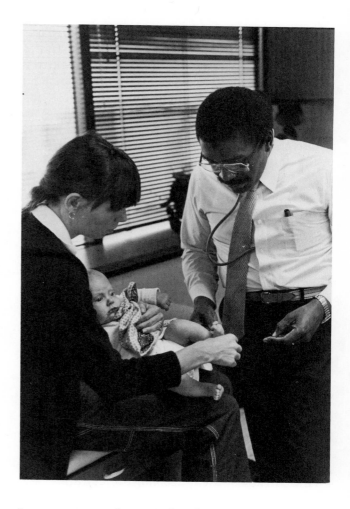

In recent years educational and occupational opportunities have enabled individual members of minority groups to achieve a high level of success in various professional careers, such as medicine, and law. The emphasis in American society merit or earned achievements regardless of race or ethnicity clearly benefits a few minority members, but the issue of what equal opportunity means remains unresolved.

black to compensate for past discrimination. Do minorities as a group have a special claim on opportunities because of past discrimination? If the schools are inadequate, should minorities be held responsible and denied opportunities for work and professional training? Should equality of opportunity be provided to all people or only to people whose characteristics or achievements match those of the dominant group?

Self-Determination or Control by the Dominant Population?

One of the basic principles of a democratic society is the right of people to participate in the establishment of their government and in the shaping of public policy. For most ethnic groups this has not posed a significant problem. For blacks and Native Americans, their participation has been compromised by a kind of colonialism.

The analogy of colonialism when applied to blacks and Native Americans is based on the fact of external control by the dominant population rather than self-determination. Blauner (1969) describes four components of colonialism. First, colonization involves forced, involuntary entry. In the case of blacks, they were forced to come to the United States as slaves. In the case of Native Americans, it was the Europeans who made a forced entry into a land already settled. Second, the culture of the indigenous people is constrained, transformed, or destroyed by the colonial power. Both blacks and Native Americans were forced to accept different languages and culture to participate, however minimally, in white society and were either left in ignorance of their own history or were taught a distorted version of it (Josephy, 1971; Salazar, 1971). Third, colonized people are regulated and administered by representatives of the dominant power. The Bureau of Indian Affairs has monitored the lives of Native Americans on reservations as closely as did any colonial administration of the British or French in Africa. The lives of blacks were closely regulated during the period of slavery. Today teachers, police, welfare workers, and shopkeepers, as white "outsiders" in black ghettos, operate as regulators. Fourth, the colonial population is seen as inferior to the dominant group—the classic basis of racism.

Clearly, a conflict is involved between economic and political self-determination and the role of the dominant power in maintaining economic and political control over the institutions of American society. This conflict is revealed in actions by blacks to gain community control over schools and police and by Puerto Ricans to force bilingual instruction in the schools. Given the assimilationist orientation of public policy, a belief in the right of self-determination that seeks to preserve ethnic or racial identity is difficult to maintain. However, the failure of assimilation of blacks has resulted in a continuation of the colonialist relationship with this group.

Can these issues be resolved? Will acceptance of cultural differences result in a shift from assimilation to pluralism as public policy? If ethnic identity provides a reference point for people in modern society, as Greeley and Novak suggest, it is unlikely that such concerns will become less important. If the role of ethnic groups in providing a source of stability and meaning in a changing world is as important as these authors believe, equality can only occur through acceptance of differences rather than the elimination of them.

SUMMARY

Minority groups are distinguished by their relative stability and powerlessness compared with the dominant groups in our society. Visibility refers to cultural, linguistic, or physical features that give evidence of a minority background. Powerlessness refers to the inability of groups to establish their own sense of identity and control over their lives. The three basic types of minority groups are racial, ethnic, and religious.

Ethnicity and race are the basic factors in dominant-minority relations in the United States. Blacks were brought to this country as slaves, while most of the whites immigrated voluntarily. Asians came for economic opportunities. Mexicans and Native Americans have seen their lands taken, their cultures destroyed, and their rights violated, though they have older claims to this country than other people. However, dominant-minority problems do not exist only in the United States.

Several patterns of contact between dominant and minority groups have developed. Avoidance may include self-imposed isolation by the minority, but usually involves expulsion or segregation imposed by the dominant group. Prejudice—negative attitudes—and discrimination—negative actions—deprive minorities of access to opportunities that would allow them full status as citizens. Acculturation involves the acceptance of dominant group values by the minority while maintaining certain ethnic or racial traits. Assimilation, or the elimination of all distinctiveness, typically through intermarriage, is the final form of integration. Rebellion and protest may be used to shock the dominant group into recognition of minority claims.

Minorities have experienced and continue to experience prejudice and discrimination. These experiences often are institutional in character: systematic denial of rights by law, tradition, or administrative rule. Black Americans, Puerto Rican Americans, Mexican Americans, Native Americans, Jewish Americans, and other immigrants continue their minority status. Assimilation, as the public expectation, is easiest for those with least physical and cultural visibility and most difficult for blacks and Orientals.

Several issues remain unresolved. What is the meaning of the newly developed emphasis on ethnicity throughout the world? Is genuine equality among ethnic groups possible? Does equality mean access based on individual merit or actions on behalf of entire minority populations?

The basic values of American society are challenged by the prejudice and discrimination that remains. A new ethnic consciousness has developed among Irish, Italians, Slovaks, and others. This ethnic identity may lead to a viable cultural pluralism that accepts the legitimacy of every ethnic group.

GLOSSARY

Accommodation   acceptance by both the minority and dominant groups of their relative positions in society.

Acculturation   acceptance of dominant group values by minority group members.

Assimilation   gradual loss of distinctiveness of minority groups absorbed into dominant population. May be of four types—cultural, structural, marital, and identificational. (Gordon)

Avoidance   strategy of controlled social contact or lack of social contact employed by either the dominant or minority group.

Black power   a concept based on the premise that the black community must preserve its racial and cultural identity and foster pride in being black to deal with white society from a position of strength.

Cultural assimilation   the process by which minority groups lose their distinctiveness and are absorbed into the dominant population.

Cultural pluralism   the coexistence of different ethnic groups based on mutual respect for cultural differences.

Discrimination   an act of unequal treatment, usually directed toward a minority population, that deprives people of political, economic, or social opportunity.

Dominant group   members of a social group that have higher status, more privileges, and greater power than members of other groups in the society.

Ethnic minorities   groups defined by national origin, language, and cultural patterns that differ from the dominant group.

Expulsion   removal by the dominant group of an undesired population from the area they have occupied; the most extreme form of avoidance.

Genocide   deliberate destruction of one group by another.

Identificational assimilation   the acquisition by minority group members of a sense of commonality with the dominant group.

Marital assimilation   assimilation through intermarriage between minority and dominant groups.

Melting pot   a concept used to describe the process by which several minority populations merge with the dominant group to form a new population, shaped primarily in terms of the attributes of the dominant group.

Minority a group or category of people distinguished by special physical or cultural traits, which are used to single them out for differential and unequal treatment. (Wirth)

Prejudice an emotional attitude that is unfavorable to an entire category of people.

Segregation setting apart or separating members of a minority group from members of the dominant group in social interactions.

Structural assimilation assimilation through large numbers of minority individuals entering into organizations and associations of the dominant society.

ADDITIONAL READINGS

Bahr, Howard M., Bruce A. Chadwick and Robert C. Day, eds., *Native Americans Today*, New York: Harper and Row, 1972.
A recent survey and analysis of the social conditions and life of American Indians.

Blauner, Robert, *Racial Oppression in America*, New York: Harper and Row, 1972.
A consideration of colonialism as it applies to American blacks.

Kitano, Harry L., *Japanese Americans: The Evolution of a Subculture*, 2nd ed., Englewood Cliffs, N.J.: Prentice-Hall, 1976.
A discussion of the circumstances of Japanese-Americans in the U.S.

Moore, Joan W., *Mexican Americans*, 2nd ed. Englewood Cliffs, N.J., Prentice-Hall, 1976.
An examination of Mexican-Americans and their situation in American Society.

Sklare, Marshall, *American Jews*. New York: Random House, 1971.
A careful consideration and analysis of Jews and Jewish life in America.

Williams, James D., editor, *The State of Black America, 1981*. New York: National Urban League, 1981.
Compares the current status of blacks to whites on various indicators and explores the reality of racism in modern America.

Wilson, William J., *The Declining Significance of Race: Blacks and Changing American Institutions*. Chicago: University of Chicago Press, 1978.
A provocative argument that social class has become more important than race for the status of black Americans.

READINGS

READING 11.1

Why Not Bring the Kids Home?
Mary McGrory

No words exist to justify the shameful treatment this country metes out to Amerasian children, those abandoned offspring of American (mostly GI) fathers and Oriental mothers. But . . . bureaucrats . . . continue to search.

They came up with their alibis at a hearing on a bill . . . to give preferential treatment to "certain children of U.S. Armed Forces personnel."

They had gone to some trouble. On one hand, they pointed out . . . the danger of "abuse and fraud" in the notion. . . .

They also offered a technological exit—a miraculous new blood test at the Communicable Disease Center, which is so fancy it can pinpoint the home state of the father. Although variously called "a breakthrough" and "still in the laboratory stage," it was meant to be light at the end of the tunnel for the outcast children, who in Vietnam are called "the dust of life." . . .

One State Department representative . . . had the grace to be embarrassed as he proffered his rationalization "that it would tend to increase our illegal alien population." He admitted that the children lead wretched lives, scorned, abused and often stoned for their freckles, their blue eyes and their telltale height.

The United States flatly refuses to recognize their existence. If they wish to come to their father's land, they must apply under sixth preference (skilled and unskilled workers in short supply). Since they are cut off from schools, housing and public assistance of any kind, their chances of qualifying are virtually non-existent. . . .

Nobody knows for sure how many of these abandoned children have been left behind as souvenirs of American foreign policy. In Vietnam, where they are officially designated "bad elements," there may be as many as 25,000. In all—Korea, Thailand and Laos are also included in McKinney's bill—there may be 80,000.

The bureaucrats . . . took off, thereby missing the testimony of the victims and heroes of their non-policy: John Slade of the Pearl Buck Foundation; Father Alfred Keane, director of St. Vincent's Home for Amerasians in Seoul; and two Amerasians who tearfully pleaded for "those we left behind."

John F. (Cho Jae Juyn), a 6-foot, slender boy with Oriental features, "thinks" he is 15. He was shaking and sighing as he read through the autobiography he had prepared himself. He does not know his father's name. His mother is Korean. She abandoned him. He had a picture of himself with his parents, but he tore it up—"It make me cry too much." He went to an orphanage, "where Americans come to pick up children, but never me." He ran away. For years, he scratched a living on the streets of Seoul, kicked, cuffed and beaten, sleeping by night in movie theaters.

Father Keane, a person of seemingly unquenchable good will, pleaded for "our forgotten children"—whose numbers are increasing, since commanders of our troops currently in Korea "mostly worry about the VD rate."

And the good father told the story that shames us most as a nation. He told how the French, who never give themselves humanitarian airs, who in fact pride themselves on their pinched practicality as a nation, treated the children their soldiers fathered in Indochina.

When they left in 1954, they took 25,000 children with them. The government paid for the schooling of those who stayed behind. When they turned 21, they had the option of French citizenship.

[Congressman] Frank said the last word: "France wasn't worried at all that some half-French, half-English child might slip in. We were in Asia for our own purposes. Therefore, it is our obligation to bring our kids home."

SUMMARY
Amerasian children have an uncertain future in Vietnam, Korea, and other countries of Southeast Asia. Because they have no official refugee status and because few fathers admit their paternity, they are excluded from the United States. Some would argue that their exclusion is an example of institutional racism, while others would describe it as the result of bureaucratic rigidity.

QUESTIONS
1. Is the refusal to accept these children a result of prejudice and hostility toward Asians?
2. Is the concern about blood tests evidence of racism?
3. What does the problem say about the United States as the land of freedom and equality?

READING 11.2
Mexican-American History Revisited and Corrected
Albert Camarillo

Mexican Americans have a long history in the United States. In the Southwest Mexicans had developed a thriving culture and pastoral economy before the arrival of Anglo Americans. The U.S. government's concern with

SOURCE: Albert Camarillo, "Mexican-American History Revisited and Corrected." *The Center Magazine*, July/August 1980, pp. 40–43. Also see the author's CHICANOS IN A CHANGING SOCIETY: FROM MEXICAN PUEBLOS TO AMERICAN BARRIOS IN SOUTHERN CALIFORNIA AND SANTA BARBARA, 1848–1930 (Harvard University Press, 1979).

illegal immigration implies that the Mexican is a poverty stricken, illiterate, landless peasant whose dream of economic success has been ruled by the vision of riches in the United States. The following reading identifies the process by which Anglos displaced Mexicans and their ways from the land.

Chicano history is much more than the old familiar story of another immigrant group waiting its turn to experience the "American dream" of upward social mobility. The historical continuity between nineteenth- and twentieth-century Mexican-American history is due largely to the developments during the half-century following the Mexican War of 1846–1848 that determined henceforth the status of Chicanos in Southern California society. Though mass immigration from Mexico in the early twentieth century significantly affected Mexican-American society, the status of those immigrants was already determined to a great extent before they entered the United States.

. . . The story of nineteenth-century Mexican-American history in California is, on the one hand, a tragic tale of the decline and subjugation of a people who became "foreigners in their native land," and on the other hand, it is a story of the cultural, linguistic, and community persistence of a people who maintained themselves as a viable ethnic group within a radically changing society. Two factors profoundly changed Mexican California: they were increased Anglo-American immigration and the loss of Mexican-owned land. Though the basis of racial conflict between Mexicans and the first small group of Americans was set in the eighteen-fifties, it was not until the following decade that Americans began to outnumber the Mexicans. Americans began to wrest control of county and municipal government from the California rancheros. By 1870, the Mexican population had experienced major political losses, although it constituted a large sector of the electorate. . . . By

1880, Anglos had achieved political hegemony.

The loss of political power by Mexicans coincided with another equally important development—the loss of Mexican land. Indeed, once Americans gained control of the political machinery, Mexican land loss increased significantly. Mexican rancho and pueblo communal lands remained relatively stable during the first decade of the American period. However, during the eighteen-sixties the forces of nature—drought and flood—and the forces of man—increased American immigration—combined to dislocate Mexicans from their ancestral lands. As a result, during the eighteen-seventies Mexican landowners lost the bulk of their lands to American speculators, unscrupulous attorneys, and squatters.

For the most part, the processes of land loss and political powerlessness had run their course by the eighteen-eighties. Those two related developments affected, in turn, two other historical patterns: barrioization and the making of the Chicano working class. Together these produced a "new Chicano reality."

Barrioization is the process by which the Mexican people in the old pueblos became a segregated, ghettoized, ethnic minority that had to adapt culturally and socially to a new, foreign environment—the burgeoning American city. The degree of barrioization was roughly proportional to the volume of American immigration. As the Anglo community expanded and became dominant, the Mexican community became subordinate and confined within the old pueblo area.

The barrio provided for its minority Chicano residents an insulated, familiar world. Here the Spanish-speaking people could carry on in a fashion similar, but not identical, to their life-style when the town was predominantly Mexican. By 1880, many traditional Mexican passtimes and customs, such as bullfights, cockfights, and other activities, had been outlawed by the Americans. Chicanos accommo-dated themselves socially and culturally to the new reality by keeping and modifying what they could of their traditional customs, at the same time creating new sources of ethnic and patriotic cohesiveness. . . . Sociocultural change and adaptation thus characterized this first generation of barrio dwellers.

The ruins of old adobe structures in and around the historic pueblo-barrio illustrate another development that dramatically affected Mexican people—the deterioration of their pastoral economy. The decline of cattle ranching had grave consequences for Mexican workers. As the traditional occupations associated with the cattle industry declined, the Mexican workers were steadily displaced, confronting the Mexican community with increasing impoverishment. Moreover, their means of livelihood declined just when their subsistence farming on communal lands was no longer possible, since those lands had been subdivided and sold to Americans.

Faced with poverty and starvation, Chicano men, women, and children began entering the capitalist labor market as menial laborers. They were not incorporated into the new labor market, however, until the number of Chinese workers had been significantly reduced as a result of anti-Chinese immigration legislation which was part of the anti-Chinese movement in general. Chicanos entered the new economy as seasonal farm workers, tourist service workers, construction laborers, cannery workers, and other unskilled and semiskilled laborers. They were a key source of labor for the expansion of urban development and agricultural production. But, underpaid and often exploited, the Chicanos have always remained an impoverished working-class element.

. . . One can plainly see in this century the continuing of nineteenth-century trends, along with changes that have occurred in the Chicano society as well as in the large society. First, residential concentration in the old pueblo-barrios continued to characterize the Chicano population, even as new barrios were being formed, some of which were extensions of the old pueblos and in newer barrios. Mexican immigrants, who arrived in increasing numbers each decade, often lived next to the native-born; if they did not live in the same barrios they at least lived under the same conditions.

Second, the working-class experience of Mexicans at the bottom of the occupational ladder—with virtually no hope for upward mobility—characterized fourth- and fifth-generation native-born as well as the most recent immigrants from Mexico. Occupational change did occur as Mexican workers were attracted to other unskilled and semiskilled jobs arising from industrialization. However, horizontal mobility did not translate into vertical mobility.

Third, the political powerlessness of the earlier generation of nineteenth-century Chicanos continued to characterize the community of Mexicans during the twentieth century. Lack of political power was exacerbated by the reluctance of the foreign-born to become naturalized citizens.

In present-day society, the historical patterns that evolved during the second half of the nineteenth century . . . still plague Chicano communities—unemployment, low wages, educational neglect, lack of effective political access, racial tension. . . . Mexican-American history cannot be understood without examining both its nineteenth-century roots and more recent twentieth-century developments.

SUMMARY
Clearly, contemporary Mexican-American society has deep roots; it is not simply the product of twentieth-century immigration. The modern problems of Mexican Americans are those created when changing laws, social rules, and economic systems destroyed the old culture and reduced the minority to a position of poverty and powerlessness. Yet the Mexican-American culture has adapted to new conditions and has forged or strengthened cultural identity among its group members.

QUESTIONS
1. Why do Anglos think of Mexican-Americans solely as immigrants?
2. How can people retain their culture and traditions in a hostile society?
3. How have Mexican-Americans accommodated to the conflict, exploitation, and stratification forced on them?

PART IV

Institutions: The Bases of Order

Institutions are clusters of norms associated with important social activities. Their validity rests upon tradition and history and they provide order and structure to social life. Many institutions might be identified, but we shall consider the normative patterns that surround family, economic, religious, political, and educational activities. Family institutions, Chapter 12 deals with relationships among people in families and with changes in family patterns. Chapter 13 examines economic life in its diverse forms, and the world of work in the modern world. Chapter 14 focuses on religious behaviors and beliefs, and the relationship of religiosity to behavior.

Political institutions are discussed in Chapter 15, especially the use of legitimate and illegitimate power in varied economic and social settings. Finally, in Chapter 16, educational institutions and their role as agents of continuity and change are considered.

CHAPTER 12

Family Institutions

CONTENTS

Is the family primarily for personal pleasure?

Would it matter to society if families did not exist? Such a question may at first seem absurd. After all, we are all born into families, and regardless of our family experiences, we tend to take families for granted.

Yet our society invests much more time, money, and concern in individuals than in family units, and some have suggested that families are out-of-date. On one side are those who suggest that families exist for individual growth and pleasure, especially in a modern society. If people no longer see family relationships as offering personal benefits, these relationships should be ended—or not begun. Others argue that families have been and continue to be the source of most of the values and ideals we cherish as Americans, and that the survival of society is dependent on family life.

YES   Families no longer are the center of society. In the past, families were the most important economic unit. Men and women who did not marry often faced economic hardship and its attendant low social status. Children were important—first to work for the family when they were part of the household and later to provide for parents if the latter survived to old age. Under such conditions, marriage was essential for individuals and if love, companionship, and genuine intimacy emerged it was an added, if unexpected, benefit.

The circumstances that made families essential for survival no longer exist. Marriage and parenthood are now matters of choice. The social and economic conditions of modern society make it possible for individuals to succeed without the burden of marriage and children. Families can be important to a person's stability and growth. Today the primary reasons for marriage and children are psychological— companionship and the emotional security that comes from intimacy. However, people change during the course of a marriage, and the family unit may at some point no longer be able to provide these benefits.

Should people stay together for the sake of children, even though research suggests that an unhappy two-parent family offers children less than what a good one-parent family can provide? A person achieves happiness through good relationships with other people. Why, then, should an individual, even if a parent, continue an unhappy, unrewarding marriage?

The family is primarily for personal pleasure!

NO   Historically, the family has been the primary social unit. Within the family children have learned work skills and attitudes, achieved growth and independence, and acquired long-lasting personal values. In terms of educational success, the family is more important than the schools. In terms of religious training, the family is a better teacher than the church. Similar findings about family influence on economic, political, and social ideals and beliefs suggests that the family is essential to any social order.

At the present time, no other social group offers an individual what the family can offer: affection, emotional support, protection against an often harsh world. For most people, life is worth living if things go well in the family but if the family fails, life falls apart.

Because of this families cannot be seen only as an arena for individual self-expression. Indeed, the give and take of family life prepares people for work and social activities outside the family. Without the family, individualism could not survive, because individualism is made possible and sustained by the unique relationships that exist in families.

It is in the family that the individual finds meaning and identity. Private life—for most people—is closely identified with family, spouse, parents, children, siblings. Stable family relationships make it possible for people to grow and achieve satisfactory relationships with friends, coworkers, lovers.

The family is not primarily for personal pleasure. The family is for society and for individuals. Neither could exist without family institutions!

How important is the marriage/ family relationship? In modern society, with its emphasis on individual growth and achievement, there is a parallel concern about personal satisfaction and happiness. Those who suggest that marriage and parenthood are for personal pleasure stress the emotional security that such ties bring. As needs change, however, family ties may need to change as well. In contrast, those who suggest that family relationships are more important than personal pleasure believe that most people can only be effective members of a society if they have strong and lasting family ties. Each view has clear implications for social life. Should we seek to reestablish economic and social conditions that support marriage and family relations? Can family institutions survive if they depend only on personal satisfaction?

QUESTIONS TO CONSIDER

- How important is the family in modern society?

- Why do different types of families exist?

- Is there a sex revolution?

- Why does abortion cause such controversy?

- Does the nuclear family have a future?

The Andersons—Betty and George—live in a high-rise apartment near Lake Michigan on Chicago's Near North side. They have no children and plan to have none. Both have careers that require frequent travel. Their marriage is a source of comfort and happiness, but both admit that their careers are too demanding for them to accommodate to the needs of children.

The Morrissey family—Louise, her sister Mary, and their mother—live in the city in a small, poorly maintained apartment. Their parents were divorced three years ago and now their mother works part time to provide for the children. On most days, Louise and Mary are alone after school. Occasionally, they see their father, but he has remarried and lives several miles away.

The Turner family includes Alice, her brother John, and their mother and father. They live together in a suburban Chicago home. Mr. Turner works in downtown Chicago and spends two hours daily traveling to and from work. Mrs. Turner, like most other mothers in the community, cooks, maintains the home, and cares for the children, who participate in scouting, clubs, and various recreational activities.

The Kotz family, Harold and his parents and grandparents, all live together in a small town just outside the Chicago area. When they married, Harold's parents moved into the big house where his grandparents had lived for many years. Several aunts and uncles live nearby, and all members of this kin group are engaged in the family business of raising vegetables for sale in Chicago markets.

WHAT IS A FAMILY?

In the past, the term family was used to define those organized activities associated with marriage and children. Families were recognized as the basic unit of social life. However, the role of families has changed, and today much emphasis is placed on personal satisfaction in marriage and family relationships. Can the family satisfy individuals and still benefit society? Or is the family no longer an important institution?

In Western society in the twentieth century, the **Nuclear Family** has been the ideal: a sexually cohabiting man and woman with children, all of whom share a common residence and cooperate economically (Murdock, 1951). However, not all families in the industrialized countries have children or live together, and many family patterns have existed and exist today in the Western and non-Western world.

Among the Nayar, who lived in nineteenth-century India, for example, ritual marriage took place between a man and his bride who was very young, often only seven to 12 years of age. Wedding ceremonies were elaborate and celebrations lasted for three or four days. The ritual husband then left his wife with her family, often without having had sexual relations with her. From then on, the husband had no sexual obligations to his wife or responsibilities for her economic support, though there might be occasional social contacts between them. The wife was supported primarily by her brother and kin group and to some degree by other men of appropriate kin relationship and caste, who also became her sexual partners. Children born to the mother were cared for by her and her kin group. Fatherhood was socially defined, and the man who paid the birth expenses was recognized as the father, whether or not the child was his biological offspring (Gough, 1959).

In the Nyoro society of Uganda a man might have several wives. Each wife has a separate house for sleeping, but they all share the kitchen and other facilities. The husband moves from house to house, and children are considered to be the responsibility of all parents equally, husband and wives. The entire family apparently shares in economic activities, and there is a high level of cooperation among all members (Beattie, 1960).

The diversity of family patterns does not hide the fact that family activities in all societies are centered on marriage and children. These activities help us define the institution of the family, either by its functions or by its kinship structure. Both definitions are useful, but each emphasizes a different aspect of family life and activities.

Family: A Functional Definition

One way to describe the family is by what it does, or its functions. Throughout history families have functioned as the principal means of socializing children, as the primary source of intimate social relationships, and as the most effective agents of transmitting culture. In some societies, such as the Nayar and the Nyoro, families are also the basis for activities of an economic, political, or religious character. In modern industrial societies, such family dominance does not exist and family functions are focused upon the individuals rather than society.

THE FAMILY AND THE SOCIAL ORDER

What are the functions of the family in modern societies? Can the institution of the family slow or speed social change? How does the family relate to other institutions?

It is a widely held view that the family has experienced a serious loss of functions, which threatens its future. One of the first efforts to describe this phenomenon was that of Ogburn (1938), who suggested that the seven functions of the family in premodern times—economic support, status conferring, education, protection, religion, recreation, and affection—the bonds that held the family together—were being eroded, and, as a result, the family's control and influence over its members

was becoming limited, even within the small conjugal unit that is the dominant pattern in Western industrial societies.

The conjugal family pattern emphasizes the husband-wife tie and a nuclear unit independent—economically, residentially, and socially—of the larger kin group. According to one argument, this conjugal system is important to industrial development because nuclear households are independent of the larger kin group and they can respond to the demands of the industrial system more quickly than larger units (Goode, 1968). The individual who has skills can accept a new job or move into a new occupation without obtaining the approval of the kin group. Neither the traditions nor the social interaction that supports the kinship structure is important for the person employed in modern industrial societies. It is merit, not family ties, that is the basis for employment and advancement; such rules also apply to women who may be employed without permission of their husbands and fathers. In short, the conjugal family facilitates Western-style industrial development by providing a labor force that is mobile, independent, and able to respond to the demands of the industrial order.

A different argument can be made to support the interpretation that traditional family structure is important for industrialization. Japan is an example. By creating an economic organization in which labor is substituted for capital, the Japanese have succeeded in integrating the larger family unit, or kinship structure, into the industrial system. The traditional values of the Japanese family have encouraged work by all members in the business, farm, trade, or profession of a family member, and have resulted in a high level of production (Wilkinson, 1962). Instead of adopting large-scale technology, the Japanese have adapted technology to their level of resources, which included strong family ties.

By contrast, evidence about the family and industrialization in India suggests that traditional family ties can prevent rather than assist industrialization. In the traditional joint family, the father asserts control, even over the married children. Decisions about employment and spending of earnings are the father's legitimate concerns. Associated with this power is an elaborate set of social behaviors and values that reinforces the traditions of the family. As a result, when faced with a choice of accepting an individual opportunity and possible achievement or remaining in the family network, a person may choose the family. The lack of the mobile, individualized, responsive work force that is found in industrialized societies hinders industrial development (Nimkoff, 1960).

These examples suggest that one way in which family patterns are important to the social order is in their relationship to industrial development. In systems of economic organization that depend on the labor potential of family units, as in Japan, the larger family may provide an unpaid labor force that makes industrial growth possible despite a lack of capital. In the West, particularly in the United States, corporate industrial structures benefit from the existence of the mobile, independent conjugal family.

Educational, religious, and political activities, which were largely controlled by the family in preindustrial eras, are interdependent with family structures in modern society. The nature of this interdependence is complex and covers a wide range of activities. For example, the early socialization of the child is a critical factor in school success, but there is also a close tie between school success and opportunities for a career and the family's ability to assist a child in achieving occupational success. Families with wealth offer a child advantages in social contacts and personal opportunities that can hardly be overemphasized; children from poor families must compete without such sponsorship.

Similarly, family background is important in shaping political and social attitudes and behavior. At the same time, political and social policies, such as those involving racial desegregation, abortion, or public education, have an impact upon decisions of the family like where to live, which school to attend, or whether to have another child. The family also is the most important source of basic religious values and activity through socialization and control. Religious institutions have traditionally defined marriage and the family as sacred and God-given forms of man-woman-child relationships. This traditional family model is undergoing change today as the opportunities for women to gain recognition and to achieve self-realization expand outside of marriage, and these changes will affect religious institutions as well.

Of all institutional patterns in the United States the family is the most traditional in character. Most of the changes that have occurred within the family are the result of changes in other institutions that affect the family, rather than of internal factors.

THE FAMILY AND INTERNAL FUNCTIONS

The basic functions internal to the family unit include sexual and economic cooperation and birth and socialization of children. For some family units, functions such as leisure, education, and religion are important, while for couples without children some of these may be unimportant. In spite of such variations a family is defined by the functions it performs for the individual, mainly emotional support, legitimate sexual relations, stable social relationships, and the pleasure of children, and for the society, notably reproduction and socialization of children.

Functional definitions of the family are widely used because of the ease of classifying family activities. The weakness of such definitions is that functions typically ascribed to families in one society may erroneously be thought of as functions of families in all societies. To avoid such assumptions, many students of family life use structural definitions.

Family: A Structural Definition

If we examine the family as a part of the kinship structure, we focus on "what it is," usually in terms of social relationships. "Kinship" refers to a network of relatives who may or may not live together and are related by marriage or birth. Theoretically, the kinship is potentially very large. In the past when large families were more common than they are today, and among the Mormons even now, uncles and aunts, brothers and sisters, grandparents, in-laws, and cousins were defined as members of the kinship groups (Kephart, 1982). In contrast, in modern industrial societies, most family units are relatively small. Large kin groups meet rarely and then usually for ritual events like weddings, funerals, and family reunions.

KINSHIP AND THE NUCLEAR FAMILY

As a kinship structure, the legally constituted nuclear family may be defined as a group composed of a married man and woman and their children. Marriage is the means by which family units are begun; thus marriage defines the relationship of the partners in kin groups and creates a new family line.

Kinship relations are most important in a society in which individual achievement is less important than family ties and parentage. Lineage, inheritance, and residence patterns also are closely related to definitions of kinship and have different meanings in modern societies dominated by small families, personal achievement, and frequent changes in residence.

PRINCIPLES OF FAMILY STRUCTURE

There are certain principles that control the creation of family units, their residence, and selection of marital partners in all societies. Normative sanctions and cultural expectations define the application of these principles in specific societies, leading to varied forms.

Marriage is a socially acceptable relationship between a man and woman for the purpose of sexual relations, procreation, and personal satisfaction. Of course, this definition applies most directly to marriage in the West, though it is valid in other societies as well.

In the United States and most modern societies, **monogamy** is the only legal form of marriage at present. In the past some subcultures, including some Mormon subgroups, practiced **polygyny**, or marriage between one man and two or more women. Most societies that practiced polygyny or **polyandry**, the reverse of polygyny, were preindustrial; few such isolated societies exist today. However, polygyny is still practiced to varying degrees in Islamic societies.

Norms governing marital selection include the incest taboo, which forbids marriage and sexual relationships between persons defined as family members. Rules of **endogamy** or **exogamy**—marrying within or outside of one's group—tend to be more explicit in preindustrial societies, which place greater emphasis upon continuity of kinship lines

or status levels, than in modern societies. However, even in the United States, spouses tend to be similar in age, religion, education, race, and occupational background, despite the lack of formal rules concerning endogamy. The structure of communities, neighborhoods, and educational institutions tends to create a pool of eligible marriage partners, defined by age and social status.

There is considerable confusion about family concepts because, for most people, the family includes all members of the household. However, some concepts help us to understand the family institution both as it was in the past and as it is at present.

The kinship relations that are created by marriage are **conjugal relationships**, that is, based upon a social tie; kinship relations that occur with the birth of children are **consanguineal relationships**, or those based upon biological ties. Both of these types of relationships are included in the concept of family in the United States, regardless of location of residence.

Most married couples in the United States have a household separate from that of either set of the couple's parents, a pattern of **neolocal** residence. At times couples may reside with or next to the parents of the wife, a **matrilocal** pattern, or with or next to the parents of the husband, **patrilocal** residence. In industrial societies, such residence with parents of either spouse occurs primarily for economic reasons and is temporary rather than permanent.

Residence arrangements help to define family and household patterns. A married couple and two or more of their married children and their children who live in the same residence is an **extended family**. Siblings who live in the same residence with their spouses and children constitute a **joint family**. (See Figure 12.1.) While these forms of families have been common in some societies, as in India among traditional Hindus and in classical China, neither of these arrangements has been common in the United States. Even in farm families, often cited as an example of the extended family, rarely did married siblings and their children live in a common residence with parents. The term **modified extended family** has been applied to closely knit fam-

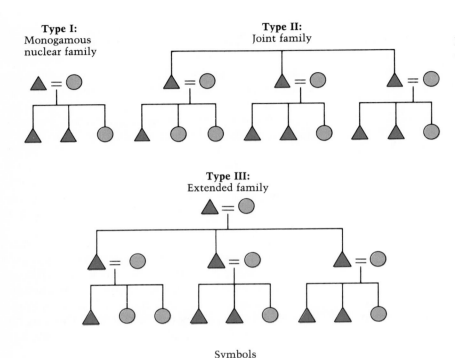

Type I:
Monogamous
nuclear family

Type II:
Joint family

FIGURE 12.1   Three Types of
Household Arrangements Based on
Consanguineal Ties

Type III:
Extended family

Symbols
▲ Male   = Marriage
● Female   ⊓ Children

Source: Bert N. Adams, THE FAMILY: A SOCIOLOGICAL INTERPRETATION, Third
Edition, © 1980 by Rand McNally College Publishing Company, Chicago, Figure 2-1, p. 21.
Used by permission.

ily units in both rural and urban areas. These family units do not share a common residence, but often live close to one another and exchange goods and services, both among siblings and between generations.

Except for neolocal residence, family residential arrangements are based on consanguineal relationships. Of course, we must remember that, despite the support of cultural norms for extended or joint families, the majority of the families in every society are nuclear units.

Authority and descent are two additional components of family structure. In modern societies the norms of authority emphasize a general **equalitarian** pattern, though subcultures of different eth-

nic or religious groups may support the patriarchal authority.

Descent is part of the kinship system, specifically the line—male or female—through which kinship is traced. **Bilateral descent** refers to descent traced through each side of the family, and it is this pattern that is followed in the United States. In the United States, however, children traditionally have been given the family name of the father, although recently, the use of both parents' family names has become more common. Patterns of descent in other societies, such as much of Latin America, have traditionally recognized surnames of both parents.

One additional set of terms often is used to define family units. The **family of orientation** is the unit into which a person is born and includes the person's parents and siblings; the **family of procreation** is the family created by the marriage and parenthood of a person and includes the spouse and children.

A Definition of the Family Institution

Given the diversity of family goals and the variations in family structure that exist in our society, is it possible to have an inclusive definition of the family? The answer to this question is obviously no if we consider only the structure of kinship relations. However, if the functions of families are also taken into account, it is possible to detail some similarities among American families, as well as families within other cultural and societal groups.

We shall define the **family** institution as a cluster of norms that surround activities associated with the marriage of a man and a woman, sexual cohabitation, affection, companionship, and the bearing and rearing of children. The family institution as the agent of early childhood socialization ideally provides the child with an environment of love, trust, and emotional support. Other aspects of the family institution that continue to be important in our society are the regulation of sexual activity, the provision of companionship and affection to spouses, and the sponsorship of children into occupations through example and support.

We must recognize that this definition does not apply to all families in the United States. Several alternative forms of family life exist, and these include an increasing number of people. However, the dominant pattern in the United States still is the conjugal family, with its emphasis on mutual satisfaction and support.

FAMILY PROCESS: THE TRADITIONAL MODEL

The traditional concept of the family in the United States was based on the following ideal: families were conjugal units, each with several children; the wife was primarily a homemaker, and the husband was the main source of economic support and authority; children were a source of pride and satisfaction; sons were expected to improve on the educational, occupational, and income levels of their father, and daughters were expected to marry, have children, and repeat the cycle of the family. In fact, this ideal was probably never achieved by most families—the poor, those on farms, those with both parents working, or those without two parents due to death, desertion, or divorce.

This concept of the ideal American family has roots in the Judeo-Christian and ancient Greek and Roman traditions, in the cultures of Africa and Asia, and in experiences on the American continent itself. In Judeo-Christian tradition, as in others derived from pastoral or agricultural societies, the family was a patriarchal unit in which goals and decisions were controlled by the father. Throughout much of Western history, male and female roles were clearly differentiated into dominant-submissive, provider-domestic, and instrumental-expressive patterns, and the family—a conjugal unit—was responsible for a wide range of economic, educational, and religious activities.

As Kenneth Kenniston has documented (Reading 12.1, "The Transformation of the Family"), the nineteenth century witnessed several changes in the family. Perhaps most significant of these changes was the development of institutions apart from the family: schools, which emphasized individual achievement; jobs in industry, which were individual rather than family positions; and courtship, in which personal choice was paramount. Slowly these changes were incorporated into the family. Patriarchal authority diminished, repression of sexual drives became less severe, and the nuclear family became virtually independent of the kin group.

In the traditional model, family life is a process that follows naturally through stages of development, from childhood through adolescence and mate selection to marriage, parenthood, and death or divorce. There are expectations about appropriate age and behavior for each of these stages and are presumed to lead to lifelong happy marriage. The stages from adolescence onward are described in the following section. Highlight 12.1 identifies the ages of most men and women at various stages of the family life cycle.

In rural areas during the first two decades of the twentieth century, families were large, and married children lived close enough to join together in a variety of economic and social activities. The couple in the front center at this family reunion in Iowa in 1914 were the parents of the men on either side, whose wives and children and grandchildren are included in the picture. All of these people lived within a few miles of each other and provided economic and emotional help to each other.

Premarital Relationships

Relationships between boys and girls in adolescence reflect the conflicting expectations of traditional patterns of mate selection and the freedom that characterizes modern social life. Dating was once governed by expectations of male dominance and female deference. Chastity and lifelong fidelity were public norms. However, some ethnic groups and some subcultures always have had different expectations about dating and marriage, and there is evidence that the dominant public norms, especially concerning sexual behavior, have not been followed for several decades by a large proportion of the population.

In the United States and in most industrialized societies, the selection of marriage partners has been governed by voluntary choice, love before marriage, and privacy in the relationship. The social activities that we describe as dating function as the chief

Marital selection is a matter of personal choice in most industrial societies. However, social structures tend to separate people by age, race, social class, and ethnic background. As a result, marital partners tend to be more similar in age, ethnic background, and marital experience than would occur by chance.

means of marital selection in our society. Dating for most people begins in early to midteen years, or roughly during junior and senior high school. Because schools have been designed to serve neighborhoods, the homogeneous character of neighborhoods in suburbs and most urban areas ensure that most dating will take place between people of similar social and economic backgrounds. The impact

---

HIGHLIGHT 12.1
The Family Life Cycle

Family experiences are closely tied to events, like marriage, birth, death or divorce, and retirement from work. Such events may be seen as experiences that begin a new stage of family life. Because of the regularity of certain patterns of family behavior across ethnic, racial, and class categories, the approximate ages at which people enter stages of the life cycle can be outlined.

	MEN	WOMEN
Beginning of dating	12–14	12–14
Marriage	22–24	19–21
Birth of first child	25	22
Birth of last (second) child	28	25
Entrance of last child in school	33	30
Marriage of first child:		
Female	45	42
Male	48	43
Marriage of last child:		
Female	48	45
Male	51	48
Retirement of husband	65–70	63–68
Retirement of wife	68–73	65–70
Death	69–71	75–77

of social cliques and ranking of students in each school also tends to limit a person's serious dating to those similar in social status, religion, and ethnicity.

Thus, structural constraints on the selection process serve to define eligibles, despite the formal freedom to choose and the voluntary nature of marriage. Evidence for the normative support of endogamy may be seen in marital choices: partners tend to be similar in age, ethnic background, religion, social status, and marital experience.

In spite of parental influence in the general selection of a pool of potential partners, a person's expectations of love are important in choosing a specific mate. Privacy in premarital relationships, including sexual intimacy, has been encouraged by the widespread use of the automobile beginning in the 1920s and more recently by the availability of apartments and college dormitories to increasing numbers of young people.

The widely discussed sexual revolution has been part of a general relaxation of behavioral constraints on adolescents and young adults in modern societies. Research findings about sexual behavior have noted considerable change over the past 20 years. During the 1960s males were more likely to have experienced premarital sex and to have had several partners than females, most of whom had had coitus only with their future husbands. In the past decade, at least three-fourths of males and three-fifths of females studied reported premarital coitus. Some studies suggest that at least 80 percent of both males and females have premarital sexual intercourse, and at ever younger ages than formerly. Clayton and Gokemeier (1980) summarize these findings:

Most studies indicate . . . (1) an increase in the overall prevalence of premarital sexual behaviors, particularly coitus, (2) an increase in the number of sexual partners among those who are experienced, and (3) a decrease in the average age at onset of coitus, [as well as] . . . a unilinear trend toward more liberal attitudes about sex before marriage. (p. 764)

The difference between expectations and behavior may be explained in part by the conflict between our belief in individual freedom and public respon-

sibility. Also, the moral standards of today lack the reinforcement of the threat of pregnancy, shame, forced marriage, and public scorn that existed in the rural, stable communities of the past. Further, the ease and availability of contraception in recent years has undoubtedly had an effect on premarital behavior. Whatever the reasons, current behavior represents a clear shift from the standard of chastity that has been supported by religious institutions throughout American history.

Marriage

The traditional view of marriage is that it is a commitment until death. It is a public announcement that the couple desires to share their lives, establish a legally and socially sanctioned sexual relationship, and have children. Most important, in modern societies, is a declaration of love for the spouse, which then serves as the basis for personal satisfaction and happiness. During 1980, nearly 2.5 million marriages took place in the United States, evidence of its continued popularity. The median age of this group was 22.1 for women and 24.6 for men.

As of March 1980 approximately 70 percent of men and 65 percent of women over the age of 18 were currently married; adding those widowed or divorced, over 80 percent of men and 85 percent of women in the United States had been married at least once (Current Population Reports, Series P-20, 1981). These figures are somewhat lower than corresponding figures of 10 years ago, but they suggest a high level of support for the institution of marriage.

Many factors are involved in the continued high rate of marriage—an effort to conform to the expectations of society, a desire to show oneself to be "normal," a concern for legitimating sex and children, a wish for companionship and intimacy. Whatever the reason for its occurrence, marriage represents a rite of passage into adulthood, by which socially approved sexual relations may occur and any children who are born will be defined as legitimate.

Children

Despite the declining birthrate in the United States and other industrialized societies in recent years,

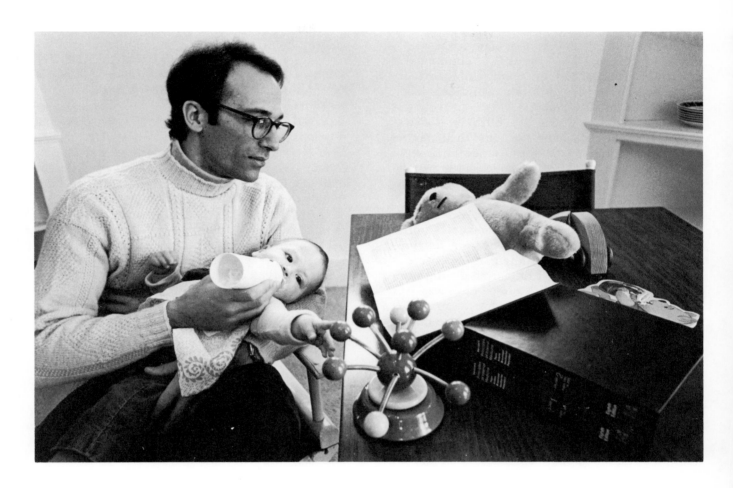

Men in traditional families only rarely assumed childcare responsibilities. In many modern families in which both husband and wife work, men have begun to assume a larger share of childcare and often experience conflicts between the demands of work or study and those of family responsibility.

children are an integral part of traditional family life. Historically, a large number of children was desirable because of high infant and child mortality and the economic benefits from children's labor, especially in agricultural areas. However, there was a long-term decline in the U.S. birthrate that was reversed between 1944 and 1957, and then another period of decline. By 1980 the **crude birthrate**—defined as the number of births per 1000 population—had dropped to replacement or even below (*Statistical Abstract*, 1980).

The decreased birthrate in industrialized societies reflects the impact of several factors. Contraceptives, despite being prohibited by some religious groups, are widely used. Children are expensive: a recent estimate of the cost of rearing a child from birth through college in the United States was over $100,000 in 1981 dollars. Later age at marriage, associated with alternatives to housewife-maternity roles for women, reduces the number of children, in part because of fewer marriage years of fertility (Marini, 1981). The increased proportion of married women who work for pay both before and after the birth of a child, combined with cost or availability of childcare, influences the birthrate. Concern about overpopulation and quality of life may also be a contributing factor. However, the traditional family model continues to emphasize children as an essential element of family life.

As societies have changed, the context of socialization of children has changed. Formerly, children were closely engaged with their parents at work, at play, and at rest. Today most activities of adults and their children are separated. There are very few children who see (or help) their parents work, and the work that can be observed by them tends to be highly specialized or difficult to understand.

Historically, "masculine" traits of men have been strength, aggressiveness, and leadership; "feminine" traits have been passivity, deference, and tenderness. Boys are taught to be aggressive and brave; girls, to be passive and defenseless. Though some aspects of traditional gender roles for men and women have been modified, current patterns of childrearing appear to be continuous with those of earlier years: parents continue to treat boys and girls differently, and as a result adults of each sex have different expectations, feelings, and attitudes.

In the traditional family the achievement of the son is emphasized; it is assumed that the daughter will marry and be a housewife, and thus fewer resources are invested in her career. Closer emotional relationships exist between mother and daughter than between son and father or son and mother (Adams, 1968), a fact consistent with the different individualizing experiences of males and females in our urban, industrial world.

The traditional family has as one of its functions in modern America the sponsorship of children into occupational roles. For daughters, the term "launching" is appropriate, since the marriage-family pattern is typical of the family's sponsorship of women. For sons, the family directs its efforts toward establishing occupational and social goals and maximizing all of the social and personal conditions for success.

Dissolution: Divorce and Death

Marriage in the traditional family is for life. As a part of the wedding ceremony, couples repeat vows that claim fidelity "till death do us part." Despite these vows, **divorce** and separation are significant factors in the termination of marital relationships. Highlight 12.2 describes some of the problems of calculating divorce statistics.

Death ends more marriages than divorce, dissolution, annulment, or separation. However, because death of a spouse is likely to occur after the children have left the home, it affects fewer people directly than other forms of dissolution. By contrast, divorce and the newer dissolution of marriage frequently occur when children are young. In 1978, more than 1,140,000 children were involved in the 1,130,000 divorces in the United States (*Statistical Abstract*, 1980).

The increase in the divorce rate is viewed by some as evidence of a decline in the strength of the traditional marriage pattern. Nevertheless, the high rate of marriage suggests that marriage is still a respected institution. Perhaps the high divorce rate would be less troubling if we viewed divorce as a way of incorporating the emphasis on individual

HIGHLIGHT 12.2
The Confusing World of Divorce Statistics

During 1981, about 1,219,000 divorces were granted in the United States. This figure can only be understood in comparison with those of earlier years. However, because birthrates change, populations and divorce statistics change. The following examples illustrate the problem:

	1960	1970	1980	1981
NUMBER OF DIVORCES	393,000	708,000	1,182,000	1,219,000
RATE PER 1000 POPULATION	2.2	3.5	5.2	5.3

Defining the divorce rate this way is an adequate measure of divorce only if the birthrates are stable. A large increase in the birthrate, as occurred during the 1940s and 1950s, will lower the divorce rate at that time because the premarriage/divorce population is increasing while the population divorcing is relatively stable. The reverse is also true: a rapid decrease in the birthrate will increase the divorce rate.

RATE PER 1000 MARRIED WOMEN, AGE 15 AND OLDER	9.2	14.9	20.4*	21.0*

This method of calculating divorce rates has the same problems as the one based on total population. Changes in the population due to increases or decreases, delayed marriage, or divorce due to wars, economic conditions, or social crises and changes in age at marriage all affect this way of computing a divorce rate.

RATE PER 1000 MARRIAGES	258	328	498	500

Though widely used in the popular literature, this calculation is practically meaningless because it varies with cultural values about marriage and divorce. Also, the divorcing population and the marrying population are different, that is, few couples marry and divorce in the same year, so no valid comparisons can be made by this approach.

The ideal way to determine the rate of divorce is to follow a group of couples married in the same year to the termination of marriage through divorce or death. One such study of couples projected that 29.5 percent of those married in 1950 would end in divorce, compared with 39.1 percent of 1960 marriages and 47.8 percent of 1970 marriages (Weed, 1980). Clearly, divorce rates have increased but the real extent of that increase remains unknown.

*Estimated by author.

happiness into a marriage-oriented social structure by providing a means of escape for individuals without destroying the institution of marriage.

Whatever the effect of divorce on institutional structures, the legal reasons for divorce and the actual reasons have often been very different. In the past, divorce actions presupposed guilt and innocence, and divorce was most often granted on charges of cruelty (*Vital and Health Statistics*, 1964–1965). Cruelty has been variously defined from physical abuse to incompatibility, making divorce possible despite rigid legal codes that would forbid it. To bring the basis for legal action more in line

with reality many states have eliminated plaintiff-defendant suits and substituted a form of **dissolution** that assumes mutual responsibility for the marital breakdown.

Thus, though traditional ideas of marriage and family life have assumed its permanency, divorce has been accepted as an alternative for individuals wishing to end the marriage relationship. However, we should note that fewer than 5 percent of people in the United States are divorced at any one time and over 90 percent of divorced people remarry. Apparently, family life is a highly acceptable pattern to most people in modern society.

FAMILY VARIATIONS: ETHNICITY AND SOCIAL CLASS

Traditional roles for men and women have been changing for several decades, and several variations on the two-parent, children, wife-as-homemaker pattern have emerged. Among these variations are single-parent families, childless families, and three-generation or communal families.

Though precise data are difficult to obtain, one recent estimate of family life, as presented in Table 12.1, suggests that the traditional family model may include only a minority of all families. If we also stipulate that the wife not be employed, fewer than

one-third of families in 1980 fit the traditional model, since about half of married women living with husbands were in the labor force. According to the data in Table 12.1, about one-fourth of all families were headed by women, most because of divorce or separation. Similarly, the proportion of families headed only by a male has increased.

What social or cultural conditions have led to these variations in the traditional family pattern? These new patterns reflect the economic and social changes of the past 50 years, especially the growth of out-of-home employment for women, fewer children, longer life expectancy, easier divorce, and greater personal choice as traditional controls have

TABLE 12.1 Family Patterns in the United States (in percent)

	1960		1970		1980*		1990*	
Married couples	74.7		68.9		60.5		54.9	
No children		33.3		33.7		30.0		27.2
One child**		14.1		12.5		11.8		11.4
Two or more children**		27.3		22.7		18.7		16.3
Male Head	8.0		9.8		13.0		16.1	
Never married		3.2		3.9		5.5		6.9
Previously married								
No children		4.3		5.2		6.8		8.3
One or more children		.5		.7		.7		.9
Female Head	17.3		21.2		26.5		29.0	
Never married								
No children		2.7		3.3		4.4		5.0
One or more children		.2		.4		1.2		1.3
Divorced/Separated								
No children		2.6		3.4		4.9		5.8
One or more children		2.1		3.0		4.6		5.1
Widowed								
No children		8.6		10.0		10.6		11.1
One or more children		1.1		1.1		.8		.7
Total: Percent	100.0		99.9		100.0		100.0	
Families (N)	52,793,000		63,394,000		79,106,000		92,711,000	
*Projected								
**Percent traditional	41.4		35.2		30.5		27.7	

SOURCE: George Masnick and Mary Jo Bane, *The Nation's Families: 1960–1990.* Cambridge, Mass.: Joint Center for Urban Studies of MIT and Harvard University, 1980. Computed from Table 2.13.

weakened. In addition to these general influences, at least two other specific factors appear to be important in shaping family patterns: ethnicity and social class.

Ethnic Variations

Several ethnic groups have maintained distinctive patterns of family life in the United States for several generations. Other groups have lost their uniqueness soon after arriving in the United States. For example, Spanish-speaking families tend to be more closely knit within the larger kin group, to be larger, to have greater differentiation between the sexes, and to be more patriarchal than Anglo or English-speaking family units. By contrast, families of Irish and Italian background are less distinguishable from other families. Clearly, the degree of access to economic and social opportunities is important in creating these differences, as are the religious traditions, the significance of the kin group in family life, and the culture of the ethnic group.

Among Spanish-speaking families, whether from Mexico, South America, Puerto Rico, or Cuba, traditional values of male dominance and authority are expressed in various ways. **Machismo** is one aspect of this dominance: a concept of masculinity built upon feats of physical prowess, daring, violence, or threats in order to master females socially and sexually. Male dominance is also expressed through a double standard for sexual behavior, which condones premarital and extramarital sex for the man but denies such freedom to the woman.

The degree of acculturation to American life also affects the family pattern. The kin group plays an important role in Spanish-speaking families in giving advice, financial aid, and services, partly because close kin are likely to live nearby through a combination of choice and discriminatory housing patterns. Spanish-speaking families also tend to begin childbearing earlier and continue it until a later age. The average number of children born per woman is 3.8, compared with about 2.7 for Anglo women.

We have selected the Spanish-speaking family as typical of ethnic families that have maintained distinctive behavior. The family is characterized by a high degree of differentiation of sex roles, a high fertility rate, and patriarchal authority. Immigrants from many other countries and ethnic backgrounds have more readily adapted to the American scene, and as a result their families no longer maintain distinct cultural patterns. Ethnic and religious subcultures of these groups may exist in some urban neighborhoods, but the factors that currently dis-

There is great variety in family traditions among Americans of different ethnic backgrounds. Among Japanese Americans, the strong emphasis on achievement and kin loyalty is evident in family activities as well as in family size and kinship relationships.

tinguish among them are economic level and social status rather than ethnicity.

Social Class Variations

Social class variations in family patterns reflect the impact of various levels of wealth and privilege. Among the very rich, the child is raised in a setting of nursemaids, governesses, and other servants. Private schools, clubs with exclusive clientele, and closely guarded social contacts effectively structure the social relationships of the rich. For rich families, primary relationships are with other rich people, often within larger kin groups. Segregated and clearly defined sex roles characterize the family and are reinforced by gentlemen's clubs and women's social clubs, with their ritual of "coming out" for the adolescent daughters. The large financial resources permit the family to structure the environment to achieve its goal, best defined as the continuity of its life style.

Among the poor, the family is often described as matricentric, or mother-centered, even if the husband-father is present in the home. A large number of births and lack of resources severely limits the ability of poor families to sponsor children in educational or occupational roles. Family roles are traditional in ideal, but women are often involved in the economic support of the family and the father's dominance appears to be qualified by the family's need of economic assistance from the mother. The conflict between cultural expectations of male dominance and economic reality often leads to desertion by the father—a significant factor in the high proportion of single-parent families among the poor. As of March 1980, about 50 percent of black families and about 25 percent of white families in the United States below the official poverty level were headed by women (Current Population Reports, P-60, 1981).

Differences in family socioeconomic level are probably most significant in planning for children, their socialization, and sponsorship of children into later life. Planning for children tends to be more common as socioeconomic status increases; the economic consequences of early parenthood and closely spaced children are considerable as children are expensive and they remove the mother from the labor force, at least temporarily.

Social class differences in patterns of socialization have been identified by many researchers. Adams (1980) summarized these findings by noting that middle-class parents are more emotionally warm and expressive toward their children, more often encourage the development of their children's verbal skills, and are more concerned to understand the reasons for their children's behavior than are lower-class parents. In general, middle-class socialization is characterized by affection and independence while lower-class socialization is focused upon neatness and control.

Early research emphasized the greater use of physical punishment by lower-class parents and its effects on personality development, such as less tolerance for delayed rewards and greater acceptance of authority. However, several recent studies have found little evidence to support such social class differences (Straus, 1980).

Differences in education, wealth, and prestige are important in shaping families, not only because of the direct impact of money and position on couples' choices, but because of the indirect effects of these factors on the socialization of children and thus on their adult lives.

ALTERNATIVES IN MARRIAGE AND FAMILY RELATIONSHIPS

Alternatives to the traditional family model have raised questions about the importance of marriage and the desirability of children. The following sections discuss these issues.

Is Marriage Important?

With the increased emphasis on individual development and satisfaction as a personal goal in modern societies, the value of monogamous marriage has become problematic for many people. The large number of opportunities for sexual intimacy and the near-perfect control of pregnancy now possible have created an important alternative to traditional marriage: unmarried cohabitation. In 1980, 1,560,000 unmarried couples were living together in the United States, about 3 percent of all male-female couples (Current Population Reports, Series P-20, 1981). Unmarried cohabiting couples, compared with married couples, tended to be younger, to live in urban areas, to have low income and high unemployment, and to be better educated (Glick and Spanier, 1980). Researchers do not agree about the significance of nonmarital cohabitation as a substitute for marriage nor about the consequences of cohabitation upon the adults, or children, or the institution of marriage. While benefits include companionship, sexual gratification, and economic benefits from sharing housing and pooling food money, conflicts tend to develop over terminating the relationships and child custody (Newcomb, 1979). Legal arrangements, spelling out the rights, duties, and benefits for each party, have been slow to develop. A movement toward legal protection of children born to cohabiting couples may have broad implications for economic support, custody, and legal status.

Another marriage alternative is open marriage, whose adherents view the monogamous relationships of traditional marriage as restrictive and limiting one's personal development. In open marriage the partners look for satisfying personal experiences, wherever and however they may be formed. These include extramarital sexual experiences and intimate social relationships, as well as the relationship within the marriage itself (O'Neill and O'Neill, 1972). Many of the supporters of open marriage view this arrangement as one that preserves both the institution of marriage and individual freedom and growth.

To maintain a relationship within the framework of open marriage, each person must sustain high desirability as a mate, including such characteristics as a pleasing personality, competence in interpersonal relations, pleasant appearance, and occupational career skills. Consequently, children not only are seen as unnecessary but may become a barrier to the full realization of the marriage's potential.

Other types of marriage models include group marriage, patterned after the Harrod experiment (Rimmer, 1966); communes, in which the social and economic advantages of living together may or may not be accompanied by sexual relationships; intentional families designed to create a supportive social network across age, sex, racial, and marital lines; and single life, by choice or by circumstances. Despite the range of possibilities, all these alternatives probably include less than 15 percent of all couples. Most young couples adhere to the traditional marriage form, although some have reservations.

Are Children Desirable?

Near-perfect control is now possible in preventing and delaying pregnancy, and new types of drugs have decreased infertility. This makes the decision about parenthood a matter of choice for nearly every couple. However, the question of whether to have children is of increasing concern to both married and unmarried people.

One alternative for married couples is to have no children. Either because both spouses are deeply involved in professional activities or because neither desires children, some couples opt for childless marriage. By chance or by design, about 25 percent of all married couples aged 18–34 were childless in 1980, and more than 10 percent of those aged 30–34 had no children (Current Population Reports, P-20, 1980). In traditional terms, marriage is the prelude to parenthood. The new concept of family based on the validity of the conjugal relationship itself defines marriage without children as an acceptable alternative to parenthood.

An alternative for both women and men is to forgo marriage, yet have children by birth or adoption. Men have become single parents through obtaining custody of children in divorce or by adoption. As of 1980 more than 5 million women and about 600,000 men in the United States were single parents, accounting for nearly one-fourth of all parent-child units. Most began parenthood in marriage but through the death or divorce of a spouse have become single parents. While not all such families are created by choice, the increasing ability of women to earn enough money to support a child makes this a viable alternative to married life.

Concerns about single parenthood have focused upon the lack of both male and female role models for young children of either sex. Men and women who act as both mother and father may be confronted with innumerable frustrations in coping with both roles, negative judgments by others, and extra demands on their time and energy. Single fathers face new tasks, often without prior preparation, such as doing laundry, housecleaning, shopping, cooking, and dealing with problems of bedwetting, finding childcare, and comforting children who are ill, hurt, or unhappy. In addition to the tasks just mentioned, single mothers face the demands of full-time employment or the expectations of social service organizations to keep the family intact. Unlike parents in the movie *Kramer vs. Kramer*, most single parents are not affluent, do not find adequate childcare easily, and do not resolve their personal problems quickly and without much difficulty. Instead, as Gordon (1981) notes, most single parents face responsibility overload, task overload, and emotional overload.

Historically, the impact of children upon marriage has been to buttress the traditional gender roles—housekeeping, nurturance, and emotional support for women and economic support and dominance for men. By contrast, some couples, seeking greater flexibility in such roles, have developed a formal marriage agreement, signed before marriage. This agreement spells out the nature of the responsibilities of each spouse regarding household activities and childcare. Reading 12.2 by Alix Shulman describes one agreement of this type. While many types of agreements exist, the one described by Shulman clearly shows the equality of responsibility that is sought through such arrangements.

The marriage agreement defines childcare and household activities as the responsibilities of both parents. Instead of limiting the masculine role to economic support and the feminine role to housekeeping and childcare, the sharing of these tasks is done on the basis of desire, convenience, and fairness. **Androgyny**, in which the person retains gender-role skills and identity but adds to these traits and skills of the opposite gender, emphasizes the sharing of such responsibilities. **Role reversal**, in which the husband becomes the homemaker and the wife becomes the provider, is another alternative to the problem of gender stereotyping.

Children are still cherished in modern societies, not for their economic contributions, but for their power to evoke our love. Few words still have the emotional impact of "mother" and "baby" in our vocabulary. However, people today have a wide range of choice regarding family and children. With increased choice has come new issues, problems, and challenges to the institution of the family.

PROBLEMS AND UNRESOLVED ISSUES

Several issues have emerged from the changing structure of family life and changes in the larger society in recent years. Birth control and abortion are common but still controversial. Employment of both parents has created a need for alternative childcare. There is growing concern about family violence, especially directed toward children. An increased number of divorces and dissolutions, combined with a new interest in caring for children by fathers, has generated issues of childcare and custody.

Each of these issues, and perhaps others, is a problem involving personal rights and public values and interest. While the form of their resolution is uncertain at present, we can explore some of these problems and identify the basis of the concerns.

Birth Control and Abortion

There have been efforts to control fertility for at least as long as human history has been recorded. While methods of birth control have taken many forms—abstinence, rhythm, mechanical devices, sterilization, and most recently, "the pill"—it has only been within the last two decades that birth control has made motherhood voluntary. Despite evidence that long-term use of oral contraceptives cause health problems for some women, the effectiveness of the pill has given women a degree of freedom and control over pregnancy unknown before (Scrimshaw, 1981).

Abortion is viewed by some people as a serious problem and an evil that should be prohibited. However, as this picture suggests, many women feel that the choice to be or not to be a mother is a matter of personal decision.

A large portion of sexually active adolescents do not use any birth control, however, either because of ignorance or inability to obtain them. As a result, one study estimated in 1976 that 30 percent of white sexually active women and 50 percent of black become premaritally pregnant by the age of 19 (Zelnick, Kim, and Kanter, 1979). Some of these pregnancies are terminated by abortion, but most result in live births.

While adults are able to obtain birth control without difficulty, adolescents may lack information about sources, fear their parents will find out, think prevention is unnecessary, or believe birth control is wrong (Zabin and Clark, 1981). Given the emphasis on sexual expression in the adolescent culture, it is not surprising that large numbers of adolescent women find themselves pregnant, unmarried, and unprepared to face motherhood, and seek abortion as a solution to their situation. Should contraceptives be easily obtained by anyone who desires them?

One of the most controversial issues in public life today is the effort to ban abortions except where the mother's life is in danger. Supporters of the ban argue that abortion is murder, since life is present from the moment of conception. Prochoice supporters argue for the right of a woman to control her own body, including termination of a pregnancy that is not wanted. Critical points of disagreement include the point at which an unborn offspring becomes human, the rights of mother versus the rights of the embryo or fetus, and the rights of individuals versus the coercive power of the state.

Since 1972 the number of legal abortions has increased from about 750,000 to a total of 7,288,000 in 1978. This represents 399 abortions for blacks and 263 abortions for whites per 1000 live births in 1978. While most legal abortions are performed on unmarried women and women under the age of 25, the ratio of abortions to live births is highest among women over the age of 35 for blacks and whites (Statistical Abstract, 1981).

For many, abortion is another form of birth control, necessary to avoid an unwanted pregnancy due to lack or failure of birth control, rape or incest, or change of circumstances like divorce or loss of income. As such, abortion means prevention of an unwanted child. The number of unwanted births was estimated at over 8 million in 1976, about 12 percent of all births, despite the relative ease of obtaining some form of birth control by most couples (Statistical Abstract, 1981).

Does society have the right to deny women access to abortion? Does the inequality of males and females in responsibility for bearing and rearing children give women unique rights to abortion?

Childcare

Childcare is a critical need for working parents, especially childcare that provides nurturance and stimulation to the young child. One estimate suggests that about 900,000 children, or about half of three to five year olds with working mothers, are presently in day care, and that by 1990, 10,400,000 children in the United States may have working mothers (Hofferth, 1979). While many of these children may be cared for by spouses, relatives, or other individuals, the growth of childcare centers has allowed 10 to 15 percent of all children to be cared for by nonfamily members. Clearly, the availability of childcare is an important factor in the entry of mothers into the labor force. Standards concerning the quality of childcare centers are not easily defined, and those standards that exist often are not enforced. There also is little information about the adequacy of care in private homes in which two, three, or four children are looked after while parents work. Despite such problems, the demand for childcare will increase as the proportion of families in which both parents work and as the number of single parents continue to rise in the United States and in other industrial societies.

Child Abuse and Neglect

The problem of family violence—here limited to child abuse and neglect—has only recently captured public attention. Abuse includes physical beatings, emotional or psychological abuse, and sexual exploitation. Neglect involves failure to provide for the physical and social needs of the child through lack of adequate food, shelter, protection, or other care. It is impossible to identify the extent of abuse, but estimates of physical abuse range from 50,000 to 1,000,000 cases annually in the United States. One estimate suggests that at least 14 percent of all children in the United States are physically mistreated seriously enough each year to be classified as abused (Straus, 1980). Sexual abuse may involve five times as many children as physical abuse, perhaps 500,000 per year, especially if child pornography is included (Finkelhor, 1979; Kempe and Kempe, 1978). Similarly, each year several hundred thousand children are victims of neglect, though precise figures are not available. There are several causes of abuse and neglect, which appear to resist elimination. First is the general cultural emphasis on the use of physical strength and violence which legitimates parents' mistreatment of children as a form of punishment (Gelles and Straus, 1979). The social and geographic isolation of families from friends or relatives that is characteristic of modern urban life also appears to be an important factor in abuse. Third, parenthood at young ages—especially early teens—and lack of knowledge and experience with infants are related to child mistreatment (Straus, 1980).

The problems in identifying and treating child mistreatment are compounded by differences in childrearing practices among various groups. The angry parent who beats his son for lying or stealing is likely to explain his actions as discipline though another parent would treat stealing by isolation or some work responsibilities. Some parents claim that sexual initiation of young children is helpful rather than harmful to them, but most parents disagree. Then, too, the experts do not agree: most childcare experts advise against physical punishment, but one recent article in a magazine for new parents advises "Only Spank When You're Angry" (Gochros, 1981). Hopefully, advice that encourages spanking is a minority view. However, child abuse—excessive punishment, exploitation, neglect, or failure to provide a child with self-understanding and self-control—will continue to be an issue as long as the social stresses to which modern families are subject continue to exist.

Marital Dissolution and Child Custody

The increase in marital dissolution during the past two decades has implications for children as well as for the married pair. In 1980 there were 120 divorces per 1000 married persons with spouse present, a rate nearly three times that of 1960 (Current Population Reports, Series P-20, 1981). Perhaps more important, these divorces involved over one million children still at home, for whom parental custody had to be decided.

In the past, custody generally was awarded to the mother unless she had serious moral or health liabilities. Recently, the improved economic opportunities that provide alternatives to homemaking for women have altered this pattern. Fathers have begun to seek and to obtain primary custody; as of 1980, about 600,000 children under 18 lived with fathers only. Fortunately, court custody battles are few, though even without conflict a large proportion of children of divorce experience guilt, trauma, and disruption of their lives (Wallerstein and Kelly, 1980). For women and men committed to their careers, the arrangement of visitation rights rather than custody may be preferred. Similarly, **joint custody**, in which divorced parents have equal responsibility for child care and major decisions, may be more desirable for both parents than primary custody.

Problems resulting from custody disputes have prompted some counselors to encourage parents to assess the most appropriate placement for the child, even if it means release of the child to a nonparent (Goldstein, Feud, and Solnit, 1979). Unfortunately, there is not yet sufficient information to answer questions about the consequences of varied custodial arrangements for children.

DOES THE CONJUGAL FAMILY HAVE A FUTURE?

Few questions have generated as much debate as that concerning the future of the family, especially the conjugal form that is common throughout much of the world. On the one side are those who argue that the family is the last bastion against dehumanization of people in modern society. As Barber (1973) suggests, the family provides an arena

where it is possible to give without reckoning emotional profit margins, to support without demanding contractual equity, to feel responsible without inquiring about compensation, to love without assuming passion is ephemeral. (p. 49)

On the other side are those who argue that the conjugal family is inherently unstable, unable to defend itself against the force of industrial society. On another level, Cooper (1970) suggests that the social experience of families essentially destroys autonomous initiative by invading its members and manipulating them by the claims of love. In this view, the unresolved problems of the family institution—dissolution, violence, child custody, personal versus family or societal control over pregnancy—are evidence of the failure of the family.

What then is the future of the family? There are several possibilities. First, the traditional pattern may continue but along with other patterns that are likely to become accepted as legitimate. Second, the family may emerge as the source of a renewal of community, both by modifying the traditional roles of spouses and by a change in governmental and economic policies to enhance family life. Third, the family may disappear from modern society, crushed by the forces of economic and social life, with its functions carried on by more efficient organizations.

Our own best guess is that the first answer will prove to be correct. The traditional family will not disappear. Instead, a variety of forms with an emphasis on the conjugal pair will become acceptable in the future. The functions of the family, particularly self-growth and child socialization, will remain dominant and continue to structure the patterns of marriage in our society.

SUMMARY

Family experiences in the United States and throughout the world are diverse. Marriage may involve more than one spouse in some societies, and families may include grandparents and married siblings as well. Patterns of marital selection, degree of kinship interaction, and types of authority relations vary from society to society. In modern societies there is no one pattern of family life: families may include single-parent heads, no children, or dual-career couples as alternatives to the traditional model.

However, despite the diversity of marital and family patterns, an institutional structure that regulates sexual behavior, socializes children, and provides emotional support to individuals in paired relationships exists in every society. The family, in these terms, is a normatively supported institution, involving marriage, sexual cohabitation, affection and companionship, and the bearing and rearing of children.

Families in the West have moved away from the Judeo-Christian tradition with its emphasis on monogamy, children, and permanency of marriage. The traditional model for families rigidly defines sex roles, encourages childbearing and rearing as a primary goal, and seeks to exert control over the marital selection, achievement, and sexual activity of its members.

Recent changes in society have created changes in family patterns. Not only do ethnic and class variations exist, but open marriage and childlessness also have become viable alternatives to the traditional model. A number of factors have created more freedom for women, who are increasingly conscious of their needs as separate individuals within the marital unit and are looking for ways to satisfy those needs. Many family-related issues have emerged in recent decades. The issue of access to birth control and abortion has divided young and old—often within families. The need for adequate and affordable childcare is increasing along with increasing numbers of working mothers. Child abuse and neglect affect millions of children each year. Child custody after divorce has been affected by changes in parent roles.

Some critics question the validity of the conjugal family. Given that it continues to be the basic source of satisfaction for most couples, its future appears to be firm, though the specific patterns of marriage will change. Can the family survive—even with changes?

GLOSSARY

Androgyny a practice in which the person retains gender-role skills and identity but adds to these traits and skills of the opposite gender.

Bilateral descent tracing of kinship through the family lines of both parents.

Conjugal relationships family relationships created by marriage and thus based on social rather than biological ties.

Consanguineal relationships family relationships that are biologically defined and based on blood ties.

Crude birthrate the number of births per 1000 population.

Dissolution a method of voiding marriages that recognizes mutual responsibility and incompatibility as valid reasons for ending the marriage.

Divorce a method of voiding marriages that requires determination of guilt or innocence of the parties.

Endogamy practice restricting marriage to persons who are both from the same group or community.

Equalitarian family a kinship structure based on the exercise of equal authority by both parents.

Exogamy practice of marrying outside of one's group or community.

Extended family kinship group sharing a common residence and including a married couple, two or more of their married children, and their children's children.

Family institution a cluster of norms that surround activities associated with the marriage of a man and a woman, sexual cohabitation, affection, companionship, and the bearing and rearing of children.

Family of orientation the kinship group into which one is born.

Family of procreation the kinship group formed through marriage and parenthood.

Joint custody divorced parents have equal responsibility for childcare and major decisions.

Joint family kinship group sharing a common residence and including two or more siblings and their spouses and children.

Machismo a concept of masculinity that involves feats of physical prowess, daring, violence, or threats to master females, socially and sexually.

Matriarchy familial authority pattern based on rule by the mother.

Matrilineal descent tracing of kinship through the wife's family line.

Matrilocality residence of married couple with the wife's parents.

Modified extended family three or more generations of a kinship group who do not share a common residence but often live close to one another and exchange goods and services.

Monogamy marriage of one man and one woman.

Neolocality residence of married couple separate from either set of parents.

Nuclear family kinship unit comprised of husband, wife, and children.

Patriarchy familial authority pattern based on control by the father.

Patrilineal descent tracing of kinship through the father's family line.

Patrilocality residence of a married couple with the husband's parents.

Polyandry marriage of one woman to two or more men.

Polygamy marriage between a person of one sex and two or more persons of the opposite sex; includes both polygyny and polyandry.

Polygyny marriage of one man to two or more women.

Role reversal a concept which when applied to marriage means that the husband becomes the homemaker and the wife becomes the provider.

ADDITIONAL READINGS

Cooper, David. *The Death of the Family*. New York: Random House, 1979.
The author examines the family in capitalist society with a view to the future and discusses the threat that exists in industrial societies that emphasize individualism.

Goode, William J. *World Revolutions and Family Patterns*. New York: Free Press, 1963.
The classic study of changing patterns, both normative and structural, of family life throughout the world.

McAdoo, Harriet Pipes, ed. *Black Families*. Beverly Hills, Calif.: Sage, 1981.
A discussion of the black family characteristics, marriage patterns, and childrearing. A special section focuses upon public policies and their impact on black families.

Pepitone-Rockwell, Fran. *Dual-Career Couples*. Beverly Hills, Calif.: Sage, 1980.
A collection of readings on the history of dual-career families, the impact of two careers on family patterns and behaviors, and the social, legal, and economic issues involved for such couples.

Shorter, Edward. *The Making of the Modern Family*. New York: Basic Books, 1975.
An examination of the changes in household, community, and marital patterns in traditional and modern societies. Changes in sexual behavior, romance, childcare, and the family group are examined within the larger social context.

Young, Michael, and Peter Willmott. *Family and Kinship in East London*. Baltimore: Penguin, 1959.
A fascinating study of working-class families in London, showing the sources and consequences of familism and the significance of the neighborhood in social life.

READINGS

READING 12.1

The Transformation of the Family
Kenneth Kenniston

Three centuries ago, almost all families resembled one part of the myth: they were largely self-sufficient agricultural units . . . Apart from nails, salt, and a handful of other goods, these family farms produced, sometimes with the help of neighbors, most of what they needed to live: their own houses, their food, bedding, furniture, clothing, and fuel. . . .

The most important difference between these early American families and our own is that early families constituted economic units in which all members, from young children on up, played important productive roles with the household. Children were essential to this family enterprise from age six or so until their twenties, when they left home. . . . Families not blessed with children usually faced economic hardship as a result, for boys were necessary to the hard work of cultivating the land and harvesting the crops, while girls were essential to the "homework" of storing and cooking food, caring for domestic animals, spinning, weaving, and sewing.

Children were, in short, economic assets. Early in life, most children began to pay their own way by working with and for their families. Many years later, when the parents were elderly, children paid another economic dividend: in a time when there was no government old-age assistance or social security, grown children were often the chief source of the parents' support. . . . As commerce and factory work became more common, family life and work were sundered: what a worker produced and what he or she consumed were increasingly not the same thing. Money—in the form of wages, salaries, or, for the wealthy, returns on speculation and investments—provided a new and more tenuous link between work and family. . . .

The economic "value" of children to families has changed as a result. If weighed in crass economic terms, children were once a boon to the family economy; now they have become an enormous economic liability. . . .

In the past then, the intrinsic pleasures of parenthood for most American families were increased by the extrinsic economic return that children brought. Today, parents have children *despite* their economic cost. This is a major, indeed a revolutionary, change. . . .

A second major change in family functions is the removal of education from the family. . . .

With the creation of public "common school" in the middle of the nineteenth century under the leadership of Horace Mann, formal education began to replace family education rather than assist it. . . . Schools, it was claimed, could do what families were failing or unable to do: teach good work habits, pass on essential skills, form good character, and, in short, Americanize.

. . . Acceptance of the doctrine of common public schooling marked another inroad on traditional family functions. A public institution, armed with the power of legal coercion, was taking over and expanding traditional family prerogatives. . . .

Even one century ago, most care of the sick was a family matter. . . . When children fell ill, their families nursed them and, if the children survived, watched over their convalescence. . . . When children died, as they did far more often than today, they died in bed, at home, with their families beside them.

Today the family plays a diminished role in health care. Parents still make the crucial first decision about whether to call the doctor, and in most cases they still give simple care. But for anything complex, the diagnosis is in the hands of experts, not parents, and one

SOURCE: "The New Role of Parents," Kenneth Kenniston and The Carnegie Council on Children, *All Our Children*. New York: Harcourt, Brace, Jovanovich, Inc., 1977, pp. 12–17.

crucial role for parents in the complicated business of nursing a sick child is to see that the child "follows the doctor's orders." . . . Most of what we expect of specialists did not exist a century ago: immunization against most life-threatening diseases, effective and accurate diagnosis of even obscure and rare illnesses, safe and hygienic surgery when needed, prompt treatment of bacterial infections, and medical correction of many handicaps. . . .

Rising expectations for what we want to give our children are crucial for understanding the transformation of families. . . .

The point is obvious: at the same time that families have been shorn of many traditional roles with children, new expectations about children's needs have arisen and, along with them, new specialists and institutions, to meet the expectations. Part of the change of family functions, which carries with it a new dependence on people and institutions outside the family, rests on the family's needs for forms of help and expert assistance that are the creations of the last century.

SUMMARY
Families have moved from an era of self-sufficiency to dependence on people and organizations outside the family. The expertise and knowledge that are a part of modern society have limited the family's ability to fulfill all their needs, desires, and expectations. Some questions remain unanswered, however.

QUESTIONS
1. Can public institutions with their bureaucratic and impersonal treatment of individuals really displace the family, even in education and health?
2. Why has the family continued to allow its functions to be taken away?
3. Can the family survive the bind between rising demands and expectations placed on it and the removal of economic and social supports it had in the past?

READING 12.2
A Marriage Agreement
Alix Shulman

Wishing to be once more equal and independent as we had been when we had met, we [my husband and I] decided to make an agreement in which we could define our roles our own way. We wanted to share completely the responsibility for caring for our household and for raising our children, by then five and seven. We recognized that after a decade of following the traditional sex roles we would have to be extremely vigilant and wary of backsliding into our old domestic habits. If it was my husband's night to take care of the children, I would have to be careful not to check up on how he was managing; if the baby-sitter didn't show up for him, it would have to be his problem.

When our agreement was merely verbal, it didn't work; our old habits were too firmly established. So we made a formal agreement instead, based on a detailed schedule of family duties and assignments. Eventually, as the old roles and habits are replaced we may be able to abandon the formality of our arrangement, but now the formality is imperative. Good intentions are simply not enough.

Our agreement is designed for our particular situation only in which my husband works all day at a job of his choice, and I work at home on a freelance basis during the hours the children are in school (from 8:30 till 3:00). If my husband or I should change jobs, income, or working hours, we would probably have to adjust our agreement to the altered circumstances. Now, as my husband makes much more money than I do, he pays for most of our expenses.

I. PRINCIPLES

We reject the notion that the work which brings in more money is the more valuable. The ability to earn more money is already a privilege which must not be compounded by enabling the larger earner to buy out of his/her duties and put the burden on the one who earns less, or on someone hired from outside.

We believe that each member of the family has an equal right to his/her own time, work, value, choices. As long as all duties are performed, each person may use his/her extra time any way he/she chooses. If he/she wants to use it making money, fine. If he/she wants to spend it with spouse, fine. If not, fine.

As parents we believe we must share all responsibility for taking care of our children and home—not only the work, but the responsibility. At least during the first year of this agreement, sharing responsibility shall mean:

1. Dividing the jobs (see "Job Breakdown" below); and
2. Dividing the time (see "Schedule" below) for which each parent is responsible.

In principle, jobs should be shared equally, 50-50, but deals may be made by mutual agreement. If jobs and schedule are divided on any other than a 50-50 basis, then either party may call for a reexamination and redistribution of jobs or a revision of the schedule at any time. Any deviation from 50-50 must be for the convenience of both parties. If one party works overtime in any domestic job, she/he must be compensated by equal extra work by the other. For convenience, the schedule may be flexible, but changes must be formally agreed upon. The terms of this agreement are rights and duties, not privileges and favors.

II. JOB BREAKDOWN

A. Children
1. Mornings: waking children; getting their clothes out, making their lunches; seeing that they have notes, homework, money, passes, books, etc.; brushing their hair; giving them breakfast; making coffee for us.
2. Transportation: getting children to and from lessons, doctors, dentists, friends' houses, park, parties, movies, library, etc.; making appointments.
3. Help: helping with homework, personal problems; projects like cooking, making gifts, experiments, planting, etc.; answering questions, explaining things.
4. Nighttime: getting children to take baths, brush their teeth, go to bed, put away their toys and clothes; reading with them; tucking them in and having night-talks; handling if they wake and call in the night.
5. Babysitters: getting babysitters, which sometimes takes an hour of phoning.
6. Sick Care: calling doctors, checking out symptoms, getting prescriptions filled, remembering to give medicine, taking days off to stay home with sick child; providing special activities.
7. Weekends: all above, plus special activities (beach, park, zoo, etc.).

B. Housework
8. Cooking: breakfasts, dinners (children, parents, guests).
9. Shopping: food for all meals; housewares; clothing and supplies for children.
10. Cleaning: dishes daily; apartment weekly, biweekly, or monthly.
11. Laundry: home laundry; making beds; dry cleaning (take and pick up).

III. SCHEDULE

(The numbers on the following schedule refer to Job Breakdown list.)

1. Mornings: every other week each parent does all.
2. and 3. Transportation and Help: parts occurring between 3:00 and 6:30 PM , fall to wife. She must be compensated (see 10 below).

Husband does all weekend transportation and pickups after 6:00. The rest is split.

4. Nighttime (and all Help after 6:30): husband does Tuesday, Thursday, and Sunday. Wife does Monday, Wednesday, and Saturday. Friday is split according to who has done extra work during the week.

5. Babysitters must be called by whoever the sitter is to replace. If no sitter turns up, the parent whose night is to take responsibility must stay home.

6. Sick Care: this must still be worked out equally, since now wife seems to do it all. . . .

7. Weekends: split equally. Husband is free all of Saturday, wife is free all of Sunday, except that the husband does all weekend transportation, breakfasts, and special shopping.

8. Cooking: wife does all dinners except Sunday nights; husband does all weekend breakfasts (including shopping for them and dishes), Sunday dinner and any other dinners on his nights of responsibility if wife isn't home. Whoever invites the guests does shopping, cooking, and dishes; if both invite them, split work.

9. Shopping: divide by convenience. Generally, wife does local daily food shopping, husband does special shopping for supplies and children's things.

10. Cleaning: Husband does all the housecleaning, in exchange for wife's extra child care (3:00 to 6:30 daily) and sick care. Dishes: same as 4.

11. Laundry: wife does most home laundry. Husband does all dry cleaning delivery and pick up. Wife strips beds, husband remakes them.

After only four months of strictly following our agreement, our daughter said one day to my husband, "You know, Daddy, I used to love Mommy more than you, but now I love you both the same."

SUMMARY
In this selection Alix Shulman describes the agreement she and her husband drew up for sharing the responsibility of home and children equally. The agreement covers both the division of jobs and the division of time. This can be a good model for many couples, although Shulman emphasizes the fact that this agreement is applicable to their particular circumstances and would have to be adapted to fit other families.

QUESTIONS
1. Can such an arrangement be used for large families as well as small units?

2. Do such arrangements solve the problem of sex-based roles?

3. What happens to these arrangements when circumstances change, such as a job, a new child, or sickness of an adult?

4. Do these definitions of responsibility create an ideal of equality that is rigid and arbitrary or do they create freedom for both parents to act independently?

CHAPTER 13

The Economic Institution: Industrialization, Modernization, and Advanced Industrial Societies

CONTENTS

Is the main responsibility of corporations to increase profits?

Private corporations are created by people who invest their money to produce goods or services for consumers. The purpose of the corporation is to make a profit in open and free competition so that those who invested their money will realize financial gain. But corporations also have a major impact on their host communities and on society in general. Their operations may affect the quality of the environment by polluting air and water. A decision to move a factory in order to increase profits can have devastating effects on a community. What, exactly, is the responsibility of corporations?

YES The chief executive officer of the modern corporation is hired by the owners of the business through the board of directors. Thus corporate executives are responsible to owners for carrying out corporate business in a way that will benefit owners. This generally means that they will try to make as much money as possible within the bounds set by law and common business practice.

If a corporate executive made decisions that furthered some social goal, such as reducing unemployment by retraining unskilled workers, and the pursuit of this goal would knowingly result in less profit for the firm, then that executive would be using other peoples' money improperly. The responsibility of the corporation, through the actions of its executives, is to increase, not reduce, the returns to owners.

Corporate executives—and owners—may have other social responsibilities which they may pursue as citizens. They may choose to use personal income in support of worthy social goals, or work to improve the quality of life in a community, or join citizens' groups wishing to clean up the environment. But as corporate executives or owners they may not use resources in any way that does not contribute to the firm's economic strength.

Individuals may have social responsibilities, but the responsibility of corporations is to increase profits.

NO Corporations must exercise voluntary restraint on the pursuit of profit when this goal conflicts with other responsibilities. There are social costs to economic activity, and the corporation that is socially responsible will attempt to balance the need for profit with other social needs. The socially responsible corporation will be concerned with how its activities affect the quality of the natural and social environment in which it exists. What are some of the things that socially responsible corporations should do?

First, they must maintain the highest ethical standards in their business operations, not simply meet the minimum standards required by law. Questionable and illegal practices by corporations do great damage to the moral climate of a nation because of the mistrust and cynicism these actions breed.

Second, they must use some of their resources for socially desirable ends even though these activities do not offer optimal economic benefits. This may involve direct financial support of community projects designed to create employment or avoiding investments that, while financially attractive, do not contribute to the quality of life.

Third, they must develop commitments to their employees that extend beyond contractual agreements. All employees should feel that the corporation cares for their security and well-being as individuals, as well as their performance as employees. Ultimately, such employees will become more productive workers and are likely to become more responsible citizens.

If corporations do not become more socially responsible, they can expect greater hostility toward their power and wealth and greater efforts by government and citizen lobbies to restrict their activities.

In this chapter we examine the modern corporation, including its goals and its key personnel. As corporations have increased in importance in modern society, the question of how they use their power and resources has assumed greater significance. The actions of giant corporations in developed societies may also influence the economic and political choices made by developing nations when trying to improve conditions in their own countries.

QUESTIONS TO CONSIDER

■ What are the main social and cultural forces favoring industrialization and modernization?

■ Does a private corporation have the right to shut down a plant, leaving people without jobs and undermining a community's economy?

■ What accounts for the emergence of giant corporations in the United States?

■ Who owns and controls corporations, and for what ends?

■ What is a multinational corporation and what are its consequences?

"Jim Farley's fellow workers at Federal Mogul Corporation's roller bearing plant on the east side of Detroit called him Big Jim—not so much because of the size of his body, they said, as because of the size of his heart.

"They liked the soft-spoken yet tough manner in which he represented them as a union committeeman. And they liked his willingness to sit down over a shot and a beer at the nearby Office Lounge and listen to the problems they had with their jobs, their wives, or their bowling scores.

"Jim Farley had come North in 1954 from eastern Kentucky, because mechanization of the mines and slumping demand for coal made finding work there impossible. The idea of leaving behind the mountains where he had grown up for the punch-in, punch-out factory life in a big city like Detroit didn't appeal to him much—but neither did the thought of living on relief, like so many unemployed miners in his hollow and most others in Pike County. . . .

"In the fall of 1971, Federal Mogul announced that it would be phasing out its Detroit operations by early 1974 and moving bearing production to a new plant in Alabama. Farley, say those who knew him, became a different man almost overnight—tense, moody, withdrawn. A month after the announcement he suffered a heart attack. Physically, he recovered rapidly. Mentally, things got worse. His family and friends called it "nerves." . . .

"With close to 20 years at Federal Mogul, the thought of starting all over again—in an unfamiliar job, with no seniority and little hope for a decent pension—was not pleasant. But Farley had little choice. Three times he found work, and three times he failed the physical because of his heart problem. The work itself posed no difficulty, but none of the companies wanted to risk high workers' compensation and health insurance premiums when there were plenty of young, strong workers looking for jobs.

"As Farley's layoff date in the first week of February 1973 approached, he grew more and more apprehensive. He was 41 years old: what would happen if he couldn't find another job? His wife had gone to work at the Hall Lamp Company, so the family would have some income. But Farley's friends were being laid off, too, and most of them hadn't been able to find work yet either—a fact that worsened his outlook.

"Farley was awake when Nancy left for work at 6:15 A.M. on January 29, but he decided to stay home. His nerves were so bad, he said, that he feared an accident at work. His sister-in-law Shirley stopped by late that morning and found him despondent. Shortly before noon he walked from the kitchen into his bedroom and closed the door. Shirley Farley recalls hearing a single click, the sound of a small-bore pistol. She rushed to the bedroom and pounded on the door. There was no response.

"Almost 20 years to the day after Jim Farley left the hills of eastern Kentucky, his dream of a secure life for his family was dead. And so was he." (Reprinted by permission of Working Papers magazine © Center for the Study of Public Policy 1978).

This tragic personal incident brings into sharp focus a broader set of social issues about how the economic institutions of our society function. As the "At Issue" question implies, the long-established practice of private corporations putting the goal of profits above all other goals is increasingly being challenged.

There are also economic questions about why the productivity and favorable competitive posture of American industry has declined relative to that of European and Japanese firms. Is it because American firms are not managed as well as those of foreign competitors? Or is it because of a declining work ethic and increased government regulation?

A related economic question is why many firms in the United States close down their operations and move to other locations. Some say it is because firms are forced to seek cheaper labor and other resources to maintain their profits. Reading 13.1 in this chapter suggests that many large corporations acquire firms, mismanage them, drain off their capital, and then shut them down in the name of efficiency.

The problems of unemployment, environmental pollution, and destruction of traditional community and family ties that are common in advanced industrial societies have given many less-developed nations second thoughts about how they should industrialize. Many nonindustrialized nations are looking for ways to improve the lives of their citizens without repeating the errors and problems of developed societies.

In this chapter we examine the process of industrialization as it was experienced by many developed nations. We also look at modernization as an alternative way to improve conditions in a society without having to follow the Western pattern of industrialization. Finally, we examine the nature of advanced industrial societies like the United States.

BASES OF INDUSTRIALIZATION AND MODERNIZATION

England was the first society to experience **industrialization,** which consisted of (1) technological

innovations such as the internal combustion engine and water power used in the manufacture of goods; (2) a shift in the labor force from agriculture to manufacturing; and (3) the standardization of the entire production process, including workers and products, for quantity production. Hand tools, simple machines, and the independent craftsworker were replaced by sophisticated mechanical processes. (See Reading 4.3 in Chapter 4 for a discussion of the factory during early industrialization in England.) In the latter part of the eighteenth century England began its transition from an agricultural and commercial society to an industrial society. For many years it stood as the single example of a society that had successfully gone through the process of industrialization. Since England was the only available model for the period, it seemed that other societies had no choice but to follow its example.

Societies today that wish to improve the quality of life for their citizens have more options available to them. In England industrialization meant the development of a manufacturing society driven by the profit motive and based on the market principles of supply and demand. The cost of labor (in the form of wages), land, and goods was determined by their scarcity. If labor is scarce but factory owners need workers to fulfill orders for their products, then workers will be offered higher wages to attract them to take vacant jobs. The role of government in this period was *not to interfere* (from the French term *laissez-faire*) with the system of supply and demand by establishing regulations or controls over wages, prices, or production goals.

Many developing nations want to enjoy the benefits of industrialization without experiencing the problems that rapid and large-scale industrialization brings. Some contemporary societies are trying to make the institutional changes that accompany economic growth and development, often referred to as **modernization,** while controlling the pace and direction of industrialization. A society undergoing modernization will try to develop its school systems, improve its level of literacy and the quality of its health care, and increase its citizens' knowledge of the national and international community by improved mass communications. The goal is to

During the early stages of industrialization, many new towns and small cities grew around a single industrial base. Mining towns, steel towns, and textile towns all show how the economic life of a community can dominate its other social institutions.

improve the quality of life without a total transformation of the traditional society. Industrialization and its accompanying changes occurred over a period of 200 years in the Western world. For many developing, or Third World, countries today, industrialization occurs all at once, bringing dramatic changes within people's lifetimes. Two cultures, the traditional and the modern, may exist side by side and frequently in conflict. It is this rapid change and culture conflict that many nations are trying to avoid.

Industrialization and modernization do have a great deal in common, however, since they both result in improved economic growth as measured by such indicators as per capita income. We will identify some economic and social factors in Western industrialization and then examine social and cultural factors aiding or inhibiting modernization in contemporary societies.

Money, Mass Markets, and Energy

Industrialization as occurred in Western nations requires a combination of economic and technological conditions. First is the need for a money economy rather than a barter system of trading with goods. Money is a universal medium of exchange, and it has the property of being easily calculable in a great variety of economic transactions. It can "move" or "attract" productive resources like land, labor, and raw materials that must be brought together to start new enterprises. If land use or wealth are tied to traditional obligations they cannot be used for new economic ventures, like building a factory. Similarly, if labor is obligated to a landlord, as it was under feudalism, rather than selling itself to the highest bidder, it is of little use as an economic resource.

It is not simply the existence of money for economic transactions that makes the difference in industrialization. Belshaw (1965) gives numerous examples of peasant societies that use money in marketplace situations. What is important is that all economic transactions are reduced to a single basis of exchange—money. If money could not obtain land, labor, and raw materials without the interference of traditional obligations, such as kinship ties, religion, or class-based relationships, industrialization as it developed in England and other Western nations could not have occurred. Indeed, Foster (1974) notes that one problem in the early capitalist industrialization of England was how to attract resources from traditional uses like building churches and maintaining feudal manors and apply them instead to building and improving new production systems and factories. One way to attract resources from other uses was to offer investors a fairly predictable high rate of profit. This probably explains in part the excessive exploitation of labor in the early phases of the factory system.

In addition to a money economy, industrialization requires a substantial, stable demand for the goods produced by the factory system, in other words, a mass market. It also needs a reliable source of energy for production. The invention of machines and new production systems did not take place overnight; the coordination of inventions with available sources of power was a gradual process. As Moore (1956) points out: "Domestic animals, wind, and water had been used for thousands of years. It was *transportable natural power* in the form of coal which was of outstanding significance for industrial expansion, for with the invention of the steam engine, heat would be transformed into energy for power-driven machinery" (p. 26).

The Labor Force

Industrialization requires a labor force that is literate, tractable, and mobile. According to Stinchcombe (1965) a literate population supports industrialization in two ways: (1) by improving the skill levels and innovation potential of the labor force and (2) by making possible the development of written law, large industrial organizations, and administrative structures. Modern organizations abound in written work rules, job descriptions, rules governing hiring and firing, and elaborate divisions of labor that require written communication for effective coordination of activities. (See the discussion of bureaucratic organization in Chapter 9.)

Literacy makes it possible for people to learn new

work roles more quickly and without role models. Schooling enables people to consider more alternatives than does an apprenticeship system, which requires commitment to a specific role model. A literate population is also more likely to form ties and establish common loyalties among widely dispersed people in similar occupations. Occupational associations that extend beyond local boundaries can be formed and they allow people to share new knowledge of work-related skills more easily.

An industrialized labor force also must be accustomed to working in organizations, prepared to follow orders and work under supervision, and willing and able to move to jobs. Each of these properties of the labor force in England was developed gradually under the guild system and the system of domestic production.

Ideology and Economic Activity

These economic, technical, and social conditions were necessary but not sufficient for the total transformation of an agricultural society to an industrial one. During any period of widespread social change like the Industrial Revolution, one can usually find a set of beliefs that serves to justify—and also to motivate—the new institutions and behaviors of individuals. These justifying beliefs, or ideology, give moral force to the new institutions that are challenging the old.

One of the most widely known studies of ideology in relation to economic activity is Max Weber's classic, *The Protestant Ethic and the Spirit of Capitalism* (1958b). Weber's task, like Karl Marx's before him, was to analyze the new economic system that had replaced feudalism in Western Europe. Both Marx and Weber sought to identify the factors responsible for the emergence of this unique economic system that called for a totally new set of social and economic relationships (Birnbaum, 1953). Marx found the reasons for expanding capitalism in the conflict among the economic and class interests of the old order, the feudal lords, the emerging financial and merchant class, and the landless proletarians. He felt that industrialization could be understood as part of objective "laws of capitalist development."

Weber's analysis of the emergence of a capitalist economic order developed partly in critical reaction to Marx's work, which had appeared some 35 years earlier. Weber held that capitalism had its roots in a system of *ideas*, namely, in the value system of Protestantism, which motivated the middle-class entrepreneur. Scholars before Weber had noted the tendency of Protestants to be entrepreneurs and artisans, while Catholics stayed in handcraft trades. What was responsible for this pattern? It remained for Weber to provide an explanation.

Catholicism in medieval Europe put its believers in a passive relationship to the Church and its representatives. "Salvation" or "achieving God's grace" was not in the hands of the individual Catholic. The priest, with his special powers, served as the intermediary between the believer and God. The priest performed the necessary rituals and prescribed specific acts, or sacraments, for the believer so that he or she might be absolved of sin and achieve grace.

The Reformation introduced a new relationship between Protestant believers and their God, emphasizing individual responsibility for salvation. The idea that "God's grace" resided in the believer and could not be conferred by an authority figure sharply reduced the power of religious leaders over the individual believer.

Weber was primarily concerned with that form of Protestantism known as Calvinism, after the teachings of John Calvin (1509–1564). In Weber's view several ideas associated with Calvinism contributed to the development of capitalism:

1. *Predestination.* Believers were either saved or damned by God's omniscient judgment. One could not discover God's decision or influence it in the course of one's lifetime. Therefore, the believers were left in doubt over whether they were headed for hell or for heaven.
2. *Work as a calling.* Uncertainty over one's standing in God's eyes led Calvinists to look for "signs" of God's grace. They came to find "evidence" of being elected, that is, predestined for heaven, in the achievements of work and in the view of work as a calling. As Samuelsson (1957) notes:

"Energy in daily work and success in his trade or vocation were signs that the individual was of the company chosen for salvation" (p. 43). Each person was encouraged to view work as "glorifying God," and therefore work in this world was a religious act.

3. *Asceticism.* The Puritan side of Calvinism led to a rejection of worldly pleasures, an emphasis on thrift, and an avoidance of excessive consumption of worldly goods. The combined virtues of hard work and asceticism are revealed in the following passage on ethics by an early Puritan writer, Richard Baxter (quoted in Hudson, 1959):

If God show you a way in which you may lawfully get more than in another way (without wrong to your soul or to any other), if you refuse this, and choose the less gainful way, you cross one of the ends of your calling, and you refuse to be God's steward, and to accept His gifts and use them for Him when He requireth it: you may labor to be rich for God, though not for the flesh and sin. (p. 59)

Following Weber's logic, the combination of (1) anxiety and uncertainty about being one of God's elect, (2) the duty to work for the glorification of God, and (3) the requirement that a person not consume wealth in worldly pleasures would lead to success in business affairs and the accumulation of wealth. However, accumulated wealth could only be spent to further glorify God. This meant that wealth was "plowed back" into economic enterprise—a central principle of capital expansion.

Weber's thesis is attractive in that it shows strong parallels between religious values and the values and behaviors required by a new economic system. The literature of industrializing England and Puritan New England abounds with examples of people who are almost caricatures of Weber's abstract capitalist Protestant.

Weber's thesis has received considerable critical attention (Green, 1959, Samuelsson, 1957). Many critics conclude that this thesis applies mainly to early commercial society in Western Europe and not to late eighteenth-century industrial capitalism. They point out that (1) Calvinism was not a strong force in England at the time of the Industrial Revolution, (2) workers did not really care about salvation by hard work, (3) capitalists did not deprive themselves of luxuries that their new wealth could buy, and (4) individual savings could not really produce the amount of capital needed to build factories.

Social scientists today continue to look for a connection between religious ideas and economic activity, asking, for example, why certain religious groups seem to have greater worldly success than others. Kennedy (1962) found important similarities between the central values of Zoroastrianism, the religion of a group of Parsis in India, and the Protestant ethic. Kennedy feels that the religious beliefs of the Parsis are responsible for their success in trade and commerce in much the same way that Weber thought the Protestant ethic was responsible for the capitalist motives of English Puritans.

Jackson, Fox, and Crockett (1970) reviewed a number of studies of modern-day American society that have compared the economic success of Protestants and Catholics. Most of these studies indicate that Protestants are more likely to enter business and professional occupations and to be more upwardly mobile than are Roman Catholics. While the statistical differences are not large, the differences persist even when Protestants and Catholics are similar in age, ethnicity, and regional and socioeconomic origin.

Recent research on Protestant-Catholic differences in socioeconomic achievement reveals the absence of consensus regarding firm conclusions (Greeley, 1981; McIntosh and Alston, 1982; Roof, 1979, 1981; Stryker, 1981). Some researchers find a convergence of Protestants and Catholics in terms of socioeconomic position, with any differences being small and insignificant. These studies have been based on broad comparisons of each religious group. Other researchers have looked at differences within each religious group to examine the experiences of Polish, Irish, and Italian Catholics in comparison to Protestants. These studies have shown that while Protestants and Catholics as a whole may have the same average years of education, some Catholic ethnic groups may have higher or lower levels of education than Protestants.

Future research on this topic will have to provide a closer examination of different ethnic groups within the larger denominations in order to see if religion has any special influence on socioeconomic attainment.

MODERNIZATION AND THE NONINDUSTRIAL THIRD WORLD*

Ferdinand Toennies (1887) used the polar terms *Gemeinschaft* (traditional community) and *Gesellschaft* (rational society) to describe the changes that eventually manifested themselves in eighteenth-century European society. Today the differences between nonindustrial and industrial societies are described as differences between tradition and modernity. Societies making the transition from traditional to modern practices in education, government, communication systems, and health care, are undergoing modernization.

Third World nations that are modernizing cannot get much guidance from the experiences of nations that industrialized in the eighteenth century. One important difference is that industrialization in countries like England was not purposely pursued; indeed, it was largely unanticipated. Modernization, on the other hand, is often consciously pursued through policies designed to encourage economic growth and development.

The situation facing most developing nations has been expressed clearly by Guy Hunter (1969). Developing nations have great difficulties in modernizing because they may have eighteenth century economies and social structures but they are surrounded by a twentieth century world. They must compete with the developed nations to gain access to markets for their products and to improve the technical capabilities of their industry. Economic resources for industrial growth compete with the needs of an expanding population for education and basic human services. Agriculture must be modernized to provide employment and raise the in-

comes of farmers, whose purchasing power supports the consumer goods industries. The temptation to borrow technology and modern institutions (like a Western educational system) from industrialized societies can produce failure because they do not fit in with established social and cultural patterns.

The difficulties facing modernizing nations can be better understood if we try to distinguish the several different meanings of modernity. Portes (1973) notes that the term modernity, as it has been used by social scientists, has three dimensions: structural, cultural, and psychological.

Structural Modernity

Degree of urbanization, literacy, population characteristics, and occupational, kinship, tribal, and political systems are some of the structural dimensions of modernity. They reflect patterns of social relationships among groups in society that influence economic life and peoples' access to important resources, such as jobs and education.

Third World nations face several structural problems in their quest for modernization:

First, strong kinship or tribal bonds inhibit the development of a central government with enough authority to enforce national policy. Strong kinship systems also can hamper market transactions that transcend kinship, class, tribal, and religious lines.

Next are the problems associated with developing a committed labor force, which is essential for modernization. Such a labor force depends on a complex occupational structure composed of many specialized roles, high levels of literacy among those who must learn to fill new occupational roles, and an educational system that prepares workers for their new roles.

Modernization is also hampered by the lack of capital resources beyond those necessary for satisfying peoples' primary needs for food and shelter. **Capital resources** can be devoted to food production, housing, education, health care, new energy sources, roads, and communication systems.

Fourth, the size, growth rate, and composition of the population in modernizing societies put an especially heavy burden on available resources. Most Third World countries will double their popula-

---

* Third World nations are those that emerged from colonial status as new nations following World War II.

Countries undergoing modernization make a major effort to improve the literacy and educational levels of their citizens. Such efforts may proceed without similar efforts at industrialization. In this photo we see the use of closed-circuit television instruction in Niger, Africa.

tions by the year 2000, assuming continuation of present birthrates and greatly decreased mortality rates that have resulted from improved health care. The combination of high birthrates and lower death rates will provide large proportions of very young and very old citizens. The young and old, outside of the labor force, are dependent rather than productive members of society.

Finally, the modernizing nations must compete in a world dominated by a handful of highly developed nations. The world's 50 largest industrial firms in 1978 held over 50 percent of the world's manufacturing assets (Fortune, 1979). Anderson (1974) says the flow of foreign capital from developed nations into Third World nations exceeded $30 billion in 1970, and the rate of profits taken from these countries far surpasses the rate of profits earned within developed countries. For example, in 1974 Mobil Oil had foreign earnings of $654 million and domestic earnings of $258 million (Eitzen, 1980). The chances for economic development in a world dominated by such a concentration of economic power are poor indeed. If England had faced such an international economic environment in the eighteenth century, it would have taken far more than the Protestant ethic to industrialize its economy!

Cultural Modernity

The cultural values of modernity emphasize an individual's achieving a social position rather than having it ascribed at birth. Thus the most valued positions in modern societies are those associated with education and occupation. Competition for educational and occupational positions is based on **universalistic standards,** that is, standards that permit all people to compete without regard to social categories. More traditional societies ascribe positions to individuals on the basis of tribal ties, religion, ethnicity, sex or caste. Such ascription of position is based on **particularistic standards,** that

is, standards that automatically exclude certain people filling a position because of certain social identities.

Sociologists disagree about the importance of cultural values in distinguishing between traditional and modern societies. To what extent do the values of traditional societies inhibit individual economic activity and, as a result, economic growth? For example, it is sometimes held that societies with religious ideologies that stress rewards in the next world or in an afterlife may not realize as much economic growth because their members are not as strongly motivated to work for a better life in this world. Or, societies that put great value on the past through ancestor worship or traditional teachings will not engage in activities that are future or change oriented.

An alternative view is that cultural values, while they are important expressions of a society, are not fixed and immutable. Values, and the goals of social action that are based on those values, develop in adaptation to particular historical circumstances. Thus the goals selected by a society conform with existing values and with subjective estimates of what is to be gained or lost by its course of action. This is true of all societies. Values change slowly

Societies in the process of modernization often contain mixtures of traditional social and economic structures side by side with elements of urban-industrial life. Here we see the use of animal transportation in the midst of an urban center in the Middle East. The technological aspects of modernization often change much faster than the social and cultural structures of society.

and they restrain certain socioeconomic innovations, but *they do change.*

Undoubtedly, cultural modernity influences modernization. However, no society, no matter how "primitive" its economic life seems, should be viewed as devoid of economically relevant values or motives. As Belshaw (1965) has pointed out, the making of the simplest tool—a digging stick—in a primitive society is an act of capital investment for some future gain. In this, the toolmaker resembles the entrepreneur in advanced industrial society.

Psychological Modernity

The third dimension of modernity is perhaps the most controversial. Psychological modernity refers to personality characteristics like mental flexibility and a high need for achievement. A leading student of psychological modernity, Alex Inkeles (1969), has described some personal qualities of "modern man":

(1) openness to new experience, both with people and with new ways of doing things such as attempting to control births; (2) the assertion of increasing independence from the authority of traditional figures like parents and priests and a shift of allegiance to leaders of government, public affairs, trade unions, cooperatives, and the like; (3) belief in the efficacy of science and medicine, and a general abandonment of passivity and fatalism in the face of life's difficulties; (4) ambition for oneself and one's children to achieve high occupational and educational goals; . . . (p. 10)

In addition, says Inkeles, modern people value punctuality and planning and have a strong sense of civic responsibility.

Inkeles and Smith (1974) note that these personal qualities are felt to be essential for a modern nation that needs well-informed citizens willing to participate in national affairs and able to operate the political, administrative, and industrial organizations of a modern economy. According to this view psychological modernity is a necessary condition for national economic growth. Much of the controversy over psychological modernity concerns two questions: (1) can psychological modernity be measured in a variety of societies? (2) Is psychological modernity essential for economic development?

Research by Inkeles and Smith (1974) and Portes (1973) indicates that the idea of modern man, or psychological modernity, can be measured in a clear and consistent manner. People's beliefs about family relationships, perceptions of what is a "small" family, religious activities, knowledge and use of contraceptives, and occupational aspirations for their children are said to be indicators of modernity. Modernity has been measured in people in a variety of countries, including Argentina, Chile, Israel, Nigeria, Pakistan, India, Guatemala, Mexico, Brazil, and Turkey. (See also Kahl, 1968, and Schnaiberg, 1970).

However, some critics maintain that often what is being measured as modernity includes many different things, some of which may be unrelated to modernity. For example, are people who say that family ties and obligations are extremely important in their lives less modern (or more traditional) than those who place less emphasis on the family? Armer and Schnaiberg (1972) in particular suggest that the techniques used to measure modernity actually do not measure a single psychological entity, but several unrelated attitudes and beliefs about traditional and modern life style. Moreover, they suggest that the aspects of modernity that *are* measured may not be valid in all cultures.

Whether psychological modernity is required for economic development is a much more interesting and important question. It is theoretically interesting because it posits a relationship between certain psychological characteristics of a population and a nation's ability to develop economically. As a practical matter, if the theory is sound, it may be used to guide those nations that are trying to "engineer" their societies toward economic development.

There have been several objections to the modernity-development hypothesis. First, the hypothesis assumes that certain social-psychological characteristics in a population will "lead to" or "produce" economic development. Critics have pointed out that economic development requires structural changes in the labor force, in the availability of capital resources, in the educational system, and in the stratification system. They also suggest that it is naive to expect that substantial structural changes will be brought about by the mere presence of psychological modernity characteristics (Muraskin, 1974).

A second objection to the modernity-development hypothesis is that it contrasts traditional and modern societies as polar opposites. Gusfield (1967) has pointed to numerous misuses of the terms tradition and modernity and the tendency to oversimplify the distinction between them. One incorrect assumption is that traditional societies are homogeneous, hostile to social change, and static. According to Gusfield the concepts of tradition and modernity fail to account for the great variety of ways in which the two mix and blend together in different societies, such as India, Japan, and Indonesia.

Third, some critics state that the modernity-development hypothesis confuses cause and effect. Rather than being a factor that leads to economic development, psychological modernity is a consequence of that development. This position is taken most directly by Portes (1973):

Defining modernity as a positive force in the socioeconomic growth of developing countries may amount to an uncritical extrapolation of consequences into causes. There is a historical naivete in believing that if the psychological product of centuries of social and economic evolution can just be reproduced in an underdeveloped context, it will bring—by association—the structural arrangements that gave rise to it in the first place. (p. 33)

We may conclude from this brief review of modernization that, first, the experience of industrialization in Western Europe and later in the United States provides few guides for nations today seeking economic growth. Second, any single set of variables—economic, ideological, or psychological—fails to account for all of the factors involved in development. Third, emphasizing traditionalism as a barrier to economic development in Third World countries may not adequately reflect their openness to social change. Fourth and finally, future research in economic development must show a

greater sensitivity to the biases and value preferences hidden in theories of development that assume Western industrial society is the standard for other societies to follow.

ADVANCED INDUSTRIAL SOCIETY

The Industrial Revolution in Western Europe and the United States led to the emergence of a new economic role—that of the capitalist entrepreneur. **Entrepreneurs** were people who used capital, generally their own, to attract and combine the other **factors of production** (land, labor, and raw materials) to manufacture a product for the market.

The Industrial Revolution saw the development of many new and diversified industrial firms owned and managed by entrepreneurs. With time some firms became very large, especially those in the steel, railroad, and petroleum industries. The heads of these firms—men like Carnegie, Mellon, Rockefeller, and Ford—were either glorified as "captains of industry" or vilified as "robber barons."

In the late nineteenth and early twentieth centuries the economic life of industrialized societies, especially the United States, changed in significant ways. First, a few industrial and financial firms were growing so large that resources increasingly became concentrated in a few hands. Second, the industrial entrepreneur as the owner and operator of the firm was being replaced by joint-stock owners and nonowning managers. Third, the federal government's fiscal policies were beginning to shape the economy, increasing the ties between business and government. Today, as a modern, industrialized society, the United States is characterized by large economic enterprises, large government, and large unions.

Many questions have been raised about the meaning of these economic changes for the United States and other advanced industrial societies.

1. What accounts for the growth in size of corporations? Are large corporations more efficient than small ones, or is growth an end in itself?
2. What are the goals of large corporations? Do

they wish solely to maximize their profits, or do they try to contribute to the larger public interest as well?

3. What is the role of government in regulating business activity? What accounts for the increasing role of federal expenditures in the total economy?

4. Has the control of large corporations actually changed with the appearance of joint-stock ownership and management appointed by stockholders?

5. What has been the effect of the large corporation on the occupational structure and the nature of work itself? Is mobility more possible in a small or large enterprise economy?

6. What is the role of organized labor in an advanced industrial society? Has the power of the labor union kept pace with that of the large corporation? What are the goals of organized labor in the face of a rapidly changing industrial system and occupational structure?

7. Do workers lose control of their unions when unions become gigantic?

8. Do corporations control national policy in dealing with other nations?

9. Are large corporations responsible for poverty and unemployment and our apparent inability to reduce either?

We will address some of these questions in the remainder of this section. Other questions should serve as guides for examining future developments in our economic institutions.

The Modern Corporation

In the United States today there are thousands of corporations producing a wide variety of goods and services. The 500 largest industrial corporations in America are reviewed each year in a survey of business conducted by *Fortune* magazine.

THE GROWTH OF THE MODERN CORPORATION

Giant corporations (the Fortune 500) are of special importance because of their influence on the economic and political life of the country. The combined decisions of the giant corporations shape wages and prices and affect levels of employment and prosperity and the very nature of work and occupational structure. Consider the following facts about the growing concentration of economic resources.*

- In 1948, the 200 largest industrial corporations controlled 40 percent of all manufacturing assets in the country; in 1978 control extended to 60 percent. The top 500 corporations accounted for 75 percent of all assets.

- Some two dozen corporations provide 15 percent of all employment in manufacturing.

- Four corporations account for 22 percent of all expenditures for research and development, much of which is underwritten by the federal government. About 85 percent of all research and development expenditures were made by 384 firms.

- A little more than 1 percent of all the industrial firms in the United States employ 75 percent of all scientists and engineers working in industry.

- Ten firms received one-third of the total dollars expended for defense contracts by the government. One hundred firms received two-thirds of the total dollars expended for defense.

- The gross annual income of a single giant corporation like General Motors has regularly exceeded $20 billion for some time. Just how extraordinary this figure is is revealed by comparison with the total revenue of some states and many countries. It equals the amount of revenue going to three million small farms in the United States.

During the twentieth century, and especially since World War II, increasing economic power has been concentrated in a relatively small number of industrial corporations. Nonindustrial firms like banks and insurance companies also reveal a concentration of resources. Zeitlin (1970) has pointed out

*This information may be found in Donovan, 1970, chap. 3; Fitch and Oppenheimer, 1970b; Galbraith, 1967, chap. 7; Horowitz, 1967; Kaysen, 1959; Perrucci et al., 1966; Statistical Abstract of the United States, 1973, 1974, 1976, 1978.

that only 14 of the 13,775 commercial banks in the United States hold 24 percent of all deposits. The largest 100 commercial banks hold 46 percent of all deposits.

A second set of changes in the modern corporation has been the decline of the owner-entrepreneur and the rise of joint-stock companies run by managers. Ownership has been separated from control; those who own the corporation, the stockholders, do not participate in its operation.

Finally, federal expenditures have played an increasing role in the economy in general and in the growth of the largest corporations in particular. In 1929 federal expenditures accounted for about 2 percent of the total economic activity in the country, while today the figure approaches 10 percent (Galbraith, 1978). Many large corporations are heavily dependent on defense-related contracts. As of July 1982 the proposed defense budget for 1983 was more than $200 billion.

Also under consideration was the project to place 200 MX missiles among 4600 underground shelters connected by roads to shuttle the missiles and keep the enemy guessing as to their location. This system, which would be located in the Great Basin of Utah and Nevada, was estimated to cost between $70 and $100 billion. The project would require major American corporations to be involved in building miles of road, providing the 1.5 million tons of cement, 400,000 tons of steel, and a fleet of newly designed transporters for the missiles.

To summarize, (1) a small number of giant corporations dominate selected sectors of the economy; (2) giant corporations are run by people who do not own them; and (3) the growth of these corporations directly and indirectly depends on a high level of government expenditures in the total economy.

THE ROLE OF TECHNOLOGY IN CORPORATE GROWTH
John Kenneth Galbraith (1978), the noted economist, believes these generalizations are interrelated and can be traced to a set of common causes. Figure 13.1, based on Galbraith's thesis, illustrates why giant corporations have grown and why the federal

government is an active partner in this growth. The following paragraphs discuss the central ideas portrayed in this figure.

1. The appearance of the giant corporation as a new creature in the history of the human race was made possible by modern technology. High speed computers, automated production, advanced communications, and rapid transportation have made the giant corporation possible. Modern technology, in contrast to earlier forms, is distinguished by its complexity. **Complex technology** has two special features. First, the cost of technology for modern production systems is high, requiring extensive capital outlay. Second, the amount of time it takes to produce something, once a decision has been made to produce it, has increased. This period is often referred to as **lead time.**

2. Complex technology, which is a combination of high cost and long lead time, leads to a certain degree of inflexibility in the behavior of modern corporations. Once a corporation decides to produce a certain product, like a new plane or car model, it cannot readily shift its objectives. So much money has been invested in production technology that change is not economically feasible. Small corporations using less complex technology, that is, with less capital outlay and less long-term planning, can shift production objectives more readily.

3. Complex technology demands a *specialized workforce* with sufficient skills to use it and to coordinate the highly interdependent activities of the production process. Scientific and technical professionals, skilled workers, and managers are essential. The costs of competing for and maintaining such personnel are greater than the same costs for a more traditional labor force with lesser skills and training.

4. *A formalized organizational structure* and professional management are needed to effectively combine the technical and human functions of the modern corporation. Therefore, large organizations are characterized by an extreme division of labor and elaborate systems of communication, coordination, and control.

5. The modern corporation must do long-range planning to maximize predictability and control of

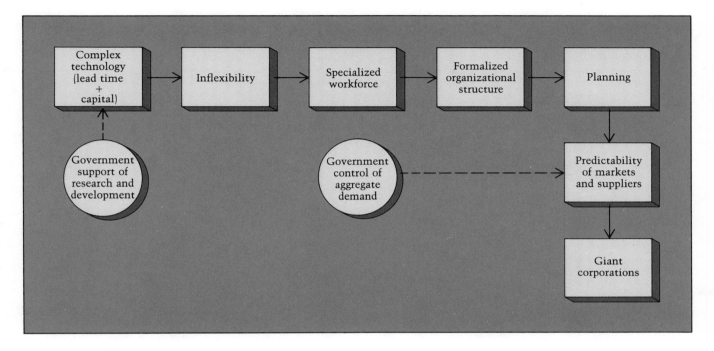

FIGURE 13.1   Growth and
Convergence of Economic Power
and Government Expenditures

its environment. The environment consists of suppliers, markets, regulatory agencies, and customers. The modern corporation will not make extensive capital outlays for technology and labor without assurance that it will be able to obtain the labor and materials needed for production. For example, General Motors will seek long-term agreements for steel or aluminum or labor at a certain price long before they actually produce a car.

6. Predictability or control over suppliers is increased if a corporation can absorb important suppliers as part of the corporation. This is known as superseding the market by **vertical integration.** For example, suppose a corporation needs chemicals in a certain quantity at a certain price for the manufacture of their products. To ensure availability they could buy a chemical plant and integrate it

with their corporation. Size can also be used to control a supplier. A steel manufacturer will be much more concerned about meeting orders at a price convenient to General Motors than it would be about meeting orders at a price convenient to American Teakettle Company.

7. Large corporations also need *predictability and control over consumers* of their products. This is achieved in two ways—by extensive expenditures for advertising and marketing and by government action to maintain high employment so that people have money to spend. Competition among giant corporations does not occur along price lines. There is very little price difference between a Ford or a Chevrolet of the same type. It is through advertising that large corporations compete for sales.

The federal government actively promotes mar-

The planning activities, coordination, and control of the modern corporation are made possible by the use of computers, with their capacity for storing and processing information. The complexity of new technology has highlighted the important role of persons with specialized scientific and technical knowledge—those that Galbraith calls the technostructure.

ket control by making sure that consumers will have enough money to buy products. It is the government that maintains a high level of consumer buying, or **aggregate demand,** for goods and services. The fiscal and monetary policies of the government can produce economic growth, high employment, high wages, and easy availability of credit for cars, homes, and other consumer items. In some cases, such as defense procurements, the federal government is the customer. For the corporation, defense contracts represent the ultimate in control over the market because the government has agreed to purchase things like planes or missiles before they are produced.

8. Finally, the complex technology that sustains the productive capacity of the modern corporation is paid for by federal expenditures for **research and development** (R&D). Support for R&D comes mainly through aerospace and defense expenditures. It is assumed that technological developments in these areas will find their way into nonmilitary production. For example, computers, which are so essential to operation of the modern corporation were first developed for military weapons systems.

THE CONSEQUENCES OF OLIGOPOLY CONTROL

Galbraith's theory suggests that complex technology inevitably leads to giant corporations and to increased corporate control over respective markets. This results in a few large corporations having most of the sales in a particular market, with many other smaller firms competing for the remainder of market sales. This form of market domination is called **oligopoly control.** The case of a single firm dominating a market is called **monopoly control.**

Some economists view monopoly or oligopoly control as detrimental to the consumer. Absence of competition allows oligopolies and monopolies to exploit their market advantage by increasing prices. The consumer, without an alternative product to purchase at a lower cost, must buy at available prices or forego the purchase. Fifty years ago there were about a dozen automobile companies. This resulted in greater competition and a greater range of automotive products from which consumers could choose. Today there are only three

U.S. auto firms and one of them has only a small part of the auto market.

Galbraith does not feel that oligopoly control by corporations is necessarily bad. He believes that giant corporations with oligopoly control are, in fact, more efficient and more interested in securing a stable profit than in exploiting their advantage and maximizing profits. Those who control the modern corporation are, according to Galbraith, not the stockholders or the board of directors but what he labels the **technostructure**—those within the corporation who have specialized scientific and technical knowledge on which the modern corporation depends.

The technostructure does not seek to maximize profits but to provide a stable, secure rate of return on investment. This lower-return-at-lower risk strategy allows the technostructure to provide sufficient dividends and growth to satisfy stockholders. It also allows the corporation to finance new growth from internal savings rather than borrowing from financial institutions. These institutions will extend credit but will also seek some degree of control over corporate decisions.

Above all, the technostructure resists all threats to its autonomy. Yet, despite its power and autonomy, the technostructure does not act against the public interest, according to Galbraith. The technostructure is restrained by its own concerns for career security and by its links with the larger educational and scientific communities that promote corporate social responsibility.

Many social scientists recognize that there is a growing concentration of economic power in a small number of corporations. Many also agree with Galbraith about the effectiveness of giant corporations and the role they play in maintaining a strong economy. However, some question who really controls the modern corporation and whether corporations seek to maximize profits.

WHO CONTROLS THE CORPORATION?

The question of who controls modern corporations is of great importance because of their immense economic and political power. In the early part of the twentieth century most corporations were owned and run by individual entrepreneurs or families. Henry Ford, along with his family, owned and managed the Ford Motor Company where he introduced mass production techniques to create a giant corporation. However, the role of the individual owner-manager was rapidly changing.

Two economists, Adolph Berle and Gardener Means (1940) were among the first to observe the separation of ownership and control of corporations. In 1929 about 44 percent of the 200 largest industrial corporations were classified as management controlled, a sharp increase from the handful of such corporations around 1900. The trend continued, and in 1963 the proportion of management-controlled firms reached 84 percent among the top 200 firms and 70 percent among the next 300 largest firms (Larner, 1970a).

Many social scientists, including Galbraith, accepted these findings as evidence that the separation of ownership and control of the large corporations was an accomplished fact. However, Zeitlin (1974) has reexamined the Berle and Means hypothesis and concludes that there is considerable evidence that those who own the corporation, that is, large stockholders, *do* control the corporation. He suggests that one does not have to own a majority of a company's stock to have working control of a corporation. Working control can be realized by individuals and families who own only 10 percent of a corporation's voting stock. Also, in some cases where the stock of a company is widely dispersed among many small shareholders, an individual or family owning less than 5 percent of the voting stock can have effective control. This means that many corporations classified as management controlled by Berle and Means, because no one owned a majority of the stock, could still be owner-controlled companies.

Other analysts have also questioned the Berle and Means hypothesis. Fitch and Oppenheimer (1970a) have pointed out how financial institutions can gain control of stock in corporations in return for extending loans. It works like this: corporations turn to the large Wall Street banks, like Morgan Guaranty Trust, Chase Manhattan Bank, or First National Bank, for the long-term capital they need to finance their operations. In return for loans that run into millions of dollars, the banks receive interest on the long-term debt. They are also offered the opportunity to purchase stock in the corporation, with the number of shares often reaching a level of working control, that is, 5 percent or more of the voting stock. Members of the financial institution extending the loan may be appointed as members of the board of directors of the corporation seeking the loan (Patman Committee, 1970). Banks are able to attach certain conditions to the loan that restrict the corporation's freedom to act, thereby giving the banks a measure of control over the borrower (Fitch and Oppenheimer, 1970a).

In addition, the work of Lundberg (1969), who has studied the wealthiest families in America, indicates that many of America's wealthiest families continue to dominate large corporations. Control may be exercised indirectly by influencing the selection of top management or directly by having family members sit on a corporation's board of directors. The wealthy may also exercise hidden stock ownership through trusts, foundations, or banks that are not required to report "beneficial owners" of a stock (the actual owners) but only those "nominated" as owners.

The power of upper-class families extends beyond the control of the nation's largest corporations. Some analysts like G. William Domhoff (1967), who has written extensively on America's upper class, suggest that the upper class controls far more than the corporate economy. More important, they control the foundations (Ford, Rockefeller, Carnegie, Danforth, and Lilly, among others), the opinion-shaping institutions (elite universities, the mass media, influential private associations like the Council on Foreign Relations), and key agencies of government (for example, the diplomatic corps and regulatory agencies). In short, not only is there no separation of ownership from control in the large corporations, but also the same families that own and control the corporations control other organizations that should be working in the public interest.

Thus there is evidence that individuals or groups that own large blocks of a corporation's stock are still in a position to control the corporation. This may mean that the managers of corporations, those that Galbraith called the technostructure, will have interests that are the same as the dominant stockholders, namely to maximize profits. As we noted, Galbraith hypothesized that the technostructure seeks only secure profits and long-term growth rather than maximum profits. This is reassuring because it suggests that giant corporations are not going to exploit their great power at the expense of the public interest.

Research by Larner (1970b) tests Galbraith's hypothesis about managerial behavior in large corporations. According to Larner if Galbraith is correct, we should expect to find "(1) profit rates of management-controlled corporations are smaller than those of owner-controlled corporations and (2) the fluctuations of profit rates are smaller for management-controlled corporations than for owner-controlled corporations" (p. 255).

Larner compared 128 management-controlled firms with 59 owner-controlled from among the top 500 nonfinancial corporations in the United States. He found little appreciable difference between the two groups in the rate of profits. Contrary to Galbraith's expectations, the management-controlled and owner-controlled firms are equally profit oriented.

In the same study Larner also examined Galbraith's contention that management is less interested in profits than in stable growth. If this view is valid the dollar amount of an executive's compensation (salary, bonuses, and stock options) should be more closely related to the size and growth of a firm than to its profitability. Larner's examination of the compensation received by 93 executives indicates that a corporation's profitability is a greater determinant of that compensation than is size and growth. Thus corporate management has a personal financial interest in profits realized by the corporations they manage. Such interests would make it hard for managers not to maximize profits when given the opportunity to do so.

The information presented in this section on the growth and power of the modern corporation suggests the following view of the possible consequences of corporate power. Giant corporations may be necessary, as suggested by Galbraith, because the demands of modern technology require cor-

porations of great size. The power of corporations, which is based on their extensive resources, can be used solely to benefit the corporation or to benefit the society at large (see the At Issue section of this chapter). The course that a corporation chooses will not be based on the good intentions of management or owners but on the existence of other forms of institutional power that can control corporate power.

Economic institutions will be unable to pursue their self-interest to the exclusion of the public interest if power and influence within the economic sphere are dispersed among many economic organizations and interests. For example, banks exist by lending money and are interested in obtaining high rates of interest on loans. Corporations that must borrow money from banks are interested in loans at low interest rates. As long as corporations and banks are in competition, it is easier for political institutions, such as the government, to offset the power of economic institutions and make decisions that benefit the public in general.

However, if power and influence are concentrated in a few organizations in any institutional sphere, those organizations are more likely to extend their influence into other institutional spheres. Thus the concentration of great economic power in the hands of relatively few corporations or wealthy families or financial institutions enables them to influence government actions to their own advantage.

Conglomerates and Multinational Corporations

In the past decade a particular kind of giant corporation has emerged. **Conglomerate** corporations, formed by the merger or acquisition of smaller firms, are made up of a number of diverse enterprises. International Telephone and Telegraph, a giant telecommunications corporation, is now a conglomerate that owns bakeries (Hostess Cup Cakes and Wonder Bread), a car rental firm (Avis), insurance companies, and a major hotel chain (Sheraton Hotels). Gulf and Western Industries started more than 20 years ago as a midwestern manufacturing corporation with 500 employees. Today it grows sugar in the Dominican Republic, produces movies (Paramount Pictures), owns the Madison Square

Garden in New York City, publishes books (Simon & Schuster), makes cigars, and in addition has holdings in the manufacture of clothing, rolled steel, and wood pulp.

The corporate activities that produce conglomerates have been steadily increasing. The Senate Antitrust Subcommittee reported that in 1973 the total value of conglomerate mergers and acquisitions was $1.5 billion. In 1978 it rose to $5 billion, and in 1980 it was around $44.3 billion. Estimates for 1982 are almost double this amount, indicating that mergers are not simply small firms being absorbed by large firms but giant firms taking over other giant firms. This pattern is seen in the recent activity of a number of large corporations competing to take over Conoco, America's ninth largest oil company.

Many of these conglomerates have become **multinational corporations,** or firms based in one country but that control business corporations based in several other countries. According to *Fortune* (1979) the world's 50 largest industrial corporations in 1978 included 21 U.S. companies. The U.S. companies were seven of the top 10 largest corporations in the world. Many U.S. multinationals conduct business in other countries because of lower wages for workers, easier access to raw materials, or more favorable environmental regulations and tax structures.

The consequences of these global corporations for the political and economic structure of nations is still a matter of speculation. One view is that multinationals will be a creative force for revitalizing national economies and establishing more liberal trade policies among nations (Macrae, 1979). There is also the possibility that they will provide a more stable basis of world order among nations than the alliances, treaties, mutual defense pacts, and international courts that have so notably failed. Global corporations will encourage nations to be less nationalistic and fearful of other nations when they are bound together in corporate groups with interests and loyalties that cross their borders. As Tannenbaum (1979) put it, "The day may well come when the majority of people in all nations will have their functional loyalties to one or more supra-national corporate bodies. They may well become conscious of basic commitments, values and interests unrelated to the state or the nation" p. 185.

It has become apparent that multinational corporations can operate outside national interests. In August 1982 President Reagan called upon the United States' European allies to abrogate their agreements with the Soviet Union to build a gas pipeline from Russia to Western Europe. It was believed that the pipeline, although benefitting Western nations in need of a stable gas supply, was against U.S. interests. The French government, among others, refused and a U.S. multinational firm located in France followed through its plans to deliver certain components for the pipeline to Russia. The firm claimed that because they were French based, they were not bound to follow policies set for U.S.-based firms.

A less optimistic view sees the global corporation leading the way to uncontrolled exploitation of labor in less-developed countries, taking advantage of the very low wages and limited benefits provided to workers (Magdoff, 1976). At the same time workers in the developed countries will also be hurt by the "runaway shops" that deprive them of jobs when firms shut down plants to move to a cheaper labor supply (Stillman, 1978).

There is also evidence that multinational corporations interfere in the internal affairs of other nations (Breckenfeld, 1976). International Telephone and Telegraph used its power to help overthrow Salvadore Allende, the democratically elected president of Chile, because they felt his policies were not in the corporation's best interests. United Brands Fruit Company paid $1.25 million in bribes to officials in Honduras to get them to reduce export taxes on bananas. Between 1970 and 1975 Lockheed Corporation paid $202 million in bribes to foreign government officials and political parties to promote sales in their countries.

Barnet and Muller (1974), in their book on multinationals, have suggested that the multinational corporation probably contributes to global poverty, unemployment, and inequality by pursuing economic policies that are contrary to the interests and needs of poor nations.

The present position and future world impact of multinational corporations is a topic of broad significance. The shape of the economic institution in the twenty-first century will undoubtedly continue to bear the mark of giant global corporations.

Work and Occupations

The effect of technological change on the nature of work in advanced industrial societies has been a concern since the beginning of industrialization. The use of the machine and new techniques of production, such as the division of labor into its smallest component activities, raised questions about the effect of repetitive, monotonous work on the worker's body and mind. Consider the following statements made more than 100 years ago by Adam Smith and by Karl Marx and Friedrich Engels (quoted in Friedman, 1955) who seem to express the same concerns despite their differences in political philosophy.

From Adam Smith:

The man whose whole life is spent in performing a few simple operations, of which the effects are perhaps always the same, or very nearly the same, has no occasion to exert his understanding or to exercise his invention in finding out expedients for removing difficulties which never occur. He naturally loses, therefore, the habit of such exertions, and generally becomes as stupid and ignorant as it is possible for a human creature to become. (p. 129)

From Marx and Engels:

Owing to the extensive use of machinery and to division of labor, the work of the proletarians has lost all individual character, and consequently, all charm for the workman. He becomes an appendage of the machine, and it is only the most simple, most monotonous, and most easily acquired knack, that is required of him. (p. 130)

The nature of work and the composition of the occupational structure have changed very dramatically in advanced industrial societies. The agricultural labor force has declined because of mechanized farming. Automated and mechanized production systems in industry have reduced the need for unskilled blue-collar workers. This has resulted in persistently higher rates of unemployment for those without skills and training.

In the United States the introduction of machine technology stimulated the development of a literature by writers like Henry Thoreau, Nathaniel Hawthorne, Ralph Waldo Emerson, Mark Twain, and Herman Melville that has since been characterized as the "pastoral tradition." In his excellent book on the pastoralists Leo Marx (1964) presents an absorbing account of the United States' response to the machine in the nineteenth century, including the literary tradition of social criticism that it spawned. The introduction of the machine was greeted with hope, optimism, and naivete by leading industrialists, educators, and political leaders. None seemed to consider the social consequences of new technology. As Marx points out, "the very notion of 'technology' as an agent of change scarcely existed" (p. 149). In addition, the new technology was seen as a force for good, which would overcome the evils of the factory system as it existed in eighteenth-century England. Marx takes the views of Thomas Jefferson, a student of the Enlightenment, as a symbol of this spirit of hope:

From Jefferson's perspective, the machine is a token of that liberation of the human spirit to be realized by the young American Republic; the factory system, on the other hand, is but feudal oppression in a slightly modified form. Once the machine is moved from the dark, crowded, grimy cities of Europe, he assumes that it will blend harmoniously into the open countryside of his native land. He envisages it turning millwheels, moving ships up rivers, and all in all, helping to transform a wilderness into a society of the middle landscape. At bottom, it is the intensity of his belief in the land, as a locus of both economic and moral values, which prevents him from seeing what the machine portends for America. (p. 150)

Most early comments on the effects of the new machine technology were overly pessimistic or optimistic. Critics of the machine were only partly correct in predicting that machine technology would downgrade the skill level of workers. Complex machine technology has, in fact, downgraded some jobs while increasing the need for more highly skilled workers in other jobs.

CHANGING OCCUPATIONAL STRUCTURE

Table 13.1 shows the distribution of the labor force among occupational groupings for each decade be-

tween 1900 and 1980. Several patterns are clear. White-collar occupations steadily expanded from 17.6 percent of the labor force in 1900 to 52.2 percent in 1980. Skilled manual work showed a small increase over this period, and service work expanded from 9.1 percent to 13.3 percent. Farm work, on the other hand, declined sharply from 37.5 percent in 1900 to less than 3 percent in 1980.

The general trend is repeated in the occupational categories within each group. The higher skill-higher education occupations show proportionate increases over time while lower skill-lower education occupations show a decline. For example, among white-collar occupations, professional, and technical and clerical positions grew more rapidly than lower level sales positions. Similarly, among manual occupations, the number of skilled positions increased while unskilled positions declined.

This pattern of change in the occupational structure reflects the increased use of mechanized and automated production systems. The sharp decline in farming is the result of mechanization, which allows fewer farmers to produce more food. It is also the result of the growth of corporate farms, sometimes referred to as **agribusiness**, which dominate farming in much the same way as giant corporations dominate manufacturing. Automated, mechanized production in industry has reduced the need for unskilled workers, since productivity can be maintained and even increased with fewer workers.

The changing occupational structure also has given rise to persistent forms of unemployment in the United States. Figure 13.2 shows many fluctuations in the unemployment rate* between 1940 and 1982. The general pattern of unemployment has almost always been above the 4 percent level,

*An unemployment rate tells you the percentage of persons in the labor force who are without employment. Being in the labor force means that you are over 16 years of age and have been actively looking for work. Thus in 1951 there were about 62 million persons in the labor force. An unemployment rate of 3.3 percent means that about 2 million persons are unemployed. In 1975 the labor force grew to about 89 million; an unemployment rate of 8.4 percent means that about 7½ million persons are seeking work but cannot find it. The annual average rate of unemployment will generally be an underestimate of the true rate for a variety of reasons (Leggett and Cervinka, 1972).

TABLE 13.1   Major Occupation Group of Experienced Labor Force for the United States, 1900 to 1980 (percent distribution)

MAJOR OCCUPATION GROUP	BOTH SEXES								
	1900	1910	1920	1930	1940	1950	1960	1970	1980
Total	100.0	100.0	100.0	100.0	100.0	100.0	100.0	100.0	100.0
White Collar	17.6	21.4	25.0	29.4	31.1	36.6	42.2	48.7	52.2
Professional, technical, and kindred workers	4.3	4.7	5.4	6.8	7.5	8.6	11.4	14.9	16.0
Managers, officials, proprietors, except farm	5.9	6.6	6.6	7.4	7.3	8.7	8.5	8.5	11.2
Clerical and kindred workers	3.0	5.3	8.0	8.9	9.6	12.3	14.9	17.9	18.6
Sales workers	4.5	4.7	4.9	6.3	6.7	7.0	7.4	7.3	6.3
Service	9.1	9.6	7.9	9.8	11.7	10.5	11.8	12.6	13.3
Private household workers	5.4	5.0	3.3	4.1	4.7	2.6	2.8	1.5	1.1
Other service workers	3.6	4.6	4.5	5.7	7.1	7.9	8.9	11.1	12.2
Manual	35.8	38.2	40.2	39.6	39.8	41.1	39.7	35.6	31.7
Craftsmen, foremen, and kindred workers	10.6	11.6	13.0	12.8	12.0	14.2	14.3	18.0	12.9
Operatives and kindred workers	12.8	14.6	15.6	15.8	18.4	20.4	19.9	17.4	10.6
Laborers, except farm and mine	12.5	12.0	11.6	11.0	9.4	6.6	5.5	4.4	4.6
Farm	37.5	30.9	27.0	21.2	17.4	11.8	6.3	3.1	2.7
Farmers and farm managers	19.9	16.5	15.3	12.4	10.4	7.4	3.9	1.8	1.5
Farm laborers and foremen	17.7	14.4	11.7	8.8	7.0	4.4	2.4	1.3	1.2

SOURCE: 1900–1950, U.S. Bureau of the Census. *Historical statistics of the United States, colonial times to 1957.* Washington: Government Printing Office, 1960, Table D 72–122, p. 74; 1960, U.S. Bureau of the Census. *U.S. census of population: 1960, general social and economic characteristics, U.S. summary.* Washington: Government Printing Office. Final Report PC(1)-1C. U.S. Census of population: 1970, general social and economic characteristics. Data for 1980 were obtained from Correct Population Reports, "Population Profile of the United States: 1980," Series P-20, No. 363, p. 36.

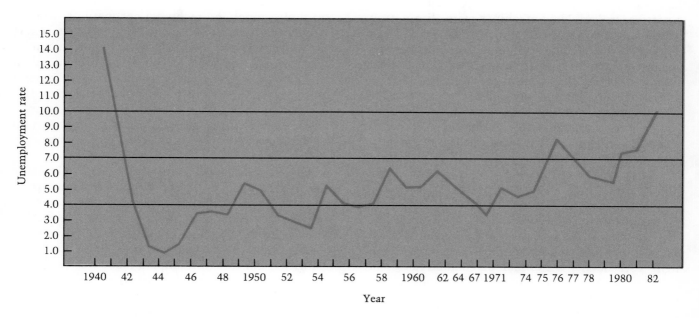

FIGURE 13.2   Unemployment
Rates, 1940–1982

with a steady increase in the last decade. In 1982 about 11 million workers were unemployed (10.3 percent of the labor force), with the rate being much higher for black males (18 percent) and black teenagers (45 percent). The rising unemployment rate may be related to the growing size of corporations and their greater use of labor-saving technology, as well as general economic conditions. Ginzberg (1979) reports that economic growth does not always result in expansion of jobs, especially good jobs, and that small rather than large firms generate a larger proportion of new jobs.

Many economists in the United States consider an unemployment rate of 3 to 4 percent to be "full employment." This means that although there are still millions of people unemployed, the reasons for their unemployment are so varied that they do not reflect a declining economy. In fact, even in a period of economic expansion it might not be possible to move below a 3 percent rate of unemployment.

The pace of industrial automation and mechanization increased in the mid-1950s. Lower skilled workers were displaced by machines, but the problem was not the elimination of a *particular* job in a *particular* firm. New machines were eliminating whole classes of jobs in entire industries. Thus workers displaced by technology in coal mining or automobile and textile manufacturing had little chance to be reabsorbed into the labor force while doing the same kind of work. The displaced workers were those with few skills and little education. The new jobs created by technology required both training and education. As a result the rate of unemployment may continue to be high, despite other effects on the economy.

WORKING WOMEN

A significant trend in advanced industrial societies, and in modernizing societies as well, is the increasing participation of women in the labor force. Highlight 13.1 details a number of characteristics of working women today. In 1920 about one out of five members of the workforce in the United States were women; in 1981 more than two out of five workers (43 percent) were women (U.S. Department of Labor, 1975). In addition, the working

woman today is distinctly different from her earlier counterpart. In 1920 the average working woman was in her mid-twenties, single, and employed as a clerk or factory worker. Today the average working woman is about 36 and, although employed in a wider variety of occupations, is concentrated in only a few (See Highlight 13.1). About 60 percent of today's women workers are married, and many of them have children. Of the 46 million women workers in 1981, 17 million were working mothers with children under 18 years of age; 7.5 million of these were mothers of children under six years of age (*Monthly Labor Review*, May, 1981).

A majority of women who work do so because of economic need. More than one-half of women workers are heads of households or are married to men who earn less than $7000 annually (1979). Nevertheless, women workers earn considerably less than men workers. For example, in 1980 the median earnings for men and women were $19,172 and $11,590, respectively. Part of the reason for these differences may be a concentration of women in certain low-wage occupations. Women are most frequently employed in clerical jobs. Even when the same proportions of men and women are found in professional and technical occupations, women are found to hold the lower paying jobs as teachers and nurses while men occupy the more lucrative professional positions. Finally, men earn more than women even when they are in the same general occupations and have had similar education. Despite their major role in the labor force, women still face discrimination in gaining entry to certain occupations and obtaining equal pay in the same jobs as men.

The problems facing nonworking women in many industrial societies is receiving increasing attention. The full-time homemaker has always worked at home without pay, making it possible for her spouse to be available for full-time paid work at lower wages than would be needed to support a family if her full-time unpaid labor was not available. The full-time homemaker is economically dependent on her spouse's success as a worker and ability to stay alive and healthy. The homemaker receives no credit for her years of unpaid work, and in her old age she may be totally dependent on her

HIGHLIGHT 13.1
Women Workers

WHERE WOMEN WORK, 1980

	% of all Women Workers
White Collar Workers	66
Professional & Technical	17
Managers & Administrators	7
Sales Workers	7
Clerical Workers	35
Blue Collar Workers	14
Craft & Kindred Workers	2
Operatives, Except transport	10
Operatives, Transport	1
Non-farm Laborers	1
Service Workers	19
Private Household	2
Service Workers	17
Farm Workers	1
Total	100%

EMPLOYED PERSONS BY SELECTED DETAILED OCCUPATIONS AND SEX, 1980

	Total Employed (in millions)	% of Each Job Held by Women
Secretaries	3.9	99.1%
Household Workers	1.0	97.5
Typists	1.0	96.9
Reg. Nurses	1.3	96.5
Bookkeeper	1.9	90.5
Nursing Aides	1.1	87.5
Cashiers	1.6	86.6
Elem. Teachers	1.4	83.7
Retail Clerks	2.3	71.1
Engineers	1.4	4.0

MARITAL STATUS OF WOMEN WORKERS, 1979

	Percent
Never married	26
Widowed, divorced or separated	19
Married-Husband's income Under $7,000	9
Married-Husband's income $7,000-$10,000	7
Married-Husband's income $10,000-$15,000	13
Married-Husband's income $15,000 and over	26
Total	100

PERCENT UNEMPLOYMENT BY SEX AND RACE, 1981

	Average 1981	Dec. 1981
Overall Rate	7.6	8.9
Males	7.4	8.1
Females	7.9	8.6
White Males	6.5	8.1
White Females	6.9	7.5
Minority Males	14.3	16.8
Minority Females	14.4	15.3
White Males 16–19	17.9	20.7
White females 16–19	16.3	17.6
Minority Males 16–19	38.3	37.6
Minority Females 16–19	38.6	41.8

SOURCE: Bureau of Labor Statistics, *Special Labor Force Report 244*, April 1981.

husband's social security benefits. The fact is that women tend to live longer than their spouses and are often without adequate financial resources. Andre (1981) reports that more than 60 percent of widows over age 65 are living on incomes below the government's official poverty line. Also, many women who choose to work parttime in order to supplement family income and still meet homemaker responsibilities find themselves discriminated against when it comes to retirement. Because they are parttime, or not in continuous employment, they are denied participation in pension programs.

Both working and nonworking women have experienced inequitable treatment in industrial societies. It is still assumed that women are primarily homeworkers and fully provided for by spouses. Such assumptions make no sense in an age when large numbers of women work out of necessity and are without a spouse because of divorce and greater longevity.

Labor Relations

The advances of industrialization and the growth of corporate capitalism in the United States has been marked by a history of struggles to establish organizations that would have the right to bargain collectively on behalf of workers. In the latter part of the nineteenth century and the early twentieth century, workers and management engaged in virtual warfare. There were numerous strikes, lockouts, incidents of industrial sabotage, strike breaking and intimidation by hired thugs, and firing of prounion workers (Kornblue, 1964; Perlman, 1937).

By 1920 the right to organize and bargain collectively seemed well established. Union membership reached five million. Although membership dropped sharply during the Depression, union strength was reestablished by 1940. Organized labor joined management and government in shaping a body of rules governing the power relations between the groups and their respective rights and obligations. Indeed, the power of organized labor was so well established that some observers believed it coequal with that of the corporation and the state, the three groups

forming a triumvirate that counterbalanced each other in the service of the public welfare (Galbraith, 1956).

Labor's role in relation to the corporation, the state, the workers, and the larger society varies considerably in industrialized societies. Kerr and his colleagues (1960) maintain that organized labor in the United States in recent decades has been moderately reformist in ideology and action. Unions have been primarily concerned with wage and benefit programs and conditions of employment. Union leaders pay much less attention to questions of control of the workplace or to the conditions of life in the larger society.

Moore (1965) has outlined what he considers the main objectives of labor unions in the United States:

1. Wage and job security for union members. Security can be achieved through control over who may enter an occupation, as in the case of apprenticeship programs. These controls are employed primarily in craft unions composed of skilled workers who protect themselves against an oversupply of labor that would depress wages. Wage and job security can also be secured by strikes against a plant or industry or boycotts against a product. Picketing and boycotting are practiced to dissuade other workers from taking jobs vacated by the strikers or to discourage consumers from buying particular products. In both cases the objective is to bring economic pressure to bear on management to recognize the union as a bargaining agent for workers or, if that recognition already exists, to obtain favorable wage-benefit contracts.

2. Fringe benefit programs. These objectives normally involve negotiations between labor and management over health plans, retirement programs, unemployment benefits, sick leave pay, and recreational programs.

3. Control of working conditions. Labor usually maintains its right to establish a procedure whereby workers can express dissatisfaction with the conditions of their employment. The grievance procedure or committee protects workers from having to complain directly to their supervisors, which might negatively affect their employment, and also offers them an opportunity to express any griev-

*The advance of industrialization
brought with it many bloody
conflicts over workers' rights to
organize, strike, and bargain
collectively. Here we see a
confrontation between police and
strikers near the Electric Auto-Lite
plant in Toledo, Ohio, in 1934.
Seven hundred Ohio National
Guardsmen were called out to
control 3,000 strikers at the plant.*

ances they may have against their supervisors. More ambitious union committees might seek the right to consult on or formally participate in decisions related to production itself or changes in plant activities. This form of union activity is resisted more vigorously by management as a serious infringement of the traditional rights of ownership and management.

The role of organized labor would seem to be at a critical point in its historical development in the United States. Labor's hard-fought battles have established its place in the corridors of power, and it has won significant wage and security benefits for workers. Today organized labor seems to be moving toward more conservative, conciliatory, and peaceful relations with corporate management. A decline in economic growth and increasing unemployment may change this conservative trend.

Despite its past successes labor's strength seems to have peaked and now to be in decline. As shown in Table 13.2 total union membership from 1956 to 1978 grew by about two million to almost 20 million members. However, in that period there was a decline in the proportion of the labor force in unions. This clearly reflects the changing character of the occupational structure. The great expansion has come in white-collar occupations, especially those that are traditionally nonunion. Thus since about 1968 union membership in numbers and in proportion of labor force has not substantially increased. However, Reading 13.2 points to the potential of unionization among white-collar workers, especially professionals. Such a development would have a very significant impact on U.S. corporations and the labor movement.

The effectiveness of labor unions in obtaining wage settlements favorable to union members may be more apparent than real. Inflation in recent years may have offset wage gains achieved by labor. For example, Table 13.3 shows substantial increases in absolute dollars in the average weekly take-home pay of employees in manufacturing. However, when we compare take-home pay in current inflated dollars and in 1967 dollars, we see little increase since about 1965. This means that wage increases have just about kept pace with the increasing cost of living. Still, maintaining wages at the same level

as inflation may be an important accomplishment of unions. It is unlikely that companies would have voluntarily provided wage increases tied to inflation without union pressure.

What the American labor movement will do in the face of this erosion of strength is not clear. Possibly, leaders will turn to more radical goals than wage and benefit contracts. Some of these goals, which are already being pursued by worker organizations in other countries, are (1) the creation of production teams on the assembly line to work on a single product rather than to repeat a single operation; (2) job enlargement, job enrichment, or job rotation, all of which are techniques designed to make the tasks of production workers more challenging; and (3) changes in the structure of authority and decision making that give workers responsibility for decisions traditionally reserved for management. Examples of structural changes include the workers' collectives in Yugoslavia, participative management in Denmark, workers' councils in Poland, and shop-floor democracy in England.* (See Chapter 9 for a fuller discussion of some of these changes.)

An added problem facing American labor is the serious decline in the country's economic growth and the growing competition from foreign corporations. The plight of the automobile industry in the face of the challenge of car imports, especially from Japan, is a special instance of a broader problem. American industry is less productive, has large amounts of unused productive capacity, invests less in newer, modernized plants, and has rising unemployment. As noted earlier, many industries have tried to solve their problems by searching for cheaper sources of industrial labor in other countries or moving plants from unionized regions of the United States (New England, the Midwest) to nonunion areas where workers can be paid lower wage rates.

Such economic problems are likely to provoke greater labor-management conflict over wage and security issues. Management will use the eco-

---

*Note, however, that European unions are traditionally class based and have been more progressive and/or radical in their programs than American unions.

TABLE 13.2   Labor Union Membership, 1958–1978

	1958	1960	1962	1964	1966	1968	1970	1972	1974	1976	1978
Total union membership (in millions)	17.0	17.1	16.6	16.8	17.9	18.9	19.4	19.4	20.2	19.6	20.2
Percentage of civilian labor force	24.2	23.6	22.6	22.2	22.7	23.0	22.6	21.8	21.7	20.3	19.7

SOURCE: Directory of National Unions and Employee Associations, 1979 U.S. Department of Labor Bulletin 2079, Sept. 1980, p. 58.

nomic crisis to get more favorable wage contracts, to defeat unionization efforts, and to obtain anti-labor legislation. On the other hand, labor militancy and increased class consciousness among workers is likely to characterize their relationships with management.

It is also possible that current economic crisis will produce a more unified and broadly based working class in the United States. In contrast to the European labor movement, the American labor movement has been more conservative and has exerted its influence within the traditional two-party political system. In the face of greater threats from corporations labor could seek to increase its efforts to bring the poor, Blacks, Puerto Ricans, Mexican Americans, and women within its ranks. It might also choose to support political parties and candidates outside of the conventional two-party structure.

Some believe that the decades ahead will see a growing interest in "economic democracy," or greater control over a corporation's economic decisions by worker-consumer groups (Carnoy and Shearer, 1980). One result might be that new legal obligations to workers and communities will prevent firms from moving their factories to another state or country.

Whether American labor will be attracted by any of these goals is a matter of speculation. Clearly, it will have to consider new goals if it is to maintain its strength and continue to be a vital force in American life.

SUMMARY

In this chapter we have dealt with some of the main features of industrialization, modernization, and advanced industrial society. The experience of industrialization in England reveals some factors that seem to be responsible for that development. A money economy, mass markets, literacy, and religious values all seem to have played a role in economic change.

Many nations of the world are still in the process of economic development, undergoing a series of changes called modernization. Conditions in nonindustrial Third World countries that are seeking to modernize are different from conditions in England and the United States during their early stages of industrialization, presenting many barriers to economic development. Social scientists have described three types of modernity essential to economic development: structural modernity, cultural modernity, and psychological modernity.

TABLE 13.3   Gross Average Weekly Earnings of Employees in Manufacturing Industries

	1955	1960	1965	1968	1970	1972	1974	1976	1978	1980
Average take-home pay (current dollars)	$75.7	89.7	107.5	122.5	133.3	154.7	176.8	209.3	249.3	288.6
Average take-home pay (1967 dollars)	$94.4	101.2	113.8	117.6	114.4	123.5	119.7	122.8	127.6	116.8

SOURCE: Monthly Labor Review, V. 106, No. 2 (February, 1982) p. 74.

Finally, we examined the economic institution in advanced industrial societies, especially the United States. The appearance of the modern corporation, with its large size and economic power, raises new questions about its goals, its centers of control, and its relationship to government and the public. The complexity and cost of modern technology has encouraged the growth of giant corporations that seek to exert control over many aspects of their economic, social, and political environment. Multinational corporations attempt to use their power to influence the political structure of foreign countries. Some see possible benefits from such tendencies, such as a decline of extreme nationalism, while others see multinationals as exploiters of less-developed countries. The modern corporation has also changed the nature of work and of organized labor in ways that might be considered to be harmful to the welfare of society.

One trend outlined in this chapter is the continued concentration of economic and political power in relatively few hands. A society dominated by economic values can transform patterns in other social institutions like the family, education, and religion. The pattern of industrialization, which started some three hundred years ago in England, is still unfolding.

GLOSSARY

Aggregate demand   amount of money available to consumers to buy products.

Agribusiness   domination of the farming industry by large corporate farms.

Capital resources   what is left over (surplus) after the primary needs of food and shelter for a population are satisfied; used to improve education, health care, etc.

Complex technology   means of producing a product characterized by high cost and long lead time.

Conglomerate   a business corporation that owns or controls a number of firms producing unrelated products.

Entrepreneur   a person who uses capital to attract and combine the other factors of production to manufacture a product for the market.

Factors of production   (in economics) money, land, labor, and raw materials.

Industrialization   in England, the development of a manufacturing society based on capitalistic profit motive and competitive market principles.

Lead time   the amount of time it takes to produce a product, once a decision has been made to produce it.

Modernization   economic and social development marked by improved school systems, literacy rates, governmental services, mass communications, and citizen participation in civic affairs; the transition from traditional to modern practices.

Monopoly control   market domination by a single firm.

Multinational corporation   a business corporation that is based in one country and owns or controls firms in a number of foreign countries.

Oligopoly control   market domination by a small number of firms.

Particularistic standards   standards that automatically exclude people in certain social categories, such as women or blacks, from filling certain educational or occupational roles.

Research and development (R&D)   invention and planning of improvements in technology that support the modern industrial and marketing complex.

Technostructure   network of scientific and technical specialists on whom the modern corporation depends.

Third World   nations that emerged from colonial status as new nations following World War II.

Universalistic standards   standards that permit all persons to compete for educational and occupational roles in a society.

Vertical integration   absorption by a corporation of its important suppliers as a means of superseding the market.

ADDITIONAL READINGS

Aronowitz, Stanley. *False Promises*. New York: McGraw-Hill, 1973.
An examination of the history of the American working class, including its formation and level of consciousness.

Birnbaum, Norman. *The Crises of Industrial Society*. New York: Oxford University Press, 1969.
A reexamination of the basic ideas of class and power in relation to what the author views as the crises of Western industrial nations. The author identifies the crises with the social and political unrest of the 1960s.

Braverman, Harry. *Labor and Monopoly Capital*. New York: Monthly Review Press, 1974.
Following upon Karl Marx's analysis of the effects of capitalism on work and workers, this book continues with a similar analysis revealed through its subtitle "The Degradation of Work in the Twentieth Century."

Coleman, James S. *Power and the Structure of Society*. New York: Norton, 1974.
A collection of four lectures by the author on the modern corporation as a "corporate actor" and the private person's loss of power in dealing with them.

Moore, Wilbert E. *The Conduct of the Corporation*. New York: Random House, 1962.
A very readable, though somewhat dated, account of the internal life of the modern business corporation. The "structures" and "characters" that make up organizations are examined thoroughly and with insight.

Polanyi, Karl. *The Great Transformation*. Boston: Beacon, 1957.
An absorbing historical analysis of the rise of the market economy along with the Industrial Revolution. The effects of the market economy are revealed through the tensions and struggles between the self-interest of the market system and a cohesive society.

Tilly, Louise A. and Scott, Joan W. *Women, Work and Family*. New York: Holt, Rinehart and Winston, 1978.
Examines the impact of industrialization on women's work in England and France from 1700 to 1950. Productive roles of women at home and in the labor market are examined to understand the jobs women did, the economic and demographic factors that influenced them to work, and the impact of working on domestic and reproductive activity.

READINGS

READING 13.1

Why Corporations Close Profitable Plants*

Barry Bluestone and Bennett Harrison

Plant closings are becoming a grimly familiar story. The parent conglomerate, usually from a remote home office, announces one day that a well-established local factory is no longer competitive. Typically, the handwriting has been on the wall for years. The machinery is outmoded; the company's more modern factories are using newer equipment—and nothing foreshadows a shutdown like failure to reinvest. The workers have been told to hold down wages or the plant will have to move; the town has been warned that property taxes must be abated or they will lose the plant altogether. Often these demands have been met.

But the dread day arrives anyway. Hundreds of jobs will be lost; the tax base will be devastated. The town elders wring their hands. Workers with seniority (those with roots in the community) are invited to pull up stakes and take lower wage jobs in company plants out of state.

A last ditch effort by workers to buy the plant fails; they can't raise the necessary capital. Although the factory is obsolete, oddly enough it is worth a king's ransom. Anyway, it must be a real lemon, or why would the company shut it down?

Why indeed?

The editorial pages of the *Wall Street Journal* suggest the reasons for plant relocation are obvious. Don't credit the sunbelt's climate, says the *Journal*. The real cause of the sunbelt's economic growth is its superior attitude toward business. Labor costs (translation: wages) are lower; tax burdens (translation: public services) are lower. Plants must relocate, therefore, because in the high-cost Northeast and Midwest workers have greedily demanded decent wages, and communities have insisted on adequate school, police, fire, and sanitation services.

And anyway, plant closings, despite their human toll, mean that the system is performing the way it should. Capital mobility is an essential ingredient in our free-market economy. The profit-maximizing entrepreneur must be free to invest capital where it will return the highest possible yield. Otherwise, we are sanctioning inefficiency: letting the economy as a whole operate below its optimum potential means allowing lower productivity and falling wages. And we surely don't want that.

Again and again, trade unions and state legislatures grappling with plant closings listen to business executives insist that plants close because they've ceased to be profitable: "If it could make money, do you really think we would shut it down?"

The contention seems plausible at first but, like so much in textbook economics, it simply fails to describe real life. Large modern corporations—and conglomerates in particular—will and frequently do close profitable branch plants or previously acquired businesses. They may do so for a variety of reasons that flow from the way conglomerates are organized. Centralized management and control produces pressure to meet corporate growth objectives and minimum annual profit targets; it also siphons off subsidiaries' profits to meet other corporate needs. Sometimes management by "remote control" actually creates the unprofitability of the subsidiary that eventually leads to shutdown—as when the home office is far removed from the production site or unfamiliar with the industry in which a subsidiary competes. Again, the textbook model of competition among entrepreneur-owned and -managed

---

* Footnotes omitted.

SOURCE: Reprinted by permission of *Working Papers* magazine © Trusteeship Institute 1980.

businesses utterly fails to explain why plants relocate.

Modern industrial theory says large corporations are under constant pressure to grow, to expand their market share. Stability is often seen as a sign of decline, no matter how well run and steadily productive the plant. In a letter to an executive of the K-Mart discount department chain, Paul McCracken, former head of the President's Council of Economic Advisors, wrote: "History suggests that companies which decide to 'take their ease' are apt to be on the route to decay."

This pressure is reinforced by the corporation's need to offer growth stock in order to attract equity capital. Investors in growth stocks make their money from capital gains realized when they sell their stock rather than from steady dividends paid out by the firm. The purchase price of the stock is thus high in relation to the dividends it earns. However, only by growing can a company keep the price-to-earnings ratio high and continue to attract investors to its stocks. In many situations it is easier for a corporation to boost its price-earnings ratio by acquiring efficient and profitable businesses—often in unrelated markets—than by developing new ventures or expanding existing operations. This option was particularly attractive during the mid-1960s and the late 1970s when the stock market tended to undervalue real assets. Then a corporation or conglomerate seeking to expand could acquire those assets at "bargain" prices.

Plants must also meet target rates of return. Many companies that are divisions or subsidiaries of parent corporations or conglomerates are now routinely required to meet minimum annual profit targets as a condition for receiving finance or executive "perks" from the home office. Many are ultimately shut down because they cannot achieve what the managers describe as the parent corporation's current "hurdle rate." . . .

Whatever the target rate in a particular company at a particular time, the existence of the corporate hurdle rate means that in the era of monopoly capital, viable businesses can be closed even though they are making a profit—because it is not enough of a profit. Perhaps the most dramatic example of this phenomenon involved Uniroyal's closing of its eighty-seven-year-old inner tube factory in Indianapolis in 1978. The *Wall Street Journal* reported the story in the following way:

The factory has long been the country's leading producer of inner tubes. It operates profitably. Its $7 million to $8 million annual payroll sustains the families of nearly 600 employees.

The company, in a formal statement cited "high labor costs" and "steadily declining demand." Union and management officials who worked at the plant tell another story. They say that Uniroyal could have kept the plant operating profitably if it wanted to but that under pressure from the securities markets management decided to concentrate its energy on higher-growth chemical lines. Interviews with securities analysts support this theory. Richard Haydon, an analyst at Goldman, Sachs and Co., says: "You have one very large entity looking at a very small entity, but the small entity being very large to those people that work there. I think it's a truism that many companies have grown too big to look at the small market.

One consultant advises his corporate clients that when the wage bill as a percent of sales rises, or when the rate of return on investment falls below some standard—he proposes the current money market interest rate—it is time to think about shutting down. "If capital does not work for you effectively it should be invested elsewhere." . . .

Uniroyal factory workers saved their jobs with the help of the presidents of the Indianapolis City Council and the Rubber Workers Union. They persuaded local financiers to put up the capital to purchase the plant from Uniroyal. The profit forecast for the first year of operation predicts that $500,000 will be distributed among the workers, and another $500,000 invested in new machinery.

The conventional wisdom about highly centralized management is that it makes possible a higher degree of efficiency in information and personnel management than ever before. But the evidence suggests that the managers of the giant corporations and conglomerates frequently "overmanage" their subsidiaries, milk them of their profits, subject them to strenuous or impossible performance standards, interfere with local decisions, and are quick to close them down when other, more profitable, opportunities appear. In 1975–76 Gulf and Western almost dumped the Brown Paper Company of Holyoke, Massachusetts, a leading producer of quality papers, and actually did sell off its most profitable product line to a Wisconsin competitor. By 1977 the plant's sales were up again to over $450 million.

Highly centralized organizations like Gulf and Western and Textron have positioned themselves so as to be able to make a profit either from a subsidiary's success or from failure that requires divestiture (since it can be treated as a tax loss and used to offset profits earned in other operations). From the point of view of capital asset management this may be the pinnacle of capitalist institutional creativity. But from the perspective of economic stability for working people and their communities, these clever-capitalist giants are a disaster. The much-discussed trade-off between efficiency and equity turns out to mean capital management efficiency, but tremendous inefficiency at the level of actual production, to go along with the inequities imposed on workers and communities.

In short, modern monopoly capitalists will sell off or shut down profitable businesses if they think they can make even more money somewhere else. This strategy is not a recent one, nor have its harmful effects ever been unforeseeable. Here is Emil Rieve, president of the Textile Workers Union of America before a Congressional committee thirty years ago:

Mr. Little is a capitalist, but in the field of finance rather than the field of production . . .

I say this in the same sense that Hitler and Stalin are in the tradition of Napoleon and Alexander the Great. We have changed our attitude toward financial conquerors, just as we have changed our attitude toward military conquerors. Success is not the only yardstick.

I do not know whether Mr. Little has broken any laws. But if he has not, our laws ought to be changed.

"Mr. Little" is Royal Little, founder of Textron, the Rhode Island conglomerate that first developed many of the strategies now in use. Textron was initially a textile company. This year the Securities and Exchange Commission has charged it with paying over $5 million in bribes to officials in eleven foreign countries in order to "stimulate" sales of its Bell Helicopters. Its chairman at the time was G. William Miller, the current Secretary of the Treasury.

Just as the law in other areas has gradually evolved over the years to recognize that property rights, though dominant, are not absolute, the law must be changed to temper arbitrary plant relocation. Fifty years ago, tenants had no rights arising from their occupancy of a building. Today, the law stipulates that a landlord must keep the building habitable, that he must provide heat and hot water, and that tenants may not be arbitrarily evicted. Some communities have authorized rent control and even rent strikes when the property is not kept in good repair.

Family law has undergone a similar evolution. A wife is no longer her husband's property, and a couple's tangible property is no longer assumed to be the fruits of the husband's labor. Even banking law has been amended to deny banks the right to shut down when the community would be denied essential banking services.

But laws dealing with plant relocation are

back in the eighteenth century. Profitability is considered an absolute right, not a relative one; and the right of a plant to relocate in the name of greater profitability is still sacrosanct, even where management's judgment or motive is specious.

As Emil Rieve observed thirty years ago, laws that sanction promiscuous relocations must be changed. A handful of states are considering requiring a year's notice before companies may shut down plants. Legislation is also under discussion to require severance pay, as well as compensation to the community. Companies could be required to pay back all tax abatements; labor contracts could also demand that the parent company not shift the production to other plants; tax write-offs for shutdowns could be prohibited. The proposed legislation to require federal chartering of the largest corporations could also include a range of sanctions against arbitrary relocations.

Far from interfering with industry's "right" to use capital optimally, these sanctions could force parent companies that acquire independent firms to operate them efficiently. As things stand now, conglomerates are being rewarded for running their subsidiaries into the ground and the employees along with them.

SUMMARY

Plant closings are often the result of large corporations mismanaging one of their subsidiaries by siphoning off profits and then shutting the plant in the name of efficiency. Giant corporations "overmanage" their subsidiaries by interfering with local operations to benefit the parent corporation. Writing off unprofitable subsidiaries as tax losses can also be used to offset profits earned in other operations. Such economic decisions may be made without considering the workers and communities affected by a plant closing.

QUESTIONS

1. How can corporations be restrained from engaging in such questionable practices?
2. Do any cities or states have legislation that requires corporations to compensate employees and communities when they shut down a plant?

READING 13.2
Professionals Go Union
Jack Golodner

Economists, statisticians and others who study our society compartmentalize economic activity in two sections—goods-producing and service-producing. Goods-producing industries are manufacturing, construction, mining and agriculture. Service-producing industries include transportation, public utilities, trade, finance, health, entertainment, recreation, communications, education, computer services and government research.

In 1950, the United States began to employ a majority of its wage and salary workers in the service-producing area. It was the first country to do so and is still the only country to do so. Since 1950, the increase in the number of service-producing employes has grown to the point where today 2 of every 3 workers are engaged in providing a service rather than a product. By 1980, 70 percent of all workers will be in the service industries.

The service industries have been and are today the largest employers of white-collar people. This shift in the relative importance of industries from goods-producing to service-producing is in large measure responsible for the rising tide of white-collar workers.

SOURCE: From Jack Golodner, "Professionals Go Union," *American Federationist* (October 1973), pp. 6–8. Reprinted by permission.

But even within the goods-producing sector, another revolution is taking place. As a result of various technological changes, the relative strength in numbers of the production worker is diminishing while the number of white-collar people is increasing at an accelerating rate. In aircraft manufacturing, for example, production workers equaled 74 percent of the workforce in 1943. But in 1968, they were down to 55 percent. The same trend is evident in machinery, electrical equipment and motor vehicles.

Recently, an official of the Steelworkers commented that the decrease of production and maintenance employees in the labor force may reach a point where some day white-collar workers might outnumber production and maintenance employes in steel. "Future membership strength of the Steelworkers," he said, "depends upon more organization of office and technical workers."

This jibes with another comment by an official of an electrical union, who says "the future life and growth of the labor movement lies with the unionization of the professional, technical and white-collar salaried workers."

The fact that unions found their first roots among the blue-collar occupations when they were the predominant employe group has been interpreted by some as an indication that unions are peculiar only to these groups of workers. This is a bit of whistling in the dark by management people and by those academicians who would like unions to wither away and stop bothering their patrician view of society.

The roots of unionism grew where the people were and where the conditions were such as to provide a need for collective action among individual employes. The people are now in the white-collar fields and the conditions for unionism—the same conditions that prompted organization by blue-collar people—are developing in the white-collar fields as well. . . .

Some of the conditions which bother professionals are susceptible to correction by management. But, by and large, many that are most crucial to the employe are beyond the means of management to change.

Among the developing conditions encouraging the growth of white-collar unions today is the growing loss of individuality by the typical white-collar employe.

Being employed in large numbers by rapidly growing and diversifying institutions or corporations means he is slowly but surely becoming removed from participation in decision-making processes. It means an individual voice—no matter how knowledgeable—no longer counts. Large areas of judgment once controlled by the individual employe are sacrificed to the logic and formalities of mass organization.

Individual bargaining power and the ability to insist on participation in the setting of salaries and working conditions is declining. When the individual white-collar worker has a share in the control of the job, the nature of the work assignment, methods and pace, his individual task can be recognized and becomes the basis for individual bargaining. Large organizations remove this control or dilute it so the individual contribution is small relative to the total enterprise. Thus, his personal stamp is obliterated.

Rationalization, specialization, and computerization all conspire to make the large employing organization both possible and necessary, but they also separate the employe from the service and from meaningful participation in the process.

In every place, in every occupation where this bureaucratization of work has occurred, there are things which management has done or is doing and must do in its own behalf which produce a counter move in the form of collective action by those who are managed.

The crafts—because they were the earliest to be affected by this process—organized into unions. We tend to forget that craftsmen of an earlier time had great status in society. Work to the pre-industrial revolution craftsman was diverse—gathering esteem by its very individuality and providing satisfaction in creative achievement. There was dignity in the act of working. But the industrial revolution brought about new institutional demands. The craftsman was subjected to the harsh disciplines of the factory. Spontaneity, exuberance, freedom to perform, identification with the product which at one time made work, play and culture virtually synonymous were lost and the status, dignity and respect of the craftsman could no longer be maintained at the work place without organization.

And in the professions, as their industries and jobs came increasingly under the control of bureaucracies, actors, musicians and other performing artists—then journalists, broadcasters, teachers, social workers and university professors—adapted the tools of unionism to their special needs. The old "Don't Tread on Me" flag was raised against management and, like the early colonists, these white-collar professionals discovered that only by organizing and uniting with others in common cause could they make this slogan meaningful.

The dignity of the worker, white collar or blue collar, faced with societal changes beyond his control, is preserved by a contract that assures him of fair treatment, rehire rights, adequate severance pay, protected pension and other retirement benefits. . . .

Another fact of contemporary life that is leading a growing number of white-collar people to unions is the steady decline in relative and real income among the unorganized in the white-collar occupations. They must live with the lag in salary increases which come after the unionized sectors of the economy get a raise and before it's passed on to them voluntarily by management. With inflation booming ahead, these people are hurting.

Furthermore, the gap between salaries paid white-collar professionals, sales and technical people and wages paid to operatives and laborers is narrowing. And the gap in net income is further reduced by taxes. . . .

Even engineers and scientists—people heretofore indifferent to unions—are slowly becoming aware of the fact that they are losing economic ground. . . .

The myth that professional people—the so-called snobs of the white-collar field—do not join unions is evaporating. The teachers and their successes in the face of anti-union laws governing public employes remind one of the early days of our largest and strongest blue-collar unions. . . .

The technicians and professionals, often highly paid, in the entertainment-arts-communications conglomerate have built strong unions in their fields and they are active in them. Professional athletes, nurses—even medical doctors—are organizing along union lines.

A major mistake that is made in the broad analysis of the "new" groups that will never join unions is in thinking of broad categories of jobs, like white-collar, as being prestigious and high-paying. They aren't—there are a lot of white-collar people who face the same frustrations and low pay that drove the craftsmen of a century ago to organize.

The Department of Labor reports that in 1970 some 21 million members of unions or employe organizations in the United States engaged in collective bargaining. Of these, nearly 22 percent, or 5 million, were in the white-collar category.

As for the myth that professional people do not join unions or engage in collective bargaining, note that nearly 3 million of the 5 million organized white-collar workers in that 1970 survey were professional and technical people. This numbers more than 20 percent of all professional and technical people in the country and approximately 40 percent of the organizable potential—that is, excluding the self-employeds, the clergy, doctors, dentists, veterinarians and judges.

A British commentator, Alan Flanders, once noted, "The value of a trade union to its members lies less in its economic achievements than in its capacity to express their dignity.

"Viewed from this angle, employes—white-collar and professional workers, no less than manual workers—have an interest in union organization, however favorable their economic circumstances or the state of the labor market, for at least two reasons.

"They are interested in the regulation of labor management because such regulation defines their rights, their status and security and so liberates them from dependence on chance and the arbitrary will of management. They are equally interested in participating as directly as possible in the making and administration of these rules in order to have a voice in shaping their own destiny."

In a world where individuals search for the strength to be a part of the action, in a society where people want again to feel important and listened to, the union has achieved new importance.

SUMMARY
The number of workers in manufacturing, construction, and agriculture is in decline, while the number of white-collar workers is increasing. This has resulted in a weakening of union strength since they have traditionally drawn on blue-collar workers for membership. However, there are increasing indications that the working conditions of many white-collar workers have become similar to production workers. Teachers, journalists, engineers, and other white-collar professionals, and sales and technical people can become the source of renewed union growth.

QUESTIONS
1. Why would professionals consider joining a union?
2. What do you gain and what do you lose by unionizing?
3. How might the general public benefit from unionization among professionals?

CHAPTER 14

Religious Institutions

CONTENTS

Is "deprogram-ming" a violation of religious freedom?

During the 1960s and 1970s, many parents saw their children join new religious groups. While these groups follow no one organizational model, isolation from parents and friends, rigorous programs of education, and emphasis upon group activities to the virtual exclusion of private life are common approaches used by these religious organizations to maintain the loyalty of their converts. Such activities have been defined as "brainwashing" by critics of the groups; the groups claim their members joined and continue membership voluntarily. Deprogramming efforts have been designed to reorient those who have been "brainwashed" by these religious groups, usually at the request of parents. Kidnapping, physical restraints, and techniques of interrogation that resemble those of the police have often been used to break down the commitment to the new faith. Do all religious groups have the protection of religious freedom, even if they use brainwashing techniques on their converts? Is religious freedom in danger?

YES   One of the basic freedoms of American society is the right to express one's religious beliefs. This right allows an individual to decide whether to join a religious group and which group to join. To take away this basic right is to deny the person religious freedom.

In recent years many religious groups have emerged in the United States. Some are Christian in origin, some have Eastern roots, some seek radical social change, some are primarily concerned with individual beliefs and practices. These marginal religious groups have endowed the lives of thousands of young people with purpose and meaning. The devotion of these youth to their new faiths often causes family conflicts leading to permanent divisions between parents and children.

At least three issues are involved. First, religion is an intensely personal matter, which parents cannot and should not control. Second, parents with only superficial commitment to their faith have difficulty understanding the loyalty and intensity of attachment that the youth feel toward their newly found faith. Third, parental efforts to destroy the child's attachment to the religious group through brainwashing is the same crime that the religious groups are accused of committing.

While these religious groups do not resemble the successful mainstream churches in the United States, they fulfill a vital social and psychological need for their adherents. To take away people's basic right to join a religious group is a violation of religious freedom guaranteed by the First Amendment.

NO   Many of the people who join marginal religious groups do so at a time of personal turmoil, frustration, and uncertainty about life and the future. For years such problems have been handled by families, schools, and churches, and when youths reach adulthood, these concerns are usually resolved.

Recently, a number of religious groups have used brainwashing techniques to convert these youth to their beliefs by providing easy answers, ready help, and a "new family" to support the person and reinforce the group's teachings. Though these conversions are technically voluntary, several questionable processes are involved. First, many groups use drugs, hypnosis, or emotional deprivation to manipulate the person to a state of conversion. Second, the psychological dependency created by the conversion decreases the convert's ability to act and think independently. Third, the convert's loyalty is maintained by isolation from all nonbelievers.

It is essential to use strong countermeasures to undermine religious brainwashing. Deprogramming does not coerce beliefs—it permits people to choose without coercion. Deprogramming allows youth to work through their programs naturally and slowly; it does not give simple answers to complex questions. Deprogramming is not a violation of religious freedom; it provides children and parents the opportunity to find religious meaning and purpose together.

The issue of deprogramming involves religious freedom, concern of parents for children, and the purpose of religion itself. Those who claim deprogramming is a violation of freedom point to the intensely personal nature of religious beliefs and commitment and to the positive benefits religious groups give to the individual. Those who deny that deprogramming violates religious freedom focus on the coercive processes that are a part of membership in such groups. Yet there are larger issues to be raised. What does religion do for individuals—and for society? Is religion a unifying or divisive factor in American life? What are the effects of the new electronic communications media and the new techniques of psychological manipulation on religious behavior?

QUESTIONS TO CONSIDER

- Why are people religious?

- Can religion exist without organized groups or churches?

- Why are Americans more religious than people in other countries?

- Does religion make a difference in people's behavior?

On November 18, 1978, over 900 persons were murdered or committed suicide in Jonestown, Guyana. The action followed the killing of a U.S. representative and four others in his party as they were leaving Jonestown after a visit to James Jones and the People's Temple. The People's Temple was a religious organization, James Jones was an ordained Christian clergyman, and the rituals—including the last one of sharing a common (though lethal) drink—were strikingly similar to Christian rituals (Richardson, 1980).

In the fall of 1975, Bo and Peep, a middle-aged man and woman, traveled around Oregon offering people eternal life if they could overcome all attachment to the world. By forsaking their jobs, possessions, and families, they could show the sincerity of their desire and UFOs would appear to take them to heaven. Perhaps 150 people followed Bo and Peep in this pilgrimage, though the group has since disappeared from public attention (Balch and Taylor, 1977).

At 4 A.M., people attending the Summer Solstice of the Healthy-Happy-Holy Organization (3HO) emerge from their tents to join in a Sikh prayer. Through a combination of exercises, chanting, and meditation, they try to gain conscious control of the processes of the body and the mind. The 3HO was founded in 1969 to prepare people in the United States for the Age of Aquarius. The roots of this movement are in northern India, but by 1973 it had gained several thousand committed members and opened a hundred centers (Tobey, 1976).

Religion is a rich and varied form of human behavior. What people in one society call religion may be seen as only superstition or ignorance in another society. Thus, while a Baptist minister in Kansas leads a local congregation in prayer asking God to destroy the insects that are swarming in the fields, a Jain priest in India sweeps the path before he walks so he will not harm an insect that may be the incarnation of a soul who behaved badly in a former life. Or, an American businessman may ask God's help in making his business profitable, while a young Buddhist priest embraces poverty and gathers up his begging bowl to roam the countryside.

WHAT IS RELIGION: THE PROBLEM OF DEFINITION

Every human society has beliefs and practices that its members see as sacred, or set apart from the profane, common beliefs and practices of everyday life. This distinction between sacred and profane (or secular) was first described by the sociologist Emile Durkheim in his efforts to identify the elementary aspects of religion. Durkheim studied the religious activities of preindustrial Australian native groups in the late nineteenth and early twentieth centuries before their religious beliefs and practices were modified by contact with the developed world.

Durkheim classified beliefs, rituals, and objects into two categories: the **profane** (the common and ordinary) and the **sacred** (the forbidden and aloof). However, his classification of, say, an object as sacred or profane was not made on the basis of its inherent characteristics but rather on the shared meanings that had emerged out of the social experiences of the members of the group (Seger, 1957). For example, the *churinga* of the Arunta people of central Australia, a polished bit of wood or stone used in rituals and religious ceremonies, was to

them an important religious symbol. But the *churinga* had no religious meaning to a non-Arunta.

Similar meanings and distinctions exist in modern societies. Perceptions of the supernatural world or views about the forces that govern human life may make the cross a sacred object to a Christian family, while it is only a secular object to their Jewish neighbors. Despite such differences, however, both families may have a deep respect and reverence for the flag. It is this diversity in the content of religious beliefs and practices that makes it impossible to focus only on content when defining religion.

The difficulty in identifying beliefs or practices that are distinctively religious has led social scientists to examine the functions that religion ful-

Religious institutions are deeply embedded in the culture. Modernistic church buildings often incorporate the symbols of the old with symbols of the new, in an effort to demonstrate the relevance of faith in the modern world.

fills both for individuals and for societies. In this approach, the content of beliefs is less important than their purpose. Similarly, religious rituals and practices are important because they occur as an organized effort to deal with the issues of human society, though their forms may be very different in various societies. Such an approach allows us to define **religion** as an institutionalized system of symbols, beliefs, values, and practices that focus on questions of ultimate meaning (Glock and Stark, 1965).

ASPECTS OF RELIGION: MEANING, BELIEFS, AND INSTITUTIONS

This definition identifies three aspects of religion in human societies: questions of meaning, systems of symbols, beliefs, values, and practices; and religious institutions. Each aspect is important in understanding how religion functions for the individual and for society.

Questions of Meaning

Why are people religious? Many answers have been given to this question. Some scholars have suggested that fear, powerlessness, ignorance, and dreams are the source of religious belief. Others, like Freud (1934), have seen religious drives as being rooted in the human heritage of guilt and anxiety about life and past deeds. Still others, Fromm (1963), for example, consider religion to be a part of the human effort to compensate for life's deprivations. These ideas may go some way in accounting for individual religious behavior, but they are not adequate to explain collective religious practices.

From a sociological perspective, religion is a product of culture, emerging from the group's social experiences. As Durkheim suggested, religion is the means by which societies most successfully exert pressure on humans to adapt to the demands of social life, uniting individuals in the face of fears about failure, injustice, the unknown, or the future, often by generating beliefs in an afterlife.

In times of crisis, like death, persecution, or natural catastrophe, religion may help people interpret these events and deal with them. Less severe crises associated with transitions in life, such as marriage or the birth of a child, traditionally have been occasions for religious celebration.

Nearly every religion emphasizes the importance of accepting others and developing self-awareness through participation in religious activities. By collective activities and worship designed to transcend everyday experiences, religion may offer an awareness of personal limitations or a sense of meaning or purpose. The desire for experiences that transcend the ordinary may be expressed in fasting, drugs, or prayer.

These consequences of religious practice help the individual cope with the problems generated by involvement in social life—insecurity, identity, and meaning. But religion may not always solve problems. Severe conflict can occur over differences in beliefs. In many societies the complexity of life and the diversity of opinion and beliefs have made it impossible for only one religious perspective to exist—and also for two or more religious perspectives to coexist. Similarly, religious beliefs and practices that have meaning in one society may have no meaning in a different social situation. Thus the variety of religious beliefs reflects the basic problems of life in different areas and cultures.

Systems of Symbols, Beliefs, Values, and Practices

Religious beliefs are of many types. **Non-theism** or **a-theism** refers to religions that do not have belief in a supernatural being. Confucianism, Taoism, Shintoism, and humanism all may be considered as nontheistic.

Theism, or the belief in a supernatural being, may be of at least two different types. **Monotheism,** which is belief in one supreme being or god, is found in Judaism, Christianity, and Islam. There are obvious variations among monotheistic religions, such as the three-persons-in-one—the Trinity—in Christianity, but all of them recognize one god who is superior to all other powers, both natural and supernatural. **Polytheism** includes religions with many gods of equal or similar power and importance, such as Hinduism. Gods of the Hindus often are tribal and village deities associated with special locations or objects.

Despite the great variation in specific beliefs and practices among these religions, there are similarities in form: each has a set of general beliefs or principles concerning the meaning of life; each emphasizes a certain quality of life and behavior; each encourages rituals and practices associated with the general beliefs; each has a set of writings or sacred scriptures to guide the believer; and each has a group of leaders who interpret, mediate, or teach.

Other patterns of beliefs and behavior that can be described as quasi-religious include rituals associated with magic, witchcraft, and mana—a supernatural power. However, **magical rituals** typically consist of a series of precisely ordered acts that are performed by individuals and directed toward a specific end, like bringing rain or recovery from illness, but are rarely concerned with questions of ultimate meaning. The practices of black magic or witchcraft, which can be used by one person against another to gain advantage over another, also fail to focus on the ultimate questions characteristic of religious beliefs and practices.

Religious symbols, beliefs, and practices reflect distinctive social conditions and cultures. Yet all religions have formalized sets of doctrines and ethical traditions and patterns of ritualistic behavior that occur among persons who share a common understanding of the symbols of the faith.

Institutions: Patterns of Religious Life

Religious institutions are the organized patterns of belief and practice that are associated with the answers to ultimate questions. Religious institutions are found throughout human societies because religion is always associated with regularized patterns of worship and with personal practices of devotion.

In early human societies religion was not set apart from family rituals and practices, which often were associated with family gods or ancestors. Such practices were eventually taken over by specialists—the headman, the chief hunter, and the shaman—who emerged in hunting and gathering so-

In recent years, many women have moved from informal leadership roles to participate as elected leaders in religious groups. Though men are dominant in leadership positions in most denominations, women now serve as pastors and elected officials in many religious bodies.

cieties. The **shaman** was a person who had special power because of his relationship with the spirit world (Malefijt, 1968).

As agricultural societies developed, certain people began to specialize in religious activities and formal religious organizations appeared. Full-time religious specialists, or priests, became identified as ritualistic leaders. Distinctions were made between priests and laymen, religious and secular activities, and compulsory and voluntary religious participation. These distinctions illustrate four basic issues in the institutionalization of religion: the problem of continuity of leadership, the development of rituals, the codification of beliefs, and the problem of organization.

CONTINUITY OF LEADERSHIP

Leadership in religious groups has often been defined in terms of two roles: prophet and priest. Weber (1963) defined a **prophet** as a person who proclaims a religious doctrine or a divine commandment and seeks to change the existing social order. A prophet derives his authority from **charisma,** exceptional qualities or unusual personal powers that command the respect and devotion of others.

Exemplary prophets seek to communicate their vision of a new order by example. Buddhist priests who burned themselves to death to protest the war in Vietnam were examples of prophets who claimed a vision of a new world.

Prophets who seek to communicate their new vision by personal example, at times suffering punishment, disgrace, or even death to present their message, are called **exemplary prophets.** Some obvious examples are Martin Luther King in the United States and the Buddhist priests who burned themselves to death in Vietnam in the 1960s. **Ethical prophets** also are critical of the existing social order but attempt to develop a new order, either by persuading people to return to traditional standards or by establishing a new ethical code. Amos and Hosea of the Old Testament and Malcolm X of the Black Muslims were ethical prophets.

Prophets provide leadership for social movements, but because their authority derives from personal religious experience or charisma, they rarely are leaders in established religious organizations. Instead, the responsibility for leadership in traditional religious activities lies with the priest. The **priest** is an individual whose religious authority comes from the sacred traditions of an organized religious group. Personal virtue is less important for the priest than for the prophet, since it is the hierarchical structure of organized religion that gives the priest religious authority. A major responsibility of the priest is leading his congregation in worship and the celebration of rituals, both of which tend to support the existing order. This function most clearly distinguishes the priest and the prophet: the priest functions to give meaning and significance to traditional religious patterns, and the prophet seeks to change the existing religious context and people's behavior.

THE DEVELOPMENT OF RITUALS

Rituals are regularly patterned acts that are imbued with sacred meaning. Rituals may be as diverse as wailing and dancing, maintaining silence, wearing special clothing, eating, or praying. They express the beliefs of the participants, and they often use symbols, such as the Christian cross, the Jewish menorah, and the Buddhist mandala.

Religious rituals create solidarity among the participants by providing a common religious experience. They also enforce a commitment to religious values. Through time, rituals may themselves take on a sacred character and develop a rigidity in form and meaning that makes change difficult.

This routinization of religious expression constitutes a major problem for religious institutions, since the social experiences that made the rituals meaningful cannot be reconstructed for following generations. This creates a dilemma. For example, forcing a child to conform to religious practices does not guarantee that the child has associated religious meaning with the practices, but not teaching a child religious rituals increases the possibility that the rituals and their meaning will not survive.

CODIFICATION OF BELIEFS

Beliefs organized into systematic form focus on the relationship of the unseen world—the world of heaven and hell, angels, and God—to the human world. For example, in the Roman Catholic tradition, codified beliefs explain the connection of bread and wine to the body and blood of Christ, and the theology of the Krishna Consciousness Society explains the relationship of a proper human life to the attainment of eternal consciousness (Ellwood, 1973).

A major consequence of the codification of beliefs is strong pressures to conform to the established doctrine, and standards for membership in a religious institution may become quite rigid. But just as religious rituals may lose their meaning over time as a result of changes in life experiences, so codified beliefs may lose their relevance.

THE PROBLEM OF ORGANIZATION

For religious groups to survive some formal organization is necessary. Recruitment and training of new members, continued satisfaction of individual members, the development of lines of authority to facilitate decision making, and the maintenance of morale all require structure and leadership, especially as the religious group grows larger. Efforts to evangelize may result in new members, new buildings, and a larger group. Such growth is seen as evidence of God's blessing, but it has several consequences and implications for organization. As the size of the group increases, there is greater diversity in group goals and norms, eventually leading to a decline in the use of sanctions against those who deviate from tradition.

Increased size also produces specialization of tasks, since individuals are not able or are no longer required to assume multiple roles. Also with growth and specialization comes the need for coordination. The members who take responsibility for coordination will have more knowledge of the group than will other members and will establish procedural rules based on their knowledge. Thus the group develops a complex division of labor, a set of procedural rules, and an administrative hierarchy. In short, it becomes a bureaucracy. Religious meaning and experience may sometimes be subordinated to religious structure. So growth brings a mixed result: organizational efficiency and organizational rigidity—and the former at the expense of religious meaning.

RELIGIOUS INSTITUTIONS IN MODERN SOCIETIES

Though religious beliefs and practices are found in all societies, the meaning of membership in a religious group varies from intense, all-inclusive involvement to general agreement on principles of ethical behavior. These differences are reflected in organizations, systems of belief, and patterns of recruitment. Some religions, such as Confucianism or Judaism, do not seek converts. Groups within Christianity and Islam, on the other hand, are often militant in their quest for converts.

Membership figures for the major religions are presented in Table 14.1. Christianity, Islam, and Hinduism claim about half of the world's population. Christianity has its greatest strength in the West. Islam and Hinduism are primarily Eastern religions.

In the Western societies of the twentieth century, the Judeo-Christian tradition has been a significant factor in shaping people's attitudes and behavior, but only two-thirds of this population at the most may be considered members of a religious group. Religious institutions in the United States and Canada are numerous, and some assessment of their importance can be made by examining statistics on membership and donations, by surveying attitudes and practices, and by comparing various characteristics of people who profess some religious commitment.

Statistics on Religion

Statistics on religious membership among United States citizens are derived from many sources and are subject to different interpretations. Because of the formal separation of church and state in the United States, no religious information may be gathered in a regular census. As a result, two basic sources provide most of the data: church records and individual responses to questionnaires or interviews.

In 1980, according to reports from religious bodies, more than 133 million people in the United States were members of some organized religious group. This accounted for about 60 percent of the entire population. This proportion has remained approximately the same for the past 20 years, having risen from about 16 percent of the citizenry who were members in the early 1800s. Unfortunately, comparisons with European societies are impossible, since formal ties between state and church in many European countries essentially create a total membership among the citizens. Table 14.2 shows membership statistics for the United States and Canada, however.

In addition to the high level of church membership in both countries, there is other evidence to support the idea that religious commitments are important in the United States and Canada. Figures provided by 44 groups with about 45 million members in the United States indicate that the average contribution to churches in 1979 was $181.42 and a total of over $8 billion. Canadian figures for 25 bodies with nearly 4 million members showed an average 1979 contribution of $102.70 and a total of $386 million (Jacquet, 1981). If data were available for all religious bodies, it is likely that the total contributions would be at least three times as large as those reported.

Attendance at religious services also appears to document the religious character of the United States and Canadian populations. According to a 1979 survey, 40 percent of Protestants and 52 percent of Roman Catholics attend services weekly in the

TABLE 14.1 Estimated Membership of the Principal Religions of the World

	NORTH AMERICA[a]	SOUTH AMERICA	EUROPE[b]	ASIA[c]	AFRICA	OCEANIA[d]	WORLD
Total Christian	237,096,500	175,114,000	342,630,400	95,987,240	128,617,000	18,058,500	997,503,640
Roman Catholic	133,489,000	162,489,000	177,087,300	55,077,000	47,024,500	4,395,500	579,562,300
Eastern Orthodox	4,750,000	516,000	55,035,600	2,428,000	13,306,000[e]	409,000	76,444,600
Protestant[f]	98,857,500	12,109,000	110,507,500	38,482,240	68,286,500[g]	13,254,000	341,496,740
Jewish	6,250,340	595,800	4,045,120	3,192,860	176,400	76,000	14,336,520
Muslim[h]	376,200	251,500	14,945,000	428,266,000	145,214,700	90,000	589,143,400
Zoroastrian	1,250	2,100	10,000	256,000	650	1,000	271,000
Shinto[i]	60,000	90,000	—	57,003,000	1,200	—	57,154,200
Taoist	16,000	10,000	—	31,260,000	—	—	31,286,000
Confucian	97,100	70,000	—	155,887,500	1,500	14,000	156,070,100
Buddhist[j]	185,250	193,200	193,000	254,241,000	20,000	35,000	254,867,450
Hindu[k]	88,500	850,000	400,000	475,073,000	1,179,800	400,000	477,991,300
Totals	244,171,140	177,176,600	362,233,520	1,501,166,600	275,211,250	18,674,500	2,578,623,610
Population[l]	369,759,000	245,067,000	750,198,000	2,557,562,000	469,361,000	22,775,000	4,414,722,000

[a] Includes Central America.

[b] Includes the U.S.S.R. and other countries with established Marxist ideology where religious adherence is difficult to estimate.

[c] Includes areas in which persons have traditionally enrolled in several religions, as well as mainland China with an official Marxist establishment.

[d] Includes Australia and New Zealand as well as islands of the South Pacific.

[e] Includes Coptic Christians, of restricted status in Egypt and in a precarious situation under the military junta in Ethiopia.

[f] Protestant statistics usually count "full members," that is, adults, rather than all family members or baptized infants, and are therefore not comparable to the statistics of ethnic religions or churches counting all constituents of all ages.

[g] Includes many new sects and cults among African Christians.

[h] The chief base of Islam is still ethnic, although missionary work is now carried on in Europe and America (through, for example, "Black Muslims"). In countries where Islam is established, minority religions are frequently persecuted and accurate statistical reports are hard to come by.

[i] A Japanese ethnic religion, Shinto has declined since the Japanese emperor gave up his claim to divinity in 1947. Neither does Shinto survive easily outside the homeland.

[j] Buddhism has produced several renewal movements in the last century which have gained adherents in Europe and America and other areas not formerly ethnic-Buddhist. In Asia it has made rapid gains in recent years in some areas, and under persecution it has shown greater staying power than Taoism or Confucianism. It also transplants better.

[k] Hinduism's strength in India has been enhanced by nationalism, a phenomenon also observable in Islam. Modern Hinduism has developed renewal movements that have won converts in Europe and America.

[l] United Nations, Department of International Economic and Social Affairs; data refer to midyear 1980.

SOURCE: Reprinted with permission from Encyclopedia Britannica 1981 Book of the Year. Copyright 1981, Encyclopedia Britannica Inc., Chicago, Ill.

United States. Comparable figures for Canada were 20 percent of Jews, 26 percent of Protestants, and 50 percent of Roman Catholics (Jacquet, 1981). These attendance figures are considerably higher than those for most other countries, especially those with state churches, though caution is required in interpreting them. Some survey information about the importance of religion in American life is given in Highlight 14.1.

An examination of denominational affiliation in the United States helps to round out the statistical picture. Information collected for the *Yearbook of American and Canadian Churches, 1981* indicates that within the United States there are over 50 million Catholics, 6 million Jews, and about 70 million Protestants, most of whom are in denominations claiming over a million members. The diversity of religious groups is evident in Table 14.3.

Despite the high level of membership in religious groups, at least one-third of the population in the United States and Canada are not church affiliated. Those who neither attend nor belong to a religious group tend to be younger, better educated, and more individualistic than church members. Further, their goals, values, and moral attitudes are often not compatible with traditional religious perspectives

TABLE 14.2   Religious Membership: United States and Canada

YEAR	NUMBER OF CHURCH BODIES REPORTING	NUMBER OF CHURCHES	INCLUSIVE MEMBERSHIP	PERCENTAGE OF POPULATION	NUMBER OF CLERGY
United States					
1975	221	330,460	131,245,139	61.6	456,258
1976	223	332,465	131,871,743	61.5	473,841
1977	223	333,114	131,012,953	60.7	473,188
1978	223	333,063	131,897,539	60.8	479,228
1979	222	333,175	132,812,470	60.7	490,360
1980	222	332,970	133,388,776	60.5	497,301
1981	219	331,065	133,469,690	57.8	494,670
Canada					
1975	60	20,176	13,890,342	61.1	30,272
1976	63	20,736	15,093,162	65.6	30,406
1977	67	19,871	14,497,842	62.5	29,679
1978	71	19,886	14,859,237	63.2	30,169
1979	74	21,672	15,204,613	64.6	30,422
1980	78	23,625	15,308,481	63.4	30,530
1981	80	23,300	15,279,301	60.4	31,378

SOURCE: From *Yearbook of American and Canadian Churches, 1981* by Constant H. Jacquet. Copyright © 1981 by the National Council of the Churches of Christ in the U.S.A. Used by permission of the publisher, Abingdon Press.

on life and morality (Perry et al., 1980; Roof and Hoge, 1980).

The nonparticipation of many younger people in traditional religious organizations is only one aspect of the modern religious scene. Many industrialized societies have much lower levels of religious participation than the United States or Canada, and few societies have as much religious activity outside traditional religious institutions. This diversity of religious activities and groups is an important aspect of life in modern societies, in which social change and personal freedom creates the conditions and opportunities for personal religious expression.

Religious Organizations

Few organizations in human society have received as much attention from sociologists as religious groups, perhaps because of their diversity. Weber, one of the first to attempt a classification of reli-

gious groups, defined two ideal types: the sect and the church. These ideal types were developed further by Troeltsch (1960), who applied them specifically to the historical analysis of Christian groups.

Sects were identified by certain features: loose organization, hostility to the dominant social order, voluntary membership, and a subjective concept of grace—that is, the belief that grace could be reached through individual religious experience. The **church,** by contrast, was a highly developed organization, closely aligned with the dominant culture. It had open and inclusive membership and an objective concept of grace, which could be achieved only through the mediation of the priestly order.

Even though Troeltsch's concept of sect does not seem to be as applicable to our industrialized world, the term sect is still used to refer to a loosely organized religious group that is antagonistic to the secular world and that is joined voluntarily through conversion or direct religious experience. A related category is the **established sect,** a religious orga-

The Texture of Social Life

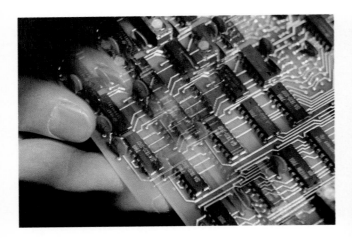

HIGHLIGHT 14.1
Religion and Life: Growing or Declining in Importance?

Question: "How important would you say religion is in your own life—very important, fairly important, or not very important?"

Percentage responding: "Very Important"

	TOTAL	PROTESTANTS	CATHOLICS	JEWS
1952	75%	76%	83%	47%
1965	70	74	76	30
1978	52	60	51	(n.d.)
1980	55	61	56	31

	MEN	WOMEN	18–24 AGE GROUP
1952	68%	79%	64%
1965	63	77	57
1978	46	58	37
1980	48	62	43

Question: "I am going to read you a list of institutions in American society. Would you tell me how much confidence you, yourself, have in each one—a great deal, quite a lot, some, or very little?"

Percentage responding: "a great deal" or "quite a lot"

	THE CHURCH OR ORGANIZED RELIGION	THE MILITARY	THE PUBLIC SCHOOLS	ORGANIZED LABOR	BIG BUSINESS
1973	66%	(n.d.)	58%	30%	26%
1975	68	58%	(n.d.)	38	34
1977	64	57	54	39	33
1979	65	54	53	36	32
1980	66	52	51	35	29

SOURCE: The Gallup Opinion Index, January 1981, Report No. 184.

nization that has all the characteristics of a sect, except that it is not antagonistic to the larger society. The established sect is the result of a compromise that accompanies the successful transition from the loose organization of the first generation of the sect to stability in the second generation (Martin, 1962; Yinger, 1970).

Sects have exercised fascination over both the general public and the researcher. Given sects' emphasis on personal religious experience and their antagonism to secular society, it is not surprising that they have emerged from a variety of social conditions and experiences. Schism, or division within religious groups, has been one source of sec-

tarianism. Another, personal, source is the need to compensate for inferior social status. Still a third perspective emphasizes deprivation—economic, social, organismic, ethical, and psychic. To develop into a sect, these deprivations must be shared among people, a leader must emerge, and there must be no institutional alternative available; even then, however, the life of the sect is tenuous. The schisms and social sources of sects are discussed in Reading 14.1.

In tracing the development of religious groups, H. Richard Niebuhr (1957) argued that sects were inevitably short-lived. Either a sect ceased to exist or it became a denomination, since it had to deal

TABLE 14.3   Membership in Religious Denominations in the United States

Catholic	51,616,000	(6)[a]
Baptist	27,026,000	(25)
Methodist	10,219,000	(7)
Lutheran	7,604,000	(12)
Jewish	5,860,000	(1)
Orthodox	3,730,000	(16)
Presbyterian	3,593,000	(9)
African Methodist Episcopal	3,100,000	(2)
Latter Day Saints	2,894,000	(2)
Episcopal	2,851,000	(3)
Churches of Christ	2,654,000	(2)
Church of God	1,870,000	(14)
Assembly of God	1,829,000	(1)
United Church of Christ	1,746,000	(1)
Disciples of Christ	1,231,000	(1)
Reformed	776,000	(4)
Pentecostal	684,000	(6)
Seventh Day Adventist	553,000	(1)
Jehovah's Witness	527,000	(1)
Nazarene	475,000	(1)
Salvation Army	415,000	(1)
Brethren	311,000	(6)
Community Churches	190,000	(1)
Missionary Alliance	174,000	(1)
Mennonite	168,000	(8)
Unitarian-Universalist	139,000	(1)
Independent Fundamental	120,000	(1)
Friends	120,000	(5)
Wesleyan	101,000	(1)
Foursquare	89,000	(1)
Full Gospel	62,000	(2)
Buddhist	60,000	(1)
Moravian	54,000	(2)
Other sects	548,000	(66)

[a] The numbers in parentheses refer to the number of groups or organized religious bodies included in the membership total.

SOURCE: From *Yearbook of American and Canadian Churches, 1981* by Constant H. Jacquet. Copyright © 1981 by the National Council of the Churches of Christ in the U.S.A. Used by permission of the publisher, Abingdon Press.

with both external threats of hostility from the larger society and from other churches as well as internal threats posed by growth, economic success, and the problem of continuity. The term **denomination** refers to a religious organization that has accommodated itself to the world, that has a professional clergy, and whose membership is based on race, class, or geography.

Successful sects, particularly evangelical ones, are thus confronted with their own possible destruction. This dilemma is admirably described by John Wesley, the founder of Methodism, and quoted by Niebuhr:

Wherever riches have increased, the essence of religion has decreased in the same proportion. Therefore I do not see how it is possible in the nature of things for any revival of religion to continue long. For religion must necessarily produce both industry and frugality, and these cannot but produce riches. But as riches increase so will pride, anger, and love of the world in all its branches. How then is it possible that Methodism, that is, a green bay tree, should continue in this state? For the Methodists in every place grow diligent and frugal; consequently they increase in goods. Hence they proportionately increase in pride, in anger, in the desire of the flesh, the desire of the eyes and the pride of life. So, although the form of religion remains, the spirit is swiftly vanishing away. (p. 70)

Thus, according to Niebuhr, the successful sect gradually loses its hostility to the secular world as a result of its growth and success. Essentially, it becomes a denomination, thereby failing to satisfy a portion of its membership. The result is a new schism and the emergence of a new sect to start the cycle again.

Recent research on sects in the United States provides additional evidence of the problems sect groups face in dealing with a hostile environment. Because of this tension, most sects do not grow and change but barely survive or slowly decline after their formation (Stark and Bainbridge, 1981). Conflict with the larger society is the most important problem of sectarian life, since the resulting tension both defines a sect's distinctiveness and also makes growth difficult.

Though Troeltsch's church model fairly described the medieval Roman Catholic Church, it clearly does not fit the pattern of religious institutions in modern industrial societies. No religious institution in the United States can hope to include all citizens in its membership, considering their widely differing social and religious experiences. However, people in modern societies share a general commitment to beliefs and symbols of the na-

Sectarian groups often emerge in periods of rapid social change. The loss of familiar family and community relationships that occurs leads to a new set of behavior patterns, responses to the threats of an unfamiliar culture.

tion. These beliefs and symbols have been described as a civil religion that functions to preserve the society despite the diversity of its population.

Civil Religion

Religion in the United States, whether individualistic or communal, active or passive, has always been pluralistic. The variety of religious traditions that the early immigrants from Europe brought with them precluded the establishment of an official state religion, and denominations and sects have flourished. However, as denominational distinctiveness has been undermined by the increasing homogeneity of American life, a civil religion has arisen to take over many of religion's functions. Herberg (1955) noted that ethnic and religious pluralism, or diversity, are now widely accepted—as long as they do not interfere with the "religion" that integrates and unifies the society.

Spiritually, the American Way of Life is best expressed in a certain kind of "idealism" which has come to be recognized as characteristically American. It is a faith that has its symbols and its rituals, its holidays and its liturgy, its saints and its sancta; and it is a faith that every American, to the degree that he is an American, knows and understands. (p. 92)

Rituals, like the Pledge of Allegiance, public prayer, and extravagant demonstrations of patriotism during elections, holidays, and times of crisis bring unity and devotion. The symbols of this religion are the flag, the capitol dome, the national anthem, the Declaration of Independence, the Constitution, and words like freedom, liberty, and honor. In Herberg's view, the ultimate claims to which Americans give their allegiance are not those of the traditional religious institutions of Protestantism, Catholicism, or Judaism but those of the nation, or the American way of life, under whose umbrella religious denominations have accommodated themselves to the society and to each other.

This religious phenomenon was described by Robert Bellah (1967) as **civil religion.** Its central idea is that a general undercurrent of religious understandings pervades society, despite the continuation and successes of traditional religious forms.

According to Bellah, in America, civil religion has existed as a set of beliefs parallel to those of the traditional religions.

The God of the civil religion is not only rather "unitarian," he is also on the austere side, much more related to order, law, and right than to salvation and love . . . He is actively interested and involved in history, with a special concern for America . . . Behind the civil religion at every point lie biblical archetypes: Exodus, Chosen People, Promised Land, New Jerusalem, Sacrificial Death and Rebirth. The civil religion is also genuinely American and genuinely new. It has its own prophets and its own solemn rituals and symbols. It is concerned that America be a society as perfectly in accord with the will of God as men can make it and a light to all nations (p. 7, 18)

Does the identification of civil religion as a binding force in American life mean that religion no longer has a special impact on people? There is considerable evidence that it continues to have an impact with positive and negative consequences for individuals and social institutions. The growth of movements that emphasize personal religious experience and small, emotionally supportive groups suggests that religious values and beliefs still represent answers to ultimate questions in certain contexts. The point is emphasized by Kelley (1972), who suggests that religious organizations that make

strict demands of their members are those that continue to grow.

DOES RELIGION MAKE A DIFFERENCE IN BEHAVIOR?

The institution of religion is shaped and changed by other social institutions, but it also has a significant impact on society, both indirectly—through the behaviors of individuals—and directly—through the interactions of institutions. As we have already noted, there has been a close tie between religious and family institutions throughout history. Similar ties have existed between religious and political institutions, notably in ancient Israel, in the Holy Roman Empire, and in modern Pakistan, Israel, and Iran. Furthermore, education has often been the responsibility of religious institutions, and religious institutions have had significant effects on economic life.

In this section we will examine the relationship of religious beliefs and practices to behavior and attitudes. Unfortunately, the exact nature of these relationships is not clear. For example, do religious beliefs produce political attitudes, or does the process work in reverse? In most cases the best we can do is to examine their interrelationships.

Individual **religiosity** refers to the cluster of beliefs and practices associated with religion in a person's life. But many studies that attempt to evaluate the effects of religion on social behavior use membership in a religious group as the only index of religiosity. Recent studies have recognized the inadequacy of that measure and have attempted to include intensity of commitment or seriousness of belief. Despite the problems in evaluating the significance of religion in the lives of individuals, social scientists tend to agree that it has profound effects on family life, social status, prejudice, political attitudes and behavior, and achievement.

Marriage and Family Life

The influence of religion on family life is reflected in several areas, like mate selection, family size, and attitudes toward abortion and divorce. Research suggests that there are differences in family life that correlate with membership in various Protestant denominations as well as with an individual's identity as Protestant, Catholic, or Jew.

On the basis of several studies from the 1950s and 1960s, it has been noted that the rates of intrafaith and intradenominational marriages, that is, marriage to a person who belongs to the same group, are much higher than expected by chance (Monahan, 1971). The level of interfaith marriages between Catholics, Protestants, and Jews, as well as between members of different denominations, reflects several conditions, especially the proportion of Catholics or Jews in a geographic area, age, and sex ratios among the population, level of religiosity, and the intensity of religious identity. Because evidence about religious intermarriage is difficult to obtain, the actual rate is unknown. However, Cohen (1977) found a higher level of intraethnic, intrareligious marriage among recent immigrants than among persons whose families have lived in the United States for several generations, suggesting the importance of family support for religious ties.

Religious membership and identification are closely associated with family size. Average family size is larger for Catholics than for Protestants, Jews, and nonmembers of religious groups. However, recent studies indicate a decreasing difference in family size among religious groups. Much of this trend seems to be a consequence of the increased use of artificial contraception by Catholics, despite the traditional Church ban on such techniques. Recent research suggests that Protestant-Catholic attitudes and use of birth control are nearly identical (Westoff and Jones, 1977).

Abortion attitudes are also related to religious affiliation, although Catholics are less likely to disapprove of abortion than might be expected on the basis of the Church's strong official position against it. A majority of nonbelievers, Jews, and liberal Protestants in a 1975 study indicated approval of abortion for reasons of health of the mother, rape, defect in the fetus, low income, and parents not married or child not wanted, while a majority of Catholics, conservative Protestants, and sect members approved abortion only for reasons of health, rape, or defect in the fetus (D'Antonio and Stack, 1980). Some studies suggest that a person's church attendance correlates more closely with his or her attitudes toward abortion than does religious affiliation. A large proportion of men and women in the United States disapproved of abortion, but opposition was most apparent among the frequent attenders, regardless of religious affiliation (Hertel, Hendershot, and Grim, 1974).

Though marriages between persons of different religious backgrounds tend to end in dissolution more often than marriages within any one religious faith, the data are sketchy. Jews married to non-Jews appear to be more likely to divorce than Jews married to Jews, and Catholics married to non-Catholics are more divorce-prone than Catholics married to Catholics. Among Protestants, divorce rates are related both to interdenominational and to interfaith marriage patterns.

Interreligious marriages are more common among previously married persons. Also, Catholics and conservative Protestants are less likely to divorce than Jews, nonattenders, and liberal Protestants. Thus the apparent impact of religious involvement on marriage may be due to a variety of factors, such as common socioeconomic, ethnic, or cultural backgrounds, a traditional approach to life, including religion and marriage, or religious beliefs that undergird the marriage by stressing its holy and sacred character (Hunt and King, 1978).

Prejudice

Research on prejudice and religious commitment has a long history, but it has produced inconsistent results. A study by Glock and Stark (1966), which obtained data from church members in the San Francisco area and from a national sample, supports earlier suggestions by many scholars that contemporary American Christianity, especially in its more traditional forms, is the major source of anti-Semitic prejudice. The fact that many Christians define Jews as responsible for the death of Jesus and also see them as potential converts is evidence for this view.

Other investigators have argued that only when certain factors are ignored can Christians be shown to be prejudiced against non-Christians and that, in fact, a large majority of religious people are opposed to prejudice and are tolerant of differences. Two of these researchers, Allport and Ross (1967), noted that church members who supported a religion for reasons that had little to do with religion (to maintain status, for example) tended to be prejudiced, but those who were committed to religion because they believe its precepts tended to be tolerant.

Much of the inconsistency in findings about prejudice derives from different definitions of religious commitment used in research studies. Researchers who have used church membership as the measure of religiosity have consistently reported that church members are more prejudiced than nonmembers (Goldsen et al., 1960; Rokeach, 1969). Cygnar, Noel, and Jacobson (1977) believe that the relationship between religion and prejudice is more complex than a single measure would indicate. Thus, while religious groups may foster prejudice, especially among nominal members, it is also possible that people with prejudices seek religious groups for legitimation of their views.

Other studies attempting to relate prejudice and religiosity have included beliefs, activities, and participation as indexes of religiosity. One finding is that the church member who attends services infrequently is more prejudiced than either nonmembers or active members (Gorsuch and Aleshire, 1974). The reasons for this relationship are not completely clear, but several interpretations can be offered. These researchers suggest that "prejudiced people are conforming to 'the great American Way of life,' a sentiment which includes strong elements of both Anglo-Saxon supremacy and Christianity, whereas nonreligious and highly religious people are selecting their values out of tradition" (p. 288).

At the highest level of group participation, religiosity and commitment tend to be associated with lack of prejudice because of the values of the faith that emphasize acceptance and equality. A superficial involvement in religion appears to be associated with prejudice, perhaps because of a lack of commitment to religious values.

Political Attitudes and Behavior

The influence of religion in politics in the United States has been indirect, often taking the form of "morality" laws—like those governing Sunday sales of beer, wine, and liquor, the sale of birth control devices, or the use of games, gambling, or betting on sports events. Conservative Protestant groups achieved great, though short-lived, success in having a moral position mandated through legislation when the Prohibition amendment outlawing the sale and public consumption of alcohol became effective in 1920. Catholics effectively maintained laws banning the sale or use of birth control devices in Massachusetts and Connecticut—laws that were put on the books by Protestants. In both cases, there was some official action or pressure by religious organizations, but most "morality" laws have been passed by legislative bodies in response to efforts of committed individuals in positions of power acting on behalf of religious groups.

National survey data from 1970 indicate that, in terms of political identification, Jews and Catholics are more likely to be Democrats than are Protestants. Protestants are at least twice as likely to be Republican as Catholics and Jews, but nearly one-fourth of each group identified themselves as independent (Johnston, 1975). Scholars have suggested that Catholics and Jews, whose families are more recent immigrants, became Democrats largely because the Republican party was dominated by earlier Protestant arrivals and less responsive to the problems of urban life. However, religion may also affect political ties. For example, Redekop (1968) noted that both extreme political conservatives and religious fundamentalists tend to define the world in absolute terms of "right" and "wrong," to have a conspiratorial political view, and to emphasize individual rights over social obligations.

Recent political activities in the United States by conservative religious groups have focused upon the selection of senators and representatives who will vote and enact legislation that reflects their views. One such organization, the Moral Majority, has identified abortion, pornography, and homosexuality as "cancers" in American life and seeks to influence federal action in these areas. Other groups have been formed to promote the teaching of "scientific creationism" in the public schools, school prayer, and other activities that the groups associate with correct moral behavior.

Achievement and Status

The question of the impact of religion on personal achievement and status motivation has long fascinated scholars. One of the first to raise the issue was Max Weber (1958) who, in the early 1900s, sought to define the relationships between Protestantism and capitalism.

Weber argued that the important connection between Protestantism—especially Calvinist Protestantism—and the rise of capitalism was the doctrine of predestination and the individual's uncertainty about salvation. The Calvinists believed that their ultimate destiny, whether salvation or eternal punishment, was predetermined by God and was independent of any actions they might take. Anxiety about their ultimate destiny was relieved through hard work. If they prospered, they felt God had favored them and had marked them for salvation. God's blessing was logically extended to the accumulation of money, or capital, which could be invested to produce even greater prosperity—and greater favor in God's eyes.

Many researchers who study achievement motivation continue to examine the connection between Protestant doctrine and achievement. Most research in the United States has focused on religion and individual achievement, specifically on the way religion affects the process of social mobility and social status.

An important study of achievement motivation is that of Lenski (1961), who reported that Protestants and Jews were more likely to demonstrate traits identified by Weber as elements of the Protestant ethic than were Catholics or black Protestants. Specifically, these traits were independence of family control and aspiration to achieve a college education, to enter business, and to succeed. Lenski's findings have been extended by several researchers (Bressler and Westoff, 1963; Glenn and Hyland, 1967; Greeley, 1977; Greeley and Rossi, 1966; Veroff, Feld, and Gurin, 1962) who have pointed out that achievement may be tied to the social situation of religious groups before they emigrated to the United States. Many Jews came from urban areas with a tradition of education and sophistication, but Catholics were predominantly peasants. However, differences have been reported in the achievement motivation of Catholics from different countries. Abramson and Noll (1966) found Italian Catholics to be more secular and to have higher economic aspirations than the devout, traditional German and Irish Catholics.

Research on achievement motivation has produced many findings that appear to be contradictory, perhaps because of the groups chosen for study or the questions asked. Ambition is an ill-defined concept, and one group's approach to success may be seen as laziness or lack of motivation by another group.

Less confusion exists about the social status of members of various religious groups. Sectarian groups that emphasize emotional support tend to attract members of lower status. Religious organizations that emphasize social participation and "churchlike" religious behaviors tend to attract persons of higher status (Demerath, 1965; Fukuyama, 1961). These patterns are reflected in findings of a national sample analyzed by Roof (1979), in Table 14.4. Perhaps the most striking finding is the similarity of socioeconomic status of Catholics and Protestants. The diversity within Catholicism and a similar pattern of differences within Judaism (Lazerwitz and Harrison, 1979) appear similar to that of Protestants.

In recent years many groups claiming large numbers of followers have emerged. Many of these would fit at the bottom of the list, especially the sectarian groups. However, the question remains: Is religion the dominant factor in achievement, or do people who have achieved success change their religious behavior?

Religion and the Social Order

What role does religion play in the larger society?

TABLE 14.4   Comparisons of Education, Occupational Prestige, and Income for Members of U.S. Religious Groups

	N	MEAN EDUCATION[a]	MEAN OCCUPATION PRESTIGE SCORE[a]	MEAN INCOME[a]
Protestants	3547	11.9	45.8	10,435
Episcopalians	175	13.6	48.6	14,250
Presbyterians	320	13.3	49.3	13,600
Congregationalists	103	13.0	48.3	12,290
Methodists	763	12.3	46.1	10,680
Lutherans	577	11.7	45.7	10,365
Baptists	961	11.1	44.6	9,595
Sectarians	332	10.5	45.1	8,120
Other Protestants	308	11.8	43.1	9,630
Catholics	1714	11.3	44.1	10,190
Irish	256	12.5	45.3	11,485
German	212	11.9	44.0	11,240
English and Welsh	63	12.0	50.1	12,010
French	53	11.6	45.5	5,595
Slavic	99	11.7	44.1	10,715
Polish	142	11.0	42.5	10,400
Italian	284	11.1	43.6	10,505
Spanish Speaking	159	9.6	43.3	7,160
Other Catholics	445	11.5	43.9	10,120
Jews	157	13.4	50.8	13,650

[a]Adjusted for age, region and size of place effects.

SOURCE: "Socioeconomic Differentials Among White Socioreligious Groups in the United States," by Wade C. Roof. Copyright © The University of North Carolina Press. Reprinted from *Social Forces* 58 (September 1979).

For one, religious organizations tend to legitimate the status quo by providing individuals with sources of status and satisfaction that may compensate for social inequalities. This role of religion was emphasized by Karl Marx (1969) in his famous statement:

Religious distress is at the same time the expression of real distress and the protest against real distress. Religion is the sigh of the oppressed creature, the heart of a heartless world, just as it is the spirit of a spiritless situation. It is the opium of the people. (p. 94)

Other scholars have emphasized religion's role as a challenge to the existing structure of society, particularly through sectarian and renewal movements. These alternative functions of religious institutions have been described as "comfort" and "challenge" or stability and change, both of which exist in the modern church. Most analyses look upon one or the other of these dimensions as the dominant function of religion in the larger society.

The influence of Emile Durkheim and also of social anthropologists Bronislaw Malinowski and Alfred Radcliffe-Brown has been dominant in the study of religion. According to their view, the function of rituals, beliefs, and practices is to create a sense of social solidarity and cohesion among members of a society so that there will be a consensus of values and attitudes among them. This consensus is assumed to be a critical prerequisite for the maintenance of a society. Failure to achieve it threatens the entire society, leading to social disorganization and collapse (Durkheim, 1961). To achieve this consensus and maintain a moral community, it is necessary to explain why certain events—such as suffering, injustice, and evil—occur in human experience.

The leading advocates of this functionalist view argue that religion is the only social institution that can provide an adequate response to these questions, since it alone has the means of grasping what is beyond the natural world. Therefore, religion is the source of human action, since only religion can give meaning to the ultimate questions that motivate men (Parsons, 1968; Davis, 1949), and is also the source of social stability.

There have been many critiques of the functionalist perspective. Typically, they focus on the functionalist emphasis on the stability of society to the neglect of conflict and social change. It is clear that in some societies religion does function to inhibit change, as in India or in South Africa or Islamic countries. Similar arguments might be made about religion's role in the lack of a "working-class consciousness" in the United States: by providing an other-worldly alternative to economic expectations, religion may function to some degree as an "opiate of the people." Some scholars have argued, however, that organized religion may support or be the cause of social change. Max Weber's theory of the role of Calvinism in the development of capitalism is one such argument. A recent example in which organized religion played a role in social change is the civil rights movement in the United States.

Churches have traditionally been the center of black community life, and black churches have been a source of leadership in the struggle for equal rights. Black churches provided a strong push for desegregation, an opportunity for young blacks to develop leadership abilities, and a context within which people could express their feelings without fear of retaliation by whites. Few white churches initially supported desegregation, though some of their national organizations applied economic and moral pressures upon local churches. However, the emergence of Martin Luther King, Jr., and the religious civil rights movement began to effect changes outside the church. In the South during the 1960s, white churches began to push for desegregation after pressure from the federal government on schools and businesses. (Earle, Knudsen, and Shriver, 1976; Thompson, 1963).

While there may be agreement that religion can offer support to certain general values in modern society, it is clear that not all religious activities or beliefs are integrative—that is, promote the stability of the society or the persons and groups involved in them (Underwood, 1957). Religious actions have different consequences in different social contexts. In some situations social change is closely related to organized religion. In most societies organized religion appears to function to provide stability and unity.

CURRENT RELIGIOUS LIFE

Does the high level of religious activity in the United States and Canada indicate deep human interest in ultimate questions? Or, as some have suggested, are current religious movements and beliefs the last remnants of a premodern belief? Although we do not have the information needed to answer these questions, there have been some important developments in current religious life that must be noted, especially secularism, the growth of Pentecostalism, the emergence of groups that focus on altered states of consciousness, and the electronic church.

Secularism

Secularism refers to a decline in religious influence. As societies develop and modernize, religious institutions become separate from other social structures, and religion loses its ability to control and dominate social life. Though at least six different conceptions of this process have been identified (Shiner, 1967), all of them describe the change from a sacred society to a secular society in which religion is only one aspect of social life and in which there is a decline of both individual beliefs and church influence.

One scholar who has made an effort to develop the general outlines of secularism, Thomas Luckmann, (1967), suggests that the symbolic world of traditional church religion appears to be unrelated to the culture of modern society. The socialization of individuals into the religious system means that they recognize the ultimate concerns, as defined by organized religion, and accept them as their own. Under such circumstances, traditional religion seems plausible to people, and beliefs and practices

remain stable. However, in modern industrial society, there is confusion in belief and practice. Not
only has organized religion become involved in secular activities, but also the diversity of doctrines
and denominations makes the idea of one official
religion implausible. Thus, while organized religion rigidifies its structure and doctrine, the individual increasingly is faced with an unbelievable
set of beliefs and with meaningless symbols and
rituals.

The effect of this inconsistency between official
church religion and individual experience is to reduce organized religion to competition with other,
alternative "packages" of ultimate meaning, including advice columns, books on pop psychology,
rock music, and the like. Luckmann does not deny
that the basic questions about the meaning of life,
death, and suffering are still present. What has
changed is the ability of modern people to find answers to such questions and meaning in the symbols of traditional religion. Instead, an "invisible
religion" has been created composed entirely of private, individual efforts to find meaning in whatever
forms are available outside the church. For Luckmann, this is the essence of secularism—privatiza-
tion and individualization of religious practices and
beliefs. Traditional religion has lost its power to
provide meaning for the individual and unity and
purpose to society.

Not all observers believe that secularism has destroyed traditional religion. A more optimistic view
is offered by Andrew Greeley (1972) on the basis
of his analyses of data from national samples. Comparing responses to questions about beliefs that were
asked in 1952 and 1965, he found a "basic continuity among gentiles in the thirteen-year period in
belief in God, in Christ, in the Trinity, in prayer,
in life after death and heaven" (pp. 137–138). Among
Jews there was a decline in belief in God, in prayer,
in life after death, and in heaven, combined with
an increase in participation in religious services.
While other changes occurred in attendance and
practices, they were generally few. Greeley summarizes his findings as follows:

The average member of a denomination who learned his
religious commitment from his earliest years, perhaps

went through some sort of crisis in his adolescence, but
presently finds his religious posture too important a part
of his life to put it aside because the theologian announces that God is dead. It is important, not because
he thinks of it all the time, or because it pervades everything he does, but because rather it provides him with
both a reassuring answer to ultimate questions and a
fellowship which enables him to find himself over against
others in society. (pp. 141–142)

HIGHLIGHT 14.2
Religion in the Media Age

What will come next and is already on the horizon
is the consumption of spiritual experiences—
personal growth cults, drug-induced ecstasy, world
traveling gurus, training in mystical meditation to
make you feel better, etc. . . . It will be subtle, and
it will be cloaked in the noble language of personal
growth . . .

It must be a simple, attractively packaged, hard-
hitting, religious message that appeals to the
already established wants and desires of the
viewers. Ambitious status seekers who are
achieving less than they wish in life will want to
buy "possibility thinking." The lonely person who
lacks intimate friendship will want to become a
"partner in faith" with the dynamic personality
who is directing an important worldwide ministry.

The 1980s will bring a new stage in the
development of television, namely, two-way or
"interactive" cable television . . . Members of the
viewing public will soon be able to sit at home and
watch the religion of their choice; and in addition,
by pushing buttons on a hand-held console, they
will be able to order a book being recommended or
make a financial pledge. It will be religion without
geographical proximity, without eye-to-eye contact,
without personal commitment, without fellowship.
It will be religion totally at the consumer's disposal.

SOURCE: Selected from Ted Peters, "The Future of Religion in a
Post-Industrial Society," *The Futurist*, October 1980, pp. 21–22.
The Futurist, published by the World Future Society, 4916 St.
Elmo Avenue, Washington, D.C. 20014.

What conclusion can we reach about the future of religion in the face of secularism? Clearly religious activities continue to be important in modern societies. Whether these activities are devoid of meaning as Luckmann suggests, or the source of strength, as Greeley suggests, remains unresolved, at least for the present.

The Growth of Pentecostalism

The meaning of the high level of church participation and membership in the United States and Canada has been a source of considerable dispute. While some theorists consider that church participation and church membership indicate the vitality of faith and belief, there is no convincing evidence that either a renewal or an expansion of established churches has occurred. In terms of recent religious activity, one of the most significant developments is that of Pentecostalism outside established Christian bodies.

Pentecostal sects long have claimed the gift of glossolalia, or speaking in tongues, and the sects are often associated with faith healing, prophecy, and ecstatic experiences. Although glossolalia and ecstatic experiences have not been limited to Pentecostal sects, members of these groups seek and interpret such experiences as unique—as "special evidence of God's visitation." Such experiences often occur in prayer groups, which also stress personal testimony or witnessing—telling about events or experiences that demonstrate God's power (McGuire, 1977).

Altered States of Consciousness

Another religious development has been the emergence of groups that focus on altered states of consciousness. These groups have both Christian and non-Christian ties. The Christian groups are exemplified by the Jesus people, who emphasize subjective personal religious experience, a denial of rationalism, and a concurrent belief that individuals—apart from religious groups—can overcome difficulties in life only through a personal relationship with Jesus. Many of the Jesus people were members of the counterculture of the 1960s. For them, a "high" experienced through the belief that Jesus "lives within the heart" may be substituted for earlier experiences with drugs, sex, and mysticism (Balswick, 1974). The intensely subjective experience of the Jesus person is in part a reaction to what is seen as an evil society and its worldly concerns.

Both the Pentecostal and the Jesus movements focus on personal and subjective experiences as a source of meaning and as evidence of contact with God. It is too early to predict the outcome of these movements. Organized denominational bodies have attempted to incorporate them in an effort similar to that made by the Roman Catholic Church, prior to the Protestant Reformation in the 1500s. If these efforts fail, the movements may develop into denominations in subsequent generations.

Other groups, whose ties are often to Eastern religious traditions, try to achieve a change in consciousness through meditation. Chanting, silent repetition of a sound or word, stylized exercises for breathing, bodily postures, or movements are means to achieve a new level of consciousness (Bird, 1978). Hare Krishna, the Divine Light Mission, Arica, Nichiren Shashu, 3HO, and Spiritualism are examples of groups which seek personal and social transformation through higher consciousness. Most followers believe that the best way to create "a fundamental change in themselves and to break out of the cycle of war, hatred, and violence in the world is to cultivate a deeper relationship to God through spriitual practice and surrender" (Downton, 1980).

A clear distinction should be drawn between groups that emphasize individual change and personal growth through altered states of consciousness and those that stress social control and resocialization, such as the People's Temple or the Father Divine Movement (Richardson, 1980). The tragic events in Jonestown, Guyana, which involved the People's Temple, have obscured the focus of that group upon communal life and social change. Other religious movements that are individualistic in character include witchcraft and some neo-Christian movements that are anti-institutional in focus. Witchcraft includes a wide range of activities that are focused on individuals: spirits, sorcery, black

Religious experiences range from quiet worship to ecstatic expressions of faith. Among many penticostal and sectarian groups, ecstatic experiences are seen as special evidence of God's visitation.

and white magic, spells, demons, and satanism. Despite the fact that sorcery and magic are still defined as solitary and charismatic rather than communal and priestly, a study of the Church of Satan in the San Francisco area found a pattern of rituals and organization similar to that of Christian groups (Alfred, 1976). Some neo-Christian groups with strong emphases on individualism, such as Christian World Liberation Front or Jews for Jesus, also have developed rituals and symbols that attract members but have not yet developed organizational structures that would perpetuate the movement (Heinz, 1976).

The Electronic Church

Religious programs have been a prominent part of radio and television programming almost from the beginning. The first regular religious program on radio aired in 1920 on KDKA in Pittsburgh. Television soon became a favorite medium for religious programs, with Bishop Fulton Sheen as the early superstar.

By the 1980s, the national television networks were broadcasting religious programs 24 hours a day. However, four early television preachers continue to dominate: Billy Graham, Rex Humbard, Oral Roberts, and Jerry Falwell, perhaps better known as the founder of the Moral Majority. Other prominent television programs include the "Hour of Power" with Robert Schuller, "The Praise The Lord Club" with Jim Bakker, "The 700 Club" with Pat Robertson, and several programs and personalities with more modest audiences: Paul Crouch, Jimmy Swaggart, "Gospel Singing Jubilee," Ross Bagley, "Day of Discovery," "At Home with the Bible," James Robison, Kenneth Copeland, Jack Van Impe, and Ernest Angley (Hadden and Swann, 1981).

The size of the audience for each of these programs is a matter of dispute. Though Jerry Falwell claimed in 1980 that an audience of 25 million people watched "The Old Time Gospel Hour" every week, a recent analysis of TV viewing suggests that the correct figure is closer to 1.5 million. In fact, the total number viewing all 66 syndicated religious programs in 1980 was 20,500,000, and if only unduplicated viewers are counted, the number is 10 to 14 million (Hadden and Swann, 1981). Such

disagreements about audience sizes are minor, however, compared with disagreements about the impact of these broadcasts.

All of the religious telecasts rely heavily upon contributions. To ensure a steady flow of funds, elaborate mailing lists are developed, cultivated by regular contact, and maintained through computer systems. The people on the mailing list are seen as the congregation by the television preacher, who seeks to involve them in his church through soliciting contributions and exhorting them by letters, by requests for money, to act against sin and evil. Some, such as Jerry Falwell and the Moral Majority, seek the defeat of elected representatives who support "evils" like the equal rights amendment and abortion and the election to public office of those sympathetic to Moral Majority views. Others may work less directly with their followers, but most view their programs as means of changing the character of American life.

These media efforts to influence public opinion and the political process have been challenged by traditional religious organizations and secular groups as well. Traditional churches have attacked the validity of private and individualistic religious experience as promoted by the electronic media, claiming that religious activities are not only private but also collective, and that participation in a religious group is an essential part of religious life. Secular groups have focused both on the rigid moral positions taken by some of the media preachers and on the use of religion to influence politics, which is seen as a violation of the principle of church and state separation.

The battle over the electronic church has begun, though some of the issues are not well defined and many questions remain. Does the electronic church threaten religious organizations? How important is the influence of religious programming on individual political action? Is the nature of religion changing in the modern society as a result of electronic technology?

SUMMARY

Religion is a universal phenomenon based on people's need to understand life, suffering, and the unknown and their desire for security and solace during periods of emotional crisis. Organized religion emerged as societies became more complex and as certain individuals specialized in religious activities. Symbols, rituals, beliefs, and behaviors associated with religion became defined as sacred phenomena, distinguished from the secular or the profane.

Religious experiences are shared through the rituals and symbols that have a common meaning for members of religious groups. These groups tend to develop from simple to complex organizations, to codify their beliefs and routinize their behaviors. The effort to institutionalize religious experiences into formal patterns of belief and practice creates tensions between individuals seeking religious meaning and organizations.

Religious organizations are diverse in character. Sects are loosely organized groups that are hostile to the secular world. Most members join sects as a result of intense religious experiences. As time passes, children of sect members may know none of the conditions which produced religious experiences for their parents. Instead, religious classes often are created to teach religious beliefs and traditions to these children, and, as a result, an organization develops to coordinate these activities. The established sect is a religious group which has successfully made the transition from a loosely organized group that relies primarily on religious experience in the first generation to an organized group which has lost much of its hostility to the secular world in the second generation. This transition is complete—in the United States—when a denomination emerges. A denomination is a religious organization that has accommodated to the secular world, is organized, has a professional clergy, and has membership based on social factors, rather than a required religious experience.

Churches, in the sense of total membership of all people in a specific area, do not exist in the United States, because a state religion is prohibited by the Constitution. However, civil religion has developed as a system of beliefs, symbols and rituals which unite citizens. The flag, the Pledge of Allegiance, and the idea of America as the "promised land" are evidence of this civil religion.

Religious institutions in the United States and Canada appear to be a dominant cultural force. About two-thirds of the United States population are members of religious groups, and many new groups emerge every year. Evidence of the importance of religion is found in studies of family life, prejudice, politics, and achievement.

Among the most important modern developments affecting religion are secularism, the growth of the Pentecostal movement, the emergence of activities focused on altered states of consciousness, and the electronic church. Some suggest that secularization is a threat to religion; others believe its influence is minimal. Pentecostalism, mind altering movements, and electronic media all have had significant impacts on individual behavior and religious organizations.

GLOSSARY

Atheism, or nontheism   lack of belief in a supernatural being.

Charisma   exceptional qualities or extraordinary powers that command the respect and devotion of others.

Church   a highly developed organization, closely aligned with the dominant culture, that has open and inclusive membership and an objective concept of grace.

Civil religion   a set of beliefs parallel to those of traditional religions, but with secular content.

Denomination   a religious organization that has accommodated itself to the world, that has a professional clergy, and whose membership is based on race, class, or geography.

Established sect   a loosely organized religious group that is joined voluntarily, emphasizes personal religious experience, but is not antagonistic toward the larger society.

Ethical prophets   people who seek to alter the existing social order by criticizing it and who attempt to establish a new ethical code or persuade others to return to traditional standards.

Exemplary prophets   people who seek to alter the existing social order by personal example, often suffering punishment, disgrace, or even death to present their message.

Magic a set of beliefs and rituals associated with a specific objective; a supernatural power.

Monotheism belief in one supreme being or god.

Pentecostal sects religious groups that seek intensely emotional, individualistic experiences, including speaking in tongues, faith healing, prophecy, and ecstasy.

Polytheism belief in many gods of equal or similar power and importance.

Priest a person who seeks to give meaning and significance to traditional religious patterns through the celebration of rituals and worship in an organized group.

Profane, or secular common beliefs and practices of everyday life.

Prophet a person who proclaims a religious doctrine or divine commandment and seeks to change the existing social order.

Religion an institutionalized system of symbols, beliefs, values, and practices that focus on questions of ultimate meaning.

Religiosity the cluster of beliefs and practices associated with a person's experience of religion.

Rituals regularly patterned acts imbued with sacred meaning.

Sacred the forbidden and the aloof.

Sect a loose organization, hostile to the dominant social order, that has voluntary membership and a subjective concept of grace.

Secularism decline in religious influence; separation of religious institutions from other social structures and loss of religious control and domination of social life.

Shaman a person with special power because of his relationship with the spirit world.

Theism belief in a supernatural being.

ADDITIONAL READINGS

Allport, Gordon W. *The Individual and His Religion*. New York: Macmillan, 1960.
A sympathetic look at the positive features of religious faith for the individual, especially in terms of religion's maturing and liberating functions.

Berger, Peter. *The Sacred Canopy: Elements of a Sociological Theory of Religion*. New York: Doubleday, 1967.
A humanistic approach to the sociology of religion, focusing upon the importance of religion in human life.

Downton, James V., Jr. "An Evolutionary Theory of Spiritual Conversion and Commitment: The Case of Divine Light Mission." *Journal for the Scientific Study of Religion* 19 (December 1980):381–96.
An examination of the emergence of a new religious group and its efforts to adapt to society.

Glock, Charles Y., and Roberta N. Bellah, eds. *The New Religious Consciousness*. Berkeley: University of California Press, 1976.
A major study of a wide range of religious and quasi-religious groups in Berkeley in the 1970s.

Hadden, Jeffrey K., and Charles E. Swann. *Prime Time Preachers: The Rising Power of Televangelism*. Reading, Pa: Addison-Wesley, 1981.
An effort to assess the impact of televised religious programs on American religion and the public.

Himmelfarb, Harold S. "The Study of American Jewish Identification: How It Is Defined, Measured, Obtained, Sustained and Lost." *Journal for the Scientific Study of Religion* 19 (March 1980):48–60.

Marty, Martin E. *A Nation of Behaviors*. Chicago: University of Chicago Press, 1976.
A summary and interpretation of current religious behavior by one of America's best known religious commentators.

Richard, Michael P., and Albert Adato. "The Medium and Her Message: A Study of Spiritualism at Lily Dale, New York." *Review of Religious Research* 22 (December 1980):186–97.
A look at a nontraditional religious practice, with a critical sociological view.

Wilson, Bryan R. "An Analysis of Sect Development." *American Sociological Review* 24 (February 1959):3–15.
A classic article, which examines religious organizations, their social sources and social context, and their development.

READING

READING 14.1

American-Born Sects

Rodney Stark and William Sims Bainbridge

INTRODUCTION

In an effort to understand religious groups, Stark and Bainbridge have examined the establishment and growth of both cults and sects. Cults are defined as emergent groups with **deviant** *or non-U.S. religious traditions. Sects are groups emerging from within traditional American religious bodies. A total of 501 cults were identified, compared with 417 native-born sects currently functioning in the United States. All of the sects are seen as existing in moderate to extreme tension with their environment; 90 percent of sects were defined as having a "high," "very high," or "extreme" level of tension.*

Some of these sects are growing, some are stable, some are declining. All of them share the experience of breaking off from another religious group, and many share common beliefs and practices as well. In the following selection, the "families" of sect groups and their location in the United States are explored.

FAMILY

It will be obvious that sects, like cults, form families. Sects break off from other bodies, and many in their turn foster additional sects. Because sects attempt to restore practices and doctrines from which the parent body allegedly drifted, sect families bear rather close resemblance in terms of theology and worship forms. Thus Baptist sects, for example, have a family likeness in terms of adult baptism by immersion.

SOURCE: Selected from Rodney Stark and William Sims Bainbridge, "American-Born Sects: Initial Findings," *Journal for the Scientific Study of Religion* 20 (June 1981):130–149.

By far the largest family, with 26.4 percent of the total, is the *Pentecostal* group. The primary characteristic distinguishing Pentecostal sects from other Protestant groups is the central emphasis given to speaking in tongues during church services. Glossolalia played a role in the earliest days of Christianity, reemerging in the late 17th century among French Huguenots during their period of intense persecution by French Catholics. Since then it has reappeared a number of times— among the Quakers during the 18th century, in the U.S. during the 19th century, and among Roman Catholics in Europe and United States in very recent years. The American family of Pentecostals began in Iowa in 1895, spread to Topeka, Kansas, then to Los Angeles, and then back to Arkansas and Tennessee. The largest contemporary group is the Assemblies of God, with well over 1 million members. Another large Pentecostal group is the Church of God (Cleveland, Tenn.) with well over 300 thousand members.

A second distinctive aspect of American Pentecostal groups is their practice of faith healing. While most Christian bodies accept the possibility of healing through divine intervention, few others than Pentecostal groups hold special healing services, and advertise the power to heal.

The second largest sect family is the *Holiness* group. The Holiness Movement that swept American Protestantism in the 19th century had its roots in Methodism. Emphasis was placed on a personal salvation experience in which the individual is "born again" in Christ and undergoes sanctification—the individual becomes personally holy and strives for perfection. As with many revival movements of the 19th century, the Holiness Movement represented the discomfort of many Americans with the constant bickering among the multitude of Christian bodies all claiming to be the one true church. The Holiness Movement aimed at a general reconciliation across

TABLE 1   Family Origins of American-Born Sects

FAMILY	NUMBER	PERCENT
1. Pentecostal	110	26.4
2. Holiness	61	14.6
3. Baptist	41	9.8
4. Adventist	27	6.5
5. Methodist	25	6.0
6. Old Catholic (Roman)	23	5.5
7. Fundamentalist	20	4.8
8. Mennonites and Amish	17	4.1
9. Eastern Orthodox	15	3.6
10. Lutheran	12	2.9
11. Disciples of Christ	12	2.9
12. Presbyterian	9	2.2
13. Quakers	7	1.7
14. Anglican (Episcopalian)	7	1.7
15. Russellites	6	1.4
16. Other Adventists	5	1.2
17. Mormons (Utah)	5	1.2
18. Pietist	4	1.0
19. Reformed	3	.7
20. Communes	3	.7
21. Congregational	3	.7
22. Jewish	2	.5
	417	100%

denominational lines. In time this led to conflicts between the holiness activists and the various denominational leaders, particularly the bishops of the Methodist church. Thus what began as a unification drive soon led to new religious bodies as internal schisms began. Today we can identify 61 different religious bodies within the Holiness family. The largest of these is the Church of the Nazarene, one of the more successful of recent sect movements, with a membership of 441 thousand members and 4,733 congregations in 1975. Another sizeable sect of the Holiness family is the Church of God (Anderson, Indiana) with more than 160 thousand members.

The *Baptists* constitute the third most numerous sect family in contemporary America, with 41 different sects, or about 10 percent of all sects. The origins of the Baptists have long been disputed by church historians. We favor those who reject direct linkage between the Baptist family of England and the United States, on the one hand, and the Anabaptists who flourished in Europe, on the other. The Anabaptists remain committed to very high tension positions and practices never found among the Baptists, such as refusing to swear oaths, to hold public office, or to serve under arms. Those practices persist among such clear descendents of European Anabaptists as the Amish and the Mennonites. But they have not existed among Baptists. The two have been linked, in our opinion, because of superficial resemblances in name, and in the practice of adult Baptism.

Modern Baptism seems to have arisen among English Puritans, perhaps during a sojourn in Holland. The first Baptist group known in America was founded in Rhode Island in 1639 by Roger Williams. The movement grew rapidly by mission work in the middle colonies where there were no established churches to impede them.

The northern and southern branches of the Baptist movement split in 1844 over the issues of slavery and of organizational centralization. The two halves, the American Baptist Churches, with more than 1.6 million members, and the Southern Baptist Convention, with more than 12.7 million, have never reunited. Each has, in turn produced a variety of sects, although the Southern Baptists have produced more.

Indeed, the Southern Baptists produced a major sect within months of their separation from northern Baptists. The group proposed that non-Baptists could not be considered as Christians and thus no relations with them could be maintained. Today, this sect is known as the American Baptist Association, and has more than a million members. Indeed, the Baptist sects tend to be larger than those in other sect families. The Baptist Bible Fellowship counts more than 1 million members, and the Baptist Missionary Association of America and the General Association of Regular Baptists Churches each have more than a quarter of a million.

The fourth most prominent sect family is in the *Adventist* tradition with 27 sect groups (6.5%). Adventists can be distinguished by their emphasis on the imminence of the Second Advent—when Christ will return to receive the saved into everlasting glory. The American Adventist Movement began with one of the most influential prophets in our religious history, William Miller, a layman who believed he had discovered that the date for the Second Coming was between March 21, 1843, and March 21, 1844. Miller aroused tens of thousands of followers. As the end of the year specified by Miller approached, thousands sold their property and gathered to be taken into heaven. The end failed to come. By May, 1844, Miller humbly admitted his error. However, his followers did not. Samuel S. Snow readjusted Miller's computations and everyone enthusiastically awaited the millennium set for October 22, 1844. This date is referred to as the "Great Disappointment" among Adventists, but still the movement did not disband. In any event, a great many very significant American sect movements originated out of the Great Disappointment. Most of these groups still await the Advent soon, but strict rules are enforced against setting any specific dates. The largest of the sects in this family is the Seventh-Day Adventist Church, with about 500 thousand members, founded by Mother Ellen G. White in the aftermath of the Millerite disappointment. This family also eventually gave raise to another sect family, the *Russelites*, whom we discuss below.

It should be no surprise that 25 sects fall within the *Methodist* family, for Methodists are second only to Baptists in terms of the denominational affiliation reported by American Protestants. Methodism arose in England under the leadership of John Wesley in 1739. The movement came to the United States with English immigrants shortly before the Revolutionary War and spread rapidly. Today the United Methodist Church, with about 10 million members, is the direct heir to the English Wesleyan movement.

Methodist sects have been especially common among black Americans. The African Methodist Episcopal Church with over 2 million members, and the African Methodist Episcopal Zion Church, with more than 1 million, are leading examples. In fact, a third of Methodist sects are black organizations.

The *Old Catholic* family has produced 23 American sects. Probably because of the historic dominance of Protestantism, the continuing emergence of sects from *Roman Catholicism* in the United States has gone almost wholly unremarked by social scientists.

The most important impetus for the formation of Roman Catholic sects in the United States was the *First* Vatican Council during the 1870s. That council declared that the Pope was infallible in matters of faith and morals. In reaction many small Catholic groups, usually led by parish priests, broke with Rome, rejected Vatican I, and based their teachings on the doctrines agreed to by earlier church councils. Often these schisms were facilitated by underlying ethnic conflicts. Thus, by far the largest of current Old Catholic sects is the Polish National Catholic Church of America with around 200 thousand members. This group not only objected to the First Vatican Council, but to the nearly universal practice of assigning non-Polish priests (usually Irish) to Polish parishes. Interestingly enough, blacks have played leading roles in the Old Catholic movement and at present the Bishop of the Old Roman Catholic Church (Marchenna), headquartered in New York, is black.

Number seven in terms of number of sects (20) is the *Fundamentalist* family. This name is the source of great confusion among observers of American religion, for often all religious groups that embrace traditional doctrines are collectively referred to as "fundamentalists." There is obvious utility in having such a short-hand term, yet there is a much more precise historical meaning to the term best describing only a few American religious groups. The Fundamentalist Movement arose at the turn of the century with one essential goal—to reassert and defend the absolute truth of a literal interpretation of the Bible. In 1890 a group of ministers, primarily from the major Baptist and Presbyterian denominations, who had for several years been holding annual meetings at Niagara, Ontario, adopted a fourteen-point statement of creed. This step soon led to major disputes within these denominations since the points of fundamentalism were not followed by the majority of clergy in these bodies. By the 1920s sects began to break away to adhere to the Niagara Creed, the largest being the Independent Fundamental Churches of America, founded in Iowa in 1922, and which today claims nearly 90 thousand members. Other sects in this family are very small.

The *Mennonite and Amish* family has many different sects (17), but has depended almost entirely on its original immigrant base and fertility to sustain membership. As mentioned earlier, splits seem to be the result of the extreme encapsulation of these groups and the consequent poor communications between centers.

Eastern Orthodox schisms have produced 15 current sects, also within ethnic communities. Often these splits have centered on relations with a state church in the nation of origins that has accommodated itself to a Communist regime.

The large *Lutheran* denominations have primarily produced small, rural sect movements, usually sustained by a single ethnic group. However, one very large sect broke off from Lutheranism in reaction to the Holiness Movement that swept through middle-America in the 19th century. This sect is the Lutheran Church-Missouri Synod which has nearly 3 million members. A second large Lutheran sect, the Wisconsin Synod, also developed as a response to the evangelical impulses of the 19th century. It counts about 400 thousand members.

The *Disciples of Christ* family includes 12 current sects, the largest being the North American Christian Convention with more than 1 million members.

The *Presbyterian, Quaker*, and *Anglican* (Episcopalian) traditions each provide a few current sects.

The *Russellite* family is the source of only six current sects, but one of them, the Jehovah's Witnesses, is among the most extreme and best known of the larger American-born sects. Charles Taze Russell picked up where the Adventist Millerites left off, reworking the Millerite doctrines and date calculations, and preaching that the end was close at hand. In 1879 Russell and his followers began to publish *Watch Tower*, which is still sold door-to-door every week by Jehovah's Witnesses.

As time passed Russell became increasingly specific about the date of the millennium. He set the "dawn period" as 1874-1914. During this time the Jews would return to Palestine (which they were already doing when the prophesy was made), and there would be a gradual overthrow of the secular leadership of Gentile nations. 1914 was the climax, when the saints would receive glorification and God would begin direct rule over the earth. The outbreak of World War I in 1914 was not seen as the failure of Russell's prophesy but as dramatic evidence of its truth. The war was interpreted as the apocalypse, and as the certain signal that God had indeed taken direct control of human events. The end would come in 1918. Russell died in 1916, so he did not face any problems with the 1918 date when the war ended but the Advent did not occur. However, his followers reinterpreted the scheme to mean that Christ began a period of "invisible rule" in 1914, which soon will end—

"Many now living will die." There is still firm belief that only those who witness for Christ before the end will live in glory, while the meek (those unconverted) will only inherit the earth.

Russell's followers have splintered a number of times, but the main body of Witnesses claims more than 500 thousand followers in the United States and another million abroad.

The *Reformed* family is rooted in the religious traditions of early Dutch settlers. Several radical rural Protestant *communes*, prominent in the 19th century, still survive. *Jewish* and *Mormon* families are small and have been discussed earlier in this paper.

LOCATION

. . . Cult movements are highly concentrated in the West, especially in the Pacific region. But where are the sects? Popular wisdom would have it that sects are very much a Southern phenomenon. Others would suggest that sects will cluster in the same fashion as cults—that all forms of religious deviance will prosper where the mainline churches are weakest. Our data belie both conclusions.

Admittedly, our data on sects, like those on cult movements, are not all that one would desire. Only one state gets credit for a sect (the state in which the headquarters of the group is located).

. . . Although our data are not the best with which to examine sect geography, they still offer useful information. . . .

Tennessee seems to deserve its reputation as an active sect state. It leads the nation with 5.48 sects per million. Utah and Indiana have the next highest rates, while Pennsylvania (which has the largest number of sects) places fourth.

It can be seen that sects, unlike cults, are not abundant in the western states. While California is home for 167 cults (a rate of 7.9 per million) it has only 29 sects for a rate of

TABLE 2   State Rates of Sects Per Million Population

STATE[a]	NUMBER OF SECTS	SECTS PER MILLION POPULATION
1. Tennessee	23	5.48
2. Utah	5	4.17
3. Indiana	20	3.77
4. Pennsylvania	39	3.72
5. Arizona	8	3.64
6. North Carolina	19	3.45
7. North Dakota	2	3.33
8. Missouri	16	3.33
9. Oklahoma	9	3.33
10. South Carolina	9	3.20
11. Mississippi	7	3.04
12. West Virginia	5	2.78
13. Montana	2	2.86
14. South Dakota	2	2.86
15. Minnesota	11	2.80
16. Georgia	13	2.65
17. Kansas	6	2.60
18. Idaho	2	2.50
19. Colorado	6	2.40
20. Arkansas	5	2.38
21. Illinois	26	2.36
22. Michigan	19	2.07
23. Kentucky	7	2.06
24. New York	35	1.94
25. Oregon	4	1.74
26. Alabama	6	1.67
27. Maryland	6	1.46
28. Washington	5	1.43
29. California	29	1.37
30. Nebraska	2	1.33
31. Wisconsin	6	1.30
32. Ohio	14	1.30
33. Texas	15	1.23
34. Virginia	6	1.20
35. Hawaii	2	1.11
36. Rhode Island	1	1.11
37. New Jersey	8	1.10
38. Maine	1	.91
39. Florida	7	.83
40. Iowa	2	.69
41. Delaware	1	.60
42. Louisiana	1	.26
43. Massachusetts	1	.17
Washington D.C.	3	4.29
NATIONALLY	416[b]	1.96

[a] Alaska, Connecticut, Nevada, New Hampshire, New Mexico, Vermont, and Wyoming had no sect headquarters.

[b] One sect omitted because of ambiguity as to location.

1.37 per million. Nevada and New Mexico are the top two states for cults, but neither has a single sect headquarters.

Perhaps even more surprising, the list of high sect states is not dominated by southern states. This is consistent with findings . . . that the South is not exceptional in terms of church membership, church attendance, or religious belief. Here we see that it is not unusually hospitable to sects.

These geographic trends come into sharp relief in Figure [14.1]. Here sect rates have been computed for the nine census regions.

The East South Central region does have the highest rate (3.19), but that is heavily influenced by Tennessee's extremely high rate. With Tennessee removed, the rate for this region drops to 2.15 per million, similar to most other regions. The map also shows that the Pacific region falls below the national average for sects, which suggests that sects and cults do *not* cluster and do *not* represent functionally alternative kinds of religious deviance. . . .

However, the most striking feature of the map of American sects is the astonishingly low

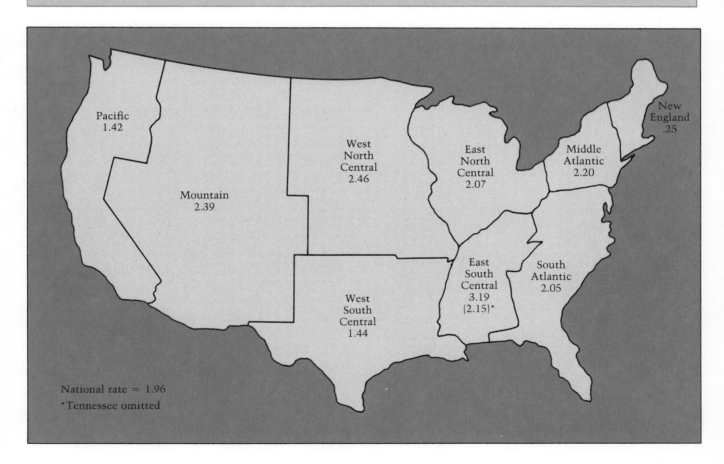

National rate = 1.96
*Tennessee omitted

FIGURE 14.1   Regional Sect Rates
per Million Population

rate of 0.25 sects per million for the New England region. What accounts for this? Here we can only offer plausible hunches.

The New England region is an area of very early settlement. Once this was a hotbed of sect formation. Some of these sects long ago died out. Many others migrated with the waves of westbound settlers that this region produced in the late 18th and early 19th century. The people who left were those most likely to have been members of sects or to have helped form new ones—people who had the least social and economic stake in staying put. Then, when new sects might have formed to replace those that died out or moved, new waves of immigrants made the region predominantly Roman Catholic. It is true that American Catholicism has produced some sects. But they are few and small. Generally speaking, Catholics have not been prone to create sects or to join them. We suspect that migration took away New England's sects and immigration prevented their replacement.

CONCLUSION

. . . One important lesson to be learned from these data is that the *United States is not unusually prolific in sects*. Nationally, there are about two (1.96) sects per million population. Work we have just begun suggests that the sect rate for many parts of Europe is about the same. In contrast, counting *only Christian* sects gives Africa a rate of 12.5 sects per million. If adequate data were available so that the large number of Muslim sects as well as those emerged out of indigenous faiths could be added, Africa's sect rate would be astonishingly high. . . . Let there be an end to the notion that America is the land of the sect.

A second important implication of these data is that most sects do not grow and do not reduce their initial high level of tension be-

cause their initial tension level was so high that they could not successfully recruit new members. Obviously, the connections among successful growth, initial level of tension, and changes in level of tension are complex and reciprocal. . . . Specifically, we must cease basing the transformation of sects into churches on what happened in a particular case, the Nazarenes, for example. Conversely, we must cease challenging the tendency of sects to be transformed merely by pointing to an apparently contrary case such as the Amish. Instead, we must ask how specific factors impede or prompt transformation and to do so we shall need to examine correlations—statistical regularities that pertain to a number of cases. That is, we need to know *probabilities* and to discard the simple-minded "on-off" logic inherent in case studies. Moreover, quantitative comparative analysis can identify important deviant cases that warrant closer inspection. Such inspection, in turn, will lead us to seek, and to test, crucial intervening variables rather than to proliferate ad hoc exception rules for individual cases.

SUMMARY
Sects are numerous and dispersed throughout the country. Some traditions—the Pentecostal, Holiness, and Baptist—have provided nearly half of all sect groups; by contrast, the Presbyterians, Episcopalians, Disciples of Christ, and Lutherans combined have produced fewer than one-tenth of these sects. These findings raise several questions.

QUESTIONS
1. Is such a pattern associated with organization, beliefs, or characteristics of members?
2. Is sectarian growth the result of intensity of beliefs or the outgrowth of close social ties?
3. Why are cults more likely than sects to prosper in the West?

454

CHAPTER 15

Political Institutions

CONTENTS

AT ISSUE

Should government spy on its citizens?

With the increase in violence and terrorism throughout the world, some leaders have advocated government spying on citizens to obtain information about threats to stability and order. The issue involves conceptions of society—why the limits of freedom, the rights of the state, the role of communities in maintaining order. There is no doubt that most governments have the power to spy on citizens. Should they?

YES   Over the last 40 years propaganda, espionage, and acts of violence have been carried out by totalitarian states against the Western democracies generally and the United States especially. Kidnappings and murders of public officials, threats, terrorist attacks, and thefts of government secrets and documents have become commonplace. While the number of such events in the United States has been small, the potential for terrorist attacks is becoming greater.

In the earlier days of our nation, citizens could—and did—take direct action to deal with external and internal threats. In today's complex world we must rely on government to protect us from subversion. Our laws grant people much freedom and privacy, which allow individuals and groups to promote violence and terrorism; the sheer size and mobility of the population make the potential number of radicals larger and the informal controls of neighbors and friends ineffective.

Under such circumstances, the development of a national intelligence network to check on the activities of individuals and groups is simply preventive action, comparable to preventive medicine. It is more effective and less expensive than responding to actions by individuals and groups after violence, death, and terror have occurred.

Those who argue that a program of spying on civilians is a violation of civil rights must face up to the fact that the world has changed and government must change too. After all, only those who are threatening the social order will be affected; law-abiding citizens have nothing to fear.

Without the protection of law and order and the prevention of violence through spying on citizens, our society may not survive at all. The greatest threat to civil liberties is terrorism and violence; surely, efforts to prevent such activities are valid. Spying must be done if we are to remain free!

NO   For centuries government leaders have justified spying on citizens on the basis of presumed violence or civil disruption. The United States is no exception: presidents, the FBI, and the military all have been involved in such activity, usually without any real threat at all.

To be sure, the Western democracies offer a high degree of freedom, including privacy, to their citizens. However, there is no evidence of a relationship between freedom and terrorism or that terrorism is increasing in the United States; even the FBI no longer considers it one of the most important issues. If a violence or terrorism problem exists it is because people have not been involved in government. The solution is a more open society—not a more closed one.

There is little reason to believe that spying on citizens will either prevent violence or terrorism or aid in the prosecution of those involved. During the 1960s the FBI infiltrated organizations in the civil rights movement, the Ku Klux Klan, and some groups like the Weathermen, which later used

456

violence to threaten and intimidate. Not only did the information obtained by these means fail to stop violence; some of the spies themselves were charged with creating violence to discredit the groups and to justify spying. Such actions should be stopped once and for all.

The right to privacy is one of the most precious of our Constitutional freedoms. To spy on people by electronic devices, use of informants, or other means that invade privacy is to destroy the strength of America. Not all people are superpatriots, and those who are not are not disloyal. Not all people respond in the same way to life experiences. To spy and to use the information gathered is to threaten and coerce people into a narrow perspective of patriotism. One of the dangers of spying is that it creates victims whose only crime is disagreement with the views of those doing the spying.

There is no evidence that spying on citizens produces benefits to anyone. Government must be built on consensus, not coercion. Spying has no place in a democratic society.

People who perceive terrorism and violence as a threat to American society see spying as an important part of self-defense. Noting that the older forms of maintaining order, such as persuasion, community ties, and closeness to government decision making, are gone, they argue that spying prevents terrorism, and the loss of civil liberties is minor compared with the threat of violence. Those who oppose spying emphasize that civil rights have been violated by such actions for years, but violence has not been stopped. They suggest that participation in decision making by all people— even radicals—is better than closing access to government and controlling citizens by the use of government power.

In this chapter we will investigate how power is used in decision making, when it is used, by whom, and for what ends. We also will explore the processes by which members of a society are socialized into the political system. Our main focus will be politics in the United States, but other societies will be included for comparison. By considering a variety of questions we hope to develop a better understanding of political institutions and the political process.

QUESTIONS TO CONSIDER

- How does power become legitimate?

- Is it possible to have democracy in developing countries?

- Is participation in politics effective in creating social change?

- How do people learn to influence political decision making?

- Is government run by a small, powerful elite or by many groups?

On March 2, 1982, Vermont citizens met to govern themselves in town meetings that are the essence of grass-roots democracy. In Newfane in southern Vermont, the proceedings got under way promptly at 9 A.M. By 11:45 A.M. 17 of the 22 items on the agenda had been discussed and voted on. Municipal officials won 50¢-an-hour raises. A local rescue squad was granted a $2,291 subsidy. Then the moderator announced that one more article would be deliberated before the lunchtime recess: item 18, which urged "a mutual freeze on the testing, production and deployment of nuclear weapons, and of missiles and new aircraft designed primarily to deliver nuclear weapons, with verification safeguards satisfactory to both countries." By noon the debate was over. Each of 124 Newfaners wrote yes or no on a paper slip and filed up to a pair of white wooden ballot boxes, and soon the moderator announced, "94 for and 30 against," to a solid wave of applause. The White House, let alone the Kremlin, is far removed from Newfane, but not, Vermont's citizens insisted last week, beyond reach. (Paraphrased from Time, March 15, 1982, p. 16)

At ten A.M. on October 1, 1979, the sun emerged through the drizzle that followed the torrents of morning rain. At that hour, Nigeria's military rulers handed political power to an elected civilian government. The symbolism of this coincidence for outsiders who had joined thousands of Nigerians to witness this historic event was one of perfection.

The head of the Federal Military government and commander in chief of the armed forces reviewed the traditional National Day parade, comprised of army, navy, and airforce units, the police and Lagos school children. About 45 minutes later, his successor, Alhaji Shehu Shagari, took the oath as the first executive president and commander in chief of the Federal Republic of Nigeria. For this nation of over 80 million—close to one-fifth of Africa's total population and the world's fourth largest democracy, this was an impressive political event.

By 11 o'clock, the inauguration was completed and the military leaders had stepped back. As President Shagari circled the parade ground at Tafawa Balewa Square, the crowd that filled some 100,000 seats cheered for their leaders and for the event itself. (Paraphrased from Foreign Policy Association, Headline Series, No. 257, January/February 1982).

The striking differences in these two events should not obscure the fact that they have a common focus: the exercise of power in decision making. Political institutions are diverse—they include all of the citizens voting on local or world issues in a small town in New England, the exercise of power by a military junta, and informal agreements about leadership in a small community or an urban area. Regardless of the diversity of governments throughout the world, all political institutions involve power, decision making, social order, and justice.

Every society has distinctive sets of norms, goals and a distinctive social context that define the appropriate action of government. Political decisions, to be effective, must take these into account. It is the social context that is of primary interest to the sociologist, rather than the decision-making structures themselves, a major focus of political science. The exercise of legitimate and illegitimate political power, political organization and conflict, voting, and community action are issues involving social relationships. Because politics occurs in social settings, sociologists are most interested in how social relations and social contexts affect political activity and political institutions. Used in a formal sense **politics** refers to the operations of government. However, we also must know what purposes a government serves and what its intentions are.

POLITICAL POWER

All political leaders, whether tribal chieftains, police commissioners, democratically elected presidents, or tyrants, share at least one common function: they exercise power. Weber (1947) defined power as the probability that one actor within a social relationship will be in a position to carry out his own will despite resistance. *Power*, then, is the ability to control actions of others through such diverse means as brute force, negotiation, promise of rewards, social exchange of goods and services, or appeals to the common good.

Politics may be viewed differently by scholarly disciplines. Political science focuses primarily on such behaviors and definitions as the functions of government, the roles of interest groups, and the nature of political parties. Sociology examines the efforts of various social groups to gain political power and particularly the social factors that shape political decision making. However, both disciplines recognize that relationships between political and other institutions are reciprocal. For example, decisions made by government officials alter relationships in social groups competing for political power, as in the case of changes in lobbying laws, tax regulations, or gun control; in turn, organized groups can influence decision-making bodies by voting and lobbying.

Power and Authority

The exercise of power is legitimated, or justified, by the norms of a society. The term **authority** describes the use of power that is consistent with the norms of society and accepted as legitimate by members of the society. Power that is not consis-

tent with norms is illegitimate and is described as **coercion** (Gerth and Mills, 1946).

By what means is authority established? Under what circumstances is one person's control over another accepted as legitimate by both? Weber (1947) concluded that authority, as the legitimate use of power, comes from three different sources: (1) tradition, (2) charisma, and (3) legal definition.

TRADITIONAL AUTHORITY

Traditional authority or, as Weber put it, "the authority of the eternal yesterday" is legitimate power that is passed down from one ruler to another—from king to king, pope to pope, or patriarch to patriarch. Loyalty is to the office or the position rather than to the individual ruler ("The king is dead, long live the king"), and tradition guarantees compliance with the rules. Precedents or rules for the exercise of traditional authority need not be written down to be effective and accepted.

CHARISMATIC AUTHORITY

Charismatic authority is based on "the extraordinary and personal gift of grace (charisma), the absolutely personal devotion, and personal confidence in revelation, heroism, or other qualities of leadership" (Gerth and Mills, 1946). The authority of a charismatic leader rests on his or her ability to inspire other people to express the leader's will. Charismatic authority has been employed, at least in part, by such leaders as Winston Churchill, Adolf Hitler, Julius Caesar, Nicolai Lenin, Golda Meier, and Indira Gandhi.

RATIONAL-LEGAL AUTHORITY

Rational-legal authority refers to the legality of and the belief in the validity of laws and rationally created rules. The willingness of the ruled to acknowledge the necessity of laws is the basis of the political order. With rational-legal authority there are usually explicit limitations to the power that leaders may wield and, in some cases, to the length of time a leader may serve in office.

The stability of a rational-legal system, independent of the fate of the leader, was dramatically illustrated twice in the United States during the recent past. On November 22, 1963, when President

John F. Kennedy was assassinated and President Lyndon B. Johnson succeeded him, and on August 9, 1974, when President Richard M. Nixon was forced to resign and President Gerald R. Ford replaced him, the transition was smooth. In both cases the leader suddenly was out of office, but government functions in general went on uninterrupted. Similarly, prime ministers may change under parliamentary forms of rational-legal political systems, but such changes rarely cause social upheaval.

All three kinds of authority may be exercised in the political institutions of a society, but one type usually dominates. In lesser developed nations rational-legal authority may be less important than traditional or charismatic authority. By contrast, in the United States the president is the head of a large bureaucratic organization based on rationally created rules; one of his major functions is to propose legislation. Other functions of the presidency, particularly ceremonial ones, are exercised by the president by virtue of tradition, including receptions for foreign heads-of-state and issuing the Thanksgiving proclamation. In addition, to rise to the presidency, an individual must become a leader in his political party. Charismatic gifts may be helpful in this rise, as in the cases of John Kennedy and Ronald Reagan, and their lack may hamper presidents in achieving their political programs, as with Woodrow Wilson and Herbert Hoover.

Power and Influence

Social decisions are made through the exercise of political power. To the extent that an individual or a group can influence a political decision they may be said to have political power. The promotion of "nuclear freeze" initiatives by peace groups, protectionist trade laws by labor unions, and antipollution controls by environmentalists are examples of attempts to influence the political decision-making process. However, the use of persuasion to influence decisions is likely to be ineffective compared with other forms of political action, such as appeals to group or party loyalty or calling in political debts.

Lane (1964) lists a variety of ways in which individuals and groups attempt to influence the political process in literate societies with political democracy. First, personal petitions may be directed at public officials. This approach suggests that the citizen is using a promise of reward or a threat of punishment to get the official to act in the desired manner. Second, a letter campaign may be waged to suggest that there is numerical strength in support of or in opposition to a particular position. Third, like-minded individuals may join in a political organization to support a program of action. All of these are attempts to exercise power over the political process and to bring about binding political decisions. Political decisions, once made, compel some degree of compliance on the part of every member of society. But who has the actual power to compel such compliance and by what means?

Authority and Shared Norms: Consensus and Conflict

In this section we will consider the means by which people are persuaded to comply with political decisions. For the exercise of legitimate authority both rulers and ruled must subscribe to the same set of social norms. For most decisions there is **consensus,** that is, widely held agreement on social values, norms, attitudes, and beliefs. If there is a law that the speed limit for automobiles is 55 mph, the authority of the police to arrest violators is legitimate only so long as the right to do so is upheld by members of that society—that is, most people feel that the law is reasonable. Similarly, the use of taxes for social services, welfare, and education is based on a well-established consensus, though disagreement may develop about the level of taxes or the amount to be spent.

The existence of normative consensus does not rule out political conflict. However, some people in positions of authority have felt that disagreement over issues of public policy indicates disloyalty to the political system. For example, President Lyndon B. Johnson suggested that people who disagreed with administration policies during the Vietnam war were disloyal Americans. Members of the Nixon Administration stated that people who

The United States, like most other industrialized nations, has formal procedures for transfer of political power and leadership. The legitimacy of these procedures is illustrated as President Reagan takes the oath of office while President Carter looks on.

disagreed with their policies were threats to national security, which they used to justify harassment of individuals and groups by governmental agencies.

Conflict may reflect a lack of agreement about either the goals or the means of achieving the goals. There is consensus about the goal of a dynamic economic system in the United States, but disagreements about the means of achieving this goal involve conflict between labor unions and corporations, Republicans and Democrats, and rich and poor. Conflict over welfare, as a basic human "right" or a "privilege" granted by the state, reflects a basic disagreement over both goals and means. Other areas about which consensus is lacking include the military draft, tax laws, and privacy against police searches.

Consensus reconciles conflicting approaches to goals. This is consensus on the "rules of the game." Within this framework political conflict is not only tolerable but also necessary for maintaining an effective and responsive government. Shared norms and values, then, establish the legitimacy of authority, define a social consensus, and set up the rules by which conflict will be mediated. Political opponents of major parties in most democratic or parliamentary governments tend to be treated as the "loyal opposition" rather than as "enemies of the state." However, most third parties or radical political organizations have been viewed as disruptive and disloyal by dominant parties.

POWER AND THE STATE

While most groups depend upon legitimate authority for survival, the state also has coercive power. In fact, the state is the only human community that successfully claims a monopoly on the legitimate use of physical force within a given territory (Gerth and Mills, 1946). In modern societies the concept of the state includes the formal governmental structure and also the entire range of institutions involved in politics.

Some scholars attach great importance to the notion of the state and describe in elaborate detail its purposes, such as regulating commerce and protecting citizens from outside aggression. These purposes suggest that the state is an all-powerful institution setting down the laws by which citizens must abide. A different and more fundamental view of the state defines it as the pattern by which members of political institutions interact in a regular manner. The fact that such interactions take place with some degree of regularity and harmony is evidence that they are governed by the same norms and values as other social institutions. The rules of the game apply to every institution in its relationship with other institutions.

LEGITIMATE FORCE VERSUS COERCION

The concept of the state helps us understand the difference between authority and coercion. Authority, or legitimate force, is used to obtain and preserve compliance with the rules of a society. Some force to guarantee compliance to rules is inevitable, even with legitimate authority. For example, the U.S. government has the authority to try draft resisters during times of war. However, coercion is the use of power that is contrary to the rules under which political institutions function. The use of wiretaps and other spying devices by government to collect information on citizens during wartime or at any other time is illegitimate, or coercive. Coercion, then, is power used in violation of the society's shared norms and values.

POLITICAL SYSTEMS

Shared norms and values establish consensus in a society. Consensus creates a legitimate order, and a legitimate order makes for political stability. Sta-

bility does not depend upon one type of political system, however. Any political structure, to function effectively over time, must be somewhat stable and can become so with the acceptance of society's members.

Authority may be exercised through different political systems. For example, many dictatorships have lasted for relatively long periods of time, creating and maintaining conditions that seem oppressive to many people in situations of greater freedom. The African nations, which until recently were colonies of European countries, had for centuries endured oppressive conditions, until nationhood was either granted by colonial powers or created out of conflict between native leaders and colonial governments. Some of these problems may be due to the fact that the shared normative orientations were not strong enough to sustain stability long enough to create a level of economic development that provides satisfaction of the basic needs of most people.

We will describe the processes and dynamics of three ideal types of political structures—totalitarianism, colonialism, and democracy. We will discuss strengths and weaknesses and give historical examples of each, though none of these is a pure type in practice. Indeed, each type should be seen as a continuum and each nation as more or less totalitarian, colonialist, or democratic.

Totalitarianism

In a **totalitarian society** all social functions are regulated by the state. Education, economic life, religion, and the family are controlled by the state. However, totalitarianism may take different forms, as in fascism and communism. Fascism, perhaps most clearly represented in Nazi Germany of the 1930s and early 1940s, allowed considerable freedom in the economic sphere, used religion to legitimate its actions, and carefully controlled the schools. Communism, as represented by the USSR, totally dominates the economic system, seeks to eliminate religion, and controls the schools. In both types of totalitarianism the social behavior of the citizen is strictly regulated from birth until death. Theoretically, the citizen has no authority to make personal decisions and no responsibility to anyone but the state. In a sense the "citizen" in a totalitarian state is not really a citizen at all; he is a "subject" (Almond and Verba, 1965).

Totalitarian societies tend to view individuals as expendable for the good of the state. Under such circumstances **genocide,** the systematic destruction of an easily identified group—ethnic, religious, cultural—by a state bureaucratic apparatus, may be directed against a population defined as a threat or an enemy. Genocide has been practiced at various times by many states, including the destruction of the Native American population by the United States during the 1800s, the destruction of the Jews by Nazi Germany under Hitler from 1935 to 1945, and the massacre of Uganda's Asian population by the dictator Idi Amin during the 1970s. The list continues to grow. Recent examples of genocide include the virtual elimination of the Moskito Indians of Nicaragua in Latin America and the annihilation of the Karens of Burma in Asia.

Usually only one party is allowed to carry on political activity in totalitarian societies. The party decides who will serve in governing capacities and how long they will serve. Through its control of government the party decides all issues of the public policy. Typically, the party makes these decisions without having to answer to other individuals or groups in the society. In short, the totalitarian society is controlled by the party. This is clearly the political pattern in the Soviet Union. Political power rests in three offices in the Soviet political structure: the president, the premier, and the general secretary of the Communist Party, although real power has most often been exercised by one of the three men filling these positions.

Elections may be held in totalitarian states, but usually only one candidate runs for each office or only candidates approved by the party if there is a choice. Thus, when the president of South Vietnam gathered more than 90 percent of the popular vote when he ran unopposed in 1971, this did not mean that he was more strongly supported than an American president is when he gets 51 percent of the vote in a two-party election. Similarly, because voting in totalitarian societies is often required by statute, an election-day turnout of 99.6 percent in the Soviet Union does not indicate that Russian citizens were more eagerly participating in decision making than the 40 to 50 percent of qualified voters that usually turn out in United States' elections (Rush and Althoff, 1981). Cross-national comparisons of political participation are of questionable value because of such wide variations in conditions of participation from society to society. Even within democratic societies elections may have little meaning when large numbers of citizens are disenfranchised, as most blacks were in the South before 1965, or when certain segments of society, such as the old or the poor, go largely unrepresented by candidates.

There have been totalitarian political systems throughout history. The Greek city-state of Sparta was highly totalitarian, as was Charlemagne's Holy Roman Empire in 866, although the means of total control were limited. Twentieth-century technology has increased the possibility of near total control of populations. Electronic methods of monitoring the activities of citizens, better techniques of manipulating citizens through propaganda, and more sophisticated nonlethal weaponry concentrated in the hands of the police and the military have made the control of social behavior much easier than it was in the past. Maintaining a totalitarian state has perhaps never been easier than it is today.

Colonialism

Colonialism may be characterized as the political and economic domination of a weak nation by a more powerful nation. All decisions are made by the dominant state, and the loyalties of the colonized are commanded by the "mother country." If a native governmental structure exists it is usually a puppet regime created to legitimize the colonial regime; its functions are to serve the interests of the dominant nation and to carry out its directives.

In most circumstances colonization gives the mother country strategic military advantage over its enemies and free access to the colony's natural resources for its own use and profit. French acquisition of the Louisiana Territory from Spain in the eighteenth century provided a colonial base from which to check British expansion in North America. Similarly, European colonization of Africa allowed older, smaller, more sophisticated nations with relatively few natural resources to become rich and powerful at the expense of less developed societies that were poorly equipped to resist foreign domination. Colonialism often has an ideological dimension as well as an economic or military one. In the nineteenth century Americans believed it was the nation's "manifest destiny" and even moral obligation to bring American influences to other lands; the "white man's burden" legitimated interference by British rule in India. At the same time colonialism also has been associated with genocide, for example, the systematic decimation of the Zulu by the British, the routine killing and displacing of Native Americans by Britain and the United States, the slave trade of the Dutch, and the recent destruction by the Vietnamese of the Laotian people.

Under colonialism, or political imperialism as it is more commonly manifested today, there must be an understanding between the dominant and subordinate states in which members of the colonialized nation submit to the rule of the colonizing state. This understanding is destroyed when the colony gathers sufficient political and economic strength to overthrow colonial rule, as did the African nations of Zaire, Mozambique, and Algiers in the 1960s.

From a historical perspective colonialism tends to be temporary. The colonizing power either generates its own destruction by becoming a political example for its colonies or finds its rule too expensive to maintain.

Democracy

A **democratic society** is one in which members share equally in the vote, thereby indirectly exercising political power and influence over the decision-making process. Power in the political system is vested in the collective citizenry, and decisions are made on the basis of the wishes of a majority of those citizens who exercise voting rights.

In a democratic society government represents individuals who vote on the basis of personal in-

terests or beliefs and also ethnic, religious, economic, or ideological groups who seek to exercise power by influencing their members to vote in a particular way. In a **pluralist society** power is sought and exercised by many groups competing on relatively equal terms and within a context of shared norms and values. According to Lipset (1960) members of a pluralist society often belong to several different groups and are faced with inconsistent "affiliations, loyalties, and stimuli" (p. 88). Simultaneous membership in different groups with different political messages has the effect of moderating the citizen's approach to political affairs and reducing the level of emotion attached to political activity.

One advantage of a pluralist society is that many groups share in the exercise of political power and make it difficult for any one group to obtain control over the society. These groups tend to have a counteracting effect on one another, providing a check that inhibits the abuse of power and promoting stability. However, complete equality of competing groups is not possible. For example, in the United States corporate lobbyists have an enormous advantage by virtue of size, organization, and capital over small business owners, poor people, and aged people. Not surprisingly, problems of large corporations are more likely to be heard by government.

What conditions are necessary for democracy? Lipset (1960) and Coleman (1960) lay heavy stress upon modernization and economic development. To test this hypothesis Lipset first compared European, English-speaking, and Latin American nations, classifying them according to the number and stability of their democratic institutions. He then used several measures to assess the economic development of the nations in each category, including per capita wealth, access to communications media, degree of industrialization, educational level, and amount of urbanization. Lipset found that stable democracies, compared with unstable democracies and dictatorships, have relatively high standards of living, higher levels of education, greater industrialization, and more urbanization.

Such data by themselves can be misleading. There is nothing inherent in democratic systems that leads inevitably to high economic development. Nor do nations with highly developed economies necessarily have democratic political systems. Rather, these data suggest that economic development supports democratic institutions by aiding in the process of democratization.

What causes a stable democratic order to develop? According to Lipset (1960) the stability of a democracy depends not only on economic development, but also upon the effectiveness and legitimacy of the political system. In his view shared democratic norms and values give a democratic system legitimacy, and a high level of economic development supports its institutions, contributes to their continuity, and helps stabilize the system.

POLITICAL STRUCTURE, POLITICAL DEVELOPMENT, AND THE THIRD WORLD

No nation exhibits characteristics of only one type of political system. The United States has been a colonial power in its annexation of other lands, yet few would deny the democratic character of the United States. The Soviet Union qualifies as a colonial or imperialistic power by its intervention into the politics of Eastern European nations, but it is also a totalitarian state. It is the structural features of governments in modern societies that permit us to classify them as one of the three types of political systems. However, the developing, or so-called Third World, nations present a unique set of problems of classification.

The *Third World* is the name given to some 80 nations of Asia, Africa, and Latin America that are industrially undeveloped or underdeveloped (by North American and Western European standards). Some Third World nations have just emerged from colony status or have just begun to industrialize. These nations otherwise exhibit a wide diversity of economic and political systems and cultural heritages. They are so heterogeneous that it is difficult to generalize about them or predict how they will develop. For example, a nation's gross national product (GNP) is frequently used as an index of its economic development but such a measure may be misleading because of the concentration and control of wealth by a small elite.

Not all of the developing nations lack economic resources. In fact, some distinctions have been made between the rich but developing nations—called the Fourth World—and the economically underdeveloped and less industrialized nations. Among the Fourth World nations are oil-producing countries like Oman, Qatar, or Kuwait, whose petroleum resources have provided vast capital, but these countries have not as yet emerged as modern, industrialized nations and do not have high levels of literacy, political participation, or consumption characteristic of older industrialized countries. By contrast, the Third World nations lack both the economic resources and technology that would permit their rapid development into industrialized nations.

Problems of the Third World

Despite wide differences in the nations that make up the Third World, they share certain problems of political and economic development, most of them related to their colonial past and to current policies of developed nations.

Colonialism did establish processes by which decisions could be made and social rewards allocated, though not equally. Also, trade and diplomatic relations established by colonizing countries provided the colonies with some stability in dealing with other nations. However, the sudden departure of the dominant state left some new nations not only with the problem of forming new processes for decision making and resource allocation but also with the immediate need to make these processes operate efficiently. The new nations' lack of political experience has sometimes led to instability and violent political conflict.

Developing nations also have had much more rapid population growth than developed nations, making increased demands upon food production, medical care, and educational facilities. These demands further destabilize the new nation that is struggling with establishing a decision-making apparatus. Without a strong sense of shared norms and values by which the government can establish legitimacy, confidence in leadership also is easily eroded.

While Third World nations are struggling to meet the minimal needs of their rapidly growing populations and to establish functioning governments, the developed nations are creating new capital, more consumer goods, and greater military strength. The widening gap between these groups of countries makes it increasingly difficult for new nations to compete with the richer nations in these areas. Developing nations then become susceptible to military and economic exploitation by their more powerful neighbors, a situation that threatens the sovereignty and stability of all Third World nations.

The Third World and Democracy

The unique history of developing nations points to a process of economic and political development that will be far different from that of most modern nations. The hope held by many Americans and some Europeans that Third World states will develop into Western-style democracies appears to be unlikely for at least two reasons. First, for a political system to govern effectively the underlying culture must be consistent with it. In a democracy citizens must share democratic values, attitudes, and beliefs that support it. Second, the problems confronting new nations are so urgent that their leaders are more concerned with solving them than they are with cultivating democratic attitudes. The old traditions, technologies, and social systems of these societies predispose them to authoritarian bureaucracy, and the political organization becomes a means to the distribution of resources to meet immediate human needs. Under such circumstances the individual freedoms typical of a Western-type democratic political system must wait until people in Third World countries can be properly fed, housed, clothed, and employed and even if this occurs, economic well-being is not always associated with political democracy, as we have noted.

The serious problems confronting these nations reflect years of economic and political exploitation by developed nations, which often left native peoples untrained to operate the industries and organizations set up by the colonial powers or left the newly independent countries without the means to develop their resources. Lacking skills and capital these countries often have had to depend upon the multinational corporations, which continue the exploitation and dependency of the past. Because of the activities of multinational corporations the high standard of living of the residents of industrialized nations is supported and subsidized in part by Third World countries that lack capital and power to control their own economic and political development.

POLITICAL PARTICIPATION AND POLITICAL CONFLICT

How does the individual affect political decisions? Are there means by which people can force government to respond to their wishes? Attempts to influence the decision-making process are acts of political participation. Broadly defined, **political participation** includes all forms of political activity, from discussing political issues to plotting the overthrow of the government—any act that affects or is intended to affect the decision-making process.

Political participation may be either routine or nonroutine. **Routine participation** involves political actions that are permitted and encouraged, although not required, like voting, holding office, or writing letters to elected officials. **Nonroutine participation** includes political acts that usually fall outside the normative values of a society and that may or may not be within the statutory limits of social behavior: strikes, passive resistance to arrest, intimidation, or acts of violence.

Routine Participation: Individual Activities

Routine political acts of the individual take many forms. Passive actions may be as simple as obtaining information about governments decisions by reading a newspaper or watching a TV news program. The most active traditional political act is to seek and hold public office. A person's choice of political activity—between, say, actively seeking office and passively watching political news on television—depends on several factors.

Voting requires that a person decide whether to vote, and if so for whom. These two decisions may lead to a third decision, depending on the intensity, duration, and extremity of a person's feeling. If he or she feels strongly about politics, the anticipated reward—the election of the desired candidate or the passage of a favored bill—will outweigh the costs of time, money, and energy that are required to campaign for candidates for office. If a person does not have this intensity, however, the costs will exceed the rewards, and he or she is unlikely to participate actively in the political process.

The range of political activities may be defined in terms of a reward-cost ratio. Analysis of several different types of political participation identified by Milbrath (1965) suggests that active participation is more costly than passive or nonparticipation. For example, public political acts, such as a speech in a public meeting, have higher social and economic costs than private acts, like a discussion of politics around a dinner table. The costs may include losing a job or even life, as the assassinations of Martin Luther King and Robert Kennedy testify.

One advantage of the higher costs of active participation may be that these costs effectively limit the number of people seeking the highest rewards offered by the system, thereby increasing its stability. Rush and Althoff (1971) propose a general hierarchy of political participation, ranging from holding public office at the top, with its high costs and few participants, to just voting at the bottom, with its low costs and many participants (Figure 15.1).

In the United States few people are active political participants. Though about 40 to 50 percent of the eligible voters cast ballots in most elections, only about 20 percent of them go so far as to write letters or send telegrams to their elected representatives. Observers have noted that most Americans do not take a serious interest in politics and in the major issues confronting their society. Those people who actively participate in politics tend to be different from the general population in socioeconomic and educational status. One study (Lane, 1964) found that although one-half to three-fourths of the sample adult population expressed an interest in writing to their congressmen or senators in Washington, only one out of seven people interviewed ever had actually written or wired a member of Congress. College-educated and professional people were about four times as likely to do so as were grade-school-educated people or those employed in manual work. Other studies of member-

FIGURE 15.1 Costs and Participation in Politics

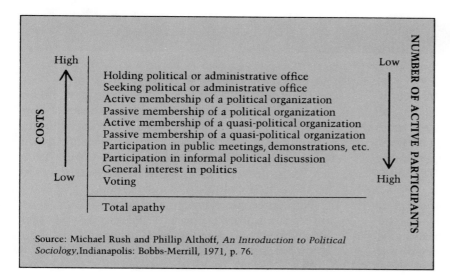

Source: Michael Rush and Phillip Althoff, *An Introduction to Political Sociology,* Indianapolis: Bobbs-Merrill, 1971, p. 76.

ship and participation in social groups have indicated few differences between people based on race, sex, age, or residence but confirmed that differences in participation in social groups are sizable between persons of different incomes, occupational training and education (Alford and Friedland, 1975; Verba and Nie, 1972; Wolfinger and Rosenstone, 1980).

From the data available we may conclude that persons with the highest levels of political participation tend to have better educations, better jobs, and make more money. They also are drawn from certain occupational groups, age, and sex categories as illustrated in Table 15.1. They also have higher costs and take greater risks for more rewards. Conversely, people with low levels of education and income have fewer resources, less influence on the political process, and less political power. Table 15.2 is a demographic profile of registered voters in the period of July to October 1980.

Why do people participate in politics? Lane (1964) offers the following reasons. People may (1) seek to advance their material well-being and their economic security through political action, (2) employ political means to satisfy needs of friendship and

Political parties seek the support of as many people as possible in order to win elections. The Democratic, Republican and other party conventions give an opportunity for citizens who represent various political constituencies and states to participate in nominations and in shaping party programs. For most citizens, however, participation is limited to voting in elections, as these New York City residents are doing.

affection, (3) want to understand the world in which they live, (4) involve themselves in politics to relieve intrapsychic tensions, (5) seek power over others, or (6) wish to defend and improve their self-esteem in political activity.

People who routinely participate in politics usually act through organizations, political parties, and interest groups. It is to these structures that we now turn.

Routine Participation of Groups

Political parties constitute the means to political power in the United States and in most industrialized nations. These organizations seek popular support for the authority to run the government or to oust those who are running it.

Most decisions in American society require a coalition of interests. The **political party** is a device for mobilizing the special interests of groups of people in the form of votes. Political parties potentially exist in all forms of groups, Key (1964). Church groups, business organizations, fraternal lodges, or antiabortion groups may organize for political ac-

TABLE 15.1 97th U.S. Congress, 1981: Member Characteristics

	HOUSE OF REPRESENTATIVES	SENATE
Sex		
Male	416	98
Female	19	2
Race		
White	415	97
Black	17	—
Other	3	3
Age		
Under 40	94	9
40–49	142	35
50–59	132	36
60–69	54	14
70–79	12	6
80 and older	1	—
Occupation[a]		
Agriculture	28	9
Business and Banking	134	28
Education	59	10
Journalism	21	7
Law	194	59
Public Service/Politics	42	13

[a]An individual may be counted in more than one category.
SOURCE: Congressional Quarterly Weekly Report, No. 4, January 24, 1981. Reprinted with permission from Congressional Quarterly Inc.

TABLE 15.2   Profile of Registered Voters (July–October 1980)

	POPULATION DISTRIBUTION	REGISTERED VOTERS		POPULATION DISTRIBUTION	REGISTERED VOTERS
NATIONAL	100%	100%	POLITICS		
SEX			Republican	24	27
Male	48	48	Democrat	46	48
Female	52	52	Southern	15	15
RACE			Non-southern	31	33
White	86	87	Independent	26	23
Southern	23	22	Other	4	2
Non-southern	63	65	RELIGION		
Non-white	14	13	Protestant	61	62
Southern	6	5	Catholic	28	29
Non-southern	8	8	Jewish	2	2
EDUCATION			Other	9	7
College	30	33	OCCUPATION		
High school	55	53	Professional & business	26	29
Grade school	15	14	Clerical & sales	7	7
REGION			Manual workers	40	36
East	27	27	Skilled	19	17
Midwest	27	28	Unskilled	21	19
South	28	28	Farmers	3	3
West	18	17	Non-labor force	21	23
AGE			CITY SIZE		
18–24 years	18	11	1,000,000 & over	20	20
25–29 years	10	9	500,000–999,999	12	12
30–49 years	34	35	50,000–499,999	26	25
50 & older	38	45	2,500–49,999	15	15
INCOME			Under 2,500, rural	27	28
$25,000 & over	25	27	Central city	32	31
$20,000–$24,999	12	13	Suburb	26	27
$15,000–$19,999	16	16	LABOR UNION		
$10,000–$14,999	18	18	Labor union families	24	25
$ 5,000–$ 9,999	18	16	Non-labor union families	76	75
Under $5,000	11	10			

SOURCE: The Gallup Poll Index, Report No. 183, December 1980, p. 69.

tion to promote their interests. Unlike national political parties, however, their activities may be single-issue oriented and stimulated by particular government decisions, economic conditions, or social changes.

National political parties also may be organized around certain special interests. The goal of the party then is to form a coalition of groups with similar interests to obtain their votes and thereby win control of the government. When interests change parties shift in response in an effort to retain public support. Party survival depends on ob-

taining the support of enough special interest groups to create a political force. Political parties, however, are expected to operate within the society's cultural and legal norms.

In the United States not all elections are carried out through the party system, especially at the local level. Nonpartisan elections for city council seats, school boards, or township offices are common. In such elections there may be several candidates for office who are not identified with a political party. In addition, parties may not nominate a candidate for every office. However, at state and national levels, the two parties that dominate the political system—Democrats and Republicans—seek to elect their candidates. Often third-party candidates are nominated for state and national office; few, however, are elected.

THE GROWTH OF POLITICAL PARTIES IN THE UNITED STATES

The United States has had a two-party system since the ratification of the Constitution. Because a state could either favor or oppose the entire document, political factions developed for and against ratification. Throughout U.S. history interest groups have aligned and realigned themselves in two parties over a variety of issues—slavery, taxation, corporate trusts, labor unions, involvement in European affairs.

Several factors have contributed to maintenance of the two-party system in the United States. First, the U.S. Constitution requires that different interests cooperate in carrying out the functions of government. Since the party in power has no authority to deprive the minority party of its congressional representatives, each party must rely on continued election of representatives from its various regional strongholds to maintain federal political control. Second, various state regulations have made it difficult for a third party to gain significant support or to obtain a place on the ballot. Third, the sheer cost of organizing a third party is so high that most people are not interested. Fourth, those third parties that have had some success eventually have allied themselves with one of the two major parties to obtain a voice in the choice of the major party's presidential candidate, or even replaced one of the major parties. Finally, in their desire to maximize public support during elections, both major parties tend to adopt many third-party policies. Parties such as the Federalists, Bull-Moose, and Dixicrats had considerable impact on major party decisions before they ceased to exist.

A significant feature of the two-party system is this adaptability to new situations. In the United States one party dominates for a time, then is replaced by the other party. After some years the pendulum swings back and the first major party

regains control of government. For example, from 1901–1932 the Republican party held the office of president of the United States, except for the nine years that Woodrow Wilson was president, 1913–1921. Similarly, from 1933–1969 a Democrat was president, except for President Eisenhower's two terms, 1953–1961. Some writers, notably Phillips (1969), have suggested that the pendulum began to swing back to the Republicans with the election of Richard Nixon in 1968.

Phillips, writing in 1969, could not have predicted the downfall of Richard Nixon or the subsequent development of substantial Democratic majorities in both houses of Congress in 1974. It still is difficult to decide whether there had been an exceptional shift in political attitudes or whether Nixon's victory represented a traditional swing in political patterns that will continue despite interruptions. The Republican party sweep of 1980 brought them control of the Senate and the presidency and a mandate for economic and social change. The long-term effects of recent elections are difficult to project, though tradition suggests that two or more decades of Republican party dominance is likely.

Both the Republican and Democratic parties are bound to certain rules of the game that are supported by the shared norms and values of the society as a whole. Indeed, Nixon's presidency ended because he and his aides violated the rules and were unable to hide the violations. Similar misdeeds of public officials in the past have been concealed more effectively, at least until their terms of office expired.

Winning elections is the job of political parties. To do so they must appeal to a majority of voters. Critics of the American two-party system say that voters have little choice in presidential elections. Such criticisms are valid in that both parties tend to take a middle stand on various issues to appeal to the largest number of people. However, because the parties are built on coalitions of different interests, their similarities appear only at the most general levels. Traditionally, the Republican party has been supported by farmers, small-town residents, residents of the Midwest and West, and those of higher socioeconomic status. Democrats, on the other hand, historically have been the party of people in the Northeast and South, in cities, of blacks and other ethnic groups, blue-collar workers, and people of lower socioeconomic status.

While it sometimes appears that traditional coalitions are breaking down and political realignments are taking place, the two-party system is most likely to continue, for it holds the following advantages for society: Competition between the parties for votes encourages a high level of responsiveness to the electorate. The two-party system promotes political compromise and therefore stability.

POLITICAL PARTIES TODAY

In 1973 a Gallup poll reported for the first time that the number of Independents exceeded the number of Republicans: 43 percent of those polled were Democrats, 24 percent were Republicans, and 33 percent were Independents (*Washington Post*, September 30, 1973). Similar findings were obtained in 1980: Democrats, 43 percent; Republicans, 26 percent; Independents, 31 percent (*The Gallup Poll Index*, Report No. 183, December 1980). What accounts for this shift away from identification with one of the two major parties?

Certainly, the Republican party lost some support following the Watergate affair, but the polls also revealed a continuing trend of increasing numbers of people who refuse to make a declaration of party preference. This does not necessarily mean a trend toward voters who examine each candidate and issue without regard to party. Independents tend to be ticket splitters, but many exhibit a clear predisposition toward one party or another. They may vote for the Republican candidate for president, the Democrat candidate for senator and governor, and the balance of the ticket for Republican candidates. Another characteristic of Independents is that they tend to participate less in the political process than do those with a party affiliation.

If, as polls have consistently shown, more people identify with the Democratic party than any other, why do Democrats not win every election? Apparently, party identification does not mean party-line voting at the polls. Also, Republicans are able to

mobilize part of the Independent vote by their stand on particular issues. Finally, the relationship of SES level, political party preference, and political participation is a factor. Because people with higher incomes and higher educational and occupational levels are more likely to participate in all phases of politics than are people from lower SES levels, and because these people traditionally vote Republican, Republicans are able to win at the polls. Table 15.3 indicates how different groups have voted in presidential elections from 1952–1980.

INTEREST GROUPS

Truman (1971) has defined an **interest group** as any group of people with similar attitudes that makes certain claims upon other groups in society to behave in ways that are consistent with these shared attitudes. By this definition virtually every social group is an interest group. However, we will focus on those groups that play a role in decision making at the national level and that try to create policy consistent with their interests.

Organized interest groups are often thought of as negative political forces representing powerful special interests who threaten democracy because they have the resources with which to bribe public officials and otherwise subvert the political process. Most interest groups, however, are only sporadically involved in politics. Organizations of ham radio operators or rifle owners usually involve themselves in politics only when debate or change of policy threatens their specific interests. Others, like the American Bar Association, while continually monitoring the political process, concern themselves primarily with issues such as professional certification or the actions of judges and lawyers. In addition, there are checks against excessive use of power by organized interest groups, including the following:

1. Federal and state regulation of lobbying by interest groups.
2. Opposition of other groups competing for support.
3. Public officials who refrain from embracing organized interests for fear of alienating other groups in their constituency.

4. Overlapping group memberships of individuals, which modify their support for positions taken by the different organized groups to which they belong.

5. Economic sanctions invoked by governmental agencies against claims made by recalcitrant interests. For example, the Government Services Administration (GSA) makes large purchases from corporations that participate in interest groups, but the GSA may buy items from other sources.

6. Congressional power to obtain information about interest groups and to expose interest group excesses and activate public concern.

Some interest groups may have excessive power and need further regulation. However, most of these groups serve useful functions. The individual consumer cannot exercise the political clout of the oil lobby, but consumers can organize into interest groups. Recently, consumer groups have challenged the oil interests in the areas of pricing, taxation, and regulation. By representing the desires and attitudes of their members, these groups exert influence on the political process and its domination by those with the most money.

Nonroutine Participation

In the United States most political activity is of the routine type, and most political actors achieve satisfactory results by working within the system or normative framework of society. However, when routine politics fails, nonroutine actions like strikes, demonstrations, and sit-downs may occur.

Nonroutine participation refers to acts that not only fall outside the formal political structure but also outside of the realm of legitimate political activity as defined by the existing order. Strikes, outbreaks of rebellion, and demonstrations are commonplace occurrences in many societies. To better understand these political acts we will consider the conditions under which they develop.

DEPRIVATION AND PARTICIPATION

Relative deprivation is the conscious experience of a discrepancy between what a person feels is a legitimate expectation from life and what he or she actually anticipates or experiences (Wilson, 1973). People who experience relative deprivation have their basic needs of food, clothing, and shelter met and have the benefit of a dependable, predictable environment. They are under no immediate threat

Many pressure groups exist to influence political action. Such groups may focus upon specific concerns, as in the case of the antinuclear energy group pictured here, or they may seek to influence a broad range of legislation. By emphasizing that their concerns are shared by many voters and potential voters, these groups force political leaders to respond to their concerns.

TABLE 15.3   Vote by Groups in Presidential Elections, 1952–1980

	1952		1956		1960		1964		1968		
	STEVENSON	IKE	STEVENSON	IKE	JFK	NIXON	LBJ	GOLDWATER	HHH	NIXON	WALLACE
	%	%	%	%	%	%	%	%	%	%	%
National	44.6	55.4	42.2	57.8	50.1	49.9	61.3	38.7	43.0	43.4	13.6
SEX											
Male	47	53	45	55	52	48	60	40	41	43	16
Female	42	58	39	61	49	51	62	38	45	43	12
RACE											
White	43	57	41	59	49	51	59	41	38	47	15
Non-white	79	21	61	39	68	32	94	6	85	12	3
EDUCATION											
College	34	66	31	69	39	61	52	48	37	54	9
High School	45	55	42	58	52	48	62	38	42	43	15
Grade school	52	48	50	50	55	45	66	34	52	33	15
OCCUPATION											
Prof. & business	36	64	32	68	42	58	54	46	34	56	10
White collar	40	60	37	63	48	52	57	43	41	47	12
Manual	55	45	50	50	60	40	71	29	50	35	15
AGE											
Under 30 years	51	49	43	57	54	46	64	36	47	38	15
30–49 years	47	53	45	55	54	46	63	37	44	41	15
50 years & older	39	61	39	61	46	54	59	41	41	47	12
RELIGION											
Protestants	37	63	37	63	38	62	55	45	35	49	16
Catholics	56	44	51	49	78	22	76	24	59	33	8
POLITICS											
Republicans	8	92	4	96	5	95	20	80	9	86	5
Democrats	77	23	85	15	84	16	87	13	74	12	14
Independents	35	65	30	70	43	57	56	44	31	44	25
REGION											
East	45	55	40	60	53	47	68	32	50	43	7
Midwest	42	58	41	59	48	52	61	39	44	47	9
South	51	49	49	51	51	49	52	48	31	36	33
West	42	58	43	57	49	51	60	40	44	49	7
Members of Labor Union Families	61	39	57	43	65	35	73	27	56	29	15

[a]Less than one percent.
Note: 1976 and 1980 results do not include vote for minor party candidates.
SOURCE: *The Gallup Poll Index*, Report No. 183, December 1980, p. 74.

of losing the means to fulfill these needs. However, they feel that their legitimate expectations for more than they are receiving are not being met and that the political system is responsible for meeting those expectations. People who act out of relative deprivation believe that a strike, demonstration, or rebellion is the most effective and efficient means to change the political system. Relative deprivation seems to be a basic condition for the development of nonroutine political participation.

In contrast, the absolutely deprived do not have even their basic needs fulfilled. While relative deprivation is strongly correlated with political action, absolute deprivation is just as strongly tied to political apathy.

While relative deprivation is an important con-

TABLE 15.3 *(cont.)*

	1972		1976			1980		
	McGOVERN	NIXON	CARTER	FORD	McCARTHY	CARTER	REAGAN	ANDERSON
	%	%	%	%	%	%	%	%
National	38	62	50	48	1	41	51	7
SEX								
Male	37	63	53	45	1	38	53	7
Female	38	62	48	51	*a*	44	49	6
RACE								
White	32	68	46	52	*a*	36	56	7
Non-white	87	13	85	15	*a*	36	10	2
EDUCATION								
College	37	63	42	55	2	35	53	10
High School	34	66	54	46	*a*	43	51	5
Grade school	49	51	58	41	*a*	54	42	3
OCCUPATION								
Prof. & business	31	69	42	56	*a*	33	55	10
White collar	36	64	50	48	2	40	51	9
Manual	43	57	58	41	1	48	46	5
AGE								
Under 30 years	48	52	53	45	1	47	41	11
30–49 years	33	67	48	49	2	38	52	8
50 years & older	36	64	52	48	*a*	41	54	4
RELIGION								
Protestants	30	70	46	53	*a*	39	54	6
Catholics	48	52	57	42	1	46	47	6
POLITICS								
Republicans	5	95	9	91	*a*	8	86	5
Democrats	67	33	82	18	*a*	69	26	4
Independents	31	69	38	57	4	29	55	14
REGION								
East	42	58	51	47	1	43	47	9
Midwest	40	60	48	50	1	41	51	7
South	29	71	54	45	*a*	44	52	3
West	41	59	46	51	1	35	54	9
Members of Labor Union Families	46	54	63	36	1	50	43	5

dition, there are other factors that contribute to nonroutine political participation. A society with a long history of nonroutine political activities may be more prone to such activities. People may use nonroutine activities to express general feelings of rejection and resentment of the social and political structures of a society. The frontier tradition in America encourages actions that are outside of the rules of the game. Vigilantism, frontier justice, and other direct actions outside of the law are treated positively in our cultural traditions. The popularity of the movie and TV "Western" gives strong support to frontier values (Goldstein and Perrucci, 1963).

A particular social structure also may affect the extent, duration, and intensity of nonroutine politics. For example, the level of socioeconomic development and existing class patterns in a society may determine the kinds of political action that are taken. If a highly skilled and educated population becomes relatively deprived, any nonroutine political action they take will be well organized and intense (Gurr, 1968b). Relative deprivation experienced by those at lower socioeconomic levels but not by those at higher levels tends to produce political action that is poorly organized, spontaneous, and of low intensity.

Another factor affecting political action involves the rapidity of social and economic changes in a society. If changes are rapid more people may engage in nonroutine politics as the relative resources of power and influence shift among existing social groups. Gradual change reduces the likelihood of great social upheaval.

Patterns of political authority, relative levels of political activity of all groups in a society, and the resources available to those in authority and their challengers also are factors in nonroutine politics. To the extent that various political organizations in a society share goals, values, and norms, the legitimacy of authority is well established. Nonroutine activities are not likely to be seen as the most effective political means. However, if there is great dissimilarity between the goals and values of various political organizations, the authority of the government is weakened and nonroutine political participation becomes more attractive.

Political participation by people from all socioeconomic levels has a moderating effect upon the development of nonroutine activities. However, if routine political participation is limited only to special groups, the chance of nonroutine political behavior increases. The resources available to authorities in their relations with their political challengers shape nonroutine politics. The challenging groups may be highly motivated, enjoy widespread support from the general population, and have the strength to inflict great costs upon traditional authorities. Alternatively, authorities possess legitimacy, effectiveness, access to channels of routine political demands, and thus a degree of coercive power. To the degree that authorities are seen as legitimate and effective, the chances of nonroutine participation decreases.

Although there are many types of nonroutine political action, the United States has experienced relatively few uncontrolled conflicts or large-scale violent incidents in its history. The ultimate nonroutine political act is revolution.

REVOLUTION

A **revolution** is the overthrow of a government by force or threat of force and replacement of the ruling class by a different set of rulers. As a social movement it seeks basic changes in the political, economic, and cultural institutions of a society. Typically, mass disaffection supplies support for revolution.

Revolutionary sentiment often is aroused by the frustration of a sizable segment of the population. When existing institutions are unable to deal with the interests and desires of the people, there often is loss of social support for traditional values and the structures representing them.

Many theorists consider economic factors to be the dynamic element in a revolution. However, as we noted earlier, it is not the absolutely deprived who give revolution its impetus but rather those who experience relative economic deprivation. This group in turn will try to mobilize the poorest segment of society.

The long-range goal of revolution is to substitute a new and just social order for the old one. However, certain short-term goals often conflict with the ultimate revolutionary purpose. Revolutionary leaders may expediently compromise with the enemy, especially at the point of taking power when they may make alliances with moderate factions, as has occurred in Kenya and Zimbabwe. Such alliances give the revolution a sense of legitimacy and neutralize the opposition moderates. Thus the revolutionary leadership gains operational flexibility. It may act within the constitution to gain support or it may act ruthlessly to establish its authority. Once revolutionary leadership is in power it remakes the legal structure. The former ruling class may be neutralized rather than eliminated; their managerial skills may be used or they may serve as scapegoats for the failures of the new regime.

While the broad outlines of revolutionary activity are clear, social scientists are in considerable disagreement over the specific issues in revolutionary behavior. Brinton (1965) and Johnson (1966) agree, however, that revolution, whatever its development, is not different in structure from other forms of nonroutine participation but is simply the most severe expression of nonroutine political activity. Strikes by labor organizations like those called by Solidarity in 1980–1982 in Poland and demonstrations against segregation like those led by Martin Luther King in the South in the 1960s were defined as illegitimate actions by political leaders, but these actions fell considerably short of revolution as we have defined it. Still, the potential for revolution exists whenever broad segments of a society become disaffected.

POLITICAL SOCIALIZATION

In our discussion of political participation, parties, and interest groups, we pointed out some of the structural aspects of the American political system that maintain our representative democracy. Legitimacy is established by normative consensus. We may assume that the values upon which this consensus is based did not develop randomly but were systematically transmitted, along with other cultural values, from generation to generation. The process by which the individual develops political attitudes within the normative context of society is called **political socialization.**

Political socialization is important to the survival of a political system. Political decision making in a democracy rests upon a broad base of support. Socialization is one means by which society develops this support; it does so through the institutions of family, church, and school.

The Family

The family provides the child's first and possibly most important experiences in political socialization (Dalton, 1980; Davies, 1965). The strength of the family's influence on the child's political attitudes rests on several conditions. First, as Lane (1959) found, the stronger the relationships between parents and children, the more profound the

political impact of the family. Second, the family's influence is the greatest when the parents agree politically. Third, the more frequently family members interact with one another, the greater their influence on each other's political attitudes. In addition, studies show that parents who are interested in politics transmit political information and party identification to their children (Beck and Jennings, 1975; Tedin, 1974). Children of politically interested families see themselves as having a greater political efficacy than average, and politically involved persons tend to come from politically interested families.

One recent study of children's reactions to Watergate and the resignation of President Nixon (Wasburn, 1977) suggests that children have a relatively well-developed political orientation by grades four, five, and six. Party identification of parents and discussions of current political events help form children's views of the political system and the legitimacy of political activities.

Such data remind us that political behaviors, like other human behaviors, both affect and are affected by social institutions. Changes in the family have political consequences, and political changes have an impact on the family as well, like changes in tax and welfare regulations or the passage of school desegregation laws.

The School

Perhaps the second most influential agency in political socialization is the school. One of its jobs is to produce "good citizens" through formal and informal interactions. Hess and Torney (1967) point out that although the family establishes a sense of political partisanship, it merely supports those institutions that actually develop political attitudes. The school teaches the history, content, and concepts of politics, expanding and elaborating the feelings of attachment to the political system that the child has developed earlier through the family.

Of the beliefs and attitudes the child learns in school, the central one is compliance with the rules and respect for authority. Very little is taught through formal educational channels about political participation other than voting—participation

Schools teach patriotism in a
variety of ways. Apart from the
formal classwork, rituals like the
pledge of allegiance, salutes to the
flag, and the national anthem
provide children with a sense of
identification and loyalty to the
nation.

in its most passive form—or about the nature or
possibilities of political conflict.

Langton and Jennings (1968) studied the effects
of giving greater stress in civics courses to loyalty
to the nation rather than to political participation.
While this emphasis seems to have had little effect
on students in general, it had a greater effect on
black students than on white students. Students
were told: "People have different ideas about what
a good citizen means. We're interested in what you
think. Tell us how you would describe a good citizen in this country—that is, what things about a
person are most important in showing that he is a
good citizen" (p. 863)? Among students who had
taken a civics course, nearly twice as many black
students gave answers emphasizing loyalty than

did whites. Whites tended to be relatively unaffected by their civics courses, since these classes tended to reinforce what they already believed to be true.

Political party preference is related to education beyond high school as well. A study by Weiner and Eckland (1979) found that increased levels of education tend to be related to increased Republican party affiliation. However, the relationship is not as clear as this finding suggests. They reported that higher education has an important effect in reinforcing the previous political orientation that appears when early socialization, especially for men, is considered.

The impact of education on political orientations appears to be complex. At the elementary and secondary school levels education seems to reinforce family values, order, and stability. At the college level education appears to create less consensus on values or political beliefs, often defined as a liberalizing effect.

The Church

The values and beliefs about politics that a child learns through religious training may be indirect, focused mainly on the importance of being a good citizen. Religious beliefs also affect political participation, and the family and the church tend to reinforce each other over a wide range of social and political values. Indeed, some churches are politically active—both directly as organized pressure groups and indirectly through actions of individual members. The close alignment of conservative political views and conservative religious beliefs is reflected in several groups, such as the Moral Majority, which seek to influence political decision making on such issues as abortion and school prayer.

Religious membership also tends to coincide with racial, ethnic, and other social groupings, which have particular political views. Lenski (1961) reports that white Protestants are more likely to become Republicans than are white Catholics, that Jews are more politically active than Catholics, and that Catholics are more politically active than Protestants, perhaps because Catholics tend to be more involved in union activities, especially at the lower socioeconomic levels. These findings suggest

that while religious beliefs may have some independent effect on participation, it is through the organization and cohesiveness of a particular group that religion has its impact.

Religious training that emphasizes the legitimacy of laws and supports public officials as valid leaders has supported public efforts to involve religion in political activities. Many feel that these efforts obscure the boundaries of church and state, as in the case of "God and Country" awards by the American Legion, prayers in the U.S. Senate, or religious invocations at political conventions.

Religious groups, like the Jews, that have suffered political oppression in the past tend to involve themselves politically more often than nonoppressed groups. However, political socialization through religion can promote either political and social change or the status quo. The Nation of Islam (the Black Muslims), until shortly before the death of Elijah Muhammad in 1975, was committed by its leader to a policy of separate nations for blacks and whites and no involvement in politics or the civil rights movement in the United States. Within a year of Elijah Muhammad's death and the succession of Wallace Muhammad to leadership, the Nation began to revise its policies. It admitted whites into membership and, if not actively seeking political power within the mainstream of American culture, certainly it no longer prohibited individual members from running for office or from voting. As of 1976, the Nation had developed a system of parochial elementary schools for the socialization of members' children. With the loosening of separatist attitudes the Nation also invited into its basically religious schools the children of nonmembers.

POWER STRUCTURES AND DECISION MAKING

There are two schools of thought in the social sciences that have occasioned considerable debate over the question, "Who runs America?" The **elitist** perspective is that power in the United States is structured like a pyramid, with the wealthiest and most powerful at the peak, controlling most resources and making all the important political decisions. The **pluralist** position is that many small and specialized elites exist in American politics, each with its own decision-making responsibility. The multiplicity of elites serves as a check against any one interest becoming too powerful. Let us examine each of these views.

The Elitist Perspective

The elitist conception of power is that the basic decisions in modern industrial society are made by a small, powerful group of political, economic, and military leaders. Through their control over money, organizations, and technological and human resources, this group has power to exert great influence over the important decisions of a society.

One of the early formulations of this view was developed by Hunter (1953), who studied how power is exercised at the local community level by a small elite. In "Regional City" (Atlanta) he found that there was a group in the power hierarchy that made most of the public policy decisions. This elite consisted mostly of businessmen, who formed committees to discuss and formulate policies. Their decisions were channeled through a fluid committee structure of institutional and associational groupings to a lower level bureaucracy that executed the policies.

Perhaps the most influential study of the power elite in America is that of Mills (1956). For Mills power is exercised by a triumvirate of corporate, military, and political interests through a series of overlapping cliques that emerged after World War II, which legitimated expansion of the military and government. In his view the power elite is shaped by the coincidence of interest between those who control the military, the corporate chief, and vested-interest politicians. Members of the elite not only share the same interests but frequently meet socially. They are personal friends, even neighbors, and they see one another on the golf course, in their clubs, at resorts, on airplanes, and in a variety of other economic and social situations. By contrast, the public, lacking access to elitist power, is "mass society," passive and disorganized, unable and unwilling to resist exploitation by the elite.

Domhoff (1967, 1978) similarly argues that an upper social class rules the United States. The top one percent of the population occupy positions of power and wealth and dominate the political decision-making process, especially where their interests are concerned. This elite group often exercises its power through middle-class executives and professionals who cooperate with them but who have no real decision-making authority. Several recent studies support this view. Useem (1979) analyzed information about the directors of the 797 largest U.S. corporations in 1969 and reported that an inner group of business leaders was greatly overrepresented in the governance of nonbusiness organizations. This elite is small, national in scope, and relies on both formal and informal associations. Moore (1979), on the basis of interviews with 545 leaders in political, economic, and social institutions, also concluded that there is a network of elite individuals who have a high potential for control through their organizational positions. Their cohesiveness allows them to exercise enormous control in decision making in various areas of public life. Similar findings have been reported by Alba and Moore (1978), Laumann and Pappi (1973, 1976), Laumann et al., (1977), and Whitt (1979).

In general, then, the elitist view is based upon the idea that a small group of people who occupy high-level positions in economic and social organizations determine basic policies and make decisions that guarantee that their power will be maintained. Critics of this view argue that there is not one but many groups that hold power in America and these groups do not agree on policies or decisions.

The Pluralist Perspective

Pluralists believe that the elitist thesis is overstated and distorted. Instead, they argue for a multiinfluence hypothesis in which the relationship between economic groups and political authority involves influence, cooperation, a division of labor, and at times conflict. Each group influences the others to some extent and each operates independently of the other. Only in the rare situations where their common interests merge is there unity of power; in most cases interests conflict and the various groups modify each other's efforts to exert power (Kornhauser, 1966; Rose, 1967).

While there may be powerless, unaffiliated individuals within the population, most people belong to groups that have varying degrees of power. These groups have common traditions and meanings and share values and concerns about life and the community. Out of such interests and concerns they develop networks of communication and action that enable them to resist control by elites. Pluralists assert that elite power is checked or modified on a regular basis by an active, informed citizenry or vetoed by conflicting interests among the elite itself.

Pluralists assert that interest groups are unequal in power and, because they have narrow goals, are not concerned with broad control of society. When these groups have different interests on the same issue, they may cancel each other's influence. In his study of politics in New Haven Dahl (1961) concluded that political influence was diffused: the economic elite had interest only in urban redevelopment and few of the social elite exerted any influence on government. The fact that elites became involved in particular issues offers some evidence of a tendency to **oligarchy,** or government by a few. However, competitive elections and the pooling of resources by individuals in the formation of interest groups thwarts elites who would seek too much power. Community power is held by a majority coalition, and groups making up the coalition shift periodically, combining and recombining into new majorities.

The Continuing Debate

How much power is exerted by elites in modern societies? Is the American power structure a "power elite" or a set of groups in competition with one another, which modify each other's efforts to control and dominate? Can an average citizen influence the political process, even at the local level?

Research continues to examine the impact of elites on political processes. Various researchers have suggested that there are multiple levels of power (Presthus, 1964), that elitist power derives from linkages among members of various organizations (Perrucci and Pilisuk, 1970), and that no single perspective gives a comprehensive view of power (Mankoff, 1970). However, each view seems to have a degree of validity, depending upon the level of government or the issue involved. Given so many conflicting hypotheses and findings in the study of power at both the national and community levels, the dispute is far from over. We cannot conclusively resolve the question of the location of power, but its answer has significance for other sociological problems, both practical and theoretical.

One finding by Walton (1966) presents an interesting puzzle. Sociologists, he reported, are more likely to embrace the elitist approach, while political scientists tend to accept the pluralist interpretation of power. Each discipline emphasizes a distinctive type of research in assessing decision-making responsibility. Such disciplinary alignment provides fertile ground for cross-disciplinary discussion and suggests that the choice of elitist or pluralist perspective will depend on the assumptions and development of the discipline, the research techniques used, and personal experiences.

Regardless of the view one holds about power and elites, it is clear that many people feel they have little impact on government. This estrangement may account for people's lack of confidence in government. A recent poll (*Society*, 1981) found that local government and state government received lower confidence ratings than churches, public schools, or the courts. Confidence in national government was less than that for local and state governments, ranking just below labor unions. There have been few attempts to involve a larger proportion of citizens in decision making at the national level. However, in recent years a large number of local and statewide groups have been organized that focus on specific issues—such as nuclear power and environmental pollution—and these groups have had considerable political impact. Undoubtedly, the next decade will see continued challenges to traditional political organizations and perhaps to the elites as well.

SUMMARY

The study of politics by political scientists tends to focus on official decision-making structures, while that of sociologists examines the context of political decisions. Both views require an understanding of power.

Political power is a means by which decisions are made and social rewards are allocated. Influence is the ability to affect the political process in the making of decisions. The legitimate exercise of power is called authority and is one of three types: traditional, charismatic, or rational-legal. Shared norms and values of a society legitimize the exercise of authority. In most societies political activities occurring within the context of shared norms and values are focused on the state.

The three main types of political systems are (1) totalitarianism, (2) colonialism, and (3) democracy. Under a democratic system the voting power of any member of the group is equal to that of any other member. For a democratic system to function its political culture must be consistent with the society's other shared democratic values.

Political participation involves acts of individuals and groups seeking to influence the political system. Routine acts of participation are those formally defined and structured; nonroutine acts of participation are disruptive and nonnormative. In the United States political parties and interest group activities are routine expressions of participation, while revolution, the ultimate expression of nonroutine politics, is uncommon.

Political socialization is the process by which members of a society become acquainted with the political system and develop political attitudes. Such socialization occurs through the transmission of political attitudes, norms, and values within the culture. The family, the school, and the church are fundamental agencies of political socialization.

Some scholars believe that power in America is exercised by a political elite, while others believe it is diffused throughout the society. Elitists see power at the national level as concentrated in the hands of political, military, and economic leaders. Pluralists find power lodged in the hands of many elites who tend to check one another and prevent any single group from dominating. In recent years challenges to elites have been made by local or state organizations focusing on issues that involve many people.

GLOSSARY

Authority   use of power that is consistent with the norms of society; legitimate use of power.

Charismatic authority   legitimation of the use of power by a leader who has personal power of the "gift of grace."

Coercion   use of power that is not consistent with the norms of society; illegitimate use of power.

Colonialism   political and economic domination of a weak nation by a more powerful nation.

Consensus   widely held agreement on the values, norms, attitudes, and beliefs of a society.

Democratic society   a society in which members share equally in the vote, thereby indirectly exercising political power and influence over the decision-making process.

Elitist politics   the perspective that power is structured like a pyramid, with the wealthiest and most powerful at the peak, controlling most resources and making all important political decisions.

Genocide   the systematic destruction of a racial or religious group by a state bureaucratic apparatus.

Interest group   any group of people with similar attitudes that makes certain claims upon other groups to behave in ways consistent with these shared attitudes.

Nonroutine political participation   political acts that usually fall outside the limits of normative social behavior and that may or may not be within statutory limits.

Oligarchy   government by a few people, usually for their own advantage.

Pluralist politics   the position that power is exercised by many small, specialized elites, each with its own decision-making responsibility.

Pluralist society a society made up of members belonging to many different groups that compete on relatively equal terms and according to mutually accepted norms and values for political power.

Political participation any attempt to influence the decision-making process.

Political party device for mobilizing the special interests of groups of people in the form of votes.

Political socialization process by which the individual develops political attitudes within the normative context of society.

Politics the operations of government; societal structures and procedures for decision making—settling disputes, distributing goods and services, defending the group, socializing members.

Rational-legal authority the legality of and the belief in the validity of laws and rationally created rules.

Relative deprivation a discrepancy between what a person feels is a legitimate expectation and what he or she actually experiences.

Revolution overthrow of a government by force or threat of force and replacement of the ruling class by a different set of rulers.

Routine political participation political actions that are permitted and encouraged although not required.

Totalitarian society a society in which all social functions are regulated by the state.

Traditional authority legitimate power passed down from one ruler to another.

ADDITIONAL READINGS

Domhoff, G. William. *Who Rules America?* Englewood Cliffs, N.J.: Prentice-Hall, 1967.
An examination of the American ruling class, which argues that a small, closely knit elite rules our society.

House, James S. "Political Alienation in America." *American Sociological Review* 50 (April 1975): 123–147.
A discussion of the impact of the political turmoil of the 1960s and an evaluation of the current alienation of citizens, which the author believes has affected all age groups and a broad segment of the population.

Kahn, Si. *How People Get Power: Organizing Oppressed Communities for Action.* New York: McGraw-Hill, 1970.
A handbook for organizing communities to influence the political process.

Nisbet, Robert A. *Community and Power.* New York: Oxford University Press, 1962.
A history of the effects of the decline of community upon political processes and decision making.

Rule, James B. *Private Lives and Public Surveillance: Social Control in the Computer Age.* New York: Schocken, 1974.
A study of the sources and uses of data that can be assembled and made available to public and private organizations with modern computer systems.

READING

READING 15.1
The Politics of Secrecy
Stanton K. Tefft

Some social scientists have suggested that political secrecy is a threat to democratic political systems; others consider it a necessary artifice of government in any society; and still others suggest that secrecy is a political strategy most characteristic of totalitarian governments. Of course, political secrecy has a moral or ideological significance to the members of any political system. Peoples' attitudes toward political secrecy reflect the political values which they hold. However, it is important to analyze secrecy as part of a political process and to assess its contribution to the political forces generating order and disorder in society. A cross-cultural analysis suggests that secrecy contributes to the social processes promoting order, change, and conflict in all political systems.

The concern of this article is with the role that political secrecy plays in the political processes promoting order and disorder. Secrecy is an important factor in politics, that is, in the political processes which determine and implement public goals as well as allocate political authority and enable political leaders to exercise their decision-making powers. Politics also involves the pursuit of public goals as they relate to the political relationships external to the political community (the autonomous, self-governing political unit).

Politics contributes to social order when the political processes operate to contain the structural and sectional conflicts characteristic of all societies or to regulate the conflicts generated by inequalities in wealth and power or by differences in group values, goals, or needs. And to the extent to which the political activities of society promote external political and economic security through peaceful or military means, then to that extent they promote order. Politics fails to promote order when it fails to actualize these fundamental political goals or creates a political climate in which powerful political groups pursue goals which aim at changing existing political structures.

Political leaders cannot maintain power through coercive methods alone. In the long run, their ability to secure compliance rests on the expectations of community members (or citizens of the state) that the leaders will fulfill the peoples' future expectations. Political leaders must either fulfill these expectations or persuade the community members that unmet demands cannot be met or are not in the best interests of the community. Political leaders will be unable to mobilize effective power or support for their decisions if community members determine that such policies are contrary to community values, laws, or economic or political interests.

At this point, secrecy plays an important role in the political process. It enables political leaders to perpetuate their power, even if their political decisions may violate community interests, values, sometimes even laws. In some cases, secrecy enables political leaders to exercise illegal coercive power against their political enemies without endangering the legitimacy of their rule.

Secret deliberations in the formulation of public policy enable political officials to mobilize public support for their plans once they are made public. Such secret discussions often hide from the citizen sharp disagreements between leaders over the formulated plans, the more desirable alternatives that were rejected by their leaders, and how the agreed upon policy may favor vested economic and political interests rather than the community at large. In this way, too, secrecy helps maintain the legitimacy of political leadership.

SOURCE: Published by permission of TRANSACTION, INC. from SOCIETY, Vol. 16, # 4, Copyright © 1979, by Transaction, Inc.

Secrecy also contributes to social order by enabling governments to carry out unpopular actions against foreign powers without generating internal discovery, to deny opponents information that would enable them to challenge the political status quo, to manipulate public opinion, to conduct espionage against internal political enemies, thereby neutralizing their potential power to subvert or challenge the existing government, and to keep constant surveillance of the community members.

While secrecy may contribute to the political processes generating social order in the ways outlined above, secrecy is also used by groups who are generating conflict and disorder. Secrecy enables groups opposed to the existing leadership to organize their opposition free of government surveillance. The counterespionage of such groups may be successful in exposing the secrets of the government, thereby undermining the legitimacy of existing political leadership. By providing protection for political dissidents, such secret organizations can provide a source of political opposition capable of effectively undermining the operations of government through terrorism or other means.

Even in the absence of opposition secret associations or revolutionary groups, the politics of secrecy can produce conflict. Various forms of bureaucratic secrecy may undermine government operations, thereby creating citizen alienation and apathy. Government secrecy may also produce policy decisions detrimental to the long-term interests of the people. Once made, these secret decisions may lead to further government actions that create citizen antagonism, opposition, and revolt.

Even the intelligence agencies created by modern governments to protect the security of the state have, in reality, undermined the ability of modern governments to carry out a rational foreign policy. In some cases, the activities of such agencies have become so secret that they carry out operations against foreign governments in ways that are at odds with the foreign policies of their own governments.

The current debate over aspects of political secrecy within Western democracies has tended to obscure the fact that political secrecy has operated to both support as well as to subvert political authority in all societies throughout human history. Political secrecy is not a monopoly of any one type of political system, though modern states have placed a higher value on certain forms of secrecy than others. Tribal chiefs, through their control of secret societies, have often utilized such associations to achieve the same political ends as modern presidents and prime ministers have reached through their intelligence organizations. In like fashion, chiefs, kings, as well as modern heads of state have used espionage against both internal and external enemies in order to maintain and defend their political power. In turn, political dissidents in all political systems have concealed their activities from the authorities in order to more effectively challenge the political leadership and to avoid persecution or destruction. The level of internal espionage and counterespionage that is characteristic of the internal politics of a political community, measures the degree of political disorder that prevails.

To be sure, there are differences between the politics of secrecy within the preindustrial society and the industrialized state. Modern governments seem to have less direct control over their secret intelligence organizations than tribal chiefs have over their secret associations. Modern intelligence agencies often subvert societal laws, while tribal secret societies tend to give support to community values. Moreover, the paramilitary activities of modern espionage agencies are not characteristic of the operations of the early espionage organizations.

Nonetheless, to understand the modern politics of secrecy, we must study the secrecy

process within a wider context, not bounded
by time or culture; thus, we must place the
modern policies of secrecy within an appropriate historical and cross-cultural perspective.

SECRECY AND POLITICAL ORDER

Within political communities, people organize
groups to pursue special interests. These are
associations. While even "open" associations
maintain some secrets, secret associations
or secret societies, by contrast, are groups
whose continued existence relies totally on
the continuous concealment of ideas, objects,
activities, plans, objectives, and/or membership from outsiders. In a few cases, the existence of the association itself may be kept secret. Some secret associations pursue goals
that are hostile to the central values and institutions of the political community. Such secret associations are *alienative* ones. Other secret organizations support or at least are in
close accord with the dominant values of the
community. These are *conformative* secret
orders. In many instances, such *conformative*
secret orders have provided political leaders
with an organization capable of not only reinforcing the legitimacy of their political status
but enabling them to expand and consolidate
their power.

Using their dominant position in the secret
societies, tribal leaders can control access to
adult rank, status, and political power. Without secret society membership, adult men and
women cannot marry, acquire property, or
assume normal sex roles. By regulating social
mobility in this way, the leaders of the secret
society make certain that individuals, before
attaining adult status, have been properly
socialized to the political and social values of
the tribe. In fact, in many of these tribal
communities, the elders perpetuate their authority over the junior members by controlling
the access of junior tribesmen to social, political, economic, magical, and religious knowledge. . . .

There are as many modern examples of
ruling-class use of secret societies for purposes
of political control. During the period of
Chinese history when the Kuomintang party
was in power (1912–1949), agents of various
secret associations were used by the government to suppress dissenters among the workers
at home and to terrorize political enemies in
the overseas Chinese communities. In eighteenth-century Ireland, the Orange Order was
formed to defend Protestant interests against
secret Catholic terrorist groups. By the end
of the nineteenth century, the Orange lodges
numbered about 90, with a total membership
of several thousand. In Tsarist Russia, after
the assassination of Alexander II, a "Sacred
Brotherhood" was organized to fight revolutionary terrorism with counterterrorism.

GOVERNMENT SECRECY

Secret societies no longer play a central role in
modern governments. Yet political leaders
still justify secrecy as necessary for efficient
government, to protect national security, and
as a means to discover and control domestic
groups which threaten state security.

The executive branches of democratic governments find further justification for secrecy.
Political leaders argue that they and their
ministers or councils cannot engage in open
and passionate debate over policy issues except
in secret. If such discussions became public
knowledge, they would be more muted and
less honest. In secret, opponents of policy may
voice their objections without fear of being
accused of disloyalty. Political leaders can
compromise original positions without loss of
prestige or political status.

Legislators make similar arguments for secret sessions. Lawmakers argue that legislative
business can be conducted more expeditiously
and efficiently in closed sessions; for, if they
were open, the legislators would dramatize
their debates for the galleries rather than carry
on business with dispatch. Others argue that

many secret sessions are needed to protect the reputations of individuals discussed by lawmakers or by witnesses called before their committees. The formal, open legislative sessions often merely confirm decisions which have been debated and decided in the closed sessions.

Secrecy, then, enables modern governments to maintain the facade of administrative competency and expertise whereas, in reality, there is much confusion and doubt in the formulation and execution of public policy. Political leaders hope that the citizens will retain confidence in the administration as long as they naively believe that their government's decisions are not based on narrow political self-interest.

Government secrecy often hides the pragmatic politics through which government agencies divulge secrets to certain groups in order to gain their cooperation and help in carrying out government policies. These executive alliances with nongovernmental bodies are necessary for effective administration in addition to partisan political support. The executive entrusts certain confidential information to legislatures and advisory bodies. Congressmen, who obtain such sensitive information through informal briefings, usually cannot put it to political advantage, for to publicly expose such secrets would subject congressmen to criticism that might prove politically embarrassing. The executive also entrusts sensitive information to established "inside lobbies." Such lobbies often represent business interests who entrust government agencies with certain business secrets partly in return for these reciprocal privileges.

The press, on the other hand, seems to have a dual role, sometimes advocating public disclosure and sometimes, as co-opted insider, sharing executive secrets. Some U.S. newspapers actually suppressed stories dealing with the Cuban invasion at the Bay of Pigs and the secret war in Laos, as well as the U.S. attempts to retrieve a sunken Soviet sub in 1975. To the extent that journalists depend on inside government sources for their important news stories, so much do they acquire a stake in the executive secrecy profiting from the relationship of trust with public officials. And, in a sense, such journalists become tools of the executive, enabling the political leadership to leak secret information to the news media in order to mobilize public opinion or to test public reaction to possible policies and plans. Thus, while often an ally of the public in advocating its right to "open" government, the news media has also conspired with the executive as well as other branches of government to keep the public misinformed about certain government acts and policies.

This process of "entrusted secrecy" seems to work to the advantage of both parties. The "inside lobbies," for example, get advance information vital to their economic or political interests, while the executive branches receive, in return, political support. Thus, some secrets are "marketed" to enhance the executive's economic or political power.

One of the strongest manipulative powers of the executive in democratic systems, then, is the ability to share or not share information with other agencies or lobbies. However, knowledge that the "marketing" of sensitive information takes place must be kept secret from the public in order that government can maintain its image as an impartial implementer of public policy. Secret politics seems to encourage deviancy from normitive [sic] rules. Secrecy provides a cloak behind which forbidden acts, legal violations, evasion of responsibility, inefficiency, and corruption are well concealed. The executive branch of modern states often uses the requirements for state secrecy as a device to hide such illegality and corruption. Closed sessions by legislative bodies, for example, may hide the influence of powerful interest groups on lawmakers' legislative decisions.

In both public and private bureaucracies, the forms of secrecy are much the same. As among the specialized divisions of a corporation, so do government agencies compete fiercely for money. They hide secret information which would damage their budget claims. The hierarchical organization of government bureaucracies prevents the downward flow of damaging information which would threaten the position of agency heads who must maintain the mystique of superior administrative leadership, and the upward flow of information which would subject experts to criticism or reveal the mismanagement and violation of formal and informal rules at the lower levels.

Thus, secrecy enables government leaders, who profess support for the dominant political values, to ignore or subvert them when required by concerns of political expediency, yet still retain their authority, which they couldn't if their lawless acts became public knowledge.

EXTERNAL AND INTERNAL SURVEILLANCE

The political community, whatever its size or complexity, being self-governing and autonomous, conducts its political transactions with similar political units in terms of its own self-interests. The usual mistrust and rivalry that marks such intertribal or international relationships makes secrecy an inevitable factor in such intercommunity affairs. The major concern of the government, in this instance, is with the protection of military, political, or economic information useful to the rival or enemy community. . . .

Foreign espionage by modern states serves much the same function today as in earlier times. However, modern intelligence units have become more involved in economic as well as new forms of political and military espionage. For example, the Soviet State Committee for Science and Technology (the Soviet agency dealing with foreign business) employs intelligence agents who covertly try to obtain technical secrets from Western businessmen. In addition, Soviet secret police organizations check on Russian emigré groups as well as place Russian diplomatic and commercial personnel under secret observation. The intelligence agencies of Western democracies conduct similar industrial espionage and, on occasion, diplomatic surveillance. Most modern intelligence services, at one time or another, appear to have intervened in the political affairs of foreign states by giving various forms of covert support to opponents of these unfriendly governments, or in some cases, by directing paramilitary operations against disfavored governments. This is a radical departure from the traditional role of foreign intelligence, that of information collector and analyzer. The security systems of state intelligence serve the function of not only advancing their own aggressive foreign espionage networks but also protecting their internal operational secrets from foreign counterespionage. Moreover, the intelligence community also must investigate possible foreign espionage against any branch of government.

Counterintelligence agencies are responsible for investigating foreign espionage. The work of counterintelligence or counterespionage agents involves a wide variety of tasks, including checking on reported disaffection cases (employees with grudges against a government organization or personnel with big financial problems), suspected leaks, routine surveillance of embassies or diplomatic residences, and suspicious incidents such as missing documents that might indicate espionage.

The great concern for state security within totalitarian systems obliterates the distinction between internal and external intelligence. Foreign intelligence is combined with domestic counterespionage. But such distinctions between internal and external intelligence operations become hazy in democratic societies during periods of major international crisis, war, or periods of political paranoia generated by hyperpatriotism and xenophobia. During these periods, intelligence agencies are quite capable of utilizing the same espionage techniques employed in foreign espionage against their own citizens.

In the Soviet Union, the GPU/OGPU, offspring of Lenin's first secret police organization, the VCheka, were concerned not only with counteracting foreign espionage within the U.S.S.R. and conducting Soviet espionage abroad (including spying on Russian émigré colonies and Soviet diplomatic and commercial representatives) but also destroying underground opposition movements and political parties and keeping watch on all commercial and industrial establishments within the U.S.S.R. to make sure they did not disobey the economic laws and regulations or fail to meet required production quotas. Even today, the Soviet KGB (Committee for State Security) continues to investigate ideological subversion, political crimes, and economic crimes. The role it plays in investigating such crimes is the basis of its powerful position in the Soviet political, legal, and administrative structures.

Historical evidence supports the view that foreign espionage services are usually co-opted by political leaders for internal surveillance. Dahomean kings also used internal espionage to maintain their authority. These monarchs employed a large body of part-time spies to keep subordinate chiefs under observation, largely to prevent the chiefs from subverting their authority or plotting against them. These spies reported to one of the Dahomean ministers who, in turn, reported their observations to the king. Both Hawaian chiefs and Zulu rulers used their intelligence agents for both internal and external espionage. . . .

MODERN SURVEILLANCE

As recent events have demonstrated, modern democratic governments have increased secret surveillance of their citizens, using the techniques of foreign espionage. Of great concern to these governments is the possible use of dissident political organizations by foreign agents for "subversive" ends. It is understandable why secret orders still provoke such suspicion. Secrecy, indeed, breeds the suspicion by outsiders that activities which must be hidden are likely illegal, immoral, or subversive. Moreover, the secret society, being a power separate and independent of state government, is often considered a threat by political leaders unless they can establish control over it or discover its true plans and have knowledge of its activities. Thus, modern secret associations are subject to much government espionage.

But even many "open" associations, ones whose goals and membership are not concealed, have become the object of state surveillance. Indeed, in some cases intelligence agents, after joining such groups, act as agent provocateurs, encouraging violent acts to bring discredit on these organizations, thus enabling the authorities to arrest and put in jail the group leaders or its other members for illegal acts. Such agents may also provoke dissension and conflict within the organization to weaken it. In the United States, for example, agents have used these tactics not only against such secret associations as the Ku Klux Klan and the Weathermen but also against the Students for Democratic Action, and Vietnam Veterans Against the War, the Black Panthers, and other campus radical organizations.

The expansion of domestic intelligence is paralleled by the erosion of citizen privacy due to the information demands of modern bureaucracy. Government and private bureaucracies, who employ thousands and serve many more, must acquire a great deal of personal information, not only on their employees, but on their clientele as well. To control and regulate both their employees and their mass clientele, modern bureaucracies accumulate as much detailed documentation as possible linking people with their pasts. Some businesses maintain constant surveillance of their employees, even after they are hired, to assure loyalty and honesty. Internal surveillance and espionage of this magnitude finds no parallel within small-scale political communities or early states.

The surprising fact about the average citizen in modern democratic states is not that he entrusts so few personal secrets to outsiders but that he entrusts so many. The public, while resisting clandestine or coercive intrusion on their privacy, nonetheless, provide much data on their personal and economic lifestyles to government agencies or large private corporations. Obviously, people provide such information in order to get jobs, apply for services, or fulfill their legal obligations to the government (tax records, for example). Computers have enabled private as well as government bureaucracies to accumulate and store a vast array of information on the private life and habits of each citizen. There have been many instances when such organizations or government agencies, unknown to the private citizen, have given such private data to third parties. On occasion, such information has been used for political purposes. During the Nixon administration, the Internal Revenue Service compiled tax information on politically suspect individuals and organizations, using its powers to audit as a politically coercive tool. The CIA has been able to obtain IRS tax files on private individuals. Moreover, many of our privileged communications have not been secure from government surveillance. For example, RCA, ITT, and Western Union for many years made copies of international cables available to the National Security Agency by allowing NSA to copy their magnetic tapes. Operations like that of NSA show how vulnerable computer storage systems are to authorized or unauthorized access by outsiders.

SECRECY AND POLITICAL DISORDER

While secrecy is a social device by which political leaders can maintain and/or expand their power, secrecy also enables certain associations or organizations to subvert the political status quo and to avoid coercive sanctions which the government sees fit to impose on them. Even "open" organizations, such as corporations and government agencies, may employ secrecy to cover up illegal acts or policies, thereby contributing to a political climate in which peoples' confidence in the conventional political process is undermined.

Secrecy as an artifice of modern government may promote political disorder in both direct and indirect ways. The concealment of information in the operation of government bureaucracy may not only promote inefficiency in the operation of government services, but also may contribute to the failure of the government's domestic and foreign policies. Continued failures of this sort result in an escalation of political dissent and conflict.

ALIENATIVE SECRET ORDERS

Secret orders may organize political rebellions or provide the secret leadership for revolutionary organizations. In either case, the existence of such secret associations has promoted political conflict. . . .

Revolutionary or subversive organizations are more well-known examples of groups who must employ forms of secrecy as a means of survival against the police forces of the governments which they hope to overthrow. One such early subversive organization, the Arab Carmathites, aimed at overthrowing the Sunni khalifs and replacing them with Ismailites, by secretly introducing atheism and impiety into the Islamic religion, thus undermining the religious authority of the existing political leaders. Their successors, the Assassins, turned to terrorism in eleventh-century Persia as a means to achieve the same ends. In the early nineteenth century, the Italian Carbonari, who opposed the Holy Alliance and were driven underground by the government, continued to function as a secret revolutionary party. . . .

In Ireland, too, down to the present day, Catholic secret association or revolutionary parties have resisted alien rule, in this case Protestant domination. Agrarian secret societies, such as the Whiteboys and the Ribbonmen of the eighteenth and nineteenth centuries, fought the economic oppression of the landowners, who were usually Protestants, and resisted the hated tithes paid to the clergy of the Established (Anglican) church. The Defenders were a Catholic secret association organized to defend Catholic peasants against Protestant secret orders, such as the Peep O'Day Boys, who raided Catholic homes to search for arms. The Defenders were later supplanted by the United Irishmen, originally a radical reform party, reorganized as a secret order toward the end of the eighteenth century, as a consequence of attempts by the Protestant government to suppress them. By 1798, 200,000 Catholics had joined the United Irishmen. By the mid-1860s, the United Irishmen had been replaced by the Irish Republican Brotherhood, a secret revolutionary group committed to the achievement of an independent republic for Ireland, as well as to restoring the land to the rural poor. Even today, secret and semisecret revolutionary organizations are part of the Irish political arena, as evidenced by the fact that the Irish Republican Army, a political heir of the IRB, while divided into two rival factions, is active and creating problems of terrorism for the present government.

In colonial situations, secret societies often oppose the spread of foreign groups who compete with them for potential "converts." In these instances, loyalty to the secret order serves to insulate the membership and prevent them from making contact with foreigners who might undermine their loyalty to the traditional associations. In Asia, such nativistic or nationalistic secret organizations may have at one time operated as money-lending societies, protectionistic organizations, mutual aid mortuary societies, and gambling groups. Yet in colonial societies they have also fostered antiforeign feeling and organized opposition to the government. In Malaya, for example, secret societies in 1825 plotted insurrection; and in 1851 and 1854 these societies led anti-Christian riots in Singapore to counter Roman Catholic influence. In like manner, the secret Bizango society and similar Haitian secret associations provided the leadership for slave revolts against French rule, conducting guerrilla warfare against the authorities. In modern Haiti, such associations organize resistance to the ruling elite's attempt to alienate peasant land.

BUREAUCRATIC SECRECY

Secrecy that reduces the accountability of private economic organizations has profound and widespread effects on public affairs and political interests. The secrets maintained by large national and international corporations give such economic organizations powerful economic and political advantages over not only their smaller rivals but also over other interest groups trying to influence governmental policy. The fact that the more powerful corporations share many secrets with government agencies makes them privy to much valuable economic information not available to smaller and less influential rivals, information vital to profitable business investment of capital. Further, these special ties with government give the heads of such corporations highly profitable knowledge about stocks and taxes not available to outsiders. Secrecy also enables multinational corporations to freely shift huge sums of money in and out of countries, often to the detriment of the countries in which they have made huge profits.

The public too may be injured, directly or indirectly, by corporation concealments. Corporation scientists may hide the fact that new products may have undesirable effects on the environment. Complex accounting practices may enable businessmen to justify price increases when these were not really necessary, given the corporation's actual profits. And often business secrecy enables these large-scale private concerns to hide illegal or highly dubious business practices. The kinds of secrets shared by big government and big corporations and concealed from smaller businesses or other interest groups may eventually create divisive political issues.

But corporation secrecy can also undermine the government's attempts to devise and carry out rational economic policies. American corporations, for example, have withheld data vital to future economic planning, such as the oil companies who refused to give the government their reserve and production data.

Modern government leaders must choose between alternative courses of action to solve problems or meet crisis situations. But, when modern governmental decisions are made in secret by a restricted body of political leaders, this secrecy increases the chances that more desirable alternatives will be ignored, or that when decisions are made, they will be less effectively carried out. Executive secrecy may close off the valuable expertise of excluded officials, experts, or agencies. Subject to no outside evaluation, these secret decision makers may make policies that are based on wrong or distorted information. They may ignore other alternatives which might prove to be more effective. Executive secrecy, therefore,

makes constructive criticism by knowledgeable outsiders impossible.

The executive branch of many modern governments often entrusts secrets to agencies, lobbies, or media interests which can be relied on to conceal them from the public and which also can serve government interests. For example, "inside" media organizations may be used for propaganda purposes. During the Yom Kippur war of 1973, the Israeli press, long conditioned to cooperate with the army in national security matters, accepted and published the military's optimistic assessment of the fighting. In reality, the Israeli army was suffering heavy casualties and once the public learned the true facts, the government, the press, and the military lost the credibility of the public.

Similarly, secrecy that surrounds the deliberations of congressional or state legislative committees, advisory bodies, and local governing boards and commissions tends to produce irrationality within the political process. Citizens have no input into the formation of legislation, exert no restraint on decisions, and have no opportunities to evaluate the performances of their representatives. Nor will the public be privy to information enabling them to appreciate the necessity for unpopular policies. Secrecy even works against the legislators themselves, in that they are not protected against any slander or false accusation which they might incur if such meetings were public.

The contributions of bureaucratic secrecy to political disorder should now be obvious. Such secrecy generates mutual suspicions and creates mistrust of government by its citizens. Policies formulated in secret receive little overall public support. The public has little chance to add its own advice and counsel to policy debate that is held in secret. Moreover, government secrecy prevents public checks on the conduct of elected and appointed political leaders. It encourages deception and illegal acts for political expediency. Secrecy creates a climate of suspicion in which even honest governmental officers may be wrongfully accused of malfeasance and misfeasance; and the security systems that demand an elaborate secrecy classification of government documents and records protects much useless information at great public expense. Moreover, secrets do get disclosed, but in such a way that the true facts are distorted or inaccurate.

Viewed from the perspective of the political community as a whole (whether state or chiefdom), the secrecy process promotes more conflict than order. More openness in both the internal and external politics of the community may have its dangers but, on the balance, secrecy, in the long run, seems to contribute more to disorderly politics than orderly politics.

SUMMARY

In this article Tefft suggests that secrecy contributes both to order and to disorder in society. Secrecy enables governments to develop public policies, to coerce enemies, and to carry out unpopular activities without public discussion. Secrecy contributes to disorder by allowing bureaucracies to ignore inefficiencies, by permitting subversive organizations to operate, and by concealing illegal activities from public knowledge. Overall, however, secrecy appears to create more conflict than order. The issue of secrecy in the United States is complex.

QUESTIONS

1. Can a free democratic society survive with secrecy about many of the operations of government?

2. What should citizens do to prevent activities that hide the operations of government from public knowledge?

3. Can our form of government and secrecy exist together?

4. What social conditions and forms of social organization encourage secrecy in government?

494

CHAPTER 16

Educational Institutions

CONTENTS

Should efforts to integrate schools be stopped?

Since the U.S. Supreme Court declared segregated schools to be inherently unequal in 1954, the federal government has used several means to enforce compliance with desegregation laws from use of the military to withholding federal funds from segregated institutions. These efforts have been largely successful. However, in the face of continued segregation based on residential patterns and the growth of private schools that are not affected by desegregation laws, state and local governments have redirected their efforts to assuring integration of minority populations by various legal and administrative means, including busing. Parents and educators who oppose these remedies believe that integration is an unrealistic goal and that the proper goal is to ensure quality education by upgrading minority schools.

YES   Desegregation has been a failure. Reactions to federal efforts to force desegregation have ranged from grudging acceptance to violence. Despite good intentions, the effectiveness of the public schools has been destroyed in many communities and all further efforts toward desegregation by integrating schools—that is, by mandating fixed minority-majority percentages of students—should be stopped.

The basic issue is quality of education—not integration. To bus children out of their neighborhoods to other schools destroys the social fabric of the community. The social relationships between minority and majority children who are bused are artificial and short term. Also, there is no easy way to involve parents in school activities when the school is miles from home. Though the Brown decision indicated that segregated schools are inherently unequal, busing also creates unequal educational experiences: participation in social programs, athletics, music, and other extracurricular activities is difficult if not impossible for students who are bused.

Desegregation has weakened the public schools. The flight to the suburbs by whites and the increased number of private schools sponsored by both blacks and whites have left the public schools without the leadership of concerned parents. Reestablishing the local school, attended by neighborhood residents, controlled by local citizens, and responsive to parents and community leaders is the only way to ensure children meaningful education.

There is little if any evidence that students—black or white—in integrated schools receive better educations than those in segregated schools. The concern about quality involves individual motivation as well as the structure of the schools; unless students want to learn, integration will not help. Mixing blacks and whites does not motivate blacks and often lowers the motivation of all students. Families are responsible for teaching people the value of education—not the schools.

Finally, if the money spent on integration were directed toward improving all neighborhood schools—whether segregated or not—the entire population would benefit. Why not improve the schools and let students attend in the neighborhood where they live, where parents and the entire community can be involved? Efforts to integrate the schools should be stopped!

NO   Since 1954, when the U.S. Supreme Court ruled that segregated schools were unequal, thousands of white and black students have had the experience of going to school with others of a different race. They have learned that people of other races are like them in their desires for a better life, in wanting to be successful and happy, and in their fears, hopes, and uncertainties about life. Because of housing patterns, many neighborhood schools are still segregated; however, busing has successfully been used to achieve integrated educational experiences, which have enriched the lives of thousands of students.

Those who would stop efforts to integrate schools often have vested interests at stake. Some teachers do not want to teach in integrated schools. Black teachers and administrators fear they may be replaced by whites, just as white teachers and administrators fear they may be replaced by blacks. Similarly, realtors and homeowners fear loss of property values if schools are integrated. However, the issue is quality, and the goal of quality education should not be thwarted by vested interests.

The desire to maintain segregated neighborhood schools on the grounds that segregation is natural—that people want to live with others of their own race— does not justify inequality. If segregated education was unequal in the 1950s, it is unequal in the 1980s. Though schools are now segregated by fact rather than by

law, and in the North as well as the South, this does not change the inherent inequality of segregation.

The results of segregation have shown that separate is never—and can never be—equal. Students who are forced into poor educational systems—black or white—face lifelong handicaps. Because neighborhood schools are stratified by race and class, blacks will continue to have poorer educational opportunities than whites unless integration is realized. Efforts to provide equal educational opportunities by integrating schools must continue!

Few issues are as controversial in the United States as efforts to integrate urban schools, especially by busing. Those who say such efforts should be stopped argue that educational experiences based on busing are artificial, that desegregation is counterproductive because many parents send their children to private schools or move, and that there is little evidence of improved education

after desegregation. Supporters of continued efforts to desegregate schools point to the benefits in learning about others, to the vested interests involved in maintaining segregation, and to the fact that race and class stratification prevents blacks from educational opportunities available to whites.

This controversy is only one phase of the general concern about education. What are the social factors that shape educational institutions in the modern world? Is there a set of functions that schools should fulfill? Does education open occupational opportunities to all or is it a means of perpetuating the status quo? These questions and others will be considered in this chapter. We shall examine the functions of education and the organization of schools in American society. Several current issues will be considered as these affect modern educational institutions—control of the schools, busing, and equal opportunity.

QUESTIONS TO CONSIDER

■ What effect do student subcultures have on learning?

■ Are teachers professionals or only employees of the school board?

■ How does grouping of students by ability affect learning?

■ Should schools teach only basics like mathematics, English, or science, or should they try to prepare students for jobs?

In West Virginia a group of parents object to the teaching of evolution in schools and insist that creation be taught as well. In a Long Island community parents, teachers, and students are divided over the school board's decision to ban Eldridge Cleaver's **Soul on Ice**, *Kurt Vonnegut's* **Slaughterhouse Five**, *and Bernard Malmud's* **The Fixer** *from the school library. In the urban North, black children attend schools that have nearly all black students just as their parents and grandparents did in the South before the 1954 Supreme Court decision declared segregated education to be unequal. Children of migrant workers in California may attend school part of the time but have to help earn a living for much of the school year. Finally, books whose titles such as* **Burn the Schools—Save the Children**, **Why Johnny Can't Read**, **Suffer Little Children**, **Death at an Early Age**, *or* **The Way It Spozed to Be** *suggest that schools are failing continue to become best sellers.*

Perhaps no institution has been criticized so severely for so many different reasons as educational institutions in the United States over the last 25 years. However, just as there are critics, there are defenders of the schools and their performance. Which view is correct? Are the schools failing to fulfill their purpose in society? To answer such questions, we must examine the functions of educational

institutions and the effects of the educational process upon individuals.

FUNCTIONS OF THE SCHOOL IN MODERN SOCIETY

In a general sense education refers to the process by which a person learns the culture of a society. However, in industrial societies at least two other functions are related to education: preparing individuals for adult roles in the society and generating social change.

Though we will discuss them separately, these three functions are related. For example, English is the basic language of schools in the United States. English is essential for people in their adult roles as workers, but learning English also involves learning the values and social norms of the society. Usually these functions do not conflict: people in their adult roles as workers are supported by the values and norms learned in school. However, at times these functions may conflict, as when values are taught that are different from local values—for example, when parents object to books or materials selected by the teacher. As one parent has put it (Melton, 1975):

I would not for one moment refute the literary merits of *Catcher in the Rye*; however, I do question its use as a textbook, not on the basis of whether or not it is good literature, but whether it is exemplary of the types of attitudes we want to present to high school students. (p. 227)

There has been much conflict in recent years about course content, values, and control of schools. We will examine these conflicts in light of the three functions of schools: transmitting culture, preparing individuals for adult roles, and acting as an agent of social change.

The Transmission of Culture

The transmission of culture is the process of learning society's values, norms, and symbols and its accumulated knowledge. For most people the family continues to be the primary agent of such learning during the early years of life. Within the family, and later within the school, the child learns what is important to the family and society. Norms, beliefs, and values are thus passed on from one generation to another.

In every society the process of learning is defined and shaped by various social institutions. Education in preindustrial societies is carried out primarily within the family and is reinforced by other social institutions. For example, Havighurst (1958) describes education in the Pueblo Indian Hopi society of the American Southwest as a largely informal process in which children learn from elders. The Hopi family is the basic economic unit, engaging in planting, herding sheep, spinning and weaving cloth, and building. The children's parents are their principal teachers. Children learn by taking part in these family activities as well as through the religious and political activities of their village. The informality of this type of education is illustrated by the following autobiographical statement of a Hopi Indian (Simmons, 1942):

Learning to work was like play. We children tagged around with our elders and copied what they did. We followed our fathers to the fields and helped plant and weed. The old men took us for walks and taught us the use of plants and how to collect them. We joined the women in gathering rabbit weed for baskets, and went with them to dig clay for pots. We would taste this clay as the women did to test it. We watched the fields to drive out the birds and rodents, helped pick peaches to dry in the sun, and gathered melons to lug up the mesa. We rode the burrows to harvest corn, gather fuel, or herd sheep. In house building we helped a little by bringing up dirt to cover the roofs. In this way we grew up doing things. (pp. 51–52)

Industrialization and urbanization, however, have radically altered the social structure of modern societies. Education has become largely independent of family and other social institutions. The family in modern societies is no longer the primary unit of production. Role socialization within the family no longer prepares children for productive adult roles; in fact, parents are incapable of doing so. The increased division of labor, which requires special knowledge and skills, makes it impossible for a child today to acquire these skills by observing par-

Small children confront new sets of cultural agents and behavioral expectations when they enter schools. These preschoolers are learning to follow the teacher and to participate in structured learning situations as preparation for later school work.

ents and other adults. Instead, formal schooling has become a necessity, bringing a new class of cultural agents—teachers—and a new social setting—the classroom—into the child's life.

Schools, being structured differently than the home, confront the child with new sets of demands, which require the child to learn new ways of dealing with others (Wheeler, 1966). Rather than learning skills and values that are particular to family or group, the child is taught skills and values that are universalistic and apply to all.

Not only are knowledge and complex skills transmitted by the schools but, nearly as important from the functionalist perspective, the child learns the cultural norms that indicate to the child how she or he ought to behave in specific situations.

The curriculum also reflects these cultural norms. History is taught, not because of its inherent value, but because it is an effective means of producing an identification with the values of American society. Learning about the hard work of the pioneers, the bravery of Washington at Valley Forge, the faith of the Pilgrims, or the courage and determination of a Ben Franklin, a Henry Ford, or a Thomas Edison develops a sense of pride and patriotism and serves as object lessons in desired behavior. At the same time, the selection of historical events that exemplify cultural values can be significant. For example, little is learned about the strength of blacks during slavery, or the creativity and culture of the Cherokee Indians, or the fierce pride and determination of Italian immigrant women in the New England mills. In short, values are taught in the historical context of dominant groups in the larger society.

Values related to the adult role of work are also taught in American schools. For example, competition and individual achievement is emphasized through the forms of testing, grading and academic, athletic, and social honors.

Not all modern societies stress individualism. Bronfenbrenner (1973), in studying Soviet education, found that Russian children, in contrast to their American counterparts, grow up in an environment that encourages them to suppress their individual gratifications and desires. Instead, they are taught to consider first the needs and expec-

tations of Soviet society. This teaching is begun by very early exposure to collective living in preschool centers. When the child enters the Soviet school at age seven, he or she becomes a member of a classroom unit that is also part of the Community Youth Organization. Major emphasis is placed on collective work effort, group competition, and collective discipline. This kind of collective upbringing appears to produce peer groups that strongly support behavior consistent with the expectations of adult society. It also induces in a child a willingness to take the initiative in assuming the responsibility for maintaining desirable behavior in others.

Some groups in the United States that have maintained distinctive cultures by isolating themselves from the larger society also have attempted to teach collectivist rather than individualist values to their children. Among the Hutterites, a group of Anabaptists who founded communal agricultural settlements in North and South Dakota and Montana, education is closely related to the unique adult roles in that subculture. The Hutterite values of cooperation, submission to authority, and sharing of responsibility are taught both formally and informally to children.

The transmission of culture is an important function of educational institutions in every society. As we will see later, it is disagreement about what should be transmitted that has created conflict among individuals, groups, and the larger society.

The Preparation of Individuals for Adult Roles

Every society has ways of assigning people to different positions in society. In preindustrial societies, ascribed characteristics or family ties often are used as the basis for assignment. For example, in India, persons were assigned occupations by caste. Brahmins, the highest caste, were educated to fill the top positions in government solely on the basis of family caste status (Bergel, 1962). By contrast, in modern industrial nations, the position a person holds in society basically depends upon personal achievement, though class, race, sex, and religion may also have an effect.

Modern industrial societies are also characterized by a highly developed division of labor and job specialization. In providing trained workers for such jobs, schools have been called on to develop individuals with specialized skills. Technical and vocational high schools train for work in such occupations as construction, printing, secretarial work, hair styling, and food service. At the college and university level, people are trained in the specialized skills necessary for occupations like medicine, law or social work.

"TRACKING"

While academic achievement is often used to predict a person's future work performance, other methods for placing students into occupational categories are also current. Tests designed to measure ability, aptitudes, and interests are widely used by guidance counselors to steer students toward certain occupations. Early decisions about courses and curricula are encouraged. As early as junior high school, boys are asked to choose between a vocational and a college preparatory curriculum and girls to choose among home economics, business and secretarial training, and college preparatory curricula. Courses within a specific curriculum are arranged sequentially, leading to a high school diploma that is assumed to verify achievement in that curriculum.

This early placement of students in various curricula is called tracking, and it has become a controversial practice in recent years. **Tracking** refers to the practice of grouping students of similar abilities and aspirations on the basis of tests or past performance in school as a means of encouraging achievement. What are the effects of tracking? Supporters of tracking argue that it benefits both the students who are low achievers by allowing them to learn at their own pace and those who are high achievers by allowing more rapid learning. Critics of tracking claim that it interferes with the goal of teaching universalistic standards and benefits those who need it least—the high achievers. In addition, they say, the tests that assign children to different

The large number of students in modern educational institutions has created various testing methods to evaluate a student's performance or potential compared to the ability and achievements of other members of the age cohort. In most classes exams are given to assess learning. In addition, standardized tests are often used for placing students in various curricula in elementary or secondary schools, or for college and professional school admission.

tracks are of doubtful value in predicting achievement and should not be used to influence life choices at such early ages.

Research on the effects of tracking is not conclusive. One researcher reviewed over 400 studies but found no clear evidence of either benefits or negative consequences for students themselves (Richer, 1976). However, middle-class children are more likely than lower-class children to have acquired aptitudes and aspirations for college and are more likely to be placed in college-bound tracks. Once identified, these college-bound students tend to receive more attention and stimulation than other students; as a result, their achievement levels increase. Tracking systems appear to work to the disadvantage of those labeled "slow" or not "college material" by encouraging a negative self-image with its consequent lack of motivation to achieve. Given appropriate attention, resources, and encouragement, tracking could produce positive benefits for all. However, the effect of tracking is often to perpetuate the social stratification already prevailing in a community and the larger society. Unless tracking is organized to benefit all classes, it cannot assist individuals to move up in the social system (Alexander, Cook, and McDill, 1978).

The organization of educational institutions reflects the social stratification of a society. The English educational system attempts to sort out the most promising students at an early age. A battery of examinations, known as the "eleven plus," personal interviews, and students' grade school records are used to select a minority of students who then are admitted to grammar schools and enter college preparatory programs. The remainder of students will enroll in secondary modern or technical schools. Early selection in this manner allows enough time for preparing the selected group of students for their elite positions. England's well-entrenched aristocracy makes use of **sponsored mobility**, in which status is conferred on the basis of family connections rather than personal achievement (Turner, 1960). In American society power, wealth, and prestige are viewed as rewards for initiative, perserverance, and achievement. Individuals are expected to aspire beyond the social status of their parents. Turner describes this pattern of

mobility as **contest mobility**, in which elite status is granted to those who earn it.

THE GOAL OF EDUCATION FOR ALL

Educational institutions of the United States espouse the principle of contest mobility and the ideal of personal choice and achievement. There is no sharp differentiation among students on the basis of ability and achievement during the early school years. Indeed, the distinctions that are made have been more for the purpose of developing remedial programs for the poorly prepared students than special programs for the gifted. Further, the comprehensive high school permits students to move from one course of study to another, though access to college is easiest through a special program of college preparation. In addition, the extensive network of junior colleges or community colleges in various states has been justified on the grounds of providing students with a "second chance" (Clark, 1960). Finally, in recent years many public colleges in the United States also have adopted an open admissions policy, accepting all students with high school or equivalent education and recruiting successful students from junior colleges as transfers. However, open admissions policies do not ensure equality in achievement. While students in junior colleges appear to be similar in ability to students in other colleges, they become discouraged more easily, drop out more often, and are less likely to achieve their stated goals. Unfortunately, the reasons for this discouragement are unclear (Alba and Lavin, 1981).

In essence, formal education in America is viewed as an open system in which students have the opportunity to demonstrate their abilities and primary responsibility for taking advantage of that opportunity. Though "tracking" has some of the same consequences for society as the system of sponsored mobility in England, the educational system in the United States assumes that individual desire and effort are the basic factors in success. However, a comparison of the educational system of the United States with those of Russia and England gives evidence that social factors are important elements in educational achievement.

In his 1973 study of the Soviet elementary schools, Bronfenbrenner notes that the primary goal of the school system is to raise the educational level of society. Group performance is rewarded. Consequently, the brightest members of the group devote a great deal of their time to helping the slower members. This is in contrast to the American elementary school classroom, where students compete against one another and slower learners are sometimes subjected to destructive criticism from their peers.

In the United States and Britain, universities differ markedly. In this country open admissions policies bring large numbers of students into college, but competitive standards result in high dropout rates for men and women, in sharp contrast to the British system. In Britain the selection process is essentially complete before the student enters college, and students are tested infrequently or not at all during the first several years of their studies. As a result, a larger proportion of students who enter college in Britain graduate than in the United States.

THE DECLINE OF COLLEGE ENTRANCE TEST SCORES

With our belief in an open-class society, we in the United States have seen education as the primary mechanism for preparing individuals for favored and rewarded positions. The United States has a much higher proportion of youth in school than most nations, and most of these youth are in academic rather than vocational programs. This high level of high school and college enrollment reflects a student population in which many appear to be ill-prepared for college, as evidenced by declining college entrance test scores among U.S. high school seniors.

During the period from the mid-1960s to 1980, scores achieved by students on the two basic college entrance examinations—the American College Testing (ACT) and the Scholastic Aptitude Test (SAT)—steadily declined. In 1967 the mean scores on the SAT were 466 (verbal) and 492 (math); by 1980 these scores were 424 (verbal) and 466 (math) (College Entrance Examination Board, 1981). Comparable declines were reported for the ACT in English, mathematics, and social studies while natural science scores remained steady (Dearman and

Plisko, 1981). Educators, government officials, and parents have expressed increasing concern about this decline; one suggested remedy is a return to "basics" in the schools. What are the reasons for such a decline?

Several social and structural factors can be identified as contributing to lowered test scores. First, more four-year colleges, junior colleges, and vocational schools are requiring either the SAT or the ACT for admission. Because these exams are standardized, schools are better able to use their results to compare and evaluate an applicant's ability rather than relying solely on grades or recommendations. Second, in response to the requirements of schools more students are taking these tests than in the past, both in absolute numbers and proportionately. This increase in test takers is largely due to the greater number of students of lower ability levels who are now electing to go to college. Their lower test scores decreases the mean score; in fact, one study estimated that without any change in the ability levels of test takers, the impact of increased numbers taking these tests would lower the mean score by 20 points (Beaton et al., 1977). Third, more students who have not pursued traditional academic paths are taking the exams, such as older persons, employed people seeking credentials, women who interrupted their education to have children, or vocationally oriented students. The increased educational opportunities offered by vocational schools and and junior colleges appear to be a significant factor in declining SAT scores, because students who choose these schools tend to have lower scores than students in college preparatory programs (Schrader, 1977). While we should also note that there appears to be a close correlation between SAT scores of high school seniors and the shift to less demanding programs during their elementary school years, especially in reading and English (Chall, 1977), much of the decline in these scores appears to be a function of expanded use of such tests by educational institutions and the expanded college population.

Comparisons between current and past educational achievement levels or with those of other countries must consider the impact of structured educational and occupational opportunities that affect these levels. To conclude that television, student disenchantment, or poor instruction is responsible for the decline in test scores ignores the effects of changes in the number and characteristics of those educated and the way education is organized in the United States.

QUALITY OF EDUCATION, STATUS, AND JOBS

Another factor that affects the preparation of students for adult roles is the variation in quality of schools and consequently of opportunities for education (Jencks, 1972). In 1979 schools in New York state spent $3180 per pupil compared with $1493 per student in Arkansas (Grant and Eiden, 1981). While money alone is not an adequate measure of quality, differences of such size are important. Schools serving wealthy families tend to be better funded than those attended by poor families, even within the same district, resulting in better facilities, better trained teachers, and better programs. Black and other minority children are more likely to attend schools in the more poorly financed school districts. Figures for per pupil expenditure indicate that as much as 20 percent more is spent per white student than per black student.

Sexton's study, *Education and Income* (1961), showed that educational opportunity is significantly affected by the student's family income. As family income goes down, the quality of education received by the child goes down. Schools in districts where the average family income was low employed three times as many teachers who were not fully qualified as schools in districts where families had higher average incomes. Similarly, nearly half of the poorer group of schools had substandard or nonexistent science facilities compared with only 2 percent of the second group. While some improvement occurred in the 1970s because of consolidation and federal pressure to improve minority facilities there are still great disparities in the quality of education among schools.

College attendance is also affected by the family's social status. While the expansion of college enrollment has resulted in the attendance of a greater proportion of working-class students in higher education, fewer than one-half of American high school graduates complete college. There is also evidence

that upward mobility and status depend not so much on the level of education attained as on the social background of one's parents. For example, in reviewing data on social stratification and mobility, Perrucci (1967) reported that, while an ever-increasing proportion of school-age children attend high schools and universities, the schools themselves are stratified. Occupation and income are tied not only to what degree one has, but also to where one got that degree. Working-class youth are overrepresented in low prestige colleges, while upper-class youth are overrepresented in high prestige colleges. Family background in combination with the prestige of the individual's college seem to work together to ensure that the person maintains the position in the social class into which he or she was born. For example, Harvard graduates, who frequently come from wealthy families, will often make more money than Big Ten graduates with higher grades. Among engineering graduates, sons from high status backgrounds held much higher positions as engineers than did sons from lower status backgrounds, even when the sons had attended the same college (Perrucci and Perrucci, 1970). In fact, father's occupation was a better predictor of son's occupation than it was for college graduates in the early part of this century. These data raise an important question. Has there been a real expansion of occupational mobility through the expansion of educational opportunity? Despite widespread beliefs that education equalizes access to occupational opportunities, it seems that all education may not be of equal value.

Perhaps too much has been made of the function of preparing students for specific jobs. A recent study of University of Pennsylvania graduates of 1964 and 1965 found a pattern of career changes (Wexler, 1980). In the 15 years since graduation, respondents averaged 1.5 changes in jobs, often to positions unrelated to formal schooling. In fact, nearly one-third of these occupational shifts involved radical moves, such as the shift from music to construction. Such findings indicate that specific training for jobs may be inappropriate and that some skills such as "sociability" or "organizational ability" are widely applicable across different occupational settings. Also, some educators have urged broader training in life skills rather than training for specific jobs that may become technologically obsolete in the current era of rapid change.

For the majority of high school students—those who do not graduate from college—high school teaches both skills and values that are important in work settings, such as promptness, personal responsibility, acceptance of authority, and cooperation. When schools fail to teach basic skills and values, when challenges to authority develop, or when students do not learn to be prompt and responsible, the schools are charged with failing their responsibilities. These charges are not surprising in a period when schools are seen both as a source of stability and a source of social change.

Schools as Agents of Social Change

Educational institutions are agents of social change. Research, technological innovations, and advanced training of skilled personnel have a direct impact on the general population and on the structure of work, the family, and other social institutions. Indirectly, schools may act as agents of social change through teaching social values and through providing students opportunities to experiment with adult roles and to examine alternative ways of filling them.

Social changes that are the result of the impact of university-based research tend to be applications of technical developments or innovations. For example, computers, household equipment, transportation vehicles, and laser beams, as well as efficiency in organizations, personal responses to stress and anxiety, and acceptance of new agricultural techniques have been the focus of university researchers and have direct implications for social organizations and social life.

Not all social change flowing from the schools is planned, however. The peer groups developed by elementary and secondary students, which are perhaps the most powerful social influence on these young people, tend to isolate them from their families and other adults. This isolation of youth is carried even further in university settings. The life of students on most campuses is contradictory: university students are generally ignored but are expected to acquire the skills and values necessary

for adult roles. Although they are as mature as their companions who graduated from high school and took jobs, they are not given the recognition of adult status that comes from work or economic independence.

Such contradictory situations often result in social change. During the 1960s many college students felt that their educational careers were being threatened by U.S. military action in Vietnam. While they were expected to study, they also were supposed to prepare for military service in a war that many opposed on moral grounds. Many students objected to these circumstances, and demonstrations were organized against the war and for student rights. These demonstrations so disrupted several institutions, like Columbia University, University of California at Berkeley, and Kent State University, that the police and the National Guard were called on to restore order. Conflict and, at Kent State and Jackson State, death resulted. However, the demands for student involvement in decision making along with other pressures, did effect social change. President Johnson decided not to seek reelection in 1968. Selective service, the draft, was eventually terminated. U.S. involvement in the Vietnam war ended. The voting age was lowered to 18. All of these changes were intended in the sense that they were goals of most of the student demonstrators. However, these changes were not intended by universities themselves; indeed, most universities sought to prevent those directly affecting their power.

Another illustration of educational institutions as agents of change is seen in the effort to equalize educational opportunity. The 1960s witnessed an unprecedented flow of federal funds into the schools for this purpose. The monies were allocated under the Elementary and Secondary Education Act and through programs initiated by the Office of Economic Opportunity. The 1970s brought widespread busing of students by court order to achieve racial balance in various school systems. The policy of busing students was based, in part, on research findings like those reported in the 1966 study, *Equality of Educational Opportunity*, often labeled the "Coleman Report" (1966), which found that black students in segregated schools had lower

College students have actively sought changes in educational institutions and in society when they felt that their lives or educational experiences were under direct attack. These Boston University students are protesting actions by the university administration and are seeking to influence decisions of the university.

achievement levels than those in integrated schools. Widespread opposition to busing students has expressed itself in the form of violence, peaceful demonstrations, and attempts to amend the U.S. Constitution to expressly ban the busing of students to achieve racial balance.

Originally, busing seemed to be an expedient and promising way to overcome racial segregation in school systems caused primarily by residential segregation in the cities. Recently, Coleman (1976) has suggested that the busing policy has caused a mass exodus of whites to suburban areas. Thus busing may create even greater amounts of residential segregation, which in turn creates more rather than less school segregation.

Research by other scholars does not support such interpretations, however. Some studies suggest that families do not move to the suburbs but choose private/parochial schools to avoid desegregation, while other evidence seems to indicate that family moves to the suburbs are affected by the racial composition and by existing level of desegregation in the schools (Marshall, 1981). One study of 104 urban school districts found that desegregation affects white enrollment in the short run, but over the period of several years, only a small percentage of the change in white enrollment is due to desegregation (Farley et al., 1980). As these authors note, desegregation may encourage some families who planned to move in a year or two to accelerate their move, but "white flight" seems an inappropriate term for the process. Other factors, such as employment opportunities, taxes, and availability of good housing are involved in these plans.

Two long-term demographic trends appear to be primarily responsible for declining white enrollment in urban schools: suburbanization and the decline in the white birth rate (Rossell, 1978). Failure to consider the impact of these factors has led to incorrect conclusions about school desegregation. The issue remains unresolved, however, and the 1980s will see continued conflict about the role of schools as agents of social change.

THE ORGANIZATION OF EDUCATION

When we consider the functions of schools, we usually focus attention on the relationship between the schools and society as a whole. However, schools can also be considered as small societies in themselves. This is especially true of schools in which students spend most of their time, such as colleges or boarding schools, but it is also true of day schools. Just as the larger society, schools have rules and roles that govern the interactions of its participants. These rules and roles affect all groups of people involved in educational institutions: school boards, administrators, counselors, teachers, students, and parents.

Most schools can be viewed as bureaucratic organizations. As we noted in Chapter 9, **Bureaucratic organizations** are characterized by a functional division of labor, organizational positions that are filled on the basis of merit and competence, a hierarchical ordering of these positions that involves authority relations, and the existence of formal rules and procedures that limit the individual's discretion in the performance of his or her duties. Within this bureaucratic structure in the schools are at least two groups of special importance: teachers and students, each of which develops a distinctive subculture. Members of both subcultures interact with one another inside and outside the classroom. The teacher subculture develops out of the teachers' common professional background. The student subculture reflects the cohesiveness of peer groups, an important reference group for school-aged children. In addition, administrators and counselors not only have special roles within the formal organization but also relate to teachers and students informally. Expectations associated with these various roles are significant factors in shaping the organization and functioning of modern educational institutions.

The Administration of Education: Control and Centralization

Since World War II schools in the United States have become increasingly bureaucratic. This has come about for a number of reasons, some of which are the increased size of schools, the growing number of functions that schools must now perform, and the longer period of time students must spend in school before assuming adult roles in society. The teacher's role has become more highly spec-

ialized, although, as Highlight 16.1 indicates, his or her old role of disciplinarian still exists. In addition, guidance counselors, school psychologists, social workers, remedial reading specialists, and psychometricians, among others, have been added to the school staff.

Within this context have developed conflicting expectations of teachers who view themselves as competent professionals and of administrators who seek control and authority over the school. This conflict of professional versus bureaucratic perspectives is centered around the authority of teach-

---

HIGHLIGHT 16.1
The Teacher's Role

There is a premium on conformity, and on silence. Enthusiasm is frowned upon, since it is likely to be noisy. The Admiral [administrative assistant] had caught a few kids who came to school before class, eager to practice on the typewriters. He issued a manifesto forbidding any students in the building before 8:20 or after 3:00—outside of school hours, students are "unauthorized." They are not allowed to remain in a classroom unsupervised by a teacher. They are not allowed to linger in the corridors. They are not allowed to speak without raising a hand. They are not allowed to feel too strongly or to laugh too loudly.

Yesterday, for example, we were discussing "The fault, dear Brutus, lies not in our stars/But in ourselves that we are underlings." I had been trying to relate "Julius Caesar" to their own experiences. Is that true? I asked. Are we really masters of our fate? Is there such a thing as luck? A small boy in the first row, waving his hand frantically: "Oh, call on me, please call on me!" was propelled by the momentum of his exuberant arm smack out of his seat and fell on the floor. Wild laughter. Enter McHabe [administrative assistant]. That afternoon, in my letter-box, it had come to his attention that my "control of the class lacked control."

SOURCE: From Bel Kaufman, *Up the Down Staircase*. New York: Avon, 1964, pp. 76–77.

ers to make decisions about textbooks, methods, and curricula. As teachers seek to achieve control over policies that govern their work, they come into conflict with bureaucratic rules that are designed to control and standardize processes.

Two major strategies are used by administrators to limit teacher discretion. The first is to develop rules and procedures that limit teachers in the performance of classroom duties like monitoring attendance, maintaining order, administering tests, setting the pace of coursework, or defining appropriate goals. The second is to maintain general control through centralized decision making and management of school facilities and schedules, thereby relieving the teacher of both responsibility for and knowledge of many facets of school life (Anderson, 1975).

The grouping of students in separate classrooms, each of which is largely under the control of a single teacher, and the highly specialized role of the teacher result in greater reliance on bureaucratic control mechanisms, especially rules and procedures that govern teacher behavior. Rules are relied upon so that the range of day-to-day problems that confront school administrators is reduced.

There is some evidence that the type and extent of administrative control has important effects on the teacher's instructional role. Washburne (1957) found that while teachers think of themselves as professionals with a right to exercise professional autonomy, they also feel severely hampered by administratively imposed goals and instructional procedures. In another study Corwin (1975) found that innovations in schools declined where rules were used to standardize procedures. He found that the most innovative schools were those in which there were few procedures governing lesson plan preparation, teacher's work hours, and topics appropriate for classroom discussion, among others. In the final analysis, teachers have little autonomy and less recognition of their professional status than they think is appropriate.

Teacher-student relations also may be affected by rules. Anderson (1975) found that an increase in instructional rules in the junior high schools of a large metropolitan school district resulted in greater resistance to innovation by teachers and in a more impersonal style of instruction. In addition, increased control over teachers' professional duties led to less time spent with individual students and fewer practices designed to individualize instruction.

Such conflicts emerge from the basic structure of the school, not from personalities or inadequate training of personnel. Most principals are former teachers often chosen because of classroom experience, maturity, and professional expertise. However, there is little evidence that such experience prepares them for the varied bureaucratic roles and responsibilities expected of a principal. Nor are principals representative of teachers. In elementary schools about 80 percent of the principals are men while men comprise only about 15 percent of teachers; in secondary schools more than 95 percent of principals are men compared with only about 55 percent of teachers (Scimecca, 1981).

Similar professional-bureaucratic conflicts exist in colleges and universities as well, though they often are less apparent due to separation of administrative and professional roles, specialization of function, and the sheer size of these institutions.

Classes and Teachers: Expectations, Reality, and Learning

While the classroom is part of the larger organization of the school, its social structural characteristics can be examined separately from the organizational characteristics of the school. For example, classes are composed of age-peers of both sexes, who ordinarily come from a relatively homogeneous neighborhood. Elementary classes are almost always taught by one teacher who instructs in all subject areas, while students face a common set of tasks. At the end of the school year pupils progress into the next grade. There they will have a new teacher in the elementary school or a new set of teachers in the junior and senior high schools. They are also presented with a new set of common tasks. Highlight 16.2 is a brief sketch of these teachers and their tasks.

Initially, there is little structural differentiation in the classroom. At the elementary level achievement is the result of living up to the expectations

HIGHLIGHT 16.2
Teachers: Who Are They?

The typical elementary school teacher teaches in a school with twenty-four other teachers and four other professional persons. She (eighty-four percent are women) has a white male principal, teaches five periods a day, with about twenty-seven students in her class. She has about forty minutes for lunch and has about a forty percent chance of eating it with the students. She is not likely to have any unassigned periods.

. . . The typical secondary school teacher teaches in a school with sixty-one other teachers and nine other professional persons. He (54.5 percent are men) has a white male principal, and teaches 134 different students in five periods a day. He has about a half hour for lunch, and has only about a twenty percent chance of eating it with students. He has five unassigned periods a week. He most likely does not teach a subject other than the one he prepared in college to teach. He is probably a teacher of either mathematics (sixteen percent), science (sixteen percent), or social studies (twenty percent) (English teachers are more likely to be women—sixty-nine percent of them are—but forty-seven percent of math teachers are women also.)

SOURCE: From Mary E. Bredemeier and Harry C. Bredemeier, *Social Forces in Education*, pp. 241–242. Sherman Oaks, California: Alfred Publishing Co., 1978.

this research has been the effect of teacher expectations on student achievement. One of the most provocative studies, done by Rosenthal and Jacobson (1966), identified the effect of high expectations on student behavior as the "Pygmalion" effect, so named because of the Greek myth of the sculptor whose statue of a beautiful woman came to life. Students were randomly assigned to groups, but the teachers were told that, on the basis of tests given earlier, some of these groups of children were likely to have large intellectual gains. Eight months later children who had been identified to teachers as "bloomers" had significantly greater gains on test scores than their classmates, especially in grades one and two. The effect of teachers' expectations and activities was to produce higher achievement, despite random distribution of talent.

Another study by Rist (1970) illustrates the process by which teachers can influence learning. Black children, during their first eight days in kindergarten, were assigned to three separate tables on the basis of the teacher's estimate of their learning potential. Assignments to the "low" table were most likely for lower-class children, regardless of test scores in reading readiness. This table was farthest from the teacher, received less attention than those closer, and progressed less rapidly than others. The performance levels of students closely followed their initial assignment, and by the second grade the students at the "low" table were labeled "the Clowns."

Despite such findings it is not clear that teachers are the most important variable in learning. Studies designed to document the effects of teacher expectations in other settings have not produced consistent results. However, few researchers would deny that the structure of the classroom gives the teacher enormous control over the behavior of students and affects the process of evaluation. It is at this point that the norms of the school and the society are interpreted and enforced by the teacher.

According to Dreeben (1968) four norms taught in school are particularly relevant in modern society. These are (1) to perform tasks by oneself and to assume personal responsibility for the result (independence); (2) to perform these tasks according to some standard of excellence (achievement); (3)

of the teacher. As the student progresses into junior and senior high schools, both expectations and evaluations become similar to those of a working adult. The teacher's role as representative of adult society is primary. As a result of these patterns of school organization and teacher control, students develop a set of norms, or principles of conduct, that are required for assuming adult positions in society.

The role of teacher in the classroom, in student performance, and in learning has been the subject of much study and evaluation. A major thrust of to have one's performance judged on universalistic criteria (universalism); and (4) to be treated as a member of a group, such as a class, a grade, a team, or a band, which is classified on the basis of several specific characteristics, for example, age, sex, ability, achievement (specificity).

These norms are often different from the norms that students learned as children in their preschool family setting. Sanctions must be used to obtain student compliance, and these sanctions are carried out in public within a homogeneous age group. Thus a student's performance is compared with that of the other students and evaluated by peers.

The process of working out the sequence of tasks that the student is given in the classroom involves several conditions controlled by the teacher. At first, students are required to work alone. Even assistance with homework by members of the child's family or others is limited. The requirement that the student work independently is reinforced by tests that measure the student against a standard of excellence set by the teacher. Consequently, students begin to become familiar with a norm of achievement.

Students learn to accept evaluation based on universalistic criteria because of the structural characteristics of the school. First, all students in a classroom are assigned essentially the same tasks. Second, classes are relatively homogeneous in terms of age and ability. This is especially true when students are grouped by ability or have been assigned to tracks in high school. Third, yearly grade promotions put the student in new situations with a new teacher or teachers and a new set of demands. The norm of specificity becomes important as students progress into junior and senior high school. There they will be taught by teachers whose interests in subject matter are more specialized than those of teachers in the elementary grades.

The goal of teaching universalistic norms in public schools has come into conflict with the fact of cultural diversity. For example, when we teach and apply universalistic norms, we must keep in mind that the norms in some ethnic and racial areas, such as the Armenian neighborhoods of Fresno, California, and the black neighborhoods of Harlem in New York City, differ from the norms of an upper-middle class suburb like Grosse Pointe, Michigan. Harlem blacks may feel that the universalistic criteria taught in the schools are detrimental to the norms of their group. Increased pressure by parents for administrative control over curricula is a part of this concern.

Although schools are organized to encourage the establishment of universalistic norms, at least two factors reduce the schools' influence. First, though teachers encourage conformity to these norms, the children may learn different norms from parents and peer groups, thereby reducing the teacher's influence in the classroom. Second, though teachers uphold these norms, they have to deal with many situations that do not clearly fit the rules and that must be met on an individual level.

Schools and Student Subcultures: Whose Values Count Most?

The existence of a separate student subculture results from the structuring of education around age groups or cohorts. An **age-cohort** is a group of people of the same or similar age. In the United States the age-cohort of six-year-olds is required to enter school and continue attending until they complete high school or reach 16 years of age. Since the activities of the secondary school years are meant to prepare students to assume adult roles in society, these activities are oftentimes viewed by students as irrelevant to their immediate interests. This, combined with the relative isolation of adolescent peer group activities from parent or teacher control, allows for the development of several student subcultures within the school, each with its own values and norms. The various subcultures are not all antiteacher or antischool; there is an achievement-oriented subculture as well as a "dropout" subculture.

According to Waller (1965) the development of an elaborate set of extracurricular activities is one of the responses of the schools to student subcultures. While these are student activities, they are guided or controlled by teachers. Most activities are age-graded and are often seen as a supplement to the school's instructional program.

Several studies have demonstrated how various student subcultures function and how they affect the school. Gordon (1957) found that status among high school students was determined primarily by what extra curricular activities the student engaged in and the student's place within that activity. Among boys athletics was a major determinant of status; among girls the highest status was accorded to yearbook queen. Within each grade like-sex friendship groups were stratified on the basis of family prestige and by the level of success by members of these groups in extracurricular activities or in academic activities.

According to Gordon, as students became socialized into the student subcultures, they learned to manipulate teachers to obtain acceptable grades, with varying degrees of success. Teachers, in turn, developed somewhat biased relations toward students who participated in extracurricular activities, and this bias resulted in a modification of the basis on which grades were assigned. Moreover, the existence of student subcultures would sometimes affect the teacher's classroom behavior. Instead of relying on the authority of his or her position, the teacher would use closer relations with particular students and student leaders to generate motivation and control behavior.

Coleman's (1961) study of 10 high schools also showed that student subcultures were usually based on nonacademic activities. Boys' membership, prestige, and influence in subgroups depended upon athletic prowess as well as dating success. Girls' membership and prestige depended upon general popularity and leadership in extracurricular activities. Further, there was a difference in the nature of the rewards derived from athletic competition and those of academic competition. Intercollegiate athletics, where competition is with rival schools, led to increased group solidarity. In contrast, academic competition, which existed primarily within one's own classroom and among one's own friends, was highly individualistic and therefore sometimes divisive. Consequently, genuine academic success sometimes resulted in a student's isolation from her or his peers and a lowering of status.

Such views of adolescent subcultures are not held by all observers of youth. Berger (1963), Turner

Student subcultures develop in small groups and provide support for various types of activities in high school and college. Fraternities provide their members with a social environment that encourages certain behaviors and values, just as athletic teams, social cliques, or academic groups do for their members.

(1964), Clark and Trow (1966), and Eve (1975) all have reported that the values of youth subcultures are much more like those of adults than suggested by Coleman and Gordon. Eve concluded that the value system of students "is primarily conventional in its orientation and differs only to a relatively small degree from the value system of the adult world" (p. 165).

Perhaps the most important factor in shaping adolescent subcultures is the family and its approval of youth values. However, the issue about level of agreement or disagreement of values of parents, teachers, and youth remains unsettled.

Teachers: Employees or Professionals?

Teachers form an important subgroup in the school. Recently, they have sought to exert collective pressure on school boards through professional associations and unions. Teacher militancy seems to stem from two trends in modern society that have also affected the schools: bureaucratization and the professionalization of work.

In 1966 there were 30 teacher strikes, almost as many as there were in the previous 10 years (Glass, 1967), and the number is increasing. In the fall of 1981, 83 different school systems across the United States were affected by teacher strikes, and several other systems had work stoppages over the issue of teacher termination. These actions have raised serious questions about whether teachers or the public will control public education and to what extent. Current teacher militancy, which expresses itself in group challenges to the authority of educational administrators and school boards, indicates that teachers are not content with the level of authority that is presently delegated to them. They are also demanding a greater role in the decision-making processes of education. This conflict between the administrative bureaucracy and the teacher, however, is due primarily to the way that the teaching profession has developed in the United States.

The professional role of elementary and secondary school teachers is shaped by the design of educational institutions in at least three ways. First, unlike other professions like law or medicine, in which occupational guidelines can be derived from a body of expertise, the teaching role involves improvisation and conjecture, especially in trying to establish the effectiveness of new technologies or methods of teaching. Second, teaching is an easy entry but limited mobility profession; it attracts many women who plan to work irregularly and many men who decide on teaching as a fall-back occupation if other plans fail to develop. This is in sharp contrast to the dominant patterns of recruitment, training, and career mobility of other professions. Third, teaching involves intensive, consistent interaction with students and near isolation from other adults. Teachers work alone, rarely observe colleagues in teaching situations, and are sheltered from the intervention of parents and people not associated with the school (Boocock, 1980). **Colleagueship,** an identification with other professionals involved in a common endeavor, has been largely absent from elementary and secondary school teaching. Isolated from one another in their separate classrooms, teachers are seldom able to develop any kind of informal social control over the actions of colleagues. Thus, the work setting constitutes a powerful barrier to the development of colleagueship and professionalization and allows administrators and school boards to define teachers simply as employees who do jobs assigned to them. Teacher militancy is partially directed toward such definitions, though the structural barriers against colleague relationships suggest limits to teacher militancy.

EMERGING ISSUES IN MODERN EDUCATION

Questions about the purposes and value of education are being asked today that challenge many of the basic beliefs of American society. Traditionally, the value placed on education by Americans could be seen in several dearly held ideas: (1) The existence of an informed, literate citizenry is the basis for the strength of our democratic institutions and is mainly due to access by all to educational opportunities. (2) The phenomenal economic growth of the United States that has made us the best fed, clothed, and housed nation in history has been made possible by a skilled and motivated work force educated in the public schools. (3) Education allows members of each new generation, regardless of social or economic origins, to rise as high as their talents will take them.

Basic beliefs about the importance of education have not often been challenged in the United States or the Western world. During economic "boom" periods, such as the 1960s, when more education usually meant more money, better jobs, and a better life, little criticism was heard. The 1970s, however, saw an intensive examination of the purposes of education by a wide spectrum of critics. Economists, historians, educators, sociologists, political scientists, and anthropologists sought to identify the sources of the problems of education. The average citizen also sensed that something was wrong; there were many public discussions of the "failures" of educational institutions at all levels: high school students who cannot read; declining scores on national achievement tests; college graduates making less money than nongraduates and sometimes unable even to find a job; Ph.D.s in history or English, often with 20 years of schooling, driving cabs or waiting on tables; the federal government engaged in a public relations effort to show high school students that there are many good jobs available that do not require a college education.

The 1980s have brought continued examination and criticism of schools. The issues concern a wide range of educational goals and practices.

Is Education Worth the Cost?

In the United States public education, free and open to all students, has been supported by taxes. Before World War II teachers were poorly paid, there was little equipment for labs, and other facilities were simple. Since that time fees, tuition, and other costs borne by students or parents have increased at all educational levels, in state-supported institutions as well as in private schools. Taxes increased as new elementary and secondary schools were built to accommodate the baby boom of the 1950s, as new technologies of teaching were developed, as the cost of keeping abreast of the "knowledge explosion"—buying books, computers, laboratory equipment, and materials—increased, and as teachers sought higher wages consistent with their education. While much attention has been directed toward the impact of federal aid to education, most money for schools is derived from state and local taxes. In 1980 about $90.5 billion was spent on education, but only $7.7 billion (8.5 percent) came

from federal sources. States contributed $42.8 billion (47.3 percent) and local taxes accounted for $39.9 billion (44.2 percent). While an individual's tax share may be greater for defense or welfare than for education, defense and welfare are not subject to local referenda; thus the public's concern about taxes often is directed toward schools because school taxes are one of the few taxes that people can vote on directly. One consequence of this voting power is to make schools vulnerable to public pressure; thus school boards and administrations seek to avoid controversies that would jeopardize public support. For college or university students, costs of education have accelerated rapidly, requiring considerable financial sacrifice by many families. In this context how does one measure the costs and benefits of education?

During the last decade, the economic benefit of education has been questioned, especially with high levels of unemployment and underemployment of recent college graduates. The large income advantage that college graduates had over nongraduates through the 1950s and 1960s has changed somewhat during the 1970s and into the 1980s. However, there is a positive relationship between education and income, as noted in Table 16.1. In a technological society there will always be a demand for highly skilled, well-trained personnel, especially when the economy is expanding. Some segments of our economic system are expected to experience rapid growth in the foreseeable future. However, some economists present a rather pessimistic view of the future, predicting a large pool of permanently underemployed college graduates who will be engaged in competition for a limited number of good jobs.

Such information is likely to discourage students who view college only as a means to obtain access to high-paying positions. The benefits of college cannot be evaluated only in economic terms, however; personal and social benefits must also be considered. In the fall of 1981, over 12 million people were enrolled in higher education in the United States—the highest number in history and the largest proportion of youth in any nation in the world. This fact has important implications for society as well as for individuals. In general, college-educated

TABLE 16.1   Median Income of Persons 18 Years Old and Over,
by Race, Sex, and Education Level, 1979

	WHITE MALE	WHITE FEMALE	BLACK MALE	BLACK FEMALE
Total Median Income	$13,168	$4,076	$8,207	$4,288
Elementary				
Less than 8 years	6,261	2,990	4,504	2,608
8 years	8,053	3,408	5,946	2,823
High School				
1 to 3 years	9,546	3,602	7,321	3,541
4 years	13,767	5,043	9,857	5,602
College				
1 to 3 years	14,160	5,459	11,334	6,374
4 years	19,365	7,850	14,530	10,596
5 or more years	23,044	11,635	19,247	14,464

SOURCE: U.S. Bureau of the Census, Current Population Reports, Series P-60., No. 129, "Money Income of Families and Persons in the United States: 1979." U.S. Government Printing Office, Washington, D.C., 1981. Table 52.

people are more likely to vote and to participate in the political process, tend to be more active in community organizations and activities, and are more likely to contribute leadership in various institutions than are less educated people. At the personal level a college education tends to develop one's ability, confidence, and creativity. Not all people experience such benefits, but these factors must be considered in any evaluation of the worth of education.

Whatever the long-term consequences to society, it is clear that a college degree does not guarantee every individual a high income, as was the expectation during the 1960s, or a rewarding job. For many, a college degree is justified in terms of its own intrinsic value. For the society, education must be viewed as a social investment. What are the social costs if higher education loses its place as a center of learning, criticism, and research in modern society?

Education: Equality or Social Control?

Life in colonial America was relatively simple, at least with respect to formal education. The family was responsible for teaching children the attitudes and skills necessary for work. With industrialization and the factory system, this role of the family as the major socializer for work declined. The new

American worker, often without ties to family or land, began to move about in his search for a place in the labor force.

For years it has been believed that the historic role of education in the United States was to extend equal opportunity to all citizens. The goal was to create a more equalitarian society in which every citizen, regardless of social origins, religion, or ethnicity, could move up the ladder of success. Some recent interpretations of the history of American education suggest that, contrary to prevailing beliefs, mass education was designed to preserve the class structure (Bowles and Gintis, 1976; Rehberg and Rosenthal, 1978). Instead of providing genuine educational opportunities, the schools have functioned to serve the labor needs of a capitalist economy and to socialize people to accept the legitimacy of existing inequalities in wealth. According to this interpretation of functions of mass education, the schools prepared children of the working class for factory labor by emphasizing discipline, punctuality, acceptance of authority outside the family, and individual accountability for one's work.

Katz (1968) suggests that the appearance of the so-called progressive education movement, which sought to develop different curricula to suit the varied needs of students, had similar results. This movement promoted vocational schools, testing, and tracking, so that those students destined for college and those destined for menial work could be distinguished. If the official purpose of the progressive movement was to meet the needs of all students, the real consequence was to maintain the class structure from one generation to the next.

What is the appropriate role of education in the modern world? The dominant view of education in industrial societies is that it imparts the skills and knowledge necessary for jobs. As technology becomes more complex, required skill levels increase, as do educational requirements. The result is a decline in the number of low-skill jobs and an increase in those with higher skill levels.

In spite of the apparent increase in higher skill jobs, there is evidence that the increase in educational levels of the labor force exceeds the skill requirements for adequate job performance (Berg, 1970). Similarly, Collins' (1971) review of available evidence indicates that outside the traditional professions of medicine, law, engineering, and scientific research, there is not strong support for the belief that education is important for job skills or productivity.

Collins has suggested that the increased educational requirements for many jobs in the United States is better explained as the result of the desire of organized occupational groups to regulate their membership to, for example, exclude people of particular ethnic origins or to maintain the prestige and high income characteristics of the group.

This poses a serious challenge to educational institutions. Is an increasing amount of education really necessary for meeting the technical requirements of jobs? Is education being used as a form of social control by the privileged and the educated?

Desegregation: Whose Children Will Be Bused?

The Equality of Educational Opportunity study, better known as the Coleman report (1966) provided evidence that minority students had higher achievement when they were in schools with a majority of white students. This finding became one basis for court-ordered busing of students to give minority students equal educational opportunities through integration.

Few issues have aroused as much hostility among parents—white and black—as busing. However, the issue is a complex one, involving traditions, racial prejudice, and control of schools.

Busing is not new: in 1937–38, one in seven children in the United States was transported to and from school. In the South busing in the 1950s and 1960s often took black children away from the nearest school, which was white, to an all-black school. In the agricultural states the consolidation of school districts during the 1950s and 1960s meant fewer schools and greater distances for students to travel. Some cities and suburbs, in response to demands for safe transportation, created systems of student busing. By the 1957–58 school year, before any busing for integration began, over 36 percent of public school students were being transported at public expense; by 1977–78, over 54 percent, or 21.8 million students, were being bused (Grant and Eiden, 1981).

The criticisms of busing focus upon the artificial character of the new school community. By moving students from their local neighborhoods, whether white or black, family and community support for education is eroded. Thus, it is argued, the emphasis should be placed on local school improvement instead of integration. However, if segregated education is inherently unequal, as the 1954 Supreme Court decision stated, most northern black students will experience unequal education, just as their southern counterparts did. Segregation in housing in urban areas leads to segregation in schools, and in many northern cities, a greater degree of segregation existed in 1976 than in 1968 (Statistical Abstract, 1981).

What can be done to provide integrated education if housing is segregated? Can busing be justified as a way to integrate schools, even if research indicates that self-esteem and tolerance are improved by interracial education (Sheehan, 1980)? Whose children should be bused?

Teaching and Values: Community Control or Professional Expertise?

Schools once claimed responsibility for students *in loco parentis* (in the place of parents). Most colleges

Busing of students has been
undertaken as a means of
integrating schools. In Boston,
police accompany buses of black
students as they are brought to
previously all-white South Boston
High Schools. Violence occurred
here and in other communities
faced with court-ordered busing,
and integrated education continues
to be an important issue in many
cities.

and universities have relinquished this role, but recent efforts to return control of elementary and secondary schools to local communities underscore society's belief in the schools' influence on the acquisition of values. Historically, most attention in this area was focused on sex education; recently, it also has involved challenges to required reading of books with "dirty words," support of secular and humanistic values, and the teaching of evolution. The controversy about evolution is an old one; however, the people—and some of the arguments—are new. Highlight 16.3 outlines the history of this controversy.

Who should define what is taught and what materials are used in schools? For parents who think that schools should reflect parental and community beliefs, payment of school taxes and concern about their children justify their involvement. For teachers whose professional expertise has been shaped by years of formal education and classroom

---

HIGHLIGHT   16.3
Evolution versus Creation: An Old Controversy

DATES

1925: Trial of John T. Scopes, a Dayton, Tennessee, high school teacher who was found guilty of violating a state law banning the teaching of evolution.

1927: Tennessee Supreme Court overturned conviction of Scopes; law later declared unconstitutional.

1929: Arkansas enacted an antievolution law; law was largely ignored and unenforced.

1968: U.S. Supreme Court declared the Arkansas law invalid.

1981 (March): Arkansas enacted a law to require the teaching of *scientific creationism* in public schools where evolution is taught; law immediately challenged in court.

1981 (December): Trial began concerning the legality of such a law.

1982 (January): U.S. District Court declared the law unconstitutional because to teach a literal interpretation of creation as presented in Genesis would require religious beliefs; thus, it is religious teaching and violates the First Amendment which prohibits establishment of a state religion; *scientific creationism* is declared nonscientific because it is dogmatic, absolutist, and never subject to revision.

BASIC ISSUES

Evolutionists argue: (1) the concept of creation requires the concept of a supernatural creator, an inherently religious belief; (2) the theory of creation has no support and that the "fit" of the explanation of change as an evolutionary process is the best possible explanation of observed facts; (3) the idea of creation requires a belief in the creation myth of the Bible; such religion is not compatible with science, which rests on facts, not myths, and is subject to testing and changing interpretations.

Creationists argue: (1) evolution essentially has become a religion that seeks to explain origins of man and life, but is unable to give adequate answers; (2) the theory of evolution requires a major jump in faith as well, and the many gaps or "missing links" of evolution are evidence of its inadequacy to explain life; (3) science cannot deal with the important question of "why" things exist; only religion can and only by adding creation to science is the full explanation of life possible.

experience, the issues are personal and academic freedom, openmindedness, and knowledge about different cultures and people. The dispute is likely to continue. No quick or easy solution appears to be possible: if parents become involved with school curricula and activities, the professional expertise of teachers is called into question; without involvement, parents can neither support nor assist in changing educational institutions.

SUMMARY

Education serves three social functions: (1) to transmit culture, (2) to prepare individuals for positions in society as adults, and (3) to serve as a change agent in society. The first two functions are conservative in nature, while the change function is progressive.

The way each function is performed depends on the nature of the society. Preindustrial societies educated primarily through the family, while modern societies educate primarily through the social organizations called schools. The schools reflect the values and beliefs of the society in which they function. The social goals of the schools are influenced by the philosophy and policies of government. These, in turn, are built into the educational system as a whole.

Schools are complex social organizations. They may be analyzed as formal organizations, with student and teacher subcultures. The increase in societal complexity has caused an increase in the bureaucratic regulation of the schools. Regulations tend to reduce innovation in all areas of teaching. On the other hand, administrators use bureaucratic rules to reduce the range of day-to-day problems and to enforce universalistic criteria.

Student subcultures often develop norms that are different from those formally defined by the schools. These student norms are often expressed through extracurricular activities. The interests of teachers center on problems related to professionalism. Parental interest may focus on social values. As a result, teachers, students, and parents all try to influence school decision making.

Challenges to education center on the most fundamental beliefs and values of American society. The idea that education provides a literate and informed citizenry, skilled and motivated workers, and social mobility based on merit for each new generation has been reviewed and challenged by many professionals as well as by the average citizen. Instead, some have argued that education has been used for social control rather than social equality and that the function of education is more to enhance status than to transmit skills.

Several issues will continue to dominate education in the 1980s in the United States. Concern about the costs of education raises complex issues, and to determine the value of education, one must consider other factors as well as economic benefits. Some important issues are whether education is to train for specific jobs or to improve the individual, determining the costs and benefits of integration, and establishing appropriate roles for parents and teachers in the schools.

GLOSSARY

Age-cohort   a group of people of the same or similar age.

Bureaucratic organizations   social groups characterized by a functional division of labor, organizational positions filled on the basis of merit and competence, a hierarchical ordering of positions involving authority relations, and formal rules and procedures which severely limit individual discretion in the performance of duties.

Colleagueship   a sense of identification with other professionals involved in a common endeavor.

Contest mobility   a way in which power, wealth, and prestige are granted as rewards by a society for individual initiative, perserverance, and achievement in competition with others.

Sponsored mobility   a way in which power, wealth, and prestige are granted to individuals who are chosen on the basis of family connections rather than personal achievement.

Tracking   the practice of grouping students of similar abilities in a specific curriculum as a means of encouraging student achievement.

READING

READING 16.1

How Schools Fail Black Children*

Harry Morgan

How do we process new information in becoming learners? There are various theories and notions which contribute to our understanding of the complexities of learning. There are theories derived from observations of growth and development as in the traditions of Freud, Erikson, and Piaget. There are also various theories of the basic nature of behavior and cognition which are derived from the work of Pavlov, Watson, and Skinner. Most theorists seem to agree that fundamental to all learning is the relationship between our nervous system and our environment. In applying this basic model to classroom children, everything within their purview—including teachers and peers—would be their environment. It is known that our nervous system is a continuum of sense organs and muscles. The receptors (sense organs) perceive the environment and, after taking in the "signals," pass them along to the appropriate effectors (muscles), which react to the impulse, and our organism undergoes change. This simple model of cause (input) and effect (output) seems to receive general agreement among researchers and practitioners alike. Once this rudimentary concept is set into place, however, various interpretations and contingencies emerge and theorists divide into extreme camps—behaviorists and humanists. Behaviorists seem to subscribe to a discrete cause-and-effect phenomenon over which the organism has little or no control. Humanistic theorists point out various modifying conditions of learning such as attitudes, values, and intuition, which they argue are

essential to the learning process. And, as in most scholarly domains, there are theorists whose beliefs fall at almost every point along the pathway between these extreme views.

To add to the aforementioned complexities, within the past 30 years an additional layer of related research has actively surfaced. It is now believed that there are approximately twelve discrete *styles* of learning. Theorists who are engaged in these studies suggest that in addition to the common basic pattern of organism change in the processing of new information, individuals have perceptual/response peculiarities which might make them more susceptible to knowledge acquisition under certain circumstances and less so under others. It is further theorized that certain teaching styles can be more or less compatible with particular learning styles.

We have also known for some time that instruments most commonly used to measure a child's intellect in reality are measures of the child's ability to do "school work" and not necessarily useful assessments of learning (or how well that individual can process new information). Because such instruments are designed to measure school achievement, they are not usually sensitive to out-of-school behavior. These behaviors, incidently, might call forth a different and/or a more complex approach to information processing than is derived from or called for in classroom tasks. Under certain conditions, an observation of behavior episodes could be more reliable than data quantification. This might have equal applicability for children of the urban underclass, migrant families, isolated farm families, and other subcultural groups in numerical minority. The extent to which classroom adaptational activities serve as a basis for planning school tasks has yet to be fully explored by educators.

Behavior, as it relates to learning, is a fundamental function of the organism, and school achievement is an inadequate index against

*References have been omitted.

SOURCE: *Social Policy* (January/February 1980: Vol. 10, No. V, pp. 49–54). SOCIAL POLICY published by Social Policy Corporation, New York, New York 10036. Copyright 1980 by Social Policy Corporation.

which to measure the effectiveness of this human function in an individual. In our imperfect attempts to quantify what an individual might have learned, we have discovered that learners have abilities available to them under certain circumstances which are not necessarily available to them under others. Also, learning-style researchers point out that certain learners who do well in a relatively static environment might not do well in a shifting terrain. It is also true that proficiency which might increase with the practice of taking tests is not the equivalent of competence in whatever the test purports to measure. Furthermore, too little is known about the conditions in which capacity matches performance.

It was Jean Piaget who taught us the value of observing and documenting behavioral episodes in early childhood. From his observations he defined certain steps and stages during the early development in a child's life. The time from birth to approximately 18 months he defined as the sensorimotor period.

... mental development during the first eighteen months of life is particularly important, for it is during this time that the child constructs all the cognitive substructures that will serve for his later perceptive and intellectual development ...

Crawling, sitting alone, standing, and walking are significant sensorimotor milestones for which norms have been established by researchers. In general, children learn to crawl by approximately nine months, sit alone by nine months, stand alone by 13 months, and walk by 14 months. Piaget rejected the notion of separate domains for perception, judgment, memory, and thought, with respect to children. He stressed a functional continuity between developing sensorimotor skills and mental functions, like concept formation.

For example, a child observing a 12-inch stick placed beside a stretched-out piece of string of equal length would learn the basic differences between these two properties by the way they behave as he attempts to pick them up. In the same manner, basic concepts about how a ball or a wheel on a toy reacts to manipulation is revealed through the child's interaction with these objects.

It has been known for some time that Black infants are more advanced during the sensorimotor period than their white counterparts. It appears that parenting and child-rearing practices as well as social class promote variations in this differentiation.

In a recent study in Syracuse we observed a series of junior high school classes and their English teacher for a period of nine months and found a differentiated style of information processing among those students. Blacks more than whites and males more than females interacted with the teacher and each other in performing academic classroom work. In this nonpunitive environment where cooperation in academic performance was encouraged, Black males were far more socially active than others. From his observations, Professor A. Wade Boykin of the Center for Advanced Study in the Behavioral Sciences at Stanford has termed this active style, "psychological/behavioral verve."

In the meantime, researchers at Yale and the University of Bridgeport exposed a sample of 58 middle-class white children to two different television programs. One program, "Mister Rogers," was described in the study as *slow paced.* The other program, "Sesame Street," was used as its *fast paced* counterpart. The researchers concluded that for the group under study, "Mister Rogers" had a more positive effect on their behavior and learning than the more "frenetic" programming of "Sesame Street." The socially reserved American classrooms—above the third grade—also seem more tuned to the needs of white children than to their Black counterparts.

We have known for some time now that most American children enter school for the first time with enthusiasm and positive spirit.

From their first day up through the third grade there are few group-measured differences in rate of achievement when whites are compared to Blacks. From the third grade through the upper grades, however, there is a steady decline in group-measured performance of Black children to do school work. Why is this condition so persistent? Teaching strategies and delivery of basic education is generally stratified according to teacher-training modes. Early childhood educators (K–3) seem to receive deeper and more concentrated training than those in elementary (K–6) and secondary (7–12) programs. Early childhood education has been a strong movement in our country for some time and receives greater attention from parents than other areas of public schooling. The nurturing environment of the early grades encourage an active role for the teacher and child. There is a higher degree of socialization and teacher-child interaction where the classroom is defined as an efficient workroom and where the child's play is viewed as work. A typical teacher will introduce a central theme of study or activities which will encourage the child to become aware of the environment. Themes are drawn first from the world around them, such as organizing chores, caring for pets and plants, building, cooking, music, etc., and then from those aspects of the community in which the children see relationships, solve problems, and use their skills. It seems that the social interaction models found in the lower grades provide an atmosphere within which Black children as a group can do well. Once out of the early childhood sphere of influence there appears to be a steady decline in group-measured academic achievement for Black children.

It is not my view that classrooms need to be redesigned for the exclusive compatibility of Black children. However, we should expand the number of ways in which all children can experience their own excellence. It seems that from birth Black children expect an environment that will be active with high levels of mother-infant interaction. At the same time, white infants expect a less active environment, and some researchers have found that lower-income Black infants have more advanced sensorimotor skills than children from upper-income families who emulate the parenting style of whites.

With the early and advanced sensori motor development theory in mind, and the *third grade syndrome* as a backdrop, I will discuss two significant display periods during the life span of the Black experience and several educational policy issues regarding the active child and our schools.

During infancy, as Black babies display certain natural characteristics, Black mothers need information and encouragement about the special needs of their infants. Significant learning patterns are already in motion at birth. It is during this early period that infants need warm acceptance, positive face-to-face eye contact, and reciprocal support. A Harvard pediatrician states:

. . . [Black babies] are strong, they are vigorous and exciting motorically. This is a real problem for Black mothers that I can take care of. . . . They often equate motor activity with aggression, with things that won't be assimilated into the culture that they are trying to assimilate into themselves. . . . I would like to give Black mothers a feeling that what they do is important . . . if the Black mother could see the strengths of her baby, and respond to them in a way that makes the baby respond back, she would feel like a better person. If Black kids could get the feeling that what they did was important early in childhood . . . that's what I'd like to give them—a feeling of their own identity.

. . . [Black mothers] often equate [their baby's] activity with aggression [being bad]. . . . They see this as bad and they often talk about it as if they were bad. They cry too much—they are bad; they are too active—they are bad. (Quote by Brazelton)

Another display which constantly invades our casual observations is the overrepresentation of Black males in certain athletic activities. This writing will not be an attempt to explain fully this phenomenon, but rather cite this as another event during the Black experience which seems to be compatible with other sensorimotor observations. Basketball especially, and football in general, require that successful participants are able to *process a tremendous amount of information in a very short span of time.* High levels of cognition (execute a play, locate opposing players and teammates, isolate play involvement from spectator noise, etc.) and physical output are required in a simultaneous manner. Could there be a relationship between the early and advanced sensorimotor development, the activeness in infancy and childhood, and athletic performance among Blacks? Not only does there appear to be such a relationship but it has critical policy implications for the school experience of Blacks.

To be sure, there are probably an infinite number of group differences which could be found if you really sought them out. However, until research can identify the nature of these differences, so that specific characteristics of intellectual functioning and how they affect academic growth can be described, their implications for teaching and learning are not particularly useful. When it comes to what we know about the advanced sensorimotor development among Black youngsters, a clear action framework suggests itself.

Urban schooling patterns, for the most part, promote quietness and docility. Such classrooms are therefore designed to suit the learning norms of children from white families and opposed to the characteristics of Black children, making it difficult for them to comply with the demands made upon them by that system. For these children to establish their own set of behavior norms to which individuals can conform should not surprise us. Their behavior can be disruptive when the planned environment for learning is lacking

in elements which could serve to defuse their buildup of sensorimotor energy. And this situation is very often intensified by the expectations of white teachers fresh out of teacher training institutions and Black teachers who expect these students to out-middle-class the middle class.

Management for docility produces reserved classrooms where many Black children—mostly males—disengage from the mainstream of academic tasks. Educators become resentful when students balk at schoolwork. A troubled teacher-pupil relationship is the outcome. The resentful teacher and the balking student's interactions erode with daily incidents. School policy leads to a compilation of a dossier on these students so as to build up a string of minor offenses, which, when presented at once, appear to be a massive campaign of misdeeds.

The Children's Defense Fund, a project of the Washington Research Project, compiled statistics directly related to this project. They reported that more than one million children were suspended from school one or more times during the 1972–73 academic year. There did not seem to be any substantial differential based on geographic location, size of school district, city, or state. More than 63 percent of the suspensions were for minor offenses such as cutting into the lunch line, smoking, truancy, and similar acts. Less than three percent were for serious acts of destruction, criminal activity, or use of narcotics. In those districts from which their statistics were derived, one out of every 24 students was suspended. For Black secondary school children, the suspension rate was *one out of every eight.*

A more devastating practice is the administration of drugs intended for children described as hyperactive. It is likely that some children attending school need help in controlling certain purposeless behavior because self-management is beyond their own capability. It is not likely, however, that a classroom teacher will have the medical knowledge necessary for diagnosis and treatment. This is further complicated by lack of knowledge in this field even by competent medical persons. Despite these circumstances, identifications and referrals are the responsibilities of the classroom teacher.

All that is really known about the practice of behavior modification by medication at this time is that the commonly used medications quiet children who are unusually disruptive and active. There are no data on the dangers of drug buildup over the years or the possibilities for future addiction. We do know that by far the larger percentage of prescribed behavior-modifying drugs are administered to Black male children. Pope has observed that unmedicated children diagnosed as hyperactive were as well controlled as normal children, when they were assigned tasks which involved well-planned forms of stimulation and were pleasurable. Rie found that if one sensitized caretakers to the cognitive and affective needs of children, their undesirable activity could be decreased without the use of drugs.

Using prescribed drugs to modify student behavior has not reached a level of accepted justification. Along with Rie, Connors, Eisenbert, and Sharpe have pointed out in their studies that medication helped produce quiet classrooms but *did not improve* the academic achievement of children. There is need for further research to explore various modes of teaching strategies and classroom management as alternatives to drug therapy for all children, even those who are chronically difficult to manage. For Black males, their natural activeness can give the false appearance of "borderline hyperactivity" and provide an excuse for schools and teachers who fail to educate them.

For some of these youthful and consistent "offenders," there are special classrooms where cognitive expectations are usually nil. Ironically, such classes are frequently referred to as "learning centers" and under the control of a tough disciplinarian. Several years ago it was a common spectacle in predominantly white schools to see the majority of Black male students herded into one room ruled over by the single Black male teacher in the school, or the assignment of a paraprofessional or teacher's aide to administer to the active Black children with whom the classroom teacher did not care to interact.

Too many of the inner-city and rural poor are powerless in encouraging our system to work for their betterment. They want a better life but their problems are too many and too large and their resources too few to change their conditions. They have too little time, not enough knowledge, too few skills, and not enough influence. For the most part they are alone with their problems: if unaided, they cannot cope with their family responsibilities or with the demands of the institutions which are designed to advance their interests. Black children from these families, and others who may appear to be somewhat better off, are often discouraged by institutions they use and from which they derive certain benefits. Too often their experience or their interpretation of an experience make them believe that these institutions (schools, hospitals, etc.) are alien and hostile.

Despite these circumstances, there are many children from upper socioeconomic Black families whose adaptation and academic achievement seem to follow a pathway similar to that of white children from middle-income families of equal status. For several generations they may have lived among white families and socialized with them in significant ways that reduced social distance—even in such taboo areas as interracial mate choice. Within opportunity and social mobility domains, Black families who are gradually becoming "better off" are also widening the gap between themselves and lower-income Blacks whose status remains the same. The better-off Blacks are often thrust into this status on the basis of a comparison between *two adult incomes* in their family and *one adult income* in a similar white family. Nevertheless, it appears that through increased sharing of jobs and social interaction of rituals (parties, holiday celebrations, marriages, and similar ceremonial occasions), certain upper-income Black children achieve in our present modes of schooling equally to their white counterparts. It is not known whether or not they might do better in a more active environment.

Then there is that recurring popular question: If *these* Black children can do well through common modes of teaching, why should we not expect others to do the same? The three implications here are that the institution is on the right track but certain learners are not. Firstly, the apparatus for adaptation and the assimilation is not available to all. Inner-city housing project dwellers, for example, hardly ever see whites outside of a power relationship where Blacks are powerless. So, one-to-one interactions are rare. Secondly, teachers need to be able to dip into the child's steady stream of consciousness without diverting or damming it up. Being insensitive to an active style of learning can very easily send the learner underground. Thirdly, adaptation to what is should not constitute the whole of what we should be striving for in the education of our young. We should be continuously searching for ways to enable children to define themselves positively as persons and as learners.

There seem to be several alternative courses of action which school personnel are likely to put into motion in dealing with Black children who are too active to learn comfortably in the entrenched school order. The education establishment will (1) assign children to special "learning centers" where only minimal learning is expected or (2) prescribe drugs to render children affectless and almost void of emotion or (3) completely separate children from their school environment by suspension. These courses of action are demeaning and hurtful.

In summary, I have proposed a framework for which there is supportive evidence in the work of other researchers. Geber and Ainsworth pioneered theories of sensorimotor differentiation among Black infants, and Piaget stressed the significance of this period in the child's development toward intellectual functioning. Furthermore, several displays along the life span of the Black experience, such as the third grade syndrome, performance in athletics, and an active pattern in early parenting and schooling (and related problems in the educational setting), call forth important issues for future research and a critical analysis of our educational policies from the child's perspective.

SUMMARY

The processes of learning for black children are the same as those for whites, but because of the differences in their cultures, blacks perceive school experiences much differently. Schools and educational programs—even on television—are more tuned to white children than to blacks, and by the third grade the effects of the schools are evident. Blacks are over-presented in sports which may require the ability to process and to respond to vast amounts of information in a short period of time, but they tend to be unresponsive to the docility expected in the classroom. In short, the pattern of early sensorimotor development is critical for determining school success of blacks, who must adapt to schools organized for whites.

QUESTIONS

1. Are schools organized to address the skills and needs of whites rather than those of blacks?

2. How can education be organized to deal with the problems Edwards identified?

3. How important is adaptation to the classroom for children to be academically successful?

4. How can schools take advantage of the high level of activity of young black children?

PART V

Developments in Modern Society

The dynamics of modern society are reflected in two important developments: growth of urban areas and population growth. These developments are consequences of social, technological, and economic changes of the past 100 years. In this section we examine the causes and consequences of these changes. Cities and City Life, Chapter 17, concerns the growth in numbers and the quality of life in modern cities. Chapter 18, Population, explores the sources of population growth in the twentieth century and discusses this growth as it affects the future of human societies.

528

CHAPTER 17

Cities and City Life

CONTENTS

Are cities worth saving?

Americans have long had a love-hate relationship with the city. On the one hand, cities exert a tremendous attraction as centers of commerce, cultural innovation, and the arts. Young men and women seeking to make their mark in the world naturally gravitate to the city with its wealth of opportunities to fulfill aspirations and to develop an interesting life style. Even those who do not live in cities come as tourists to enjoy the richness and diversity of city life. On the other hand, people decry the pollution, congestion, and disorder of urban life; many claim that cities are unlivable. The attractions of clean air, open space, and less congestion have led millions to flee the cities for the peace and tranquility of the suburbs. Some social scientists see this exodus as evidence that the economic, political, and social problems of the city are intractable and that the city is destined to become the dinosaur of our age.

YES Where else but in the cities of the United States can one find such a tremendous variety of work to do, places to live, foods to eat, clothes to wear, cultural events to attend, and political and philosophical opinions to argue. Cities have historically been the centers of intellectual life and vitality of a nation. The innovations that are the basis of a society's progress are first tested in the marketplace of ideas that exists in the city. People of many cultures, languages, races, and ages live together in cities, producing the social bonds that makes a country strong. These bonds, with their pull of tension and accommodation, are not likely to be forged in the small communities of our land, where homogeneity of people and ideas is valued over diversity. The essence of America is in the diverse and sometimes chaotic culture of the city. A country such as the United States will survive in its cities or not at all.

But what of the city's problems? What about the budget deficits that have brought many cities to the brink of bankruptcy? What about the declining quality of city services in education, health and recreation, fire and police protection? Answers to these questions are complex, but we can identify two overriding factors responsible for the plight of cities today. First is the fact that decisions by the federal government since the 1950s have been responsible for the flight of people and jobs out of the cities and into the suburbs. Government subsidies for home mortgages and highway systems are the basis of suburban growth. At the same time support for cities has been "off again, on again" depending upon the particular party in power or person in the White House. Second is that the cities have been left with a major responsibility in caring for those Americans who remain in cities: older citizens, the poor, and others disadvantaged by race, mental illness, and other handicaps. These vulnerable citizens are the responsibility of all Americans.

But things are changing. Many who fled the cities' streets to raise their children in the suburbs are finding the crabgrass and crickets hard to take now that the kids are gone. And others are finding that crime can be found on Bluebird Lane as well as on Flatbush Avenue. Cities will survive, because they fulfill needs that cannot be met elsewhere.

NO At one time cities were vital centers in our nation's life. Millions of immigrants who came to our shores could settle in urban areas, finding jobs suitable to their limited skills. They could also enjoy the emotional and social support of others who spoke the same language and faced the same problems of settling in a new land. Industries sprang up close to these centers of cheap and abundant labor. Many of the great cities of our nation flourished in these conditions.

But times have changed. The children and grandchildren of the early immigrants have grown up and find they no longer need the ethnic communities that sustained their parents. Second-generation Americans have become educated, and their talents and training have carried them to jobs and communities throughout the land. Industry finds that it no longer has to be in close proximity to the sources of energy, labor, and capital. Advanced transportation and communication have encouraged the relocation of factories in the suburbs. Workers can more easily commute 50 or 60 miles a day to get to work. Business transactions can be completed with the aid of computerized information systems.

While these changes have been underway many cities are approaching bankruptcy because of their inability to meet the rising cost of city services with shrinking tax revenues. The industries that have left the city for the lower taxes, cheaper land, and better services of the suburbs have taken a good portion of the city's tax base with them. Cities find themselves with a large population of unemployed persons, such as the aged, welfare families, and the unskilled poor, and less money to provide traditional services.

The solution to this problem is not to bail out cities with federal aid. It should be obvious that many people no longer want to live or work in the city. The pollution, crime, high cost of living, and declining services have made them look elsewhere for homes and jobs. Even those who are still trapped in cities would move if they had the chance. Instead, they will simply live out their lives there as a diminishing population. The large, densely populated city has outlived its usefulness. Let it pass out of existence and be replaced by a more adaptive form of human habitat.

The city is a complex human invention that has survived successfully for over 5000 years. Perhaps in its present form it is no longer a suitable environment for human populations. Many of the questions raised in this "At Issue" are discussed in this chapter. The pros and cons of city life are examined, along with the theories that attempt to explain the growth patterns of cities. The closing section of the chapter returns to the question: "Are cities worth saving?"

QUESTIONS TO CONSIDER

- Do cities develop in a haphazard or predictable way?

- Is the urban dweller an isolated, alienated individual?

- How do urban life styles differ from rural ones?

- What are the advantages and disadvantages of suburban living?

Humans, unlike other animals, play an active role in restructuring the environments in which they reside. This level of environmental activism has been most apparent since the development of cities nearly 5500 years ago. In one sense, at least, cities may be described as the most human of environments, for no other environment bears such a distinct human imprint. Cities are human-made containers of human population and activity in which temperature, light, climate, and other elements of the physical environment are directly controlled by the decisions of humans. Yet in spite of this fact, cities are often described as unlivable and dehumanizing. Indeed, enthusiasm for the city has not been typical, particularly in American intellectual and cultural history. Here are but a few examples of this distaste for urban living:

I view great cities as pestilential to the morals, the health and the liberties of man.—Thomas Jefferson

New York was difficult and revolting. The police and politicians were a menace; vice was rampant; wealth was shamelessly showy, cold and brutal. In New York the outsider or beginner had scarcely any chance at all, save as a servant. The city was overrun with hungry, loafing men of all descriptions.—Theodore Dreiser

. . . cities degrade us by magnifying trifles. The country-man finds the town a chop-house, a barbershop. He has lost the grandeur of the horizon, hills and plains, and with them sobriety and elevation. He has come among

a supple, glib-tongued tribe, who live for show, servile to public opinion.—Ralph Waldo Emerson

. . . the turbid air . . . the whole quality and allure [of New York], the consummate monotonous commonness of the pushing male crowd, moving in its dense mass—with the confusion carried to chaos for any intelligence, any perception; a welter of objects and sounds in which relief, detachment, dignity, meaning, perished utterly and lost all rights.—Henry James

Still, peoples in the West have flocked to cities for the last several centuries, lured by jobs, diversity, and the promise of wealth and personal freedom.

What are cities and why have they encouraged such an ambivalence? Before we can begin to formulate an answer to such questions and others about the city we must examine the terminology sociologists have used to describe areas of residence.

THE URBAN AREA: SOME DEFINITIONS

In this section we will first discuss the differences between communities and cities and then describe that more recent invention—the metropolitan area.

The Community

Humans are by nature and necessity social creatures. Long before the evolution of the city as a place of residence, people sought satisfaction of their psychic, economic, social, and cultural needs in human settlements, which sociologists term *communities*. The community is a group that resides in a relatively permanent area. More specifically, "a community exists (1) when a set of households is relatively concentrated in a delimited geographical area; (2) their residents exhibit a substantial degree of integrated social interaction; and (3) have a sense of common membership, of belonging together, which is not based exclusively on ties of consanguinity [blood ties]" (Inkeles, 1964, p. 68). Thus a community is identified by its territorial boundedness, its sustained ties of interaction, and the sense of group identity that it encourages. It is a socially and culturally cohesive unit. Such cohesiveness is possible only if the group is relatively small and homogeneous. In this sense, then, we cannot speak of the city as an urban community, for cities are too large and too diverse to permit this cohesiveness.

The City

Most of the people who have ever lived on earth have lived in some form of rural community. In fact, even in the contemporary world, over 60 percent of the population resides in rural communities. Such communities far outnumber cities. It is estimated that there are currently over 880,000 rural hamlets and villages, and only around 1,777 cities (Golden, 1981). Even though the most common place of residence worldwide has been, and still is, the rural community, we live in an age dominated by the city's influence. In the politically and economically powerful industrial nations, urban areas contain a majority of the population. In all nations they are the centers of wealth, innovation, and social change.

Everyone in the modern world has some understanding of what a city is. How have sociologists distinguished between the city and the rural community? The most obvious features of the city are its large size, its dense concentration of people and activities, and the tremendous social and economic diversity of its occupants. The kind of cohesion that exists in the city is due to the interdependence that characterizes its economic, political, and cultural life, rather than to the homogeneity of its residents.

The official censuses of most nations define cities as population aggregates that exceed a minimum size or density. This minimum cutoff point is arbitrary and varies greatly among nations. For example, Denmark and Sweden require a minimum size of 200, whereas in the United States it is 2500, and in Japan the figure is set at 30,000 (Hawley, 1981). The use of such numbers is obviously somewhat problematic. In some areas the minimums established are too low; in all cases size minimums do not isolate the qualities of the city that make it a unique residential community. When such quantitative features, however, are coupled with qualitative criteria, specifically the occupational specialization of the urban population, we have sufficient information to distinguish cities from rural communities. **Cities** are large, dense, permanently settled territories whose population engages primarily in nonagricultural pursuits. These "pursuits" are normally quite diverse, making the city population heterogeneous in terms of its social, economic, and cultural interests.

The diversity of the urban division of labor creates a situation of economic and social dependency for the average urban resident. Because occupations are specialized, individuals must rely on a variety of other people simply to survive on a daily basis. This condition of dependence is characteristic of the city resident but uncharacteristic of the rural dweller.

The Metropolitan Area

The dependencies so characteristic of the urban dweller also accurately describe the modern city itself. Industrial cities are not independent social or economic units. With the tremendous advances in communication and transportation technology of the twentieth century—the telephone, automobile, subway, and the like—city populations have spilled over into suburban and rural areas. In so doing they have expanded their influence well beyond the bounds of the local political unit, and at the same time have come to rely on the populations of these areas to staff and support the local economy. The local urban area, then, cannot be accurately described by the political boundaries of the city, for in the auto age the urban place is a much more extensive territory.

In recognition of this fact two terms, metropolitan area and megalopolis, are often used to describe contemporary urban territories. A **metropolitan area** describes an urban area that extends far beyond the legal city limits, most of whose residents carry out their daily activities in the central city or metropolis of the area (Hawley, 1981). This zone of daily activity usually involves an enlarged area of about 25 to 30 miles in radius. The U.S. Census Bureau has created the concept **Standard Metropolitan Statistical Area** (SMSA) to provide a readily identifiable metropolitan area for statistical purposes. An SMSA includes (1) a city of 50,000 or more (the central city or metropolis), (2) the entire county in which this city is located, and (3) all contiguous counties in which residents have close economic links with the "central county." These close economic links are determined by employment figures on the nonagricultural segment of the county (no more than 25 percent of the population works in agriculture) and the daily commuting habits of the county's residents (at least 30 percent must work in the central county).

The SMSA more clearly describes the enlarged urban territories characteristic of mid-twentieth century cities. It does not, however, fully capture the significance of urban sprawl for the urban residential unit. A considerable number of SMSAs do not exist in isolation but rather form a **megalopolis,** or a number of contiguous metropolitan areas. Because of this situation the Census Bureau recognizes **Standard Consolidated Areas** (SCAs), which are several contiguous SMSAs and additional counties that have strong social and economic interrelationships. Recognizable SCAs include the New York-northeastern New Jersey and the Chicago-northwestern Indiana megalopolises, and the lower coastal area of California. It is estimated that by the year 2000 these three areas will comprise a majority of the American population (Report of the Commission on Population Growth and the American Future, 1972).

THE URBAN EXPLOSION: A HISTORY OF THE CITY

Humans have resided on earth for nearly three million years; they have lived in cities for only one-fifth of one percent of that time. The city is thus a recent development in human cultural evolution, the first cities having arisen in about 3500 B.C. in Mesopotamia. Even more recent are the metropolitan area and the megalopolis, which appear in the mid-twentieth century. What factors gave rise to the first cities and how has the urban area changed over time?

Ancient Cities

The essential condition for the development of cities was the ability to produce stable, relatively large food surpluses. Levels of food production had to be high enough so that people produced more food than was required for survival. This surplus was used by city dwellers who did not produce their own food. To extract that surplus from the agriculturalist required a strong political and military organization. The prehistoric and historic record suggests very clearly that ancient cities, to survive, had to gain the food surplus from rural areas through coercion, in the form of taxes or tribute to a ruler. Ancient cities had not established the commerce or production necessary to exchange goods and services for food. Thus early cities arose by virtue of rural agricultural primacy and urban piracy (La Gory and Pipkin, 1981). The first such concurrence of these events was in the fertile river valleys of the Tigris and Euphrates in Mesopotamia, in the Nile valley of Egypt, in the Indus valley of India, and in the Yellow River valley of China.

The strong political and military organization necessary to coerce food supplies from farmers stimulated the emergence of an elaborate social class system in the new cities. At the top warrior kings controlled the military establishment and a class of administrators that included priests, accountants, astronomers, scribes, and overseers. Lower down the scale were a variety of artisans, laborers, and a class of slaves. Marx (1848) points out that with the birth of the city class conflict emerges for the first time in human history. Class conflict occurred at two levels: between the urbanite and the relatively impoverished agriculturalist and between the urban political elite and the urban laborers and slaves. Indeed, because early cities represented such intense concentrations of wealth they were likely targets for indiscriminate raids by poor peasants and nomadic groups. For defense all cities before the Industrial Revolution were surrounded by thick walls.

In fact, the Industrial Revolution serves as a watershed between two types of cities. Cities before the growth of industrial production shared a number of basic features, which allow us to refer to ancient cities, Greco-Roman cities, and medieval

Preindustrial cities were relatively small and organized around residential neighborhoods. There was little spatial separation of activities, as patterns of living, working, and recreation took place in the same area. The preindustrial city did not attract significant migration from rural areas and thus had little physical change and growth.

and Renaissance cities as a single type—the preindustrial city (Berry, 1973; Sjoberg, 1960).

Reading 17.1 provides a composite picture of the ancient, preindustrial city as we might experience it if we were transported across time. Early cities had a heterogeneous population, with rich and poor, beggar and merchant, brought into almost daily contact. In contrast the modern city has spatial segregation patterns that keep social groups and people of different social classes apart from each other.

What Did the Preindustrial City Look Like?

The best way to answer this question is to organize the characteristics of the preindustrial city into several general categories (La Gory and Pipkin, 1981).

POPULATION SIZE AND GROWTH

With few exceptions preindustrial cities were small in terms of both the area inhabited and the number of inhabitants. The population of the earliest cities is estimated at around 30,000 (Hawley, 1981). During the preindustrial period the great bulk of people were nonurban. In both the United States and England immediately before industrialization, no more than 5 percent of the population was urban.

The small size of cities was due essentially to the relatively inefficient economy and technology characteristic of preindustrial societies. The preindustrial city did not attract significant migration from rural areas. Cities were dangerous places to live, mortality was high, and the immigration that did occur merely served to balance the high death rates. Because of this lack of growth the use of specific areas in the city for such activities as living, working, and recreation became traditional and permanent. This contrasts vividly with the modern city where physical change and growth are a characteristic feature.

ECONOMIC ORGANIZATION

Economic activity occurred on a relatively small scale in the preindustrial period. As a result cities were spatially organized in a manner quite different from cities today. Economic activities, including the various stages of the production process, were

The study of modern cities by sociologists has attempted to discover the spatial form of urban places. Three theories are used to describe the urban space and how it is shaped by the processes of population growth and areal expansion. One theory sees growth occurring in circular bands or zones from the city center. Another emphasizes growth along transportation routes. The thrid sees the city growth pattern reflected in its unique history and economic activities.

carried out under one roof—usually in the home. Masters, craftworkers, laborers, and merchants frequently lived and worked on the same premises. The spatial separation of home and work site with its complicated and often tedious commuting patterns was absent.

The economic functions of the city increased in scope throughout the period. In the ancient city-states, cities controlled the surrounding agricultural communities by religious and military means. In later periods the city's dominance over the surrounding territory became more explicitly economic. Trade became a well-established activity in Roman, medieval, and Renaissance cities, and changes in the city's physical form reflected its growing significance. The marketplace and the guildhall occupied a prominent place beside the church and the palace in medieval and Renaissance Europe.

SOCIAL ORGANIZATION

The major unit of the preindustrial social organization was the extended family. Because such units are not very mobile, residential neighborhoods were not likely to change. In addition to this stability, neighborhoods displayed a social mix uncharacter-

istic of their later industrial counterparts. Since different portions of the production process were carried out in a single household, in many cities rich and poor lived side by side. This is not to imply that social segregation did not exist, but segregation was more likely to be by function than social station alone. Typically, the most prestigious locations were close to the symbolic centers of urban life like public squares. Successively poorer groups lived farther away from these centers or even beyond the city's walls in the first "suburbs." This pattern of residence is of course very different from that of modern cities.

Another signficant difference between the preindustrial and contemporary city is the nature of citizenship status. Until about the second century A.D. citizenship was a right jealously guarded by kinship and religious groups. Many urban dwellers, in fact all females, were not given the privilege of citizenship, and indeed some groups were even barred from city residence.

CONTEMPORARY PREINDUSTRIAL CITIES

The preindustrial city is still common in many unindustrialized countries of Latin America, Africa, and Asia. Historically, they have been fairly small and compact; social and physical changes have been minimal. They are ill-equipped to handle growth. Recently, however, rural overpopulation has forced many new migrants into the city. The urban economy of these nations is not growing fast enough to provide jobs for these great waves of new urbanites, nor do the cities have the resources necessary to house them. Many new residents are either forced to live in the streets or in ill-constructed, makeshift housing on the outskirts of the city. Such cities are faced with a serious problem of "over-urbanization," which shows no signs of abatement. As a result urban densities are high and poverty is intensely concentrated, leading to the likelihood of future social unrest and violence.

The Industrial Revolution and the Modern City

The distinguishing features of modern cities were determined by the technology and population changes that occurred during the Industrial Revolution, which began in England in the mid-eighteenth century. The significance of this revolution for the modern city can best be understood by considering the nature of industrial production itself. Economists speak of two ways industries can increase the efficiency of their production: (1) by increasing the size of the production system and (2) by locating close to the sources of energy, raw materials, and labor.

Industrial machinery is bulky and expensive. To increase profits industries had to increase the size of their production facilities. For example, one large blast furnace is much cheaper to operate than two or three smaller ones with the same capacity. Working the new large-scale factories required an extensive pool of hired labor. As a consequence factories located in areas where population densities were high—usually in areas near the city's center.

This location strategy produced rapid urban growth and a radical reordering of the city's spatial arrangement. The industrial city attracted vast numbers of migrants from rural areas because of the new employment opportunities. During most of the nineteenth and early twentieth centuries urban populations grew significantly through migration. Weber (1899) found that in the large cities of

the nineteenth century as much as 80 percent of the adult population had been born outside the city and two-thirds of these had lived in these cities less than 15 years. It is only in the last 30 to 40 years that these large migrant streams have ceased in industrialized countries.

The rural to urban migrants settled near the factories, resulting in an increasing concentration of large numbers of working-class people around the city's center. These centrally located ghettos, and the soot and grime that were by-products of the factories, became characteristic of the industrial city. For the first time in urban history the city became repugnant to the upper classes. The upper classes moved away from the city's center as factories and the working class moved in. Thus the distribution of social classes was reversed: the city turned inside out. This trend was further accelerated by continuing transportation innovations—the railroad, streetcar, and automobile—which led to the urban sprawl of the modern city.

These changes in the city resulted from large-scale production and migration. In addition, industries found they could save money by locating their facilities close to other related industries, to the raw materials used in production, to specialized transport facilities, and to a trained labor pool. Because of these savings, clusters of industrial cities sprang up near these resources. In preindustrial times such a clustering would not have been economically feasible; however, in modern times these concentrations of cities are not only viable but characteristic. Figure 17.1 shows projected urban concentrations for the year 2000.

THE FORM OF THE CITY: THEORIES OF HUMAN ECOLOGY

The history of the city from preindustrial to modern times suggests that the spatial form of urban places has undergone radical transformation. Since the 1920s sociologists who call themselves human ecologists have spent a great deal of effort in analyzing the city's spatial structure. The earliest ecologists (sometimes called the Chicago School because they taught at the University of Chicago) were interested in urban space because they felt that knowledge of the urban environment could

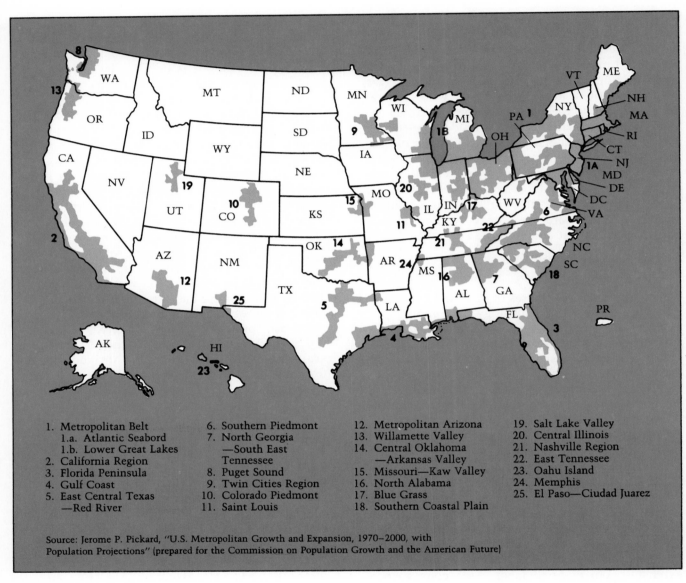

1. Metropolitan Belt
   1.a. Atlantic Seabord
   1.b. Lower Great Lakes
2. California Region
3. Florida Peninsula
4. Gulf Coast
5. East Central Texas
   —Red River
6. Southern Piedmont
7. North Georgia
   —South East
   Tennessee
8. Puget Sound
9. Twin Cities Region
10. Colorado Piedmont
11. Saint Louis
12. Metropolitan Arizona
13. Willamette Valley
14. Central Oklahoma
    —Arkansas Valley
15. Missouri—Kaw Valley
16. North Alabama
17. Blue Grass
18. Southern Coastal Plain
19. Salt Lake Valley
20. Central Illinois
21. Nashville Region
22. East Tennessee
23. Oahu Island
24. Memphis
25. El Paso—Ciudad Juarez

Source: Jerome P. Pickard, "U.S. Metropolitan Growth and Expansion, 1970–2000, with
Population Projections" (prepared for the Commission on Population Growth and the American Future)

FIGURE 17.1   Urban
Concentrations By the Year 2000

*Megalopolitan regions are forming in many
areas of the United States. The most notable
clusters include the New York-Northeastern
New Jersey, Chicago-Northwestern
Indiana, Lake Michigan, Gulf of Mexico,
Florida, and Lower Coastal California regions.*

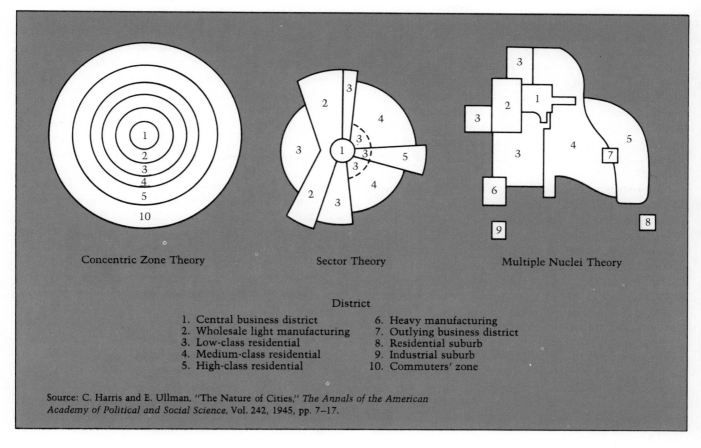

Concentric Zone Theory   Sector Theory   Multiple Nuclei Theory

District

1. Central business district
2. Wholesale light manufacturing
3. Low-class residential
4. Medium-class residential
5. High-class residential
6. Heavy manufacturing
7. Outlying business district
8. Residential suburb
9. Industrial suburb
10. Commuters' zone

Source: C. Harris and E. Ullman, "The Nature of Cities," *The Annals of the American Academy of Political and Social Science*, Vol. 242, 1945, pp. 7–17.

FIGURE 17.2   Ecological Theories of the Urban Form

The three ecological theories of the urban form are shown. Each depicts a somewhat different urban arrangement.

lead to a better understanding of the behavior of urban residents. They noted that people living in different areas of the city had different life styles and cultures and behaved in different ways. For example, patterns of neighboring, crime, mental illness, and educational and occupational mobility varied by locality. Such spatial variation led Wirth (1938) to describe the city as a "mosaic of social worlds," an area of great diversity characterized by an equally intensive pattern of residential segregation.

Many urban scholars have attempted to define this "pattern" or mosaic of segregation. Three theories in particular describe the urban space and how it is shaped by the processes of population growth and areal expansion. **Concentric zone theory** suggests that the city expands in a pattern of circular bands or zones that grow from the city center outward, much like the ripples created by throwing a stone in a pond. **Sector theory** emphasizes the significance of transportation routes in encouraging growth and change in specific areas of the city. **Multiple nuclei theory** suggests that the pattern of growth in a given city is influenced by specific geographic and historical conditions. Figure 17.2 shows the urban mosaic as depicted by each of the three theories. The following sections examine the three views.

Concentric Zone Theory

In 1923 Ernest Burgess wrote "The Growth of the City: An Introduction to a Research Project." Burgess, in that article, suggested that the unplanned city grew in a patterned way, as a series of concentric circles each with its own distinctive groups of population and activities. In this idealized form cities were composed of five basic zones:

Zone 1: The central business district. This area is the focus of the city's commercial, cultural, and social life. At its center is the downtown shopping area. Surrounding this area is a wholesale district with its warehouses and public markets. Zone 1 is the city's central public space. Activity and population is highly concentrated here, with lots of people and buildings occupying a rather small amount of land.

Zone 2: The zone in transition. This area is characterized by an inner district of factories and an outer area of deteriorated housing. A ghetto area, it consists of a highly mobile population usually first-generation migrants to the city, bad housing, high crime, and severe poverty. At one time it had been a suburban fringe housing many of the city's wealthy members. As the city grew, however, business and industry expanded into the area making it an undesirable place to live. Much of the land was bought up by speculators who anticipated eventual profits from expanding commerce and industry. These absentee landlords did little to improve residences since they hoped for greater profits when the site would be sold for commercial use.

Zone 3: The zone of workingmen's homes. This is predominantly an area of blue collar, two-family houses. Residents of this area have achieved enough occupational mobility to escape zone 2, but they cannot afford the costs of the long daily commute to work that the more affluent residents of zones 4 and 5 can.

Zone 4: The zone of better residences. This area consists of apartments as well as single-family dwellings with spacious yards. Zones 4 and 5 contain the great heartland of urban America—the middle class.

Zone 5: The commuter's zone. Outside the legal boundaries of the city, this area consists of a ring of smaller-sized cities, towns, and villages, most of which are "bedroom" communities rather than employing suburbs. The commuter's zone is the least homogeneous area of the metropolis, each suburb having a somewhat different residential character, government, and so forth.

The zonal theory describes the spatial structure resulting from urban growth. As the central commercial district expanded outward it initiated ripple-like waves of change in population and activities as each zone extended its area by invading the next outer zone. This growth had its most serious consequences for zone 2, which experienced social and physical decline rather than benefit from economic and population expansion. In fact, there is a general tendency for the economic and social status of zones to decline as closeness to the source of growth (zone 1) increases.

Sector Theory

Burgess, attempting to portray the spatial structure

of cities, used the city of Chicago as his laboratory for observation. Hoyt (1939), who first developed sector theory, studied a much larger sample of cities—(142 cities in the three years of 1900, 1915, and 1936). His analysis led him to disagree with two basic concepts of concentric zone theory: (1) growth always originated in the center and initiated uniform change in all directions outward, and (2) the spatial pattern produced by this growth process was a series of zones, each with a distinctive social status.

Hoyt argued that the growth pattern in the 142 cities of his sample was not uniform in all directions, and thus the spatial pattern of cities and social classes was not zonal. Instead, growth and spatial structure is strongly influenced by existing routes of transportation. This pattern of growth creates pie-shaped wedges, or sectors, of like-status residential areas rather than zones. Because residents depend on transportation into and out of the central commercial and civic area of the city, major trunk routes of travel determine the clustering of residential areas. In turn, the pattern of clustering is determined by the original spatial form of the city. Because of certain location advantages, industry and commerce are likely to concentrate in different sectors of the city. Residential development will depend on where these sectors concentrate.

The location tendencies produce the following pattern: (1) The high-rent sector originates near the retail, financial, and office districts. This point is always farthest removed from the side of the city with industrial concentrations. Over time this area moves out along the major transportation route in the sector, generally locating in a wedge on the city's outskirts. (2) Middle-class areas are usually found on either side of the highest rent areas. (3) Low-rent areas are frequently found on the opposite side of town from high-rent areas. Usually low-rent areas are in relatively central locations.

Multiple-Nuclei Theory

One of the assumptions common to concentric zone theory is the existence of single-centered cities, that is, cities in which business and production activity is located at a common point. In many cities, however, the pattern of land use is not built

around a single center but rather many such centers or nuclei. This pattern of multiple centers is the result of the new modes of transportation of the twentieth-century city, particularly the automobile.

The domination of the central business district over retail sales and commerce in general has been seriously weakened by the growth in automobile usage. With the auto suburbia became an ideal location for retail establishments as well as factories. The auto permitted vast numbers of consumers and workers to move farther away from the urban core; as a result the city became multinucleated.

Harris and Ullman (1945) proposed the multiple nuclei theory to describe the pattern encouraged by automobile usage. The theory suggests that cities develop a number of districts that grow up around distinct centers, each specializing in a particular activity. The reasons for this are as follows:

1. Certain activities need special facilities. Manufacturing districts require lots of space and access to regional and national transportation routes, whereas retail districts require less space and more accessibility to local markets.

2. Certain like activities attract one another. Financial and office districts require close communication with other offices in the area. Retail stores of a particular type also increase potential customers by clustering. Thus in cities we find "automobile row," furniture and carpet districts, and so forth.

3. While some like activities attract one another, certain unlike activities repel one another. Heavy industry districts require close proximity to rail facilities and truck terminals. These transport facilities cannot concentrate in retail areas, which depend upon heavy pedestrian traffic.

4. Not all activities can afford the expense of locating in the most desirable areas. Warehousing and heavy manufacturing require lots of space. In areas where space is at a premium these activities cannot function economically.

Inherent in the multiple nuclei theory is the view that no two cities look alike. The number, variety, and arrangement of districts in the city depend upon the city's history, its current population, and its economic activity. While the urban shape is highly variable from city to city, Harris and Ullman do believe that certain districts commonly arise in all cities. All cities have a central business district, but because cities tend to grow unevenly (as Hoyt suggests) this district is hardly ever at the city's geometric center. Near the central business district an area of wholesale and light manufacturing usually develops. This district locates close to interregional transportation routes, which historically are near the commerical center. Heavy industry, on the other hand, locates near the present or former boundaries of the city because of its need for large tracts of land and its undesirable effects on the environment. Lower-class residential districts are found near the heavy industry district because of the district's undesirable residential character. Upper-class residential districts will be established in areas far removed from this industry.

Of the three theories the multiple nuclei theory is certainly the most flexible, taking into account the unique characteristics of cities. Its flexibility, however, is in some ways a disadvantage since it is not capable of predicting a characteristic pattern of activity and population.

What is the Urban Residential Pattern?

Which of the three theories correctly describes the residential pattern of modern city? The answer is that each is correct to a point. Certainly, as multiple nuclei theory suggests, no two cities are alike. Each has a unique political, demographic, and economic history. This uniqueness, however, does not imply an absence of pattern. What does the urban residential pattern appear to be?

Research indicates that all three theories simplify the patterns of social and therefore residential, segregation in cities. All of the theories tend to assume that residential segregation occurs along only one social dimension—socioeconomic status. This assumption is incorrect. As a variety of studies indicate, residence is spatially structured according to at least three dimensions (Timms, 1971). City residents are segregated by their socioeconomic characteristics, by their age, and by ethnic group.

Berry (1965), summarizing information collected on the internal structure of a number of cities, suggests that concentric zone theory and sector theory can be used to describe different dimensions of res-

idential segregation. Socioeconomic characteristics of residents (income, education, occupation) are distributed according to a sector pattern. The education, occupation, and income levels of neighborhoods are arranged along lines drawn from the center to the periphery. Areas of homogeneous socioeconomic status are thus most like Hoyt's pie-shaped wedges.

Areas with residents of similar age, however, are best described by the concentric zone pattern. The age of the population in an area, the type of housing (single-family versus multiple housing units, rental versus owner occupied), the size of the family, and the percentage of women in the labor force vary by zones. At the edge of the city are family-oriented neighborhoods that consist of single-family homes, in which larger, younger families reside and where women are less likely to be employed. Toward the city center one is more likely to find neighborhoods consisting of older, smaller households living in multiple-family dwellings.

Ethnicity is distributed neither by sector nor by zone. Indeed, the concentration of ethnic groups appears to be without pattern. Since cities are heterogeneous this is not surprising. Because there is a variety of ethnic groups it is likely that these groups will reside in different sectors and zones.

To summarize, when sector and zonal patterns are overlaid on a city we can note the following residential pattern. Within each zone there is a variety of status areas but much similarity in the age characteristics of the residents. At the same time, in each sector there is great similarity in socioeconomic status but a mix of life styles, some areas being family oriented while others are career or age oriented.

Why Does This Pattern Emerge?

The answer to this question must be sought in the sector and concentric zone theories themselves. Each theory identifies a different growth pattern in the modern city. Zone theory suggests that urban growth is initiated by changes occurring in the city's central district, which set off waves of ripplelike expansion. Why does this affect life-cycle patterns in cities? Students of the urban scene believe that central growth is significant because of certain factors that people take into consideration when deciding where to live (Casetti, 1967). On the one hand, people would like to be as close as possible to major city activities (employment, culture, civic life, and so on). On the other hand, people do not like to be crowded. They do not like congested streets, cramped living space, and the like. Depending on their life style, people will assign more or less weight to each of these factors. For the family-oriented person congestion is very costly. It is hard to raise a family under crowded conditions. Thus residence away from the center will be desirable. The career-oriented or older household finds congestion less costly and location near the center more desirable. Thus a concentric pattern by life cycle is likely to occur.

At the same time a sectorlike pattern of socioeconomic status emerges. The status of residential neighborhoods has for the most part been set by the history of the city's development. Because certain economic activities locate in specific areas of the city, these places will develop an image that is difficult to change. These images in turn will determine the value of real estate in an area. Since economic activities arrange themselves around existing transportation routes, residential status patterns will follow.

URBAN LIFE STYLES: THE SOCIAL AND PSYCHOLOGICAL SIGNIFICANCE OF THE URBAN FORM

To this point we have discussed what cities look like without considering the city's impact on people. We now turn to this issue of *urbanism*—the distinctive social and psychological characteristics of city life.

The urban experience differs fundamentally from the rural. Because of the city's large size, density, and social diversity, social organization and interaction are more complex and difficult. The sheer immensity of the modern urban setting encourages unique experiences. These include the following:

1. *Complex interaction patterns.* The city dweller has the potential for initiating an enormous number of social relationships.
2. *Exposure to strangers.* Because of the city's large

population the urbanite shares the community with a great many unknown others.
3. *Exposure to unconventional norms.* The size and diversity of the city makes it more likely than other community types to foster unconventional behavior patterns (La Gory and Pipkin, 1981).

These unique urban experiences have a number of possible consequences for urban life styles. Individual choice and freedom of action will be greater in the city. People can choose among a variety of life styles and friends. At the same time, people may find the characteristic heterogeneity of the city confusing; they may become alienated or isolated. This variety of possible consequences has led to two differing views of urban life. Louis Wirth (1938) tends to see the urban experience as potentially alienating, impersonal, and chaotic, while Claude Fischer (1976) views urban life as an orderly composition of diverse and vital subcultures. Let us consider these competing views.

Urban Alienation: The Views of Louis Wirth

The complex patterns of interaction and exposure to strangers and unconventional behaviors characteristic of the urban experience led Wirth to see the city as a seedbed for distrust and pathology. He discussed the negative consequences of urban life in an article entitled "Urbanism as a Way of Life" (1938). Wirth argued that the city's characteristic size, density, and diversity encouraged the expansion of secondary relations and the decline of intimate personal ties. The loss of personal ties in turn bred social isolation and distrust. This view of the city as a corrupting force has been shared by a great many intellectuals and has been supported, and indeed enhanced, by media reports that characterize city life as dangerous and demoralizing.

There are several reasons why the urban environment may lead to the pathological conditions predicted by Wirth. First of all, in the city the number of stimuli—sights, sounds, and smells—is overwhelming. Milgram (1972) claims that the urban experience produces *stimulus overload*, a situation in which the individual finds it impossible to manage all of the stimuli emanating from the environment either because there are too many stimuli or they are coming too fast. When overload occurs the person can adapt by blocking out certain stimuli entirely and by giving as little attention to others as possible. This encourages a posture of aloofness and superficiality. For urbanites most of the people sharing public space with them, whether it be on a sidewalk, in a marketplace, elevator, or subway, are nonpersons—objects to be maneuvered around.

The diversity of the city's people also contributes to the city's potential for breeding anonymity and impersonalism. In a diverse residential area, consisting of people from different class and ethnic backgrounds who also perform a variety of social and economic roles, people have less in common. With such diversity it is difficult to maintain a consensus of interests, values, and life styles. As a result social cohesion is precarious.

Vital Urban Subcultures: The Views of Claude Fischer

Several sociologists have criticized Wirth's view of the city as a pathological social environment (Fischer, 1976, 1981; Lofland, 1973; Reiss, 1955). Fischer's work in particular provides an important clarification of Wirth's theory. Wirth sees anonymity, impersonalism, and distrust as major effects of dense, heterogeneous communities. Fischer's research, however, shows that these effects are not uniformly true of all urban social relations. Social relations can be divided into public and private spheres. City dwellers do not mistrust their neighbors (private sphere), but they do mistrust unknown, socially dissimilar groups in the wider residential area (public sphere). Small town people are not necessarily any friendlier with their neighbors than city residents; however, they are friendlier in public with those they do not know than are urbanites.

Urban life is not impersonal. In fact, Fischer points out that in the city personal relationships can often be more intense and intimate than in the small town. Large size can provide the *critical mass* that permits what would otherwise be a small group of unrelated people to become a vital, active group. This is especially true for ethnic subcultures. For a subculture to survive, certain minimum numbers of people must be present to support the institu-

tions that give the group its identity. In the case of an ethnic community this critical mass might simply mean enough people to keep alive the specialty shops, churches, newspapers, and clubs necessary to satisfy the group's cultural requirements. Certainly in this instance large size breathes life into such groups, rather than breeding social disintegration and isolation.

It seems clear that Wirth's picture of the urbanite as socially isolated and culturally alienated is exaggerated. The city can be described as a collection of close-knit subcultures that are spatially separated from one another (Berger, 1978). While the tightly segregated spatial pattern increases interaction and common values and works against social isolation and mistrust, it is obviously not without its costs. For segregation also promotes discrimination and creates a mosaic of cultural "islands" separated by fear and mistrust.

CITY VERSUS SUBURB: THE NEGATIVE CONSEQUENCES OF SPATIAL SEGREGATION

What is the effect of the overall pattern of segregation for the metropolitan area and its residents? At the neighborhood level segregation engenders trust among the residents in the local area, but at the metropolitan level segregation appears to produce a clear-cut division between the central city and its suburbs. The demography of these two areas is quite different. Cities generally contain an older population and more blue-collar and lower level white-collar workers. As a result, the inner portion of the central city has been variously characterized as a "geriatric ghetto" (Clark, 1971), a "chocolate city with vanilla suburbs" (Farley et al., 1976), and an "unheavenly city" in which the population's skills do not match well with the available jobs (Banfield, 1974). In contrast, residents of suburbs are younger, better educated, and predominately white.

These descriptions indicate real social differences between the cultural and social groups who reside in inner city areas and suburbs. The descriptions, however, do not do justice to the complexity of life styles in each area.

Gans (1968) has described five basic subcultural groups that are usually found in inner-city areas. These include (1) professionals with good educations and high paying jobs, (2) unmarried or childless couples, (3) ethnic villagers who live in their own separate areas, (4) the elderly who remain trapped in old areas because they cannot afford to live elsewhere, and (5) deprived groups of the very poor, emotionally disturbed, and members of broken families.

Of these groups the first three live in the inner city by choice and thus benefit from the inner-city environment. The latter two groups, however, reside there simply because there is no other place for them to go. Their choices with regard to life style, services, and residence are extremely limited. Consequently, they are often victims of the inner-city environment.

Urban renewal programs were designed to attack the problems of the inner city by destroying slum areas and replacing it with new housing and a revitalized economic community. Unfortunately, renewal projects often resulted in destroying neighborhoods with intimate and long-standing social networks, and displacing the poor to find housing elsewhere. Here we see the early stage of an urban renewal effort in the heart of the city.

While the inner city is made up of diverse populations, suburbia is more homogeneous. As Gans suggests, they are younger, more of them are married and have children, their incomes are higher, and they hold proportionately more white-collar jobs. These demographic characteristics clearly indicate that the suburbanite will possess a life style different from those in the inner city. Bell (1958) suggests that suburbanites place great value on the nuclear family and believe that suburban residence provides a better environment for raising children. In addition, their orientation is local rather than cosmopolitan (Fava, 1975). Their span of interests is limited principally to the immediate area and their family, and their interest in the problems and offerings of the entire metropolis is narrow. This fact often puts the interests of central city residents and suburbanites in conflict.

What are the social consequences of this division between inner city and suburb? The impact is substantial and complex. We will explore only a few of its results, specifically its influence on patterns of crime, job opportunities, and the delivery of services.

Patterns of Crime: The Case of the Urban Slum

Just as human ecologists have shown that the pattern of local life styles changes with distance from the city's center, students of deviance have found that crime rates vary with distance. Generally, a spatial pattern of crime can be observed in contemporary industrial cities, with the lowest rates in the suburbs and a peak at the center. Early studies of Chicago's crime statistics (Shaw and McKay, 1942) found that delinquency and adult criminality increased in areas closer to the city center. Crime, in short, is most often a problem of the inner-city slum. Table 17.1 contains more recent evidence on the rates of different crimes in central cities and suburbs.

The invisible walls of the slum—its social barriers and physical segregation—intensify the isolation of the slum resident from the rest of society. Within the slum this feeling of isolation leads to a generalized suspicion of those who live outside its boundaries. But the suspicion and uncertainty is directed inward as well. Their residential transiency, characteristic of slum dwellers, intensifies their distrust. The psychological coping strategies available to the slum dweller include (1) taking refuge in a familiar ethnic subculture, (2) withdrawing into a private world in which social relationships are exclusively kin based, (3) taking a more independent stance and establishing new personal relationships, and (4) embracing one or more

TABLE 17.1 Rates of household and personal victimization (per thousand households) by place of residence of victim and type of victimization, 1977

	HOUSEHOLD VICTIMIZATION		
	Burglary	Household Larceny	Motor Vehicle Theft
Central cities	111.5	141.0	24.3
Suburbs and rural-urban	86.7	135.8	18.3

	PERSONAL VICTIMIZATION					
	Crimes of Violence	Rape	Robbery	Assault	Theft	Personal Larceny
Central cities	47.2	1.2	12.0	34.1	112.9	157.9
Suburbs and rural-urban fringe	33.7	1.0	4.9	27.9	107.2	107.2

SOURCE: T. Flanagan, M. Hindelang, and M. Gottfriedson. *Sourcebooks of Criminal Justice Statistics—1979.* Albany, New York: Criminal Justice Research Center, 1980.

of the deviant roles found in the community and using this strategy to gain entry into the deviant subculture (Suttles, 1968). This variety of strategies makes for a diverse community, but here diversity fosters normative confusion and mistrust. Indeed, if there is a place in the city that comes close to Wirth's view of urbanism, it is the slum. Here isolation, impersonalism, and distrust are adaptations to an unhealthy environment.

Job Opportunities

The negative effects of segregation are not limited to crime. More than a decade ago the Kerner Commission suggested that the United States was moving toward two separate societies—one black and one white (National Advisory Commission on Civil Disorders, 1969). The boundaries of these societies are already apparent in the metropolitan area: large cities are becoming increasingly black, while suburbs remain white (Farley et al., 1976).

This clear-cut separation of blacks and whites exacerbates the already existing racial inequalities in education and occupation. As Coleman has shown (1966), racial segregation in the schools promotes significant disparities between the races in educational achievement. Also, school and residential segregation affect accessibility to employment and information about job opportunities. Kain (1968) argues that the underemployment of inner-city blacks is due to the spatial mismatch between job opportunities and the skills of workers. In the last 30 years cities have lost a large number of manufacturing jobs to the suburbs, while new jobs have generally been higher skilled or service-oriented positions. The trend toward the relocation of manufacturing to the suburbs has produced a serious problem of underemployment for the inner-city resident. Those least able to bear the daily cost of transportation to work find that the available jobs are located at points farthest removed from their homes.

Delivery of Services

We can view the metropolitan area "as a gigantic man-made resource system which contains an abundance of resources for individuals to exploit to their own benefit" (Harvey, 1972, p. 3). These resources, however, are spatially structured; they occur in fixed locations, which are more accessible to some than others. Perhaps the most obvious result of resource segregation is unequal retail services for residents of different areas of the city. The Kerner Commission summarized the problem for the black ghetto resident:

Residents of low-income Negro neighborhoods frequently claim that they pay higher prices for food in local markets than wealthier white suburbanites and receive inferior quality meat and produce. . . . There are significant reasons to believe that poor households generally pay higher prices for the food they buy and receive lower quality food. Low-income consumers buy more food at local groceries because they are less mobile. Prices in these small stores are significantly higher than in major supermarkets because they cannot achieve economies of scale, and because real operating costs are higher in low-income Negro areas than in outlying suburbs . . . In addition, it is probable that genuinely exploitative pricing practices exist in some areas. (National Advisory Commission on Civil Disorders, 1969, pp. 274–277)

This same problem exists for the highly centralized urban elderly. The aged, living on fixed incomes and relatively limited in their ability to move around in the local community, must seek services close by. As a result, they generally pay more for these services.

While relatively poor inner-city populations may find the results of metropolitan segregation costly, the better-off suburban resident often benefits. The middle class have, for the last couple of decades, abandoned the city in droves, attracted by plentiful jobs, cheaper land, new housing, and lower tax rates of suburbia (Marshall, 1979). Suburbanization has resulted in a diminishing central city tax base. Because of the lowered per capita revenues, central city taxes have had to increase substantially. At the same time, while revenues have declined, expenses have increased. As former mayor of New York John Lindsay states, "Our cities have become the guardian of the country's unwanted stepchildren" (quoted in Pettengill and Uppal, 1974, p. 7). Cities must carry, and pay for, this tremendous economic and social burden while maintaining services and facilities that are used by the entire metropolis. Suburban residents can take advantage of such services as museums and public transportation without carrying their share of their cost.

Hawley (1956) claims that suburbs represent a basic cost to the city resident and contribute directly to the city's current fiscal plight:

The [cities] are carrying the financial burden of an elaborate and costly service installation, i.e., the central city is used daily by a noncontributing population that in some instances is more than twice the size of the contributing population (pp. 781–782).

Reading 17.2 suggests that the problems of the city are the result of conservative political policies that have reduced federal subsidies to cities. The author, Richard Morris, is critical of conservative arguments that these are problems of rising social welfare costs, powerful labor unions with high wage contracts, and government regulations. Rather, as Dorman (1972) states, "the people holding the purse strings of federal and state governments are essentially anti-urban" (p. 196).

ARE CITIES WORTH SAVING?

These seem to be hard times for cities. The new austerity ushered in by the Reagan Administration in 1981 has severely affected cities, cutting general revenue funds for local programs and welfare funds for the urban poor. In addition, the well-publicized "tax revolt" of the middle-class has resulted in states and municipalities adopting tax-cutting measures, like California's Proposition 13, which have further reduced funds available to cities. What can be done to improve the city's prospects? Since World War II one group of professionals, the urban planners, has been actively involved in reshaping the city. What effect have they had?

Urban Renewal

The Housing Act of 1949 created the urban renewal program. The philosophy of urban renewal was

simple: the best way to attack the problems of the inner city was to destroy the slum and replace it with new housing and a revitalized economic community. This bulldozer solution was ill conceived. It aimed primarily to improve the quality of neighborhoods, but did not explicitly address the problem of rehousing the poor who were displaced as the buildings came tumbling down. Indeed, urban renewal projects often forced the poor into playing a game of "musical houses" (Gans, 1965). A study of Boston's West End showed that 41 percent of the residents lived in adequate housing that should not have been destroyed (Hartman, 1964). These households were moved from adequate housing to adequate housing, but their situation did not remain constant. Rather, rents nearly doubled, while people were forced to leave their communities and friends.

By no measure can urban renewal be judged successful. Even in terms of simply increasing housing for the poor it failed. Its social impact, however, has been far more devastating. Renewal destroyed the intimate and long-standing social networks of inner-city areas and offered nothing to replace it. Many ghetto residents were relocated in high-rise buildings, which did provide more living space and newer facilities. However, these advantages did not offset the social costs. High-rise design made it impossible for parents to supervise children's play once children left the interior confines of the apartment. In the older neighborhoods, where apartment buildings were usually low rise and near to the sidewalks, alleys, and streets where children played, parents had easy access to their children.

They also had easy access to their neighbors. In high rises, which were built to save money, there was no wasted space, and thus no space that could be used for socializing or for recreation. Yancey (1971) states:

In lower and working-class slums, the littered and often trash-filled alleys, streets, and backyards provide the ecological basis around which informal networks of friends and relatives may develop. Without such semipublic space and facilities, the development of such social networks is retarded, the resulting atomization of the community can be seen in the frequent and escalating conflict between neighbors . . . (p. 17)

While urban renewal failed to improve the plight of the urban slum dweller, it did revitalize the central business district. Its success here was often at the expense of inner-city residents who saw their apartments and their community's stores and businesses replaced by hotels and high-rise office buildings. Like much of American planning the benefits went to those who were already well off.

The most successful planning efforts have stimulated suburban home ownership and added to the suburbanization of metropolitan areas. Federal support of middle- and upper-class home ownership takes several forms. Indirectly, suburban residence has been made possible by a marvelously engineered system of expressways and freeways that often gets the suburbanite to work quicker than the city dweller. Directly, home ownership has been subsidized by a variety of government acts, which have reduced down payment requirements, insured mortgages, and provided large tax deductions, making new homes in the suburbs more attractive financially. In this sense federal planning actually encouraged the trend toward suburbanization and the eventual impoverishment of the central city. Thus the federal government's tacit solution to the urban problem has been to finance the abandonment of cities.

New Towns

For many planners the most feasible solution to the urban problem was simply to start all over again and build new cities. This practice was first implemented in Western Europe. Great Britain started a concentrated effort to build new towns right after World War II. A total of 15 new cities were built, of which eight formed a ring around London. Each was designed to be economically self-sufficient. Population densities were low and neighborhoods were planned as cohesive social entities with schools, parks, churches, and shopping nearby.

In the United States several new towns have been developed around the British model. Unlike the United Kingdom, however, these have been supported by private developers. The two most successful projects are Reston, Virginia, and Columbia, Maryland. Each planned town emphasized the close-knit neighborhood unit. The developer of Columbia, James W. Rouse, expressed this philosophy most succinctly:

> Personally, I hold . . . that people grow best in small communities where the institutions which are the dominant forces in their lives are within the scale of their comprehension and within reach of their sense of responsibility and capacity to manage. (quoted in Eichler and Kaplan, 1967, pp. 55–56)

The strong neighborhood, with its emphasis on local decision making and community commitment is, however, not uniformly viewed as desirable. This is illustrated by the following comment from a newcomer to Reston:

> It didn't take long to find out what it was about. We were burdened with several layers of government which we felt were not necessary. We lived among 27 attached houses which was called a cluster. The cluster association bought the street and made it private. They also planted trees in our yard and didn't tell us anything about it. We didn't want the trees. There was a terrible imposition into our life. (quoted in Wilson and Schulz, 1978, p. 331)

The diversity of life styles characteristic of the urban community suggest that such settings are not appropriate for all urban residents. In addition, while many urban scholars judge these projects desirable, they are costly. In American society these costs are borne primarily by the individual home owner. Thus in the Columbia project less than 10 percent of the homes are affordable to middle-income groups. Perhaps more to the point, however, the philosophy of the new town is based on a questionable assumption—that cities are not worth saving.

A Look Into the City's Future

The political and economic climate of the 1980s suggests that few dramatic steps will be taken to alleviate the urban crisis. However, there is reason for optimism about the urban future (La Gory and Pipkin, 1981).

At present several trends in the societies of Western nations signal the resurgence rather than the

Suburbs are more homogeneous than cities. Residents are younger, married with children, have higher incomes, and hold white-coller jobs. These characteristics suggest that suburbanites have a life style that puts great value on nuclear family and that they believe suburban residence provides a better environment for raising children.

demise of the city. These trends include increasing energy costs, the decline in the proportion of the married population, the general reduction in median family size, and the growth of the female labor force. While the suburbs were attractive to the parents of the "baby boom" generation, couples today are electing to have fewer or none at all. The interest in child bearing and-rearing exhibited in the 1950s and 1960s has been tempered in the 1980s by the crises of unemployment and inflation. Because of this shift in life style concerns away from the home and toward the career, city residence is likely to become more attractive.

Cities are good environments for career-oriented and consumption-minded life styles. The life-style attraction of the urban environment has already stimulated neighborhood revitalization in many medium- and large-sized older cities in the Northeast and North Central regions of the United States. In some communities the lure of easy access to central city shopping and cultural facilities has encouraged a trend of **regentrification**, in which middle-class, career-oriented couples have purchased and rehabilitated deteriorated housing in zone 2 areas of the city.

Supporters of regentrification believe it should be encouraged because cities and the urban poor alike may benefit. The tax base should expand in a regentrified city. If the tax base expands, the city will be able to expand its services to the poor. Also, if suburbia begins to be a less desirable residential area for a portion of the middle class, the urban poor may find housing available in the older suburbs of the metropolis. When this happens the mismatch between the underemployed's skills and the availability of jobs may partially resolve itself. These presumed benefits of regentrification remain to be demonstrated. It is true that an expanded tax base can result in improved services to the poor. But will the new revenue be so used?

While it is still too early to tell, it is possible that a new period of urban revitalization is on the horizon. Perhaps it will soon be possible to respond to the critics who have pronounced the city dead by paraphrasing Mark Twain: "We have heard the news of the city's death and can say that it is much exaggerated."

SUMMARY

The city is different from the community, because the city lacks cultural cohesiveness, and it is also different from the metropolitan area, which is the larger area (including suburbs) that is tied economically to the city. Cities have existed for over 5000 years, although the preindustrial is different from the industrial city. Before industrialization cities were smaller, less diverse economically, and poorer residents lived farther away from the center of the city.

There are a number of theories that try to explain how cities grow. Concentric zone theory states that cities grow in concentric bands or zones starting at the city center and working outward. Sector theory sees cities growing along major transportation routes. Multiple nuclei theory suggests that the pattern of growth in a given city is influenced by specific historic and geographic conditions, making it unlikely for cities to grow in similar ways.

The social and psychological significance of urban life for its residents may be viewed in two ways. One view sees urban dwellers as isolated and alienated, because of the transient population, the large number of strangers, and the diversity of behavior patterns. Another view sees strong, supportive subcultures built around ethnic neighborhoods. The urbanite is not alone but has close, personal relationships while living surrounded by a larger number of strangers.

Major differences exist today between cities and their surrounding suburbs. The city contains a more diverse population, including educated professionals, childless people, and ethnic subgroups who live there by choice. It also includes the elderly and poor who are trapped in the city. Suburbia is more homogeneous, containing young, educated, higher-income families with children.

The interests of central city residents and suburbanites are often in conflict. There are also differences between the two areas in terms of their patterns of crime, job opportunities, and quality of services. Some analysts have noted that the city continues to pay for many of the services that suburbanites use but do not pay for.

The future of the city and the suburb will require

a new set of economic and political relationships between the two areas. It is also possible that the city will begin to lure middle-class, childless people back to a life style that is only possible in the city.

GLOSSARY

City   a large, densely populated, permanently settled territory whose population engages primarily in nonagricultural pursuits.

Concentric zone theory   cities grow in concentric bands or zones starting at the city center and working outward.

Megalopolis   a number of contiguous metropolitan areas.

Metropolitan area   an urban area extending beyond the legal city limits, the residents of which carry out their daily activities in the central city.

Multiple nuclei theory   the pattern of growth in a given city is influenced by specific historic and geographic conditions, making it unlikely for cities to grow in similar ways.

Regentrification   upgrading of a city neighborhood by middle-class, career-oriented people who purchase and rehabilitate deteriorating housing.

Sector theory   cities grow along major transportation routes from the city center outward.

Standard Consolidated Area   several contiguous SMSAs and additional counties that have strong social and economic relationships.

Standard Metropolitan Statistical Area (SMSA)   a city of 50,000 or more including the county in which it is located and all contiguous counties in which residents have close economic ties with the central county.

ADDITIONAL READINGS

Dorman, Michael. *The Making of a Slum*. New York: Delacorte Press, 1972.
A series of brief, personal accounts of people living in Hunts Point, a section of New York City that is described by the author as "perhaps the worst urban jungle in the United States— teeming with filth, misery, narcotics addicts, thieves, looters, and killers."

Geller, Evelyn, ed. *Saving America's Cities*. New York: H. W. Wilson Company, 1979.
A collection of readable papers dealing with the economic, political, and social problems of cities, including the shift of industry and population from the snowbelt to the sunbelt and the role of the federal government in solving these problems.

Hannerz, Ulf. *Exploring the City: Inquiries Toward an Urban Anthropology*. New York: Columbia University Press, 1980.
A look at the city from the perspective of an anthropologist. The author reexamines the work of the early Chicago school of urban sociology, and the studies of urban areas of Central Africa by British social anthropologists. A chapter dealing with the city as a complex web of social networks is especially valuable.

Meadows, Paul, and Ephraim H. Mizruchi, eds. *Urbanism, Urbanization, and Change*. Reading, Mass.: Addison-Wesley, 1976.
An extensive collection of articles on urban life. Especially valuable are Parts 3, 4, and 5, which deal with the character of life in the city.

Smith, Michael P. *The City and Social Theory*. New York: St. Martin's Press, 1979.
Examines many of the so-called "urban problems" as societywide problems. The work of five major theorists of urban culture is analyzed according to their view of urban conditions as frustrating or fulfilling basic human needs. Each theorist presents a different answer to the question: "What can be done to render the urban environment nonalienating?"

Vidich, Arthur, and Joseph Bensman. *Small Town in Mass Society*. Princeton, N.J.: Princeton University Press, 1968.
A study of small town life and its relationship to the influences of an urban society.

READINGS

[L]et us take a brief journey backward in time and visit a preindustrial city, not an actual one, but a kind of composite city—a mythical sort of place that brings together many of the sights and sounds we might have seen and heard had we been able to visit a wide range of settlements across a broad spectrum of time. This will be, by no means, a complete tour. We shall not enter the homes or other private sectors of the city but shall concentrate our attention on what is happening in its public parts, especially in its streets. And even after so limiting ourselves, we shall not have time to see and hear everything that might be seen or heard. We must be content with merely "getting a sense" of the flavor of a kind of city living very unlike anything we are apt to have known.

Picture yourself then, a modern urban human, dropped by means of a time machine, in the midst of some mythical composite preindustrial city. You are struck, first of all, by the sheer amount of activity there. Merchants, operating out of little cubbyholes, have spread their wares in the street. Next to them, a school of some type appears to be in session and you wonder how the students can concentrate. A wandering vendor is coming toward you, shouting out the wonders of his wares, and out of the hubbub of the street noises, you can just make out the shouts of other wandering vendors moving through the other streets. A man stops the vendor and they begin haggling over the price of an item. Then you notice that the more immobile merchants are also engaged in such haggling, some of it of

SOURCE: From A WORLD OF STRANGERS: ORDER AND ACTION IN URBAN PUBLIC SPACE, by Lyn H. Lofland, Copyright © 1973 by Basic Books, Inc., New York. Reprinted by permission of the publisher.

long duration. Here and there, such an encounter has drawn a crowd and bystanders have involved themselves in the interaction. Everyone is shouting, with many insults passing back and forth.

Down the street, a beggar, his eyes obviously sightless, his face scarred by burns, keeps up a steady stream of requests for aid. As you pass through the streets you note that they are teeming with beggars. Some appear to be members of religious orders, others are lame or maimed, but many seem to have no bodily afflictions. Of the beggars, many are children; some are with adults, but large numbers "work" alone.

You turn a corner and are struck with a sight repulsive to your modern eyes: a man has been nailed by his ear to a door. Upon inquiry, you discover that this is his punishment for cheating his customers. He is a merchant and he has been nailed to the door of his own establishment. Now a huge cry attracts your attention and you turn another corner to discover three people, stripped naked, being driven through the streets with whips and brushes. Later, at the outskirts of the city, you see the remains of bodies hanging in chains in some sort of elevated cage. One or two of the chains support whole bodies, from the rest, hang only "quarters."

Back in the city itself, a wandering actor or street singer or story teller has attracted a crowd and is in the midst of a performance. In one plaza, you note a public reader who is droning on and on about absolutely nothing and you marvel at the patience of his listeners.

Suddenly a town crier appears, shouting to all he passes that a fire is underway at such and such a place. You follow the crowd and, arriving at the scene, watch the citizenry attempt to cope with the flames. No one special seems to be in charge, and efforts to either contain or put out the fire appear hopeless. People are bringing things from their houses to help—bowls or buckets—running to the well with them and running back to toss the water on the flames. All is chaos. Eventually, after destroying many of the buildings in the area where it started, the fire burns itself out.

Watching the people running for water, you follow them and stop awhile at a nearby well or fountain, where you see men and women bathing, washing clothes, exchanging gossip. You see men with large buckets come by to fill their containers and then hurry off to deliver the water to nearby houses. And you see women coming with jars to get their own water.

The initial shock of this strange place having begun to wear off, you begin to note things that at first did not attract your attention. The sheer filth of the streets appalls you. Everywhere there seems to be refuse, garbage, human and animal excrement. And then you note for the first time the large numbers of animals in the streets—pigs eating the garbage, insects attracted to the excrement, dogs tearing at bones. There are larger animals too, horses and oxen drawing carts through the crowded, narrow streets, and other animals being driven to the marketplace. And everywhere children: playing in the streets, running up and down the narrow alleyways; taunting the lame and maimed beggars, poking sticks at an obviously feeble-minded man who is helpless to protect himself. Here and there they are joined in their ''games'' by an adult, and your modern ''sensitivities'' are stung by the discovery that human beings can find the suffering of others so amusing.

Suddenly, pushing its way through the crowd comes an enclosed litter. It is being carried by four huge men and is richly appointed. Surrounding it are four other men carrying weapons. Much of the crowd makes way for the litter as it passes. Those who do not do so voluntarily are pushed aside roughly by the guards. You cannot see inside but you are told by one of the passersby that this litter is carrying one of the city's elite.

Night begins to fall and more and more people disappear from the streets. No lamps light the impending darkness. The sounds diminish with the light and you are suddenly afraid. For a while, nothing stirs. You can hear the occasional step of the night-watch, patrolling the deserted streets, the occasional cry of the watchman that all is well. You move along. Suddenly you note that a huge gate within the city that had been open earlier in the day is closed and that a whole section of the city has been sealed off. You cannot enter that section for it is walled. Now, should this city you are visiting be like Rome, new sounds begin, and the carts and wagons banned from the streets during the day make their appearance, bringing into the city the supplies it needs to stay alive. The lanterns of these trains of wagons provide a welcome glow in the oppressing darkness, and the sounds of the ''teamsters' '' voices are comforting. But if this city is not like Rome, it is probable that very little beyond an occasional scream breaks the darkness and stillness of the night. Somehow you avoid the lurking men, waiting in the darkness to rob you if possible, to kill you if necessary. You move from place to place, stumbling here and there across the outstretched legs of sleeping men. These are the homeless ones, huddled against walls and doorways, seeking warmth and shelter from the night.

At last, morning comes. Life begins with daybreak. And now it seems that there are even more people on the streets than there were the day before. You learn that today is a holiday, one of the many throughout the year, a day of public ceremony and festivity. The actors, street singers, storytellers, readers, and beggars are out in even greater numbers and are attracting even greater crowds. Again, if this city is a ''Roman'' sort of place, you might go to the Coliseum or to the Circus Maximus to enjoy the amusements provided you by the rich and mighty of the city. But if it is not a "Roman" sort of city, the streets and plazas and squares themselves are likely to be turned into places of amusement. Perhaps there is some religious ritual; perhaps the elites will show themselves by parading through the streets. Perhaps there will be dancing or human sacrifice or animal sacrifice or battles between men or between men and animals or between animals. Or perhaps the spectacle will be as simple as watching someone beat a dog with a stick. But whatever there is to be seen, it will be enjoyed with great gusto. And it will be free.

Suddenly you feel tired. The multiplicity of sights and sounds, the pushing and shoving and shouting of the crowd, the smells—particularly the smells—all of this begins to seem "too much." Too many people are crowded into too small a space; too many odors, most of them offensive; too many sights, most of them vile. You can't get away from the beggars and vendors. They accost you wherever you go. You can't escape the crippled limbs, the scarred faces, the running sores. Your person seems never safe from the constant assaults of the pickpockets. Everything seems jumbled together. Rich and poor, health and disease, young and old, house and business, public and private. All seems disorder. All seems chaos. Dizzy, frightened, confused, you step back into the time machine and are returned again to what now seems the orderliness and cleanliness of your own crowded, carcongested, smogridden, crime-obsessed modern city.

SUMMARY
The preindustrial city contains great diversity of people and activities. Business and commerce are carried out in streets teeming with children and animals. Street singers and beggars move in the streets with the city's elite. Human sacrifice and animal sacrifice take place amidst scenes of incredible filth and unsanitary conditions. The chaos and disorder of the ancient city make our modern cities models of orderliness and cleanliness.

QUESTIONS
1. Are there any features of the preindustrial city that seem worth having in modern cities?
2. What are the disadvantages of modern cities that segregate different economic and racial groups, and different social and economic activities into separate areas?

READING 17.2
The Real Causes of Urban Decay
Richard S. Morris

[O]nce America's cities were her economic core. To their streets came millions of Americans in search of jobs, cultural opportunities, and a new life as well as tens of millions of immigrants from impoverished foreign shores. As recently as 1968, New York, Boston, and dozens of other cities had unemployment rates below the national average. Now almost every northeastern city experiences joblessness well above the national norm, some as much as 70 percent higher. From Newark to Minneapolis and Buffalo to Milwaukee, the cities of the Northeast were in desperate trouble. Unemployment was only one of their problems. Increasingly, inflation had devastated them far more than it had affected the rest of America. The same energy that costs $15 in Houston, one of the new cities of the Sun Belt, costs $37 in New York and $25 in Philadelphia and Boston. It costs $27,000 to live in New York or Boston at a life-style that costs only $18,500 in a rural southern town. . . .

SOURCE: From the book, BUM RAP ON AMERICA'S CITIES: THE REAL CAUSES OF URBAN DECAY by Richard S. Morris © 1978 by Richard S. Morris. Published by Prentice-Hall, Inc., Englewood Cliffs, NJ 07632.

This book argues that liberals are, indeed, taking a bum rap in shouldering the blame for the fiscal and economic decay of the American city. In attacking permissivism, labor unions, consumerism, social welfare, environmental concerns, and other favorite targets of the right, we miss the point. The cities are being punished by a very different cast of villains and are suffering at their hands far more profoundly and far more permanently:

□ *The Welfare Profiteers:* Eighty percent of all money spent on welfare in New York City in 1976 did not go to poor people but went instead to middle-class providers of service, many of whom overcharged for providing the poor with medical care, nursing homes, housing, and social services. They are the true welfare cheats, and it is to reducing the cost of their services that we must look to contain the social welfare budget.

□ *The Banks.* Right-wing mythology argues that the banks decided to withdraw from lending to American cities in 1975, recoiling in horror at the imbalance of the New York City budget and determined to protect their depositors from loss. The facts indicate that the banks withdrew from the cities in *1973*, well before there was any basis for concluding that cities were in trouble. The data indicates that banks more precipitated the urban fiscal crisis by driving up debt service costs than reacted to it once it was in full swing.

□ *Mortgage Lenders.* Urban real estate is in desperate trouble not because of rent control laws— most cities don't even have them—but because of redlining, the refusal of mortgage lenders to invest in inner-city neighborhoods. Behind redlining lies the federal government. In 1975 Washington channeled 29 percent of its loan insurance to three states—Florida, California, and Arizona—which had, together, 15 percent of the country's population. By insuring loans in the Sun Belt and not in the Northeast, Washington led the way for the bank redlining of American cities.

□ *The Income Tax System.* So prejudicial are the deductions and exemptions afforded in the federal tax law to urban taxpayers that the citizens of New York City paid 6.8 percent of all federal income tax collections while they comprised only 3.6 percent of the national population. Renters cannot deduct property taxes and mortgage interest payments; homeowners can. Gasoline taxes are deductible, but urban energy-use taxes are not.

□ *The Pentagon.* The federal defense budget is a subsidy to the South. With only 38 percent of the nation's population, the Sun Belt states get 50 percent of the defense budget. But the states of the Northeast, with 45 percent of the people, must be content with only 28 percent of the defense budget. These allocations drain wealth away from the Northeast and encourage the Sun Belt boom.

□ *The Social Security System.* By failing to adjust its benefits for the radical differences in the regional cost of living in the North and in the Sun Belt which have arisen in recent years, federal programs such as Social Security, veterans' benefits, and food stamps pay more to the South, in real dollars, than they do to the North.

□ *Energy Policy.* The Northeast faces a dire energy crisis. The rest of America has realized an energy bonanza as their cost of power has dropped far below that of the Northeast, bringing jobs, migrants, and corporations to the South in search of cheaper gas and oil.

Together, these problems saddle the Northeast with an insufferable economic and fiscal burden. They militate for a higher cost of living in the Northeast, higher taxes, fewer jobs, less income, and fewer government services. The fifteen states of the Northeast send to Washington $44 billion more in taxes than they get back in spending. The fifteen states of the Sun Belt get back from Washington $36 billion more in *spending* than they pay in *taxes*. Such a gap between the regions is the true cause of the urban fiscal and economic crisis. It is the true area in which we must make progress if we are to allow our cities to survive and recover. It is time to stop embracing slogans about welfare cheats and liberal excesses that have no meaning. We must rivet our attention on the real enemies of our cities and move ahead from there.

SUMMARY
The problems of the city are the result of conservative political policies that have reduced federal subsidies to cities. Many economic problems can be traced to actions of banks that withheld loans, from unfair antiurban tax laws, and from federal spending that flows disproportionately to the Sun Belt. These policies contribute to a higher cost of living, high taxes, fewer jobs, and fewer government services for cities in the Northeast.

QUESTIONS
1. How can American cities be revitalized through actions of the government?
2. Do the Republican and Democrat parties differ in their support for cities?

CHAPTER 18

Population

CONTENTS

Are fertility control programs the answer to the problems of less-developed nations?

During the last 30 years many organizations in the United States and other modern nations have provided birth control education and technology for many countries throughout the world. These programs are based on the belief that population growth should and must be stopped if poor nations are ever to achieve a decent standard of living and, indeed, if such growth is not to outstrip the world's resources.

There is not complete agreement about these programs, however, either in the United States or in less-developed nations. Those who support birth control programs and those who think they are unimportant or unnecessary have convincing arguments to support their views.

YES The world faces a crisis of unbelievable proportions. The world's population has doubled in 50 years; at present rates of population growth it will double again—to nine billion people—by the year 2025. Research has made control of fertility not only possible but easy, inexpensive, and effective. Evidence from people in many nations indicates concern about improving the quality of their lives and a real desire for contraceptives to limit births. Clearly, a worldwide emphasis on fertility control is essential, for several reasons.

First, the world has limited resources for supporting human life. Estimates vary, but most experts suggest that seven billion people is the maximum number that can be supported with adequate supplies of food, shelter, and other necessities of life. This limitation of size is absolute. If we are to avoid a world catastrophe of starvation, disease, and death, the absolute number of people on earth must be limited.

Second, the countries that have lower birthrates and less crowding tend to be the developed countries. This is not an accident of history but indicates the importance of small populations for economic and social development. The overwhelming impact of population on the lesser-developed countries will prevent them from achieving the quality of life for their people that would be possible with fewer numbers.

Third, there is a moral issue. One of the basic beliefs of Western societies is that people should have control of their lives, and contraceptives are one important means of achieving control over the burden of childbearing for women. Fertility control is important because it increases the range and number of choices for people and allows them to develop and to achieve both personal and family goals that uncontrolled fertility prevents.

NO Predictions of world catastrophe through overpopulation have been made for nearly 200 years. The most recent efforts to persuade people of future catastrophe have included worldwide programs of education about the value of birth control and distribution of contraceptives to women, especially in poorer, less-developed countries. Such programs should be resisted for at least three reasons.

First, the emphasis on overpopulation and scarcity of resources underestimates the adaptive abilities of humans. Not only has population increased dramatically since 1950 but so have new, more efficient ways to produce food, to distribute goods and resources, and to organize human life. Thus the known world resources are greater now than in 1950; more people are sharing in the medical and economic benefits of modern research with the result that they are healthier and have longer life expectancy than ever before; the world's population has more food for consumption than in 1950—all of which is due to the creativity, intelligence, and adaptability of humans.

Second, the emphasis on population control comes from the developed countries and is an effort to maintain their privileges and advantages. The most important resource for economic development in any society is its people. A larger population will enable less-developed nations to challenge the current distribution of wealth and power more effectively than a small population. Naturally, then, the developed nations want to keep these populations small.

Third, the export of birth control programs that developed nations justify as a moral necessity are really acts of coercion, or efforts to control other countries. History suggests that people will lower their fertility as their societies achieve economic and social stability. Developed nations—if they wish to be involved with issues of population—should help less-developed countries achieve economic levels that will reduce fertility naturally.

Advocates of fertility control programs cite the limits of our planet to support human life, the importance of quality of life for individuals, and the increased choices that such control provides. Those who do not support such programs emphasize human adaptability, the desire to maintain advantages for the developed countries, and the coercive aspects of contraception programs.

This chapter attempts to answer some of the questions raised by these arguments.

Why does population grow more rapidly in less-developed nations? Is there really a natural order that limits population size? What factors affect population growth? Can human ability overcome the survival problems that will come with populations twice as large as the world presently has?

QUESTIONS TO CONSIDER

- Why has world population grown so rapidly since 1950?

- Why do developed nations have lower birthrates than less developed nations?

- What are the effects of uncontrolled fertility?

- What are the natural limits to population growth?

Polly, a former student of one of the authors, who graduated in 1982, was married recently. In talking with the author before the wedding she proudly announced that she and her future husband had agreed to have a lot of children—at least 10—if possible. Though it remains to be seen if they will have 10 children, Polly and her husband have decided that the value of having several children is greater than the cost. Companionship among siblings, a desire for love, happiness and fulfillment, a wish to continue the family line, a need for help in old age, or recognition from friends and kin are often motives for having more than one child (Espenshade, 1977).

Ideals and social pressures are important elements in determining fertility levels. In the United States, where the ideal family often includes a son and a daughter, the birth of a second son or a second daughter may encourage a couple to have a third child, or a fourth if the third is also of the same sex as the first two. How many children would you have to fulfill your ideal? If you wanted at least one son and one daughter, would you have four or five—or even seven—children to reach that goal?

Such questions are at the heart of population concerns. Attitudes toward children, government policies that raise or lower the costs of having children, and expectations about the future are significant factors in population growth or decline.

During most of human history the prevailing idea in most societies was that large and growing populations were both desirable and possible. Population size typically was equated with political power and military strength, and the potential for population growth was believed to be limitless because of the abundance of natural resources.

After World War II this view began to change when it was recognized that many nations were growing at rates more rapid than ever before in human history. Most of these nations were poor, economically underdeveloped, and had just emerged from years of colonial rule. As the imbalance of food supplies and growing population continued, evidence of severe malnutrition and poverty—even starvation—in large areas of Asia and Africa and in pockets of Latin America has created concern about an ever-expanding population. This awareness of the problems brought by a growing population has also stimulated the study of factors that affect population, called demography.

THE DEMOGRAPHIC PERSPECTIVE

The objective study of population began in the seventeenth century (Thomlinson, 1976), and since that time it has developed into a specialized discipline characterized by a distinctive set of concepts, analytic techniques, and explanatory theories. **Demography** is the analysis of a population by size or number of people, territorial distribution or where they live, and composition or social characteristics, such as occupation and marital status. Demographers also study the components of population change—natality (birthrates) and mortality (death rates). Population change also occurs from territorial movement or migration.

Basic Demographic Variables

The significant features of a population may be divided into two categories: population structure and population processes.

Population structure variables includes size, distribution, and composition. The definition of population size is simply the number of people in an area. The concepts of population distribution and composition are somewhat more complex. Population distribution refers to the pattern of people's location in physical space. Although it is conceivable that members of a population might be evenly distributed throughout the area available to them, such a pattern almost never occurs. Instead, people tend to cluster together and to organize social activities for purposes of collective survival. A population may also be described in terms of the characteristics of its members. This feature, typically labeled population composition, includes such diverse attributes as age, sex, marital status, occupation, education, and religion.

If a population could be "frozen" at a given moment, as in a snapshot, it could be described to an outsider by identifying its structural features—how many members it contains (size), how those members are dispersed in space, whether they are in villages, towns, or cities (distribution), and what kinds of people it contains, identified by sex, ratio of women to men, their ages, marital status, occupation and income, and the like (composition).

Demographic analysis typically goes beyond the mere description of population structure to the factors directly influencing size, distribution, and composition. These factors are the **population processes** of natality (more often labeled fertility), mortality, migration, and social mobility. To illustrate the use of these concepts in the analysis of a population, we will use an isolated area with fixed geographic boundaries, like the island of Tahiti. The size of its population can change only through four processes: birth, death, in-migration or immigration, and out-migration or emigration. The **distribution** of the population—its location in physical space—similarly is a function of these four variables. The **composition** of the population is also influenced by births, deaths, and migrations, but a more significant factor in composition change is change in the inhabitants' characteristics. When people marry, divorce, or separate, when they change their jobs or religion, or when they receive advanced training or education, they become socially mobile—they move from one marital, occupa-

tional, religious, or educational group to another—altering the composition of the population.

The relationship of the various demographic variables to population change may be summarized in a simple equation:

$$P_1 + (B - D) + (I - E) + e = P_2$$

In this equation P_1 is the size of the population at one time and P_2 is the size of the population at some later time. B is the number of births and D is the number of deaths that occurred between the two times. I refers to the number who immigrated and E to the number of people who emigrated. Error in recording these figures is e, though this is usually unknown. Any real difference in the size of the population between two dates will be due to natural change, or the balance of births and deaths, and net migration. Suppose that the size of a population is 10,000 in 1970 and 11,000 in 1980, and that during this decade there were 800 births and 400 deaths. Net migration could then be determined as follows (N is the net number of migrants):

$$10,000 + (800 - 400) + N = 11,000$$

We see that 600 people were added to the population through migration.

The principal use made of the demographic equation is to estimate one unknown component of population change when data are given for the other components. It is also possible to use this equation in assessing changes in population composition. Finally, by estimating the number of future births, deaths, migrations, and compositional changes, future population characteristics can be predicted.

Data and Methods of Population Analysis

Demographic data are obtained from four primary sources. National governments conduct **population censuses** periodically to record the number of inhabitants, their characteristics, and their location. However, the nations of the world vary considerably in the periods for which census data are available, the number of years between censuses, the types of information collected, and the completeness and accuracy of the counts (Thomlinson, 1976).

Information about populations and their characteristics are essential to adequate planning and preparation for human services. Most nations combine various types of data collection by recording marriage licenses registration of births and deaths, and divorce decrees as these events occur, and taking periodic censuses of the entire population.

Although a few European nations and the United States began systematic census taking during the eighteenth century, most nations of the world began collecting such data only within the last 100 years. The United States took the first official census in 1790, and a new census has been taken every 10 years since that time.

Vital registration systems record certain population events as they occur. They typically include aggregate data on live births, deaths, marriages, divorces, legal separations, annulments, and adoptions. Unfortunately, except in the more indus-

trialized nations, these systems do not always give accurate information. Uncounted births and deaths continue to be a major problem.

Population registers are used in some countries, for example, Denmark, Israel, Norway, Sweden, and the U.S.S.R. for the continuous recording of individual events and changes in individual characteristics. Such registers are an ongoing source of data about marriages, divorces, births, deaths, or other changes, which enables governments to plan services as these changes occur.

The fourth major source of population data is the

sample household survey, which is used increasingly to supplement and check information provided by censuses and vital registration systems. These surveys are especially useful in nations for which standard sources of demographic data are known to be unreliable. In the United States current population surveys are conducted to provide data about the population between the censuses.

In spite of recent attempts to expand and improve the collection of demographic information, our knowledge of the size, rate of growth, distribution, and composition of populations is not precise. This is especially true in the less well-developed nations where 70 percent of the world's population lives. Demographers use a variety of measures, including distributions, rates, and ratios, to analyze population characteristics and events.

Distributions show the absolute numbers or percentages of a population with various characteristics, for example, the number or percentage of people married, divorced, or separated; employed or unemployed; of teenage, childbearing, or retirement age. **Rates** represent the number of times an event like birth, death, marriage, or migration occurs in a population over a period of time. Crude rates show incidence of an event for a specified period, typically one year. For example, **crude birthrate** (CBR) is the number of births in a year divided by the number of people in the total population. For ease of reporting and comparisons, this percentage is usually stated as a rate of births per 1000 people in the population being described. So if 6207 babies are born in one year in a population of 245,693, the CBR would be

$$\frac{6027}{245,693} \times 1000 = \frac{24.5 \text{ births}}{\text{per 1000 population}}$$

The problem with crude birthrates is that total population shown in the denominator includes men, children, and old women—people who either do not or are not likely to bear children. To get around this problem specific rates are limited to subgroups that are more likely to experience the particular event. For example, the **age-specific birthrate** (ASBR) for a population is the number of births in a year per number of women of certain ages. Usually, this

rate is calculated for women of childbearing age, generally those who are between 15 and 44. If, in our example population, there are 63,880 women ages 15–44, the ASBR for the same number of births in a year would be

$$\frac{6027}{63,880} \times 1000 = \frac{94.3 \text{ births per 1000}}{\text{women of childbearing age}}$$

This ratio of births for all women of childbearing age in a population is also often referred to as the **fertility rate.**

Finally, **ratios** are used to indicate the relative sizes of various population categories. For example, the sex ratio describes the number of males per 100 females, the child-woman ratio shows the number of children under age 5 per 100 women of childbearing age, and the dependency ratio identifies the number of younger and/or older persons in the population per 100 of the middle-age groups.

THEORIES OF POPULATION

Demographic analysis involves more than a description of population characteristics and trends. A variety of theories have been developed to explain the causes and consequences of variations in population size, growth, distribution, and composition (Eversley, 1959; Goldscheider, 1971; Hutchinson, 1967; United Nations, 1973). In this section we will briefly summarize some of the more influential theoretical approaches to the study of population change.

The Malthusian and Marxian Approaches

In 1798 the Reverend Thomas Malthus published his now famous "Essay on the Principle of Population." By 1826 the book had gone through five revisions. The final edition was published posthumously in 1872 (see Malthus, 1963). The Malthusian argument is based upon two basic assumptions: (1) that food is necessary to the existence of man and (2) that the passion between the sexes is necessary and will remain in its present state. The substance of Malthus's concern was the relationship between population growth and the food supply, although he recognized that other resources were necessary for human survival. He based his views on three propositions:

1. Population is necessarily limited by the means of subsistence.
2. Population invariably increases where the means of subsistence increase, unless prevented by some very powerful and obvious checks.
3. These checks, and the checks which repress the superior power of population and keep its effects on a level with the means of subsistence, are all resolvable into moral restraint, vice and misery (p. 3–6).

The "preventive checks" of moral restraint and vice included delayed marriage, sexual abstinence to prevent the birth of children, extramarital relations, and prostitution. The "positive checks" of misery included epidemics, wars, plagues, and famines. Malthus concluded that without these checks human population would increase geometrically, that is, by doubling (1, 2, 4, 8, 16, 32, 64), while the means of subsistence would increase arithmetically, or by simple addition (1, 2, 3, 4, 5, 6, 7).

The essay provoked substantial controversy. Malthus was criticized for (1) unduly emphasizing the limited supply of land, (2) underestimating the potential of inventions and technological innovations for counteracting the effects of population growth, (3) overlooking non-European countries as sources of markets, labor, and raw materials, and (4) failing to recognize the possible benefits of widespread birth control (Thomlinson, 1976). Nevertheless, the issues raised by Malthus set the stage for the development of modern population theories. Furthermore, the food/population dilemma remains and is becoming more serious, as Malthus suggested it would (Hartley, 1972).

Among the more influential reactions to Malthusianism is the position formulated by Karl Marx and amplified by his followers (Meek, 1971). Marx argued that overpopulation is an apparent consequence of the capitalist economic system. Because it depends on surplus labor and needs an ever-expanding pool of consumers, capitalism can survive only so long as population continues to grow. For

For many years, world relief organizations have attempted to provide food to many people living in countries that are unable to produce enough for their citizens. Such activities are often necessitated by war and famine, and are cited by some people as evidence that Malthus was right.

Marx and his followers overpopulation does not constitute a major problem; rather, the problem is unequal distribution of goods and services under the prevailing capitalist system of ownership.

The Demographic Transition and Multiphasic Response Theories

Both the Malthusian and Marxian approaches to problems of population growth were based on imperfect understanding of demographic trends and relationships. Modern theorists examine the data gathered about population change and attempt to arrive inductively at a set of broad explanatory principles. One such principle, generally referred to as the "theory of the demographic transition," was developed in the early part of this century (Thompson, 1929) and was subsequently reformulated as new knowledge became available (Abu-Lughod, 1964; Beaver, 1975; Cowgill, 1963; Davis, 1945; Taeuber, 1966; Weinstein, 1976).

The **demographic transition theory** postulates three types of societies defined in terms of the balance between birth and death rates. In *traditional* societies both birth and death rates are high, and thus population growth (natural increase) is minimal. *Transitional* societies are characterized by high birthrates but declining death rates, and it is this change in death rates that produces population growth. *Modern* societies, in which both birth and death rates are low, again show a low rate of natural increase.

The demographic theory is evolutionary in that it hypothesizes that all societies are initially traditional, then transitional, and ultimately modern. This model is based on the demographic experience of Western societies and mirrors their historical development. Modern industrialized societies currently exhibit low rates of growth, and in all of them the sequence of population events showed a decline in the death rate before a decline in the birthrate.

The explanation for the demographic transition is a series of changes in the technological, social, cultural, economic, and demographic bases of society. Mortality rates declined because of improvements in sanitation, nutrition, medical treatment, and standards of living. The reduction in birthrates is harder to explain but involves changes accompanying the rise of urbanization, industrialization, social mobility, individualism, and female emancipation. Figure 18.1 illustrates the Malthusian and demographic transition approaches to population growth.

One attempt to expand the demographic transition theory of population change is Davis's (1963) multiphasic response theory. This theory emphasizes the active role of people in altering their demographic circumstances. Davis cites post-World War II Japan as an example of a nation whose leaders, recognizing that Japan's population was growing too rapidly for its limited land area and resources, offered families options and inducements for controlling fertility. Population policy in contemporary China also offers inducements for small families. For example, families with one child receive a government allotment to assist with additional costs, with a second child the allotment is one-half of that received with the first child.

There is no single comprehensive theory of population change. Malthus correctly recognized that, if left unchecked, population will grow faster than the means of subsistence, but he did not foresee that technological and economic innovations could forestall the time of crisis. Marx argued that a more equitable distribution of goods and services would eliminate overpopulation, but he did not consider the increased demands for goods and services and consumption of resources in modern societies. Thus, he failed to recognize that even under socialism or communism the earth's resources ultimately would become scarce. The transition theorists developed through observation and experience a model of demographic changes that followed the Industrial Revolution, but the applicability of the model may be limited to societies undergoing early industrialization. Davis's explanation accurately portrays the experience of one modern nation, and perhaps even a few others, but multiphasic response does not describe the experiences of many nations.

The demographer, then, attempts to quantify, describe, and explain a limited set of population var-

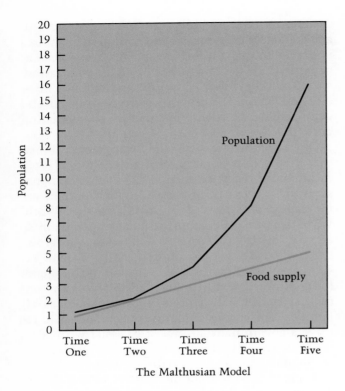

FIGURE 18.1   The Malthusian and
the Demographic-Transition
Approaches to Population Growth

iables. The significance of population size and
growth is that satisfaction of basic human needs
occurs in a larger system of relationships involving
natural resources, environmental conditions, and
social organization.

POPULATION TRENDS

The world now faces a problem of providing a balance between the human population and its demands on the food supply, water, and and other

natural resources. To understand this problem better and to evaluate alternative solutions, it is necessary to examine demographic trends, particularly
those of the past three centuries.

The size of a population is significant because it
tells us how many people depend on available resources. The rate of growth tells us the speed at
which population size is changing and gives us a
clue to future demands for food, housing, jobs, and
so on. Population distribution measures the degree
to which people are concentrated in particular environmental settings. In short, these variables, examined historically, are indicators of the changing

pressure of population on the ability of a society to provide for that population. Other demographic variables—fertility, mortality, migration, and population composition—will be considered here only as they influence population size, rate of growth, and distribution.

Population Size and Growth: World Patterns

World population figures are incomplete, especially for the less-developed areas. The best source of figures is the United Nations Population Division through its annual publication, *The Demographic Yearbook*, and various special reports. According to figures gathered by the United Nations (1981) the earth's inhabitants totalled over 4,415,000 in 1980. While the first billion was not reached until

about 1850—after all of recorded history to that time—the second billion was achieved by 1925—in only 75 years! The three billion figure came in 35 years, 1960, and by 1975—only 15 years later—world population reached four billion.

Nearly three-fourths of the world's people live in the less-developed nations, as noted in Table 18.1. The most populated area is the continent of Asia. Asia, including China and India but not Russia, has a population of more than two and one-half billion—nearly 60 percent of the world's people. Approximate figures for other areas are as follows: Europe, 485 million; Africa, 470 million; Latin America, including Mexico, Central America, and the Caribbean, 370 million; North America, 250 million; and Oceania, including Australia and New Zealand, 23 million. The U.S.S.R., which covers areas of both Asia and Europe has about 266 million people (United Nations, 1981).

TABLE 18.1   World Population for Selected years, 1750–1980, Distinguishing the More Developed from the Less-Developed Regions

YEAR	POPULATION (MILLIONS)			ANNUAL RATE OF INCREASE SINCE PRECEDING DATE (PERCENT)[a]		
	WORLD TOTAL	MORE-DEVELOPED REGIONS	LESS-DEVELOPED REGIONS	WORLD TOTAL	MORE-DEVELOPED REGIONS	LESS-DEVELOPED REGIONS
1750	791	201	590	---	---	---
1800	978	248	730	0.4	0.4	0.4
1850	1262	347	915	0.5	0.7	0.5
1900	1650	573	1077	0.5	1.0	0.3
1910	1775	650	1125	0.7	1.3	0.4
1920	1837	682	1155	0.3	0.5	0.3
1930	2044	759	1285	1.1	1.1	1.1
1940	2267	821	1446	1.0	0.8	1.2
1950	2560	857	1649	0.9	0.4	1.2
1960	2995	976	2019	1.8	1.3	2.0
1970	3621	1074	2537	1.9	1.1	2.3
1980	4415	1120	3295	2.2[b]	0.4	3.0

SOURCE: Figures for 1750–1900 are from John D. Durand, "The Modern Expansion of World Population," *Proceedings of the American Philosophical Society 111* (June 22, 1967), pp. 136–159. Figures for 1900–1970 are reported in United Nations Secretariat, "Demographic Trends in the World and Its Major Regions, 1950–1970," Background Paper for World Population Conference, Bucharest, Romania, August 1974. Figures for 1980 are from *World Statistics in Brief*, United Nations, 1981.
[a]Exponential rates.
[b]Estimated rate of growth for 1980.

Another way of considering the distribution of the world's population is by political units or nations. As shown in Table 18.2 the 10 largest nations in 1980 had nearly two-thirds of the world's population. In fact, China and India alone account for more than 35 percent of the world total.

While the absolute size of the human population is an important consideration, a better indicator of the current population dilemma is the rate of growth. From Table 18.1 it is evident that, for the world as a whole, the annual rate of growth averaged less than 0.5 percent from 1750 through 1920 and about 1.0 percent for the period 1920–1950. Since 1950 this figure has averaged about 2.0 percent and has been gradually increasing.

We can note the wide variations in the rate of population change among the world's regional and national populations. Until 1930 the more-developed nations grew more rapidly, but since that year the less-developed nations have shown a faster rate of increase and the differential between the more- and less-developed areas has widened. As of 1980 the most rapidly growing regions were Africa and Latin America. Many less-developed nations like Algeria, Ecuador, Ghana, Honduras, Jordan, Mexico, and Zimbabwe have current annual rates of population growth of more than 3 percent. Most of the developed nations are increasing at rates below one percent. As of 1980 only five nations, Austria,

the Democratic Republic of Germany (East Germany), the Federal Republic of Germany (West Germany), United Kingdom of Great Britain and Northern Ireland, and Lebanon, exhibited a negative growth rate (United Nations, 1981).

It is useful to consider rates of growth and population size together. For example, the less-developed nations, with approximately 75 percent of the world's population and an average annual growth rate of 3.0 percent, will double in size in less than 25 years. The doubling time for the slower growing, more-developed nations will be more than 75 years at the current rate. Thus by the year 2000, the less-developed nations probably will have at least 75 to 80 percent of the world's six to eight billion inhabitants. However, population projections must be interpreted cautiously as they are based on the assumption that current patterns will continue.

Population growth is directly influenced by three demographic processes: fertility, mortality, and migration. With the exception of a few countries (Australia, Brazil, Canada, Israel, and New Zealand), net migration is not a major contributor to national population increase today. The influence of the other two variables, fertility and mortality, is best understood in the context of the demographic transition model. Figure 18.2 summarizes 200 years of birth and death rates for the more- and less-developed countries of the world. The more-

TABLE 18.2   The World's 10 Largest Nations (1980)

	POPULATION (MILLIONS)	PERCENTAGE OF WORLD TOTAL	CUMULATIVE PERCENTAGE
China	956.8	21.7	21.7
India	663.6	15.0	36.7
USSR	265.5	6.0	42.1
U.S.	227.6	5.2	47.9
Indonesia	151.9	3.4	51.3
Brazil	123.0	2.8	54.1
Japan	116.8	2.6	56.7
Bangladesh	88.7	2.0	58.7
Pakistan	82.4	1.9	60.6
Nigeria	77.1	1.7	62.3

SOURCE: United Nations *World Statistics in Brief*, 1981.

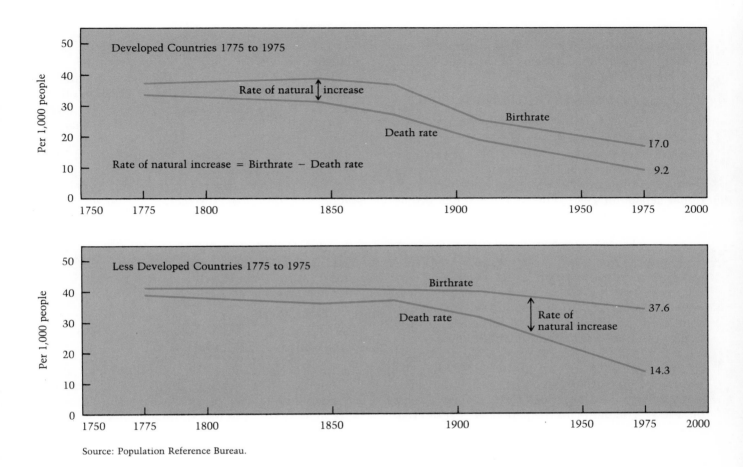

Source: Population Reference Bureau.

FIGURE 18.2   World Birth and Death
Rates (estimated)

developed nations show a gradual decline in the death rate beginning near the middle of the eighteenth century and a parallel, though slightly delayed, drop in the birthrate. The result has been that population growth, as indicated by the rate of natural increase, has slowly declined during the last 100 years. The demographic experience of the less-developed countries shows some important differences. First, mortality did not begin to drop until about 1875, but since that time the drop has been rapid, especially during the last 50 years. Second, birthrates for these countries have remained high and are currently at a level comparable with the birthrates of the more developed nations around 1875. Third, this combination of sharply declining death rates and high birthrates has resulted in the explosive rate of natural increase characteristic of the less-developed world during the twentieth century. The major factor underlying rapid world population growth today is the high birthrate in the poorer, less-developed nations of the world.

Population Growth in the United States

The first national census taken in the United States in 1790 showed a total population of fewer than four million inhabitants. A little more than a century later the census of 1900 recorded slightly more than 76 million people, while the most recent national census in 1980 showed 226,504,825 people (*Statistical Abstract*, 1981). U.S. population size has almost tripled in the last 80 years. It is estimated that by the year 2000, depending upon future birth trends, there will be between 245 and 287 million Americans (*Statistical Abstract*, 1981).

Growth rates for the U.S. population have fluctuated considerably. From 1790 to 1860 the average annual rate of increase was about 3 percent. At the beginning of this century the population was growing at a rate of just under 2 percent and reached an all-time low of 0.6 percent in the mid-1930s. The average rate for the "baby boom" years of the 1950s was 1.7 percent; this dropped to 1.2 percent during the 1960s. The figure for the period 1975–1980 was approximately 0.9 percent.

Two factors account for the uneven pattern of population growth in the United States: fluctuation in the birthrate and in the number of inhabitants gained through immigration. At the beginning of the twentieth century the crude birthrate was about 32 per 1000 population, declining to a low of 18.7 per 1000 by 1935. There followed a gradual upswing in this rate, which averaged 25 per 1000 from 1947 to 1957. Since then the crude birthrate decreased to a low of 14.8 in 1975, but by 1979 it had risen to 15.9 (*Statistical Abstract*, 1981). The effects of these changing birthrates are evident in Figure 18.3. Not only does the age pyramid indicate the higher death rates at older ages, but the low birth rate during the 1930s is reflected in the size of the population aged 40 to 49. This cohort has had some distinct advantages and benefits because of its smaller size relative to older and younger cohorts. This idea is explored at greater length in Reading 18.1.

Net migration reached its peak at the beginning of this century when 6.3 million people were admitted into the country between 1900 and 1910. The volume of immigrants dropped to 2.5 million during the next decade, rose to 3.2 million during the 1920s, and then fell sharply to 140,000 during the 1930s. The number of immigrants has increased during each decade since 1940. Immigrants totalled about 2.9 million between 1960 and 1970, and between 1970 and 1980 about 4 million people immigrated to the United States, many as political refugees (*Statistical Abstract*, 1981). Nevertheless, though the proportion of total population increase due to immigration has risen recently (17 percent for the period 1970–1980 compared with 9 percent for 1940–1950), it is still relatively small. As in most other countries population growth in the United States is primarily a function of the excess of births over deaths.

Distribution of Population

Although there are a number of ways in which population distribution patterns can be measured (Arriaga, 1975), two of the most useful indicators are density (the number of inhabitants per square kilometer) and degree of urbanization. Because the world's land area is relatively fixed (excluding minor gains from drainage and minor losses from flooding), population growth is translated into increased density, or more people per square kilometer. The more-developed areas had about 10 persons per square kilometer in 1920 and about 18 in 1970. A density of 22 per square kilometer is projected for the year 2000. Comparable figures for the less-developed areas are 16 and 34, with 62 predicted by the turn of the century (Hartley, 1972; United Nations, 1973). Obviously, population density is higher and is increasing at a much faster rate in the poorer nations.

The most dramatic shift in population distribution in modern times may be seen in the growth of urban communities (Figure 18.4). The proportion of the world's population living in communities of 5000 or more grew from a little more than 3 percent in 1800 to approximately 41 percent in 1980. For cities of 100,000 or more the increase from 1800

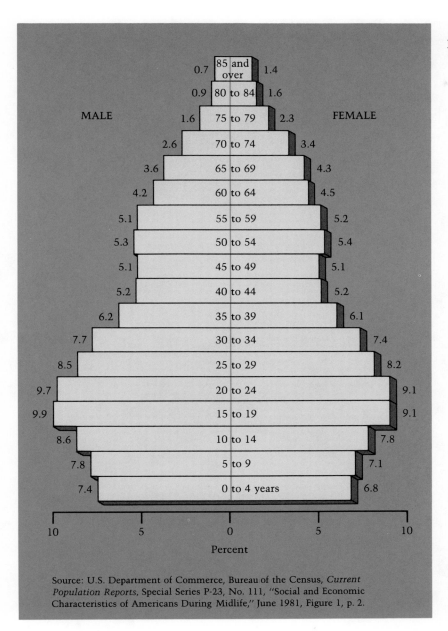

Source: U.S. Department of Commerce, Bureau of the Census, *Current Population Reports*, Special Series P-23, No. 111, "Social and Economic Characteristics of Americans During Midlife," June 1981, Figure 1, p. 2.

FIGURE 18.3 Distribution of the Population, by Age and Sex: July 1, 1979

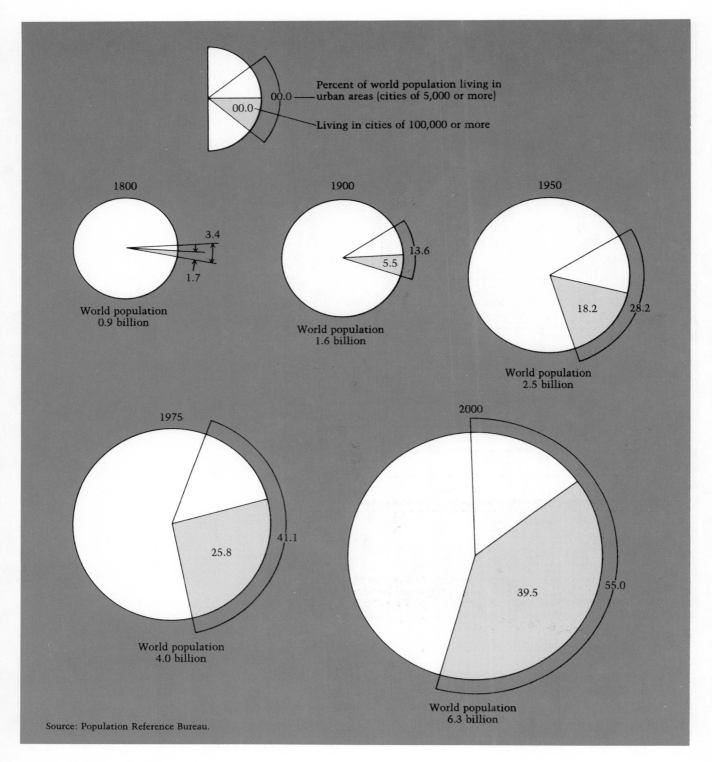

FIGURE 18.4   World Urbanization,
1800–2000

to 1980 was from slightly less than 2 percent to nearly 26 percent.

Not only is the proportion of the human population residing in urban areas growing but so is the absolute number of urban areas. For example, between 1950 and 1970 the number of urban areas with 20,000 or more inhabitants increased from 4973 to 9341, while the number of cities of 100,000 or more grew from 962 to 1777 (Davis, 1972). In short, the world is becoming increasingly urbanized, and there is no evidence to suggest a reversal in this trend.

While residence in large cities (populations of 100,000 or more) is still more characteristic of the more-developed nations, the rate of change is higher for those that are less developed. In the more-developed regions the proportion of the population in large cities grew from 30 percent in 1950 to 42 percent in 1970. The corresponding figures for the less-developed regions are 8 and 15 percent. By the year 2000 it is estimated that at least 10 cities—most of which are in less-developed countries—will have over 15 million people: Mexico City, 31.0 million; São Paulo, 25.8 million; Shanghai, 23.7 million; Tokyo-Yokohama, 23.7 million; New York, 22.4 million; Peking, 20.9 million; Rio de Janeiro, 19.0 million; Bombay, 16.8 million; Calcutta, 16.4 million, and Jakarta, 15.7 million (Population Reference Bureau, 1981).

Although the pattern of population distribution may be somewhat influenced by geographic features, government policies, and opportunities for employment, the most direct causes of population concentrations in urban areas are natural increase and net migration. In the past natural increase has generally been lower in urban areas due to lower birthrates, but, as a 1973 United Nations report noted, "it is now quite possible that the levels may be more nearly the same in both urban and rural areas" (p. 197). Where there is little or no rural-urban differential in natural increase, urban growth is accounted for by net migration.

In recent years less-developed nations have experienced a virtual flood of migrants from rural areas to the cities. For example, the net volume of rural-to-urban migration in Latin America between 1950 and 1960 has been estimated at 14.6 million

people (Ducoff, 1965). Sizable movements from villages and towns to the cities have also been reported for Africa (Hance, 1970), and similar patterns doubtless hold true for most of the other less-developed areas of the world (see United Nations, 1973). A more recent source (Eckholm, 1982) notes that between 1970 and 1980 the urban population of less-developed countries increased by 320 million city dwellers, an annual growth rate of 4 percent. The comparable growth rate for cities in the developed world is 1.2 percent.

Population density in the United States increased from just fewer than 2 persons per square kilometer in 1790 to 12 in 1920 and about 24 in 1980. By 2000 this figure will probably range between 28 and 31 persons per square kilometer. Thus, while U.S. population density is slightly greater than the average for the more-developed nations, it is considerably less than that for the less-developed areas of the world.

During the past 200 years the United States has undergone a drastic change in population distribution. The census of 1790 showed only 5 percent of the population living in urban areas of 2500 or more. By 1850 this figure had increased to only 15 percent. At the beginning of the twentieth century fully 40 percent of the population was classified as urban, and this trend has continued to the present. About three out of four Americans live in urban areas, according to the 1980 census.

A more realistic assessment of urbanization in the United States can be made by using the concept of the **standard metropolitan statistical area (SMSA)**. First used in conjunction with the 1960 census, the SMSA may be roughly defined as a central city of 50,000 or more inhabitants and any surrounding territory and residents that are metropolitan in character and economically and socially integrated with the central city (Bogue, 1969). In 1980 more than 70 percent of the U.S. population was living within an SMSA. While this was a small increase from 1970, the rural population also increased during the 1970s, signalling a future United States of several large urban areas that contain most of the population with a few rural areas between these cities.

During the early part of this century, the growth

of metropolitan areas was accounted for largely by rural-to-urban migration. In recent years, however, such growth has been primarily due to natural increase. "In the 1940's, net migration accounted for over 44 percent of total metropolitan increase, but in the 1950's this dropped to about 35 percent, and in the 1960's to 26 percent" (U.S. Bureau of the Census, 1974, p. 124).

POPULATION AND THE FUTURE

These demographic trends have important consequences for human societies. The larger the size and the higher the rate of growth of human populations, the greater are the demands for resources and the pressures placed on natural and social environments. Conversely, environmental limitations place constraints on the capacity for a territory to absorb future population growth and concentration.

The problems created by population growth are related to the inability of the world to absorb unlimited numbers of people. Increasing population size and concentration contributes to the growing scarcity of resources, to the degradation of life support systems, and to the breakdown of social institutions and services. The simultaneous occurrence of population growth and scarcity of resources point to future problems for the entire world.

Can the Relationship Between Growth and Scarcity Be Changed?

Perhaps the most important issue facing humankind today is whether the circular relationship between growth and scarcity be broken by human intervention. Biologist Rene Dubos (1976) suggests that a creative response to human needs and the requirements of the natural environment is possible—that human activities can be organized to promote long-term goals of both environmental protection and human survival. Generally, this will require collective efforts to interrupt the worldwide trends toward growth and scarcity. Specifi-

cally, there is a need to identify and evaluate the alternative organizational mechanisms through which stability between population levels and environmental resources might be achieved.

To assess the possibilities for change Micklin (1973) proposes that we examine the organizational processes through which a territorially based population adapts to the constraints of its demographic and environmental situations. The process of adaptation may involve an alteration of these demographic and environmental conditions either by conserving resources through growth limitation or by adjusting the internal social organization, that is, by changing patterns of distribution of wealth, food, or other resources in the population. In either case the goal of adaptation is to maximize conditions favorable to survival of the population.

Developments in science and technology have provided humankind with powerful means for influencing fertility and thus population growth. Most significant has been the demographic impact of improvements in nutrition, sanitation, and the prevention and treatment of disease. These advances have resulted in drastic reductions in the death rate and dramatic increases in life expectancy. These results are most evident in the less-developed countries, where mortality has declined during the past 40 to 45 years to a point comparable with that reached in 75 to 150 years in the more industrialized nations.

The widespread application of science and technology to fertility control—the development of oral contraceptives and intrauterine devices (IUDs) and surgical sterilization—is a relatively recent phenomenon (Thomlinson, 1975). During the past 25 years scientists have made great strides in providing relatively safe and effective means of preventing births (Hatcher et al., 1976; Kols et al., 1982). Recent evaluations suggest that modern contraceptives have been a major cause of sizable reductions in fertility in several less-developed nations (Freedman and Berelson, 1976). The desire to control family size is mediated partly by culture. As societies receive new influences and opportunities, collective cultural traditions that influence societal functioning may change, however slowly. These transformations of societal ideologies, norms, and values constitute another form of adaptation to the population-resources problem.

Death and illness are universally defined as undesirable conditions. Throughout history humans have tried to reduce the rate of death, increase the length of life, and eliminate disease and illness. The upper limit of the human life span may now have been reached, "because of inevitable biological deterioration of the organism at advanced ages" (United Nations, 1975, p. 188). For comparisons among populations deaths are usually defined in terms of *mortality rates*, or the number of deaths per 1000 population, and illness is usually defined by *morbidity rates*, a measure of amount of illness per 1000 population. Less-developed countries have higher mortality and morbidity rates than developed nations, because of lack of health care, poor nutrition, and generally poor economic conditions, though the gap has decreased in recent years. The desire to prolong life will continue to have demographic impact as the less-developed nations seek levels of health and lower death rates comparable with those enjoyed by industrialized nations.

ABORTION

In the United States conflicts about abortion and what constitutes life are evidence of the strong symbolic meanings attached to life. Some nations, like Japan, have a very liberal policy on abortion. In the United States there are two polar positions on the issue. On the one side is what has been described as the "prochoice" position, which states that abortion should be a private act based on the woman's decision. This view assumes that it is not possible to define life as beginning at conception or at any single point during pregnancy. On the other side is the "prolife" position, which states that abortion should be permitted only under very limited conditions, for pregnancies that have occurred by rape or incest or that are a threat to the woman's life. This view assumes that life is present at the moment of conception.

It should be recognized that because the sperm and the egg also are living, life is present in the components of reproduction itself. As a result there

can be no clear, empirical definition of when life begins because life is not produced, but is reproduced, by living sperm and living ova. This rationalization of fertility control that has been achieved through contraception as well as abortion is supported by general cultural values of equality for men and women.

Abortion, whatever the rationale for public policy, continues to have great symbolic significance in many societies. Because of contradictory cultural values—those that emphasize life and those that emphasize personal control—abortion is sure to be a point of controversy for many years.

FERTILITY CONTROL

There is much greater variation in normative orientations toward fertility than abortion. In traditional societies children, motherhood, and the family are highly valued. In part, these values reflect high infant and child mortality rates and the lack of social services for the aged. If one must depend on children for support in old age, it may be necessary to have seven or eight to guarantee that two or three will be alive to provide that support. As a result preferred family size is invariably large and the "normal" number of children in these societies may be quite high (Micklin and Marnane, 1975; Simmons, 1974). In industrialized societies norms favor considerably smaller families (Ryder and Westoff, 1971). Some students of population change (Davis, 1963; Micklin, 1969) have argued that an important component of the demographic transition observed in industrialized societies is a widespread redefinition of the value of children in relation to competing personal goals and motivations. Indeed, modern family-planning programs are based in part on changing the social meaning of reproductive behavior in ways that will lower fertility rates. The social meaning of children varies throughout the world. As Table 18.3 illustrates, children are more likely to be valued for their economic contributions in underindustrialized areas and for the satisfaction and fulfillment they bring to parents in industrialized settings. Class levels also affect how children are valued: rural parents are more likely to emphasize the economic cost of

TABLE 18.3 Advantages of Having Children
(Percentage of respondents who assigned first ranking to each of specific major code categories,
by socioeconomic group and country)

SES GROUP AND COUNTRY	HAPPINESS, LOVE, COMPANIONSHIP	PERSONAL DEVELOPMENT OF PARENT	CHILDREARING SATISFACTIONS	ECONOMIC BENEFITS, SECURITY	BENEFITS TO FAMILY UNIT	KIN GROUP BENEFITS	OTHER ADVANTAGES[a]
Urban Middle							
Korea	34	10	29	3	9	10	4
Taiwan	62	4	5	3	13	10	4
Japan	37	19	24	2	14	3	1
U.S. (Hawaii)							
Japanese	26	18	18	1	20	1	12
Caucasian	37	21	16	2	14	1	4
Philippines	38	11	4	30	12	1	3
Thailand	34	17	3	6	28	9	3
Urban Lower							
Korea	42	8	18	11	8	12	2
Taiwan	39	1	4	9	3	40	4
Japan	54	10	14	3	17	1	2
U.S. (Hawaii)							
Japanese	29	16	21	3	20	1	4
Caucasian	33	17	18	2	16	2	2
Filipino	62	3	3	15	11	2	2
Philippines	24	9	7	46	7	4	3
Thailand	15	4	1	66	3	8	3
Rural							
Korea	27	9	19	21	2	17	5
Taiwan	19	1	11	36	4	25	3
Japan	44	9	20	11	5	7	3
U.S. (Hawaii)							
Filipino	25	4	1	63	4	1	1
Philippines	23	6	7	60	2	*	2
Thailand	14	2	*	60	3	17	3

additional children, while urban middle-class families emphasize the restricting effects of children on activities.

Lowered fertility in many countries is a national or government goal, rather than simply a matter of personal choice. The accomplishment of lowered fertility levels frequently depends on the degree to which individual interests and activities can be co-ordinated. In most modern societies, where many groups pursue their interests through collective action, there have recently been coordinated attacks on the problems of population growth and the environment.

Associations dedicated to reductions in population growth include international bodies like the United Nations Fund for Population Activities (UNFPA) and the International Planned Parenthood Federation (IPPF), national family-planning associations, like the Planned Parenthood Association, and regional or local groups. An organization called Zero Population Growth (ZPG) is active in many parts of the United States and in Australia and Canada as well. Other organizations involved in population activities are the U.S. Agency for International Development (AID), the Ford Foundation, the Rockefeller Foundation, the Population

TABLE 18.3   (*cont.*) Disadvantages of Having Children

SES GROUP AND COUNTRY	FINANCIAL COSTS	EMOTIONAL COSTS	PHYSICAL DEMANDS ON PARENTS	RESTRICTIONS ON ALTERNATIVE ACTIVITIES	OTHER DISADVANTAGES[b]
Urban Middle					
Korea	20	35	4	28	13
Taiwan	17	53	5	25	*
Japan	10	30	2	50	8
U.S. (Hawaii)					
Japanese	8	26	1	35	2
Caucasian	16	25	2	39	7
Philippines	29	54	3	12	2
Thailand	32	51	8	7	2
Urban Lower					
Korea	41	41	3	13	2
Taiwan	35	47	5	14	*
Japan	8	41	3	48	*
U.S. (Hawaii)					
Japanese	22	18	3	38	4
Caucasian	20	30	*	21	*
Filipino	30	32	7	20	*
Philippines	34	50	1	13	2
Thailand	50	32	5	12	2
Rural					
Korea	42	44	4	8	2
Taiwan	49	34	9	9	*
Japan	14	53	2	28	3
U.S. (Hawaii)					
Filipino	81	11	2	1	1
Philippines	39	51	4	6	*
Thailand	42	21	28	9	*

[a]Includes social and religious influences, and the general and intrinsic value of children.

[b]Includes marital problems, kin group costs and problems of inheritance, societal costs and overpopulation.

*Less than 1 percent.

SOURCE: Thomas J. Espenshade, "The Value and Cost of Children," *Population Bulletin*, Vol. 32, No. 1 (Population Reference Bureau, Inc., Washington, D.C., 1977). Courtesy of the Population Reference Bureau, Inc., Washington, D.C.

Council, the Population Reference Bureau, the Population Crisis Committee—all based in the United States—and the Swedish Development Foundation.

These associations seek to curb population growth in one or more ways. First, they provide financial support for population research and the development of contraceptive technology. Second, they offer technical assistance to governments of less-developed countries that wish to initiate or reorganize family-planning programs. Third, they may partially or totally underwrite the costs of operating family-planning clinics, for example, by paying personnel or supplying contraceptives. Finally, during the past few years these organizations have increased their educational activities, especially through the schools.

POPULATION GROWTH AND PUBLIC POLICY

While interest groups have an obvious impact on the formulation and realization of societal goals, governments have an even more direct influence. Governments may commit their constituencies to goal-oriented actions through the establishment of social policies. Moreover, governments have the power to enforce policy choices through the appli-

Women in many lesser-developed nations have been encouraged to practice birth control through use of an IUD, as pictured here, voluntary sterilization, or the pill to lower the birth rate and ultimately the population. Such programs are supported by many organizations in developed countries. However, not all countries endorse these efforts, and little success has been achieved without considering cultural factors as well.

cation of sanctions against people who do not comply with the rules.

Population policy refers to "measures and programmes designed to contribute to the achievement of economic, social, demographic, political and other collective goals through affecting critical demographic variables, namely the size and growth of the population, its geographic distribution . . . and its demographic characteristics . . ." (United Nations Economic and Social Council, 1972, p. 6). Although this definition goes much beyond fertility control, such control is the primary concern of most nations that have adopted a population policy.

A study prepared for the 1974 World Population Conference (United Nations Secretariat, 1975) summarizes the current population policies of all but two of the world's 150 sovereign states, excluding only Grenada and the Democratic Republic of Vietnam. Eighty-eight countries define their level of fertility as "acceptable" and are not intervening to change it. Forty-two countries label their fertility rate "excessive" and are explicitly intervening to limit births. The other 18 countries find their fertility rate "deficient" and are explicitly intervening to stimulate it. Governments that wish to lower fertility overwhelmingly respond to the problem with family-planning programs. Eighty-eight percent of those that perceive their birthrates as "excessive" sponsor family-planning services.

Public policies also often reflect concern over international migration. The same study also suggests that international migration is a matter of governmental policy in many nations. Permanent emigration is "encouraged" by 15 countries, "permitted" by 61, and "discouraged" by 72. On the other hand, permanent immigration is "restricted" by 116 nations and "encouraged" by only 32. In addition, few governments explicitly encourage or restrict migration of people to metropolitan areas. However, 76 countries have policies formulated to divert migration into urban centers in nonmetropolitan regions.

The relationship between population policy and law has only recently received detailed attention (UNFPA, 1975). All nations have laws regulating international migration. Legal restrictions on fertility have been proposed as a solution to the problem of excessive growth (Berelson, 1969; Davis, 1967), but only a few countries (for example, India) have taken steps toward implementing such laws. Reduced to their most elementary level many population-environment problems involve an imbalance between the size of a population and the availability of resources needed to sustain that number of people. One way of directly adjusting the imbalance is to redistribute people or the components of the life-sustaining environment, such as resources, jobs, and services.

Historically, people have migrated to find new sources of sustenance. Frontier settlements and industrializing regions typically receive immigrants from older, more populated areas and nations. At the national and regional levels people continue to migrate in response to environmental pressures and opportunities, but the relationship between population and environment at this level is complicated by the influence of other factors (Sly, 1972).

International migration is a limited means of adjusting imbalances between population and resources because of government policies. Many people living in densely populated, resource-poor nations obviously would migrate to countries with higher standards of living if they were free to do so, and, as indicated by the United Nations 1975 survey of population policies, a number of the less-developed nations encourage temporary or permanent emigration. However, the high cost of international resettlement and the legal restrictions on immigration tend to minimize the potential of migration as a solution.

The materials and services needed by human populations for sustenance also can be redistributed. Indeed, international trade, development assistance, and industrialization have just such a result. However, such adaptive redistribution is also subject to severe constraints. Primary among these constraints is the exploitation of human and natural resources in less-developed nations by governments and private businesses. Legal and informal restrictions impede the reallocation of materials and services to needy populations. Resistance to the establishment of an international food bank, described by Eckholm (1976), is evidence of these barriers to redistribution.

Through social organization human beings have developed a number of mechanisms for survival within the constraints set by demographic and environmental circumstances. However, the long-run consequences of the organizational forces they have set in motion are only now being recognized. Heretofore adaptation was seen as an immediate problem, involving response to the isolated needs of individual societies. Population growth was generally advocated to stimulate economic development and to provide for national defense. Exploitation of the environment was pursued with abandon because resources appeared to be infinite.

Increasingly, we recognize the folly of our past actions. There are limits to the size of the population the world can sustain. Resource depletion and environmental degradation are direct consequences of population growth. Can we reverse these processes? Can we create a habitat that is responsive to our needs, yet conserves the life-support system on which we all depend? Science and technology can have both beneficial and detrimental effects on population growth and resource scarcity. Similarly, cultural norms can stimulate or depress the birthrate and work for or against environmental conservation. The coordinating, regulatory, and distributive processes of social organization also have consequences for population and the environment.

How Can Population Growth Be Slowed?

Although the question of the optimum size and distribution for world and national populations has never been settled (Singer, 1971), a consensus seems to be emerging that continued population growth and increased density would have disastrous consequences for the quality of life. Advocates of zero population growth are seeking to rally support among world leaders. Whether and how the ZPG goal can be achieved, however, are still subjects of debate. The answers to these two questions are crucial to our prospects for managing the future.

First, short of a drastic increase in mortality, world population is not likely to cease growing before the next century. The effects of two factors—the built-in inertia of current rates of growth and the reproductive potential of the disproportionately large group of young people in most nations—cannot be reversed in the immediate future (Frejka, 1973). Even if the people of the world had achieved replacement level fertility, that is, the number of births each year equaled the number of deaths each year during the 1970s, population growth would continue through the next century. By 2100 the earth would have approximately 5.7 billion inhabitants (Peck, 1974). In contrast, if replacement level is not reached until the middle of the next century, zero growth would be delayed until 2200 when world population would be about 15 billion. An intermediate projection would be that attainment of replacement fertility by the year 2005 would lead

to a growing population through 2100, and result in leveling off at more than eight billion people. These projections highlight the significance of when fertility at the replacement level is reached. "Immediately" would result in a stationary (nongrowing) world population of just under six billion; "slowly" would lead to two and one-half times that number, or 15 billion people.

The size of future world population depends primarily upon a second issue: the means through which replacement level fertility is sought. The dominant approach to reducing fertility has been through family planning (Berelson, 1969). Davis (1967, 1973, 1976), among others, has argued that voluntary limitation of reproduction is an ineffective means of controlling population. "People want families and children. . . . That being the case, they are not wholehearted about population control. They do not want runaway population growth either, but they want to avoid it painlessly. They want a solution that leaves them free to have five children if they wish. In short, they want a miracle" (1974, pp. 28–29). Davis advocates that other, more drastic measures, such as later marriage, increased attractiveness of nonfamilial roles for women, and restrictions on the number of children a family can produce, be made part of enforceable national population policies.

World population is likely to grow for many years to come. Whether and when that growth can be halted will depend on the effectiveness of organized efforts to employ all means at our disposal—technology, normative change, coordinated action, and governmental regulation—toward that end. Even if the human population stabilizes near the low projected figure of six to seven billion, or 50 percent more than presently live on earth, people will have serious problems obtaining the materials and services we now consider necessary to a desirable standard of living.

A Look at the Future

The future shape of society has been dreamed and argued about throughout the ages. Plans for utopia are recorded in the writings of scholars, statesmen, and philosophers from Plato through the present generation of futurists (Bernari, 1950; Manuel, 1966; Toffler, 1972). Only in recent years, however, have the goals of utopian futures reflected a widespread concern with the demographic and ecological effects of societal organization.

What will the future be like? In spite of the many revolutionary techniques and ideas that have altered the course of human history—toolmaking, agriculture, urbanization, centralized government, mass communication, nuclear energy—there have been many continuities in human affairs from one epoch to the next. The organization of contemporary society imposes constraints on change that will be felt in the centuries to come.

The problem of scarcity applies to more than the absolute abundance of materials, products, and services that sustain human societies. Of obvious importance is the size of the population among whom these goods and services are distributed. Increases in world population can only contribute to scarcity. Similarly, rates of consumption are important. Apart from population growth, increased resource consumption is due primarily to rising levels of affluence among favored groups.

We should also note that the threat of scarcity varies among the nations of the world. Food is not scarce for most citizens of the United States, whereas most inhabitants of India are engaged in a daily struggle to get enough to eat. Iran is not likely to face an oil shortage in the near future, but the United States is. Such examples remind us that the problem of population and its impact is worldwide and that the preservation of civilized society beyond the next century or two requires a concerted attack on problems of excessive population growth and depletion of environmental resources.

SUMMARY

The future of human society may well rest with us and our solutions to the imbalance created by population growth and resource scarcity. Demographers, the students of human populations, say there may soon be too many of us for this planet to support. Demographers collect data on the distribution and composition as well as the size of human groups, and through censuses, surveys, and the like they record the life events that most affect those figures—births, deaths, and migrations. The analysis of demographic data produces statements and predictions about variables of vital interest to social theorists and planners.

In the nineteenth century Malthus hypothesized that humankind would produce more people than it could feed. Although he failed to anticipate the effects of technology, migration, and social organization that would delay the dilemma for about a hundred years, he correctly identified two major threats to survival today. Marx, another nineteenth-century theorist, rightly recognized a related problem, that of unequal distribution of goods and services within and among the populations of the world.

Twentieth-century demographic theorists have approached the population problem from two angles. In the first, the demographic transition model, theorists have distinguished types of societies by their birth and death rate patterns. Traditional societies tend to have high birth and high death rates and therefore fairly stable populations. However, so widespread has been the dissemination of life- and health-protecting information and technology in this century that only a few societies have failed to enter the transitional phase, marked by rapid population growth. This phase occurs when birthrates remain high while death rates decline, a circumstance that now prevails in most developing nations of Latin America, Africa, and Southeast Asia.

The developed nations of the world have reached modern society status—that is, low birth and low death rates. Most industrialized societies, apparently with no greater motivation or incentive than lack of economic need for more children or personal convenience, have reduced fertility rates considerably within the past decade. Population growth, such as that exhibited now by the United States, results largely from the prolongation of life.

Davis maintains in his multiphasic response theory that societies can change their demographic circumstances. He suggests, for example, that societies can and must intervene directly in population processes affecting future growth, as Japan has done.

As of 1980 there were 4.4 billion people in the world. The rate of population growth in less-developed nations is increasing rapidly; growth in developed nations is slowing and even stabilizing. The number of people who live in urban areas in both developing and developed nations continues to increase. By the year 2000, at present rates, about 80 percent of the population of the United States will live in urban areas. Approximately 75 percent already do.

Industrialized nations demand and receive far more than their share of world resources based on percentage of work population supported. Inequalities are apparent in the distribution of goods and services that we identify as indices of quality life—housing, employment, education. Even within the United States, which is the best fed, best clothed, and best housed country in the world, not all people have adequate food, clothing, and shelter.

If humankind is to halt runaway population growth and regulate use and distribution of resources, adaptations will have to be made. Our survival on this planet depends on learning how to influence future outcomes.

GLOSSARY

Age-specific birthrate (ASBR)　number of births in a year per number of women of certain ages in a population.

Crude birthrate (CBR)　number of births in a year divided by the number of people in the total population; usually stated as rate of births per 1000 population.

Demographic transition theory　defines three types of societies in terms of the balance between birth and death rates: traditional, transitional, and modern.

Demography　the analysis of a population by size, territorial distribution, and composition; also the study of population changes—natality, mortality, territorial movement, and social mobility.

Distributions　in demographic studies, measures showing various characteristics of a population, such as marital or employment status or age grouping.

Fertility rate　age-specific birthrate for all women of childbearing age in a population.

Morbidity rate　the amount of illness in a population, usually calculated on the basis of illness among 1000 people in a population.

Mortality rate　the number of deaths per 1000 population.

Population census　a record usually made periodically by national governments of the number of its inhabitants, their characteristics, and their location.

Population composition　social characteristics of a group, including attributes like age, sex, marital status, occupation, education, and religion.

Population distribution　pattern of people's location in physical space.

Population processes　factors affecting the structure of a population, namely, natality, mortality, migration, and social mobility.

Population registers　an ongoing record of individual events and changes in individual characteristics—divorce, birth, death, and the like.

Population structure　the size, distribution, and composition of a group of people.

Rates　in demographic studies, measures showing the number of times an event, like birth, death, marriage, or migration, occurs within a population.

Ratios　statements of the relative sizes of various population categories, such as the sex ratio (number of males to females) and the dependency ratio (number of younger and/or older persons to those in the middle-age groups).

Sample household survey　method of collecting population data from randomly selected households on a face-to-face basis; used to supplement and check data from more formal sources.

Standard metropolitan statistical area (SMSA)　a central city of 50,000 or more inhabitants and any surrounding territory and residents that are metropolitan in character and economically and socially integrated with the central city.

Vital registration systems records of certain population events, typically live births, deaths, marriages, divorces, legal separations, annulments, and adoptions.

ADDITIONAL READINGS

Anderson, Charles H. *The Sociology of Survival: Social Problems of Growth.* Homewood, Ill.: Dorsey, 1976.
Examines the meaning of the growth society, its ideology and mystique. The problems of growth in developed capitalist and socialist societies and underdeveloped societies make up the core of the book.

Ehrlich, Paul, and Anne H. Ehrlich. *Population, Resources, Environment: Issues in Human Ecology.* San Francisco: Freeman, 1972.
An examination of the ecological crisis facing the world and a call for action by two environmental activists and scholars.

Micklin, Michael, ed. *Population, Environment, and Social Organization: Current Issues in Human Ecology.* Hinsdale, Ill.: Dryden, 1973.
A good collection of papers introducing the study of human ecology. Emphasizes the role of human social organization as the connecting link between a population and its environment.

Peterson, William. *Population.* New York: MacMillan, 1975.
A textbook on the general topic of population, including the theory and methods of study. For the student who wishes to develop a serious interest in the area.

Spengler, Joseph J. *Population and America's Future.* San Francisco: Freeman, 1975.
This book combines a scholarly analysis of past and prospective population trends with an examination of declining world resources. The author considers possible policy decisions to deal with these trends including the "no-growth society" and zero population growth.

READING

READING 18.1

The "Good Times" Cohort of the 1930s: Sometimes Less Means More (and More Means Less)
Carl L. Harter

Many of the things we do or need in life are age specific. We go to elementary school between the ages of 6 and 14, so that is the age at which we need an elementary teacher and a school building. Most of us leave our parents and set up our own home between the ages of 18 and 25, so that age range is when we need our first job and a house or apartment of our own. From several months before birth (the need for an obstetrician) to several days after death (the need for a mortician), our lives are filled with age-specific activities and needs. How much of each age-specific need is required or expected at any one time is determined by the number of us who are at each age.

Obviously the number of persons who are at any particular age is related to the number of births that occurred that many years previously. In demographic jargon, persons who share the same year of birth are referred to as the "birth cohort" for that year. In common usage, the "birth" portion of the term is dropped and only the word "cohort" is used. For example, the 1936 cohort means all persons born in calendar year 1936, and the 1930s cohort means all persons born between January 1, 1930, and January 1, 1940. Technically the term cohort can be applied to any group whose members have some demographic characteristic in common, such as the same year of first marriage, same year of first parenthood, such as the same year of death, etc.; but, unless otherwise specified, cohort is used to refer to a group who are the same age—a birth cohort.

SOURCE: *PRB Report*, Vol. 3, No. 3, April 1977 (Courtesy of the Population Reference Bureau, Inc., Washington, D.C.)

Once the birth year is past, births can no longer be used to increase the cohort size—one cannot enter a group by birth at age 5 or 25 or 50. Accordingly, the original size of cohorts in any nation can only be changed by deaths or migration. With each passing year deaths diminish the absolute size of each cohort; but in the U.S.—indeed in most of the developed world—age-specific death rates before 50 years or so are quite low and stable, and hence deaths at these ages do not alter the relative size of cohorts or even account for much absolute decrease in their size. For the past quarter of a century in the U.S., for example, more than 98 percent of the people who reached age 5 were still alive at age 20.

Both the absolute and relative size of cohorts in any nation could be affected by international migration, the people who leave and enter a country. A host of social-economic-political factors can differentially stimulate members of certain cohorts to want to leave their country and/or to enter a specific country. In actual practice, however, most nations have very low annual rates of immigration and emigration. Since most nations have policies that restrict the number and the type of persons who can enter, we are not likely to see any large international migrations in the near future.

"BABY BOOMERS" GROW UP

Thus, if international migration does not significantly increase or decrease the size of a cohort at any age and if deaths do not differentially affect cohorts, then the original size of birth cohorts is the main factor that determines how many people there will be at each age each year. So in a very real sense, the number of people retiring in 1977 is related to what happened 65 years ago—to the number of births that occurred in 1921—just as the number of youngsters entering junior high school this year was predetermined 13 years ago by the number of births that occurred in 1964.

In this "age of relativity" the absolute power or value of something does not always increase or decrease as the absolute number or cost or size of that thing increases or decreases. For example, a society with 250 million people will not necessarily be "better off" than a society with only 50 million, nor will a family with ten members necessarily be "better off" than a family of four. We tend to be more concerned with how developed a nation is, compared to other nations, than we are with how many people it has, or with how well off a family is, compared to other families, than we are with how large the family is.

There are instances, though, in which the absolute size or number of something is an important consideration. Using a boat and a lake as an analogy, neither a small, slow boat, nor a fast, large boat will be affected by a calm lake, but the different boats will have vastly different effects on the lake: A small, slow boat will hardly cause ripples on the lake whereas a large or fast boat will create high waves. On the other hand, a very rough lake will be largely unaffected by either small or large boats, but the boats in turn will be differentially affected by the rough lake: The small boat will be tossed to and fro by the lake while the large boat will more likely be able to weather the storm. In some respects an age cohort and a society have this boat-lake relationship to each other.

When a particular age group accounts for only a small proportion of the population, that age group will probably not create many "ripples" or "waves" in the society. But if that same age group, at some later date, accounts for a considerably larger proportion of the total population, it may "rock the boat" of society. In discussing the political consequences of population change, for example, Dr. Myron Weiner, Professor of Political Science at MIT, has pointed out that "It is necessary to distinguish between the political role of a particular age group when it constitutes a small portion of the population and its role when its numbers have sharply increased"[1] In 1970, Dr. George H. Brown, then Director of the Bureau of the Census, indicated that one-third of our nation's total population increase between 1970 and 1985 would be in the 25-to-34 age group, and as a consequence "By 1985 we may expect to see more young leaders in government, private industry and politics than ever before."[2] This increase in young leaders by 1985 is expected because their cohort constituency, the "baby boom" cohorts born after World War II, are much larger than the young adult cohorts were in 1970. In 1970 some 25 million (12 percent) Americans were aged 25 to 34, but by 1985 almost 40 million (17 percent) Americans will be 25 to 34.[3] Not only will the cohort increase by about 15 million in just 15 years, but by 1985 every sixth American will be between 25 and 35 whereas in 1970 every eighth American was in that age group.

Since these "baby boomers" constitute an increasing proportion of the voting population, we can expect them to have an increasingly significant say-so in the running of the "ship of state." At the same time, though, they have created some "stormy seas" or "tidal waves" for society. As Dr. Robert C. Cook, past president of PRB, has commented, "Wherever these children have gone, from kindergarten to college, into massive developments of three- and four-bedroom houses, into the labor market, their progress has caused a shaking of heads over crowding, split school sessions, bulldozing of green acres, and job openings."[4]

There are also instances in which a big increase in the size of a cohort can lead to seemingly contradictory conditions. For example, during the debate between the presidential candidates on September 23, 1976, the Republican candidate stated that more people were currently employed than ever before in our history. In apparent contradiction, the Democratic candidate said that the number of unemployed people was larger than ever before and the unemployment rate was at one of the highest points since the Great Depression. Actually both candidates were correct, and one of the phenomena responsible for these curious employment statistics is the baby boom cohorts. Those large cohorts (plus an increase in the proportion of women seeking jobs) have now reached "employment age" and have greatly increased the size of the labor force (a term which includes the employed plus the unemployed who are seeking employment). In a recent report on the aging of the baby boom cohorts, Denis F. Johnston, Director of the Social Indicators Project in the Office of Management and Budget, points out that in the ten years prior to 1964, the labor force was increasing by about 880,000 per year, but in the ten years from 1964 to 1974 when the baby boom cohorts began entering the job market, the annual net growth of the labor force nearly doubled—to about 1,740,000 per year.[5] Many of these new job seekers are finding employment, but in the absence of sufficient new jobs to provide work opportunities for all of those large cohorts recently entering the labor force, we have seen increases both in the total number employed (some 88 million) and in the total number unemployed (some 7.5 million).

Since we know that the original size of a birth cohort has a direct bearing on the amount of future age-specific needs and activities of that cohort, it should be possible for people and societies to prepare to provide for those various needs and activities. In many cases, however, it takes years of lead time for a society to develop the jobs or services required to meet the specific needs generated by each cohort. And the problems become greatly compounded if there are large year-to-year or decade-to-decade changes in the number of people at each age. For example, the slightly more than 3.5 million births in 1950 required x number of pediatricians between 1950 and 1960, but the slightly more than 4.3 million births in 1960 required x plus 18 percent pediatricians between 1960 and 1970. Since it

takes at least ten years from the time a student decides to become a physician until he or she is a practicing pediatrician, in order to have had enough pediatricians for the 1960 cohort, some students in the 1950s would have had to anticipate (or hope) that there would be enough children for them to take care of when they finished their training. In 1970 the number of births (3.7 million) declined to about the 1950 level, so the extra pediatricians required in the sixties are no longer needed in the seventies.

Year-to-year or decade-to-decade fluctuations in the size of successive cohorts can indeed make it difficult for businesses, educational institutions, or any group to make long-range plans. Yet such fluctuation seems to be occurring. In his 1969 discussion of an emerging fertility pattern in the U.S., Professor Norman Ryder, who was then at the University of Wisconsin, stated that "The future of fertility is likely to be increasingly bound up with questions of fluctuation rather than of trend."[6] In his discussion of future populations in 1972, Professor Nathan Keyfitz of the University of Chicago indicated that the more developed nations "will have an endless series of ups and downs in their births . . ."[7] More recently Professor Ronald Lee of the University of Michigan has provided evidence suggesting that the fluctuations in U.S. fertility in the twentieth century may represent fertility control cycles that peak about every 40 years or every other generation.[8] At any rate, fluctuations in cohort size make it difficult to anticipate how many teachers or jobs or houses, etc., will be required at some future date.

Sometimes business or governmental managers can correctly anticipate the number of people who will be needing age-specific services or doing age-specific activities. But even with such foresight these managers often will not accept the risk of guessing wrong, particularly if the risk involves investing a lot of money or time. Instead, they wait until the anticipated demand or need arrives and then attempt to meet it. As a consequence, when cohorts are followed by ever larger cohorts, there are always demands or needs that, at least temporarily, remain unmet or unfilled.

THE "GOOD TIMES" COHORT

There is however, a cohort of currently middle-aged Americans—the 1930s cohort—that is smaller, not larger, than the cohort that preceded it. We might therefore consider whether being fewer in number has made the cohort members' life easier—a case, perhaps, in which "less means more." By virtue of their smaller number, the thirties cohort, upon encountering each important life cycle event, have experienced relative abundance—a legacy from the larger cohort that preceded them. Thus, this cohort, born during the "bad times" of the 1930s, have received advantages and "good times" at every new period in their life.

The stage was set for this relatively small "good times" cohort in the following way. For a century and a half preceding the 1930s, the country's fertility rate declined steadily—in each decade women on the average had fewer children than did women in the previous decades. Nonetheless, each decade always saw more babies produced than the decade before, as fertility (production), though declining, was still considerably above replacement level. The result was that when the female babies of each decade grew up and produced their own children, in their numbers they more than made up for the lower production per woman, so that total production was always greater than before. Immigration also added to the ranks of the producers, which helped to push total production each decade higher than production in the previous decade.

Throughout our nation's history each generation has tended to be larger than its predecessors. In keeping with the "bigger means better" philosophy that prevailed in business and industry and in keeping with the "expansion" psychology that accompanied the settling of the nation and the growth of cities, we gener-

ally viewed population growth and ever-larger cohorts as more or less natural. Until the 1930s our whole history had been one of more and ever more. Every decade had more people at each age or stage in life than the previous decade; there were more first graders, more high schoolers, more college students, more young adults seeking their first jobs, more young marrieds needing their own homes, more middle-aged adults to climb occupational career ladders, more old folks to provide for, and finally, even more deaths which called for more mortuaries and cemeteries. This relentless increase in the size of birth cohorts meant that we could never really catch up with their needs. We produced more pediatricians, or schools, or jobs, or houses, or cemeteries; but there was a seemingly never-ending supply of larger cohorts followed by even larger ones. With each cohort needing a larger supply than the one just before it, there was never quite enough for everyone.

But all that changed with the cohort born in the 1930s. For the first time we had a decade in which there were fewer births than in the decade that preceded it. For example, as indicated in Figure [18.5], the number of children age 5 in 1940 (the 1935 cohort) was about 25 percent less than it had been ten years earlier. For the first time in our history we had smaller cohorts following larger cohorts instead of the other way around.

What advantages have the thirties cohort enjoyed because of their fewer numbers? For one thing, compared to their immediate predecessors, they have needed less from society. They did not find overcrowded delivery rooms, insufficient classrooms, burgeoning universities, scarce job offers, a big housing shortage. With their fewer numbers, they have also had greater opportunity for career mobility. Relatively speaking, in all their important life cycle events the 1930s cohort has "had it made."

In 1950 when the thirties cohort was age 11–20, there were about a quarter million fewer 15-year-olds than there had been in 1940 (Figure

590

READING

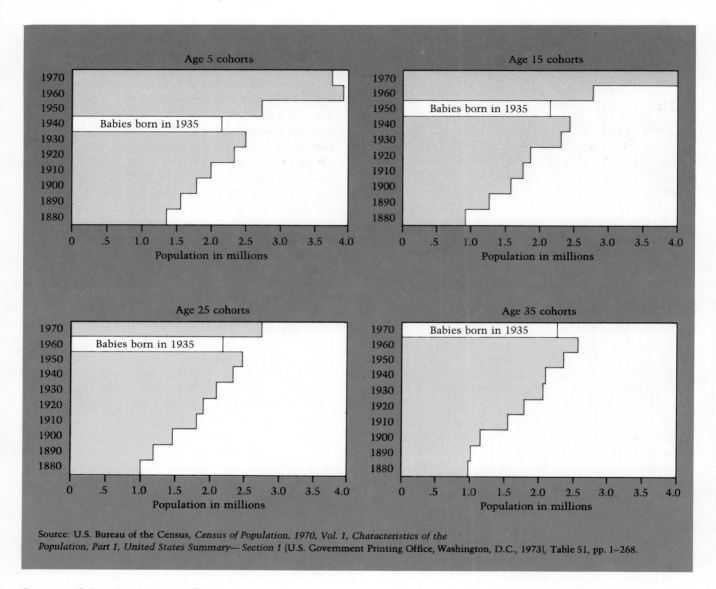

FIGURE 18.5 Comparisons of
Cohorts Ages 5, 15, 25, and 35 for
Each Decade from 1880 to 1970 in
the U.S.

[18.5]). Insofar as the number of high-school classrooms, glee clubs, athletic teams, debate squads, class officers, etc., had not diminished, then the 1950 fifteen-year-old had a greater chance than did the 1940 fifteen-year-old of being in a smaller-size class, of being a class officer, of being a member of the glee club and athletic team and debate squad, etc. Similarly in 1960, when the thirties cohort was 21–39, they required fewer new jobs and housing units than did their predecessors ten years earlier.

At their current age of 37–46 the thirties cohort are presumably in their most productive years—in positions of seniority, decision making, and leadership. (Parenthetically, we might well ask if the cohort's uninterrupted "good times" have prepared them to make appropriate decisions and provide the leadership required by the greatly increased cohorts of the forties and fifties—the "baby boomers"—who are following in their shadow.) Even at this middle-age stage in their life, the thirties cohort may largely escape a problem encountered by those a decade or two older than they. Technological unemployment and job obsolescence have been serious problems for persons who were trained for the pre-World War II and pre-Sputnik vocations. The thirties cohort, however, was the first cohort to be trained in the modern postwar era. While they may now be beginning to feel some job insecurity from the host of precocious young adults nipping at their heels, the thirties cohort with their modern training, relatively small number, and advanced seniority, are reasonably assured of more than subsistence income and positions until they retire some 20 to 30 years from now.

Even at retirement the thirties cohort will probably still have relatively "good times." In the U.S. today the largest age concentration of poor people are those in retirement—the 65s and over. Inflation continues to render them ever poorer when they live on fixed income retirement plans, and Social Security benefits (a program which began during the bad times of the 1930s) seem inadequate to keep up with the cost of living. Nevertheless, during the next 20 years there will be more people retiring each year than the year before, and by 1995 about one of every eight Americans will be age 65 or older.

Perhaps this landslide of retirees during the next 20 years will stimulate a variety of programs to assist the elderly so that retirees will indeed have some gold for their "golden years." If so, by the time the cohort of the thirties retires, during 1995–2005, they will once again have benefitted from the trials and tribulations of the larger cohort that preceded them.

The cohort of the thirties began life during bad times, but by being fewer in number than the cohort they followed, they have had the advantage of experiencing relatively good times throughout their lives. Similarly the past decade in this nation also produced a cohort some 17 percent smaller than the one which preceded it. Thus perhaps another advantaged cohort is on its way through life, and the good times of the thirties cohort will not have been a once and only occurrence.

REFERENCES

[1]Weiner, Myron, "Political Demography: An Inquiry into the Political Consequences of Population Change," in Roger Revelle (Ed.), *Rapid Population Growth: Consequences and Policy Implications* (Baltimore: Johns Hopkins Press for the National Academy of Sciences, 1971), p. 582.

[2]Brown, George H., "1985," *PRB Selection* No. 34 (November, 1970), p. 5.

[3]U. S. Bureau of the Census, *Current Population Reports*, Series P-25, No. 601, "Projections of the Population of the United States: 1975 to 2050," (U. S. Government Printing Office, Washington, D.C., 1975), pp. 8–9.

[4]*PRB Population Profile*, "Marriage Gaps and Gains," (June 26, 1967), p. 4.

[5]Johnston, Denis F., "The Aging of the Baby Boom Cohorts," *Statistical Reporter*, No. 76–9, (Government Printing Office, Washington, D. C., March 1976), pp. 161–165.

[6]Ryder, Norman B., "The Emergence of a Modern Fertility Pattern: United States, 1917–66," in S. J. Behrman, Leslie Corsa, Jr., and Ronald Freedman (Eds.), *Fertility and Family Planning: A World View* (Ann Arbor: The University of Michigan Press, 1969), p. 116.

[7]Keyfitz, Nathan, "On Future Population," *Journal of the American Statistical Association*, Vol. 67 (June 1972), p. 361.

[8]Lee, Ronald, "The Formal Dynamics of Controlled Populations and the Echo, the Boom and the Bust," *Demography*, Vol. 11 (November 1974), pp. 563–585.

SUMMARY
Harter argues that the people born during the 1930s have received special benefits and advantages because they are a smaller cohort than the ones in the decades of the 1920s and the 1940s. Not only did this group benefit from the schools, public programs, and the expansion of economic opportunities of the late 1940s and 1950s, but they were at the appropriate age to assume leadership in planning for the postwar baby boom.

QUESTIONS
1. Are such benefits unique, or will the cohort of the 1970s experience similar advantages?
2. Are the factors identified by Harter as important as he suggests in a modern society?
3. Is this situation properly described as "social inequality"?

REFERENCES

Abramson, Harold J., and Noll, C. E. "Religion, Ethnicity and Social Change." *Review of Religious Research* 8 (Winter 1966):11–26.

Abu-Lughod, Janet. "Urban-Rural Differences as a Function of the Demographic Transition: Egyptian Data and an Analytical Model." *American Journal of Sociology* 66 (March 1964):476–90.

Adams, Bert N. *The Family: A Sociological Interpretation.* Third Edition. Chicago: Rand McNally, 1980.

———. *Kinship in an Urban Setting.* Chicago: Markham, 1968.

Adorno, T. W.; Frenkel-Brunswick, Else; Levinson, D. J.; and Sanford, R. N. *The Authoritarian Personality.* New York: Harper, 1950.

Alba, Richard D., and Lavin, David E. "Community Colleges and Tracking in Higher Education." *Sociology of Education* 54 (October 1981):223–37.

Alba, Richard D., and Moore, Gwen. "Elite Social Circles." *Sociological Methods and Research* 7 (1978): 167–88.

Albrow, Martin, *Bureaucracy.* New York: Praeger, 1970.

Aldrich, Howard E. *Organizations and Environments.* Englewood Cliffs, N.J.: Prentice-Hall, 1979.

———. "Technology and Organizational Structure: A Reexamination of the Findings of the Aston Group." *Administrative Science Quarterly* 17 (March 1972):26–43.

Alexander, Karl; Cook, Martha; and McDill, Edward L., "Curriculum Tracking and Educational Stratification: Some Further Evidence." *American Sociological Review* 43 (February 1978):47–66.

Alexander, Karl L., and McDill, Edward L. "Selection and Allocation Within Schools: Some Causes and Consequences of Curriculum Placement." *American Sociological Review* 41 (December 1976):963–80.

Alford, Robert, and Friedland, Roger. "Political Participation." In Alex Inkeles, et. al, eds. *Annual Review of Sociology*, Palo Alto, Calif.: Annual Reviews, 1975.

Alfred, Randall H. "The Church of Satan." In Charles Y. Glock and Robert N. Bellah, eds. *The New Religious Consciousness.* Berkeley: University of California Press, 1976.

Alland, Alexander, Jr. *To Be Human.* New York: John Wiley and Sons, 1980.

Allport, Gordon. *The Nature of Prejudice.* New York: Doubleday, 1958.

Allport, Gordon W., and Ross, J. M. "Personal Religious Orientation and Prejudice." *Journal of Personality and Social Psychology* 5 (April 1967): 432–43.

Almond, Gabriel A., and Verba, Sidney. *The Civic Culture.* Boston: Little, Brown, 1965.

Alves, Wayne H., and Rossi, Peter H. "Who Should Get What? Fairness Judgements of the Distribution of Earnings." *American Journal of Sociology* 84 (November 1978):541–64.

Alwin, Duane F., and Luther B. Otto. "High School Context Effects on Aspirations." *Sociology of Education* 50 (October 1977):259–73.

Anderson, Charles H. *The Political Economy of Class.* Englewood Cliffs, N.J.: Prentice-Hall, 1974.

Anderson, James G. "Strategies of Control and Their Effects on Instruction." *Journal of Research and Development in Education* 9 (1975):115–22.

André, Rae. *Homemakers: The Forgotten Workers.* Chicago: University of Chicago Press, 1981.

Arafat, Ibithaj and Yorburg, Betty. *The New Women: Attitudes, Behavior, and Self-Image.* Columbus, Ohio: Charles E. Merrill Publishing Co., 1976.

Aramoni, Aniceto. "Machismo." *Psychology Today* 5 (January 1972):69–72.

Armer, Michael, and Schnaiberg, Allan. "Measuring Individual Modernity: A New Myth." *American Sociological Review* 37 (June 1972):301–16.

Arriaga, Eduardo, and Davis, Kingsley. "The Pattern of Mortality Change in Latin America." *Demography* 6 (August 1969):223–42.

Balswick, Jack. "The Jesus People Movement: A Sociological Analysis." In Patrick H. McNamara (ed.), *Religion American Style.* New York: Harper & Row, 1974.

Bandura, A., and Huston, A.C. "Identification as a Process of Incidental Learning." *Journal of Abnormal and Social Psychology* 63 (1961):311–18.

Banfield, Edward. *The Unheavenly City Revisited.* Boston: Little, Brown, 1974.

Baran, Paul A., and Sweezy, Paul M. *Monopoly Capital.* Pelican Books, 1966.

Barber, Benjamin. "Man on Women." *Worldview* 16 (1973):48–49.

Barber, Bernard. *Social Stratification.* New York: Harcourt, Brace, 1957.

Barber, Bernard, and Fox, Renée. "The Case of the Floppy-eared Rabbits: An Instance of Serendipity Gained and Serendipity Lost." *American Journal of Sociology* 65 (September 1958):128–36.

Barber, Richard J. *The American Corporation: Its Money, Its Power, Its Politics.* New York: Dutton, 1970.

Barnet, Richard J., and Muller, Ronald E. *Global Reach: The Power of the Multinational Corporations.* New York: Simon & Schuster, 1974.

Beaton, Albert E.; Hilton, Thomas L.; and Schrader, William B. *Changes in the Verbal Abilities of High School Seniors, College Entrants, and SAT Candidates between 1960 and 1972.* Educational Testing Service, 1977.

Beattie, John. *Bunyoro, An African Kingdom.* New York: Holt, 1960.

Beaver, Stephen C. *Demographic Transition Theory Reinterpreted.* Lexington, Mass.: Heath, 1975.

Beck, Paul A., and Jennings, M. Kent. "Parents as Middlepersons in Political Socialization." *Journal of Politics* 37 (February 1975):83–107.

Becker, Howard. *Outsiders: Studies in the Sociology of Deviance.* New York: Free Press, 1963.

———. "Social Class Variations in the Teacher-Pupil Relationship." *Journal of Educational Sociology* 25 (1953):451–65.

———. "Whose Side Are We On?" *Social Problems* 14 (Winter 1967):239–47.

Bell, Wendell. "Social Choice, Life Styles, and Suburban Residence." Pp. 225–47 in Dobriner, W. (ed.) *The Suburban Community.* N.Y.: Putnam 1958.

Bellah, Robert N. "Civil Religion in America." *Daedalus* 96 (Winter 1967):1–21.

Belshaw, Cyril S. *Traditional Exchange and Modern Markets.* Englewood Cliffs, N.J.: Prentice-Hall, 1965.

Bennis, Warren. "The Decline of Bureaucracy and Organizations of the Future." *Transaction* (July 1965).

Berelson, Bernard. "Beyond Family Planning." *Studies in Family Planning* 38 (February 1969):1–16.

Berg, Ivar. *Education and Jobs.* New York: Praeger, 1970.

Bergel, Egon. *Social Stratification.* New York: McGraw-Hill, 1962.

Berger, Bennett. "On the Youthfulness of Youth Cultures." *Social Research* 30 (Autumn 1963):319–42.

Berger, Peter L. "Sociology and Freedom." *American Sociologist* 6 (February 1971):1–5.

Berger, Peter L., and Berger, Brigitte. "Becoming a Member of Society," in Peter I. Rose, ed. *Socialization and the Life Cycle.* New York: St. Martin's Press, 1979.

Berle, Adolph A., and Means, Gardener C. *The Modern Corporation and Private Property.* New York: Macmillan, 1940.

Bernari, Marie Louise. *Journey Through Utopia.* London: Routledge and Kegan Paul, 1950.

Berry, Brian. "Internal Structure of the City." *Law and Contemporary Problems* 30 (1965):111–19.

Bettelheim, Bruno. "Feral Children and Autistic Children." *American Journal of Sociology* 54 (1959):458–67.

Bibb, Robert, and Form, William H. "The Effects of Industrial, Occupational, and Sex Stratification on Wages in Blue-Collar Markets." *Social Forces* 55 (June 1977):974–96.

Bird, Frederick. "Charisma and Ritual in New Religious Movements" In Jacob Needleman and George Baker, eds. *Understanding the New Religions.* New York: The Seabury Press, 1978.

Birnbaum, Norman. "Conflicting Interpretations of the Rise of Capitalism: Marx and Weber." *British Journal of Sociology* 4 (1953):125–41.

Blau, Peter M. *Exchange and Power in Social Life.* N.Y.: Wiley, 1964.

———. "A Formal Theory of Differentiation in Organizations." *American Sociological Review* 35 (April 1970):201–18.

———, and Scott, W. Richard. *Formal Organizations: A Comparative Approach.* San Francisco: Chandler, 1962.

Blauner, Robert. *Alienation and Freedom: The Factory Worker and His Industry.* Chicago: University of Chicago Press, 1964.

Blumberg, Paul. *Industrial Democracy: The Sociology of Participation.* N.Y.: Schocken Books, 1968.

Blumer, Herbert. *Symbolic Interactionism.* Englewood Cliffs, N.J.: Prentice-Hall, 1969.

———. "What is Wrong With Social Theory." *American Sociological Review,* 19 (February 1954):3–10.

Blundell, William E. *Swindled.* N.Y.: Dow Jones Books, 1976.

Bogue, Donald J. *Principles of Demography.* New York: Wiley, 1969.

Bohannon, Paul. *Social Anthropology.* New York: Holt, Rinehart and Winston, 1963.

Bolsh, Robert, and Taylor, David. "Seekers and Saucers: The

Role of the Cultic Milieu in Joining a UFO Cult." *American Behavioral Scientist* 20 (1977):839–60.

Bonacich, Edna. "Advanced Capitalism and Black/White Race Relations in the United States: A Split Labor Market Interpretation." *American Sociological Review* 41 (February 1976):34–51.

Bonjean, Charles M.; Hill, Richard, J.; and McLemore, S. Dale. *Sociological Measurement: An Inventory of Scales and Indices.* San Francisco: Chandler, 1967.

Boocock, Sarene S. *Sociology of Education: An Introduction.* Second ed. Boston: Houghton-Mifflin, 1980.

Borland, Dolores Cabic. "A Cohort Analysis Approach to the Empty-Nest Syndrome Among Three Ethnic Groups of Women: A Theoretical Position." *Journal of Marriage and the Family* 44 (February 1982):117–29.

Bowles, Samuel, and Gintis, Herbert. *Schooling in Capitalist America: Educational Reform and the Contradictions of Economic Life.* New York: Basic Books, 1976.

Breckenfeld, Gurney. "Multinational Corporations at Bay." *Saturday Review* (January 24, 1976):12–22.

Bressler, Marvin, and Westoff, Charles F. "Catholic Education, Economic Values and Achievement." *American Journal of Sociology* 69 (November 1963):225–33.

Brim, O. "Socialization Through the Life Cycle." In O. Brim and S. Wheeler (eds.) *Socialization After Childhood.* New York: Wiley, 1966.

Brinton, Crane. *The Anatomy of Revolution.* New York: Random House, 1965.

Brofenbrenner, Urie. *Two Worlds of Childhood: U.S. and U.S.S.R.* New York: Pocket Books, 1973.

Bryan, James H. "Occupational Ideologies and Individual Attitudes of Call Girls." *Social Problems* 13 (Spring, 1966):441–50.

Burgess, Ernest W. "The Growth of the City: An Introduction to a Research Project." *Proceedings of the American Sociological Society* 18 (1923):85–89.

Burt, Ronald S. "Cooptive Corporate Actor Networks: A Reconsideration of Interlocking Directorates Involving American Manufacturing." *Administrative Science Quarterly* 25 (December, 1980):557–82.

Cameron, Mary. *The Booster and the Snitch.* New York: Free Press, 1964.

Carmichael, Stokely, and Hamilton, Charles V. *Black Power, The Politics of Liberation in America.* New York: Random House Vintage, 1967.

Carneiro, Robert L. "Slash and Burn Cultivation Among the Kuikuru and Its Implications for Cultural Development in the Amazon Basin." In Yehudi A. Cohen (ed.), *Man in Adaptation: The Cultural Present.* Chicago: Aldine, 1968.

Carnoy, Martin and Derek Shearer. *Economic Democracy: The Challenge of the 1980's.* N.Y.:M.E. Sharpe, 1980.

Casetti, E. "Urban Population Densities: An Alternative Explanation." *Canadian Geographer* 11 (1967):96–100.

Centers, Richard. *The Psychology of Social Classes.* Princeton, N.J.: Princeton University Press, 1949.

Chafe, William. *The American Woman.* New York: Oxford University Press, 1972.

Chall, Jeanne S. *An Analysis of Textbooks in Relation to Declining SAT Scores.* New York, N.Y.: College Entrance Examination Board, 1977.

Chatfield, Walter F. "Economic and Sociological Factors Influencing Life Satisfaction of the Aged." *Journal of Gerontology* 32 (September 1977):593–99.

Chinoy, Ely. *Automobile Workers and the American Dream.* New York: Doubleday, 1955.

Christensen, James A., and Yang, Choon. "Dominant Values in American Society: An Exploratory Analysis." *Sociology and Social Research* 60 (July 1976):461–73.

Clark, Burton R. *The Open Door College.* New York: McGraw-Hill, 1960.

———, and Trow, Martin. "The Organizational Context" in Theodore M. Newcomb and Everett K. Wilson, eds. *College Peer Groups: Problems and Prospects for Research.* Chicago: Aldine, 1966.

Clark, M. "Patterns of Aging Among the Elderly Poor of the Inner City." *The Gerontologist* 11 (1971):58–66.

Clark, Ramsey. *Crime in America.* N.Y.: Simon and Schuster, 1976.

Clayton, Richard R., and Bokemeier, Janet L. "Premarital Sex in the Seventies." *Journal of Marriage and the Family* 42 (November 1980):759–75.

Clinard, Marshall. *Sociology of Deviant Behavior,* rev. ed. N.Y.: Holt, Rinehart and Winston, 1963.

Cloward, Richard A., and Ohlin, Lloyd. *Delinquency and Opportunity: A Theory of Delinquent Gangs.* Free Press, 1960.

Cohen, Albert. *Delinquent Boys.* New York: Free Press, 1955.

Cohen, Steven Martin. "Socioeconomic Determinants of Intraethnic Marriage and Friendship." *Social Forces* 55 (June 1977):997–1010.

Cohen, Yehudi A., ed. *Man in Adaptation: The Cultural Present.* Chicago: Aldine, 1968.

Coleman, James S. "The Political Systems of Developing Areas." In Gabriel A. Almond and James S. Coleman (eds.), *The Politics of Developing Areas.* Princeton, N.J.: Princeton University Press, 1960a.

———. "The Adolescent Subculture and Academic Achievement." *American Journal of Sociology* 65 (January 1960b):337–47.

———. *The Adolescent Society.* New York: Free Press, 1961.

———. "Liberty and Equality in School Desegregation." *Social Policy* 6 (Jan./Feb. 1976):9–13.

Coleman, James S., et al. *Equality of Educational Opportunity.* Washington: United States Government Printing Office, 1966.

Collins, Randall. "Functional and Conflict Theories of Educational Stratification." *American Sociological Review* 36 (December 1971):1002–19.

Commission on Population Growth and the American Future. *Population and the American Future.* Washington, D.C.: U.S. Government Printing Office, 1972.

Cooley, Charles H. *Social Organization.* N.Y.: Scribner and Sons, 1909.

Cooper, David. *The Death of the Family.* New York: Pantheon, 1970.

Corwin, Ronald G. "Innovation in Organizations: The Case of Schools." *Sociology of Education* 48 (Winter 1975):1–37.

Coser, Lewis A. *The Functions of Social Conflict.* Glencoe, Ill.: Free Press, 1967.

———. *Masters of Sociological Thought.* New York: Harcourt Brace Jovanovich, 1971.

Cowgill, Donald O. "Transition Theory as General Population Theory." *Social Forces* 41 (March 1963):270–74.

Current Population Reports. U.S. Bureau of the Census. U.S. Government Printing Office, Washington, D.C.

Series P-20: Population Characteristics

No. 329: "Persons of Spanish Origin in the United States: March 1977." (September 1978).

No. 358: "Fertility of American Women: June 1979." (December 1980).

No. 363: "Population Profile of the United States: 1980." (June 1981).

No. 365: "Marital Status and Living Arrangements: March 1980." (October 1981).

No. 366: "Household and Family Characteristics: March 1980." (September 1981).

No. 371: "Household and Family Characteristics: March 1981." (May 1982).

Series P-60: Consumer Income

No. 105: "Money Income in 1975 of Families and Persons in the United States." (June 1977).

No. 127: "Money Income and Poverty Status of Families and Persons in the United States: 1980." (August 1981).

No. 129: "Money Income of Families and Persons in the United States: 1979." (November 1981).

No. 133: "Characteristics of the Population Below the Poverty Level: 1980." (July 1982).

Cygnar, Thomas E.; Noel, Donald L.; and Jacobson, Cardell K. "Religiosity and Prejudice: An Interdimensional Analysis." *Journal for the Scientific Study of Religion* 16 (June 1977):183–91.

Dahl, Robert. *Who Governs?* New Haven, Conn.: Yale University Press, 1961.

Dahrendorf, Ralf. *Class and Class Conflict in Industrial Society.* Palo Alto: Stanford University Press, 1959.

Dalton, Melville. *Men Who Manage.* N.Y.: Free Press, 1959.

Dalton, Russell J. "Reassessing Parental Socialization: Indicator Unreliability Versus Generational Transfer." *The American Political Science Review* 74 (June 1980):421–31.

Daly, Mary. *Beyond God the Father: Toward a Philosophy of Women's Liberation.* Boston: Beacon Press, 1973.

D'Antonio, William V., and Stock, Steven. "Religion, Ideal Family Size, and Abortion: Extending Renzi's Hypothesis." *Journal for the Scientific Study of Religion* 19 (December 1980):397–408.

Davie, Maurice. *William Graham Sumner: An Essay of Commentary and Selections.* New York: Crowell, 1963.

Davis, James A. "The Campus as a Frog Pond: An Application of the Theory of Relative Deprivation to Career Decisions of College Men." *American Journal of Sociology* 72 (July 1966):17–31.

Davies, James C. "Toward a Theory of Revolution." *American Sociological Review* 27 (February 1962):5–19.

———. "The Family's Role in Political Socialization." *Annals* 361 (September 1965): 10–19.

Davis, Jerome. "The Sociologist and Social Action." *American Sociological Review* 5 (April 1940):171–76.

Davis, Kingsley. "Extreme Social Isolation of a Child." *American Journal of Sociology* 45 (January 1940):554–64.

———. *Human Society.* New York: Macmillan, 1948.

———. "The Migration of Human Populations." *Scientific American* 231 (September 1974):93–105.

———. "The World Demographic Transition." *Annals of the American Academy of Political and Social Science* 237 (January 1945):1–11.

———. "Final Note on a Case of Extreme Isolation." *American Journal of Sociology* 52 (1947):432–37.

———. *Human Society.* New York: Macmillan, 1949.

———. "Sexual Behavior." In R. Merton and R. Nisbet (eds.), *Contemporary Social Problems.* New York: Harcourt, Brace and World, 1961.

———. "The Theory of Change and Response in Modern Demographic History." *Population Index* 29 (October 1963):345–66.

———. "Population Policy: Will Current Programs Succeed?" *Science* 10 (November 1967):730–39.

———. *Analysis of Trends, Relationships and Developments.* World Urbanization 1950–1970, vol. 2. Population Monograph Series, no. 9. Berkeley, Cal.: Institute of International Studies, University of California, 1972.

———. "Zero Population Growth: The Goal and the Means." *Daedalus* 102 (Fall 1973):15–30.

———. "The World's Population Crisis." In Robert K. Merton and Robert Nisbet (eds.), *Contemporary Social Problems.* 2d ed. New York: Harcourt, Brace, Jovanovich, 1976.

———, and Moore, Wilbert. "Some Principles of Stratification." *American Sociological Review* 10 (April 1945):242–49.

Davis, Nanette J. *Sociological Constructions of Deviance.* Dubuque, Iowa: William C. Brown Company, 1975.

Dearman, Nancy B., and Plisko, Valena White. "Test Scores and Attainment Rates." *American Education* 17 (August/September 1981):15–20.

Deckard, Barbara. *The Woman's Movement: Political, Socioeconomic and Psychological Issues.* New York: Harper and Row, 1975.

DeJong, Peter Y.; Brewer, Milton J.; and Robin, Stanley S. "Patterns of Female Intergenerational Occupational Mobility." *American Sociological Review* 36 (December 1971):1033–42.

Demerath, N. J., III. *Social Class in American Protestantism.* Chicago: Rand McNally, 1965.

Dentler, Robert, and Erikson, Kai. "The Functions of Deviance in Groups." *Social Problems* 7 (1959):98–102.

Denzin, Norman K. *Childhood Socialization.* San Francisco: Jossey-Bass, 1977.

Deutsch, Morton. "The Effects of Cooperation and Competition

Upon Group Process." In Dorwin Cartwright and Alvin Zander (eds.), *Group Dynamics*. 3d ed. New York: Harper & Row, 1968.

Dobzhansky, Theodosius G. *Genetic Diversity and Human Equality*. New York: Basic Books, 1973.

Domhoff, G. William. *Who Really Rules?* New Brunswick, N.J.: Transaction Books, 1978.

———. *Who Rules America?* Englewood Cliffs, N.J.: Prentice-Hall, 1967.

Donovan, James A. *Militarism, U.S.A.* New York: Scribner's, 1970.

Downton, James V., Jr. "An Evolutionary Theory of Spiritual Conversion and Commitment: The Case of Divine Light Mission." *Journal for the Scientific Study of Religion* 19 (December 1980):381–96.

Dreeben, Robert. *On What Is Learned in School*. Reading, Mass.: Addison-Wesley, 1968.

Dubos, René. "Symbiosis Between Earth and Humankind." *Science* 193 (6 August 1976):459–62.

Ducoff, Louis J. "The Role of Migration in the Demographic Development of Latin America." Components of Population Change in Latin America. *Milbank Memorial Fund Quarterly* 43 (October 1965), Part 2: 197–207.

Durkheim, Emile. *Rules of the Sociological Method*. Translated by S. Solovay and J. Mueller. Edited by G. Catlin. New York: Macmillan, 1938.

———. *The Elementary Forms of the Religious Life*. Translated by Joseph W. Swain. New York: Collier, 1961.

Dwiggins, Dan. *The SST: Here It Comes, Ready or Not: The Story of the Controversial Supersonic Transport*. Garden City, N.Y.: Doubleday, 1968.

Earle, John R.; Knudsen, Dean D.; and Shriver, Donald W., Jr. *Spindles and Spires*. Atlanta: John Knox Press, 1976.

Eckholm, Erik P. *Losing Ground: Environmental Stress and World Food Prospects*. New York: Norton, 1976.

Eichler, E. P., and Kaplan, M. *The Community Builders*. Berkeley, Cal.: University of California Press, 1967.

Eisenstadt, S. N. *From Generation to Generation*. New York: Free Press (paper), 1956.

Eitzen, D. Stanley. *Social Problems*. Boston: Allyn and Bacon, 1980.

Elkins, Stanley. *Slavery*. Chicago: University of Chicago Press, 1959.

Ellwood, Robert S., Jr. *Religious and Spiritual Groups in Modern America*. Englewood Cliffs, N.J.: Prentice-Hall, 1973.

Erikson, E. *Childhood and Society*. New York: Norton, 1950.

Espenshade, Thomas J. "Value and Cost of Children." *Population Bulletin* 32 (April 1977):2–47.

Etzioni, Amitai. *A Comparative Analysis of Organizations*. New York: Free Press, 1961.

———. *Modern Organizations*. Englewood Cliffs, N.J.: Prentice-Hall, 1964.

Eve, Raymond A. " 'Adolescent Culture', Convenient Myth or Reality? A Comparison of Students and Their Teachers." *Sociology of Education* 48 (Spring 1975):153–67.

Eversley, David E. *Social Theories of Fertility and the Malthusian Debate*. London: Oxford University Press, 1959.

Farley, Reynolds; Richards, Toni; and Murdock, Clarence. "School Desegregation and White Flight: An Investigation of Competing Models and Their Discrepant Findings." *Sociology of Education* 53 (July 1980):123–39.

———; Schuman, H.; Branchi, S.; Colasanto, D.; and Hatchett, S. "Chocolate City, Vanilla Suburbs: Will the Trend Toward Racially Separate Communities Continue?" Presented at the Annual Meetings of the Population Association of America, 1976.

Faunce, William A. "Automation and the Automobile Worker." *Social Problems* 6 (Summer 1958a):68–78.

———. "Automation in the Automobile Industry: Some Consequences for In-Plant Social Structure." *American Sociological Review* 23 (August 1958b):401–7.

Fava, Sylvia. "Beyond Suburbia." *Annals of the American Academy of Political and Social Sciences* 422 (1975):10–24.

Featherman, David. "Opportunities are Expanding." *Society* 16 (March/April 1979):4–11.

Festinger, Leon, and Freedman, J. L. "Dissonance Reduction and Moral Values." In P. Worchel and D. Byrne (eds.), *Personality Change*. New York: Wiley, 1964.

Finkelhor, David. *Sexually Victimized Children*. New York: The Free Press, 1979.

Fischer, Claude S. *The Urban Experience*. N.Y.: Harcourt Brace, Javanovich, 1976.

———. "The Public and Private Worlds of City Life." *American Sociological Review* 46 (June 1981):306–16.

Fitch, Robert, and Oppenheimer, Mary. "Who Rules the Corporations? Part 2." *Socialist Revolution* 1 (September–October 1970a):61–114.

———. "Who Rules the Corporations? Part 3." *Socialist Revolution* 1 (November–December 1970b):33–94.

Fitzpatrick, Joseph R. *Puerto Rican Americans*. Englewood Cliffs, N.J.: Prentice-Hall, 1971.

Form, William H. "Auto Workers and Their Machines: A Study of Work, Factory, and Job Satisfaction in Four Countries." *Social Forces* 52 (September 1973):1–15.

———. "Technology and Social Behavior of Workers in Four Countries: A Sociotechnical Perspective." *American Sociological Review* 37 (December 1971):727–38.

Form, William, and Stone, Gregory. "The Social Significance of Clothing on Occupational Life." East Lansing, Mich.: Michigan State University Agricultural Experiment Station Technological Bulletin 262, 1967.

Fortune. "The Fifty Largest Industrial Companies in the World." (August 13, 1979).

Foster, John. *Class Struggle and the Industrial Revolution: Early Industrial Capitalism in Three English Towns*. New York: St. Martin's, 1974.

Freedman, Ronald, and Berelson, Bernard. "The Record of Family Planning Programs." *Studies in Family Planning* 7 (January 1976):1–40.

Friedan, Betty. *The Feminine Mystique*. New York: Norton, 1964.

Friedmann, Georges, *Industrial Society: The Emergence of the Human Problems of Automation*. Glencoe, Ill.: Free Press, 1955.

Freud, Anna, and Burlingham, D. *War and Children*. New York, Medical War Books, 1943.

Freud, Sigmund. *The Future of an Illusion*. London: Hogarth, 1934.

Fromm, Erich. *The Dogma of Christ*. New York: Holt, Rinehart and Winston, 1963.

Fukuyama, Yoshio, "The Major Dimensions of Church Membership." *Review of Religious Research* 2 (Spring 1961):154–61.

Galaskiewicz, Joseph. "The Structure of Community Organizational Networks." *Social Forces* 57 (June 1979):1346–64.

Galbraith, John Kenneth. *American Capitalism: The Concept of Countervailing Power*. Boston: Houghton Mifflin, 1956.

———. *The New Industrial State*. Boston: Houghton Mifflin, 1967. Revised, 1978.

Gallagher, James, and Burke, Peter J. "Scapegoating and Leader Behavior." *Social Forces* 52(1974):481–88.

Gallup Poll, The. *Gallup Opinion Index.*
Report No. 198, March 1982. "What's Important to Americans?"
Report No. 184, January 1981. "Religion and Life: Growing or Declining in Importance?
Report No. 183, December 1980. "Profile of Registered Voters" and "Vote by Groups in Presidential Elections Since 1952."

Gans, Herbert. "The Failure of Urban Renewal: A Critique and Some Proposals." *Commentary* 39 (1965):29–37.

———. "Urbanism and Suburbanism As Ways of Life." Pp. 70–84 in Gutman, R. and Popenoe, D. (eds.) *Neighborhood, City and Metropolis*, N.Y.: Random House, 1968.

———. *The Urban Villagers: Group and Class in the Life of Italian-Americans*. New York: Free Press, 1962.

Garfinkel, Harold. "Conditions of Successful Degradation Ceremonies." *American Journal of Sociology* 61 (1956):420–24.

Gelfand, Donald E. "The Challenge of Applied Sociology." *American Sociologist* 10 (February 1975):13–18.

Gelles, Richard J., and Straus, Murray A. "Violence in the American Family." *Journal of Social Issues* 35 (No. 3, 1979):15–39.

Gergen, Kenneth, and Gergen, Mary. "Encounter: Research Catalyst for General Theories of Social Behavior." Unpublished manuscript. Swarthmore College, 1971.

Gerth, Hans, and Mills, C. Wright, eds. *From Max Weber: Essays in Sociology*. New York: Oxford University Press, 1946.

Gilbert, Dennis and Kahl, Joseph A. *The American Class Structure: A New Synthesis*. Homewood, Ill.: Dorsey, 1982.

Gilder, George. "The Suicide of the Sexes" *Harpers* 248 (July 1973):42–43.

Ginzberg, Eli. *Good Jobs, Bad Jobs, No Jobs*. Cambridge, Mass.: Harvard University Press, 1979.

Gist, Noel P., and Fava, Sylvia F. *Urban Society*. New York: Crowell, 1969.

Glass, Ronald W. "Work Stoppages and Teachers: History and Prospects." *Monthly Labor Review* (1967):43–46.

Glenn, Norvel D., and Hyland, Ruth. "Religious Preference and Worldly Success—Some Evidence from National Surveys." *American Sociological Review* 32 (February 1967):73–85.

Glenn, Norval D., and McLanahan, Sara. "Children and Marital Happiness: A Further Specification of the Relationship." *Journal of Marriage and the Family* 44 (February 1982):63–72.

Glick, Paul C., and Spanier, Graham B. "Married and Unmarried Cohabitation in the United States." *Journal of Marriage and the Family* 42 (February 1980):19–30.

Glock, Charles Y., and Stark, Rodney. *Religion and Society in Tension*. Chicago: Rand McNally, 1965.

———. *Christian Beliefs and Anti-Semitism*. New York: Harper & Row, 1966.

Gochros, Jean S. "Only Spank When You're Angry." *American Baby* 43 (March 1981):38–45.

Goffman, Erving, *Asylums: Essays on the Social Situation of Mental Patients and Other Inmates*. Garden City, N.Y.: Doubleday, 1961.

———. *Stigma: Notes on the Management of Spoiled Identity*. Englewood Cliffs, N.J.: Prentice-Hall, 1963.

———. *Interaction Ritual: Essays on Face-to-Face Behavior*. Garden City, N.Y.: Doubleday Anchor, 1967.

———. *The Presentation of Self in Everyday Life*. N.Y.: Doubleday, 1959.

———. *Relations in Public: Microstudies of the Public Order*. N.Y.: Basic Books, 1972.

Golden, Hilda H. *Urbanization and Cities*. Lexington, Mass.: Heath, 1981.

Goldscheider, Calvin. *Population, Modernization, and Social Structure*. Boston: Little, Brown, 1971.

Goldschmidt, Walter. *Man's Way: A Preface to the Understanding of Human Society*. New York: Holt, Rinehart and Winston, 1959.

Goldsen, Rose; Rosenberg, Morris; Williams, Robin M.; and Suchman, Edward A. *What College Students Think* New York: Van Nostrand, 1960.

Goldstein, Bernice, and Perrucci, Robert. "The TV Western and the Modern American Spirit." *Southwestern Social Science Quarterly* (March 1963):357–66.

Goldstein, Joseph; Freud, Anna; and Solnit, Albert J. *Before the Best Interests of the Child*. New York: The Free Press, 1979.

Goldstein, Michael. "Exposure to Erotic Stimuli and Sexual Deviance." *Journal of Social Issues* 29 (1973):197–219.

Goldstein; Sidney; and Goldscheider, Calvin. *Jewish Americans: Three Generations in a Jewish Community*. Englewood Cliffs, N.J.: Prentice-Hall, 1968.

Goode, William J. "A Theory of Role Strain." *American Sociological Review* 25 (1960):483–96.

———. "The Role of the Family in Industrialization." In Robert F. Winch and Louis W. Goodman (eds.), *Selected Studies in Marriage and the Family*. 3d ed. New York: Holt, Rinehart and Winston, 1968.

Gordon, C. W. *The Social System of the High School.* New York: Free Press, 1957.

Gordon, Judith Bograd. "Single Parents: Personal Struggles and Social Issues," in Peter J. Stein, ed. *Single Life.* New York: St. Martin's Press, 1981, pp. 278–88.

Gordon, Milton M. *Assimilation in American Life.* New York: Oxford University Press, 1964.

Gorsuch, Richard L., and Aleshire, Daniel. "Christian Faith and Ethnic Prejudices: A Review and Interpretation of Research." *Journal for the Scientific Study of Religion* 13 (September 1974):281–307.

Gough, Kathleen E. "The Nayar and the Definition of Marriage." *Journal of the Royal Anthropological Institute of Great Britain and Ireland* 89 (1959): Part I.

Gouldner, Alvin W. *Patterns of Industrial Bureaucracy.* Glencoe, Ill.: Free Press, 1954.

———. "Cosmopolitans and Locals: Toward An Analysis of Latent Social Roles, I and II." *Administrative Science Quarterly* (December 1957 and March 1958):281–306 and 444–80.

———. "The Sociologist as Partisan: Sociology and The Welfare State." *American Sociologist* 3 (May 1968):103–16.

Grant. W. Vance, and Eiden, Leo J. *Digest of Education Statistics 1981.* National Center for Educational Statistics, February, 1981.

Gray, Susan H. "Exposure to Pornography and Aggression Toward Women: The Case of the Angry Male." *Social Problems* 29 (April 1982):387–98.

Grebler, Leo; Moore, Joan W.; and Guxman, Ralph C. *The Mexican-American People.* New York: Free Press, 1970.

Greeley, Andrew. *Ethnicity, Domination, and Inequality.* Beverly Hills, Calif.: Sage, 1976.

———. *The American Catholic: A Social Portrait.* New York: Basic Books, 1977.

———. "Catholics and the Upper Middle Class: A Comment on Roof." *Social Forces* 59 (1981):825–30.

———. *The Denominational Society.* Glenview, Ill.: Scott, Foresman, 1972.

———. *Ethnicity in the United States.* New York: Wiley, 1974.
Greeley, Andrew M., and Rossi, Peter H. *The Education of Catholic Americans.* Chicago: Aldine, 1966.

———. *Why Can't They Be Like Us? America's White Ethnic Groups,* New York: Dutton, 1971.

Green, Robert W., ed. *Protestantism and Capitalism: The Weber Thesis and Its Critics.* Boston, Heath, 1959.

Gruenberg, Barry. "The Happy Worker: An Analysis of Educational and Occupational Differences in Determinants of Job Satisfaction." *American Journal of Sociology* 86 (September 1980):247–71.

Guetzkow, Harold, and Simon, Herbert A. "The Impact of Certain Communication Nets Upon Organization and Performance in Task-Oriented Groups." *Management Science* 1 (1955):233–50.

Gulliver, Philip H. "The Jie of Uganda." In Yehudi A. Cohen Man in Adaptation: The Cultural Present. Chicago: Aldine, 1968.

Gurr, Ted Robert. "Psychological Factors in Civil Violence." *World Politics* (January 1968b):245–78.

Gusfield, Joseph. "Social Structure and Moral Reform: A Study of the Women's Christian Temperance Union." *American Journal of Sociology* 61 (1955):221–32.

———. "Tradition and Modernity: Misplaced Polarities in the Study of Social Change." *American Journal of Sociology* 72 (January 1967):351–62.

Hackenberg, Robert A. "Economic Alternatives in Arid Lands: A Case Study of the Pima and Papago Indians." In Yehudi A. Cohen, Man in Adaptation: The Cultural Present. Chicago: Aldine, 1968.

Hadden, Jeffrey K., and Swann, Charles E. *Prime Time Preachers: The Rising Power of Televangelism,* Reading, Pa. Addison-Wesley, 1981.

Hall, Richard H.; Haas, J. Eugene; and Johnson, Norman J. "Organizational Size, Complexity, and Formation." *American Sociological Review* 32 (December 1967):903–12.

Hallowell, Irving A. "The Size of Algonkian Hunting Territories: A Function of Ecological Adjustment." *American Anthropologist* 51 (1949):33–45.

Hamby, Russell. "Effects of Motivational Orientation on Deindividuation." *Human Relations* 29 (July 1976):687–97.

Hammond, Phillip E., ed. *Sociologists at Work.* New York: Doubleday, 1967.

Han, Wan Sang. "Two Conflicting Themes: Common Values Versus Class Differential Values." *American Sociological Review* 34 (October 1969):679–90.

Hance, William A. *Population, Migration, and Urbanization in Africa.* New York: Columbia University Press, 1970.

Hannerz, Ulf. *Soulside: Inquiries into Ghetto Culture and Community.* New York: Columbia University Press, 1969.

Hare, Paul A. *Handbook of Small Group Research.* N.Y.: Free Press, 1976.

Harlow, H. "Love in Infant Monkeys." *Scientific American,* June 1959, pp. 68–74.

———, and Harlow M. "Social Deprivation in Monkeys." *Scientific American,* November 1962.

Harris, Chauncey C., and Ullman, Edward L. "The Nature of Cities." *Annals of The American Academy of Political and Social Sciences,* 242 (1945):7–17.

Hartley, Shirley Foster. *Population: Quantity vs. Quality.* Englewood Cliffs, N.J.: Prentice-Hall, 1972.

Harvey, D. "Social Justice and Spatial Systems." *Antipode Monographs in Social Geography* 1 (1972).

Hatcher, Robert A.; Stewart, Gary K.; Guest, Felicia; Finkelstein, Richard; and Godwin, Charles. *Contraceptive Technology 1976–1977.* 8th rev. ed. New York: Irvington, 1976.

Hauser, Robert M.; Sewell, William H.; and Alwin, Duane F. "High School Effects on Achievement." In William H. Sewell, Robert M. Hauser and David L. Featherman (eds.), *Schooling and Achievement in American Society.* N.Y.: Academic Press, 1976.

Havighurst, Robert J. "Education, Social Mobility and Social Change in Four Societies." *International Review of Education* 4, 1958.

Hawley, Amos. "Metropolitan Population and Metropolitan Government Expenditure in Central Cities." Pp. 773–83 in

Hatt, Paul K., and Reiss, Albert (eds.), *Cities and Society.* Glencoe, Ill.: Free Press, 1956.

———. *Urban Society.* N.Y.: Wiley, 1981.

Hayghe, Howard. "Families and the Rise of Working Wives— An Overview." *Monthly Labor Review* 99 (May 1976):12– 19.

Heinz, Donald. "The Christian World Liberation Front." In Charles Y. Glock and Robert N. Bellah, eds. *The New Religious Consciousness,* Berkeley: University of California Press, 1976.

Herberg, Will. *Protestant-Catholic-Jew.* Garden City, N.Y.: Doubleday, 1956.

Herzog, A. Regula. "High School Seniors' Occupational Plans and Values: Trends in Sex Differences 1976 Through 1980." *Sociology of Education* 55 (January 1982):1–13.

Hertel, Bradley; Hendershot, Gerry E.; and Grim, James W. "Religion and Attitudes Toward Abortion: A Study of Nurses and Social Workers." *Journal for the Scientific Study of Religion* 13 (March 1974):23–24.

Hess, Robert D., and Torney, Judith V. *The Development of Political Attitudes in Children.* Chicago: Aldine, 1967.

Himes, Joseph S. *Racial and Ethnic Relations.* Dubuque, Iowa: Brown, 1974.

Hobbs, Daniel. "Parenthood as Crisis: A Third Study" *Journal of Marriage and the Family* 27 (August 1965):367–72.

Hobbs, Daniel, and Cole, Sue. "Transition to Parenthood: A Decade Replication" *Journal of Marriage and the Family* 38 (November 1976):723–31.

Hodge, Robert W.; Trieman, Donald J.; and Rossi, Peter H. "A Comparative Study of Occupational Prestige." Pp. 309–21 in Bendix Reinhard and Lipset, Seymour M. *Class, Status and Power,* 2d ed. N.Y.: Free Press, 1966.

Hofferth, Sandra L. "Day Care in the Next Decade: 1980–1990." *Journal of Marriage and the Family* 41 (August 1979):649– 58.

Hollinger, Richard C., and Clark, John P. "Formal and Informal Social Controls of Employee Deviance." *Sociological Quarterly* 23 (Summer, 1982):333–43.

Hollingshead, August B. *Elmtown's Youth.* New York: Wiley, 1949.

Homans, George C. *Social Behavior: Its Elementary Forms.* New York: Harcourt and Brace, 1961.

Horowitz, Irving Louis. "The Conflict Society: War as a Social Problem." In Howard S. Becker (ed.), *Social Problems: A Modern Approach.* New York: Wiley, 1967.

———. "The Life and Death of Project Camelot." *Trans-action* 3 (November 1965):3–7.

Hoselitz, Bert F. "Economic Growth: Noneconomic Aspects." In *International Encyclopedia of the Social Sciences* 4. New York: Macmillan and Free Press, 1968.

Howard, James; Liptzin, M.; and Riefler, C. "Is Pornography a Problem?" *Journal of Social Issues* 29 (1973):133–45.

Hoyt, Homer. *The Structure and Growth of Residential Neighborhoods in the United States.* Washington, D.C.: Federal Housing Administration, 1939.

Huber, Joan, and Spitze, Glenna. "Wives' Employment, House-

hold Behaviors and Sex-Role Attitudes." *Social Forces* 60 (September 1981):150–169.

Hudson, Winthrop S. "Puritanism and the Spirit of Capitalism." In Robert W. Green (ed.), *Protestantism and Capitalism.* Boston: Heath, 1959.

Humphreys, Laud. *Tearoom Trade.* Chicago: Aldine, 1970.

Hunt, Richard A., and King, Morton B. "Religiosity and Marriage." *Journal for the Scientific Study of Religion* 17 (December 1978):399-406.

Hunter, Floyd. *Community Power Structure.* Chapel Hill, N.C.: University of North Carolina Press, 1953.

Hunter, Guy. *Modernizing Peasant Societies.* New York: Oxford University Press, 1969.

Huntington, Richard, and Metcalf, Peter. *Celebrations of Death: The Anthropology of Mortuary Ritual.* Cambridge: Cambridge University Press, 1979.

Hurwitz, Jacob; Zander, Alvin; and Hymovitch, Bernard. "Some Effects of Power on the Relations Among Group Members." In Dorwin Cartwright and Alvin Zander (eds.), *Group Dynamics.* 3d ed. New York: Harper & Row, 1968.

Hutchinson, Edward P. *The Population Debate.* Boston: Houghton Mifflin, 1967.

Hyman, Herbert H. "The Value Systems of the Direct Classes: A Social Psychological Contribution to the Analysis of Stratification." In Reinhardt Bendix and Seymour M. Lipset (eds.), *Class, Status and Power.* New York: Free Press, 1953.

Hymer, Stephen H. *The Multinational Corporation: A Radical Approach.* N.Y.: Cambridge University Press, 1979.

Inglehart, Alfreda P. *Married Women and Work, 1957 and 1976.* Lexington, Mass.: D.C. Heath and Co., 1979.

Inkeles, Alex. "Making Men Modern: On the Causes and Consequences of Individual Change in Six Developing Countries." *American Journal of Sociology* 75 (September 1969):208– 25.

———. *What is Sociology?* Englewood Cliffs, N.J.: Prentice-Hall, 1964.

Inkeles, Alex, and Rossi, Peter H. "National Comparisons of Occupational Prestige." *American Journal of Sociology* 61 (January 1956):329–39.

Inkeles, Alex, and Smith, David H. *Becoming Modern: Individual Change in Six Developing Countries.* Cambridge, Mass.: Harvard University Press, 1974.

Itard, Jean. *The Wolf Boy of Aveyron.* Translated by George Humphrey and Muriel Humphrey. New York: Appleton-Century-Crofts, 1962.

Jackson, Elton F., and Crockett, Harry J. "Occupational Mobility in the United States: A Point Estimate and Trend Comparison." *American Sociological Review* 29 (February 1964):5– 15.

Jackson, Elton R.; Fox, William S.; and Crockett, Harry J., Jr. "Religion and Occupational Achievement." *American Sociological Review* 35 (February 1970):48–63.

Jacquet, Constant H., Jr. ed. *Yearbook of American and Canadian Churches, 1981*. Nashville and New York: Abingdon Press, 1981.

Janis, Irving L., and Mann, Leon. *Decision Making: A Psychological Analysis of Conflict, Choice, and Commitment*. N.Y.: Free Press, 1977.

Janowitz, Morris. "Professionalization of Sociology." *American Journal of Sociology* 78 (July 1972):105–35.

Jencks, Christopher. *Inequality*. New York: Basic Books, 1972.

Jensen, Arthur R. "How Much Can We Boost I.Q. and Scholastic Achievement?" *Harvard Educational Review* 39 (1969):1–123.

Johnson, Chalmers. *Revolutionary Change*. Boston: Little, Brown, 1966.

Johnston, Ronald L. National Opinion Research Center Survey conducted for the Lutheran Council in the U.S.A., 1970. Cited in Ronald L. Johnston, *Religion and Society in Interaction: The Sociology of Religion*. Englewood Cliffs, N.J.: Prentice-Hall, 1975.

Jones, Edward E. *Ingratiation*. N.Y.: Appleton-Century-Crofts, 1964.

Jones, Edward E.; Gergen, Kenneth; Gimpert, Peter; and Thibaut, John. "Some Conditions Affecting the Use of Ingratiation to Influence Performance Evaluation." *Journal of Personality and Social Psychology* 1 (1965):613–25.

Josephy, Alvin M., Jr. "Indians in History." In R. Perrucci and M. Pilisuk (eds.), *The Triple Revolution Emerging*. Boston: Little, Brown, 1971.

Kahl, Joseph A. "Educational and Occupational Aspirations of 'Common Man' Boys." *Harvard Educational Review* 23 (Summer 1953):186–203.

———. *The Measurement of Modernism*. Austin: University of Texas Press, 1968.

Kain, J. "The Distribution and Movement of Jobs and Industry." Pp. 1–43 in J. Q. Wilson, (ed.), *The Metropolitan Enigma*. Cambridge, Mass.: Harvard University Press, 1968.

Kanter, Rosabeth. *Commitment and Community*. Cambridge, Mass.: Harvard University Press, 1972.

Katz, Daniel, and Kahn, Robert. *The Social Psychology of Organizations*. New York: Wiley, 1966.

Katz, Michael B. *The Irony of Early School Reform*. Cambridge, Mass.: Harvard University Press, 1968.

Kaysen, Carl. "The Corporation: How Much Power? What Scope?" In Edward S. Mason (ed.), *The Corporation in Modern Society*. Cambridge, Mass.: Harvard University Press, 1959.

Keesing, Roger M. *Cultural Anthropology: A Contemporary Perspective*. Second Edition. New York: Holt, Rinehart, and Winston, 1981.

Kelley, Dean M. *Why Conservative Churches are Growing*. New York: Harper & Row, 1972.

Kempe, Ruth S., and Kempe, C. Henry. *Child Abuse*. Cambridge, Mass.: Harvard University Press, 1978.

Kennedy, Robert E., Jr. "The Protestant Ethic and the Parsis." *American Journal of Sociology* 68 (July 1962):11–20.

Kephart, William M. *Extraordinary Groups: The Sociology of Unconventional Life-Styles*. New York: St. Martin's Press, 1982.

Kerckhoff, Alan. "The States Attainment Process: Socialization or Allocation." *Social Forces* 55 (December 1976):368–381.

Kerr, Clark; Harbison, F. H.; Dunlop, J. T.; and Myers, C. A. *Industrialism and Industrial Man*. Cambridge, Mass.: Harvard University Press, 1960.

Kessler, Ronald C., and McRae, James A. Jr. "The Effect of Wives' Employment on the Mental Health of Married Men and Women." *American Sociological Review* 47 (April 1982):216–27.

Key, V. O. *Politics, Parties and Pressure Groups*. New York: Crowell, 1964.

Kluckhohn, Clyde. *Culture and Behavior*. New York: Free Press, 1962.

Knox, Robert E., and Douglas, Ronald L. "Trivial Incentives, Marginal Comprehension, and Dubious Generalizations from Prisoner's Dilemma Studies." *Journal of Personality and Social Psychology* 20 (1971):160–65.

Koestler, Arthur. *Act of Creation*. New York: Macmillan, 1964.

Kols, Adrienne; Rinehart, Ward; Piotrow, Phyllis T.; Doucette, Louise; and Quillin, Wayne F. "Oral Contraceptives in the 1980s." *Population Reports*. Series A, Number 6 (May–June 1982). Population Information Program, the Johns Hopkins University, Baltimore, Md.

Kornblue, Joyce L. *Rebel Voices: An I.W.W. Anthology*. Ann Arbor: University of Michigan Press, 1964.

Kornhauser, Arthur. "Toward an Assessment of the Mental Health of Factory Workers." *Human Organization* 21 (Spring 1962):43–46.

Kornhauser, William. " 'Power Elite' or 'Veto Groups'?" In Rein hard Bendix and Seymour M. Lipset, eds. *Class, Status, and Power*. 2nd. ed. New York: Free Press, 1966.

———. *Scientists in Industry*. Berkeley: University of California Press, 1963.

Kozol, Jonathan. *Death at an Early Age*. New York: Bantam Books, 1967.

Kriesberg, Louis. *Mothers in Poverty: A Study of Fatherless Families*. Chicago: Aldine, 1970.

Kroeber, Alfred Louis. *The Nature of Culture*. Chicago: The University of Chicago Press, 1952.

Lafargue, Paul. "Souvenirs Personnels." *Neue Zeit*, 1890.

LaGory, Mark, and Pipkin, John. *Urban Social Space*. Belmont, Cal.: Wadsworth, 1981.

LaGory, Mark; Ward, Russell A.; and Mucatel, Marc. "Patterns of Age Segregation." *Sociological Focus* 14 (January 1981):1–13.

Lane, Harlan. *The Wild Boy of Aveyron*. Cambridge, Mass.: Harvard University Press, 1976.

Lane, Robert E. "Fathers and Sons: Foundations of Political Belief." *American Sociological Review* 24 (June 1959):502–511.

———. *Political Life*. New York: Free Press, 1964.

Langton, Kenneth, and Jennings, M. Kent. "Political Socialization and the High School Civics Curriculum in the United States." *American Political Science Review* 62 (September 1968): 852–67.

Larner, Robert J. *Management Control and the Large Corporation.* New York: Dunellen, 1970a.

———. "The Effect of Management-Control on the Profits of Large Corporations." In M. Zeitlin (ed.), *American Society, Inc.* Chicago: Markham, 170b.

Laumann, Edward; Marsden, Peter; and Galaskiewicz, Joseph. "Community Elite Influence Structures: Extension of a Network Approach." *American Journal of Sociology* 83 (November 1977):594–631.

Laumann, Edward O., and Pappi, Franz. "New Directions in the Study of Urban Community Elites." *American Sociological Review* 38 (April 1973):212–30.

———. *Networks of Collective Action: A Perspective on Community Influence Systems.* N.Y.: Academic Press, 1976.

Lawrence, Douglas H., and Festinger, Leon. *Deterrents and Reinforcement: The Psychology of Insufficient Reward.* Stanford, Calif.: Stanford University Press, 1962.

Lazerwitz, Bernard, and Harrison, Michael. "American Jewish Denominations." *American Sociological Review* 44 (August 1979):656–66.

Leavitt, Harold J. "Some Effects of Certain Communication Patterns on Group Performance." *Journal of Abnormal and Social Psychology* 46 (1951):38–50.

Lee, Gary R. "Kinship in the Seventies: A Decade Review of Research and Theory." *Journal of Marriage and the Family* 42 (November 1980):923–34.

———, and Ellithorpe, Eugene. "Intergenerational Exchange and Subjective Well-being Among the Elderly." *Journal of Marriage and the Family* 44 (February 1982):217–24.

Leggett, John, and Cervinka, Claudette. "Countdown: Labor Statistics Revisited." *Society* 10 (November/December 1972):99–103.

LeMasters, E. E. "Parenthood as Crisis." *Marriage and Family Living* 19 (November 1957):352–55.

Lemert, Edwin. *Social Pathology.* New York: McGraw-Hill, 1951.

———. *Human Deviance, Social Problems, and Social Control.* Englewood Cliffs, N.J.: Prentice-Hall, 1967.

Lenski, Gerhard. *The Religious Factor.* Garden City, N.Y.: Doubleday, 1961.

———. *Power and Privilege: A Theory of Social Stratification.* New York: McGraw-Hill, 1966.

———. *Human Societies.* New York: McGraw-Hill, 1970.

Lenski, Gerhard, and Lenski, Jean. *Human Societies: An Introduction to Macrosociology.* N.Y.: McGraw-Hill, 1982.

Lewis, Michael. "Culture and Gender Roles: There's No Unisex in the Nursery." *Psychology Today* 5 (May 1972):54–57.

Lewis, Oscar. *La Vida: A Puerto Rican Family in the Culture of Poverty—San Juan and New York.* New York: Random House, 1966.

Lieberman, Stanley. "The Effects of Changes in Roles on the Attitudes of Role Occupants." *Human Relations* 9 (1956):385–402.

Liebow, Elliot. *Tally's Corner: A Study of Negro Streetcorner Men.* Boston: Little, Brown, 1967.

Lipset, Seymour M. *Political Man: The Social Bases of Politics.* New York: Doubleday, 1960.

Lipset, Seymour M., and Bendix, Reinhard. *Social Mobility in Industrial Society.* Berkeley and Los Angeles: University of California Press, 1962.

Loehlin, J. D.; Lindzey, G.; and Spuhler, J. N. *Race Differences in Intelligence.* San Francisco: W. H. Freeman, 1975.

Lofland, John. *Doomsday Cult.* Englewood Cliffs, N.J.: Prentice-Hall, 1968.

Lofland, Lynn. *A World of Strangers.* N.Y.: Basic Books, 1973.

Logan, Rayford W. *The Betrayal of the Negro from Rutherford B. Hayes to Woodrow Wilson.* New York: Collier, 1965.

Luckmann, Thomas. *The Invisible Religion.* New York: Macmillan, 1967.

Lundberg, Ferdinand. *The Rich and the Super-Rich.* New York: Bantam, 1969.

Maccoby, Eleanor, and Jacklin, Carol. *The Psychology of Sex Differences.* Palo Alto, Calif.: Stanford University Press, 1974.

Malefijt, Annemarie de Waal. *Religion and Culture.* New York: Macmillan, 1968.

Malson, Lucien. *Wolf Children and the Problem of Human Nature.* New York: Monthly Review Press, 1972.

Malthus, Thomas Robert. *On Population.* Edited by Gertrude Himmelfarb, New York: Modern Library, 1960 (originally published 1798–1872).

Mankoff, Milton. "Power in Advanced Capitalist Society: A Review Essay on Recent Elitist and Marxist Criticism of Pluralist Theory." *Social Problems* 17 (Winter 1970):422–30.

Manuel, Frank E., ed. *Utopias and Utopian Thought.* Boston: Houghton Mifflin, 1966.

Marcson, Simon. *The Scientist in American Industry.* New York: Harper & Row, 1960.

Marini, Margaret M. "Effects of the Timing of Marriage and First Birth on Fertility." *Journal of Marriage and the Family* 43 (February 1981):27–46.

Marsden, Peter V. "Introducing Influence Processes into a System of Collective Decisions." *American Journal of Sociology* 86 (May 1981):1203–35.

Marshall, Harvey. "White Movement to Suburbs." *American Sociological Review* 44 (December 1979):975–94.

Marshall, Harvey. "Social Segregation, Percent Black, and the Suburbanization of White Children." Unpublished Manuscript. Purdue University, 1981.

Martin, David. "The Denomination." *British Journal of Sociology* 13 (October 1962):1–14.

Marx, Karl. *Capital: A Critique of Political Economy.* New York: Modern Library, 1906.

———. *The Communist Manifesto.* Chicago: Regnery, 1954. (Originally published 1848.)

———. "Religious Illusion and the Task of History." In Norman Birnbaum and Gertrud Lenzer (eds.), *Sociology and Religion,*

A Book of Readings. Englewood Cliffs, N.J.: Prentice-Hall, 1969.

Marx, Leo. *The Machine in the Garden: Technology and the Pastoral Ideal in America.* New York: Oxford University Press, 1964.

Mason, Karen O.; Czayka, John L.; and Arber, Sara. "Change in U.S. Women's Sex Role Attitudes, 1964–1974." *American Sociological Review* 41 (August 1976):573–96.

Matthews, Donald R., and Prothro, James W. *Negroes and the New Southern Politics.* New York: Harcourt, Brace and World, Inc. 1966.

Matza, David. *Delinquency and Drift.* New York: Wiley, 1964.

McGuire, Meredith. "Testimony as a Commitment Mechanism in Catholic Pentecostal Prayer Groups." *Journal for the Scientific Study of Religion* 16 (June 1977):165–68.

McIntosh, William, and Alston, Jon. "Lenski Revisited: The Linkage Role of Religion in Primary and Secondary Groups." *American Journal of Sociology* 87 (1982):853–83.

Mead, George H. *Mind, Self and Society.* Chicago: University of Chicago Press, 1934.

Mead, Margaret. *Coming of Age in Samoa.* New York: William Morrow and Co., 1928.

———. *Sex and Temperament in Three Primitive Societies.* Magnolia, Mass.: Peter Smith, 1935.

Mechanic, David. "Sources of Power of Lower Participants in Complex Organizations." *Administrative Science Quarterly* 7 (December 1962):349–64.

Medsker, L. L., and Trent, J. W. "The Influence of Different Types of Public Higher Institutions on College Attendance from Varying Socioeconomic and Ability Levels." Berkeley, Calif.: Center for Research and Development in Higher Education, 1965.

Meek, Ronald L., ed. *Marx and Engels on the Population Bomb.* Berkeley, Calif.: Ramparts, 1971.

Meggitt, M. J. *Desert People.* Sydney, Australia: Angus and Robertson, Ltd., 1962.

Melton, David. *Burn the Schools Save the Children.* New York: Crowell, 1975.

Merker, M. *Die Masai.* Berlin: Dietrich Reimer, 1904.

Merton, Robert K. *Social Theory and Social Structure.* Glencoe, Ill.: Free Press, 1957.

Micklin, Michael. "Urban Life and Differential Fertility: Specification of an Aspect of the Theory of the Demographic Transition." *Sociological Quarterly* 9 (Fall 1969):480–500.

Micklin, Michael, ed. *Population, Environment, and Social Organization: Current Issues in Human Ecology.* Hinsdale, Ill.: Dryden, 1973b.

Micklin, Michael, and Marnane, Patrick J. H. "The Differential Evaluation of 'Large' and 'Small' Families in Rural Colombia: Implications for Family Planning." *Social Biology* 22 (Spring 1975):44–59.

Milbrath, Lester W. *Political Participation.* Chicago: Rand McNally, 1965.

Milgram, Stanley. "The Experience of Living in Cities." *Science* 167 (1972):1461–68.

Miller, D., and Swanson, G. *Inner Conflict and Defense.* New York: Holt, 1960; Schocken, 1966.

Miller, Delbert C. *Handbook of Research Design and Social Measurement.* New York: McKay, 1964.

Miller, Seymour M. "Comparative Social Mobility." *Current Sociology* 9 (1960):81–9.

Mills, C. Wright. *The Power Elite.* New York: Oxford University Press, 1956.

———. *The Sociological Imagination.* New York: Oxford University Press, 1959.

Monahan, Thomas P., "The Extent of Interdenominational Marriage in the United States." *Journal for the Scientific Study of Religion* 10 (Summer 1971):85–92.

Money, John, and Ehrhardt, Arke A. *Man and Woman, Boy and Girl.* Baltimore: Johns Hopkins Press, 1972.

Moore, Gwen. "The Structure of a National Elite Network." *American Sociological Review* 44 (October 1978):673–92.

Moore, Joan W. *Mexican Americans.* 2d ed., Englewood Cliffs, N.J.: Prentice-Hall, 1976.

Moore, Wilbert E. *Industrial Relations and the Social Order.* New York: Macmillan, 1946.

———. *The Impact of Industry.* Englewood Cliffs, N.J.: Prentice-Hall, 1965.

Morgan, Marabel. *The Total Woman.* Old Tappan, N.J.: Fleming H. Revell Co., 1973.

Mueller, Carol, and Dimieri, T. "The Structure of Belief Systems Among Contending ERA Activists." *Social Forces* 60 (March 1982):657–75.

Muraskin, William. "The Moral Basis of a Backward Sociologist: Edward Banfield, the Italians, and the Italian-Americans." *American Journal of Sociology* 79 (May, 1974):1484–96.

Murdock, George Peter. *Social Structure.* New York: Macmillan, 1949.

Myrdal, Gunnar. *An American Dilemma: The Negro Problem and Modern Democracy.* Volume 2. New York: Harper, 1944.

Nash, Manning. "Economic Anthropology." In *International Encyclopedia of the Social Sciences* 4. New York: Macmillan and Free Press, 1968.

National Advisory Commission on Civil Disorders. *Report of the National Advisory Commission on Civil Disorders.* Washington, D.C.: U.S. Government Printing Office, 1969.

National Crime Panel. *Crime in Eight American Cities, Advance Report.* Washington, D.C.: U.S. Department of Justice, 1974.

Neugarten, Bernice; Moor, Joan; and Lowe, John. "Age Norms, Age Constraints, and Adult Socialization." *American Journal of Sociology* 70 (May 1965):710–17.

Neugarten, Bernice, and Weinstein, Karol. "The Changing American Grandparent." *Journal of Marriage and the Family* 26 (May 1964):199–204.

Neugarten, Bernice; Wood, Vivian; Kraines, Ruth; and Loomis, Barbara. "Women's Attitudes Toward the Menopause." *Vita Humana* 6 (1963):140–51.

Newcome, Paul R. "Cohabitation in America: An Assessment of Consequences." *Journal of Marriage and the Family* 41 (August 1979):597–603.

Niebuhr, H. Richard. *The Social Sources of Denominationalism.* New York: Living Age Books, 1957.

Nielsen, Joyce McCarl. *Sex in Society: Perspectives on Stratification.* Belmont, Calif.: Wadsworth, 1978.

Nimkoff, Meyer F. "Is the Joint Family An Obstacle to Industrialization?" *International Journal of Comparative Sociology* 1 (1960):109–18.

Nixon, Howard L. *The Small Group.* Englewood Cliffs, N.J.: Prentice-Hall, 1979.

Novak, Michael. *The Rise of the Unmeltable Ethnics.* New York: Macmillan, 1971.

Ogburn, William F. "The Changing Family." *The Family* 19 (1938):139–43.

Olmstead, Michael S. *The Small Group.* New York: Random House, 1959.

O'Neill, Nena, and O'Neill, George. "Open Marriage; A Synergic Model." *The Family Coordinator* 21 (1972):403–9.

Oppenheimer, Valeria K. *The Female Labor Force in the United States: Demographic and Economic Factors Governing Its Growth and Changing Composition.* Population Monograph Series, No. 5. Berkeley: University of California, 1970.

O'Toole, James. "The Reserve Army of the Underemployed: I— The World of Work." *Change* 7 (June 1975):26–33, 60–3.

Ouchi, William. *Theory Z: How American Business Can Meet the Japanese Challenge.* New York: Avon Books, 1981.

Padilla, Elena. *Up From Puerto Rico.* New York: Columbia University Press, 1958.

Palazzolo, Charles S. *Small Groups: An Introduction.* New York: D. Van Nostrand, 1981.

Parsons, Talcott. "On the Concept of Value-Commitments." *Sociological Inquiry* 38 (Spring 1968):135–60.

———. *Structure and Process in Modern Society.* New York: Free Press, 1960.

———. *The Social System.* Glencoe, Ill.: Free Press, 1951.

———. *Societies: Evolutionary and Comparative Perspectives.* Englewood Cliffs, N.J.: Prentice-Hall, 1966.

———. *The System of Modern Societies.* Englewood Cliffs, N.J.: Prentice-Hall, 1971.

Parsons, Talcott, and Bales, Robert. *Family, Socialization and Interaction Process.* Glencoe, Ill.: Free Press, 1955.

Patman Committee. "Investments and Interlocks Between Major Banks and Major Corporations." In Maurice Zeitlin (ed.), *American Society, Inc.* Chicago: Markham, 1970.

Peck, Jennifer Marks. "World Population Projections: Alternative Paths to Zero Growth." *Population Bulletin* 29, no. 5 (1974):1–32.

Perez, Galo Rene. "Traditions in Conflict." *Americas* 32 (May 1980):40–4.

Perlman, Selig. *A History of Trade Unionism in the United States.* New York: Macmillan, 1937.

Perrow, Charles. *Complex Organizations: A Critical Essay,* 2nd edition. Glenview, Ill.: Scott, Foresman, 1979.

———. "The Analysis of Goals in Complex Organizations." *American Sociological Review* 26 (December 1961):854–66.

———. "A Framework for the Comparative Analysis of Organization." *American Sociological Review* 32 (April 1967):192–208.

Perrucci, Carolyn C., and Perrucci, Robert. "Social Origins, Educational Contexts, and Career Mobility." *American Sociological Review* 35 (June 1970):451–63.

Perrucci, Robert. "Education, Stratification, and Mobility." In D. Hansen and J. Gerstl (eds.), *On Education: Sociological Perspectives.* New York: Wiley, 1967.

———. *Circle of Madness: On Being Insane and Institutionalized in America.* Englewood Cliffs, N.J.: Prentice-Hall, 1974.

———. "Engineering: Professional Servant of Power." *American Behavioral Scientist* 14 (March/April 1971):492–506.

———. "Social Distance, Bargaining Power and Compliance With Rules on a Hospital Ward." *Psychiatry* 29 (February 1966):42–55.

———. "Social Distance Strategies and Intraorganizational Stratification." *American Sociological Review,* (December 1963):951–62.

Perrucci, Robert; Anderson, Robert M.; Schendel, Dan E; and Trachtman, Leon E. "Whistle-Blowing: Professionals' Resistance to Organizational Authority." *Social Problems* 28 (December 1980):149–64.

Perrucci, Robert, and Pilisuk, Marc. "Leaders and Ruling Elites: The Interorganizational Bases of Community Power." *American Sociological Review* 35 (December 1970):1040–57.

Perrucci, Robert, and Targ, Dena B. *Mental Patients and Social Networks.* Boston: Auburn House, 1982.

Perrucci, Robert et al. "The Engineer in Industry and Government." *Journal of Engineering Education* 56 (March 1966):237–73.

Perry, Everett L.; Davis, James H.; Doyle, Ruth T; and Dyble, John E. "Toward a Typology of Unchurched Protestants." *Review of Religious Research* 21 (Supplement 1980):388–404.

Pettengell, R., and Uppal, J. *Can Cities Survive? The Fiscal Plight of American Cities.* New York: St. Martin's Press, 1974.

Pettigrew, Thomas F. "Forward." In Elizabeth W. Miller (compiler), *The Negro in America: A Bibliography.* Cambridge, Mass.: Harvard University Press, 1966.

Pfeffer, Richard M. *Working For Capitalism.* New York: Columbia University Press, 1979.

Phillips, Derek L. "Rejection: A Possible Consequence of Seeking Help for Mental Disorders." *American Sociological Review* 28 (December 1963):963–72.

Phillips, Kevin. *The Emerging Republican Majority.* New Rochelle. N.Y.: Arlington House, 1969.

Pollack, Otto. "Unfinished Life Tasks on Retirement." *Proceedings of the Eighth Annual Volunteer Venture Conference,* Connecticut State Department of Health, 1969.

Polsby, Nelson W. "City." In David L. Sills (ed.), *International Encyclopedia of the Social Sciences.* Vol. 2. New York: Macmillan and Free Press, 1968.

Polsky, Ned. *Hustlers, Beats, and Others.* Chicago: Aldine, 1967.

Population Reference Bureau. *PRB Report.* Vol. 7, 1981.

Portes, Alejandro. "The Factorial Structure of Modernity: Empirical Replications and a Critique." *American Journal of Sociology* 79 (July 1973):15–44.

Presthus, Robert. *Men at the Top: A Study in Community Power.* New York: Oxford University Press, 1964.

Psathas, George, "Ethnomethods and Phenomenology." *Social Research* 35, No. 3 (1968).

Quinney, Richard. *Criminology*, 2nd edition. Boston: Little, Brown, 1979.

———. *The Social Reality of Crime.* Boston: Little, Brown, and Co., 1970.

Rabiner, Sylvia. "How the Superwoman Myth Puts Women Down." *The Village Voice.* May 24, 1976.

Ray, Marsh. "The Cycle of Abstinence and Relapse Among Heroin Addicts." *Social Problems* 9 (1961):132–40.

Redekop, John H. *The American Far Right.* Grand Rapids, Mich.: Eerdmans, 1968.

Rehberg, Richard A., and Rosenthal, Evelyn R. *Class and Merit in the American High School.* New York: Longman, 1978.

Reiss, Albert. "The Social Integration of Queers and Peers." *Social Problems* 9 (1961):102–19.

———. "The Social Integration of Queers and Peers." In Howard Becker (ed.), *The Other Side: Perspectives on Deviance.* New York: Free Press of Glencoe, 1964.

Reiss, Albert J. "The Analysis of Urban Phenomena." Pp. 41–54 in R. M. Fisher (ed.), *The Metropolis in Modern Life.* N.Y.: Doubleday, 1955.

Richardson, James T. "People's Temple and Jonestown: A Corrective Comparison and Critique." *Journal for the Scientific Study of Religion* 19 (September 1980):235–55.

Richer, Stephen. "Reference Group Theory and Ability Grouping: A Convergence of Sociological Theory and Educational Research." *Sociology of Education* 49 (January 1976):65–71.

Ridgeway, Cecelia. "Status in Groups: The Importance of Motivation." *American Sociological Review* 47 (February, 1982):76–88.

Rimmer, Robert. *The Harrod Experiment*, Los Angeles: Sherbourne Press, 1966.

Rist, Ray C. "On Understanding the Processes of Schooling: The Contributions of Labeling Theory." In *Power and Ideology in Education*, J. Karabel and A. H. Halseys, eds., N.Y.: Oxford University Press, 1977.

———. "Student Social Class and Teacher Expectations: The Self-Fulfilling Prophecy in Ghetto Education." *Harvard Educational Review* 40 (August 1970):411–51.

Robinson, Robert V. and Kelley, Jonathan. "Class As Conceived by Marx and Dahrendorf: Effects on Income Inequality, Class Consciousness, and Class Conflict in the United States and Great Britain." *American Sociological Review* 44 (February 1979):38–58.

Rodgers, Harrell R. *Community Conflict, Public Opinion and the Law.* Columbus, Ohio: Merrill, 1969.

Rodman, Hyman. "The Lower Class Value Stretch." *Social Forces* 42 (December 1963):205–15.

Roethlisberger, Fritz J., and Dickson, William J. *Management and the Worker.* Cambridge, Mass.: Harvard University Press, 1939.

Rogoff, Natalie. *Recent Trends in Occupational Mobility.* Glencoe, Ill.: Free Press, 1953.

Rokeach, Milton. "Value Systems in Religion." *Review of Religious Research* 11 (Fall 1969):24–39.

Roof, Wade C. "Socioeconomic Differentials Among White Socioreligious Groups in the United States." *Social Forces* 58 (September 1979):280–89.

———. "Unresolved Issues in the Study of Religion and the National Elite: Response to Greeley." *Social Forces* 59 (1981):831–836.

Roof, Wade C., and Hoge, Dean R. "Church Involvement in America: Social Factors Affecting Memberhsip and Participation" *Review of Religious Research* 21 (Supplement 1980):405–26.

Rose, Arnold. *The Power Structure.* New York: Oxford University Press, 1967.

Rosenbaum, James E. "The Stratification of Socialization Processes." *American Sociological Review* 40 (February 1975):48–54.

———. "The Structure of Opportunity in School." *Social Forces* 57 (September 1978):236–56.

———. "Track Misperceptions and Frustrated College Plans: An Analysis of the Effects of Tracks and Track Perceptions in the National Longitudinal Survey." *Sociology of Education* 53 (April 1980):74–88.

Rosenberg, Morris, and Pearlin, Leonard I. "Social Class and Self-Esteem Among Children and Adults" *American Journal of Sociology* 84 (July 1978):53–77.

Rosenhahn, David L. "On Being Sane in Insane Places." *Science* 1979 (January 19, 1973):250–58.

Rosenthal, Robert, and Jacobson, Lenore. *Pygmalion in the Classroom.* New York: Holt, Rinehart and Winston, 1968.

Rossell, Christine H. "School Desegregation and Community Social Change" *Law and Contemporary Problems* 42 (Summer 1978):133–83.

Rossi, Peter. "The Challenge and Opportunities of Applied Social Research." *American Sociological Review* 45 (December 1980):889–904.

Rossi, Peter H., and Blum, Zahara. "Class, Status and Poverty." In Daniel Moynihan (ed.), *On Understanding Poverty.* New York: Basic Books, 1968.

Rush, Michael, and Althoff, Phillip. *An Introduction to Political Sociology.* Indianapolis: Bobbs-Merrill, 1971.

Ryan, William. *Blaming the Victim*, N.Y.: Random House, 1976.

Ryder, Norman B., and Westoff, Charles F. *Reproduction in the United States: 1965.* Princeton, N.J.: Princeton University Press, 1971.

Rytina, Joan Huber; Form, William H.; and Pease, John. "Income and Stratification Ideology: Beliefs About the American Opportunity Structure." *American Journal of Sociology* 75 (January 1970):703–16.

Safa, Helen I. "Runaway Shops and Female Employment: The Search for Cheap Labor." *Signs: Journal of Women in Culture and Society* 7 (Winter 1981):418–33.

Sagarin, Edward. *Odd Man In: Societies of Deviants in America.* Chicago: Quadrangle, 1969.

Salazar, Ruben. "Stranger in One's Land." In R. Perrucci and M. Pilisuk (eds.), *The Triple Revolution Emerging.* Boston: Little, Brown, 1971.

Samuelsson, Kurt. *Religion and Economic Action: A Critique of Max Weber.* New York: Harper Torchbooks, 1957.

Sander, Jack; Myerson, Marilyn; and Kinder, Bill N. *Human Sexuality: Current Perspectives* Tampa, Florida: Mariner Publishing Co., 1980.

Saville, John. *Working Conditions in the Victorian Age.* Westmead, England: Gregg International Publishers, 1973.

Sayre, Ann. *Rosalind Franklin and DNA.* New York: Norton, 1975.

Schachter, Stanley. "Deviation, Rejection and Communication." *Journal of Abnormal and Social Psychology* 46 (1951):190–207.

Schaefer, Richard T. *Racial and Ethnic Groups.* Boston: Little, Brown, and Co., 1979.

Schafer, W. E., and Polk, K. "Delinquency and the Schools." In *Task Force Report: Juvenile Delinquency and Youth Crime.* President's Commission on Law Enforcement and Administration of Justice, pp. 222–77. Washington, D.C.: U.S. Government Printing Office, 1967.

Scheff, Thomas J. "Control Over Policy by Attendants in a Mental Hospital." *Journal of Health and Human Behavior* 2 (1961):93–105.

Schnaiberg, Allan. "Measuring Modernism: Theoretical and Empirical Explorations." *American Journal of Sciology* 76 (December 1970):399–425.

Scholzman, Kay L., and Verba, Sidney. *Inquiry to Insult: Unemployment, Class and Political Response.* Cambridge: Harvard University Press, 1979.

Schrader, William B. *Distribution of SAT Scores as an Indicator of Changes in the SAT Candidate Population.* New York, N.Y.: College Entrance Examination Board, 1977.

Schulman, Harry M. "The Measurement of Crime in the United States." *Journal of Criminal Law, Criminology and Police Science* 57 (December 1966):485–86.

Schumacher, E. F. *Small is Beautiful: Economics as If People Mattered.* N.Y.: Harper and Row, 1973.

Schur, Edwin. "Drug Addiction under British Policy." In H. Becker (ed.), *The Other Side: Perspectives on Deviance.* New York: Free Press, 1964.

———. *Labeling Deviant Behavior.* New York: Harper & Row, 1971.

Schur, Edwin M. *Crimes Without Victims.* Englewood Cliffs, N.J.: Prentice-Hall, 1965.

———. *Interpreting Deviance: A Sociological Introduction.* N.Y.: Harper & Row, 1979.

Schwartz, Richard, and Skolnick, Jerome H. "A Study of Legal Stigma." *Social Problems* 10 (1962):133–38.

Scimecca, Joseph A. *Education and Society,* New York: Holt, Rinehart and Winston, 1980.

Scott, Marvin B., and Lyman, Stanford. "Accounts." *American Sociological Review* 33 (1968):46–62.

Scrimshaw, Susan C. M. "Women and the Pill: From Panacea to Catalyst" *Family Planning Perspectives* 13 (November/December 1981):254–62.

Seger, Imogen. *Durkheim and His Critics on the Sociology of Religion.* Columbia University: Bureau of Applied Social Research, 1957.

Sennett, Richard, and Cobb, Jonathan. *The Hidden Inuries of Class.* N.Y.: Random House, 1972.

Sewell, William H. "Inequality of Opportunity for Higher Education." *American Sociological Review* 36 (October 1971):793–809.

Sewell, William H.; Haller, Archie O.; and Straus, Murray A. "Social Status and Educational and Occupational Aspiration." *American Sociological Review* 22 (February 1957):67–73.

Sewell, William H., and Shah, Vimal P. "Parents' Education and Children's Educational Aspirations and Achievements." *American Sociological Review* 33 (April 1968):191–209.

Sexton, Patricia. *Education and Income.* New York: Viking, 1961.

Shanas, Ethel. "Social Myth as Hypothesis: The Case of the Family Relations of Old People." *The Gerontologist* 19 (February 1979):3–9.

Sheehan, Daniel S. "A Study of Attitude Change in Desegregated Intermediate Schools." *Sociology of Education* 53 (January 1980):51–59.

Sheppard, Harold L., and Herrick, Neal Q. *Where Have All the Robots Gone? Worker Dissatisfaction in the '70s.* New York: Free Press, 1972.

Sherman, Howard J., and Wood, James L. *Sociology: Traditional and Radical Perspectives.* N.Y.: Harper and Row, 1979.

Shibutani, Tamotsu. *Society and Personality.* New York: Prentice-Hall, 1961.

Shibutani, Tamotsu, and Kwan, Kian M. *Ethnic Stratification: A Comparative Approach.* New York: Macmillan, 1965.

Shils, Edward, and Janowitz, Morris. "Cohesion and Disintegration in the Wehrmacht in World War II." *Public Opinion Quarterly* 12 (1948):280–315.

Shiner, Larry. "The Concept of Secularization in Empirical Research." *Journal for the Scientific Study of Religion* 6 (Fall 1967):207–20.

Siegal, Alberta, and Siegal, Sidney. "Reference Groups, Membership Groups and Attitude Change." *Journal of Abnormal and Social Psychology* 55 (1957):360–64.

Sills, David L. "Voluntary Associations: Sociological Aspects." In David L. Sills (ed.), *International Encyclopedia of the Social Sciences.* Vol. 16. New York: Macmillan and Free Press, 1968.

Silver, Marc L. "Worker Management: A Power-Dialectic Framework." *Sociology of Work and Occupations* 8 (May 1981):145–64.

Simmons, Alan B. "Ambivalence Toward Small Families in Rural Latin America." Social Biology 21 (Summer 1974):127–43.

Simmons, Leo W., ed. *Sun Chief.* New Haven: Yale University Press, 1942.

Simpson, George E., and Yinger, J. Milton. *Racial and Cultural Minorities.* 4th ed. New York: Harper & Row, 1972.

Singer, S. Fred, ed. *Is There an Optimum Level of Population?* New York: McGraw-Hill, 1971.

Sivard, Ruth L. *World Military and Social Expenditures, 1980.* Leesburg, Va.: World Priorities, 1980.

Sjoberg, Gideon. *The Preindustrial City: Past and Present.* Glencoe, Ill.: Free Press, 1960.

Skolnick, Arlene. "The Family and Its Discontents." *Society* 18 (January/February 1981):42–27.

Slater, Philip. *The Pursuit of Loneliness.* Boston: Beacon Press, 1976.

Sly, David F. "Migration and the Ecological Complex." *American Sociological Review* 37 (October 1972): 615–28.

Smith, Joel; Form, William H.; and Stone, Gregory P. "Local Intimacy in a Middle-Sized City." *American Journal of Sociology* 60 (November 1954):276–84.

Society. "Social Science and the Citizen." *Society* 18 (March/April 1981):2

Spanier, Graham, and Lewis, Robert A. "Marital Quality: A Review of the Seventies" *Journal of Marriage and the Family* 42 (November 1980):825–39.

Spilerman, Seymour. "Careers, Labor Market Structure, and Socioeconomic Achievement." *American Journal of Sociology* 83 (November 1977):551–93.

Spitz, Rene. "Hospitalism." In R. S. Eissler et al. *The Psychoanalytic Study of the Child*, vol. 1. New York: International Universities Press, 1945.

Spitze, Glenna, and Huber, Joan. "Changing Attitudes Toward Women's Nonfamily Roles: 1938 to 1978." *Sociology of Work and Occupations* 7 (August 1980):317–35.

Spock, Benjamin M. *Baby and Child Care.* New York: Pocket Books, 1961.

Stark, Rodney, and Bainbridge, William S. "Networks of Faith: Interpersonal Bonds and Recruitment to Cults and Sects." *American Journal of Sociology* 85 (May 1980):1376–95.

Stark, Rodney, and Bainbridge, William S. "American-Born Sects: Initial Findings." *Journal for the Scientific Study of Religion* 20 (June 1981):130–49.

Statistical Abstract of the U.S. The Bureau of the Census. Washington, D.C.: U.S. Department of Commerce, 1973, 1974, 1976, 1978, 1980, 1981.

Stephenson, Richard M. "The CIA and the Professor: A Personal Account." *The American Sociologist* 13 (August 1978):121–33.

Stillman, Don. "The Devastating Impact of Plant Relocations." *Working Papers* (July/August 1978):42–53.

Stinchcombe, Arthur. "Social Structure and Organizations." In James G. March (ed.), *Handbook of Organizations.* Chicago: Rand McNally, 1965.

Stone, Gregory. "Appearance and the Self." In A. Rose (ed.), *Human Behavior and Social Processes.* Boston: Houghton Mifflin, 1962.

Stouffer, Samuel A., et al. *The American Soldier, Studies in Social Psychology in World War II.* Vol. I–II. Princeton, N.J.: Princeton University Press, 1949.

Straus, Murray A. "Stress and Physical Child Abuse." *Child Abuse and Neglect* 4 (No. 2, 1980):75–88.

Stryker, Robin. "Religio-Ethnic Effects on Attainments on the Early Career." *American Sociological Review* 46 (1981):212–31.

Study Commission on U.S. Policy Toward South Africa. *South Africa: Time Running Out*, University of California Press, 1981.

Sutherland, Edwin. Criminology, 4th Ed., Philadelphia: J. B. Lippincott Company, 1947.

———. *White Collar Crime.* New York: Dryden Press, 1949.

Suttles, Gerald D. *The Social Order of the Slum: Ethnicity and Territory in the Inner City.* Chicago: University of Chicago Press, 1968.

Sykes, Gresham, and Matza, David. "Techniques of Neutralization: A Theory of Delinquency." *American Sociological Review* 22 (1957):667–70.

Taeuber, Irene B. "Demographic Modernization: Continuities and Transitions." *Demography* 3, no. 1 (1966):90–108.

Tannenbaum, Frank. "The Survival of the Fittest." In George Modelshi (ed.) *Transnational Corporations and the World Order.* San Francisco: W. H. Freeman, 1979.

Taylor, Lee. *Urbanized Society.* Santa Monica, Calif.: Goodyear Publishing, 1980.

Tedin, Kent L. "The Influence of Parents on the Political Attitudes of Adolescents." *American Political Science Review* 68 (December 1974):1579–92.

Thomlinson, Ralph. *Demographic Problems* 2d ed. Belmont, Calif.: Dickenson, 1975.

Thompson, Daniel C. *The Negro Leadership Class.* Englewood Cliffs, N.J.: Prentice-Hall, 1963.

Thompson, John R. "Women and Religion: Psychic Sources of Misogyny." *Christianity and Crisis* 39 (April 2, 1979):73–7.

Thompson, Warren S. "Recent Trends in World Population." *American Journal of Sociology* 34 (May 1929):959–75.

Time. August 2, 1982, July 12, 1982, March 15, 1982.

Timms, D. W. G. *The Urban Mosaic.* New York: Cambridge University Press, 1971.

Tobey, Alan. "The Summer Solstice of the Healthy-Happy-Holy Organization." In Charles Y. Clock and Robert N. Bellah, eds. *The New Religious Consciousness.* Berkeley: University of California Press, 1976.

Toennies, Ferdinand. *Community and Society.* Originally published in 1887. New York: Harper Torchbooks, 1957.

Toffler, Alvin. *Future Shock.* New York: Random House, 1970.

Treiman, Donald J. *Occupational Prestige in Comparative Perspective.* New York: Academic Press, 1977.

Treiman, Donald J., and Terrell, Kermit. "Sex and the Process of Status Attainment." *American Sociological Review* 40 (April 1975):174–200.

Tripplett, N. "The Dynamogenic Factors in Peace-Making and

Competition." *American Journal of Psychology* 9 (1898): 507–33.

Troeltsch, Ernst. *The Social Teachings of the Christian Churches.* Vol. 1. Translated by Olive Wyon. New York: Harper Torchbooks, 1960.

Truman, David. *The Governmental Process.* New York: Knopf, 1971.

Turner, Ralph H. "Sponsored and Contest Mobility and the School System." *American Sociological Review* 25 (December 1960):855–67.

———. "Collective Behavior." In Robert E. Faris (ed.), *Handbook of Modern Sociology.* Chicago: Rand McNally, 1964, pp. 382–425.

Underwood, Kenneth, *Protestant and Catholic.* Boston: Beacon, 1957.

United Nations. *The Determinants and Consequences of Population Trends. New Summary of Findings on Interaction of Demographic, Economic and Social Factors,* vol. 1. Department of Economic and Social Affairs, Population Studies No. 50, New York: United Nations, 1973.

———. *1974 Report on the World Social Situation.* New York: Department of Economic and Social Affairs, 1975.

———. *World Statistics in Brief.* 1981.

United Nations Economic and Social Council. *Population Commission Report of the ad hoc Consultative Group of Experts on Population Policy* (E/CN. 9/297), 1972.

United Nations Educational, Scientific, and Cultural Organization. *Statement on the Nature of Race and Race Differences* 26 May 1952.

United Nations Fund for Population Activities. "Law and World Population." *The Population Debate: Dimensions and Perspectives.* Papers of the World Population Conference, Bucharest, 1974. Vol. 2. New York: United Nations, 1975.

United Nations Secretariat. "Population Policies and Programmes." *The Population Debate: Dimensions and Perspectives.* Papers of the World Population Conference, Bucharest, 1974. Vol. 2. New York: United Nations, 1975.

United States Bureau of the Census. *Current Population Reports.* Series P-20, No. 99, 226, 274, 280, 363.

U.S. Department of Health, Education and Welfare. *A Study of Selected Socio-Economic Characteristics of Ethnic Minorities Based on the 1970 Census.* Volume 1: Spanish Speaking Peoples. Washington, D.C.: U.S. Government Printing Office, 1974.

———. *A Study of Selected Socio-Economic Characteristics of Ethnic Minorities Based on the 1970 Census.* Volume 2: Asian Americans. Washington, D.C.: U.S. Government Printing Office, 1974.

U.S. Immigration and Naturalization Service. *Annual Report.* (Yearly.)

Useem, Michael. "The Social Organization of the American Business Elite and Participation of Corporation Directors in the Governance of American Institutions." *American Sociological Review* 44 (August 1979):553–72.

Van den Berghe, Pierre L. "Bridging the Paradigms: Biology and the Social Sciences," in Michael S. Gregory, Anita Silvers, and Diane Sutch, eds. *Socio-biology and Human Nature.* San Francisco: Jossey-Bass, 1978.

Van Gennep, Arnold. *The Rites of Passage.* Translated by Monika B. Vizedom and Gabriel L. Caffee. Chicago: The University of Chicago Press, 1960.

Vanneman, Reeve, and Pampel, Fred C. "The American Perception of Class and Status." *American Sociological Review* 42 (June 1977):422–37.

Verba, Sidney, and Nie, Norman H. *Participation in America.* New York: Harper and Row, 1972.

Veroff, Joseph; Feld, Sheila; and Gurin, Gerald. "Achievement Motivation and Religious Background." *American Sociological Review* 27 (April 1962): 205–17.

Vincent, George F., and Small, Albion W. "The Family as a Primary Social Group." In Edgar F. Borgatta and Henry J. Meyer (eds.), *Sociological Theory: Present-Day Sociology from the Past.* New York: Knopf, 1961.

Vital and Health Statistics. "Divorce Statistics Analysis, United States." Washington, D.C.: U.S. Department of Health, Education and Welfare, 1964–1965.

———. *Divorce Statistics Analysis, United States,* 1964 and 1965. Washington, D.C.: U.S. Department of Health, Education, and Welfare, Public Health Service, 1969.

von Hoffman, Nicholas. "The Solid Gold Cornflake." *The New York Review of Books,* 26 (1979):21–3.

Vroom, V. *Motivation in Management.* American Foundation for Management Research, 1965. [15]

Waite, Linda. "Working Wives: 1940–1960." *American Sociological Review* 41 (February 1976):65–80.

Walker, Charles R., and Guest, Robert H. *The Man on the Assembly Line.* Cambridge, Mass.: Harvard University Press, 1952.

Waller, Willard. *The Sociology of Teaching.* Science ed. New York: Wiley, 1965.

Wallerstein, Immanuel M. *The Capitalist World Economy.* New York: Cambridge University Press, 1979.

Wallerstein, Judith S., and Kelly, Joan B. *Surviving the Breakup.* New York: Basic Books, 1980.

Walters, R. H., and Demkow, L. "Timing of Punishment as a Determinant of Response Inhibition." *Child Development* 34 (1963):207–14.

Walton, John. "Discipline, Method and Community Power: A Note on the Sociology of Knowledge." *American Sociological Review* 31 (October 1966):684–89.

Ward, Lester Frank. *Dynamic Sociology.* 2d ed. New York: Appleton, 1911.

Wasburn, Philo. "Children and Watergate: Some Neglected Considerations." *Sociological Focus* 10 (October 1977):341–51.

Washburne, Chandler. "Teacher in the Authority System." *Journal of Educational Sociology* 30 (1957):390–94.

Washington Post. "Only 24% of Voters and Non Republican." 30 September 1973, A-31.

Watson, James. *Double Helix.* New York: Atheneum, 1968.

Wax, Murray L. *Indian Americans, Unity and Diversity.* Englewood Cliffs, N.J.: Prentice-Hall, 1971.

Weber, Adna F. *The Growth of Cities in the Nineteenth Century.* New York: Free Press, 1955. Originally published in 1899.

Weber, Max. *General Economic History.* Glencoe, Ill.: Free Press, 1927.

———. *The Theory of Social and Economic Organization.* Translated by Talcott Parsons. Glencoe, Ill.: Free Press, 1947.

———. *Essays in Sociology.* Translated by H. H. Gerth and C. Wright Mills. New York: Oxford University Press, 1958*a*.

———. *The Protestant Ethic and the Spirit of Capitalism.* Translated by Talcott Parsons. New York: Scribner's, 1958*b*.

Weed, James A. *National Estimates of Marriage Dissolution and Survivorship: United States.* U.S. Department of Health and Human Services, National Center for Health Statistics. Vital and Health Statistics—Series 3, No. 19. November 1980.

Weinberg, Martin. "The Nudist Management of Respectibility." In Jack Douglas (ed.), *Deviance and Responsibility.* New York: Basic Books, 1970.

Weiner, Terry S., and Ecklund, Bruce K. "Education and Political Party: The Effects of College or Social Class?" *American Journal of Sociology* 84 (January 1979):911–28.

Weinstein, Jay A. *Demographic Transition and Social Change.* Morristown, N.J.: General Learning, 1976.

Weitzman, Lenore J.; Eifler, Deborah; Hokada, Elizabeth; and Ross, Catherine. "Sex-Role Socialization in Picture Books for Pre-School Children." *American Journal of Sociology* 77 (1972):1125–50.

Westoff, Charles, and Jones, E. F. "The Secularization of U.S. Catholic Birth Control Practices." *Family Planning Perspectives* 9 (1977):203.

Wexler, Henrietta. "Research Developments: Coed Practical Arts." *American Education* 16 (April 1980):32–3.

———. "Occupational Shifting Among College Grads." *American Education* 16 (October 1980):63.

Wheeler, Stanton. "The Structure of Formally Organized Socialization Settings." In Orville G. Brim, Jr., and Stanton Wheeler (eds.), *Socialization After Childhood.* New York: Wiley, 1966.

White, Ralph, and Lippitt, Ronald. *Autocracy and Democracy.* New York: Harper & Row, 1960.

Whitt, J. Allen. "Toward a Class-Dialectical Model of Power: An Empirical Assessment of Three Competing Models of Political Power. *American Sociological Review* 44 (February 1979):81–100.

Whyte, William F. *Street Corner Society: The Social Structure of an Italian Slum.* Chicago: University of Chicago Press, 1943.

Wiggins, James A.; Dill, Forrest; and Schwartz, Richard. "On Status-Liability." *Sociometry* 28 (1965):197–209.

Wilhelm, Sidney. *Who Needs the Negro?* Garden City, N.Y.: Doubleday Anchor, 1971.

Wilkinson, Thomas O. "Family Structure and Industrialization in Japan." *American Sociological Review* 27 (October 1962):678–82.

Williams, J. H. *Psychology of Women: Behavior in a Biosocial Context.* New York: Norton, 1977.

Williams, Robin. *American Society.* 3d ed. New York: Knopf, 1970.

Wilson, Edward O. *On Human Nature.* Cambridge, Mass.: Harvard University Press, 1978.

———. *Socio-biology: The New Synthesis.* Cambridge, Mass.: Harvard University Press, 1975.

Wilson, John. *Introduction to Social Movements.* New York: Basic, 1973.

Wilson, William J. *The Declining Significance of Race: Blacks and Changing American Institutions.* Chicago: University of Chicago Press, 1978.

Wilson, R., and Schulz, D. *Urban Sociology.* Englewood Cliffs, N.J.: Prentice Hall, 1978.

Winick, Charles, "Physician Narcotic Addicts." In H. Becker (ed.), *The Other Side: Perspectives on Deviance.* New York: Free Press, 1964.

Wirth, Louis. "Urbanism as a Way of Life." *American Journal of Sociology* 44 (July 1938):3–24.

Witt, Shirley Hill. "Pressure Points in Growing Up Indian." *Perspectives* 12 (Spring 1980):24–31.

Wolfinger, Raymond E., and Rosenstone, Steven J. *Who Votes?* New Haven: Yale University Press, 1980.

Woodward, Joan. *Industrial Organization.* London: Oxford University Press, 1965.

Woodworth, Warner. "Forms of Employee Ownership and Workers' Control." *Sociology of Work and Occupations* 8 (May 1981):195–200.

Yancey, William. "Architecture, Interaction, and Social Control." *Environment and Behavior* 3 (1971):3–21.

Yinger, J. Milton. *The Scientific Study of Religion.* New York: Macmillan, 1970.

Yogev, Sara. "Do Professional Women Have Egalitarian Marital Relationships?" *Journal of Marriage and the Family* 43 (November 1981):865–71.

Young, Donald. "Sociology and the Practicing Professions." *American Sociological Review* 20 (December 1955):644–48.

Zabin, Laurie S., and Clark, Samuel D., Jr. "Why They Delay: A Study of Teenage Family Planning Clinic Patients." *Family Planning Perspectives* 13 (September/October 1981):205–17.

Zajonc, Robert. "Social Facilitation." *Science* 149 (1965):269–74.

Zeitlin, Irving M. *Ideology and the Development of Sociological Theory.* Englewood Cliffs, N.J.: Prentice-Hall, 1968.

Zeitlin, Maurice. "Corporate Ownership and Control: The Large Corporation and the Capitalist Class." *American Journal of Sociology* 79 (March 1974):1073–1119.

———, ed. *American Society, Inc.* Chicago: Markham, 1970.

Zelnick, Melvin; Kim, Young J.; and Kantner, John F. "Probabilities of Intercourse and Conception Among U.S. Teenage

Women, 1971 and 1976." *Family Planning Perspectives* 11 (May/June 1979):177–83.

Zey-Ferrel, Mary, and Aiken, Michael, (eds.). *Complex Organizations: Critical Perspectives.* Glenview, Ill.: Scott, Foresman and Co., 1981.

Zimbardo, Philip. "The Human Choice: Individuation, Reason, and Order versus Deindividuation, Impulse and Chaos." In W. Arnold and David Levine (eds.), *Nebraska Symposium on Motivation.* Lincoln, Neb.: University of Nebraska Press, 1969.

GLOSSARY

Accommodation   acceptance by both the minority and dominant groups of their relative positions in society.

Acculturation   acceptance of dominant group values by minority group members.

Age-cohort   a group of people of the same or similar age.

Ageism   prejudice against older persons.

Age-specific birthrate (ASBR)   number of births in a year per number of women of certain ages in a population.

Aggregate demand   amount of money available to consumers to buy products.

Agribusiness   domination of the farming industry by large corporate farms.

Agriculture   domestication of food supplies with the use of the plow and the use of animals as an energy source.

Analytic research   a study to test hypotheses about the relationship between two or more variables and to identify causal connections.

Androgyny   role that is characterized by behavior appropriate to a situation, regardless of traditional gender definition.

Anticipatory socialization   the learning of parts of a role by an individual who expects to occupy the role in the future.

Applied research   attempts to use sociological knowledge to conduct research of interest to a specific client. The objective is more practical because it may result in social change.

Aspirations   goals and hopes shared by group members that they wish to realize.

Assimilation   gradual loss of distinctiveness of minority groups absorbed into dominant population. May be of four types—cultural, structural, marital, and identificational.

Atheism, or nontheism   lack of belief in a supernatural being.

Authority   use of power that is consistent with the norms of society; legitimate use of power.

Avoidance   strategy of controlled social contact or lack of social contact employed by either the dominant or minority group.

Basic research   attempts to contribute to a body of theoretical knowledge about human society. The audience is usually other scientists in the researcher's field.

Bilateral discent   tracing of kinship through the family lines of both parents.

Black power   a concept based on the premise that the black community must preserve its racial and cultural identity and foster pride in being black to deal with white society from a position of strength.

Bureaucratic organizations   social groups characterized by a functional division of labor, organizational positions filled on the basis of merit and competence, a hierarchical ordering of positions involving authority relations, and formal rules and procedures which severely limit individual discretion in the performance of duties.

Capital resources what is left over (surplus) after the primary needs of food and shelter for a population are satisfied; used to improve education, health care, etc.

Caste system a social order that is made up of religiously sanctioned and hierarchically ranked groupings in which membership is fixed at birth and is permanent.

Charisma exceptional qualities or extraordinary powers that command the respect and devotion of others.

Charismatic authority legitimation of the use of power by a leader who has personal power of the "gift of grace."

Church a highly developed organization, closely aligned with the dominant culture, that has open and inclusive membership and an objective concept of grace.

City a large human collectivity with recognized territorial boundaries and a common political system.

Civil religion a set of beliefs parallel to those of traditional religions, but with secular content.

Class consciousness the recognition of class-related interests by members of a class, and the belief that such interests are in conflict with those of all other economic classes.

Class system a social order with hierarchical economic groupings based on similarities in occupation and wealth and in which people may move up or down over their lifetime.

Coercion use of power that is not consistent with the norms of society; illegitimate use of power.

Colleagueship a sense of identification with other professionals involved in a common endeavor.

Colonialism political and economic domination of a weak nation by a more powerful nation.

Communication structure the set of relationships defined by who communicates with whom; three types of structures are all-channel, wheel, and circle.

Community a collectivity similar to a city but smaller in size, with a lesser degree of institutional completeness, a more homogenous population, and more intimate social relationships.

Complex technology means of producing a product characterized by high cost and long lead time.

Comte, Auguste founder of sociology (1798–1857). He stressed the importance of obtaining factual data about society.

Concentric zone theory cities grow in concentric bands or zones starting at the city center and working outward.

Conflict model a view of society as made up of antagonistic groups with different amounts of economic power

that relate to each other in patterns of dominance and subordination.

Conformity acceptance of culturally approved goals and means as a mode of adaptation.

Conglomerate a business corporation that owns or controls a number of firms producing unrelated products.

Conjugal relationships family relationships created by marriage and thus based on social rather than biological ties.

Consanguineal relationships family relationships that are biologically defined and based on blood ties.

Consensus widely held agreement on the values, norms, attitudes, and beliefs of a society.

Constraints pressures that groups exert on their members to make sure that their ideas and behavior are consistent with the groups' norms.

Contest mobility a way in which power, wealth, and prestige are granted as rewards by a society for individual initiative, perserverance, and achievement in competition with others.

Correlation a relationship between two variables; if, when one variable increases, the other variable increases, they are positively or directly correlated; if, when one variable increases, the other decreases, they are negatively or inversely correlated.

Cosmopolitan a person low on loyalty to the employing organization, high on commitment to specialized role skills, and likely to use an outer [professional] reference group orientation.

Craft guilds protective associations of independent artisans or craftworkers.

Crude birthrate (CBR) number of births in a year divided by the number of people in the total population; usually stated as rate of births per 1000 population.

Cultural accommodation the process by which a subculture satisfies the demands of the dominant culture while maintaining its own identity as a group.

Cultural assimilation the process by which minority groups lose their distinctiveness and are absorbed into the dominant population.

Cultural integration the way in which the elements of a culture, such as values, beliefs, and symbols, are related to each other.

Cultural pluralism the coexistence of different ethnic groups based on mutual respect for cultural differences.

Cultural relativity a concept that encourages examination of a culture in terms of its internal cohesion; not its differences from other cultures; acceptance of validity of all cultures.

Culture shared knowledge, meanings, concepts, rules, and ideas that are acquired by humans through social learning.

Deindividuation loss of individual identity, which occurs when people working in large organizations ignore individual differences in their coworkers or clients.

Democratic society a society in which members share equally in the vote, thereby indirectly exercising political power and influence over the decision-making process.

Demographic transition theory defines three types of societies in terms of the balance between birth and death rates: traditional, transitional, and modern.

Demography the analysis of a population by size, territorial distribution, and composition; also the study of population changes—natality, mortality, territorial movement, and social mobility.

Denomination a religious organization that has accommodated itself to the world, that has a professional clergy, and whose membership is based on race, class, or geography.

Dependent variable a variable measured by a researcher that follows in time, and changes as a result of changes in, an independent variable.

Descriptive research a study to obtain accurate information about some social phenomenon, for example, crime rate.

Deviance the process by which those who violate group norms are so identified and whose behavior receives negative sanctions by the group.

Deviants those who violate group norms and are so identified and whose acts are negatively sanctioned by the group.

Deviates those who violate group norms but are not identified as norm violators and whose acts are not negatively sanctioned by the group.

Disavowal refusal by a deviant to perceive self as deviant, particularly in the absence of any group support for deviant behavior.

Discrimination an act of unequal treatment, usually directed toward a minority population, that deprives people of political, economic, or social opportunity.

Dissolution a method of voiding marriages that recognizes mutual responsibility and incompatibility as valid reasons for ending the marriage.

Distributions in demographic studies, measures showing various characteristics of a population, such as marital or employment status or age grouping.

Divorce a method of voiding marriages that requires determination of guilt or innocence of the parties.

Domestic or shop production system system whereby a merchant-entrepreneur brings raw materials and sometimes tools to craftworkers in their homes or gathered in shops and then collects the finished products for sale on the market.

Dominant group members of a social group that have higher status, more privileges, and greater power than members of other groups in the society.

Elitist politics the perspective that power is structured like a pyramid, with the wealthiest and most powerful at the peak, controlling most resources and making all important political decisions.

Endogamy practice restricting marriage to persons who are both from the same group or community.

Entrepreneur a person who uses capital to attract and combine the other factors of production to manufacture a product for the market.

Equalitarian family a kinship structure based on the exercise of equal authority by both parents.

Established sect a loosely organized religious group that is joined voluntarily, emphasizes personal religious experience, but is not antagonistic toward the larger society.

Ethical prophets people who seek to alter the existing social order by criticizing it and who attempt to establish a new ethical code or persuade others to return to traditional standards.

Ethnocentrism an evaluation of other cultures on the basis of familiar and commonly shared ways of thinking and acting.

Exchange theory a version of the interaction model that sees interaction in terms of transactions in which social goods like favors, time, or ideas are exchanged.

Exemplary prophets people who seek to alter the existing social order by personal example, often suffering punishment, disgrace, or even death to present their message.

Exogamy practice of marrying outside of one's group or community.

Expressive role a set of expectations, behaviors, or norms that provide emotional satisfaction, warmth and support to others; traditionally seen as more appropriate for a woman than for a man.

Expulsion   removal by the dominant group of an undesired population from the area they have occupied; the most extreme form of avoidance.

Extended family   kinship group sharing a common residence and including a married couple, two or more of their married children, and their children's children.

Factors of production   (in economics) money, land, labor, and raw materials.

Factory production   shop production with wage labor and fixed capital.

Family institution   a cluster of norms that surround activities associated with the marriage of a man and a woman, sexual cohabitation, affection, companionship, and the bearing and rearing of children.

Family of orientation   the kinship group into which one is born.

Family of procreation   the kinship group formed through marriage and parenthood.

Feminists   people who believe that sex or gender is not a legitimate basis for social roles and who seek to change current patterns of inequality.

Feral children   children whose mental, physical, and social growth has been cut off because of being reared in total, or nearly total, isolation from other humans.

Fertility rate   age-specific birthrate for all women of childbearing age in a population.

Feudalism   an agrarian socioeconomic system based on an elaborate system of rights and obligations existing between landed lords and those who serve them.

Formal organization   two or more persons in a deliberately constructed social unit whose explicitly coordinated activities are directed toward the attainment of a specifically stated goal.

Gender   social aspects of sex, such as the expectations, roles, feelings or concepts associated with being male or female.

Genocide   deliberate destruction of one group by another.

Group   an aggregate of people who define themselves as belonging together.

Group cohesion   the degree to which members feel positively about the group.

Group structure   positions of members of a group relative to each other and differentiated according to criteria relevant to the group's activities.

Horticulture   gardening with primitive hand tools, such as a digging stick or a hoe.

Hunting and gathering   foraging for available game and plant foods in an environment.

Hypothesis   a prediction about the relationship between two or more variables that is derived from a system of explanation called a theory.

Ideal-type bureaucracy   a large organization characterized by a clearly ordered hierarchy of positions or offices with clearly defined "spheres of competence" that are filled on the basis of expert training. Bureaucratic activities are carried out in a spirit of impersonality, carefully recorded in writing, and guided by general rules.

Identification   in socialization, the internalization by the learner of beliefs and behaviors characteristic of a model who is unusually attractive to the learner (compare with *imitation*).

Identificational assimilation   the acquisition by minority group members of a sense of commonality with the dominant group.

Identity   a commitment to normative standards that allow observers to place us in relation to others and to expect certain behaviors from us.

Imitation   the copying of beliefs and behaviors characteristic of a model who is unusually attractive to the person doing the copying (compare with *identification*).

Independent variable   a variable that may be manipulated by a researcher and that precedes in time, and produces changes in, a dependent variable.

Industrialization   a shift in the labor force from agriculture to manufacturing.

Industrial Resolution   a shift from hand labor to the use of machine tools and mechanized production of goods, generally assumed to have started in late eighteenth-century England.

Inference   a statement about a research population based on information obtained from probability sample of that population.

Innovation   use of illegitimate means to achieve cultural goals.

Instincts   inborn tendencies within a species to perform a complex set of behaviors in a predetermined, systematic way.

Instrumental role   a set of expectations, behaviors or norms that emphasize achievement, leadership, dominance and self-assertion; traditionally seen as more appropriate for a man than a woman.

Insufficient deterrence   mild punishment, insufficient to inhibit prohibited social behavior; may lead to internalization of positive value for not performing the behavior.

615

Interactionist model a view of society as composed of elementary patterns of social interaction among persons.

Interest group any group of people with similar attitudes that makes certain claims upon other groups to behave in ways consistent with these shared attitudes.

Intergenerational mobility the income, occupational, or educational attainments of children relative to their parents.

Intermittent or delayed reward reward for making a desired response that is given only part of the time or after a delay; leads to slower learning but greater internalization.

Internalization willingness of individual to perform socially approved role behaviors in the absence of any external rewards.

Interorganizational network a set of organizations that are directly and indirectly linked to each by formal and informal ties.

Intragenerational mobility social mobility of an individual during his or her own lifetime.

Joint custody divorced parents have equal responsibility for childcare and major decisions.

Joint family kinship group sharing a common residence and including two or more siblings and their spouses and children.

Latent structure a collection of persons who have a socially significant attribute in common that can become the basis for group formation, for example, age, sex, religion, race-ethnicity, or socioeconomic status.

Law of marginal utility condition of loss of effectiveness of frequently applied punishment; to maintain effectiveness, severity of the punishment may have to be increased over time.

Leader someone who has more influence in the group than most of the other members.

Lead time the amount of time it takes to produce a product, once a decision has been made to produce it.

Life chances opportunities, determined by income and wealth, for long life expectancy, good health care, adequate food and housing, and quality education.

Local a person high on loyalty to the employing organization, low on commitment to specialized role skills, and likely to use an inner [organizational] reference group orientation.

Machismo a concept of masculinity that involves feats of physical prowess, daring, violence, or threats to master females, socially and sexually.

Magic a set of beliefs and rituals associated with a specific objective; a supernatural power.

Marital assimilation assimilation through intermarriage between minority and dominant groups.

Master status firmly established identity as a deviant attached to individual who has been caught and punished for deviance.

Matriarchy familial authority pattern based on rule by the mother.

Matrilineal descent tracing of kinship through the wife's family line.

Matrilocality residence of married couple with the wife's parents.

Megalopolis a number of contiguous metropolitan areas.

Melting pot a concept used to describe the process by which several minority populations merge with the dominant group to form a new population, shaped primarily in terms of the attributes of the dominant group.

Methodology the total set of procedural rules used in collecting, organizing, and analyzing data in scientific research.

Metropolitan area an urban area extending beyond the legal city limits, the residents of which carry out their daily activities in the central city.

Minority a group or category of people distinguished by special physical or cultural traits, which are used to single them out for differential and unequal treatment.

Modernization economic and social development marked by improved school systems, literacy rates, governmental services, mass communications, and citizen participation in civic affairs; the transition from traditional to modern practices.

Modified extended family three or more generations of a kinship group who do not share a common residence but often live close to one another and exchange goods and services.

Monogamy marriage of one man and one woman.

Monopoly control market domination by a single firm.

Monotheism belief in one supreme being or god.

Morbidity rate the amount of illness in a population, usually calculated on the basis of illness among 1000 people in a population.

Mortality rate the number of deaths per 1000 population.

Multifunctional (or functionally diffuse) role structures the existence of only a small set of differentiated roles in a society that cover a wide range of activities.

Multinational corporation a business corporation that is based in one country and owns or controls firms in a number of foreign countries.

Multiple nuclei theory the pattern of growth in a given city is influenced by specific historic and geographic conditions, making it unlikely for cities to grow in similar ways.

Neighborhood the immediate environment within a community or city in which one lives covering territory that is usually subjective and personal in nature.

Neolocality residence of married couple separate from either set of parents.

Nonindustrial society a society that has a labor force whose members are primarily directly involved in food provision and that has a simple division of labor and little differentiation between the production and consumption units.

Nonroutine political participation political acts that usually fall outside the limits of normative social behavior and that may or may not be within statutory limits.

Nonverbal communication behavior that is understood without verbal explanation.

Norms rules or expectations defining acceptable or required behaviors of individuals in social situations.

Nuclear family kinship unit comprised of husband, wife, and children.

Oligarchy government by a few people, usually for their own advantage.

Oligopoly control market domination by a small number of firms.

Organization a deliberately constructed, goal-directed collectivity based on impersonal social relationships and run by a hierarchy of authority whose purpose it is to produce something that is ultimately used or consumed by an individual or other groups or organizations.

Organizational societies societies in which the health and welfare of most of the population is defined and controlled by large organizations.

Particularistic standards standards that automatically exclude people in certain social categories, such as women or blacks, from filling certain educational or occupational roles.

Pastoral a type of society based on the use of domesticated animals as a food supply.

Patriarchy familial authority pattern based on control by the father.

Patrilineal descent tracing of kinship through the father's family line.

Patrilocality residence of a married couple with the husband's parents.

Pentecostal sects religious groups that seek intensely emotional, individualistic experiences, including speaking in tongues, faith healing, prophecy, and ecstasy.

Pluralistic politics the position that power is exercised by many small, specialized elites, each with its own decision-making responsibility.

Pluralistic society a society made up of members belonging to many different groups that compete on relatively equal terms and according to mutually accepted norms and values for political power.

Political participation any attempt to influence the decision-making process.

Political party device for mobilizing the special interests of groups of people in the form of votes.

Political socialization process by which the individual develops political attitudes within the normative context of society.

Politics the operations of government; societal structures and procedures for decision making—settling disputes, distributing goods and services, defending the group, socializing members.

Polyandry marriage of one woman to two or more men.

Polygamy marriage between a person of one sex and two or more persons of the opposite sex; includes both polygyny and polyandry.

Polygyny marriage of one man to two or more women.

Polytheism belief in many gods of equal or similar power and importance.

Population all persons who have one or more social characteristic in common; for example, college freshmen, bankers, snake handlers, blue-collar workers.

Population census a record usually made periodically by national governments of the number of its inhabitants, their characteristics, and their location.

Population composition social characteristics of a group, including attributes like age, sex, marital status, occupation, and religion.

Population distribution pattern of people's location in physical space.

Population processes factors affecting the structure of a population, namely, natality, mortality, migration, and social mobility.

Population registers an ongoing record of individual events and changes in individual characteristics—divorce, birth, death, and the like.

Population structure the size, distribution, and composition of a group of people.

Position a social location in a system of activities undertaken by a group to attain its formal or informal objectives.

Poverty the condition of living below an income that provides minimum satisfaction of basic needs for food, shelter, and clothing.

Power the ability of a person to achieve his or her own purposes by controlling others.

Prejudice an emotional attitude that is unfavorable to an entire category of people.

Prescriptive norms social rules that require certain behavior.

Priest a person who seeks to give meaning and significance to traditional religious patterns through the celebration of rituals and worship in an organized group.

Primary deviance initial act of deviation from group norms.

Primary groups social structures that have intimate face-to-face association and cooperation among their members and which, because of their more permanent nature, give the individual his or her earliest and most complete experience of social unity.

Profane, or secular common beliefs and practices of everyday life.

Prophet a person who proclaims a religious doctrine or divine commandment and seeks to change the existing social order.

Proscriptive norms social rules that prohibit certain behavior.

Random sample selection of persons from a population in such a way that each person has an equal chance of being selected. Such a sample is believed to represent the population.

Rates in demographic studies, measures showing the number of times an event, like birth, death, marriage, or migration, occurs within a population.

Rational-legal authority the legality of and the belief in the validity of laws and rationally created rules.

Ratios statements of the relative sizes of various population categories, such as the sex ratio (number of males to females) and the dependency ratio (number of younger and/or older persons to those in the middle-age groups).

Rebellion rejection of existing cultural goals and means, combined with endorsement of cultural goals in general; attempts to establish a new institutional order.

Recidivism conviction for a crime committed after a first conviction.

Reference group a group whose norms an individual uses to evaluate and judge her or his own beliefs and behaviors.

Reference group, comparative a group used by individuals to judge the relative distance between their own and the group's beliefs and behaviors.

Reference group, normative a group to whose norms a nonmember conforms because he or she would like to belong.

Reflex an inborn tendency to specific, simple, and undifferentiated behavior.

Regentrification upgrading of a city neighborhood by middle-class, career-oriented people who purchase and rehabilitate deteriorating housing.

Relative deprivation a discrepancy between what a person feels is a legitimate expectation and what he or she actually experiences.

Religion an institutionalized system of symbols, beliefs, values, and practices that focus on questions of ultimate meaning.

Religiosity the cluster of beliefs and practices associated with a person's experience of religion.

Research and development (R&D) invention and planning of improvements in technology that support the modern industrial and marketing complex.

Research design the plan for a scientific study that designates the unit of analysis, the method of data collection, and the method of data analysis. Three common research designs are the sample survey, the experiment, and direct observation.

Retreatism rejection of both institutionalized goals and the means to them.

Revolution overthrow of a government by force or threat of force and replacement of the ruling class by a different set of rulers.

Ritualism adherence to institutionalized means long after cultural goals have been forgotten or have declined in importance.

Rituals regularly patterned acts imbued with sacred meaning.

Role behavioral expectations associated with a person's social position.

Role behavior the actual behavior of people in positions.

Role conflict contradictory expectations placed upon a person in a single position, or contradictory expectations from occupying two incompatible positions.

Role engulfment acceptance by deviant of others' perceptions and definitions of self.

Role reversal a concept which when applied to marriage means that the husband becomes the homemaker and the wife becomes the provider.

Roles expectations about appropriate behavior for occupants of positions.

Routine political participation political actions that are permitted and encouraged although not required.

Sacred the forbidden and the aloof.

Sample household survey method of collecting population data from randomly selected households on a face-to-face basis; used to supplement and check data from more formal sources.

Secondary deviance use of deviant behavior or a role based on it as a means of defense, attack, or adjustment to the overt and covert problems created by the consequent societal reaction to one's deviance.

Sect a loose organization, hostile to the dominant social order, that has voluntary membership and a subjective concept of grace.

Sector theory cities grow along major transportation routes from the city center outward.

Secularism decline in religious influence; separation of religious institutions from other social structures and loss of religious control and domination of social life.

Segregation setting apart or separating members of a minority group from members of the dominant group in social interactions.

Self A person's identity, which develops when an individual sees or experiences his or her behaviors as they appear to other individuals as well as how they appear to the person.

Serendipity the chance discovery of positive outcomes that were not being sought.

SES abbreviation for the term *socioeconomic status.*

Sex biological differences or characteristics that distinguish males and females.

Shaman a person with special power because of his relationship with the spirit world.

Significant others those people who are particularly important in influencing the development of self-identity.

Small group a group of no more than 15 people, characterized by some emotional commitment, intimacy and face-to-face contact.

Social class a collection of individuals with the same relationship to the means of production, with an awareness of their common interests, and who engage in political action to advance their interests.

Social control influences on individual behavior that increase the probability that a person will behave similarly to other group members.

Social differentiation the process by which activities in a society are allocated to different persons, such as a division of labor based on age and sex. Such differentiation is not vertical since the positions do not have unequal rewards.

Social facilitation the degree to which an audience facilitates a person's performance on a task; also, the effects on a person of working with others on a task.

Social institutions clusters of values, norms, positions, and social roles dealing with a basic problem facing members of a society, such as producing and distributing goods.

Socialization process of learning by which members of a society acquire the behaviors and skills that are essential for social living.

Social mobility changes in position in the stratification system over time that is measured by occupation, income, prestige, or other measure of social standing.

Social network a set of people who have direct and indirect ties to each other but not all of whom necessarily know each other or have face-to-face relationships.

Social stratification a hierarchy of positions with different amounts of wealth, power, and prestige and intergenerational transmission of advantage or disadvantage stemming from one's location in the hierarchy.

Social structure the patterned and recurrent social relationships among persons in organized collectivities as well as the patterned and recurrent interrelationships of the various parts (not persons) of organized collectivities.

Social values goals and standards in which people have great emotional investment.

Society interacting individuals and interrelated groups sharing a common culture and territory.

Sociobiology a perspective that emphasizes the biological basis of human behavior.

Sponsored mobility a way in which power, wealth, and prestige are granted to individuals who are chosen on the basis of family connections rather than personal achievement.

Standard Consolidated Area several contiguous SMSAs and additional counties that have strong social and economic relationships.

Standard Metropolitan Statistical Area (SMSA) a city of 50,000 or more including the county in which it is located and all contiguous counties in which residents have close economic ties with the central county.

Statistical norm the number of people in a society who actually behave in accordance with a cultural norm.

Status amount of social honor or prestige a group member receives for filling a position in the group.

Status group a group of people with a similar life style and a strong sense of group identity.

Structural assimilation assimilation through large numbers of minority individuals entering into organizations and associations of the dominant society.

Structural-functional model a view of society as made up of interdependent parts and common values, existing in stability and equilibrium.

Subculture values, norms, and ideals associated with smaller units of population that emerge as a result of that group's unique experiences in achieving particular goals or satisfying particular needs.

Sufficient deterrence severe punishment sufficient to justify inhibiting behavior as long as the threat of punishment is present; condition for compliance.

Superwoman model the ideal which encourages women to combine the roles of nurturant, supportive wives and mothers, career women, and socially active people.

Symbolic interaction a version of the interaction model that sees interaction taking place through socially constructed symbols such as language and gestures.

Symbols words, actions, body movements, and visual cues that stand for ideas and objects and to which members of a culture attach similar meanings.

Technostructure network of scientific and technical specialists on whom the modern corporation depends.

Territorial social structures human collectivities based upon spatial and social factors, such as city, community, or neighborhood.

Theism belief in a supernatural being.

Third World nations that emerged from colonial status as new nations following World War II.

Total institution an organization like prisons or mental hospitals where members live in isolation from the rest of society for periods of time and whose lives are subject to the control of the organization.

Totalitarian society a society in which all social functions are regulated by the state.

Tracking the practice of grouping students of similar abilities in a specific curriculum as a means of encouraging student achievement.

Traditional authority legitimate power passed down from one ruler to another.

Universalistic standards standards that permit all persons to compete for educational and occupational roles in a society.

Value-free sociological research uncontaminated by influence of the investigator's personal values.

Values abstract standards that persist over time and identify what is right and proper for people in a society.

Vertical integration absorption by a corporation of its important suppliers as a means of superseding the market.

Vital registration systems records of certain population events, typically live births, deaths, marriages, divorces, legal separations, annulments, and adoptions.

Voluntary association a group of persons organized to further some common interest of its members and who participate on a voluntary, spare-time basis.

Women's movement a general term encompassing both formal and informal efforts by women to achieve equal rights.

NAME INDEX

SUBJECT INDEX

†